O N S

ault Ste. Marie

L HURON

L ONTARIO

Buffalo

L ERIE

GEORGE CATLIN'S
TRAVELS IN THE WEST
1830-1836

▪▪▪▪▪▪▪▪▪▪▪▪ 1830	1835 ••••••••••••••		
▬▬▬▬▬▬▬ 1832	1836 ▬▬▬▬▬▬		
▬▪▬▪▬▪▬▪ 1834	■ MILITARY POSTS		
	▲ FUR TRADING POSTS		

The Natural Man Observed:

A Study of Catlin's Indian Gallery

WILLIAM H. TRUETTNER

Published in cooperation with the

AMON CARTER MUSEUM OF WESTERN ART, FORT WORTH,

and the

NATIONAL COLLECTION OF FINE ARTS, SMITHSONIAN INSTITUTION,

by the

Smithsonian Institution Press

Washington, D.C. 1979

Library of Congress Cataloging in Publication Data

Truettner, William H.
The natural man observed: a study of Catlin's Indian gallery.

Bibliography: p.
Includes indexes.
1.   Catlin, George, 1796-1872.   2.   Painters—United
States—Biography.   3.   Indians of North America—
Pictorial works.   4.   The West in art.   I.   Title.
ND237.C35T78   759.13   [B]   78-15152
ISBN 0-87474-918-2

First Edition

Endpapers: Itinerary of Catlin's travels, 1830-1836.

Published simultaneously by Volair Limited,
Kent, Ohio, in a deluxe leatherbound edition
limited to 500 copies

To my wife

and to Laura, Madeline, Josephine, and Hadley

Contents

Foreword

Indians and their lifeways have provided one of the most popular themes in American art since the discovery of the New World. Sixteenth- and seventeenth-century artists who accompanied exploring expeditions to the East and West coasts sought to create pictures which would satisfy the curiosity of stay-at-home Europeans about the appearances and customs of the Indians they encountered.

By the second quarter of the nineteenth century another motive began to encourage artists to picture Indians—a growing fear that those tribes who still lived beyond the rapidly advancing frontier of white settlement would be destroyed by white men's diseases, wars, and liquor, or that their traditional picturesque customs would be immutably altered through contacts with civilization before artists could compile visual records of those Indians' great leaders and of their strange customs.

No artist felt that urgency more strongly than did George Catlin, who traveled westward to St. Louis in 1830, determined to visit the Indians beyond the frontier of settlement in their own country and to become their historian. And no artist of the precamera period traveled more widely among as many different tribes, or made as many portraits and scenes of Indians from life, as did Catlin. Nor did any other artist of that time devote the greater part of his life to interpreting Indians to non-Indians on both sides of the Atlantic.

Even so, George Catlin's accomplishments tended to be lost sight of during the early decades of this century. Even some of the anthropologists who were responsible for the preservation of major collections of his work seldom consulted his paintings or reproduced them in their own writings. A rebirth of interest in Catlin followed World War II as part of the phenomenal growth in popularity of drawings and paintings which portrayed the Old West prior to 1900. Research since the middle 1940s has brought to light a host of small collections of drawings and/or paintings of Indians and the West executed by George Catlin from life or after his own earlier works. William Truettner's work in providing a catalogue of the 607 paintings in the original Indian Gallery and the more than 2,000 works derived from them should be a welcome aid to future scholars.

In this book the author first provides a concise and accurate account of George Catlin's remarkably active career as both a recorder and an interpreter of American Indian life and customs. He tells of Catlin's childhood interest in collecting Indian relics, of the motives which led him to abandon law for art, and to give up a rather promising career as a painter of portraits of prominent whites to devote the rest of his life to gathering and disseminating verbal and pictorial knowledge of American Indians. The author traces Catlin's extensive travels among more than fifty Indian tribes, in the course of which he painted portraits of tribal leaders and members of their families, as well as scenes of activities in the Indians' camps and villages, including games, dances, and complex religious rituals.

These paintings provided the basis for Catlin's famed Indian Gallery, which he exhibited to many thousands of people in major cities of the United States and England, as well as in Paris and other centers on the continent. Most of these viewers probably had never seen a live Indian. Catlin reached an even wider audience on both sides of the Atlantic through his popularly written books, which were lively accounts of his travels and observations on Indian life, lavishly illustrated with engravings of his best or most popular paintings.

The author's review of Catlin's life provides a solid background for his closer look at the man's achievements as an artist. This he offers in a systematic, illustrated catalogue of all the known pictures from Catlin's Indian Gallery that are preserved in museums, libraries, and archives in the United States, Canada, and western Europe. Here is revealed the oeuvre of an amazingly productive and versatile graphic artist, who not only painted hundreds of original portraits and scenes, but who copied and recopied many of his original subjects in pencil, pen and ink, watercolors, or oils over a period of four decades. This portion of the book will be of special value to students who want to know not only what subjects Catlin painted, but when particular subjects were first executed and what replicas of those works the artist later produced with his own hand. This should also be very helpful in distinguishing copies of Catlin's works by other artists from those he executed himself.

It appears especially fitting that this book is a product of the patient labors of an art historian from the Smithsonian Institution, and that this volume is published by the Smithsonian Institution Press. The Catlin-Smithsonian relationship has been a long and uniquely close one. Not only have the majority of the paintings George Catlin showed in his famed Indian Gallery been preserved in the Smithsonian for a century, but Joseph Henry, the Smithsonian's first Secretary, was the first American scientist to recognize the importance of Catlin's works. Catlin's later years had been saddened, even embittered, by the failure of the United States Congress to approve the purchase of his Indian

Gallery for the nation. But Joseph Henry invited the aging Catlin to hang what proved to be the last exhibition of his works during his lifetime in the upper hall of the Smithsonian's red stone castle on the Mall in Washington. Indeed, Catlin lived in one of the towers of that building while his works were displayed. It was also Joseph Henry who, shortly after Catlin's death on December 23, 1872, sagely prophesied, "His paintings will grow in importance in advancing years."

That they have done—not only for anthropologists and art historians, but for descendants of those Indians whom George Catlin pictured from life in their own homelands more than 140 years ago, and for all men, women, and children who are interested in American history, science, and art.

John C. Ewers

Preface

It is with some misgivings that I add to the already formidable bibliography on George Catlin. We seem ready to drown in the quantity of current publications on the American West, and Catlin has received ample space in each one. His story has been told and retold in periodicals, exhibition catalogues, survey texts, and monographs until one no longer bothers to distinguish between the various sources. If they all sound too much alike, it is because most are based on Catlin's own account of his western travels, *Letters and Notes on the Manners, Customs, and Condition of the North American Indians* (London, 1841). Only a few have dug beyond the adventures that he served up in these two volumes, adventures that often obscure as much as they tell us about the man and his work.

Catlin was one to shape his image and to define his mission with a dramatic flair. To be sure, he was deeply concerned over the condition of North American Indians and committed to the task of rescuing them from a predictable oblivion. One cannot for a moment fault his ideals. But somehow Catlin—the intrepid traveler, the prolific artist, the consummate promoter—was a bit too conspicuous in arguing his cause. Historians, perhaps understandably, have been so fascinated by the magnitude of his activities and accomplishments, with the story he sought to leave behind, that they have been remarkably uncritical in assessing his work.

The time has come, therefore, to think more about why Catlin pursued his singular career. The artist would have us believe that philanthropy was his foremost objective, and that he was indebted to no individuals, institutions, ideas, or traditions in the pursuit of his career. This cannot be the case, however. He was much more aware of Philadelphia natural history studies and prevailing literary trends than he perhaps realized or wished to admit. On the other hand, Catlin has never been given just credit for his most significant contribution—the beguiling veil of primitivism that he cast across the American West.

His account of his artistic training is a related problem. He was not entirely self-taught, as he claimed; his early works fall easily into accepted period styles. But he was not noticeably successful, before embarking for the West, in competing with his colleagues, a fact he conveniently forgets when recalling his sudden conversion to painting Indian portraits. Yet he accomplished much more as an artist than his contemporaries realized (and much more than his ambiguous commitment to high art might have allowed). Only recently have we begun to understand the total statement the Indian Gallery was intended to make.

Apart from these questions of interpretation, there is the practical need to distinguish between paintings Catlin actually did in the West and the many studio versions that followed. Too often his dates and intineraries are accepted at face value, the original and cartoon collections are confused, and the numerous albums of drawings he produced in Europe are called field sketches. Since we can hardly make a clear judgment of Catlin's work while such a situation exists, I have tried to explain, in the catalogue that follows the introductory chapters, where and when each example in the original collection was painted.

The South American cartoons and those painted west of the Rockies in the mid-1850s have not been my concern in this publication, nor have I attempted a definitive biography of Catlin. I have made corrections that I felt would permit a more accurate and revealing account of his career, but it seemed unnecessary to repeat factual information that could easily be found in previous publications on the artist, or in studies solely concerned with history or anthropology. These are briefly mentioned in the text or the footnotes, and can be followed according to the reader's inclination. My intention has been to supply an interpretation of the artist's work, one that would explain the wellsprings of Catlin's ambition, and give us a clearer understanding of the image he developed of Plains Indians and the American West.

In the many years I have been at work on this project I have accumulated any number of debts. Countless institutions have supplied photographs, and as many curators and librarians have searched their files in response to my requests. At the outset I must pay tribute to the splendid cooperation I received from three former staff members of the Gilcrease Institute, David Hunt, Mrs. Carolyn Bradshaw, and Mrs. Marie Keene. With much patience and a true professional concern, they replied to each of my letters and phone calls until at last there were no more questions left to ask. My own colleagues at the Library of the National Collection of Fine Arts and National Portrait Gallery have been no less forthcoming with their assistance. For years William Walker has allowed me to make the library my second home, and more recently Katharine Ratzenberger, Alison Abelson, and Gailya Osborne have traced obscure volumes and kept in order my numerous loans.

Among other individuals and institutions to whom I am grateful, I should like to name the following: Stanley A. Freed of the American Museum of Natural History; Max Terrier of the Musée de la Coopération Franco-Américaine de Blérancourt; Penny Bateman of the Ethnography Department, British Museum; Mrs. Elmer S. Forman of the Cincinnati Historical Society; Charles Millard of the Hirshhorn Museum; Mildred Goosman, formerly of the Joslyn Art Museum; Joseph G. Gambone of the Kansas State Historical Society; George B. Brooks and Frances H. Stadler of the Missouri Historical Society; the late William P. Campbell of the National Gallery of Art; Neville Public Museum; Boyd Cruise and Mrs. Ralph Platou of the Historic New Orleans Collection; New York Public Library; Helmuth Fuchs of the Royal Ontario Museum; Richard G. Carrott of the University of California, Riverside; Richard E. Kuehne and Michael Moss of the West Point Museum; Mrs. Marie P. Kapps of the U.S. Military Academy Library; and Harold McCracken, formerly of the Whitney Gallery of Western Art.

Dealers have been extremely helpful in calling to my attention paintings in private collections and those in their own stock. I wish to thank in particular Richard Finnegan and Mrs. Ann Fernández of Knoedler; Larry Fleischman, Irving Levitt, Norman Hirschl, Stuart Feld, James Graham, and M. R. Schweitzer.

I must also acknowledge the consideration I have received from the National Collection of Fine Arts, other Smithsonian staff members, and colleagues who share an interest in nineteenth-century American art. David Scott and Richard Wunder encouraged me to undertake this project many years ago, and sent me to the late Marvin Ross, who made available his extensive file of Catlin material. Joshua Taylor granted me several informal sabbaticals to complete the manu-script and recommended the project to the Smithsonian Institution Press. Publication was not assured, however, until the Amon Carter Museum, at the request of Mitchell Wilder and Ron Tyler, made a generous contribution toward the color plates. Felix Lowe, Hope Pantell, and Stephen Kraft took over from there. With a long supply of patience and good judgment, they supervised the production of the manuscript.

John Ewers was my anthropological mentor and much else besides. Not only was his previous work on Catlin the basis for much that appears in the catalogue, but he gave my numerous queries prompt and courteous attention, and shared with me every scrap of Catlin material that came his way. One could not ask to be associated with a more decent and generous man.

Roger Stein's experienced eye caught numerous passages in the manuscript that needed clarification or strengthening—or just plain untangling. Paul Reddin, of Adams State College in Colorado, supplied several important references from his current study of Wild West shows, and Col. Merl Moore, a former NCFA Intern, convinced me there were several George Catlins in New York City directories. Lois Fink and Herman Viola gave me copies of many Catlin items they came across in their respective searches of NCFA records and the archives of the Bureau of Indian Affairs. Thomas Carter and Stefano Scafetta recently examined each of the Catlin paintings in the Smithsonian collection and advised me which have been significantly altered by past restoration. And for the past year, the Office of Slides and Photography has been patiently culling negatives to produce the best possible prints of the Catlin collection. I hope each member of that office, Eleanor Fink, Rachel Allen, Michael Fischer, and Martin Curry, knows how much I appreciate their efforts.

My own office staff has proved over the last several years that they can manage very well without me. I take this as a compliment, as a mark of their sympathy and understanding. They did my work for months on end, enabling me to write in a leisurely, uninterrupted fashion, and never once complained. Robin Bolton-Smith took over the major responsibilities of the office, and a hundred other details, in my absence. Meryl Muller was an invaluable research aide and editor, and organized the manuscript for publication. Paula Ganzel and Terri Echter were able proofreaders, and former staff members Camille Larson and Cindee Perlis contributed much to earlier stages of this project. My deepest thanks to each of you for your supportive attitude (and for politely concealing your indifference to the life and works of George Catlin).

I

At Home: Pursuing the Vanishing Race

When George Catlin was born, on July 26, 1796, his family had lived in Hartford, and then Litchfield, Connecticut, for some 150 years, long enough to establish themselves as members of that moderately prosperous professional class called New England gentry. Putnam, his father (fig. 1), after six years in the Continental Army, had moved west in 1787 to Wilkes-Barre, Pennsylvania, where he had begun practice as a country lawyer. Reasonably well educated, and with determined Federalist sympathies, he had achieved some local success by 1800, and he continued to hold responsible public offices throughout most of his career. As the years passed, however, failing health, an accumulation of children, and a rather genteel indifference to personal affairs, led to frequent moves and increasing financial difficulties.

George's happiest childhood years were spent on a farm on the banks of the Susquehanna River in Broome County, New York, where the family removed after Putnam closed his practice in Wilkes-Barre. Polly Sutton (fig. 2), the daughter of a local Pennsylvania family, whom Putnam had married in 1789, had produced six or seven children by the time the family settled on the farm in 1800 or 1801, and five more were born during the ten years they lived there.[1] With his numerous brothers and sisters, George led an ideal rural existence, hunting, fishing, searching for Indian remains, and absorbing the colorful backwoods tales of the old settlers and trappers who shared the Catlins' hospitality.

After another move to nearby Hopbottom, Pennsylvania, in 1810, George and several brothers were apparently sent to an academy in Wilkes-Barre, where they were instructed in English grammar, geography, history, classical languages, rhetoric, logic, mathematics, and natural philosophy by "a Yale man of sound learning and eloquent expression," according to Loyd Haberly.[2] Such grim subjects must have been a shock after the idyllic days beside the Susquehanna, but even if Haberly exaggerates the curriculum, George did gain a fluent command of written and spoken English in the course of his education, and an acquaintance with classical authors that surfaced, not surprisingly,

when he first encountered the Indians of the Upper Missouri. George later recalled that he spent five years at the academy, and this must have been supplemented to some extent by reading and instruction from his father, whose public offices and correspondence indicate that he had intellectual interests beyond those of his New York and Pennsylvania neighbors.[3]

Putnam Catlin was also very much involved in his sons' choice of careers. When George's turn came he was sent off, after mild protest, to study with Tapping Reeve and James Gould at the Litchfield Law School, an advantage his older brother, also a lawyer, had not received. Reeve and Gould, Putnam knew, offered at the time the foremost course of legal instruction available in this country. The list of prominent politicians, Supreme Court judges, and successful lawyers trained there reads like a Who's Who of the early Republic. George, who was a bright, if somewhat reluctant, student, remembered the time as a difficult "siege with Blackstone and Coke."[4] His education was apparently less "finished" than that of his more prosperous colleagues, but in spite of this handicap he did successfully complete the fourteen-month course of instruction (July 1817-September 1818) and pass the Connecticut bar exam. He must also have taken advantage of the civilized refinements of Litchfield, where several uncles, aunts, and cousins remained, and the local population included notables who ranged from the pious clergyman Lyman Beecher to the itinerant miniature painter Anson Dickinson. Several portraits or miniatures are supposed to have been painted by Catlin during this year, including one of Tapping Reeve. Promising or not (none have been located), they prove that legal studies had not dampened his enthusiasm for art, and the two interests would remain in conflict after Catlin returned to Pennsylvania, to begin law practice with his older brother in Montrose. He later recalled that during the next three years "another and a stronger passion was getting the advantage of me—that for painting, to which all of my love of pleading soon gave way; and after having covered nearly every inch of the lawyer's table . . . with penknife, pen and

Figure 1. *Putnam Catlin,* 1840s. Marjorie Catlin Roehm, Portland, Oregon.

Figure 2. *Polly Sutton Catlin,* 1828, miniature. National Collection of Fine Arts.

ink, and pencil sketches of judges, juries, and culprits, I very deliberately resolved to convert my law library into paintpots and brushes, and to pursue painting as my future, and, apparently more agreeable profession."[5]

Neither of Catlin's parents passed on to him any such talents, and it is not certain he had even seen a painting before his arrival in Litchfield. His interest must have developed rapidly during those years, and probably in opposition to the wishes of his father, who would have urged him to remain with the law. Nevertheless, we find Catlin in Philadelphia in 1821, exhibiting his work, in distinguished company, at the Pennsylvania Academy of the Fine Arts. His activities must have centered in that city for at least the next four years, since his address is given as Walnut Street through 1825 in the Pennsylvania Academy catalogues, but whom he studied or associated with, other than Thomas Sully, John Neagle, and several of the natural scientists, remains a mystery.[6] He became a member of the academy in 1824, and most likely supported himself as a miniature painter during those years, since miniature portraits constitute the majority of his entries in the annual academy exhibitions.

Even before 1825, however, Catlin's activities had taken him beyond Philadelphia. At the request of William Stone, publisher of the *New York Commercial Advertiser,* he painted Governor DeWitt Clinton in Albany in 1824. The next year Stone apparently employed Catlin to make lithographs of prominent construction sites along the Erie Canal, which were published in an official souvenir booklet, *Narrative of the Festivities Observed in Honor of the Completion of the Grand Erie Canal* (fig. 3).[7]

By 1826 Catlin had all but ceased to exhibit at the Pennsylvania Academy, which probably means that New York, rather than Philadelphia, had become his principal residence.[8] He was a member of the National Academy of Design in 1826 and 1827, and exhibited twelve paintings at the American Academy of Fine Arts in 1828. He traveled extensively in upstate New York during those years, painting portraits and fulfilling commissions for the Niagara Falls and West Point lithograph series. Red Jacket (fig. 4; no. 263), Catlin's first Indian subject, whom he probably met at the home of a mutual friend near Buffalo, was painted in 1826, various landscapes of Niagara Falls (fig. 76) and the West Point parade ground (fig. 5) must have been done in 1827 or 1828, and a full-length portrait of Clinton (fig. 6), comissioned by the New York Common Council, was completed in the spring of 1828.[9]

While Catlin was engaged in these travels, however, he had his mind on other plans. In 1826, the painter George Harvey remembered, Catlin had called at his Wall Street studio and "disclosed the ambition of his [Catlin's] life to become the historian and limner of the aborigines of the vast continent of North America."[10] This was followed (or perhaps preceded) by the resignation from the Army of George's younger brother Julius, who was to join George in New York late in 1826 to plan for a western expedition.[11] Several years later Catlin was still attempting to find a suitable way to realize his ambition. In a letter of 1829 to Gen. Peter B. Porter, Secretary of War, he makes no secret of his distaste for the kind of portrait and miniature painting he has been practicing for the last several years. "My feelings," Catlin writes,

are becoming too enthusiastic for the limited and slavish branch of the arts which I am now pursuing, and in which I am wasting my life and substance for a bare living, without the possibility of attaining in this country, to the higher & more exalted walks of my profession. . . . Life is short, and I find that I have already traveled over half of it without stepping out of the beaten path in the unshackled pursuit of that Fame for which alone, the Art, to *me*, is valuable, and for the attainment of which I wish to devote the whole energies of my life.

His ultimate ambition, Catlin continues, is to become a history painter, and he asks Porter to appoint him to the professorship of drawing at West Point, where he might have "time to devote to the prosecution of my exalted views in the Arts"; or, failing that, to "some little agency among the savage Indians" where he "could have the benefit of the finest school for an Historical painter now to be found in the world, where, among the naked savage [he] could select and study from the finest models in Nature, unmasked and moving in all their grace and beauty." In two years, Catlin assures Porter, he

could return with such a collection of portraits of the principal chiefs of different nations and paintings representing all their different manners and customs, as would enable me to open such a gallery, first in this country and then in London, as would in all probability handsomely repay me for all my labours, and afford me the advantage of a successful introduction beyond the Atlantic.[12]

Catlin never lacked ambition. He wanted desperately to get ahead, at the age of thirty-three, and he aspired to the highest branch of painting that a young artist could practice in those days (although one

Figure 4. *Red Jacket*, Seneca, 1826 (see no. 263). Gilcrease Institute, Tulsa.

Figure 3. *Buffalo from the Light House*, lithograph, 1825. American Antiquarian Society, Worcester, Massachusetts.

suspects that his concept of history painting would have struck Reynolds as a rather desperate attempt to qualify an American theme). Some years later, Catlin traced his desire to paint Indians back to having witnessed a delegation passing through Philadelphia, presumably before 1826. His oft-quoted remark in *Letters and Notes* describing the dignity and grace of the warriors, and his immediate resolution to paint

Boston. In the decade of 1820-1830, there were, perhaps, more good portrait painters at work in this country than at any time before or since, and according to William Dunlap, the most knowing critic of the period, Catlin was not among them. In fact, Dunlap considered him "utterly incompetent," and the DeWitt Clinton portrait "the worst full-length which the city of New York possesses." Dunlap laments

Figure 5. *West Point Parade*, ca.1828. West Point Museum.

them in their native surroundings, is a romantic fable of sorts that telescopes many direct and indirect influences into one convenient, dramatic moment.[13] He discounts, of course, the scientific environment of Philadelphia, in which he had been living for the last several years, in touch with the leading naturalists of his day. He says nothing of the large body of literature that had conditioned Americans to believe in the virtue of their wilderness environment and its native inhabitants, and he gives no hint of the boredom and frustration with which he was pursuing his professional career.

Most of Catlin's recent biographers have treated the years 1821 through 1829 as a succession of triumphs, and the artist himself wrote to William Stone in January 1827, "I have had within the last year more orders than I could handle."[14] But the 1829 letter to General Porter makes clear that Catlin did not consider these orders the basis for a challenging career, and he must also have had doubts about his ability to compete with better-known artists in New York, Philadelphia, and

that a man of established reputation was not chosen for the job, and then dismisses Catlin as one who has since become

better known as a traveller among the western Indians, and by letters published in the *Commercial Advertiser*. He has had an opportunity of studying the sons of the forest, and I doubt not that he has improved both as a colorist and a draughtsman. He has no competitor among the Black Hawks and the White Eagles, and nothing to ruffle his mind in the shape of criticism.[15]

Dunlap's critical estimate of Catlin's portraits must have been shared by others. Catlin was surely not immune to these opinions, and his decision to leave the beaten path was probably based as much on removing himself from stifling competition, as it was on finding meaningful work. One may read Dunlap's remarks, in this respect, as more of a comment on Catlin's future than his past. As far as the critic was concerned, roaming the wilderness and painting Indians was a pursuit that placed the artist outside of traditional academic boundaries;

Figure 6. *DeWitt Clinton*, 1828. City Hall, New York.

Figure 7. *Clara Gregory Catlin*, 1828, miniature. National Collection of Fine Arts.

therefore, he was not entitled to serious professional consideration. But by this time, one concludes, Catlin wanted to be out of bounds. In spite of the high purpose he espoused to General Porter, there is enough in the rest of the letter to indicate that he longed to try his hand at a fresh endeavor, beyond the restrictions of a conventional career. If he encountered further disapproval from critics like Dunlap, no matter; he was safely out of the arena. He could insist, as he did in his catalogues and later writings, that his work not be judged on its artistic merit, but as a record of a vanishing race.[16]

In June 1828 Catlin married Clara Gregory (fig. 7), the daughter of a prosperous and presumably well-connected family of Albany, New York. He returned with his bride to New York City, where they remained, on and off, for the next three years.[17] Haberly and subsequent scholars claim that before and after his marriage, Catlin was busily painting upper New York State tribes, but a careful check of the location of these tribes and the style of the portraits indicates that they were done out West at a later date. In fact, the only Indians Catlin seems to have painted between the Red Jacket portrait of 1826 and his first summer in the West, were the Winnebago delegation (nos. 209-17) he encountered in Washington, D.C., in the fall of 1828. Catlin and his wife spent that winter in Washington or Richmond, and the next summer in Albany, presumably with the Gregorys. The following winter (1829-30), in poor health, they went south again. Catlin remarked in a letter to his father that there were many artists ahead of him in Washington, an indication of the difficulty of obtaining portrait commissions.[18] He was more successful in Richmond, where the Virginia Constitutional Convention was meeting, and he was engaged to make a group portrait of all 101 delegates (fig. 8). But the tedious process of recording that chamber of worthies was perhaps the last straw. In the spring of 1830, against his family's wishes, Catlin set out for St. Louis. For the next six years, over many thousands of miles, his dream never faded. In that time he crossed and recrossed the vast rolling wil-

Figure 8 *(top right). Virginia Constitutional Convention,* 1829-1830, watercolor. New-York Historical Society.

Figure 9 *(bottom right). General William Clark,* 1830. National Portrait Gallery, Washington, D.C.

derness between the Mississippi and the Rockies, from North Dakota to Oklahoma, gathering the nucleus of his Indian Gallery.

Catlin's mentor in St. Louis would be Gen. William Clark, Governor of the Missouri Territory, Superintendent of Indian Affairs, and a man whose knowledge of western travel and Plains Indian tribes was second to none. Catlin claims that the Secretary of War, presumably Porter or his successor, John Eaton, had provided him with a letter of introduction to Clark and to "the commander of every military post and every Indian agent on the western frontier."[19] Whatever his means, he seems to have received splendid cooperation from all parties, and in particular from Clark, whose portrait he painted that summer (fig. 9). "My works and my design have been warmly approved and applauded by this excellent patriarch of the Western world; and kindly recommended by him in such ways as have been of great service to me," Catlin later wrote, in appreciation of Clark's services.[20]

St. Louis (fig. 10; no. 311) became the base of Catlin's operations, as it was for most frontier activity in those days. Making use of fur-trading expeditions, outposts, and Army surveillance when available, in addition to his natural talent for wilderness travel, Catlin covered an astonishing amount of territory west of the Mississippi in the next six years. Scholars differ as to where he was each year, and to prove that he painted a certain tribe at a given location is no easy matter. Catlin has further complicated the sequence of his travels by scrambling the few chronological references in *Letters and Notes,* and by issuing itineraries later in his life that clearly do not correspond with certain documented travels between 1830 and 1836.[21] In spite of this confusing situation, one can determine a clearer outline of his travels than has been proposed before if one carefully notes his increas-

Figure 10. *St. Louis, from the river below,* 1832-1833, no. 311.

Figure 11. *Grizzly Bear, chief of the tribe,* Menominee, 1831, no. 218.

ing skill with a brush and the location of certain tribes through these years.

One of the many favors General Clark granted to Catlin in the summer of 1830 was to allow the young artist to accompany him up the Mississippi to Fort Crawford at Prairie du Chien, where Clark negotiated a treaty on July 15 between the Sioux and Sauk and Fox on the one hand, and the Omaha, Iowa, Oto, and Missouri on the other. Catlin claims to have been present at the ceremony, although his name does not appear as a witness to the treaty, and his portraits of those tribes all appear to have been painted at a later date. Nevertheless, the experience must have led him to attempt his first series of Indian portraits in the West, those painted near Fort Leavenworth in northeastern Kansas (he may have detoured on his return from Fort Crawford) in the late summer or early fall of 1830 (see no. 237). These would include the Delaware (nos. 274-76), Kaskaskia (nos. 246, 247), Kick-

apoo (nos. 240-45), Peoria (nos. 251-53), Piankashaw (nos. 254, 255), Potawatomi (nos. 237-39), Shawnee (nos. 277-82), and Wea (nos. 248-50) tribes. The style of this series is reasonably consistent, and much improved over previous work, but the portraits cannot compare to those that followed in 1832.

Several subjects in the Leavenworth group were known to have been living west of the Mississippi in 1830 (see nos. 248, 279) and remnants of each of the tribes had settled near the fort by this time, making it a logical center for Catlin's activities.[22] Haberly and other scholars contend that Catlin went with Clark as far west as the Kansa villages that same fall, but Clark makes no reference to such trip in his journals and the Kansa portraits (nos. 22-28) are more accomplished than those painted in the summer of 1830.

Catlin's movements through the next year are even more difficult to trace. He apparently had come back east in the late fall of 1830, probably dividing his time between New York City and Albany with Clara, and Washington, where he pursued his professional interests. Putnam's letter of January 21, 1831, asks about the result of his son's "Southern labors and travels," and there is ample evidence that George painted Menominee and Seneca delegations in Washington in January and February of 1831 (see fig 11; nos. 218-31, 264-69).[23] According to Putnam's next letter, dated June 23, George was in New York and expected to visit his parents, who now lived in Great Bend, Pennsylvania, in July.[24] An earlier visit, scheduled for April, had been postponed, but Putnam does not say that a western trip intervened, and little more than three months could have elapsed between George's portrait session in Washington and his presence in New York on June 23. Haberly maintains, however, that in the early spring of 1831, Catlin accompanied the Indian agent John Dougherty up the Missouri and Platte rivers to visit the Pawnee, Omaha, Otto, and Missouri tribes, a journey for which there is no documentary evidence (see no. 99), and which could not have begun in Washington and ended in New York in the space of three months.[25] Haberly's version of the trip (in effect, an attempt to correct Catlin's stated itinerary for 1833) has been accepted by subsequent scholars who, presumably, were unaware of the impossible time frame.

Putnam concluded his June 23 letter by advising his son to bring "brushes and painting apparatus, as you will where ever you go have many calls, and feel justified in making a long visit." In fact, Putnam may have been lining up business for George, who must have supported himself when not in the field by painting portraits during his various stops in the East. But another pattern was beginning to emerge: after a season of intensive field work, during which he would briefly sketch dozens of portraits (see no. 119), Catlin would take the next year off, or at least reduce his schedule, in order to finish as many of them as possible. Putnam's reminder, therefore, may have also applied to the unfinished canvases of the previous summer, which he hoped George would bring to Great Bend to justify a long visit.

By December 1831 Catlin was back in St. Louis, painting portraits of an Assiniboin and a Cree chief (fig. 12; nos. 176, 179, 474)

Figure 12. *Pigeon's Egg Head (The Light) going to and returning from Washington,* Assiniboin, 1837-1839, no. 474.

Figure 13. *Fort Pierre, mouth of the Teton River, 1200 miles above St. Louis,* 1832, no. 384.

who were among a delegation of Upper Missouri Indians bound for Washington.[26] He must have remained there for the next three months, making arrangements for what would be the most absorbing and productive summer of his entire career, a 4,000-mile odyssey among the primitive tribes of the Upper Missouri. On March 26, 1832, the American Fur Company steamboat *Yellowstone* (fig. 10) left St. Louis with Catlin and a host of fur trappers and Indians on board, its upriver destination the mouth of the Yellowstone (at the western border of present-day North Dakota), where the fur company had constructed a sizable fort. Prior to this voyage, no steamboats had attempted to navigate the Missouri north of Council Bluffs. Seated on the deck day after day, Catlin made the first record of the high bluffs and strangely eroded banks of the giant river in spring flood, and when the boat's progress was halted by snags or visits to fur company outposts, he went ashore to paint the tribes encamped nearby. Numerous Western Sioux (nos. 69, 71, 72, 76-89, 91) and two Cheyenne visitors (nos. 143, 144) were painted at Fort Pierre (fig. 13), for example, an outpost midway between St. Louis and the mouth of the Yellowstone, where Catlin spent several weeks in late April and early May on the upriver voyage. He took extensive notes on Sioux dances and tribal

activities, and joined Pierre Chouteau, owner of the American Fur Company, and Major John Sanford, Indian agent of the Upper Missouri, as an honored guest at a Dog Feast (fig. 14; no. 494). An earlier stop had been made at the Ponca village, some three hundred miles southeast of Fort Pierre, and close enough to the frontier to be threatened by whisky and smallpox. Catlin painted the chief (no. 95), whom he described as a "Caius Marius, weeping over . . . the poverty of his ill-fated community," and other portraits of members of his family (nos. 96-98).[27]

None of these preliminary efforts, however, measured up to the opportunities available at Fort Union, 2,000 miles northwest of St. Louis, where the artist believed he had at last found the perfection of aboriginal life. The American Fur Company maintained a well-appointed outpost there, in the heart of the Blackfoot and Crow country. Fort Union became Catlin's base of operations for a month or more (approximately mid-June through mid-July) during which he painted an imposing portrait of Buffalo Bull's Back Fat (fig. 15; no. 149) and other leading members of the surrounding tribes (Assiniboin, nos. 180, 181; Blackfoot, nos. 150-61; Crow, nos. 162-70; Plains Cree, nos. 177, 178; and Plains Ojibwa, nos. 182, 183, 195). He also took part in and sketched details of several buffalo hunts (nos. 406, 407), and greatly

Figure 14. *Sioux Dog Feast*, 1832-1837, no. 494.

Figure 15. *Buffalo Bull's Back Fat, head chief, Blood tribe*, Blackfoot, 1832, no. 149.

enjoyed the informal hospitality of his rough-hewn Scottish host, Kenneth McKenzie. Manager of the fort and keeper of a table that groaned "under the luxuries of the country," McKenzie provided his guests with such oddly disparate fare as buffalo tongues, beaver's tails, and marrow fat, and excellent bottles of Port and Madeira that were "set in a pail of ice every day, and exhausted at dinner."[28]

Catlin's grandest expectations were fulfilled by every aspect of life in this remote outpost, and by the appearance and manners of the proud savages encamped nearby. "I am now in the full possession and enjoyments of those conditions on which alone I was induced to pursue art as a profession," he wrote back to William Stone's *New York Commercial Advertiser* in July.

My enthusiastic admiration of man in the honest and elegant simplicity of nature, has always fed the warmest feelings of my bosom, and shut half the avenues to my heart against the specious refinements of the accomplished world. This feeling, together with the desire to study my art, independently of the embarrassments which the ridiculous fashions of civilized society have thrown in its way, has led me to the wilderness for a while, as the true school of the arts.[29]

By mid-July, in a canoe packed with provisions and painting equipment, and paddled by two French Canadian voyageurs, Catlin had begun the long downriver journey to St. Louis. He stopped frequently, climbing bluffs to paint an occasional view (fig. 16; nos. 366, 390) and to speculate upon the geology of the "unsystematic and unintelligible mass of sublime ruins" that lined the Upper Missouri.[30] But the greater part of his time he devoted to painting tribes he had missed on the upriver voyage. Principal among these were the Mandan (nos. 127-42), whose comfortable and civilized way of life so intrigued him that he devoted over half of the first volume of *Letters and Notes* to describing it (see fig. 17; no. 502). The Mandan, in turn, pronounced the artist a great medicine man and lined up for their portraits in awe and respect of his powers. Much of Catlin's information came from the hospitable Four Bears, second chief of the tribe and perhaps the best-known Indian on the Upper Missouri (fig. 18; no. 128). Catlin spent hours with the chief in the latter's spacious earth lodge, listening to tales of Indian warfare and learning the intricate symbolism of O-keepa, the sacred Mandan torture ceremony, which the artist was the first white man to record (see fig. 19; nos. 504-7).

Catlin's stay at Fort Clark, adjacent to the Mandan village, must have lasted for almost a month, from July 20 to the middle of August. Then he backtracked slightly to the Hidatsa villages on the Knife River, where he encountered an old chief (fig. 88; no. 171), who recalled the visit of "Red Hair" and "Long Knife," better known as Lewis and Clark, some thirty years earlier. Catlin's next stops were the Arikara village (see nos. 123-26, 386), a few miles downriver from the Mandan, and Fort Pierre, which he had visited for several weeks on the upriver voyage. If one can trust *Letters and Notes*, the portraits and sketches of Sioux tribal activities had been done in the spring, and after a few hurried notes Catlin was off again to admire the long stretch of prairie and river (fig. 113; no. 399) between Fort Pierre and Fort Leavenworth, the westernmost garrison on the United States frontier. "I often landed my skiff," he writes,

and mounted the green carpeted bluffs, whose soft grassy tops, invited me to recline, where I was at once lost in contemplation. Soul melting scenery that was about me! A place where the mind could think volumes; but the tongue must be silent that would *speak* and the hand palsied that would *write*. A place where a Divine would confess that he never had fancied Paradise—where the painter's palette would lose its beautiful tints—the blood-stirring notes of eloquence would die in their utterance—and even the soft tones of sweet music would scarcely preserve a spark to light the soul again that had passed this sweet delirium. I mean the prairie, whose enamelled plains that lie beneath me, in distance soften into sweetness, like an essence; whose thousand thousand velvet-covered hills, (surely never formed by chance, but grouped in one of Nature's sportive moods)—tossing and leaping down with steep or graceful declivities to the river's edge, as if to grace its pictured shores, and make it 'a thing to look upon.'[31]

Several miles above Leavenworth, Catlin passed Belle Vue (no. 381), the frontier estate of his friend John Dougherty, Indian agent for the surrounding tribes. About mid-September, some two years after his previous visit, Catlin began work at the fort among tribes he had not observed before. In spite of his claims for a separate trip to the Kansa villages, a close reading of *Letters and Notes* shows that both the semicivilized tribes living a short distance east of the fort, and the primitive tribes that occupied their original villages to the north and west, came frequently to trade at Leavenworth. Presumably it was the latter group (Iowa, nos. 256-62; Kansas, nos. 22-28; Missouri, no. 122; Omaha, nos. 112-16; Oto, nos. 117-21; and Pawnee, nos. 99-111), many of whom were camped about the fort at the time, that he painted during the 1832 visit (see nos. 22, 99). Besides the evidence offered in *Letters and Notes*, one need only observe the vigorous modeling of such portraits as that of Horse Chief (fig. 20; no. 99) to prove that Catlin had the experience of the Upper Missouri behind him.

One problem does arise, however, in adding this second Leavenworth series to the end of the Upper Missouri trip. The total production for the summer swells beyond even the generous estimate (135 paintings in 86 days) of Smithsonian anthropologist John C. Ewers,[32] to a figure of about 170 paintings in five months. Before we dismiss such a possibility, we must remember that Catlin took no more than a brief likeness in the field, and that the buffalo hunts and scenes of Indian life included in the summer's total were probably studio productions of the succeeding winter and spring.

Leavenworth appears to have been Catlin's final downriver stop, but his painting activities continued after his arrival, about October 20, in St. Louis. Several miles away, imprisoned in Jefferson Barracks, were the leaders of the Black Hawk War, including the Sauk and Fox chief (fig. 21; no. 2) and his two sons (nos. 3, 4). Catlin took portraits of each of the defiant prisoners (nos. 7, 8, 12-15, 18) and continued to work on previous paintings until late December, when he headed back east to spend the winter with Clara.

The next year, 1833, Catlin did not travel in the West, despite

Figure 16. *Big Bend on the Upper Missouri, 1900 miles above St. Louis*, 1832, no. 390.

Figure 17. *Bird's-eye view of the Mandan village, 1800 miles above St. Louis*, 1837-1839, no. 502.

Figure 18. *Catlin Feasted by the Mandan Chief,* 1865-1870, cartoon 133,
National Gallery of Art, Washington, D.C. Paul Mellon Collection.

the lengthy itinerary he devised in later years.[33] Instead, he followed the pattern of taking a year off to finish the previous season's work, as he apparently had done in 1831. Too restless to remain in his studio for long, however, and probably hoping for some additional income, he began showing his unfinished collection in Pittsburgh in April, moved it to Cincinnati in May for the summer, and perhaps completed the tour in Louisville, where he and Clara were registered in a hotel for several weeks in November and December. Most of the paintings in the Pittsburgh exhibition lacked background and costume details, according to the *Pittsburgh Gazette* of April 23, 1833, and there were still a great many unfinished examples mentioned in the favorable review of Catlin's collection that appeared in the November issue of *Western Monthly Magazine.* About 140 paintings exhibited in Cincinnati were finished and framed, however, including many from the travels of the previous summer. "These are not the portraits of the depraved savages who linger upon the skirts of our advanced settlements," wrote James Hall, editor of the magazine and a leading commentator on frontier history. "They are those of the manly Indian, as he exists in his own wide plains, joint-tenant with the buffalo, the elk, and the grisly bear; and they exhibit in a striking manner the distinctive features of the tribes to which they belong."[34] When Hall joined Thomas McKenney several years later to publish *The Indian Tribes of North America,* he remembered these paintings and urged Catlin to join the project. By that time, however, the artist had publishing plans of his own.[35]

Catlin writes in *Letters and Notes* that he spent the winter of 1833-34 in Pensacola, but it seems likely that he confused dates again, because Marjorie Catlin Roehm has proved that he was there the following winter.[36] Perhaps he and Clara went only as far as New Orleans in late December and remained there for the winter. In any case, Catlin was off that spring (1834) on a well-documented adventure that would take him deep into Comanche country with the first United States military expedition to contact the Indian tribes of the Southwest.

His initial stop was Fort Gibson, a remote outpost far up the Arkansas River, which he reached by steamboat in early April. For about the next two months he painted the neighboring tribes (Cherokee, nos. 284-87; Choctaw, nos. 294-99; Creek, nos. 288-93; and Osage, nos. 29-45) and witnessed the unique ball-play scenes of the Choctaw (fig. 22; nos. 427-29). The grueling part of the journey began in mid-June, when he set off with the dragoons on a cross-country march of several hundred miles to the Comanche villages in present southwestern Oklahoma. The distance was shorter than the Upper Missouri venture of 1832, but the mission was comparable in that it again enabled Catlin to observe tribes that had been only infrequently touched by civilization. The dragoons hoped to establish friendly relations with the Comanche and neighboring tribes, who frequently harassed the few ranchers and traders who crossed their path, and the artist saw much during the four-month journey that would considerably broaden and deepen his experience. He watched Comanche attack buffalo herds

Figure 19. *The Cutting Scene, Mandan O-kee-pa ceremony*, 1832, no. 506. Harmsen Collection, Denver.

Figure 20. *Horse Chief, Grand Pawnee head chief, 1832,* no. 99.

Figure 21. *Black Hawk, prominent Sauk chief,* 1832, no. 2.

Figure 22. *Ball-play of the Choctaw —ball up,* 1834-1835, no. 428.

with even more skill than the Crow, Blackfoot, or Sioux, and he marveled at the luxuriant landscape as the dragoon column moved southwest toward the Red River, crossing high bluffs that offered a sweeping view of the horizon, and then "trailing through broad and verdant valleys" choked with vegetation. Oftentimes we "find our progress completely arrested by hundreds of acres of small plum-trees," he wrote,

so closely woven and interlocked together, as entirely to dispute our progress . . . every bush that was in sight was so loaded with weight of its delicious wild fruit, that they were in many instances literally without leaves on their branches, and bent quite to the ground. Amongst these . . . were intervening beds of wild roses, wild currants, and gooseberries. And underneath and about them . . . huge masses of the prickly pears, and beautiful and tempting wild flowers that sweetened the atmosphere above.[37]

After many days of hard travel, the dragoons encountered a party of Comanche who had ridden out to observe their approach. With a display of horsemanship that left Catlin and the officers stunned, the Comanche welcomed the troops and escorted them back to their village at the base of the Wichita Mountains (see fig. 23; no. 353). Catlin set to work recording the chief and principal warriors of the tribe (nos. 46-54), several visiting Kiowa and Waco (nos. 62-68), the appearance of the village (no. 346), and the skill with which the Comanche conducted mounted warfare (nos. 471, 487). Before his job was complete, however, he came down with a fever, caused by intense heat and foul water, that had already decimated the ranks of the dragoons, and he was forced to leave a survey of the Wichita village (nos. 55-61, 343) to his civilian friend from St. Louis, Joe Chadwick. The dragoons returned to Fort Gibson along a northern route that ran for a distance beside the Canadian River. Many of the men, including Catlin, were confined to stretchers, and when the regiment arrived at its destination in late August only two-thirds of the 455 men who had begun the expedition were still alive. The others had died on the trail of the same fever Catlin had contracted.

After several weeks of recuperation at the fort, Catlin embarked alone on a remarkable endurance test, riding his mustang Charley across corners of Oklahoma and Arkansas, and the breadth of Missouri, to St. Louis, some five hundred miles away, to meet his wife. Together the Catlins sailed for New Orleans and then on to Pensacola, where they spent the winter with James Catlin, one of the artist's younger brothers. George painted several landscapes nearby (nos. 349, 354), worked on the portraits and field sketches from the past summer, and met John Howard Payne, author of "Home, Sweet Home," with whom he went north to protest the removal of the Cherokee from Georgia.[38] For several weeks in late March and early April, Catlin was back in New Orleans, lecturing and exhibiting his collection to enthusiastic audiences, according to local newspapers.[39] From there he went north to Fort Snelling, Minnesota (fig. 24; no. 332), where the next reliable account of his travels begins in early July 1835.

Catlin had planned a more relaxed program for that summer—a cruise on the Mississippi. He and Clara boarded a steamboat in New Orleans and proceeded up the length of the river to the Falls of St. Anthony (fig. 25; no. 321), admiring, among other sights, the imposing bluffs north of Rock Island. They celebrated the Fourth of July at the fort among "several hundreds of the wildest of the Chippeways [nos. 184-194], and as many hundreds of the Sioux" (nos. 70, 73-75, 90, 92-94), who prepared them with "material in abundance for the novel—for the wild and grotesque,—as well as for the grave and ludicrous."[40] It was not the Upper Missouri, Catlin implied, and his portraits reflect a relative indifference to semicivilized tribes. But he took notes on the Sioux version of Indian ball-play and the numerous dances performed at the fort (nos. 443, 445, 447, 452), while he and Clara enjoyed the hospitality of Major Laurence Taliaferro, the Indian agent.

The Catlins began their downriver voyage separately, George by canoe, making sketches and taking notes on the passing scenery (nos. 315-20), and Clara by steamer, to Prairie du Chien (no. 333), where they met several weeks later. Fort Crawford, the military outpost at Prairie du Chien, had long been a gathering place for the Winnebago and Menominee tribes, and Catlin added to the group of portraits he had painted earlier, in Washington, of each tribe. But he was disturbed by conditions at the fort. The local Indians, who could not make the transition from hunting to an agricultural life, were gradually being corrupted by the white men on the frontier. One almost senses the relief with which he regained his canoe after these stops, content to dream along the green banks of the river and put aside the changing world. Yet he was not unaware of the potential of the rich land upon which he was gazing. "A few years of rolling time," he wrote, would cover the banks with "splendid seats, cities, towers and villas," along with "new institutions, new states, and almost empires."[41] And when he landed his canoe at Dubuque, the next stop after Prairie du Chien, the future of the lead mines in the region again caused his imagination to take flight.

Catlin's last stop of the summer was at the village of Keokuk, chief of the Sauk and Fox, located about sixty miles up the Des Moines River from where it joined the Mississippi. Here he painted two portraits of the portly chief (fig. 26; no. 1) and other members of the tribe (nos. 5, 6, 9-11, 16, 17) he had not encountered among Black Hawk's warriors at Jefferson Barracks in 1832.

Except for the few scattered subjects Catlin painted the next summer, this would be the final sequence of Indian portraits west of the Mississippi. He carried them back to St. Louis, where much of his collection had been stored, and shipped the lot to Pittsburgh that fall, following with Clara for another long visit to his parents at Great Bend. Clara, expecting her first child, went off to Albany at the end of February 1836, and George returned to Pittsburgh to prepare and exhibit his paintings. The foul air of the city, he claimed, would tone down the colors to a more "realistic tint."[42] In late spring the collection was repacked and shipped to Buffalo, where an elaborate opening was planned for early July.

Plans were changed in June, however, when Clara lost her child. George decided, somewhat abruptly, to cancel the exhibition and make one last trip west to visit the legendary Pipestone Quarry, the

Figure 23. *Comanche warriors, with white flag, receiving the dragoons, 1834-1835, no. 353.*

Figure 24 *(facing page, top). Fort Snelling, United States garrison at the mouth of the St. Peter's River, 1851-1853* (see no. 332). Gilcrease Institute, Tulsa.

Figure 25 *(facing page, bottom). Falls of St. Anthony, 900 miles above St. Louis, 1865-1870* (see no. 321). Collection of Mr. and Mrs. Paul Mellon, Upperville, Virginia.

Figure 26. *Keokuk on horseback*, Sauk and Fox, 1835 (see no. 1).

Figure 27. *Pipestone Quarry, on the Coteau des Prairies*, 1836-1837, no. 337.

source of the soft red stone from which many of the Plains tribes fashioned their pipebowls. Leaving his father and brothers to dismantle the collection, Catlin boarded a steamer at Buffalo for Sault Ste. Marie and Green Bay. At the former he painted several Ojibwa (nos. 185, 191-94) and local scenery (nos. 338, 339); at the latter, an old Menominee chief (no. 232) and two civilized Mohegan (nos. 272, 273) who were about Fort Howard. By August 1 he was at Prairie du Chien, having paddled down the Fox and Wisconsin rivers (nos. 347, 360) with Washington Irving's nephew and the Englishman Robert Serrill Wood. Catlin and Wood went on by canoe to the mouth of the St. Peter's (Minnesota) River, then changed to horses for the overland journey to the Coteau des Prairies, the long, bare ridge in the southwestern corner

of the state that divides the watersheds of the Missouri and Minnesota rivers. At the crest of the ridge, deep in Sioux territory, Catlin found the sacred quarry (fig. 27; no. 337). He spent several days collecting rock samples and speculated at length about the formation of the area. The quarry product, he proudly tells us, was named Catlinite and eventually was declared a new mineral compound, but the pages of *Letters and Notes* reveal that geology was not the sole aim of the artist's investigation. His imagination was equally stirred by the legend and mystery surrounding the area, and he gave several interpretations of myths the Sioux and their ancestors had invented to explain the presence of this bountiful source of pipestone.

On the return trip, Catlin sketched scenes along the St. Peter's

River (nos. 314, 340, 341) and then paddled down the Mississippi, where he witnessed a Sauk and Fox treaty at Rock Island on September 28.[43] By late December he was in Utica, New York, with Clara and his collection, planning to spend the winter finishing up "numerous sketches" and preparing his letters and notes for publication. He hoped to open his collection in New York City, with his paintings "more completed," he wrote in a letter to his brother Francis, perhaps revealing one reason why he had canceled the Buffalo exhibition. George also admitted to Francis that he was "too *poor* to do *anything*," which is not surprising after six years of supporting himself by an occasional portrait commission and selling a few copies of his Indian subjects.[44] Catlin seems to have survived these years generally by spending nothing, except for his exhibition tour in 1833. Otherwise, he begged passage for his Indian travels, spent winters with relatives, and left Clara at home with her father and her brother, both reasonably wealthy men, who probably made up the difference when the Catlins got too far behind.

In the spring George shipped his collection to Albany, exhibiting it there intermittently from May 15 through June, and then moving it to Troy for July.[45] After these two trial runs, he felt better prepared for New York City audiences, who acknowledged the opening (September 25) of the Indian Gallery at Clinton Hall with praise, astonishment, confusion, and hostility. The Far West and its inhabitants, one must remember, were mostly a mystery to the people of the East in the fall of 1837. Few graphic representations of either the Indians or the landscape had been circulated, and written accounts, other than those compiled by Lewis and Clark, Major Stephen H. Long, Washington Irving, and an occasional trapper, tended to be highly fanciful. Catlin presented for the first time an extensive and relatively accurate account of portions of the country which, Bernard DeVoto has written, were "exercising an exceedingly powerful influence on the national imagination."[46] Audiences responded with a combination of surprise and disbelief, in that they could conceive of the Indian only as one of two stereotypes: a noble warrior or a menacing, bloodthirsty savage. Lecturing at Clinton Hall night after night, and later at the Stuyvesant Institute on Broadway, where he moved after the crowds increased, Catlin attempted to show that Indians were more human and complex than these polar attitudes indicated. They had a legitimate culture of their own, he maintained, suited to a range of ideals and interests as worthy as any standards of civilization existing east of the Mississippi. But the cutting edge of Catlin's argument went deeper. White men who disregarded this culture were destroying the Indian's traditional means of livelihood, forcing an inevitable conflict. He knew from experience the debauching practices of the fur companies, and the effect of appropriating Indian lands through treaties that tribal leaders had difficulty understanding and the government rarely honored.

Catlin's first catalogue, published that fall, contained 494 entries, but fewer paintings, as he sometimes assigned more than one number to each.[47] Many portraits, some still unfinished, were generously documented by statements from General Clark, John Dougherty, Kenneth McKenzie, James Schoolcraft, and other Indian authorities whom the artist had met on his travels. Catlin also spent time that fall on *Letters and Notes,* which was progressing rapidly, he said in the catalogue commentary, although it would not appear for another four years. Promoting the Indian Gallery was his major concern, however. When he was not lecturing, or attending to exhibition matters, he was entertaining visiting dignitaries with a flair and style all his own. Philip Hone, the observant, all-purpose New Yorker, wrote in his diary on December 6, 1837:

I went this morning by invitation of the proprietor, Mr. Catlin, to see his great collection of paintings, consisting of portraits of Indian chiefs, landscapes, ceremonies, etc., of the Indian tribes, and implements of husbandry, and the chase, weapons of war, costumes, etc., which he collected during his travels of five or six years in the great West. The enthusiasm, zeal, and perseverance with which he has followed up this pursuit are admirable. I have seldom witnessed so interesting an exhibition. Among the invited guests were Mr. Webster, some of the members of the Common Council, the mayor, and some of the newspaper editors. We had a collation of buffaloes' tongues, and venison and the waters of the great spring, and smoked the calumet of peace under an Indian tent formed of buffalo skins.[48]

Catlin ceased lecturing and closed his exhibition late in December when he learned of the imprisonment of Osceola (fig. 28; no. 308) and his warriors in Fort Moultrie, South Carolina, at the conclusion of the Seminole War. Responding to a commission from the Bureau of Indian Affairs, and deeply concerned over the fate of the prisoners, the artist sailed down to Charleston to interview and paint portraits of the Seminole leaders (nos. 300-310), the last such effort he would make in the United States.[49]

In late January, after about two weeks at Fort Moultrie, Catlin returned to New York with the portraits more or less complete, and promptly placed them on display at the Stuyvesant Institute.[50] He intended, no doubt, to use the public sympathy generated by Osceola's death to call attention to the severe Indian policy of the Jackson Administration. But he also knew that the controversy, and the addition of the unique Seminole portraits, would make his collection more valuable. A full-length print of Osceola, copyrighted February 27, 1828, had been selling well during the exhibition, and the time must have seemed right to press his advantage in Washington.

Catlin had begun his campaign a year earlier. In the previous session of Congress the purchase of the Indian Gallery had come up for discussion, most likely at his instigation, although Daniel Webster and others may have already been working for him. Catlin's aggressive position had become clear in his response to a *National Intelligencer* editorial of September 29, 1837, describing the reluctance of Sioux delegates in Washington to pose for the artist Charles Bird King. It made no difference, Catlin claimed, as he had most of their portraits in his collection anyway.[51] On April 9, 1838, Catlin opened his combined exhibition and lecture series at the Old Theater on Louisiana Avenue, according to the multitude of broadsides that were distributed at the time (fig. 29). Initial attendance was less than anticipated, one learns

Figure 28. *Osceola, the Black Drink (full length),* Seminole, 1838, no. 308. American Museum of Natural History, New York.

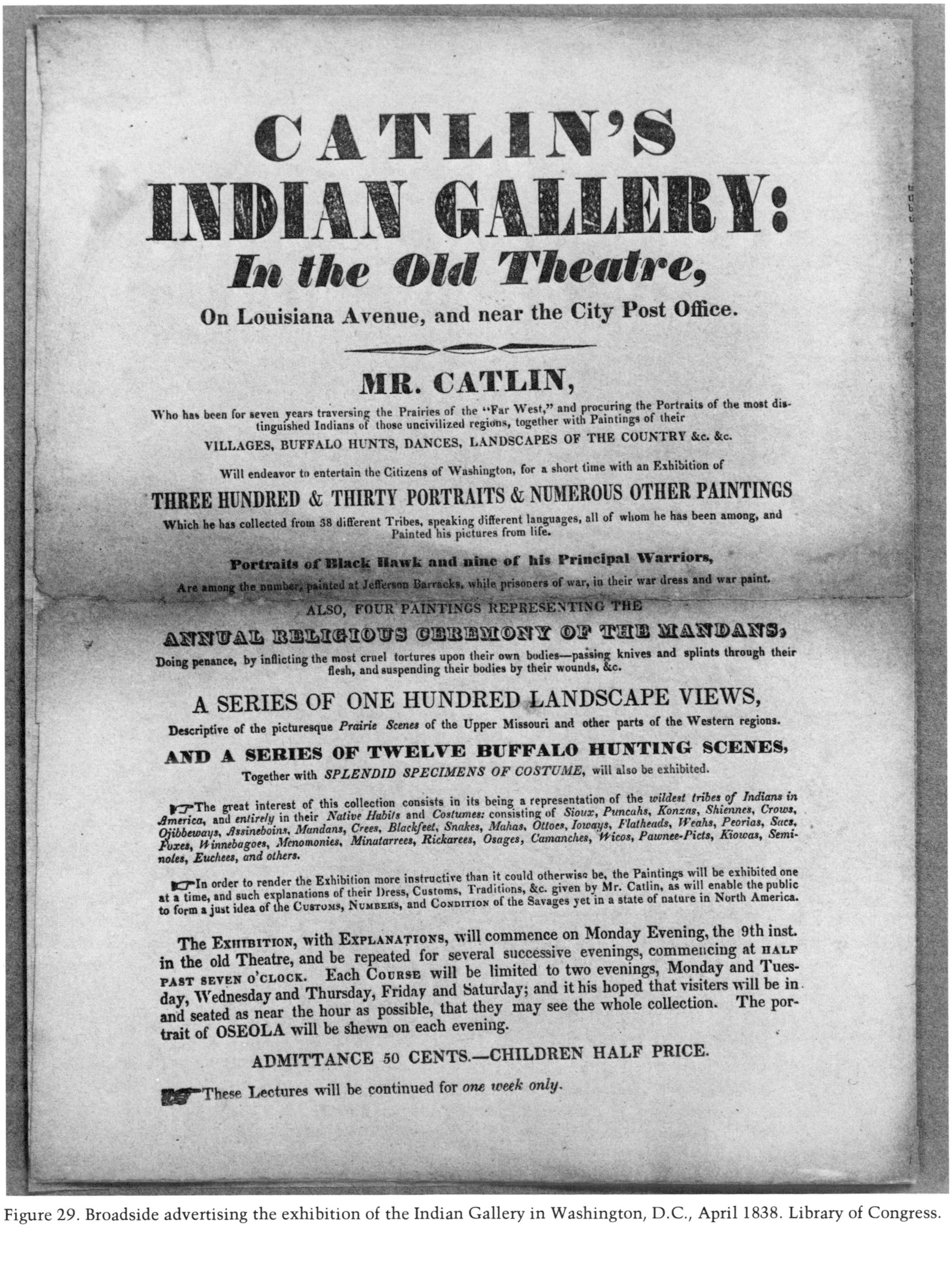

CATLIN'S INDIAN GALLERY:
In the Old Theatre,
On Louisiana Avenue, and near the City Post Office.

MR. CATLIN,

Who has been for seven years traversing the Prairies of the "Far West," and procuring the Portraits of the most distinguished Indians of those uncivilized regions, together with Paintings of their

VILLAGES, BUFFALO HUNTS, DANCES, LANDSCAPES OF THE COUNTRY &c. &c.

Will endeavor to entertain the Citizens of Washington, for a short time with an Exhibition of

THREE HUNDRED & THIRTY PORTRAITS & NUMEROUS OTHER PAINTINGS

Which he has collected from 38 different Tribes, speaking different languages, all of whom he has been among, and Painted his pictures from life.

Portraits of Black Hawk and nine of his Principal Warriors,

Are among the number, painted at Jefferson Barracks, while prisoners of war, in their war dress and war paint.

ALSO, FOUR PAINTINGS REPRESENTING THE

ANNUAL RELIGIOUS CEREMONY OF THE MANDANS,

Doing penance, by inflicting the most cruel tortures upon their own bodies—passing knives and splints through their flesh, and suspending their bodies by their wounds, &c.

A SERIES OF ONE HUNDRED LANDSCAPE VIEWS,

Descriptive of the picturesque *Prairie Scenes* of the Upper Missouri and other parts of the Western regions.

AND A SERIES OF TWELVE BUFFALO HUNTING SCENES,

Together with *SPLENDID SPECIMENS OF COSTUME*, will also be exhibited.

☞The great interest of this collection consists in its being a representation of the *wildest tribes of Indians in America*, and *entirely* in their *Native Habits* and *Costumes:* consisting of *Sioux, Puncahs, Konzas, Shiennes, Crows, Ojibbeways, Assineboins, Mandans, Crees, Blackfeet, Snakes, Mahas, Ottoes, Ioways, Flatheads, Weahs, Peorias, Sacs, Foxes, Winnebagoes, Menomonies, Minatarrees, Rickarees, Osages, Camanches, Wicos, Pawnee-Picts, Kiowas, Seminoles, Euchees, and others.*

☞In order to render the Exhibition more instructive than it could otherwise be, the Paintings will be exhibited one at a time, and such explanations of their Dress, Customs, Traditions, &c. given by Mr. Catlin, as will enable the public to form a just idea of the CUSTOMS, NUMBERS, and CONDITION of the Savages yet in a state of nature in North America.

The EXHIBITION, with EXPLANATIONS, will commence on Monday Evening, the 9th inst. in the old Theatre, and be repeated for several successive evenings, commencing at HALF PAST SEVEN O'CLOCK. Each COURSE will be limited to two evenings, Monday and Tuesday, Wednesday and Thursday, Friday and Saturday; and it his hoped that visiters will be in and seated as near the hour as possible, that they may see the whole collection. The portrait of OSEOLA will be shewn on each evening.

ADMITTANCE 50 CENTS.—CHILDREN HALF PRICE.

☞These Lectures will be continued for *one week only*.

Figure 29. Broadside advertising the exhibition of the Indian Gallery in Washington, D.C., April 1838. Library of Congress.

from the *National Intelligencer,* perhaps because Catlin had so often criticized the administration's Indian policy. But his father reported from Utica that George had had "as much applause as he could expect or wish," and Washington insiders claimed that the government was prepared to pay $150,000 for the Indian Gallery.[52] No offer was forthcoming, however; Congress failed to act and Catlin decided to take the collection on tour for the remainder of the summer and early fall. He began in Baltimore on July 4, moved on to Philadelphia, July 23, where his collection received more praise from the press than in Washington, if we can judge from the collected notices at the end of Catlin's London catalogue of 1848. One reviewer, referring either to the July 1838 exhibition, or the one that followed in April 1839, stated that the Indian Gallery was "not merely a minute and thorough description of a nation whose situation and history render everything that relates to it in the highest degree curious and personal to Americans, but it addresses itself to the admiration and instruction of every philosophic mind as an encyclopedia picture of the savage state."[53]

The tour ended in Boston. Catlin commenced a series of lectures at Amory Hall on August 16, according to Haberly, but he could not find space to hang the Indian Gallery until mid-September, when he obtained use of Faneuil Hall, rent free, for one month. The mayor had apparently urged Catlin to seek space in the historic building, implying that it would be granted as a public benefit and as a tribute to the artist's mission.[54] The collection remained there until mid-October, when Catlin packed it off to rooms in New York he had rented for the winter.

In spite of the critical success of the tour, Catlin had done no better than break even on expenses over the summer, and prospects had not improved for selling his collection to the government. He considered again the public threats he had made in Washington to take his collection abroad—threats that were, in fact, part of a scheme he had developed long before, perhaps recalling how the acclaim received by James Fenimore Cooper and Washington Irving during their visits to England had served their reputations in America.[55] But he was not anxious to depart until he had tested the ground once more. After a winter spent touching up paintings and editing his notes, he reopened the collection in New York in March, and then sent it to Philadelphia in April for a much-praised return engagement. In each case he announced that he would soon take it abroad. Newspaper editors reacted as he had hoped, expressing dismay that the government would allow the collection to be disposed of to a foreign party. On the side, Catlin lowered the price to $60,000, but still the government was not interested.[56]

The collection was back in New York in June for a final showing at the Stuyvesant Institute, and then Catlin packed it aboard the steamer *Roscius,* which sailed for Liverpool on November 25, 1839. The departure was marked by more extravagant praise in the New York newspapers, but none of it was as effective as the simple words Philip Hone penned in his diary on November 29: "Mr. Catlin, the Indian traveler, sailed on Monday last . . . for London. . . . He will shew the greatest and most interesting collection of the raw material of America that has ever been on their side of the water."[57]

2

Abroad: For European Audiences

The eight tons of freight that comprised the Indian Gallery were finally deposited in Egyptian Hall (fig. 30), a popular London exhibition gallery, in early January 1840. The hall has been secured by Catlin at the suggestion of his English friend Charles Murray, a fellow traveler on the Great Plains, who would, in his position as Master of the Queen's Household, render many services to the artist.[1] On February 1, after a private viewing for members of the nobility and the press, Catlin opened the exhibition to the public. A new catalogue had been issued, with the tribes rearranged and the entries expanded and renumbered.[2] On the walls were banked some 485 portraits, landscapes, and scenes of Indian life, more finished by this time, one would assume, than for his American tour. In the center of the room stood a tall, white, Crow tipi, beautifully decorated with a series of hunting and battle scenes, and around this the artist had arranged, perhaps on screens, several thousand Indian costumes, weapons, and domestic utensils.

Catlin was elated by the initial response to his Indian Gallery and his lectures. European scientists and men of letters, whose distance from American shores made them both more objective and more extravagant in their theories about savage cultures, were eager to learn whatever they could from the artist and his collection. But no less satisfying to the "backwoodsman" from America was his triumph in London society. He had prepared carefully for the trip with letters of introduction from Henry Clay, Thomas Sully, Benjamin Silliman, and probably numerous others, and once reports of his engaging charm and the colorful stories of his travels began to circulate, he was embraced by the fashionable world. Catlin became, in effect, as much of a show as his collection, and after a month as a celebrity he wrote home to his parents, scarcely able to conceal his pride:

You will rejoice to hear that I am well, although almost half crazy with the bustle and excitement I have been continuously under in this great and splendid city—amongst nobody but strangers. . . . I have had the trembling excitements and fears to contend with which beset & besiege a green horn from the backwoods when making his *Debut* & his bow to the most polite and fastidious part of the whole world—I have kept as cool as possible—have pursued steadily and unflinchingly my course, and have at last succeeded in making what they call a "decided hit."'

Unhappily, this euphoria could not last. Catlin was spending the admission fees as quickly as they came in to meet overhead expenses, to repay a debt to "Mr. Gregory" (Clara's father or brother), and to carry on a social life he could not afford.[4] When Clara arrived in London at the end of June with their two daughters (the first was born in December 1837, the second a year later), he rented expensive rooms, just at the time attendance at Egyptian Hall was dropping off. His letter of June 29 tells optimistically of purchase prospects and exhibition plans in France, Edinburgh, or St. Petersburg, making one suspicious that he had already gone into debt on expectations. And the company he was keeping could only add to his problems. The last half of the letter to his parents describes an elaborate reception that he and Clara had recently attended in the Grand Hall of Buckingham Palace.[5]

During the fall, Catlin was able to make progress on *Letters and Notes*, now less than a year from publication, and to devise a means of reviving interest in the Indian Gallery. Clara wrote in October that he was lecturing at night by gaslight, with dummies in Indian costume serving to illustrate his text.[6] This was supplemented later in the fall by what Catlin called *Tableaux Vivants* (fig. 31), staged recreations of Indian dances, songs, and war-making ritual. Twenty white men, including Burr Catlin, the artist's nephew, took part in these events—dressed, shaved, and painted to imitate as nearly as possible the appearance of Plains Indians (fig. 32).[7] The tableaux became even more effective several years later when Ojibwa and Iowa warriors took over for their white counterparts, anticipating the Wild West shows that would tour Europe in the 1880s.

Despite Catlin's efforts, receipts from Egyptian Hall continued to decline. Clara had written home that the exhibition would never do more than break even, but George, certain that he would eventually succeed, was careless of debt and determined to carry out his plans.[8]

Figure 30. *Egyptian Hall*, lithograph from *London As It Is* by Thomas Shotter Boys, 1842. The elaborate facade of the hall, with banners advertising the Indian Gallery, stands just behind the street construction in the right foreground. Library of Congress.

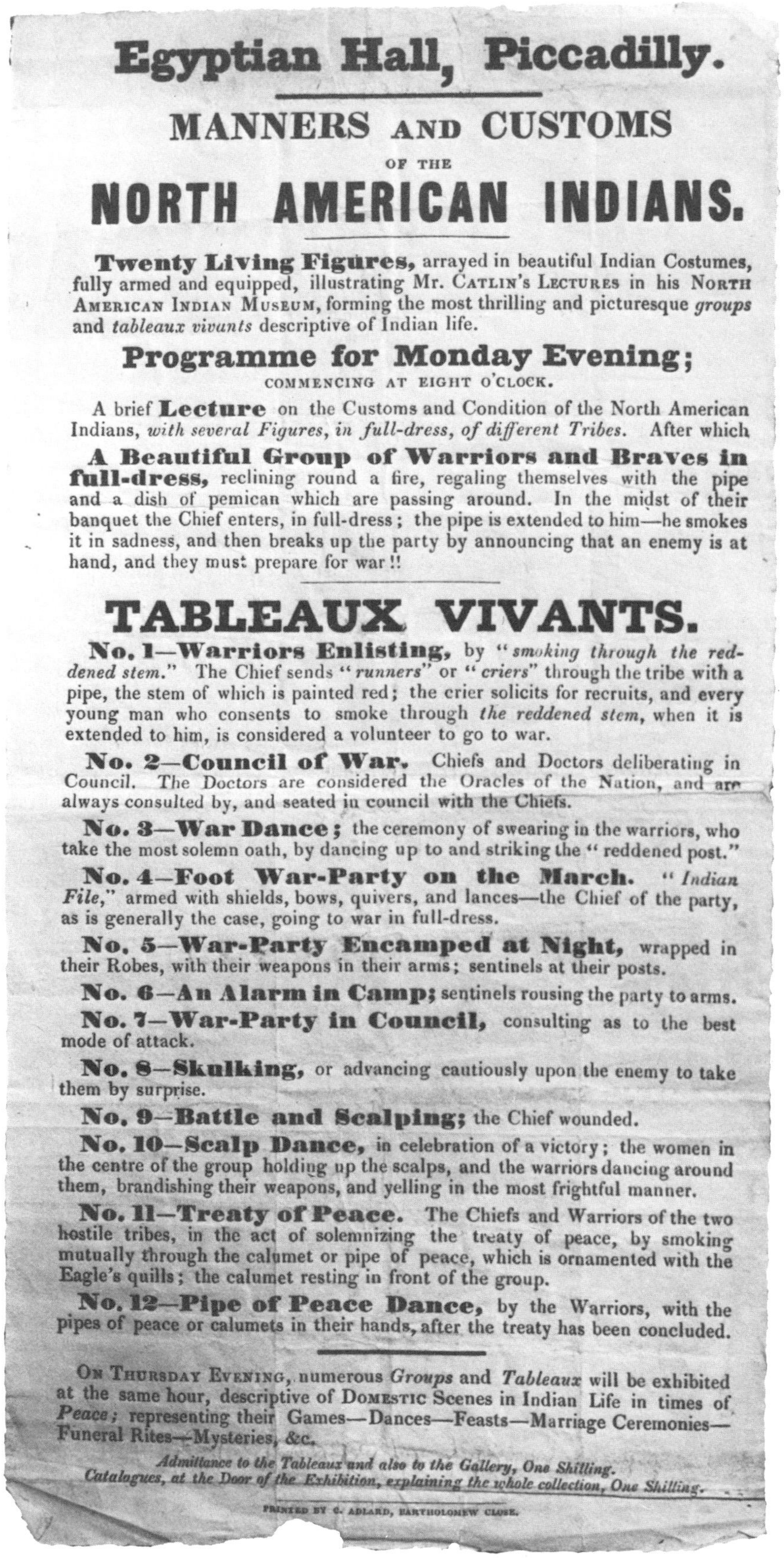

Egyptian Hall, Piccadilly.

MANNERS AND CUSTOMS OF THE NORTH AMERICAN INDIANS.

Twenty Living Figures, arrayed in beautiful Indian Costumes, fully armed and equipped, illustrating Mr. CATLIN'S LECTURES in his NORTH AMERICAN INDIAN MUSEUM, forming the most thrilling and picturesque *groups* and *tableaux vivants* descriptive of Indian life.

Programme for Monday Evening;

COMMENCING AT EIGHT O'CLOCK.

A brief **Lecture** on the Customs and Condition of the North American Indians, *with several Figures, in full-dress, of different Tribes.* After which

A Beautiful Group of Warriors and Braves in full-dress, reclining round a fire, regaling themselves with the pipe and a dish of pemican which are passing around. In the midst of their banquet the Chief enters, in full-dress; the pipe is extended to him—he smokes it in sadness, and then breaks up the party by announcing that an enemy is at hand, and they must prepare for war!!

TABLEAUX VIVANTS.

No. 1—Warriors Enlisting, by "*smoking through the reddened stem.*" The Chief sends "*runners*" or "*criers*" through the tribe with a pipe, the stem of which is painted red; the crier solicits for recruits, and every young man who consents to smoke through *the reddened stem,* when it is extended to him, is considered a volunteer to go to war.

No. 2—Council of War. Chiefs and Doctors deliberating in Council. The Doctors are considered the Oracles of the Nation, and are always consulted by, and seated in council with the Chiefs.

No. 3—War Dance; the ceremony of swearing in the warriors, who take the most solemn oath, by dancing up to and striking the "reddened post."

No. 4—Foot War-Party on the March. "*Indian File,*" armed with shields, bows, quivers, and lances—the Chief of the party, as is generally the case, going to war in full-dress.

No. 5—War-Party Encamped at Night, wrapped in their Robes, with their weapons in their arms; sentinels at their posts.

No. 6—An Alarm in Camp; sentinels rousing the party to arms.

No. 7—War-Party in Council, consulting as to the best mode of attack.

No. 8—Skulking, or advancing cautiously upon the enemy to take them by surprise.

No. 9—Battle and Scalping; the Chief wounded.

No. 10—Scalp Dance, in celebration of a victory; the women in the centre of the group holding up the scalps, and the warriors dancing around them, brandishing their weapons, and yelling in the most frightful manner.

No. 11—Treaty of Peace. The Chiefs and Warriors of the two hostile tribes, in the act of solemnizing the treaty of peace, by smoking mutually through the calumet or pipe of peace, which is ornamented with the Eagle's quills; the calumet resting in front of the group.

No. 12—Pipe of Peace Dance, by the Warriors, with the pipes of peace or calumets in their hands, after the treaty has been concluded.

ON THURSDAY EVENING, numerous *Groups* and *Tableaux* will be exhibited at the same hour, descriptive of DOMESTIC Scenes in Indian Life in times of *Peace;* representing their Games—Dances—Feasts—Marriage Ceremonies—Funeral Rites—Mysteries, &c.

Admittance to the Tableaux and also to the Gallery, One Shilling. Catalogues, at the Door of the Exhibition, explaining the whole collection, One Shilling.

PRINTED BY C. ADLARD, BARTHOLOMEW CLOSE.

Figure 31. Broadside advertising *Tableaux Vivants,* performed in Egyptian Hall, 1840-1841. Gilcrease Institute, Tulsa.

When in the spring of 1841 he was unable to find a publisher for *Letters and Notes,* he decided to finance the venture himself. Most of the $8,500 needed to produce the two volumes would go to cover the cost of the 312 illustrations Catlin had carefully drawn after examples from the Indian Gallery.[9] Much of the money he raised by subscription, and he saved more by managing the layout, printing, and distribution of the book himself. When it finally appeared in October 1841, it consisted of a curious blend of storytelling and perceptive reporting. Loyd Haberly's criticism is much to the point when he calls it "unbalanced," "hasty," and "wordy."[10] Its accuracy is questionable on many counts, and the chronology seems designed to confuse the reader at every turn. Yet *Letters and Notes* remains one of the seminal texts of the period. Much of Plains Indian ethnology is still based on what Catlin observed and recorded during his travels, and his literary talents often surpassed his skill with a paint brush. His descriptions of the endless prairie landscape, of wild chieftains and sacred tribal rituals, are as lucid and compelling as any to be found in journals of that phase of western history. And this was only one aspect of his talent. In the midst of a sublime passage, Catlin could lapse into a droll dialogue between two French Canadian trappers that was not much beneath the vernacular effects achieved later on by Mark Twain or Bret Harte. But the more substantive portions of the text, for purposes of this study, are those rambling soliloquies in which he reveals his motives for painting savages and describing the life they led. Nowhere in contemporary literature does one find a more forceful exaltation of the American wilderness and its inhabitants, of nature and the natural order as a fundamental guide to divine truth. What attracted Americans to their native environment in the 1830s, one learns from these passages, is implicit in every picture Catlin painted and every line he wrote.

The book was generously received by the British press, Catlin reported later in his *Notes of Eight Years' Travels and Residence in Europe,* citing pages of reviews from prominent literary journals and newspapers. Among the group is one from the *London Morning Chronicle* that begins with a humorous parody of the author's own words: "Mr. Catlin ventures alone and unaided before the public," and then continues with praise for the author's vivid style:

> What he has seen in the prairie, and noted down in its solitude, he sends forth, with all the wildness and freshness of nature about it. This, together with his free and easy conversational style, plentifully sprinkled with Americanisms, gives a peculiar charm to his descriptions, which are not merely animated or life-like, but *life* itself. The reader is made to believe himself in the desert, or lying among friendly Indians in the wigwam, or hurried along in the excitement of the chase. He is constantly surrounded by the figures of the red man, and hears the rustle of their feathers, or the dash of their half-tamed steeds as they bound by him.[11]

The American press was apparently no less enthusiastic about the book, but a bit more perceptive in judging its merits. The *United States Democratic Review,* for example, noted that Catlin "paints in glowing colors the high spirits and noble traits of the savages," but "hardly does justice to the bold and untiring backwoodsmen." Yet there was great

Figure 32. *Theodore Burr Catlin in Indian Costume,* 1840-1841.
National Collection of Fine Arts.

value in Catlin's "strong Indian partiality," the reviewer conceded, and he ended by endorsing *Letters and Notes* as "the most valuable work on the inhabitants of the vast untrodden west which has been as yet produced."[12]

Favorable press notices did not sell a fifty-shilling book, however. Catlin was obliged to place many copies in the hands of publishers in England and America for distribution, thus ending any chance of the profit he had hoped for. Returns from Egyptian Hall were also disappointing, and the lease was not renewed for a third year. In the spring of 1842, to reduce living expenses, he moved his growing family to a small but comfortable cottage in Waltham Green (he now had three children, another daughter had been born July or August 1841), and then took advantage of an invitation to show the Indian Gallery at the Mechanics Institute in Liverpool, where it remained through the summer of 1842. From late fall until May 1843, leaving his collection behind, Catlin barnstormed through provincial towns with

his London troupe of Indian dancers. They performed, with "varied success," the mock ritual of the *Tableaux Vivants* in Chester, Manchester, Leamington, Rugby, Stratford-on-Avon, Cheltenham, Sheffield, Leeds, York, Hull, Edinburgh, Glasgow, Paisley, Greenock, Belfast, and Dublin, according to the order of Catlin's list.[13]

At the conclusion of the tour Catlin returned to Manchester and reopened the Indian Gallery. This would be the last showing before he took the collection back to America, he told the press and promised his family, but instead he succumbed to a somewhat unscrupulous Canadian promoter, Arthur Rankin, who came to England with a troop of Ojibwa during the spring of 1843. Rankin argued that authentic *Tableaux Vivants* would again make the Indian Gallery a paying proposition, and Catlin wanted very much to believe him.

One might point to this episode as an ominous sign for the future, as the moment in Catlin's career when he became less a spokesman than a promoter. He returned to London, arranged for the Ojibwa to perform before Queen Victoria (fig. 33; P. T. Barnum did the same for Tom Thumb a year later), and took a six-month lease on Egyptian Hall, which must have lasted almost to the end of the year. The Ojibwa did prove to be a popular attraction (see fig. 34; nos. 508-16), and Catlin worked hard to make the most of their routine. Charles Dickens, who visited the collection one evening, was impressed by the persuasive talents of the artist, if not by the performances themselves. With evident distaste, he described the Indians as "squatting and spitting" on a table in the center of the Hall, or "dancing their miserable jigs, after their own dreary manner," while Catlin, "in all good faith, called upon his civilised audiences to take notice of their symmetry and grace, their perfect limps, and the exquisite expression of their pantomime; and his civilised audience, in all good faith, complied and admired."[14] After a month or two, however, the audiences were not so easily convinced. Many resented the changed aspect of the Indian Gallery, and Catlin for the first time was accused of exploiting his collection. A disagreement with Rankin ended the engagement three months early, and Catlin retired to the country (a letter of September 1843 places him outside of Manchester) to work on the text and lithographs of his *North American Indian Portfolio*, a selection of hunting scenes, dances, and sporting contests, based on examples from the Indian Gallery, that he published early in 1844 (figs. 35, 128).[15]

Catlin promised his family (which now included his young son George, born November 1843) that the *Portfolio* would be his last attempt abroad to recoup his finances, and Clara wrote to her mother-in-law (Putnam was now dead) that she hoped they would all come home in the autumn of 1844.[16] The arrival of a party of Iowa Indians (fig. 36) changed Catlin's mind, however. His chance to cash in on the Indian Gallery, despite his family's wishes, was even more tempting this time. He remembered several of the Iowa from his western travels, and he sensed that the warriors, a proud and colorful group whom he painted with unusual care (see nos. 517-24), would be effective on stage. He engaged their services in the summer of 1844, his hope renewed, and soon the Indian Gallery was back in Egyptian Hall, the

Figure 33. Ojibwa Dancing before Queen Victoria, engraving. *Travels in Europe,* 1848, plate 6.

Figure 34. Ojibwa Troupe in London, 1844, watercolor. Gilcrease Institute, Tulsa.

Figure 35. *Indian Scalp Dance,* lithograph. *Catlin's North American Indian Portfolio,* 1844, plate 31.

Iowa performing at night in place of the Ojibwa and visiting the usual sights about London by day. This lasted until late autumn, when Catlin and G. H. Melody, their American sponsor, took the Iowa on tour to Birmingham, Newcastle-on-Tyne, Edinburgh, Dundee, Perth, Glasgow, Greenock, Dublin, Liverpool, and Manchester. Because of the tight schedule, Catlin was forced to regret a "friendly" invitation from Sir William Drummond Stewart, whose Murthly Castle and collection of Alfred Jacob Miller paintings (fig. 37) were located only a few miles from Perth.[17]

Although the Iowa suffered much illness during the winter of

1844-45 (two Indians died; one in Scotland, the other in Liverpool), they agreed to accompany Catlin to Paris in the spring. There they would find, one can hear him promising, a suitable climate, lively entertainment, and more supportive audiences. Unhappily for the Iowa, none of this quite came true, and for Catlin, the decision to extend the tour of the Indian Gallery to France was ultimately a disaster. His initial success in Paris, however, probably made him think his troubles were over (fig. 38). Following his arrival in early April 1845, he engaged the Salle Valentino in the rue St. Honoré, put out a French edition of his catalogue (which included the Iowa portraits), and opened his exhibi-

Figure 36. Iowa Indians with interpreter and sponsor. Engraving after a daguerreotype, from *The Iowa,* by W. H. Miner, 1911.

Figure 37. Alfred Jacob Miller, *Scene at "Rendezvous,"* 1859-1860, watercolor. Walters Art Gallery, Baltimore.

Figure 38. *Les Indiens à Paris,* 1845. Lithograph advertising music composed in honor of Catlin's Indian troupe. Library of the National Collection of Fine Arts and National Portrait Gallery.

tion on June 3 to the acclaim of the French press, which seemed most intrigued by Catlin's straightforward method of recording his Indian subjects:

Il est très heureux que M. Catlin ait été seulement assez peintre pour faire tout bonnement sur la toile ce qu'il voyait, sans parti pris d'avance et sans convention européenne. Nous avons ainsi des steppes dont nous ne nous faisions pas une image, des buffles prodigieux, des chasses fantastiques, et une foule d'aspects et de scènes plus intéressantes l'une que l'autre. Ici, c'est un marais vert tendre, entouré d'arbres sveltes et légers. Là, c'est la plaine infinie avec ses grandes herbes mouvantes comme les vagues d'une mer sans repos, et l'on aperçoit une course diabolique de quelques animaux dont on a peine à distinguer la forme et qui fendent l'immensité.[18]

Louis Philippe, who had spent two years of exile (1797-99) traveling in America and was familiar with Catlin's publication, received the Iowa at the Tuileries (fig. 39) even before the exhibition opened, and talked at length with the artist about his past experiences among the Indians. George Sand and Victor Hugo came several times to the Salle Valentino, Catlin toured the Louvre with Baron von Humboldt, and Prosper Mérimée tried to persuade the French government to purchase the collection.[19] Further recognition came when long passages from *Letters and Notes,* accompanied by engraved copies of the plates, appeared in the weekly *l'Illustration,* and the young critic Charles Baudelaire singled out for praise two portraits (figs. 15, 40; nos. 149, 521) that Catlin entered in the Salon of 1846.[20] Amid these triumphs, however, Catlin lost his wife, who died of pneumonia in July 1845, and the Iowa, having had their fill of European travel, returned home. The Indian Gallery thus remained a liability until late summer, when a group of Ojibwa (nos. 531-42) from England took over the stage at the Salle Valentino, but even so the receipts were dwindling. Fortunately, the Ojibwa were invited to entertain the royal family at Saint-Cloud (fig. 41) in early October, and Louis Philippe was so pleased with the performance that he offered Catlin, whose lease on the Salle Valentino expired at the end of the month, gallery space in the Louvre. The

Figure 39. Karl Girardet, *Louis-Philippe, assistant, dans un salon des Tuileries, à la danse des Indiens Novas,* 1845. Musée de Versailles.

artist reinstalled the collection in the Salle de Séance (fig. 42), and subsequent visits by the King led to a commission for fifteen copies of Indian Gallery subjects.[21] At the close of the Louvre exhibition, which was apparently of six weeks' duration, Catlin stored his collection and took the Ojibwa on the road, scheduling performances in Brussels, Antwerp, and Ghent.[22] However, the tour never got farther than Brussels, where eight of the Indians contracted smallpox. Two died, and Catlin stayed with the others until they recovered. In January 1846 they departed for England, the artist remaining behind, greatly relieved and much the wiser. He never again attempted to stage these Wild West performances.

Catlin returned to Paris, took rooms for himself and his four small children, and set to work on the replicas ordered by Louis Philippe. This commission and others that followed appear to have been his sole means of support from the beginning of 1846 to the end of his career, and he must have been particularly pressed between 1846

Figure 40. *Little Wolf, a famous warrior,* Iowa, 1844, no. 521.

Figure 41. Ojibwa at Saint-Cloud, engraving. *Travels in Europe*, 1848, plate 21.

Figure 42. Catlin's Collection in the Salle de Séance, engraving. *Travels in Europe*, 1848, plate 22.

Figure 43. Thomas P. Rossiter, *A Studio Reception, Paris, 1841* (including John F. Kensett, Daniel Huntington, G. P. A. Healy, Asher B. Durand, and possibly John Vanderlyn). Albany Institute of History and Art.

and 1852, when the care of his children was his foremost concern. The sale of his collection, of course, was still his chief hope for financial salvation, and he cast about again for potential customers. A letter of February 17, 1846, to Sir Thomas Phillipps, who amassed one of the largest book and manuscript collections in Victorian England, asks for help in placing the Indian Gallery with the British Museum, or an interested nobleman, at a suggested price of $35,000. This may have been an indirect means of asking Phillipps himself if he were interested, or simply an attempt to follow up an earlier offer the artist supposedly had received from an English peer.[23] Catlin also sent off a memorial to the United States Congress on April 2, once again offering his collection for $65,000. Two additional memorials followed in support of Catlin's cause, the first sent by a group of American artists then working in Paris, whom, oddly enough, Catlin never once mentions in his writings (fig. 43). Among the signers were such impressive figures as John Vanderlyn, William Morris Hunt, and John F. Kensett. Perhaps only a question of national patronage could have caused three such

disparate artists to place their names on the same document. The second memorial, from a group of American citizens resident in London, included such prominent signers as Thomas Aspinwall, George Peabody, John Lord, and George Palmer Putnam. The Joint Committee on the Library, to whom the memorials were submitted, proposed amending the recent bill that had established the Smithsonian Institution to include the purchase of Catlin's collection, but there the matter seems to have rested for the next two years.[24]

In the meantime, Catlin's work on Louis Philippe's paintings was interrupted by the death of his young son, of typhoid, in the late summer of 1846. He refers to the occasion in *Travels in Europe* as a sad twist of fate, never once admitting that his obsession to publicize the Indian Gallery had caused unaccountable hardship for his family. Equally blind to his dismal prospects in the fall of 1846, he refused an offer made to him in London by Henry Schoolcraft that would have solved just about all his immediate problems. With sanction from Congress all but guaranteed, Schoolcraft was compiling a major work on the North American Indians in which he wished to use a number of Catlin's paintings as illustrations. Schoolcraft's publication was bound to be a success, and he had influence enough at home to secure passage of the stalled proposal to purchase Catlin's collection. Catlin chose not to bargain, however. He was reluctant to share his work, and he apparently felt confident that congressional action was assured without Schoolcraft's help. Two and a half years later, the bill to purchase the Indian Gallery failed in the Senate by one vote.

Louis Philippe's first commission (see nos. 428, 449; the fifteen paintings were probably delivered by the end of the year) was followed by an order for a series of twenty-nine paintings commemorating the voyages of LaSalle in North America (figs. 44, 45). The King promised Catlin about $100 apiece, but payment was never made.[25] After seven months' work, with the series nearly complete, mobs once again took over the streets of Paris.[26] The King and Queen fled the country in February 1848, and Catlin was advised to follow. Although his studio was broken into, he did manage to escape to England with his three daughters and his collection. He later retrieved the LaSalle paintings, and probably a number from the previous commission (see no. 449), an indication that the King had paid little or nothing on any of the forty-four paintings he had ordered.

Catlin had been busy with other projects in 1846 and 1847, however. He claims to have submitted a design for a mural, *Boone's Entrance into Kentucky*, for the rotunda of the United States Capitol, after Henry Inman's death, and he continued to add to his original collection.[27] Six hundred and seven titles (representing about 585 paintings) appear in the final catalogue of his Indian Gallery, published in 1848 at Number 6, Waterloo Place, London, where the artist maintained a combined residence, studio, and showroom after he fled France (fig. 46).[28] Numbers 543 through 607, which follow the Ojibwa and Iowa portraits, are mostly hunting and battle scenes designed to appeal to European audiences (fig. 47; see nos. 558, 585, 603). Catlin also published in 1848 his account of *Eight Years' Travels and Residence in Europe*, intended as a sequel to *Letters and Notes*.[29] The former, however, has none of the careful observation or sustained narrative impact of the latter. *Travels in Europe* is a careless, windy series of anecdotes, describing the bewildered reaction of the Ojibwa and Iowa to European civilization. The subject had great potential, but Catlin's treatment lacks the thoughtful interpretation he gave to *Letters and Notes*, in which he had developed the opposite theme—the compatability of the savage to his native surroundings. Perhaps the most objectionable aspect of the book, the author's pandering to what he supposed was his countrymen's insatiable curiosity about European nobility, was simply a tasteless stratagem to boost sales. The book was not a critical success, according to Haberly,[30] and if the author's intention was to make money, he was probably disappointed by the modest return.

From all accounts, Catlin was seeking any means to relieve his debts as the years passed. He was not forgotten by the public, but his attempts to convert his reputation into a comfortable living had mostly failed. The first signed and dated copies of his original collection began to appear in the late 1840s, along with the specialty items Catlin called "Albums Unique." These were handsomely bound sets of reduced line drawings (sometimes tracings) taken from subjects in the Indian Gallery. Each consisted of a short introduction and a number of illustrations, accompanied by handwritten texts of varying lengths. In 1851—with two costumed figures from the Indian Gallery on display, beside Hiram Powers's *Greek Slave*, at the Crystal Palace (fig. 48)—he agreed to paint fifty-five copies, at the modest price of two pounds (or about ten dollars) each, to repay a debt to his friend Sir Thomas Phillipps. To be sure, these were smaller (11 by 14 inches) than standard sizes, but even larger copies were not selling for more than fifty dollars each. That must have been one reason why Catlin wrote the next year (June 24, 1852) from Paris to the Library Committee of the United States Senate, urging reconsideration of the Indian Gallery at the reduced figure of $50,000.[31] The other was necessity. By then the artist desperately needed the money to save his collection and to stay out of debtor's prison should he ever return to England.

In the early spring of 1852, Catlin's debts, speculation, bad judgment, and misguided ambition had finally caught up with him. One learns from the Phillipps correspondence that he had been living on credit for many years, borrowing against his collection with the expectation that someday it would be sold to the government. But what brought matters to a crisis in the early 1850s was the collapse of a Texas land company in which he had invested heavily several years before.[32] Creditors closed in, Catlin was thrown in jail, and Dudley Gregory came abroad to escort his nieces back to New Jersey.[33] When Catlin was released from prison, probably at Gregory's request, he retreated to Paris and issued the urgent appeal to the Senate Library Committee to prevent an auction sale, already once postponed, of the Indian Gallery. Despite strong efforts by Daniel Webster and William H. Seward, the Senate once again rejected Catlin's proposal, and had the American locomotive manufacturer Joseph Harrison not stopped in London that summer, on his return from Russia, the collection might well have been dispersed.[34] Fortunately, Harrison was able to pay off the major creditors in time and gain possession of the collection, which he shipped back to his boiler factory in Philadelphia. Catlin had apparently rescued a number of paintings, sketches, notebooks, and perhaps some watercolors from his studio before the contents were packed, and with these he remained in Paris, most likely to avoid other creditors (his collection had been mortgaged several times over) who had not received satisfaction from Harrison.

A year or two later, seeking refuge in the wilderness, Catlin set sail for South America, where he remained for most of the next seven years, looking for gold, painting Indians, and, it has been suggested, running out the statute of limitations. Once during this period (probably 1854) he crossed the western slopes of the Rockies, and in 1855 he returned briefly to Europe—to London and Berlin. In the latter city he reported his geological findings to Baron von Humboldt, who had explored South America many years earlier. In November 1857, Catlin

Figure 44 *(above). The Expedition Leaving Fort Frontenac on Lake Ontario,* 1847-1848. National Gallery of Art, Washington, D.C. Paul Mellon Collection.

Figure 45 *(right). La Salle Taking Possession of the Land at the Mouth of the Arkansas,* 1847-1848. National Gallery of Art, Washington, D.C. Paul Mellon Collection.

Figure 46. William Fisk, *George Catlin*, 1849. National Portrait Gallery, Washington, D.C.

Figure 47. *Portraits of a grizzly bear and mouse, life size*, 1846-1848, no. 603.*

was in Brussels, and three years later he returned there, taking a small apartment in which he lived as a recluse for the next ten years, attempting to reconstruct his past and his collection.

During his South American wanderings, Catlin had recorded the native tribes and scenery with the same technique he had employed earlier on the Albums Unique. Only the support varied. Outlines of the South American subjects were drawn in pencil or ink on small paperboard panels, easy to manage in the damp climate. If time permitted, the artist filled in details of the composition and added touches of flat, thin color to the costumes and background (fig. 49). The North American tribes west of the Rockies (fig. 50) were also painted in this unique, shorthand style, so that when Catlin finally settled in Brussels he had over 300 of these cartoons, as he called them, in various stages of completion. They formed the basis of his second collection, which grew over the next ten years to twice that number with his decision to reconstitute the original collection in the new medium. Using notes, sketches, and watercolors that still remained in his possession, and illustrations from *Letters and Notes*, he combined and duplicated many of the subjects he had lost to Harrison in 1852. Thus he completed two separate collections during his lifetime, the Indian Gallery and the cartoon collection, consisting of about 600 paintings each. To determine his total production, however, one must add the hundreds of copies he made of these Indian subjects between 1830 and 1870, and many more portraits and miniatures of white men and women done during his travels in the United States.

Catlin continued to write as well as paint during the years in Brussels, publishing new accounts of his travels among the Indians of

North and South America. *Life Amongst the Indians* (1857 and 1861) was a series of tales for "youthful readers," mined from the store of adventures in *Letters and Notes* and the South American journals, and polished with a care unusual for the author. Haberly says that for many years it was regarded as a children's classic. *The Breath of Life* (1865) told of the dangers of sleeping with one's mouth open, instead of closed, as the Indians did, and *Last Rambles Amongst the Indians* (1867) traces the artist's wanderings through South America (and North America west of the Rockies) with a disregard for chronology that easily surpasses the lack of dates in *Letters and Notes*. Perhaps the most important publication from the Brussels years was *O-Kee-Pa* (1867), a detailed account of the Mandan torture ceremony written in response to earlier criticism by Henry Schoolcraft, who had challenged Catlin's account of the ceremony in *Letters and Notes*.[35] One last essay, *The Lifted and Subsided Rocks of America* (1870), presents novel theories to explain geographical phenomena observed during his travels in the 1850s.

Neither the copies of the paintings he was preparing nor his publications seemed to bring in much income, however. In a letter of 1863 or 1864 to George Harvey, he writes, "In my whole life I was never so near starving to death as now. . . . I have a great many paintings ready for sale but here one may as well try to sell the hair from his head as to sell a picture, unless it is a representation of the Miraculous Bambino or the likeness of the holy Virgin, or something of that class."[36] Some of this must have been humorous exaggeration, but Catlin's modest circumstances were also noted by Gen. A. L. Cheltain, American Consul in Brussels in the winter of 1869-70 (fig. 51). "Mr. Catlin was then in good health," he recalls,

and active for one of his advanced years. He was a charming talker, but his hearing was so impaired that it was with great difficulty one could talk to him. He often . . . breakfasted or dined at my hourse *en famille*. His studio was in an obscure street near the Antwerp railroad station, in the northern part of the city. It occupied two rooms on the second floor, one a large front room, in which he exhibited his paintings and did his work; the other, a rear and smaller room, used as a sleeping and store room. Both were scantily furnished. He lived in a frugal way, taking part of his meals in an adjoining restaurant. His expenses were light, not exceeding, I judged, rent and living combined, over five francs per day. He seemed to have few acquaintances, even among his brother artists, many of whom I knew. . . .

He talked to me often about his collection or collections of Indian paintings and sketches, and expressed a hope, as I now recollect, that all his works might be brought together and placed in the hands of the Government of the United States. . . . He evidently felt more anxiety for the future of his life-long work than to execute orders, some of which came from England and a few, I think, from Germany.[37]

The concern Catlin expressed to Cheltain that winter involved more than the future of his two collections. Despite age and reduced circumstances, the artist had launched an elaborate publishing scheme that would, he assured his younger brother Francis, make them both a fortune and convince Congress to purchase the cartoon collection.[38] Catlin had planned a deluxe, folio-size catalogue (perhaps something

Figure 48. United States section of the Great Exhibition. Lithograph by John Absolon, from *Recollections of the Great Exhibition of 1851*, Lloyd Brothers & Co., ed., London, 1851. University of Illinois Library, Urbana.

Figure 49. *Entrance to a Lagoon, Shore of the Amazon,* 1853-1854, cartoon 554. National Gallery of Art, Washington, D.C. Paul Mellon Collection.

Figure 50. *Archery of the Apaches,* 1854-1855, cartoon 178. American Museum of Natural History, New York.

in the form of an expensive Album Unique) to illustrate many of the North American Indian subjects he had lately redone as cartoons. He prepared outlines and captions, which he hoped to reproduce by photolithography, and persuaded Francis to promote the publication in Washington.[39] The scheme, surprisingly, took many months to fail, but in the meantime Catlin had completed his cartoons, and now turned his attention to designing a grand European and Asian tour, including Belgium, Italy, Prussia, Persia, and Russia, before making a triumphant return to his native land.[40] His dreams were such that when the New-York Historical Society asked the price of his collection in February 1870, he replied that he would sell the original and cartoon collections together for $120,000. Not only was the price a fantasy, but he assumed he still had the option to dispose of his original collection, which for the past eighteen years had been rotting away in Harrison's boiler factory in Philadelphia.

By the summer of 1870 Catlin was determined to make a comeback with the cartoons, which he mounted, floor to ceiling, in a "splendid Hall" in Brussels. The exhibition was well received, he wrote Francis, but no further mention was made of a lengthy grand tour.[41] Instead, he packed the collection and sailed for the United States, arriving in New York late in 1870, after an absence of some thirty-two years. The following October he installed his cartoon collection and the LaSalle paintings in the Somerville Gallery on Fifth Avenue, and issued a complete catalogue of the collection. Six hundred and three entries, with "descriptive and instructive" comments, are followed by a notorious itinerary, in which hardly a date or an event corresponds to those in other published sources.[42]

The press generally paid little attention to the exhibition; the interest Catlin had generated in 1837 and 1838 had largely disappeared by 1871. The following February he moved to Washington, where his old friend Joseph Henry, Secretary of the Smithsonian Institution, had invited him to hang the cartoons on the second floor of the Smithsonian building. Catlin and Henry were still hopeful that Congress would take an interest in the paintings, displayed, as they were, so close to the Capitol. It was even proposed in another memorial that the government acquire both the Indian Gallery and the cartoon collection, but the issue never came to a vote. Congress, like the public, no longer considered Indians a desirable complement to the western wilderness. Legislation to create the first national park passed both Houses by unanimous vote in 1872, but the concept Catlin had preached in the 1830s, the preservation of a naturally ordered sphere of savage life, had become anathema to white men in the course of western expansion.

Catlin remained in a small tower room at the Smithsonian, tending his collection, until October 1872, when he fell seriously ill. He lasted two months under the care of his daughters in Jersey City, and then died on December 23, 1872, at the age of seventy-six. He was buried in Brooklyn, in Greenwood Cemetery, beside his wife and son.

Figure 51. Catlin in Brussels, 1868. Original photo in Library of the National Collection of Fine Arts and National Portrait Gallery.

3

Philadelphia Science and the Artist-Naturalist

Pioneers of American science had long found a home in Philadelphia. Since Revolutionary times it had been the acknowledged center for training and research in the field, and by the early nineteenth century, when the study of natural history had become a major concern of learned men everywhere, the city could boast of an impressive concentration of scholars and institutions. A spirit of progress and impending discovery seemed to pervade the atmosphere, and a remarkably sophisticated exchange of information marked the daily course of events in this restless intellectual community. Scientific gatherings were the medium for presenting a variety of topics, from recent advances in medicine to obscure geological theories, but inevitably the discussion would turn to the theme that most intrigued the major talents of the community: the need to discover and classify the mysteries of the New World. Even those adventuresome professionals found it an awesome task. Naturalists were often obliged to travel for months or even years over thousands of miles in order to observe the unique range of flora and fauna on the American continent, and those in control of local societies and museums, committed to the expanding role of science, were constantly seeking more funds and larger quarters to keep pace with this extensive field activity.

Best known among these institutions was the museum that had been founded in 1786 by the self-styled mechanic, inventor, artist, and naturalist, Charles Willson Peale. By the time George Catlin arrived in Philadelphia some thirty-five years later, Peale's Museum had twice outgrown its quarters and was located on the top floor of Independence Hall (fig. 52). There, Peale and his sons had constructed a "world in miniature," a skillfully designed combination of natural history and portrait exhibits that the father dared hope would someday expand to cover the full range of human knowledge. Futile as it may now seem, Peale aimed at nothing less than demonstrating a favorite principle of Enlightenment philosophers—the "inevitable" relationship between man and all aspects of the natural world.

Even in its early years, the museum had a national reputation, and Peale, who was fond of showing the exhibits to all manner of people who passed through Philadelphia, had stories to tell about their various reactions. One of his favorites had to do with separate delegations of Indians who unwittingly paid a visit to the museum on the same day in December 1796. Despite everyone's fears, the sudden encounter was not hostile, Peale tells us, because each of the delegations was too absorbed by the surrounding exhibits.[1] He does not burden us with the moral of the story; it was easily apparent to his contemporaries, if not to us. The Indians, it was believed, as children of nature, would intuitively relate what they observed in the museum to the harmony of the environment from which they had come. Therefore, such higher motives as they possessed, conditioned by natural law, would govern their behavior.

Surely Catlin would have thought the same, and been equally fascinated by the expanded "world in miniature" that filled the top floor of Independence Hall twenty-five years later. Peale often acknowledged his intention to design his exhibits according to a master plan that would reveal how each had a part in the grand system of nature. "My Collection of natural curiosities are increasing," he wrote John Beale Bordley in 1786.

I have, I believe, nearly compleated the class of wild Ducks belonging to this river, ducks & Drakes which I have disposed in Various attitudes on artificial ponds, some Birds & Beasts on Trees and some Birds suspended as flying. . . . if my life is preserved for any length of time, it is most likely that my labours will make a museum that will be considered of more consequence than anything of this sort in America.[2]

The range and ingenuity of these exhibits came to be truly remarkable as the years passed. A visitor in 1794 described the exhibition room as

about 50 feet long, and 20 high. On the floor, and near the door, the American Buffaloe stands in its huge and natural shape. . . . Every portion of this spacious apartment exhibited objects to excite wonder and admira-

Figure 52. John Lewis Krimmel, *Election Day at the State House,* 1816, watercolor. Historical Society of Pennsylvania, Philadelphia.

tion . . . a vast variety of monsters of the earth and main, and fowls of the air are seen, in perfect preservation and in their natural shape and order. . . . Over them are suspended 50 portraits, being complete likenesses of American and French patriots. . . . At the further extremity of this room are to be seen a great collection of the bones, jaws, and grinders of the incognitum, or non-descript animal, royal tyger, sharks, and many other land and marine animals, hostile to the human race: shields, bows, arrows, petrifactions, Indian and European scalps, &c.[3]

Fortunately, we need not depend on a written description of the appearance of these exhibition rooms in 1822, when Catlin might have visited them (and perhaps noted for the future how successfully the older artist had combined portraits and field specimens). Peale has left, instead, a visual record of how his many talents and interests were channeled into the orderly scheme of natural history. *The Artist in His Museum* (fig. 53) is a portrait so revealing of the man and his age, of sustained faith in reason and human progress, that generations of change have failed to dim its message.

In addition to demonstrating his system, Peale intended the painting to show off the range of his collections: the portraits hanging high above the neat geometry of the fowl cases, and on the right, the skeleton of the famous mastodon excavated by him and his sons near Newburgh, New York, in 1801. What Peale could not include, among other exhibits, was the variety of natural history specimens and Indian

artifacts that had come his way from the expeditions of Lewis and Clark, and Major Long. Through Jefferson's influence, Peale had received, in 1809, Indian costumes, leggings, tobacco pouches, ornamental belts, and a magnificent beaver mantle "fringed with 140 ermine skins and studded with 'prismatic coloured shells' " that Lewis had worn on the journey.[4] Titian Peale returned home from the Long expedition in January 1821 with additional specimens and sketches of Indian life observed during his extensive western travels. The Indian collections at the museum grew still further in 1826 when Titian's father purchased a collection of Indian costumes from the Missouri and Mississippi regions, "the most complete ever seen in Philadelphia."[5]

To interpret the collections and to broaden the scientific and educational appeal of the museum, Peale had introduced a lecture series in 1821, selecting for speakers several of the most distinguished scientists in Philadelphia. Thomas Say, veteran of the Long expedition and soon to become professor of natural history at the University of Pennsylvania, was to lecture in zoology, and John D. Godman, a young physician with a scholarly interest in anatomy and a facility for languages, was given the field of physiology. The series was typical of the benefits offered by the Philadelphia community. If the subjects were too narrow for Catlin in 1821, the work of Say and Godman would be a valuable resource in years to come, and there were other institutions through which he might have access to more pertinent scientific topics and reports from field investigations in the western United States. The Academy of Natural Sciences, founded in 1812 by a small group that included Say, had grown by 1820 to a membership of one hundred. Every leading scientist in the city belonged and others participated at a distance as correspondents. William Bartram, Thomas Jefferson, Baron Georges Cuvier, Chevalier de Lamarck, and Benjamin Silliman were among those in the latter category. Weekly meetings were held, at which papers were presented, a major journal was published, and the library and collections grew steadily. Academy members also staffed numerous expeditions of the period. Say and Titian Peale, for example, had gone west with Long (and much of the material gathered by the former eventually appeared in the academy *Journal*). Other members accompanied Long on his subsequent expedition to the St. Peter's (Minnesota) River, and several more went through the Northwest with Henry Schoolcraft in 1831.

Both the academy and the American Philosophical Society, a much older institution, founded by Franklin in 1743, were, in effect, training centers in geology and natural history for the parade of scientists and explorers who headed West in the wake of Lewis and Clark.[6] After some relatively dormant years, the society began publishing its *Transactions* in 1769, and had established its impressive library and collections in Philosophical Hall twenty years later. Joseph Priestly was its brightest star at the turn of the century, but at the same time the society reaffirmed its interest in "the antiquity, changes, and present state" of the country and resolved to investigate "the customs, manners, languages and character of the Indian Nations and their migrations."[7] More positive steps were taken in 1815, under the guidance of the statesman and linguist Peter S. DuPonceau, who is thought to have established the Historical and Literary Committee of the society and requested that it collect historical documents and manuscripts recording Indian languages.[8] DuPonceau also persuaded the Moravian missionary John Heckewelder to work with the committee and to donate his large collection of Indian manuscripts. A member of the society since 1797, Heckewelder was probably the foremost authority on American Indians in the country. His major publication, *Account of the History, Manners, and Customs of the Indian Nations who once inhabited Pennsylvania and the neighboring States* (1818), not only argued for the intelligence, ability, and moral worth of the Indian, but provided a historical context for Cooper's Leatherstocking Tales. It was also a source well known to Catlin and Schoolcraft.

In addition to these activities, DuPonceau and others at the society had petitioned Congress in 1816 to undertake scientific exploration west of the Mississippi, an action that paved the way for the government-sponsored Long expedition several years later. Long and his companions conducted the first survey of the Great Plains in the summer of 1820, following the Platte River to the base of the Rockies, and returning home, along the banks of the Arkansas, after being the first to ascend Pike's Peak. Catlin, who was destined to cover some of the same territory (and paint the same tribes Long encountered), would have had ample opportunity to see and hear the results when the spoils

Figure 53. Charles Willson Peale, *The Artist in His Museum*, 1822. Pennsylvania Academy of the Fine Arts, Philadelphia.

came back to Philadelphia. And two years later (1823) he could have sampled the scientific flavor of Edwin James's two-volume account of the journey.[9]

Although Catlin was not a member of the society, its pervasive influence would soon affect his plans for the future, and eventually determine, along with other local institutions, the method he would use to study the Plains tribes. Not surprisingly, letters Catlin wrote from the Upper Missouri ten years later found their way back to the society's official publication.[10]

⟶ Stressing as they did the importance of direct observation, scientists of the period ranged over thousands of miles of magnificent wilderness to locate the rare plants and animals of the New World. They were a learned group, on the whole, familiar with a generation of

Figure 54. Alexander Wilson, *Black Hawk*, ca. 1812, pencil, ink, and watercolor. Houghton Library, Harvard University.

Romantic poetry and landscape theory, and often passionately fond of natural beauty. The practical necessity alone of recording the appearance of their discoveries demanded careful prose descriptions and accurate sketches to insure proper classification when the time came for publication. Such close scrutiny was bound to develop a heightened aesthetic response to the objects under examination, and, in turn, to the surroundings from which they came. As a result, these early naturalists rarely made a sharp distinction between science and art; accuracy and beauty were to go hand in hand in pursuit of their professional concerns. Charles Willson Peale saw nothing unusual in a museum combining natural history and the fine arts, nor did he frequent the American Philosophical Society less often than the Pennsylvania Academy. And his scientific colleagues were quick to admit the aesthetic inspiration that often guided their rambles through the countryside.

From such a rare and unified intellectual spirit was born the tradition of the traveling artist-naturalist, a tradition that dominated the activities of Philadelphia science for more than two generations. William Bartram, second-generation botanist and friend of Thomas Jefferson, was perhaps the first to practice this approach. Touring the southern states in the 1770s in search of rare plants and trees, he could not resist climbing an occasional mountain and commenting upon the view that lay before him. So entranced was he on one occasion, his "imagination . . . wholly engaged in the contemplation of . . . [a] magnificent landscape," that he admits to having almost missed a new species of rhododendron.[11] Alexander Wilson, happily leaving behind the "stinking sewers of Philadelphia," had written an epic poem about a journey to Niagara Falls in 1804, and then ranged from Maine to Georgia compiling his extraordinary *American Ornithology* (1808-1814), a nine-volume study that he illustrated with his own skillful drawings (fig. 54).

Although John Godman was less of a traveler than Bartram and Wilson, one can be certain that he had observed each of the examples he patiently describes in *American Natural History* (1826-1828), his pathfinding effort to classify the animals of North America. Apologizing for the delay in publishing his work, which he had begun in 1823, Godman tells us in the preface of the frequent necessity to suspend writing for "weeks and months, in order to procure certain animals, to observe their habits in captivity, or to make daily visits to the woods and fields for the sake of witnessing their actions in a state of nature. On other occasions," Godman continues,

we have undertaken considerable journies, in order to ascertain the correctness of statements, or to obtain sight of an individual subject of description. It would be far more agreeable thus to obtain materials for the whole work from nature, than to depend in the slightest degree upon books . . . a long lifetime spent in this way on such a work would not be too much to give it the requisite degree of perfection.[12]

The two volumes begin, appropriately enough, with a full discussion of the American Indian ("When free, in his native wilds," the author says, he "displayed a form worthy of admiration, and a conduct which secured him respect").[13] Godman then devotes himself to lengthy descriptions of various native animals. Facts and personal observations abound; one can hardly doubt his claim to diligence and accuracy. But what stands out for us is an occasional description in which the author betrays a further dimension of his appreciation. "The size and appearance of elk are imposing," Godman writes in the second volume.

His air denotes confidence of great strength, while his towering horns exhibit weapons capable of doing much injury when offensively employed. The head is beautifully formed, tapering to a narrow point; the ears are large and rapidly movable; the eyes full and dark; the horns rise loftily from the front, with numerous sharp pointed branches, which are curved forwards, and the head is sustained upon a neck at once slender, vigorous and graceful.

There is but one species of American Elk, Godman concludes, and "in beauty of form, grace and agility of movement, and other attributes of its kind, it is not excelled by any deer of the old or new world."[14]

Among the first of this Philadelphia circle to travel in the West was Thomas Nuttall, an English botanist who had gone up the Missouri in 1811, and deep into the Arkansas Territory in 1819. On the latter trip he kept a journal that is as much a record of his astonishing range of interests as it is an observation of the natural history of the area. Nothing escaped Nuttall's attention, from the attitude of slaveholders, to the religious and linguistic practices of the Indian tribes. The breadth and complexity of his approach, in fact, seems almost in conflict with the simplicty of his inspiration. "For nearly ten years I have travelled throughout America, principally with a view of becoming acquainted with some favourite branches of the natural history," Nuttall remarks in the preface of his *Journal* (published in 1821). "To converse, as it were with nature, to admire the wisdom and beauty of creation, has ever been, and I hope ever will be, to me a favourite pursuit."[15] Like most traveling naturalists, Nuttall was trained (or compelled, one might say) to see the endless connecting links of natural history: he could not begin one subject without being led to another. He was intrigued by the fact that so many aspects of the natural world were interrelated, as if planned by some unseen hand. Thus he firmly believed, as did his colleagues, that the inspirational effect of scenery and natural objects was paralleled by another aesthetic, manifest in the beauty of the sytem.

When Major Long set out for the Rockies, he took with him an impressive array of Philadelphia scientists. Long himself was an experienced Army topographical engineer; Say and Titian Peale were, respectively, naturalist and assistant naturalist; and the group included, as well, a geologist, a botanist (later replaced by Edwin James, who compiled the *Account* of the expedition), and a journalist. Although the party was somewhat reduced after the first winter, Say and Titian Peale went the full distance to the Rockies, collecting and sketching whenever possible. Peale returned with a number of finely detailed studies of animals (fig. 55) encountered along the way, and broader sketches of Indian life on the Great Plains (fig. 56). Samuel Seymour,

Figure 55. Titian Peale, *Plains Pocket Gopher*, 1819, watercolor. American Philosophical Society, Philadelphia.

the official painter of the expedition, contributed a number of appealing watercolors of the Rockies (fig. 57), much in the spirit of James's narrative. Describing the view gained by a small detachment that had climbed to an intermediate point between the mountains and the prairie, James begins:

They could trace the course of the Platte, and number the streams they had crossed, and others which they had before passed near, by the slight fringing of timber or bushes which margined their banks, and by an occasional glimpse of their streams, shining like quicksilver, and interrupting and varying the continuity of the plain, as they pursued their serpentine course. The atmosphere was remarkably serene, and small clouds were coursing over the surface of the heavens, casting their swiftly-moving shadows upon the earth, and enhancing the beauty of the contrast, which the long lines of timber afforded, to the general glare of light.[16]

Seymour was also under instructions to "paint miniature likenesses, or portraits if required, of distinguished Indians, and exhibit groups of savages engaged in celebrating their festivals, or sitting in council, and in general illustrate any subject, that may be deemed appropriate in his art."[17] Unhappily, few of Seymour's Indian subjects survive (fig. 58), but large portions of James's text are taken from the notes of Say and John Dougherty, the Indian agent at Council Bluffs who would later become a great friend of Catlin. During the winter of 1819-20, before departing for the Rockies, Say and Dougherty visited the Pawnee, Oto, Iowa, Missouri, and Omaha, compiling an extraordinary ethnological record of the various tribes. In the expedition report one finds detailed descriptions of Indian dress, hunting methods, habitations, dances and ceremonials, standards of behavior, and religious beliefs. No better basic guide could have been devised for Catlin, even when it came to describing the primitive attributes of certain Indian leaders. The chief of the Cheyenne, James wrote,

Figure 56. Titian Peale, *Pawnee Indian Fort on the Platte River*, 1820, watercolor. American Philosophical Society, Philadelphia.

Figure 57. Samuel Seymour, *Distant View of the Rocky Mountains*, 1820, engraving. Rare Book Division, New York Public Library.

seemed to be a man born to command, endowed with a spirit of unconquerable ferocity, and capable of inflicting exemplary punishment upon any one who should dare disobey his orders. He was tall and graceful, with a highly ridged aquiline nose, corrugated forehead, mouth with the corners drawn downward, and rather small, but remarkably piercing eye, which when fixed upon your countenance, appeared strained in the intenseness of its gaze, and to seek rather for the movements of the soul within, than to ascertain the mere lineaments it contemplated.[18]

By the time Catlin found his way to the mouth of the Yellowstone, twelve years later, the tradition of the artist-naturalist was solidly established. Letters extolling the virtues of the Blackfoot and Crow, and telling of the conditions under which he painted their portraits in the summer of 1832, appeared shortly afterward in *The Cabinet of Natural History and American Rural Sports*, a Philadelphia journal published by the landscape painter Thomas Doughty and his brother.[19] Another letter of 1832 informs a friend from whom Catlin sought help to join a military expedition that "the sciences of Geology, Mineralogy, Botany and Natural History . . . embrace an important part of my travels to the Indian country," and two years later, so much was he indebted to this tradition that he could call himself both an artist and a scientist within the short space of a few sentences.[20] Having set off with the dragoons in the summer of 1834 to locate the Comanche village in southwestern Oklahoma, Catlin justifies "the toil, the privations, and the expense of traveling to these remote parts of the world" to seek Indian subjects by proclaiming that he is "practicing in the true school of the arts." Besides, he continues,

The landscape scenes of these wild and beautiful regions are, of themselves, a rich reward for the traveller who can place them in his portfolio: and being myself the only one accompanying the dragoons for scientific purposes, there will be added pleasure to be derived from these pursuits.[21]

Catlin was not only inspired by the Philadelphia scientific community, and the complement of naturalists who went forth to explore the virgin continent, but he learned from both the more difficult task of putting his imagination and interest to work. In the early pages of *Letters and Notes*, he sums up his accomplishments by stating:

I have visited forty-eight different tribes, the greater part of which I found speaking different languages, and containing in all 400,000 souls. I have brought home safe, and in good order, 310 portraits in oil, all painted in their native dress, and in their own wigwams; and also 200 other paintings in oil, containing views of their villages—their wigwams—their games and religious ceremonies—their dances—their ball plays—their buffalo hunting, and other amusements (containing in all, over 3000 full-length figures); and the landscapes of the country they live in, as well as a very extensive and curious collection of their costumes, and all their other manufactures, from the size of a wigwam down to the size of a quill or a rattle.[22]

One is struck by the statistics Catlin puts forth in support of his project, by the numbers and categories of subjects he has painted and collected, by the systematic range of his interests, and the orderly progression of his method. Why, one might ask, did not an artist so conditioned by every romantic sentiment that favored his subject simply wander about the West and paint the most colorful Indians he could find? Or, having found them at the mouth of the Yellowstone, why did he not return year after year to take his subjects from what he considered the perfection of aboriginal life? The answer, of course, is that Catlin had set out to preserve the image of a vanishing race. His interest was not only in proud individuals or primitive tribes, but in a total inventory of the Indian civilization then existing on the Great Plains (years later he would extend this to include the tribes of the Rockies and the West Coast). What he meant to do, in effect, was to classify the principal tribes: to describe the chiefs, warriors, medicine men, and other noteworthy members of each; to examine and compare habits, amusements, and religious beliefs; and to collect a representative group of costumes, weapons, and domestic articles. His paintings were to serve as illustrations for the extensive notes he was taking; the result would be a full account of all he had observed and learned from other sources in the course of his travels. Thus he could demonstrate, in the manner of his Philadelphia colleagues, why Plains Indians were so admirably suited to the life they led. Say, Godman, or Nuttall might have organized an expedition in much the same way.

In truth, Catlin's inspired sentiment never conflicted with his compulsive need to gather facts. He proclaimed Four Bears (no. 128) the most impressive chief on the Upper Missouri, and then devoted four pages to a description of his costume—from the arrangement of feathers in the headdress to the pattern of beads on his moccasins. It took Catlin a full chapter to recount the chilling ritual of O-kee-pa, the sacred Mandan torture ceremony, and parts of several more to tell all he knew about the appearance and habits of the buffalo. Nor did he slight the landscape. After running off from his family and risking his life among hostile Sioux to locate the mysterious Pipestone Quarry (fig. 27; no. 337), he described it with the eye of a geologist:

The principal and most striking feature of this place is a perpendicular wall of close-grained, compact quartz, of twenty-five and thirty feet in elevation, running nearly North and South with its face to the West, exhibiting a front of nearly two miles in length, when it disappears at both ends by running under the prairie, which becomes there a little more elevated, and probably covers it for many miles, both to the North and the South. . . . At the base of the wall, and within a few rods of it, and on the very ground where the Indians dig for the red stone, rests a group of five stupendous boulders of gneiss, leaning against each other; the smallest of which is twelve or fifteen feet, and the largest twenty-five feet in diameter, altogether weighing, unquestionably, several hundred tons. These blocks are composed chiefly of felspar and mica. . . . [23]

And so on for another four pages, at which point Catlin terminates the discussion with a chemical analysis of the pipestone that had appeared in Silliman's *American Journal of Science and Arts.*

To account for Catlin's method, one must recall that Philadelphia science in the early nineteenth century still operated under the principles handed down by Bacon and Newton to the natural philosophers of the Englightenment. Bacon had called for an end to speculation and hypothesis, and preached instead the study of facts. All science was to be based on observation, on an empirical method that guaranteed a carefully built system of knowledge, each level of which was based on a simple and rational formula. What could not be confirmed by observation or direct sense impression, was questionable as evidence. Under such a system, scientists were more likely to gather an exhaustive supply of information on a subject than to attempt a theory. The Academy of Natural Sciences, for example, issued an appeal "to exclude entirely all papers of mere theory" in the early issues of its *Journal.* The academy wished instead "to confine their communications as much as possible to facts . . . [to abridge] papers too

Figure 58. Samuel Seymour, *Kiowa Apache, Cheyenne, and Arapaho,* 1820, sepia wash. Beinecke Library, Yale University.

long for publication in their original state, to present the facts thus published, clothed in as few words as are consistent with perspicuous demonstration."[24]

While this puts matters much too simply in regard to the heritage of Bacon and Newton, it does help to explain the mission of those early Philadelphia naturalists, who felt obliged to record everything of scientific interest in the New World. Their haste to do so in a few short decades was an added burden. Much of the flora, fauna, mineral wealth, and native population of America was virtually unknown, and had remained undisturbed for centuries. Before civilization expanded westward, before local environments changed, each plant or animal must be examined in its natural habitat, its relation determined to the natural order. Scholars went off to the far corners of the continent, gathering specimens and compiling information, preoccupied with the need to close the gaps in the finite system of nature. Collecting and classifying were the acknowledged aims of science: Peale had envisioned just such a role for his museum and Catlin had followed a similar pattern in assembling the Indian Gallery.

The net result of such activity did not end in a pyramid of scientific data, however. While each of the naturalists was serving himself and his colleagues, he was also untangling the mysteries of the universe, making manifest natural and divine law. Striving to repudiate the atheism of Enlightenment scientists, Philadelphia naturalists combined their learning with a more devout conception of nature. The physical beauty of the objects and the abstract beauty of the system were sufficient to reveal a guiding hand, they believed. It was the duty of the scientist to add the discoveries of the New World to the already formidable body of knowledge from the Old. Piecing both together would add greater glory to their mission, natural law would more truly reveal divine law. Numerous statements by Catlin in the following chapter support such a belief, but Godman provided the most direct testimony in 1829, when urging the benefits of natural history upon a Philadelphia lecture audience:

We desire, as far as practicable, to solicit your attention to the study of nature through some of her most interesting works; to excite your wishes to become acquainted with the living beings scattered in rich profusion over the earth, to call forth your admiration at the endless variety of form, the singular contrivance, the beautiful adaptation, the wonderful perfection exhibited throughout animated nature, and thence to win your observation to their habits and manners, the benefits they confer upon mankind, their relations to each other, and their subordination in the system of the universe. . . . the enlighted student of nature can never forget the omnipresence of Deity—it is everywhere before his eyes, and in his heart—obvious and palpable;—it is a consciousness, not a doctrine; a reality, not an opinion, identified with his very being, and attested to his understanding by every circumstance of his existence.[25]

4

Plains Indians as the Primitive Ideal

The love of science in the early 1800s did not flourish in cold hearts. We have seen that Philadelphia natural history studies of the period had few limitations, that the scholars involved had the widest possible range of interests, and that even the most specialized investigation was based on a broad humanistic concern. Aesthetics and religion were as much a part of scientific inquiry as a knowledge of the Linnean system or the writings of Buffon. The unifying spirit, revered above all, was a generous variety of nature, tempered and well ordered, and a model from which man could learn and aspire to the perfection of his surroundings.

The study of natural history was not the only means for developing such an attitude of mind, however. Most educated men of the period would have been familiar with a body of Romantic literature that had already prepared them to appreciate nature, and Catlin, a student of the classics, a lawyer, and an accomplished writer, was no exception. *Letters and Notes* abounds with a variety of references that range from Caius Marius and Shakespeare to Irving, Cooper, and the picturesque and sublime. Whether literary ideals or scientific interests came first in Catlin's case, and which had the greater influence on his subsequent career, we cannot know. The one would have complemented the other, and both approaches might have yielded finally almost the same result. Yet there was something in the combination that made Catlin's career unique, in spite of his great debt to contemporary science. To distinguish him from those involved in similar pursuits, one must somehow account for the theories of wilderness virtue and the natural man that comprise the central theme of *Letters and Notes.* Their influence upon Catlin was profound, and they establish the background, ultimately, that gives shape and meaning to his achievement.

Except for a few pages of notes in which he lists the dates and principal characters of the Leatherstocking Tales and several texts having to do with the history or exploration of North America (Jefferson's *Notes,* James's *Expedition to the Rocky Mountains,* the writings of John Heckewelder, John Dunn Hunter, and Thomas Nuttall, for example), we know little of the source of Catlin's interests.[1] Presumably his travels and his lean finances prevented him from owning a library, but his activities in the 1820s and 1830s led to frequent contact with learned men and institutions in the East. From them, and what books he got hold of, and from a childhood spent in "Nimrodical" pastimes, he fashioned a mode of cultural primitivism that enabled him to understand and interpret the American Indian with a remarkable degree of sympathy.

No one who has browsed through *Letters and Notes* can fail to experience the sheer joy that Catlin felt when drifting down some untouched stretch of river, pursuing buffalo at a mad pace across a wild prairie, or observing an Indian ritual at some remote village on the Upper Missouri. For much of his life he yearned to be free of the social customs, laws, and institutions of society. He wished to roam the wilderness at will, to live only by nature's law, uninhibited in the pursuit of happiness and freedom. He could not, of course, because he was also ambitious for fame and for other satisfactions that could be gained only in society, but the vast expanse of wilderness that lay west of the Mississippi forever intrigued him. Like many others of his time who followed an essentially urban career, he conceived of the West and its native inhabitants as a spiritual refuge, a place of green fields, abundant game, and innocent savages. The vices of civilization—political and commercial intrigue, and the unattractive environment of large eastern cities—were constantly compared to the virtue and beauty of life on the Upper Missouri. If Catlin and his contemporaries could not abandon the lives they were leading, they could in very real terms envision an Edenic opposite, and from this they formed the beliefs (or the myths) that governed their attitude toward Indians and the West, or, for that matter, toward every wilderness area that remained in North America.

"How I hate to dwell in those accumulated and crowded cities," Crévecoeur had written in the 1770s, after finding refuge on a farm in Orange County, New York.[2] By the time his fellow countryman Chateaubriand arrived, several years later, something infinitely more rustic than a farm was needed to quiet the latter's nerves. "Every one boasts of loving liberty," he wrote,

and hardly any one has a just idea of it. When I travelled among the Indian tribes of Canada—when I quitted the habitations of Europeans, and found myself, for the first time, alone, amidst boundless forests, having all nature, as it were prostrate at my feet, a strange revolution took place in my sensations. I was seized with a sort of delirium, and followed no track, but went from tree to tree, and indifferently to the right or left, saying to myself: 'Here there is no multiplicity of roads, no towns, no confined houses, no Presidents, Republics and Kings, no laws and no human beings.— Human beings! Yes—some worthy savages, who care nothing about me, nor I about them; who like myself wander wherever inclination leads them, eat when they wish it, and sleep where they please. . . .

Released from the tyrannical yoke of society, I comprehended the charms of that natural independence, far surpassing all the pleasures of which civilized man can have an idea. I comprehended why a savage was unwilling to become an European, why several Europeans had become savages. . . . It is incredible to what a state of littleness nations and their boasted institutions were reduced in my eyes. It appeared to me that I was looking at the kingdoms of earth with an inverted telescope, or rather that I myself was enlarged, exalted, and contemplating, with the eyes of a giant, the remains of my degenerate fellow creatures.[3]

Although Chateaubriand sincerely appreciated the rural delights of America, his remarks are couched in that mode of primitivism—the belief that remote and simple societies offered a happier, more fulfilling existence—that was standard fare for many European writers in the second half of the eighteenth century. As a literary convention, primitivism reached back to the Renaissance, when European explorers began the long series of voyages that would acquaint them with exotic tribes living in what was regarded as a bountiful, New World paradise. Through the eighteenth century, the character of that paradise gradually changed, as German and English writers, seeking to establish a moral and spiritual base in nature, revealed divine inspiration in the forests, mountains, and waterfalls in remote areas of their native landscapes. At the same time, French philosophers and English romantics were engaged in a similar campaign to transform the role of the "noble savage." By tradition, the term had been applied to any representative of a foreign or exotic people whose appearance was reminiscent of the grace and dignity of classical sculpture. But James Boswell and his contemporaries, who willingly misread the limitations Rousseau had placed on savage life, and missionaries hard at work in the New World had soon burdened the noble savage with all the simplicity and virtue of his natural surroundings (fig. 59).[4] By the end of the eighteenth century, he emerged from the pristine wilds of America with a new role, designed to establish him as the model whom civilized man must never forget. As an innocent primitive, untouched by the corrupt ritual of European society, he was proclaimed the chief exponent of natural law, the one splendid example who remained close to

God's original image of mankind.

The high point of primitivism in England coincided, not by chance, with the vogue for the picturesque and sublime, a means of appreciating landscape that some years later would enable Catlin and certain contemporaries to see the prairies as an endless rolling garden, one more symbol of the abundant grace that had shaped the American continent. The Indian was made to preside over this natural setting, indeed to personify the spirit of what was deemed a verdant paradise. "The great and almost boundless garden-spot of earth," Catlin called it,

Over whose green, enamelled fields, as . . . free as the ocean's wave, Nature's proudest, noblest men have pranced on their wild horses, and extended, through a series of ages, their long arms in orisons of praise and gratitude to the Great Spirit in the sun, for the freedom and happiness of their existence.[5]

The Great Plains, of course, were not the only aspect of America that appealed to primitivist sensibilities in the early nineteenth century. Except for a narrow strip along the East Coast, the country was still a vast natural preserve, only sparsely settled and relatively untouched by commerce. Already this heritage had become an overwhelming presence in the minds of European and native artists and writers, who sought to resolve in some way its significance for the future. In one sense the wilderness was an immense laboratory, in which man might ultimately discover the mystery of creation, or it was the opposite, a force to test the skill and ingenuity of the pioneers. More often than not, a balance was sought between the two; the raw edge of nature was traded off to slow the wheels of progress. But the most ardent primitivists would not compromise; they yearned for a simpler world in which they could reestablish an innocent relationship with their surroundings and their fellow man.

Primitivism seems to have come to this country as an approved mode of social criticism, a polite and reasonable argument in favor of ideal societies.[6] Those who believed in this concept did not wish to revert to a savage state, of course; they simply saw it as a means to reform certain institutions that had come to dominate and restrict their lives. Once Americans began to realize the vast resources of their continent, however, the argument broadened into moral, spiritual, and preservation concerns, and decade by decade through the nineteenth century it became more germane to the question of our expansion than to events in Europe. Curiously enough, as the debate continued, most people chose to forget that the concept of primitivism had never been based on any actual study of primitive people. It was simply assumed that Indians represented that wonderful paradox: their conduct was ultimately more civilized than white men's because they were uncorrupted by civilization.[7] This meant that tribal units were thought to function successfully without fixed laws or a cumbersome political and economic system, without courts and legislatures, commerce and private property, without the host of institutions that bred evil among white men. The customs and beliefs of the Indians were solely a product of their natural environment. They were dignified, courageous, and

Figure 59. Joseph Wright of Derby, *The Indian Widow,* 1783-1785. Derby Museum and Art Gallery, Derby, England.

honorable, the theory went, because they had never been taught to be otherwise.

Much had been said before and during Catlin's time about other attitudes associated with primitivism. Jedidiah Morse and Timothy Flint had attacked the wretched conditions that already prevailed in some American cities, and Cooper, William Cullen Bryant, Thomas Cole, and Asher B. Durand had praised the contrasting benefits of the American wilderness. Jefferson, with great insight and eloquence, had challenged the opinions of Buffon and the Encyclopedists, who dismissed American savages as a feeble race; and Hunter, Heckewelder, and Schoolcraft had greatly added to our knowledge of other tribes on the fringes of civilization. Emerson, Thoreau, and Margaret Fuller had urged the study of nature and savage cultures as a means of attaining a higher degree of self-realization, but it was Catlin, borrowing from many of these sources, who concentrated his energies solely on the study of the Indian in "the honest and elegant simplicity of nature." Seeking his experience among those tribes far removed from civilization, studying their habits and customs as a part of their natural surroundings, painting portraits that would reveal a more searching range of character, Catlin at last provided a study of the Indian that was meant to justify the ideal of primitivism. Indeed, it becomes clear that he wished to bolster the arguments in favor of nature and savage life that prevailed in the eighteenth century, to update them, in effect, with more advanced scientific methods and an abundance of personal testimony that spoke passionately of his high regard for the inhabitants of the Great Plains. If a number of his contemporaries wrote with more depth and concentration about these same problems, we need not apologize. Catlin exceeded them all as a dedicated spokesman for Indian culture, and as an energetic and imaginative interpreter of the American West.

When Gulian Verplanck, William Ellery Channing, and their colleagues began a campaign for a national literature in the 1820s, feeling too much the burden of debt to European men of letters, they searched for themes that would reveal the distinctive traits of the people and the landscape. The resourceful character of our pioneers was celebrated, the extent and beauty of the New England landscape (its virgin character making up for its lack of historical associations)

Figure 60. Robert Weir, *Red Jacket,* 1828. New-York Historical Society.

were vividly described, and the Indians were glorified as an ancient race whose traditions had long since incorporated the freedom and democratic spirit sought by men of the New World. Fitz-Greene Halleck said as much when describing a portrait of Red Jacket (fig. 60) by Robert Weir:

If he were with me, King of Tuscarora!
Gazing, as I, upon thy portrait now,
In all its medalled, fringed, and beaded glory,
Its eye's dark beauty, and its thoughtful brow—

Its brow, half martial and half diplomatic,
Its eye, upsoaring like an Eagle's wings;
Well might he boast that we, the Democratic,
Outrival Europe, even in our kings![8]

In the course of writing the Leatherstocking Tales, Cooper (the absent authority in Halleck's poem) became much concerned with the creation of an American legend, incorporating all these ingredients in a series of novels that would reveal the dilemma surrounding our natural environment. Through his principal character, the peripatetic Natty Bumppo, Cooper expressed the basic conflict between primitivism and progress: Natty stood for the wisdom and bounty of the forest, where he had learned, or been provided with, everything he deemed worthwhile; against him were arrayed a legion of civil authorities who, in the name of private property and commerce, constantly interrupted his peaceful habits. Indians, at least those on the side of Heckewelder's Delaware, were very much involved in this conflict, complementing Natty's position, and facing a similar challenge from civilized authority. Cooper deeply sympathized with the woodsman's plight, but he saw the advance of the pioneers into unsettled land as an inevitable consequence of the growth and prosperity of the nation.

As Natty was forced to retreat, he more and more symbolized the dilemma of the Indians, whose forests and hunting grounds were also disappearing. The theme was too ripe for Catlin to miss. Cooper was the central interpreter of the period and several of the Leatherstocking Tales had been written in the 1820s, when Catlin was planning his new career. The detailed outline, mentioned earlier, of the plots and characters of each of the novels shows his careful attention to Cooper's work, and when it came to writing *Letters and Notes,* Catlin used for the central theme of the two volumes just the arguments Bumppo had used to justify his own stubborn desire to remain free.

While Catlin's general notion of primitivism probably came from issues Cooper defined in the course of the Leatherstocking Tales, issues the author had planted so securely in an American context, there was one novel in the series that dealt specifically with the West. In *The Prairie* (1827) Cooper had attempted a description of the Indians and the landscape of the Great Plains, where Bumppo (Leatherstocking) had finally come to live after the pressures of civilization had dislodged him from the forests of New York. Although Cooper had no firsthand knowledge of the area, he used reports from Lewis and Clark, Long, and other western explorers to devise a background that blends some authenticity with his energetic imagination. Calling on "the truant eyes of Allston and Greenough" to turn their gaze from the models of antiquity to a handsome Pawnee brave, Cooper gives a description of one that might well have inspired Catlin:

> The Indian in question, was in every particular a warrior of fine stature and admirable proportions. . . . The outlines of his lineaments were strikingly noble, and nearly approaching to Roman, though the secondary features of his face were slightly marked with the well known traces of his Asiatic origin. The peculiar tint of the skin, which in itself is so well designed to aid the effect of a martial expression, had received an additional aspect of wild ferocity from the colors of the war-paint. . . . His head was, as usual, shaved to the crown, where a large and gallant scalp-lock seemed to challenge the grasp of his enemies. . . . His body, notwithstanding the lateness of the season, was nearly naked, and the portion which was clad bore a vestment no warmer than a light robe of the finest dressed deer-skin, beautifully stained with the rude design of some daring exploit, and which was carelessly worn, as if more in pride than from any unmanly regard to comfort. His leggings were of bright scarlet cloth, the only evidence about his person that he had held communion with the traders of the Palefaces. But as if to furnish some offset to this solitary submission to a womanish vanity, they were fearfully fringed, from the gartered knee to the bottom of the moccasin, with the hair of human scalps. He leaned lightly with one hand on a short hickory bow, while the other rather touched than sought support, from the long, delicate handle of an ashen lance.[9]

Cooper went on to describe the prairie landscape in equally compelling terms, the sight of buffalo herds moving in great black columns over hills of waving grass, and Pawnee horsemen who rode with a grace and agility no white man could match. If Catlin was attracted by these vigorous scenes, however, he could not have missed the deeper message Cooper planted between in the poignant soliloquies of Bumppo. "How much has the beauty of the wilderness been deformed in two short lives," the great hunter lamented.

> My own eyes were first opened on the shores of the Eastern sea, and well do I remember that I tried the virtues of the first rifle I ever bore, after such a march, from the door of my father to the forest, as a stripling could make between sun and sun; and that without offence to the rights or prejudices of any man who set himself up to be the owner of the beasts of the fields. Natur' then lay in its glory along the whole coast, giving a narrow stripe, between the woods and the ocean, to the greediness of the settlers. And where am I now? Had I the wings of an eagle, they would tire before a tenth of the distance, which separates me from that sea, could be passed; and towns and villages, farms and highways, churches and schools, in short, all the inventions and deviltries of man, are spread across the region.[10]

Catlin, however, was not only concerned about preserving the wilderness for Natty Bumppo and his kind. Bumppo, after all, was still a Christian and maintained some few connections with the civilized world. Catlin envisioned the primitive spirit as residing more securely in the hearts and minds of those Indians still far up the Missouri, untouched by intercourse with the whites. Cooper, in fact, knew very little about Indians other than what he had gleaned from Heckewelder and a few other sources. He followed delegations from New York to Philadelphia and Washington, to learn more of their customs and individual traits, but he rarely managed to portray them in a convincing manner. Catlin, on the other hand, based his career and reputation

upon having observed the Indians on their home ground, upon a firsthand study that enabled him to judge, in effect, whether savages actually lived up to their reputation. After this experience, he was convinced that primitivism in its purest form rested not with the Bumppos of America, but with those few tribes of Indians in the far West who still roamed free. So forcefully did he argue his case that he managed to revitalize the image of primitivism we had inherited from Europe, to transfer it to a greener garden, and to restore it at last to the bosom of an actual savage.

It is a less difficult task, perhaps, to demonstrate Catlin's inspiration than to explain how his paintings reflect such beliefs. But one can with confidence turn to *Letters and Notes* to illustrate how much his admiration of savage life guided his travels. He was convinced, for example, that savage models were superior to any that could be found in academic circles. "I have for a long time been of the opinion," he wrote,

> that the wilderness of our country afforded models equal to those from which the Grecian sculptors transferred to the marble such inimitable grace and beauty; and I am now more confirmed in this opinion, since I have immersed myself in the midst of thousands and tens of thousands of these knights of the forest; whose whole lives are lives of chivalry, and whose daily feats, with their naked limbs, might vie with those of the Grecian youths in the beautiful rivalry of the Olympian games. . . . Of this much I am certain—that amongst these sons of the forest . . . I have learned more of the essential parts of my art in the last three years, than I could have learned in New York in a life-time.[11]

Stay clear of the tradition-bound academies of New York and Europe, Catlin was saying, and the studios in which his colleagues made dry copies of plaster casts and old master compositions. Under such restrictions, he was convinced that "a painter must modestly sit and breathe away in agony the edge and soul of his inspiration."[12] Nature, not art, had revitalized his notion of antiquity. In the wilderness he had found the source of true inspiration, of that perfection of form manifest in all great models of the past. Like many of his contemporaries, Catlin sought the guiding hand of tradition not in the conventions or "refinements" of society, but in the midst of nature's enduring system.

With "indescribable pleasure," he returned to the West year after year, not only to select and paint his cherished models, but to escape, to seek refuge in the broad expanse of landscape that lay beyond the Mississippi. His happiest moments often occurred at some particularly appealing campsite, where in solitude he could absorb the full effect of nature's offering. One evening, riding his mustang Charley from Fort Gibson to St. Louis, after the conclusion of the long and tiring dragoon expedition, he chanced upon a bit of Missouri prairie as bountiful as Eden.

> Charley and I stopped in one of the most lovely little valleys I ever saw, and even far more beautiful than could have been *imagined* by mortal man. An enchanting little lawn of five or six acres, on the banks of a cool and rippling stream, that was alive with fish; and every now and then, a fine brood

Figure 61. George Romney, *Portrait of Joseph Brandt,* ca. 1776. National Gallery of Canada, Ottawa.

of young ducks, just old enough for delicious food, and too unsophisticated to avoid an easy and simple death. This little lawn was surrounded by bunches and copses of the most luxuriant and picturesque foliage, consisting of the lofty bois d'arcs and elms, spreading out their huge branches, as if offering protection to the rounded groups of cherry and plum-trees that supported festoons of grape-vines, with their purple clusters that hung in the most tempting manner over the green carpet that was everywhere decked out with wild flowers, of all tints and of various sizes, from the modest wild sun-flowers, with their thousand tall and drooping heads, to the lillies that stood, and the violets that crept beneath them. By the side of this cool stream, Charley was fastened, and near him my bear-skin was spread in the grass, and by it my little fire, to which I soon brought a fine string of perch from the brook; from which, and a broiled duck, and a delicious cup of coffee, I made my dinner and supper, which were usually united in one meal, at half an hour's sun. After this I strolled about this sweet little paradise, which I found was chosen, not only by myself, but by the wild deer, which were repeatedly rising from their quiet lairs, and bounding out, and over the graceful swells of the prairies which hemmed

in, and framed this little picture of sweetest tints and most masterly touches.[13]

Letters and Notes abounds in like passages (conveniently "framed" and "tinted" by the author) that describe the idyllic atmosphere of a wild bower, but these are interspersed with sterner statements, reminiscent of appeals from Concord (and Philadelphia), in which Catlin acknowledges the moral obligation to sort out the facts of nature into some intelligible form. To do justice to the Indian, one needed to correct "many theories and opinions which have, either ignorantly or maliciously, gone forth to the world in indelible characters; and gather and arrange a vast deal which has been but imperfectly recorded. . . . The world knows generally," Catlin continues,

that the Indians of North America are copper-coloured; that their eyes and their hair are black, &c.; that they are mostly uncivilized, and consequently unchristianized; that they are nevertheless human beings, with features, thoughts, reason, and sympathies like our own; but few yet know how they *live,* how they *dress,* how they *worship,* what are their actions, their customs, their religion, their amusements, & c. as they practise them in the uncivilized regions of their uninvaded country, which it is the main object of this work, clearly and distinctly to set forth.[14]

In spite of the seeming paradox, Catlin's exalted view of Indian life actually encouraged him to take a serious look at what it was really like. After proceeding west, fired by an ideal notion of primitives, he settled down to observe all aspects of their society, to write a balanced opinion of what he saw, and to paint pictures that would illustrate the true nature of individuals and events on the Great Plains. His portraits, so distant from the classical images of eighteenth-century savages (fig. 61), might stress the bold authority of a Crow chief, the curious gray hair of a Mandan child (fig. 62), or the mixed blood of a Comanche warrior. If he painted his share of potboilers, the majority of his sitters were treated with sympathy and understanding. Few other portrait painters in the nineteenth century achieved as much with Indian subjects, and those who painted as many as Catlin inevitably fell short of the inspired range of the Indian Gallery.

Much the same mixture of emotion and objectivity is evident when Catlin describes Indian ritual or hunting scenes. He celebrates the courage, strength, and endurance of young Mandan candidates, about to submit to the gruesome torture of O-kee-pa (fig. 63), but then records the subsequent ceremony with the eye of a modern anthropologist; he expresses awe at the reckless skill of Sioux running down buffalo, but observes, in the process, the curious quarter-moon of white above the dark irises of the frightened animal's eyes (fig. 64). The prairie landscape, which Catlin thought almost as impressive as its savage inhabitants, he read with a similar breadth of interest. He was one of the first western travelers to characterize it as a vast ocean of waving grass (perhaps again following Cooper's lead), and to give glowing accounts of the potential richness of the land and the unusual appearance of the Missouri shores. Some stretches of the river he thought might be called the "Hell of waters," and he described in sublime terms banks "where . . . mighty forests of stately cottonwood stand, and frown in horrid dark and coolness over the filthy abyss below." Other

Figure 62. *Mint, a pretty girl,* Mandan, 1832, no. 134.

Figure 63. *Bull Dance, Mandan O-kee-pa ceremony,* late 1830s (see no. 505).

Figure 64. *Buffalo bull, grazing on the prairie,* 1832-1833, no. 404.

stretches could not be more picturesque, he says, challenging those who have reported the scenery as monotonous:

The eye is delightfully relieved by wandering over the beautiful prairies; most of the way gracefully sloping down to the water's edge, carpeted with the deepest green, and, in distance, softening into velvet of the richest hues, entirely beyond the reach of the artist's pencil.[15]

The fantastic shapes into which the banks of the river had been carved by spring floods reminded Catlin of the standard array of "ramparts, terraces, domes, towers, citadels, and castles" that one was expected to see in a landscape lacking architectural ruins (figs. 65, 66), but the artist was equally fascinated by the combination of erosion and geology that had caused the phenomenon.

The landscapes Catlin painted on the Upper Missouri (and those that he described) are by far the most accurate and interesting of all that he did during his western travels. Any number of current theories enabled him to appreciate the river's awesome beauty, and he was excited by the mystery of geological change visible at every bend. As a result, the broad path of the Upper Missouri, like the proud savages who lived beside it, brought forth some of his most revealing thoughts, those that began as a transcendental reverie and ended as an ominous vision of the

Figure 65. *View in the Grand Detour, 1900 miles above St. Louis,* 1832, no. 372.

Figure 66. *Picturesque clay bluff, 1700 miles above St. Louis,* 1832, no. 380.

future. What gave Catlin's mission of recording the Plains Indians its poignant urgency was the knowledge that their primitive livelihood was doomed. When it disappeared, he wondered, would there still be faith that civilization could be kept in check by the example of its opposite, or would the cyclical theories of the Comte de Volney and others be fulfilled?

The best summary of these thoughts came forth one clear day in 1832, after Catlin had climbed the high bluff on which Sergeant Floyd of the Lewis and Clark expedition lay buried (fig. 67). "I . . . sat upon his grave, overgrown with grass and the most delicate wild flowers," he recalled,

and contemplated the solitude and stillness of this tenanted mound; and beheld from its top, the windings infinite of the Missouri, and its thousand hills and domes of green, vanishing into blue in distance, when nought but the soft-breathing winds were heard, to break the stillness and quietude of the scene. Where not the chirping of bird or sound of cricket, nor soaring eagle's scream, were interposed 'tween God and man; nor aught to check man's whole surrender of his soul to his Creator. I could not *hunt* upon this ground, but I roamed from hill-top to hill-top, and culled wild flowers, and looked into the valley below me, both up the river and down, and contemplated the thousand hills and dales that are now carpeted with green, streaked as they *will* be, with the plough, and yellow with the harvest sheaf; spotted with lowing kine—with houses and fences, and groups of hamlets and villas . . . wholesome and well-earned contentment and abundance—and again, of wealth and refinements—of idleness and luxury—of vice and its deformities—of fire and sword, and the vengeance of offended Heaven, wreaked in retributive destruction!—and peace, and quiet, and loveliness, and silence, dwelling *again*, over and through these scenes, and blending them into futurity![16]

Unhappily, there was at the very heart of the concept of primitivism a hopeless paradox. Since it was an attitude of mind, or indeed, a cherished dream, it was ever so vulnerable. Either the glimpse of Eden did not match expectations, or, in the case of Catlin, having discovered a primitive society in full flower, he could at once spot the seeds of destruction. The frontier was just over the horizon, inexorably advancing westward, and bringing with it the worst of all aspects of civilization, the demimonde that lay between the comparative light of the East and the perfection of savage life at the mouth of the Yellowstone. Jefferson had noted the changing aspect of society as one proceeded west—it was, he said, like descending through various stages of civilization, until at the frontier one encountered the most barbarous aspects of the white race.[17] Irving lamented that "The current opinion of the Indian character . . . is too apt to be formed from the miserable hordes which infest the frontiers and hang on the skirts of settlements,"[18] and Catlin, more vigorously opposed to westward expansion, saw the frontier as a place "where the genius of natural liberty and independence [of the Indian] have been blasted and destroyed by the contaminating vices and dissipations introduced by the immoral part of *civilized* society . . . My heart has sometimes almost bled with pity for them, while amongst them, and witnessing their innocent amusements, as I have contemplated the inevitable bane that was rapidly advancing upon them."[19]

Figure 67. *Floyd's Grave, where Lewis and Clark buried Sergeant Floyd in 1804*, 1832, no. 376.

Catlin was not alone in his fear that frontier society would destroy all vestiges of Indian culture. His lament echoed similar expressions in Freneau's poetry and the noble speech of Chief Logan from Jefferson's *Notes*. Jedidiah Morse had made an eloquent plea for Indian rights in an 1822 *Report to the Secretary of War*, and this was followed by the prophetic words of Metamora, central character in the play of the same name by John Augustus Stone. Edwin Forrest was a sensation in the leading role when *Metamora* opened in New York, December 15, 1829, and one is tempted to picture Catlin in the audience listening to the following passage:

The pale-faces are around me thicker than the leaves of summer. I chase the hart in the hunting grounds; he leads me to the white man's village. I drive my canoe into the rivers; they are full of the white man's ships. I visit the graves of my fathers: they are lost in the white man's cornfields. They come like the waves of the ocean forever rolling upon the shores. Surge after surge, they dash upon the beach, and every foam-drop is a white man. They swarm over the lands like the doves in winter, and the red men are dropping like withered leaves.[20]

Andrew Jackson as much as sealed the fate of the American Indian by making official in his Second Annual Message (1830) what had been unofficial government policy up until then. We still live with the shame of his chilling logic:

Humanity has often wept over the fate of the aborigines of this country, and Philanthropy has been long busily employed in devising means to avert it, but its progress has never for a moment been arrested, and one by one have many powerful tribes disappeared from the earth. To follow to the tomb the last of his race and to tread on the graves of extinct nations excite melancholy reflections. But true philanthropy reconciles the mind to these vicissitudes as it does to the extinction of one generation to make room for another. . . . What good man would prefer a country covered with forests and ranged by a few thousand savages to our extensive Republic, studded with cities, towns, and prosperous farms. . . .[21]

The Indian Removal Act followed, shunting hapless tribes across the Mississippi and leaving others at the mercy of government officials and private interests who were more determined than ever to seize their lands. Tribal holdings, rich in natural resources the Indians refused to exploit, still blocked westward expansion in many areas, a situation that was thought harmful to the health and prosperity of the nation. Moreover, the majority of Americans had little sympathy with their nomadic and hunting society, which Common Sense philosophy implied was inferior to an agricultural system. Some years later, with profound self-righteousness, Horace Greeley addressed himself to the distinction:

It needs but little familiarity with the actual, palpable aborigines to convince any one that the poetic Indian—the Indian of Cooper and Longfellow—is only visible to the poet's eye. To the prosaic observer, the average Indian of the woods and prairies is a being who does little credit to human nature—a slave of appetite and sloth, never emancipated from the tyranny of one animal passion save by the more ravenous demands of another. As I passed over those magnificent bottoms of the Kansas which form the reservations of the Delawares, Potawatamies, etc., constituting the very best corn-lands on earth, and saw their owners sitting around the doors of their lodges at the height of the planting season and in as good, bright planting weather as sun and soil ever made, I could not help saying, 'These people must die out—there is no help for them. God has given this earth to those who will subdue and cultivate it, and it is vain to struggle against His righteous decree.'[22]

Much of this prejudice might have been overcome had the Indians been willing to accept Christianity. Some conversions were made by Heckewelder and other sympathetic missionaries, but in general the tribes were suspicious of a religious belief that enabled white men to teach one set of values and practice another. In rejecting Christianity, however, they raised an issue that made even the most ardent primitivists uncomfortable. Few believed, in spite of the apparent contradiction, that ultimate happiness and perfect sympathy with nature were possible in a pagan society. Atala could not marry René until he accepted the sacrament. Natty Bumppo admitted the wisdom of only one book, the Bible, and Catlin, about to propose that savage life was more fulfilling than his own, stopped to wonder if the word "happiness" could be "properly applied to the enjoyments of those who have not experienced the light of the Christian religion."[23]

If Catlin finally balked at paganism, however, he did not for a moment lessen his efforts on behalf of the vanishing Indian nations.

His faith in the virtue of primitive people was more than sufficient to make a moral obligation of his mission to record their appearance and customs. It was his duty as an artist to direct his energies toward a noble cause, he was reminded by his colleagues on all sides—but as a lover of justice and freedom, of the proud and independent spirit of primitive man, it may be that he reached for an even higher goal. Something of Thomas Paine's radical zeal comes through in the passionate words he used to justify his choice of a profession:

Justice to a nation who are dying need never be expected from the hands of their destroyers. . . . Long and cruel experience has well proved that it is impossible for enlightened governments or money-making individuals to deal with these credulous and unsophisticated people . . . but the humble biographer or historian, who goes amongst them from a different motive, may come out of their country with his hands and his conscience clean, and himself an anomaly, a white man dealing with Indians, and meeting out justice to them. . . . I have flown to their rescue—not of their lives or of their race (for they are "doomed" and must perish), but to the rescue of their looks and their modes, at which the acquisitive world may hurl their poison and every besom of destruction, and trample them down and crush them to death; yet, phoenix-like, they may rise from the "stain on a painter's palette," and live again upon canvass, and stand forth for centuries yet to come, the living monuments of a noble race. For this purpose, I have designed to visit every tribe of Indians on the Continent, if my life should be spared; for the purpose of procuring portraits of distinguished Indians, of both sexes in each tribe, painted in their native costume; accompanied with pictures of their villages, domestic habits, games, mysteries, religious ceremonies, &c. with anecdotes, traditions, and history of their respective nations.[24]

Even this elaborate program did not entirely ease Catlin's restless conscience, however, and there was at least one occasion when he was unwilling to admit that extinction was inevitable. Having reviewed his reasons for painting savages, and mourned the passing of their splendid primitive world, he had one final dream. Why not set aside a park

where the world could see for ages to come, the native Indian in his classic attire, galloping his wild horse, with sinewy bow, and shield and lance, amid the fleeting herds of elks and buffaloes. What a beautiful and thrilling specimen for America to preserve and hold up to the view of her refined citizens and the world, in future ages! A nation's Park, containing man and beast, in all the wild and freshness of their nature's beauty.

The further we become separated from the wilderness, he argued,

the more pleasure does the mind of enlightened man feel in recurring to those scenes, when he can have them preserved for his eyes and his mind to dwell upon. . . . I would ask no other monument to my memory, nor any other enrolment of my name amongst the famous dead, than the reputation of having been the founder of such an institution.[25]

5

The Artist and His Work

Catlin never says when the delegation of Indians that all but sealed his destiny passed through Philadelphia. Cooper had followed several imposing Pawnee, and representatives from neighboring tribes, from New York to Washington in the fall of 1821, and were one to succumb to historical fantasy, it would be tempting to think that they were the same "lords of the forest" the artist had observed, strutting about the city streets "in silent and stoic dignity." By that time, we have noted, Catlin was established in Philadelphia, and it continued to be an important center for his interests over the next five years. Not only was it the home of a distinguished community of natural scientists, but opportunities were available there, second only to New York, for the training of young artists.

Even before he arrived in Philadelphia, Catlin must have been, as he says, "dabbling" with a brush. During his Litchfield days he attempted several portraits or miniatures of relatives and professors at law school, and after he returned to Pennsylvania his pencil turned more often to sketching than to legal briefs. As a result, he claims, he "commenced the art of painting in Philadelphia, without teacher or adviser."[1] In fact, Catlin did exhibit, perhaps only a short time after his arrival in 1821, four miniatures at the Pennsylvania Academy. But if his training up to that point had been independently gained, it is difficult to believe that he did not fall under the influence of one or more of Philadelphia's able portrait painters in the years that followed. In 1822 and 1823 he exhibited more miniatures at the academy, and then, in 1824, a *Self-Portrait* (fig. 68), which carries the additional inscription in the catalogue: "1st attempt in Oil from life painted by Himself."[2] On the basis of this achievement, presumably, he was elected to academy membership that same year, along with several better-known contemporaries: John Longacre, John Neagle, Bass Otis, Anna Peale, Sarah Peale, and William Strickland.

After a late start, Catlin was probably still trying to catch up with this group of talented professionals, but the *Self-Portrait* was ac-

Figure 68. *Self-Portrait*, 1824. Gilcrease Institute, Tulsa.

Figure 69. Thomas Sully, *Portrait of the Artist*, 1821.
Metropolitan Museum of Art, New York.

have direct access to the master's studio, he might have learned the substance of Sully's method from another artist who did, his fellow academician John Neagle. *Portrait of an Artist*, painted by Catlin but owned by Neagle, was exhibited at the Artist's Fund Society in 1840, probably a testament to a friendship formed in the early 1820s when both artists, exact contemporaries, were struggling together. Neagle, not incidentally, was painting an occasional Indian (fig. 71) from the delegations passing through Philadelphia (one of which was shepherded by a future patron of Catlin, Major Benjamin O'Fallon of St. Louis), and in 1823 he exhibited at the academy *Portrait of Red Jacket, a rapid sketch in oil*, which must have made a deep impression on Catlin, who attempted the same subject (no. 263) three years later. In addition to all this, Neagle was a frequent visitor to Sully's studio in the early 1820s, where he developed his own deft technique and at the same time pursued Sully's stepdaughter, whom he married in 1826. Thus Neagle, as an agent of Sully, may well have helped Catlin through these difficult years. With no other training, the latter's first attempt in oil (if the inscription can be trusted) would indeed have come as something of a triumph.

The Peales have been mentioned as an alternate source from whom Catlin may have gained artistically during his Philadelphia years, but this seems to be confusing the activities of the museum with the father and sons as painters. The neoclassical clarity of their styles presumably would not have appealed to Catlin, although he did not necessarily hold academic theories in disdain, in spite of his later pronouncements. He may have taken a turn at drawing the collection of antique casts that remained in the academy, even though no instruc-

complished enough for one who had been seriously at work for only three or four years. Its mood of youthful romanticism says much about the artist's thoughts and ambition for the coming years, and the brushwork that sets off the handsome features and tousled hair is as bold and free as the artist's gaze. Sully comes to mind at once, of course (fig. 69). Catlin could not have spent three years in Philadelphia without the style of the city's most prominent painter having had some effect upon him. If he were fortunate, he might even have been offered a corner of the large studio Sully (noted for his generosity to students) maintained in Philosophical Hall, or in houses nearby, during this time. The dashing technique of a miniature *Bacchanal* after Rubens (fig. 70), another of Catlin's entries in the 1824 academy exhibition, also suggests that he benefitted from the older artist's instruction, but proof of a relationship is difficult to find. Catlin's copy after Sully, exhibited at the American Academy of Fine Arts in 1828, and two letters written in 1839 are all we have to depend upon.[3] Yet, if Catlin did not

Figure 70. *Bacchanal*, 1824, miniature. Kennedy Galleries, New York.

Figure 71. John Neagle, *Big Kansa (Oto) and Angry Chief (Pawnee)*, 1821. Historical Society of Pennsylvania, Philadelphia.

tion was then available, and he most probably cribbed his expression studies, which must also date from this period, from a copy of Le Brun, perhaps left over from the days when the French neoclassicist Denis Volozan directed the life class.[4] These studies, some twenty self-portraits showing the artist in various stages of wonder, pain, despair, and ecstasy (figs. 72-75), are just the sort of exercise an aspiring portrait painter of the period would practice. Moreover, they are quite carefully executed, in charcoal, with delicate shading and attention to linear detail. Even so, one can hardly miss the exuberance of Catlin's drawing, or the vivid personal interpretation he gives to the characterization of each mood.

Had Catlin's official portraits succeeded as well, he might never have undertaken his western travels. As William Dunlap notes, however, Catlin was in trouble soon after he got to New York. Samuel F. B. Morse had sponsored him for membership to the National Academy of Design, along with Durand and Browere, in April 1826, and Catlin had intended to show at least three portraits in the spring exhibition—a half-length version of the DeWitt Clinton portrait, one of Mrs. Clinton, and the Red Jacket "sketch." Accounts vary as to what happened, but it seems certain that the paintings did not receive the attention

Catlin had anticipated (which may mean that they were hung in an obscure gallery) and he indignantly withdrew the lot.[5] This was followed by his resignation from the academy the next year. Loyd Haberly also came across unfavorable criticism of the Red Jacket portrait (it was apparently condemned as "brutal and ugly"), which may have occurred at the same time.[6] In any case, Catlin did not venture before the New York public again for another two years.

Except for *Bacchanal*, Catlin exhibited only portraits during these years, but he had also attempted a history painting or two and had worked on several important landscape commissions. In addition to the Erie Canal lithographs (1825), William Stone had asked the artist for two murals to decorate the cabin of the *Seneca Chief*, the steamboat upon which Clinton was to preside over the ceremony opening the canal. One was simply a view of Buffalo Harbor, showing the *Seneca Chief* about to depart, but the other was "a classic emblematical production of the pencil," presumably of Catlin's own design. "On the extreme left," we are told in Stone's *Narrative*, was

a figure of Hercules in a sitting posture, leaning upon his favorite club, and resting from the severe labor just completed. The centre shows a section of the Canal, with a lock, and in the foreground is a full length figure of Gov.

Figure 72. *Smile*, 1821-1824, charcoal and white chalk.
Neville Public Museum, Green Bay, Wisconsin.

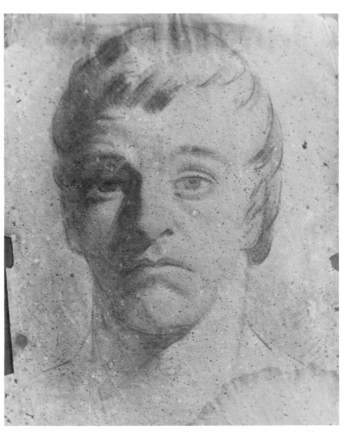

Figure 73. *Sadness*, 1821-1824, charcoal and white chalk.
Neville Public Museum, Green Bay, Wisconsin.

Figure 74. *Wonder*, 1821-1824, charcoal and white chalk.
Neville Public Museum, Green Bay, Wisconsin.

Figure 75. *Anger*, 1821-1824, charcoal and white chalk.
Neville Public Museum, Green Bay, Wisconsin.

Clinton, in Roman costume; he is supposed to have just flung open the lock gate, and with the right hand extended, (the arm being bare,) seems in the act of inviting Neptune, who appears upon the water, to pass through and take possession of the watery regions which the Canal has attached to his former dominions; the God of the Sea is upon the right of the piece, and stands erect in his chariot of shell, which is drawn by sea-horses, holding his trident, and is in the act of recoiling with his body, as if confounded by the fact disclosed at the opening of the lock; Naiades are sporting around the sea-horses in the water, who, as well as the horses themselves, seem hesitating, as if half afraid they were about to invade forbidden regions, not their own.[7]

Catlin's imagination probably far exceeded his ability to compose or paint such an elaborate allegory, but one need not fault him for lack of ambition. Besides, the mural probably flattered and impressed Clinton, who in turn may have prevailed upon Morse to sponsor Catlin at the National Academy the following spring.

The portrait of Red Jacket started out as a history painting, according to Haberly, who says that Catlin had asked his father and Timothy Pickering for a description of their first meeting with the Seneca chief during the Revolutionary War.[8] Putnam replied with a detailed account of the meeting, but Pickering said he could recall nothing of interest for such a painting, and that apparently ended the matter. Catlin mentioned his interest in history painting several years later in his letter to General Porter, but by then, as we have seen, the term was used to dignify the practical scheme he had devised to get himself closer to Indian country.

There is better evidence remaining upon which to make a judgment of the artist's early landscapes. The Erie Canal lithographs (his first known series of landscapes, fig. 3) are primitive efforts, but have a certain vitality and charm as native "view paintings." Lithographs of Niagara Falls (fig. 76) done several years later, but not published until 1831, show an ability to compose on a grander scale, although Catlin may have simply profited from the work of more accomplished artists who had preceded him to the site. Several of the panoramas are marred by improper scale relationships and by Catlin's technique, still inadequate for such full scenic effects. A related series of oil paintings (which have often been mistaken for the originals, but more likely date from the late 1840s), show how much he improved in twenty years (fig. 77). The scenes of the West Point Parade Ground (fig. 5) are the only original oils known to survive from these three series of lithographs. They were painted at about the same time as those of Niagara Falls, but they appear more accomplished in every respect. The technique is smoother, space and perspective sequences are relatively coherent, and the compositions are based on a few simple, traditional formulas. They are by no means major accomplishments, but they do place Catlin squarely in the tradition of the picturesque view painting that the Englishmen Joshua Shaw and William Guy Wall had brought to America just before the 1820s. Shaw, who cut something of a figure in Philadelphia art circles, may have been known to Catlin before the latter left for New York, and Wall's popular *Hudson River Portfolio*, published in several editions between 1820 and 1828, actually included views of

Figure 76. *View from the Canada Shore, one mile below,* lithograph from *Views of Niagara . . .* by George Catlin, 1831, plate 3. U.S. Military Academy Library, West Point.

Figure 77. *View of Both Falls from the Canadian Side, one-half mile below,* late 1840s. Hirschl & Adler Galleries, New York.

West Point (fig. 78) painted in the same broad and slightly primitive style as Catlin's. Wall, of course, was a more imaginative painter, capable of a far more sophisticated definition of space and atmosphere, but these were grafted upon an essentially factual approach to landscape. His rolling hills, peaceful rivers, and secluded villas were usually a fair equivalent of the scene that had inspired the painting. If Cat-

Figure 78. William Guy Wall, *West Point*, 1820-1825, watercolor. New-York Historical Society.

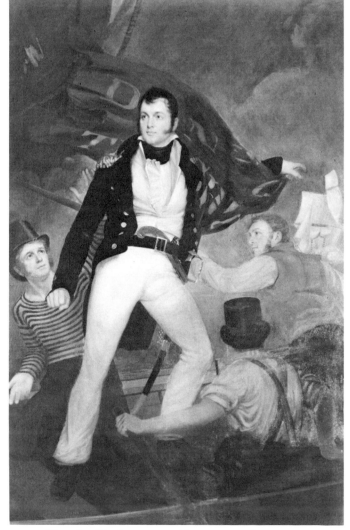

Figure 79. John Wesley Jarvis, *Oliver Hazard Perry*, 1816. City Hall, New York.

lin understood little else about this continental tradition, he did seem to know what was required of him when he first saw the green hills of the Upper Missouri.

Despite such landscape commissions, the majority of Catlin's income must have come from portrait painting during these years. In the spring of 1828, he exhibited twelve works at the American Academy of Fine Arts, all but two of which were portraits. Included were the full-length version of Clinton (fig. 6) and the Red Jacket "sketch" (as Catlin referred to it, fig. 4), one copy after Sully, and nine unidentified subjects. He fared better critically than in 1826, the *New-York Mirror* commenting that the merits of the Clinton portrait were "well known."[9] Hindsight, however, makes Dunlap's adverse remarks seem closer to the mark. The rigid planes of Clinton's face and costume must have been a harsh contrast to the suave performances of Jarvis (fig. 79), Sully, or Inman, whose portraits shared with Catlin's the chambers of the New York Common Council. The crude technique of the Red Jacket sketch showed as little promise, although it had been painted two years earlier. In the fall of 1828, Catlin tried again with Indian subjects, painting a Winnebago delegation (nos. 209-17) he met in Washington, but the results were gruesome (fig. 80). All of this is a bit surprising when one recalls the talent he had demonstrated in his 1824 *Self-Portrait*. Not even the Indian portraits of Charles Bird King, which he could have seen in the old office of Thomas McKenney, Superintendent of Indian Trade, at the War Department, nor the examples of his Philadelphia colleagues, Neagle and the Peales, seemed to offer him any guide, and his talent seemed doomed until he arrived in St. Louis a year and half later. His last effort before heading west, a portrait of the Virginia Constitutional Convention (fig. 8) painted in the winter of 1829-30, can only be seen as an exercise in frustration. The august legislators, whose outsized heads pivot on scrawny dark bodies, are perched around the chamber like so many magpies. Perhaps they began to appear that way to the artist, who must have wearied of the task long before it was over.

Two and a half years after Catlin completed the Virginia Convention, he was painting some of his finest portraits. Much traveling and many portraits intervened, but only inspiration can account for such a dramatic change. What follows, therefore, is more an attempt to measure that inspiration than to provide an annual progress report on Catlin's years out West. The many distinctions of style and quality in the works that compose the Indian Gallery are more properly discussed in the catalogue that follows. Evidence has been given there to document the artist's growth from year to year, to explain when and where he painted each tribe listed in the 1848 catalogue. Catlin's notes on each entry have been included, along with critical comments on individual paintings; and the accuracy of his work, insofar as it concerns art historical problems, has been carefully examined. But 607 catalogue entries tend to magnify differences, and it is more important that we see the Indian Gallery as a work of art in itself. Stylistic problems fall away before the broader aspect of Catlin's accomplishment—the number and range of his subjects and the various attitudes outlined in the previous chapters that are reflected in his work. We must realize, in addition, that splendid individual portraits and lively village scenes were just one aspect of illustrating Indian life on the Great Plains. Other items from his collection, and his many publications, are almost as necessary to understanding the full significance of the Indian Gallery.

One must not imply, however, that Catlin's talents were equal in all fields. He will be remembered as a portrait painter, whose Indian subjects began with Red Jacket and reached full expression in the somber and powerful image of Little Wolf (fig. 40; no. 521), singled out for praise by Baudelaire at the Salon of 1846. Once the artist arrived on the Upper Missouri, his subjects gained a dignity and meaning that would have seemed impossible two years earlier, and each succeeding year he capitalized more on the color and variety of savage life. He could make the most of the different headdresses of One Horn (fig. 81; no. 69) and The Surrounder (fig. 82; no. 117), the graceful topknot of the former complementing his impassive features and the roach of the latter doing the same for the massive line of his jaw. He urged sitters to display handsome pipes (fig. 83; no. 122), decorated weapons, and domestic accessories (fig. 84; no. 186), and to dress in their most distinctive costumes. Bust portraits and half-lengths were interspersed with standing figures, some posed like classical statues, every symbol of their office draped about them (nos. 114, 152), and others less formally presented, like the numerous females who cling tenderly to their children (no. 177). The assortment of characters included Bloody Hand (fig. 85; no. 123) and Little Spaniard (fig. 86; no. 51), whose wild appearance was a mark of their skill and daring in battle. The latter, a half-breed, was obliged to lead Comanche war parties to prove his courage, but peaceful and eloquent John W. Quinney (fig. 87; no. 273) preached to his people that their days of fighting were over. Catlin noted every line in the aged faces of Wee-tá-ra-shá-ro (no. 55), a Wichita chief, and Black Moccasin (fig. 88; no. 171), who remembered Lewis and Clark, but the portraits still manage to convey that great respect Indians have for the elders of their tribes. Children, whom Catlin sometimes portrayed as shrunken adults (no. 181), more often have the pleasing corpulence of baroque putti (fig. 89; no. 159), and females vary from ageless aboriginal types (fig. 90; no. 195) to soft and provocative maidens like Thighs and Wild Sage (fig. 91; nos. 58, 59), who make one suspicious of the artist's objectivity.

Not only did Catlin paint a variety of subjects, but he took care to suggest individual characteristics and attributes when they seemed appropriate. The round and pleasant features of Sam Perryman (fig. 92; no. 289), for example, tell us much about his personality, and the shy smile of Kay-a-gís-gis (fig. 93; no. 183) indicates a slight discomfort and uncertainty at suddenly becoming the center of attention. Mick-e-no-páh (no. 300) was part black and owned 100 slaves, Catlin wrote in the 1848 catalogue and confirmed in the portrait of the Seminole chief. The artist was also interested in the unusual cranial contour of male Crow Indians. Several he painted in profile (nos. 163, 168) to emphasize their receding foreheads, the dominant genetic trait in the appearance of the tribe.

Figure 80. *He Who Comes on the Thunder,* Winnebago, 1828, no. 211.

Costumes and poses were further variables. Subjects were dressed in every conceivable article, from the briefest of loin cloths to the most elaborate deer and buffalo-hide garments. The decoration of these garments was as distinctive as the taste of each warrior (fig. 94; no. 145) or squaw (fig. 95; no. 144) who wore them. Civilized tribes often mixed white and native costumes to great advantage (fig. 96; no. 284), but some Indians preferred to appear in white men's clothes (fig. 97; no. 271). The latter, typically, are more conservative in pose and manner, as if the atmosphere of the studio had taken its toll. (In spite of their native costumes, certain Indians Catlin painted in Europe suffered a similar fate; see no. 538.) Poses came from any number of sources. Many were based on classical prototypes (fig. 98; no. 170), and others must have been improvised at the last moment. None are elabo-

Figure 81. *One Horn, head chief of the Miniconjou tribe,* Teton Dakota (Western Sioux), 1832, no. 69.

Figure 82. *The Surrounder, chief of the tribe,* Oto, 1832, no. 117.

Figure 83 *(above left). He Who Kills the Osages, chief of the tribe,* Missouri, 1832, no. 122.

Figure 84 *(above right). Jú-ah-kís-gaw, woman with her child in a cradle,* Ojibwa, 1835, no. 186.

Figure 85 *(bottom right). Bloody Hand, chief of the tribe,* Arikara, 1832, no. 123.

Figure 86 *(facing page). Little Spaniard, a warrior,* Comanche, 1834, no. 51.

Figure 87. *John W. Quinney (The Dish), a missionary preacher,* Mohegan (Stockbridge), 1836, no. 273.

rate, and most are between bust and half-length, but angles and positions constantly change. Routine poses are more often repeated in standing male portraits. Each figure assumed the dignity of its classical ancestor in a different way, however, despite a few hasty adaptations (nos. 45, 80). When the artist chose to abandon antiquity, which he frequently did, he took a more direct approach to subjects (fig. 99; no. 129), or used a characteristic activity as the basis for their design (fig. 100; no. 299).

While variety may have been one of Catlin's chief assets, the different techniques (and the borrowed poses) he uses in his portraits raise other issues, less easily resolved, about the nature of his work. At first glance, considerations of time and interest seem to take precedence over style; yet one cannot help but notice that important subjects (and commissions) are usually more carefully finished than other paintings in the collection. When he insisted in the 1848 catalogue that his work consisted of "true and fac-simile traces of individual life and

historical facts," he meant, apparently, that he prized an accurate record above all other representations of a subject.[10] A photograph would have done as well, he implies, and asks to be forgiven the present "unfinished and unstudied condition" of his paintings. Not only was this a calculated retreat from academic criticism, as we have seen, but it was a theory of necessity for Catlin, whose schedule was so demanding at times that he was obliged to rough in half a dozen portraits per day. The fact that his technique does vary, however, suggests some ambivalence on his part as to how he regarded his work. He did, after all, enter in the Salon of 1846 two portraits that he must have thought of as more than "fac-similes." Since they are both relatively finished paintings, one would judge that he thought this a requisite condition for a work of art. To be sure, a minimum of careful brushwork was needed for an accurate transcription of any subject, but beyond such immediate considerations, there is ample evidence to prove that Catlin was making distinctions between high art and production. How fine these distinctions were and how often they were practiced is another problem; we can only guess by considering a few obvious contrasts.

Corn (fig. 101; no. 78) and *Round Island* (fig. 102; no. 265), for example, are among the most broadly brushed works in the collection. The former, in particular, shows every indication of having been painted with remarkable speed, but with a sureness that brings off a distinct image—or, perhaps one should say, a "sureness" that appeals to us today. Presumably, Catlin would have relegated both to the category of mere transcriptions, but *Osceola* (fig. 103; no. 301), modeled with neoclassic perfection, was obviously a bid for public acceptance. It was as far as he could go in the opposite direction toward meeting the demands of what he considered reigning academic taste. If we were to decide his *juste milieu* today, we would probably place it somewhere between, with portraits such as *The Six* (fig. 104; no. 182) and *Horse Chief* (fig. 20; no. 99). In which category would he have classified these, one wonders, or the handsome group of female portraits (nos. 124, 134, 144) in which he finished costume decoration and jewelry with a dazzling touch. While we cannot be sure of his answers, we need not be too indulgent, either, of his professed intentions.

Catlin was no more consistent when it came to modifying the details of his portraits. Many of the weapons held in the hands of male sitters, one suspects, were calculated additions of a later date, and he could not have spent countless hours in the field copying the colorful array of beads worn by female sitters. On the other hand, the artist admits that he did not include all the detail he described in *Letters and Notes* as part of Four Bears's costume (fig. 105). "Such trappings and ornaments as interfered with the grace and simplicity of the figure," were omitted, he says, a statement that hardly squares with his claim that his paintings were "unstudied . . . as works of art."[11] In fact, Catlin undoubtedly made many such changes, not only in costume details, but in posing and arranging his figures. He borrowed from classical sources, made the most of the stern countenances and exotic trappings of his sitters, and employed every other convention of traditional portraiture. While these practices do not necessarily contradict his pro-

Figure 88. *Black Moccasin, aged chief,* Hidatsa, 1832, no. 171.

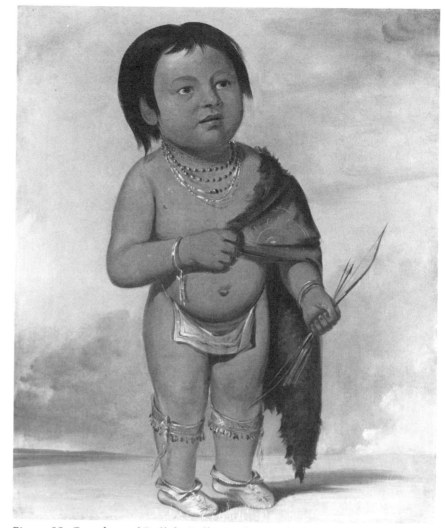

Figure 89. *Grandson of Buffalo Bull's Back Fat,* Blackfoot, 1832, no. 159.

fessed concern for accuracy, they do indicate that he was not nearly so indifferent to academic methods as he wished people to believe.

The variation of Catlin's style is made more confusing by the uneven quality of his work. Except for his first year in the West (1830), when he was occasionally groping for control, and his perennial bouts with anatomy, he was capable of a convincing likeness during the entire course of his travels. If he did not always achieve one, it can usually be attributed again to lack of interest or a busy schedule. Protocol made it necessary for him to paint certain individuals in each tribe to whom he was blandly indifferent (no. 185), and he made no secret of his preference for the proud savages of the Upper Missouri over those tribes whose customs had been compromised by civilization. One glance at *The Dog* (fig. 106; no. 85) and *The Crow* (fig. 107; no. 193) reveals the difference, although Catlin could if he wished show the hopeless plight of frontier Indians with great sympathy and compassion (fig. 108; no. 198). Catlin's lack of training in anatomy was a more serious problem.

He seemed to have a natural ability to grasp the dimensions and planes of facial structure, but his methods of coping with the rest of the figure were decidedly less adequate. There was often a discrepancy in finish between the two, since the likeness was carefully taken in the field, and the rest of the portrait only roughed in (and sometimes never finished). Wa-ho-béck-ee (fig. 110; no. 33), for example, has a polished head, but his ill-positioned arms and his costume have been given only cursory definition. Often the scale of arms and hands was never corrected (no. 41), and seated figures have torsos and legs that do not properly connect (fig. 111; no. 102). If proportions were reasonably accurate in full-length figures, the draftsmanship might be so weak as to make them appear incapable of natural movement (nos. 38-40). Yet under different circumstances, Catlin could arrange the components of a seated figure with some grace and assurance, he could draw standing figures that seemed ready to spring into action, and tribal leaders of genuine merit he could endow with full dignity and authority.

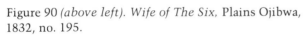

Figure 90 *(above left). Wife of The Six,* Plains Ojibwa, 1832, no. 195.

Figure 91 *(above right). Wild Sage, a Wichita woman,* 1834, no. 59.

Figure 92 *(bottom right). Sam Perryman.* Creek, 1834, no. 289.

Figure 93. *Kay-a-gís-gis, a young woman,* Plains Ojibwa, 1832, no. 183.

Figure 94. *Rabbit's Skin Leggings, a brave,* Nez Perce, 1832, no. 145.

Figure 95. *She Who Bathes Her Knees, wife of the chief,* Cheyenne, 1832, no. 144.

Figure 96. *Dutch, a war chief,* Cherokee, 1834, no. 284. Collection of Mr. and Mrs. Paul Mellon, Upperville, Virginia.

Figure 97. *Cú-sick, son of the chief,* Tuscarora, probably 1837-1839, no. 271.

Figure 98. *He Who Jumps over Everyone,* Crow, 1865-1870 (see no. 170). Collection of Mr. and Mrs. Paul Mellon, Upperville, Virginia.

Figure 99. *Old Bear, a medicine man,* Mandan, 1832, no. 129.

Figure 100 *(top left). Drinks the Juice of the Stone, in ball-player's dress,* Choctaw, 1834, no. 299.

Figure 101 *(above). Corn, a Miniconjou(?) warrior,* Teton Dakota (Western Sioux), 1832, no. 78.

Figure 102 *(bottom left). Round Island, a warrior,* Seneca, 1831, no. 265.

Figure 103. *Osceola, the Black Drink, a warrior of great distinction,* Seminole, 1838, no. 301.

Figure 104. *The Six, chief of the Plains Ojibwa,* 1832, no. 182.

Figure 105. *Four Bears, second chief, in full dress,* Mandan, 1832, no. 128.

Figure 106 *(above left). The Dog, chief of the Bad Arrow Points Band,* Teton Dakota (Western Sioux), 1832, no. 85.

Figure 107 *(above right).The Crow, a dandy,* Ojibwa,1836, no.193.

Figure 108 *(bottom). Big Sail, a chief,* Ottawa, probably 1836, no. 198.

No matter what method the artist used to compose and paint his portraits, however, their ultimate success was determined by the drama of his palette. Traveling with only a dozen or so colors, and canvases he kept rolled in a large cylinder, he wasted no time with preliminary sketching. The outlines of the figure were placed on the canvas with broad, sepia strokes, and then the bust was modeled directly in warm earth tones (see nos. 100, 119). Depending on the time remaining, he would begin to fill in costume details with unmixed touches of vermilion, ultramarine, prussian blue, and various ochres and umbers, until a scheme was established that would enable him to complete the portrait after he returned home (fig. 109). Pigment was originally applied in thin strokes, so that it would dry quickly and not crack when the canvases were rerolled for storage, but once back in the studio Catlin filled in the broad, flat areas of costume with colors of sufficient strength to balance the details. Heads were finished with middle tones, but folds and contours of the robes and blankets were treated with primitive simplicity. An alternate slash of color barely provided the necessary dimension, and suggested the texture of the material. Smaller accessories were carefully gauged for contrast and pattern, the colors chosen, it would seem, as much for display as for an authentic record. Yet boldness of color was not a characteristic of Catlin's style before 1830, and his subsequent talent strikes one as genuinely inspired by his encounter with red men and their exotic costumes. To duplicate their appearance, he forged a palette that would have shocked most of his colleagues in New York, but which was, in fact, the most effective ingredient in his vivid portrayal of the Indian. What remains remarkable is how quickly this talent emerged. In the space of a few years he learned to balance raw tones and contrasting values with enough skill to impress one of the great critics of nineteenth-century France.

Had Catlin worked consistently at his painting, had there been a clear development in his portrait style from 1832 to 1844 (when he painted the Iowa troupe in London), perhaps we could now assess his position among his peers with some confidence. As it stands, however, his interests were too broad to perfect any one of his talents, and such uneven results leave one at a loss, finally, to account for his ability. Energy and devotion made him a brilliant interpreter of savage life, but expediency often robbed him of ultimate artistic success. Yet some half dozen portraits in the Indian Gallery are such masterful interpretations of mood and character that they easily surpass the efforts of Charles Bird King and Karl Bodmer, his two most challenging contemporaries, and bring him close to the moving portrait of *Black Hawk and His Son* by Jarvis (fig. 112). Not one of those who followed Catlin painted more Indians as successfully, nor did they produce portraits so memorable that they transcended the genre. Perhaps the greatest tribute we now pay Catlin is to place his work in the context of all serious artists of his time, not just those who went west. He has, inevitably, outgrown the category he set for himself.

As a landscape painter, Catlin never reached a comparable level, although he produced much imaginative and original work during the

Figure 109. *Buffalo Bull, a Grand Pawnee warrior*, 1832, no. 100.

1830s. He ascended the Missouri with the full vocabulary of the picturesque at his command, noting ruins, the gentle conformation of the green hills, and the sublime aspect of prairie fires (nos. 374, 375). The artful view painting of Wall was soon modified, however, to describe the fascinating array of geological formations that appeared at every bend. In search of a means of capturing quickly the changing scenery, Catlin followed his portrait method, painting directly on small canvases (11 by 14 inches) from the deck of the steamboat or from the top of strategic bluffs on his way downriver. Not even Cole or Doughty had ventured to paint from nature at that time, and the first of Durand's outdoor oil sketches date from the mid-1840s. Yet there was Catlin in 1832, stating that he had stopped many times along the banks of the Missouri, "clambered up their grassy and flower decked sides, and . . . carefully traced and fastened them in colours on [his] canvass."[12] While one must regard Catlin's claims with a skeptical eye, he repeats this story so often, even embellishing it with the struggles of Batiste

Figure 110. *Wa-ho-béck-ee, a handsome brave,* Osage, 1834, no. 33.

Figure 111. *Little Chief, a Tapage Pawnee warrior,* 1832, no. 102.

and Bogard, the two voyageurs who carried his easel up the steepest bluffs, that one must accept the method or categorically doubt every page of *Letters and Notes.*

Certain landscapes seem little more than a pleasant record of the scenery—the endless variety of the conical mounds, the intense green of prairie grass, and the pattern of shadows that softened the river vista. Catlin says as much when he recalls the circumstances under which *River Bluffs, 1320 miles above St. Louis* (fig. 113; no. 399) was painted.

We landed our canoe at the base of a beautiful series of grass-covered bluffs . . . I took my easel, and canvass and brushes . . . to their summits [and painted] even to a line . . . two views from the same spot; the one looking up, and the other down the river. The reader, by imagining these hills to be five or six hundred feet high, and every foot of them, as far as they can be discovered in distance, covered with a vivid green turf, whilst the sun is gilding one side, and throwing a cool shadow on the other, will be enabled to form something like an ade-

quate idea of the shores of the Missouri. From this enchanting spot there was nothing to arrest the eye from ranging over its waters for the distance of twenty or thirty miles, where it quietly glides between its barriers, formed of thousands of green and gracefully sloping hills, with its rich and alluvial meadows, and woodlands—and its hundred islands, covered with stately cottonwood.[13]

On another occasion he climbed to a vantage point above *Big Bend on the Upper Missouri* (fig. 16; no. 390), requested his canvas and easel, and set to work. Again he marveled at the expansive view and its picturesque qualities, but he noted that the cause of all he admired was the rather spectacular channel carved by the Missouri through a *"super* surface" of "tabular hills" he carefully outlined in the background. The clear light that crosses the river and casts delicate colors and shadows across the bluffs, one would also like to attribute to Catlin's direct methods, although he appears to have had a more positive interest in geology than atmosphere in the Upper Missouri landscapes. At the

Figure 112. John Wesley Jarvis, *Black Hawk and His Son*, 1833. Gilcrease Institute, Tulsa.

"Brick Kilns" (fig. 114; no. 366), for example, he gives a reasonably scientific explanation of how their unique form and color came about:

By the action of water, or other power, the country seems to have been graded away; leaving occasionally a solitary mound or bluff, rising in a conical form to the height of two or three hundred feet, generally pointed or rounded at the top, and in some places grouped together in great numbers . . . the sides of these conical bluffs (which are composed of strata of different coloured clays), are continually washing down by the effect of the rains and melting of the frost; and the superincumbent masses of pumice and basalt are crumbling off, and falling down to their bases; and from thence, in vast quantities, by the force of the gorges of water which are often cutting their channels between them—carried into the river, which is close by. . . .

The upper part of this layer of pumice is of a brilliant red; and when the sun is shining upon it, is as bright and vivid as vermilion. These curious bluffs must be seen as they are in nature; or else in a painting, where their colours are faithfully given, or they lose their picturesque beauty, which consists in the variety of their vivid tints.[14]

Thus the painting is both a record of geological change and a varied arrangement of forms and colors that constitute, in the eyes of the artist, a pleasing effect.

Catlin may also have had a larger plan in mind when he painted this series of forty small canvases. Joshua Shaw had earlier called attention to the picturesque character of American rivers, and Wall's *Hudson River Portfolio* had been, in effect, a portrait of the river between New York and Albany (and in addition, perhaps, a stepping stone toward the river panoramas of the mid-nineteenth century). Catlin's series was a similar concept—a continuous narrative of the Missouri from the mouth of the Yellowstone to its entry into the Mississippi. Many of the landscape titles have an indication of mileage above St. Louis, and others designate particular geographic points along the river. One could follow its course and the changing appearance of the countryside in a remarkably consistent fashion, acquiring in the process a knowledge that might serve a variety of interests. It

Figure 113. *River Bluffs, 1320 miles above St. Louis,* 1832, no. 399.

Figure 114. "Brick Kilns," clay bluffs 1900 miles above St. Louis, 1832, no. 366.

Figure 115. Karl Bodmer, *Remarkable Eminences on the Banks of the Missouri*, 1833, engraving. Reuben Gold Thwaites, ed., *Early Western Travels*, volume 25, plate 67.

was, after all, the first comprehensive view of western landscape offered to the population back East, and it represented something vastly more tangible than the fanciful reports it replaced.

Bodmer's fragmentary glimpses along the banks of the Missouri (fig. 115) illustrate best, perhaps, what Catlin's series was not. Bodmer concentrated on isolated formations in all but a few of his river views, while Catlin attempted a full panorama as he traveled from St. Louis to Fort Union, and back again. Technically, Bodmer was a far superior artist. His broad vistas of the Missouri (fig. 116) are superb topographical documents; Catlin's, by comparison, are primitive, repetitious, and

moonlike in appearance. With a limited supply of pigments, and too great a fondness for the verdant carpet of the prairie, the latter was undoubtedly guilty of some distortion and simplification. Yet his faults become a virtue when the scenes are taken together. The merging of the endless sequence offers a compelling vision, a unity of design and mood that makes a silver path of the river, winding through the green hills of Eden. The artist would later be criticized for taking liberties with the landscape, but for us they make his account of the Missouri as valuable as that of any of his contemporaries.

Catlin was eloquent in his appreciation of the Mississippi, too,

Figure 116. Karl Bodmer, *Missouri River, with Bear Paw Mountains in the Distance,* 1833, watercolor. Joslyn Art Museum, Omaha. Northern Natural Gas Company Collection.

Figure 117. *Prairie du Chien, United States garrison,* 1835-1836, no. 333.

Figure 118. *Picturesque bluffs above Prairie du Chien,* 1835-1836, no. 317.

Figure 119. Seth Eastman, *On the Mississippi, 30 Miles above Prairie du Chien, Indians Moving to a New Camp,* 1847-1849, watercolor. St. Louis Art Museum.

but his statements were never followed by the direct paintings or the careful notes that he made on the Missouri. Only a pencil and sketchbook were used from his canoe on the Mississippi (see fig. 157; nos. 312, 327) and the oils that came later are doubtless studio products of the following winter. Such views as *Prairie du Chien* (fig. 117; no. 333) or the *Picturesque Bluffs* (fig. 118; no. 317) above the town are probably accurate enough, but they do not have the concentrated vision of his earlier efforts, nor, for that matter, the freshness and economy of Seth Eastman's wash drawings of similar subjects (see fig. 119; no. 320). Such southwest prairie scenes as *View on the Canadian River* (no. 351)

are even less inspired, although in one instance Catlin added a portion of Hudson River monumentality to a mountainside near the Comanche village (fig. 121; no. 352). In general, however, the written descriptions of his canoe trips down the Mississippi and his visit to the Comanche country are far more interesting than any landscapes he sketched during these travels (see no. 488).

Catlin's landscape technique followed much the same pattern (or lack of it) that we saw in his portraits. Time and interest often determined finish, there was no consistent attempt to improve his style, and the results are uneven. The Missouri River landscapes are his

finest accomplishment, but he also painted a detailed cityscape of St. Louis (fig. 10; no. 311), the first view of the sacred Pipestone Quarry (fig. 27; no. 337) in southwestern Minnesota, and early versions of many important frontier outposts, such as Fort Snelling (fig. 24; no. 332) on the Upper Mississippi. At the opposite pole from such documentary pictures are a group of landscape backgrounds (so called for want of a better term) that place a different light on Catlin's artistic interests. During conservation treatment some years ago, they were found attached to the backs of original canvases, presumably as liners. They appear to be abstract landscape settings that the artist prepared for the series of hunting scenes he painted in Europe to round out the Indian Gallery. He would probably object strongly to our giving them independent status, but they are, nevertheless, tantalizing arguments for the potential of his technique (figs. 120, 122). Only an obscure horizon line reminds us that they were intended as landscapes; otherwise, they might pass as a scheme for an exotic stage on which Catlin had thought to compose a tableau of primitive life (see nos. 543, 558, 596). Arrangements of bright pastel tones, softened and merged by delicately

Figure 120 *(facing page, top)*. Landscape background,
1846-1848.

Figure 121 *(facing page, bottom). Ta-wa-que-nah, or the Rocky
Mountain, near the Comanche village,* 1834-1835, no. 352.

Figure 122 *(above).* Landscape
background, 1846-1848.

Figure 123. *Wounded buffalo, strewing his blood over the prairies,* 1832-1833, no. 406.

Figure 124. *Buffalo bulls fighting in running season, Upper Missouri,* 1837-1839, no. 424.

Figure 125. *Catlin and his Indian guide approaching buffalo under white wolf skins,* 1846-1848, no. 590.

textured brushstrokes, begin as interpretations of atmospheric phenomena and end as luminous visions of the artist's fancy. The scenes are related, perhaps, to European and American sky studies of the early and mid-nineteenth century, but in the final analysis Catlin seems more intent on simply inventing independent patterns of brushwork and color.

When Catlin turns to describing the habits and appearance of buffalo in *Letters and Notes,* he gives us, for once, a clear account of his method of taking field sketches. Having wounded a large bull in a hunt near the mouth of the Yellowstone, he followed the animal until, on the verge of death, it turned and challenged him to advance another step (see fig. 123; no. 406). At that point the artist drew forth his notebook and began sketching the besieged model, which "stood stiffened up . . . swelling with awful vengeance." He made a full circle to observe the "numerous attitudes" of the bull, and when it collapsed from exhaustion and loss of blood, Catlin would throw his cap, "rousing him on his legs, rally[ing] a new expression, and sketch him again."[15] The description reminds us of the careful (if less gruesome) scrutiny John Godman gave to many of the animals he discussed in *Natural History.* The reward for such patient field work is evident in Godman's publication and in the oil paintings Catlin composed from his sketchbooks. Not only had the artist mastered the anatomy of the buffalo, but he noted other characteristic traits, such as the dark color of the animals' summer coats, and the curious appearance of their eyes (see fig. 64; no. 404), which were always "strained quite open . . . the ball rolling forward and down; so that a considerable part of the iris is hidden behind the lower lid."[16] He distinguishes between the coats and

horns of the male and female, shows bulls fighting in running season (fig. 124; no. 424), and "wallowing" in the summer (no. 425) to avoid the fierce heat of the prairie. Even methods of stalking the beasts or chasing them to death are illustrated in considerable detail (fig. 125; no. 590), despite Catlin's concern for the diminishing herds.

Buffalo hunts were a means of displaying the power and endurance of the animal, and the courage of his Indian pursuer. They were high drama on the Plains, a raw test of primitive survival in which the buffalo was pitted against the hunter in a race to death. Usually the Indian was victorious, but when he suffered defeat it was gory and painful in the extreme (fig. 126; no. 423). While Catlin studied the sport carefully, never failing, for example, to have the rider approach the buffalo from the right side, he often had difficulty representing animals moving at a fast pace or grouping them effectively in a composition (no. 413). Buffalo and horses in the hunting scenes of the 1830s are given the appearance of running by simply repeating the fixed position of their legs. Not until the lithographers at Day and Hague corrected his style (see figs. 127-29; nos. 411, 413) was Catlin able to simulate more realistic action. He did less well, in general, with the anatomy of horses and grizzly bears than with buffalo. The linear elegance of the former was more difficult to represent, and he would have been hard pressed to make a leisurely study of the latter.

A different problem arises with the hunting scenes Catlin painted in Europe (fig. 130; nos. 543-607), which at best are only nostalgic recollections of actual events from the artist's past. Those he produced shortly after returning from the Upper Missouri are usually regarded as more legitimate interpretations of Indian life. Yet if we

Figure 126. *Dying buffalo in a snowdrift*, 1837-1839, no. 423.

Figure 127. *Buffalo chase over prairie bluffs*, 1832-1833, no. 411.

Figure 128. *Buffalo Chase*, lithograph. *Catlin's North American Indian Portfolio*, 1844, plate 6.

Figure 129. *Buffalo Hunting with Bow, Arrow, and Spear*, mid-1850s (see no. 411). Royal Ontario Museum, Toronto.

exalt the spirit of the latter, and dismiss the former as studio fabrications, how do we judge *Buffalo chase in snowdrifts* (fig. 131; no. 417), in which the snowy background fades into a harmony of tones as delicate and beguiling as any Catlin painted. Plunging over drifts in the foreground are two hunters in summer war dress, adequate testimony that the artist had never experienced a winter on the Great Plains.

Except for the original versions of the Mandan O-kee-pa series (nos. 504-7), one can safely assume that the remaining Indian dance and ritual scenes are studio paintings, composed from fragmentary notes and sketches. The dance scenes (nos. 436-54), in fact, are simply amusing variations of one another, all based on the same composition and the same lively repetition of essentially static dancers (see figs. 132, 133; nos. 440, 451). Figures, costumes, and accessories vary in an attempt to give each an individual authenticity. Draftsmanship prevails over direct painting, anticipating the style Catlin would use in his European copies and in the cartoon series. Many of these comments apply as well to the ball-play scenes (fig. 22; nos. 427-30), which were painted at about the same time. Once again, running figures repeat one another's position to effect the equivalent of motion. Catlin marshalls the great numbers of figures together in effective patterns, and sets these off against droll incidents that show players grappling with one another, or drunken observers on the sidelines, who writhe on the ground in laughter or retch and fall asleep.

A Mandan archery scene (fig. 134; no. 435), an encyclopedia of classical poses Catlin used in standing portraits, has a quite different emphasis. Individual figures in the friezelike composition are carefully played off against one another, creating an exaggerated rhythm that carries one's eye from left to right down the line of warriors. It is the closest Catlin came to illustrating the familiar parallel (not much changed since Benjamin West's first encounter with classical sculpture) between Indian sports and "Grecian youths in the beautiful rivalry of the Olympian games." In the process, he demonstrates his knowledge of anatomy in a highly self-conscious manner, as if to prove that his own variety of classical training might indeed flourish in the wilderness. It is no less "unstudied as a work of art" than the portrait of Four Bears, and suffers too much perhaps from advance planning. On the other hand, scenes like *Dance of the chiefs* (no. 436) become a grotesque charade, so hastily and crudely are the figures drawn. Catlin did paint the series for Louis Philippe with extreme care (fig. 135; see no. 449), embellishing costumes and backgrounds for dramatic effect, and occasionally he arranged the compositions of other Indian rituals with amusing invention (fig. 14; no. 494).

More important than the criticism of Catlin's technique, however, is the fact that he chose to paint these scenes at all. Only Peter Rindisbacher and Titian Peale had turned their attention earlier to aspects of Indian life other than portraits and landscapes, and their efforts had been minor. Like Heckewelder and Schoolcraft, who had studied the myths and legends of the eastern tribes in order to gain a deeper knowledge of their society, Catlin was unwilling to limit his investigation to mere likenesses of tribal leaders. If the complexity and richness

Figure 130. *Elk and buffalo making acquaintance, Texas,* 1846-1848, no. 581.

of Indian life were to be understood, he argued, there must be a record of their games and amusements, hunting and war-making activities, and their sacred rituals. It was a mark of his sympathy and respect for these vanishing tribes, an attitude that enabled the artist to probe more deeply into Plains Indian culture than all but a few of his contemporaries. In a word, Catlin honored their primitive existence as a source from which civilized men could learn again the lessons of the wilderness. No aspect of it should be denied to those who sought the ideal among tribes still living in simple harmony with nature.

At the end of Catlin's 1848 catalogue is a section called "Opinions of the Press." It consists of forty pages of clippings from a variety of American and European newspapers, carefully selected by Catlin to publicize the reception given his collection from its first exhibition in New York to the final days in Paris. They are mostly puffs, of course, and all say about the same thing. They praise the artist for bravely assaulting the wilderness to carry out his mission, for his skill and energy in rescuing the image of a vanishing race, and for bringing to the public such an accurate and vivid account of Plains Indian life. It will remain, they agree, a work of permanent historical interest, and the artist/author is to be congratulated for his noble sentiments on behalf of the American savage. In addition to the clippings already quoted, *The American Daily Advertiser* offers a concise summary of these opinions:

> The collection embraces a wonderful extent and variety of national history, likewise an exact and discriminating range throughout the different tribes. They are all classed with the method and arrangement of a philosopher, developed and associated with the vivacity of a dramatist, and personated, defined, and coloured with the eye and hand of a painter.

Figure 131. *Buffalo chase in snowdrifts, Indians pursuing on snowshoes,* 1832-1833, no. 417.

Figure 132. *Buffalo Dance, Mandan,* 1835-1837, no. 440.

Rarely, indeed, would one man be found who could do all this; still more rarely a man, who to these various offices and talents would add the courage, the patience, and the taste to become an eyewitness of his subjects, and above all, would possess the industry and the veracity to represent them to others, and thus to command credibility and admiration.[17]

While one is reluctant to accept the artist's selection of press opinions, especially in view of his talent for self-promotion, negative comments do seem to be almost nonexistent. To be sure, Dunlap and others had been hard on Catlin's pre-Indian Gallery work, but once the artist launched his career in the West, he moved beyond the realm of their criticism. Whatever shortcomings were discovered among the paintings of the Indian Gallery were simply attributed to the difficult circumstances under which the artist had worked, and neither the public nor prominent citizens could do other than applaud the general nature of his accomplishment. It is only among other artists and writers of the period that we find an undercurrent of doubt, and their comments again deal not so much with Catlin as an artist, as with the accuracy of his reports. Alfred Jacob Miller, writing from London the year after *Letters and Notes* was published, says "Catlin is here and visits me sometimes. . . . There is in truth . . . a great deal of humbug about [him]. . . . He has published a book containing some extraordinary stories and luckily for him, there are but few persons who have travelled the same ground."[18] Audubon was another detractor. On a steamboat voyage up the Missouri in 1843, he noted in his journal:

Figure 133. *Snowshoe Dance, at the first snowfall*, 1835-1837, no. 451.

"Oh! Mr. Catlin, I am now sorry to see and to read your accounts of the Indians *you* saw—how very different they must have been from any that I have seen! We saw here no 'carpeted prairies,' no 'velvety distant landscape'; and if these things are to be seen, why, the sooner we reach them the better" (see nos. 388, 502).[19] The same year, in an unsigned preface to F. O. C. Darley's *Scenes in Indian Life,* Catlin was assaulted as "vain, self-sufficient and arrogant" and the source of "a host of speculations" about the Mandan tribe.[20] Presumably, Darley did not necessarily agree with all this, because Ewers has shown that many of his subsequent illustrations of Indian buffalo hunts are based on Catlin's subjects (see no. 412).

The debate continued with Seth Eastman and John Mix Stanley.

In the late 1840s the former was assured by the nature writer Charles Lanman and others that his work was superior to Catlin's, the implication being that Catlin had exaggerated his subjects, while Eastman had given an accurate account of everyday life (fig. 136).[21] Eastman, in turn, testified in favor of Stanley's work (fig. 137) at the expense of Catlin. When the Senate was debating the purchase of Stanley's collection in 1852, Eastman was asked by Stanley to submit an opinion comparing his paintings (Stanley's) to Catlin's. "It affords me pleasure," Eastman replied, "to say that I consider the artistic merits of yours far superior to Mr. Catlin's; and they give a better idea of the Indian than any works in Mr. Catlin's collection."[22] Years later, in 1871, Clarence King added the final insult by calling Catlin an "erratic amateur Indian" whose

Figure 134. *Archery of the Mandan,* 1832-1833, no. 435.

description of Shoshone Falls (from *Last Rambles*) failed "to give an adequate idea of their formation and grandeur."²³

While much evidence can be gathered in support of the Indian Gallery, and Bernard DeVoto, Robert Taft, and John Ewers have substantially resolved the question of Catlin's accuracy, it is evident that a number of his colleagues challenged the credibility of his work. Only Eastman, however, mentioned the problem of artistic merit; the rest were content to question the content of the paintings and *Letters and Notes.* Each one was a skillful artist, better trained in every respect than Catlin, but none came west with the latter's deep commitment to the superior virtue of Indian life. Catlin, after all, wished to preserve the proud spirit of Upper Missouri savages, and the look of the impos-

ing wilderness in which they reigned. Miller could go as far as sharing the sport of the trapper's rendezvous (fig. 37), but the others expressed no firm resolve to sustain the primitive ideal. They wished as fervently as Catlin to create a lasting record of vanishing tribes, but theirs was to be a more objective, methodical account of their western travels. Catlin, a decade earlier, had been entranced by the fresh new world he had encountered. If his savages were handsomer and his landscapes greener than those seen by his more sober followers, it was all part of his message. Unhappily, the meaning of Catlin's rhetoric was not always apparent to his colleagues. His vision was framed in a world they could not share, and they came to regard his occasional exaggerations as evidence that his standards were much different from their own.

Figure 135. *Eagle Dance, Iowa,* ca. 1846 (see no. 449).

Figure 136. Seth Eastman, *Sioux Indians Breaking Up Camp*, 1847. Museum of Fine Arts, Boston; M. and M. Karolik Collection.

Figure 137. John Mix Stanley, *The Buffalo Hunt*, 1853. Hirschl & Adler Galleries, New York.

quoting the current opinion that the artist was a worthy man "who could neither paint nor draw." He quickly added, however, that this was an unfortunate "blunder," and proceeded with an analysis of the paintings more sympathetic and revealing than any Catlin had received at home. The direct and passionate response of the great French critic was just the sort to unsettle his counterparts in America, who, predictably, sought firmer standards to support their less confident notion of high art. "M. Catlin has captured the proud, free character and noble expression of these splendid fellows in a masterly way," Baudelaire wrote.

The structure of their heads is wonderfully well understood [see figs. 15, 40; nos. 149, 521]. With their fine attitudes and their ease of movement, these savages make antique sculpture comprehensible. Turning to his colour, I find in it an element of mystery which delights me more than I can say. Red, the colour of blood, the colour of life, flowed so abundantly in his gloomy Museum that it was like an intoxication; and the landscapes —wooded mountains, vast savannahs, deserted rivers—were monotonously eternally green.[24]

Delacroix and George Sand, whose names have always been used in the past to bolster Catlin's reputation abroad, were in fact more interested in the *Tableaux Vivants* than the Indian Gallery. The Ojibwa, whom Delacroix sketched on the stage of the Salle Valentino (fig. 138), brought to mind "the noble and mysterious poise" of Greek gods and classical sculpture.[25] Sand, on the other hand, was entranced by the raw passion of the performances. She imagined herself watching one of the lurid scenes from *The Last of the Mohicans*, the dancers displaying a range of primitive emotion that made them "more dangerous and implacable than wolves or bears." The performance began as a giant warrior rushed forward on the stage, shaking his bow and tomahawk. "Others followed him," she wrote,

some throwing off their cloaks and showing their panting breasts and their arms as supple as snakes were still more terrifying. A kind of delirious rage seemed to transport them; raucous cries, barks, roars, shrill whistles and the war-cry which the Indian makes by putting his fingers on his lips and which uttered far off in the deserts freezes the strayed traveler with fear, interrupted the song creating an infernal concert. A cold sweat came over me; I believed I was witnessing the real scalping of some vanquished enemy or some still more horrible torture.[26]

After the mystery had worn thin, however, only Baudelaire remained to call attention to Catlin's artistic merits. The rest, including Rosa Bonheur, were more taken by the contents of his paintings or the activities he devised to promote the Indian Gallery. They were quick to applaud his travels and the range of his collection, but only tolerant and forgiving of an imperfect style. Baudelaire, fortunately, had a more progressive approach. As a critic of considerable dimension, and an admirer of Chateaubriand and Cooper, he was uniquely equipped to sense the image Catlin was after, and he justly praised the artist's two entries in the Salon of 1846. But then, one must ask, did he err in the opposite direction with his blanket endorsement of Catlin's style? Did he examine a cross section of paintings in the Indian Gallery, the hasty and the uninspired, as well as the superior examples? Did he mean to

Figure 138. Eugène Delacroix, *Two Ojibwa Indians,* 1845, pencil. Amon Carter Museum, Fort Worth.

Praise for Catlin's work came from so many quarters that it is difficult to know just how sincerely it was meant, or what aspect of the Indian Gallery appealed to each. Sully introduced the artist to several English friends, but commended his work only in the most general terms. Reports drifted back from England that Mulready, Leslie, and Wilkie were favorably impressed by Catlin's painting, but was this a polite acknowledgment or an expression of genuine interest? In their Memorial of 1846, American artists in Paris seemed more intent upon reminding Congress of its patronage obligations than lauding Catlin's work, and even Baudelaire began his review of the Indian Gallery by

ignore the former in order to praise Catlin's few masterpieces and his stirring palette, or was he simply refreshed by Catlin's lack of sophistication, by his distance from the intellectual refinement of mid-century French artists and critics? Sadly enough, it appears that Catlin never received a balanced judgment from the one prominent critic who understood his work, nor a just appraisal from those Americans who missed the flavor of his primitivism.

Many years later, when Catlin was all but forgotten, Henry Tuckerman tried to make up for it in his *Book of the Artists.* Or, more precisely, he appears to have slighted the artist on the first pass and then wished to redress the balance. After a perfunctory third of a page on Catlin, Tuckerman launched into a four-page discussion of Charles Deas's paintings (fig. 139). Halfway through he must have recalled that Catlin had been a major influence on Deas, and found it necessary to include more material on the former. The second time around Catlin was treated with considerably more enthusiasm:

With the tastes and habits we have described, it is not difficult to fancy the effect produced upon the mind of Deas by the sight of Catlin's Indian Gallery. Here was a result of art, not drawn merely from academic practice or the lonely vigils of a studio, but gathered amid the freedom of nature. Here were trophies as eloquent of adventure as of skill, environed with the most national associations, and memorials of a race fast dwindling from the earth. With what interest would after-generations look upon these portraits, and how attractive to European eyes would be such authentic "counterfeit presentments" of a savage people, about whose history romance and tradition alike throw their spells! To visit the scenes whence Catlin drew these unique specimens of art, to study the picturesque forms, costumes, attitudes, and grouping of Nature's own children; to share the grateful repast of the hunter, and taste the wild excitement of frontier life, in the very heart of the noblest scenery of the land, was a prospect calculated to stir the blood of one with the true sense of the beautiful, and a natural relish for woodcraft and sporting.[27]

It all sounded as if it had been written much earlier, not four years before Catlin's final exhibition would be ignored by New York critics. Tuckerman was one of the last nineteenth-century writers to pay tribute to the artist; few others chose to remember his work or take an interest in the fate of his collections. The New-York Historical Society had made only a half-hearted bid in 1870 for the cartoons, and it may have been the chance intervention of Thomas Donaldson several years later that saved the original collection from total destruction. Once the collection came under the eye of Smithsonian anthropologists, however, its value as a document began to be more clearly understood (fig. 140). The critics G. W. Sheldon, Sadakichi Hartmann, and Royal Cortissoz might not take notice, but the anthropologists maintained a measure of interest in the collection until the late 1940s, when historians once more turned their attention to Catlin's activities. DeVoto was first, then Haberly, Taft, and McCracken slowly reconstructed the course of his travels and determined the effect of his career on the development of the West. The most serious study published in this period, however, was by Ewers.[28] In this and subsequent writings, he carefully distinguishes which aspects of Catlin's work can be taken as an accurate reflection of Plains Indian

Figure 139 *(top).* Charles Deas, *The Voyageurs,* 1846. Museum of Fine Arts, Boston; M. and M. Karolik Collection.

Figure 140 *(bottom).* Catlin Collection installed in the Arts and Industries Building, Smithsonian Institution, ca. 1900.

culture, and traces the lasting impact of the Indian Gallery on all those who followed in the artist's footsteps.

Catlin's painting and writing became the inevitable standard of comparison, whether his successors agreed with his interpretation or not. He had no students or followers, and he trained no one to continue his mission, but it was impossible to escape the influence of his iconography. He had, after all, seen most of it first, and one could hardly begin a buffalo hunt, an Indian dance, or a prairie landscape without being aware of Catlin's original image. Many had seen his collection during the two years it toured the East, and those who missed it had another chance when he published *Letters and Notes* in 1841 with over 300 illustrations. His endless curiosity, his natural rapport with the tribes he visited, and his field procedure were such that he rarely missed a scene with any potential. His successors might adjust the technique or the composition, but it was Catlin who had first deemed it worthy to set down on canvas. Not until cavalry and Indian conflicts began after the Civil War did the course of western iconography change from what he had prescribed in the Indian Gallery.

In addition to the pervasive influence of Catlin's work, one can point out instances in which he directly affected artists about to travel west. In the spring of 1833, for example, Bodmer and his German patron, Prince Maximilian, saw a group of Catlin paintings at the home of General Clark's nephew, Benjamin O'Fallon, before they set off for the Upper Missouri. Ewers thinks this might explain why Bodmer painted so few of the same subjects.[29] The Canadian artist Paul Kane struck up a friendship with Catlin in London in 1843, and later that year returned to Canada to begin painting the tribes of the western provinces. Tuckerman has already connected Deas and Catlin for us, and Eastman and Stanley could not have criticized his work without being fully acquainted with it. George Caleb Bingham is supposed to have copied several of Catlin's buffalo hunts, Carl Wimar was at Fort Union thirty years after Catlin, and one could continue with lesser figures—Kurz, Sohon, Möllhausen, Hays, and Trotter. Others borrowed figures and compositions from Catlin for illustrations and lithographs. Alvan Fisher, Darley (fig. 141), Ranney, Tait, and many more are among this group, but the list is too long to repeat.

The ground has been covered often by Taft, Ewers, and others

Figure 141. Felix O. C. Darley, *Hunting Buffalo,* 1842, ink. Beinecke Library, Yale University.

who have examined the subject with great care. One need only accept the evidence of Taft, who after reviewing the contents of the Indian Gallery and the number of Catlin publications available between 1841 and 1860, says, "It is no small wonder . . . that I find Catlin's name the most frequently mentioned in biographical accounts of later artists of the West or for that matter one of the most frequently referred to authorities on the early history of the Upper Missouri country."[30] Yet even this does not fully explain the significance of Catlin's role. The strength of his position ultimately rests on his having been the first major painter to seek the Indian in his own territory. Whatever his faults, Catlin had seen the West with his own eyes; from that time on, no self-respecting artist could paint Indian life without venturing forth from his eastern studio.

Notes

CHAPTER 1

1. Marjorie Catlin Roehm, *The Letters of George Catlin and His Family*, p. 2. Nine of the fourteen children born to Polly and Putnam Catlin survived their early twenties.
2. *Pursuit of the Horizon*, p. 15.
3. George Catlin, *Catlin's Notes of Eight Years' Travels and Residence in Europe*, vol. 2, p. 317. (Hereafter referred to as *Travels in Europe*.)
4. Ibid.
5. *Life Amongst the Indians*, pp. ix-x.
6. Anna Wells Rutledge, ed., *The Pennsylvania Academy of the Fine Arts: Cumulative Record of Exhibition Catalogues 1807-1870*, p. 45.
7. Marie Hewett, "Pictorial Reporter: George Catlin in Western New York," p. 100.
8. He is listed as a portrait painter in New York City directories from 1827 through 1830.
9. Hewett, p. 101. The West Point lithographs were published in 1828, and Catlin's model of Niagara was mentioned by William Stone in 1829 (see Hewett, p. 102), although the lithographs did not appear until 1831.
10. Thomas Donaldson, "The George Catlin Indian Gallery," *Annual Report of the Smithsonian Institution for 1885*, part 5, p. 715.
11. Roehm, p. 31.
12. Catlin to Gen. Peter B. Porter, Feb. 22, 1829, Buffalo and Erie County Historical Society, Buffalo. Thomas Gimbrede was then serving as drawing master at West Point.
13. *Letters and Notes on the Manners, Customs, and Condition of the North American Indians*, vol. 1, p. 2. (Hereafter referred to as *Letters and Notes*.)
14. Harold McCracken, *George Catlin and the Old Frontier*, p. 25.
15. William Dunlap, *History of the Rise and Progress of the Arts of Design in the United States*, vol. 3, p. 172.
16. *A Descriptive Catalogue of Catlin's Indian Gallery*, Egyptian Hall, London, 1840, p. 3 (see McCracken, p. 212).
17. Roehm, p. 32.
18. Roehm, p. 46.
19. *Letters and Notes*, vol. 1, p. 16.
20. *Letters and Notes*, vol. 2, p. 30. Clark's Indian museum must also have made a great impression on Catlin. In a large council chamber beside his home in St. Louis, the general had on display in 1830 what many considered the finest collection of Indian artifacts in the country (see Ewers, "William Clark's Indian Museum").
21. Donaldson, p. 425; Catlin, *Catalogue Descriptive and Instructive of Catlin's Indian Cartoons*, New York, 1871, pp. 90-91. (Hereafter referred to as the "1871 catalogue.")
22. Catlin may also have encountered members of these Leavenworth tribes passing through St. Louis that summer.
23. Roehm, p. 50.
24. Roehm, p. 54.
25. Roehm, p. 56.
26. John C. Ewers, *Indian Life on the Upper Missouri*, p. 78.
27. *Letters and Notes*, vol. 1, p. 213.
28. *Letters and Notes*, vol. 1, p. 21.
29. Catlin's thirteen letters to Stone's *Commercial Advertiser* give a brief account of his travels from July 24, 1832, to September 30, 1837. They were later edited and expanded into *Letters and Notes*.
30. *Letters and Notes*, vol. 1, p. 69.
31. *Letters and Notes*, vol. 2, p. 3.
32. "George Catlin, Painter of Indians and the West," p. 493.
33. McCracken, pp. 129-34; Roehm, pp. 55-57.
34. *Western Monthly Magazine* 2 (November 1833): 536.
35. Hall wrote to Catlin, Feb. 12, 1836 (see Donaldson, pp. 766-67).
36. *Letters and Notes*, vol. 2, p. 35; Roehm, p. 76.
37. *Letters and Notes*, vol. 2, p. 46.
38. William H. Goetzmann, *Exploration and Empire*, p. 190.
39. *New Orleans Courier*, April 2, 1835, p. 3.
40. *Letters and Notes*, vol. 2, p. 135.
41. *Letters and Notes*, vol. 2, pp. 148-49.
42. *American Turf Register and Sporting Magazine* 7 (August 1836): 554-55. The exhibition apparently took place at the museum established by the portrait painter James Reid Lambdin (see Bruce W. Chambers, *David Gilmour Blythe (1815-1865): An Artist at Urbanization's Edge*, unpublished Ph.D. dissertation, University of Pennsylvania, 1974, p. 32).
43. Charles J. Kappler, *Indian Affairs. Laws and Treaties*, vol. 2, p. 475.
44. Roehm, p. 102.
45. McCracken, p. 184.
46. *Across the Wide Missouri*, p. 396.
47. *Catalogue of Catlin's Gallery*, New York, 1837 (see McCracken, p. 212).
48. Allan Nevins, ed., *The Diary of Philip Hone 1828-1851*, pp. 290-91.
49. Roehm, p. 125
50. *New York Evening Star*, Feb. 1, 1838, p. 2.
51. Herman J. Viola, *The Indian Legacy of Charles Bird King*, p. 107.
52. *Daily National Intelligencer*, April 16 and May 18, 1838; Roehm, p. 133. Putnam Catlin also said that the expenses of the Washington exhibition were "enormous," and "possibly beyond" the receipts.
53. *A Descriptive Catalogue of Catlin's Indian Collection*, No. 6, Waterloo Place, London, 1848, p. 80. (Hereafter referred to as the "1848 catalogue.") See McCracken, p. 213.
54. Haberly, p. 111; Roehm, p. 139.
55. Catlin first mentioned an English tour in his 1829 letter to General Porter (see n. 12).
56. Roehm, p. 145. The original price had been $65,000.
57. Nevins, p. 434.

CHAPTER 2

1. Murray, grandson of Lord Dunmore, last English governor of Virginia, had met Catlin at the Falls of St. Anthony in the summer of 1835.
2. See n. 16, chap. 1.
3. Marjorie Catlin Roehm, *The Letters of George Catlin and His Family*, pp. 156-57.
4. Roehm, p. 175.
5. Ibid.
6. Roehm, p. 196.
7. Roehm, p. 206; *Travels in Europe*, vol. 1, p. 95.
8. Roehm, pp. 207, 208. After the first year in Egyptian Hall, during which 32,500 visitors had paid $9,433 to see the Indian Gallery, Catlin's nephew noted that the receipts were "all spent."
9. Ibid., p. 222.
10. *Pursuit of the Horizon*, p. 126.
11. *Travels in Europe*, vol. 1, p. 55. Letters praising the book came from Benjamin Silliman, Michael Faraday, and many others (see National Collection of Fine Arts/ National Portrait Gallery Library files).
12. *United States Democratic Review* 11 (July 1842): 44, 45. The *North American Review* (vol. 54, April 1842, pp. 283-99) also praised *Letters and Notes*, while acknowledging that Catlin was too much on the Indian's side, but the *Southern Literary Messenger* (vol. 11, April 1845, pp. 202-11) saw the book only as a critical attack on American society.
13. *Travels in Europe*, vol. 1, p. 100.
14. "The Noble Savage," *The Works of Charles Dickens*, vol. 17 (New York, 1922), p. 233.
15. Roehm, p. 278. Sales of the *Portfolio* were disappointing, Catlin wrote to Sir Thomas Phillipps, April 7, 1845 (Gilcrease Institute, Tulsa), which is probably why plans to publish three additional volumes were never carried out. According to a prospectus in the files of the National Collection of Fine Arts/National Portrait Gallery Library, the subjects of the proposed volumes were: II Portraits and Costumes, with Biography, of American Indians; III Religious Rites and Ceremonies, and Domestic Scenes, of American Indians; IV Warfare and its Cruelties, of American Indians. See Harold McCracken, *George Catlin and the Old Frontier*, p. 213, for a bibliography of subsequent editions, including one by Currier & Ives, of the *Portfolio*.
16. Roehm, p. 290.
17. *Travels in Europe*, vol. 2, pp. 172-73.
18. *Travels in Europe*, vol. 1, pp. 237-38. The success of the opening must also have come from plans laid much earlier. A letter warmly endorsing Catlin's activities was sent from Edward Everett, Minister to Great Britain, to W. R. King, his counterpart in France, Dec. 2, 1844 (New York Public Library).
19. Brasseur de Bourbourg, *Quatre Lettres sur Le Mexique*. p. xx.
20. Robert N. Beetem, "George Catlin in France: His Relationship to Delacroix and Baudelaire," p. 130.
21. *Travels in Europe*, vol. 2, pp. 316-17.
22. Catlin to Sir Thomas Phillipps, Feb. 19, 1846, Gilcrease Institute, Tulsa.
23. McCracken, p. 197; Roehm, p. 310.
24. Memorial of R. R. Gurley, *Senate Miscellaneous Documents*, vol. 511, no. 152, July 1848, pp. 1-9. Following the memorial are letters of support from G. P. A. Healy and Samuel F. B. Morse.
25. McCracken, p. 202.
26. Roehm, p. 370. Louis Philippe had apparently ordered the LaSalle series two years earlier (see Catlin to Phillipps, Feb. 19, 1846, Gilcrease Institute, Tulsa).
27. Ibid. Neither a design for the mural nor related correspondence can be found in the Capitol archives.
28. See n. 53, chap. 1.
29. The full title is *Catlin's Notes of Eight Years' Travels and Residence in Europe, with His North American Indian Collection* (see n. 3, chap. 1).
30. *Pursuit of the Horizon*, p. 177.
31. Roehm, p. 317.
32. Catlin to Phillipps, Aug. 12, 1851, Gilcrease Institute, Tulsa. The artist besieged Sir Thomas with loan requests from 1840 to 1860.
33. *North American Miscellany and Dollar Magazine* 4 (July 1852): 271.
34. In 1851 Catlin had acted as an agent for Harrison, purchasing *Penn's Treaty with the Indians*, so the two must have already been acquainted (see Nicholas B. Wainwright,

"Joseph Harrison, Jr., a Forgotten Collector," *Antiques* 102 [October 1972]:665). Harrison redeemed the Indian Gallery for $40,000 (see Thomas B. Donaldson, "Events of 1879 Leading to the Conservation of the George Catlin Indian Gallery," unpublished MS, National Collection of Fine Arts/National Portrait Gallery Library).
35. Catlin was still smarting from Schoolcraft's criticism a year later when he petitioned Congress to purchase the cartoon collection (see National Collection of Fine Arts/National Portrait Gallery Library files). Schoolcraft, he charged, had unfairly damaged his reputation and had led Congress to believe that Seth Eastman would donate his Indian collection to the government. These actions, Catlin claimed, had prevented the sale of his own collections.
36. Heritage Book Shop, Catalogue No. 2, p. 5.
37. Thomas Donaldson, "The George Catlin Indian Gallery," *Annual Report of the Smithsonian Institution for 1885*, part 5, pp. 715-16.
38. Roehm, pp. 348-49, 383, 445.
39. See Roehm, pp. 445-47. The several albums of cartoons at the Henry E. Huntington Library, San Marino, Calif., may be the remains of this project.
40. Roehm, p. 360.
41. Roehm, p. 402.
42. See n. 21, chap. 1, and McCracken, p. 214. The exhibition was advertised in New York newspapers as taking place from October 22 to November 14.

CHAPTER 3

1. Charles Coleman Sellers, *Charles Willson Peale*, pp. 281-82.
2. Ibid., p. 216.
3. Ibid, pp. 262-63.
4. Jessie Poesch, *Titian Ramsay Peale 1799-1885*, p. 10.
5. Sellers, p. 426.
6. William H. Goetzmann, *Exploration and Empire*, p. 184.
7. Clark Wissler, "The American Indian and the American Philosophical Society," p. 189.
8. Ibid., p. 192. In 1838 or 1839 Catlin and DuPonceau met in Philadelphia to discuss the latter's dictionary of Indian languages (see *Travels in Europe*, vol. 1, pp. 83-85).
9. Edwin James, *Account of an Expedition from Pittsburgh to the Rocky Mountains*.
10. Wissler, p. 202, cites Catlin as a contributor, but the letter did not turn up in a search of American Philosophical Society publication indices.
11. Roderick Nash, *Wilderness and the American Mind*, p. 54.
12. John D. Godman, *American Natural History*, Preface, p. v.
13. Godman, vol. 1, p. 28.
14. Godman, vol. 2, p. 108.
15. *A Journal of Travels into the Arkansa Territory*, p. vi.
16. James, vol. 2, p. 9.
17. Poesch, p. 24.
18. James, vol. 2, pp. 177-78.
19. *Cabinet of Natural History and American Rural Sports* 2 (1832): 184-86.
20. Catlin to Major J. H. Hook, Dec. 24, 1832, National Archives, Quartermaster's Consolidated Correspondence File, Record Group 92.
21. *Letters and Notes*, vol. 2, p. 37.
22. *Letters and Notes*, vol. 1, p. 4.
23. *Letters and Notes*, vol. 2, pp. 201-2.
24. George H. Daniels, *American Science in the Age of Jackson*, p. 16.
25. *Addresses Delivered on Various Public Occasions*, pp. 110, 128-29.

CHAPTER 4

1. These pages are in the North American Indian (NAI) sketchbook, Gilcrease Institute, Tulsa.
2. Hans Huth, *Nature and the American*, p. 22.
3. François-René Vicomte de Chateaubriand, *Recollections of Italy, England and America*, pp. 138-39.

4. Hoxie N. Fairchild, *The Noble Savage*, pp. 328-38. A critic reviewing *Letters and Notes* for the *Athenaeum* (London, Feb. 12, 1842, p. 142) actually stated that Catlin "Boswellizes savage life almost as accurately as he paints it."

5. *Letters and Notes*, vol. 2, pp. 155-56.

6. Roy Harvey Pearce, *The Savages of America*, p. 136.

7. Ibid.

8. *The Poetical Works of Fitz-Greene Halleck*, p. 47. See also N. F. Adkins, *Fitz-Greene Halleck*, pp. 235-40.

9. *The Prairie*, pp. 213-14.

10. Ibid., p. 290.

11. *Letters and Notes*, vol. 1, p. 15; vol. 2, p. 37.

12. *Letters and Notes*, vol. 2, p. 37.

13. *Letters and Notes*, vol. 2, p. 91.

14. *Letters and Notes*, vol. 1, p. 5.

15. *Letters and Notes*, vol. 1, p. 18.

16. *Letters and Notes*, vol. 2, pp. 4-5.

17. Merrill D. Peterson, ed., *The Portable Thomas Jefferson*, p. 273.

18. *The Sketchbook*, p. 273.

19. *Letters and Notes*, vol. 1, p. 60.

20. Albert Keiser, *The Indian in American Literature*, p. 78.

21. Pearce, p. 57.

22. *An Overland Journey, from New York to San Francisco*, pp. 151-52.

23. *Letters and Notes*, vol. 1, p. 61.

24. *Letters and Notes*, vol. 2, p. 225; vol. 1, p. 16.

25. *Letters and Notes*, vol. 1, pp. 260, 261-62.

CHAPTER 5

1. *Letters and Notes*, vol. 1, p. 2. Putnam's letter to George, March 26, 1821 (National Collection of Fine Arts/National Portrait Gallery Library), is the first proof we have of the latter's move to Philadelphia. Putnam writes that he is pleased his son has resolved to attempt portraits. This apparently represented a change from the previous fall, when the artist had expressed to his father a preference for miniatures.

2. Anna Wells Rutledge, ed., *The Pennsylvania Academy of the Fine Arts: Cumulative Record of Exhibition Catalogues 1807-1870*, p. 45.

3. Sully to James Wright, June 12, 1839; Sully to Catlin, July 16, 1839, National Collection of Fine Arts/National Portrait Gallery Library. The first is a letter of recommendation to Sully's friend, the English artist Wright. In the second, Sully thanks Catlin for assisting with the New York exhibition of the Queen Victoria portrait, and requests a sketch of an Indian cradle board.

4. David Sellin, "Denis A. Volozan, Philadelphia Neoclassicist," pp. 119-28.

5. H. W. French, *Art and Artists in Connecticut*, p. 55, is the earliest source of this story. The author is confused on at least one point, however. Catlin was admitted to the academy May 3, 1826, the date French gives for his resignation.

6. *Pursuit of the Horizon*, p. 30.

7. For Stone's *Narrative* see Cadwallader D. Colden, *Memoir Prepared at the Request of a Committee of the Common Council of the City of New York*, p. 296.

8. *Pursuit of the Horizon*, p. 27.

9. Mary Bartlett Cowdrey, *American Academy of Fine Arts and American Art-Union*, vol. 1, p. 47.

10. 1848 catalogue, p. 4. Leo Marx, when discussing *Walden*, accuses Thoreau of a similar indulgence (i.e., demonstrating a seeming preference for facts over artistic form), calling it "the national art of disguising art" (see *The Machine in the Garden*, pp. 244-45).

11. *Letters and Notes*, vol. 1, p. 147.

12. *Letters and Notes*, vol. 2, p. 5.

13. *Letters and Notes*, vol. 2, p. 8.

14. *Letters and Notes*, vol. 1, pp. 69, 70.

15. *Letters and Notes*, vol. 1, pp. 26-27.

16. *Letters and Notes*, vol. 1, p. 248.

17. 1848 catalogue, p. 77.

18. Bernard DeVoto, *Across the Wide Missouri*, p. 409.

19. Donald C. Peattic, cd., *Audubon's America*, p. 282.

20. *Scenes in Indian Life*, p. 5.

21. John Francis McDermott, *Seth Eastman: Pictorial Historian of the Indian*, pp. 40, 105.

22. W. Vernon Kinietz, *John Mix Stanley*, p. 17.

23. *Mountaineering in the Sierra Nevada*, p. 202.

24. *The Mirror of Art*, p. 73.

25. Hugh Honour, *The New Golden Land*, p. 237.

26. Hugh Honour, *The European Vision of America*, no. 298.

27. *Book of the Artists*, pp. 426-27.

28. "George Catlin, Painter of Indians and the West."

29. Ibid., p. 504.

30. *Artists and Illustrators of the Old West 1850-1900*, p. 38.

A Descriptive Catalogue of the Indian Gallery

INTRODUCTION

Had Catlin been able to spend more time out West and less promoting the Indian Gallery, he would have left far fewer problems for art historians. As it stands, he produced a bewildering array of replicas and adaptations during his lifetime—so many, indeed, we often fail to notice that almost every one can be traced back to a source in either the original or the later cartoon collection. Once this repetition becomes apparent, however, the task of sorting out the later versions becomes less formidable. There are, in fact, only a handful of Catlin's Indian paintings that cannot be identified as subjects in his catalogues of 1848 or 1871. Furthermore, at least 300 of a total of 603 cartoons listed in the latter catalogue are simply adaptations or outright copies of paintings in the original collection. Only the West Coast, Rocky Mountain, and South American tribes (and related scenes), painted in the 1850s, represent new material in the cartoon collection, despite the artist's somewhat ambiguous assertion to the contrary in the "Remarks" introducing his 1871 catalogue.

The original collection, composed mainly of paintings done between 1830 and 1836, forms the nucleus of what ultimately became known as the Indian Gallery. In the six years Catlin traveled on the Great Plains, he completed (or finished enough to exhibit) the approximately 470 paintings listed in the 1837 catalogue (there are more entry numbers than paintings in all of Catlin's catalogues). By 1840 he had added about fifteen to this number, which appear in the first catalogue published at Egyptian Hall in London. Subsequent catalogues were not renumbered, and those published after 1843 but before 1848 sometimes include addenda that enumerate portraits he painted of the three delegations that performed with the Indian Gallery between 1843 and 1845 (see nos. 508, 517, 532). The group of hunting scenes that follow these portraits in the 1848 catalogue (nos. 543-607) were produced for European audiences between 1846 and 1848. They were the last additions to the Indian Gallery, and the last of Catlin's western subjects that can be called in any sense original, in that they are not duplicates of any previous paintings. When one understands how this "original" collection grew—that it was the first consistent group of Indian subjects the artist painted, that all the portraits were taken from life, and many other scenes from field notes and sketches, and that work continued on it, sporadically, until 1848—the relationship of Catlin's subsequent inventions is easier to follow.

At first Catlin seemed content with simply copying his own paintings in both oil and watercolor. The O'Fallon collection (see nos. 3,182) is the earliest example we have of the former, a group of thirty-five Upper Missouri subjects (figs. 142, 143) Catlin painted for Major Benjamin O'Fallon of St. Louis between 1832 and 1835. The O'Fallon paintings, sold to the Field Museum of Natural History, Chicago, in 1894, are easily dated by contemporary accounts, but the eighty-seven watercolors in the Gilcrease Institute, Tulsa, are a more difficult problem. In a letter of January 23, 1853, to Sir Thomas Phillipps,[1] Catlin maintains that every one was taken from life: "I painted thus many of my pictures in water colours during my 8 years travels, and most, though not all of them I enlarged onto canvass, wishing my collection to be all in oil painting." He did no such thing, of course. The statement directly contradicts all the evidence in his *Letters and Notes,* and the numerous certificates of authenticity signed by people more reliable than the artist in 1853, when he was dodging English bailiffs in Paris. Furthermore, comparisons between the watercolors and the oils indicate the former to be copies in every case but four (nos. 41, 192, 285, 286). One suspects that Catlin added dates to some at the time they were sold to Phillipps (November 1853), and they are about as reliable as the itinerary he included at the end of the 1871 catalogue. To condemn the artist, however, is not to condemn his works. Many of the watercolors are fresh and appealing in their own right (figs. 144-47), and the technique of most suggests they were painted not long after the

Figure 143. *Interior of a Hidatsa Lodge,* 1832-1833 (see no. 503). Field Museum of Natural History, Chicago.

Figure 142. *He Who Ties His Hair Before,* 1832-1833 (see no. 163). Field Museum of Natural History, Chicago.

Figure 144. *Cock Turkey, repeating his prayer,* 1832-1839 (see no. 241), watercolor. Gilcrease Institute, Tulsa.

original. The few dates that appear range from 1826 to 1844, both too early and too late to have any real meaning. There is evidence, however, that Catlin was painting watercolor copies of his collection by 1832 or 1833, and he claims that the Gilcrease examples were left with his sister in New York when he went abroad.[2] He also says that he sold twenty-five watercolor copies to his friend Charles Murray in 1834 or 1835, and he submitted the same number to the Art Union in 1847.[3] In any case, the Gilcrease watercolors are the next most important to the original collection, and in several instances they have served as guides to lost originals (see nos. 239, 252).

Catlin probably made a good many replicas of Indian Gallery subjects during his first stay in England, and Louis Philippe commissioned fifteen more in 1845, only two of which can now be identified with any certainty (see fig. 135; nos. 428, 449). Phillipps ordered an additional fifty-five small paintings in 1851 and received them in 1853. They also belong to the Gilcrease, along with a number of larger oil

Figure 145. *Black Coat, a chief*, 1834 (see no. 286), watercolor. Gilcrease Institute, Tulsa.

Figure 146. *Cól-lee, a Band chief*, 1834 (see no. 285), watercolor. Gilcrease Institute, Tulsa.

replicas, some of which may be from the group of twenty oils Catlin had deposited with Phillipps in 1851 as security for a loan. Since Phillipps still had this group in 1854, we know they were not confiscated in the 1852 debacle.[4]

The North America Indian (NAI) sketchbook at the Gilcrease Institute is the last item Catlin seems to have copied exclusively from Indian Gallery subjects, or more precisely in this case, from the plates in *Letters and Notes.*[5] Catlin was apparently planning a larger and more fully illustrated publication on the Indian Gallery, and the sketchbook may have served as a tentative layout. From one to eight ink drawings appear on almost every page (fig. 148); the pages are of uniform size (ca. 9 by 14 inches) and ruled margins separate the drawings, each of which has a number(s) that sometimes designates the page of the original plate in *Letters and Notes.* The date 1859, which appears on the cover of the book, is probably a bit late, since the project was most likely begun soon after Catlin lost his original collection. Some-

one (probably Phillipps) has bound the material with miscellaneous broadsides and earlier sketches that presumably were not intended as part of the original scheme. These sketches, however, are the most dazzling of the entire group. Catlin reveals a talent for using a flexible pen and ink wash that considerably raises our estimate of him as a draftsman (figs. 149, 150).

Even before Catlin lost his original collection in 1852, he had been experimenting with other means of reproducing the subjects of the Indian Gallery. Although he continued to make direct copies through the 1850s, he had adopted a new technique and a method of editing and combining his original subjects in an 1849 album called *Souvenir of the North American Indians as They Were in the Middle of the Nineteenth Century.* This album, which also came to the Gilcrease from the Phillipps collection, is composed of fifty outline drawings (ca. 8 by 10¼ inches) that have been carefully tipped in with watercolor. Individual portraits from the Indian Gallery are grouped three to a

Figure 147. *The Open Door, known as The Prophet, brother of Tecumseh,* 1832-1839 (see no. 279), watercolor. Gilcrease Institute, Tulsa.

Figure 148. *Ojibbeway Tribe, Mandan Tribe,* mid-1850s (see nos. 182, 195, 130, 132), ink. North American Indian sketchbook, p. 5. Gilcrease Institute, Tulsa.

drawing, with positions and garments somewhat altered (fig. 151). Most hunting and dance scenes have been copied directly from the originals, but others have been invented (fig. 152) that match cartoons in the 1871 catalogue. Since no earlier examples of this technique of free adaptation of subject matter can be found, the Gilcrease *Souvenir* album appears to be Catlin's first step toward the numerous Albums Unique of the 1850s, and the subsequent cartoon collection. The same formula was used in each, although the albums contained only North American Indian subjects, and many of the cartoons were done in South America. There are twelve or more extant albums, ranging in date from 1849 to 1863, and having from eleven to 219 plates.[6] They are "unique" only in the sense that they contain different numbers and combinations of outline drawings, but each was based on a master copy that Catlin must have maintained in his studio. The same figures and activities were duplicated time and again, sometimes in pencil, less often in ink (figs. 153, 154), and only rarely with watercolor tints. Cat-

lin advised Lady Phillipps in 1848 of his special method of preparing tracing paper, and there is evidence that many of the albums were reproduced by a similar method.[7] Some are more detailed than others, but the outlines of figures and backgrounds are about the same size, and almost every plate can be identified as a cartoon in the 1871 catalogue. As Catlin got deeper in debt in the early 1850s, the albums must have been a quick means of reproducing his work. There is little evidence of inspiration about them, except in the separate introductions, where the artist makes a pitch to convince potential buyers of the original material contained in each.

Catlin used the same technique to record South American and West Coast tribes in the 1850s, substituting paperboard for the lighter stock on which the albums had been produced, and using a thin wash of oil instead of watercolor. Oil on canvas copies that included subjects from both the albums and the South American cartoons were acquired in the mid-1850s by Frederick Wilhelm IV of Prussia and Leopold I of

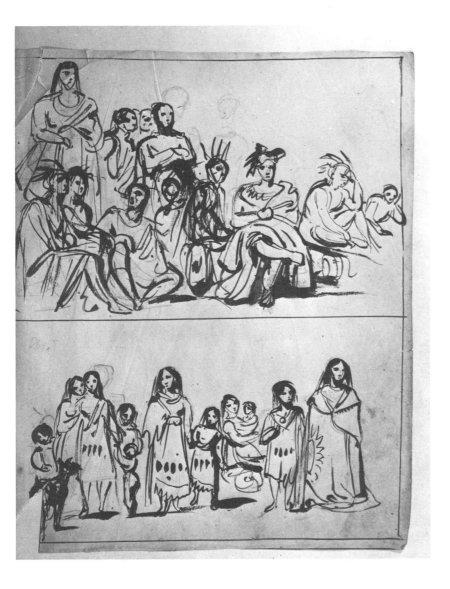

Figure 149. Indian Troupe, 1844-1845, pen and ink wash. North American Indian sketchbook, p. 87. Gilcrease Institute, Tulsa.

Figure 150. Tree Study, 1845, pen and ink wash. North American Indian sketchbook, p. 125. Gilcrease Institute, Tulsa.

Belgium (see no. 411). The ten paintings commissioned by the King of Prussia, probably at the suggestion of Alexander von Humboldt, have come to rest in the Museum für Völkerkunde, Berlin. The King of the Belgians' thirty-three hunting and camp scenes eventually got to the Royal Ontario Museum, Toronto, which disposed of half of them in 1954.[8]

Sometime after Catlin settled in Brussels in 1860, with the South American cartoons and master designs from the Albums Unique, he resolved to duplicate the latter and add additional scenes from the original collection to make the cartoon collection a truly representative survey of North and South American tribes. This was mostly accomplished during the mid- and late 1860s,[9] and after a trial showing at a Brussels gallery, Catlin brought the collection to New York for the ill-fated exhibition of 1871. After his death, ownership of the cartoons passed to his daughters, who left them in storage at the Smithsonian Institution until 1876, when 126 were sent to Philadel-

phia for exhibition in the Art Annex of the Centennial.[10] Some years later (1893), the entire collection was returned to Catlin's daughters in New York, from whom it was purchased by the American Museum of Natural History (AMNH) in 1910, with a grant of $10,000 from financier Ogden Mills.

The Indian Gallery had a less happy fate from 1852 to 1879. Joseph Harrison stored it for most of those years in two of his boiler factories in Philadelphia, where it underwent fire and water damage, and many of the Indian artifacts were destroyed. Several letters that passed between Smithsonian Secretary Joseph Henry and Harrison in the early 1870s indicate both wished to see the collection in government hands, and Harrison did offer the Institution some of Catlin's "Indian relics" in 1873.[11] But the paintings he seemed determined to sell, and Congress was no more willing to purchase them than they had been many years earlier. Fortunately, a local taxidermist came across the cache after Harrison's death and mentioned it to Thomas

Figure 151 *(top). Black Dog, Tál-lee, and Big Crow* (see nos. 31, 32, 35), ink and watercolor. *Souvenir of the North American Indians,* 1849, plate 36. Gilcrease Institute, Tulsa.

Figure 153 *(bottom). Clermont, Wáh-chee-te, He Who is Not Afraid, Man of the Bed* (see nos. 29, 30, 34, 36), pencil and ink. *North American Indians and Their Customs,* plate 52. New-York Historical Society.

Figure 152 *(top). Dying Moose,* cartoon 254, ink and watercolor. *Souvenir of the North American Indians,* 1849, plate 100. Gilcrease Institute, Tulsa.

Figure 154 *(bottom). Mandan village, women and children bathing,* cartoon 131, pencil and ink. *North American Indians and Their Customs,* plate 123. New-York Historical Society.

Figure 155. Condition of catalogue number 477, after storage in Joseph Harrison's factory.

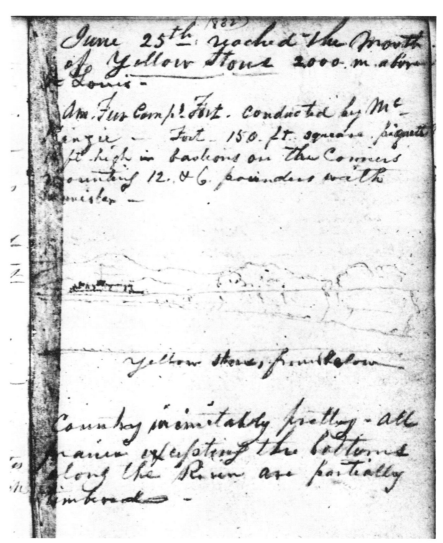

Figure 156. Fort Union, mouth of the Yellowstone, 1832, pencil. SI sketchbook, Smithsonian Institution.

Figure 157. *Eagle Bluff*, 1835, pencil. NCFA sketchbook, National Collection of Fine Arts.

Donaldson, a federal official and commissioner to the Centennial from Idaho, whom he had met through their mutual friend, Spencer F. Baird of the Smithsonian (Baird succeeded Henry as Secretary in 1878). The next step was probably a collaboration between Donaldson and Baird, both of whom wished to preserve what remained of the Indian Gallery. Donaldson served as an able diplomat, and Baird promised a suitable exhibition area in the newly planned Arts and Industries Building. Together, they persuaded Mrs. Harrison and the executors of her husband's estate to donate the collection to the Smithsonian in 1878. The following spring, Donaldson arranged for the battered contents to be packed aboard a freight car and shipped to Washington (fig. 155).[12] Only 445 of some 585 original paintings remained, the rest having disappeared when the collection was appropriated in London. Catlin must have had a few stored elsewhere, as they turn up in the cartoon collection (see nos. 284, 517), and Donaldson apparently retained a small group which he sold to John Wanamaker, who later donated them to the University Museum in Philadelphia (see no. 504). The museum disposed of these paintings in 1971.

When the original collection was unpacked at the Smithsonian, Donaldson began sifting through all of Catlin's writings to find information appropriate to each painting. The result was published in a monumental catalogue that constitutes most of the Smithsonian Annual Report for 1885, and will remain the basic work on the Indian Gallery. It is over 900 pages long, and densely packed with Catlin's findings and statistics compiled by Donaldson on the North American tribes visited by the artist. In preparing the publication, Donaldson relied heavily on Catlin's *Letters and Notes* and the catalogues issued by the artist between 1837 and 1871. The sequence of these catalogues

Figure 158. Rosa Bonheur, Page from a sketchbook (see nos. 46, 57, 58, 68), after 1876, pencil and watercolor. M. Knoedler & Co., New York.

and the significance of the one published in 1848, which is the basis for the entries that follow, will be more clearly understood by a selective reading of the first two chapters of this book.

Two small sketchbooks that appear in the entries, but have not been mentioned thus far, both belong to the Smithsonian.[13] In one of them, the SI sketchbook (see nos. 366, 388), Catlin recorded notes and

scenes on the Upper Missouri in 1832 (fig. 156). The other, the NCFA (National Collection of Fine Arts) sketchbook (see no. 312), contains a few brief views of the Upper Mississippi, probably done in 1835 (fig. 157).

The copies by Rosa Bonheur (more precisely, a group of fifty-three drawings from her estate, usually stamped "Rosa B-" at the lower right of each 6¼-by-9½-inch page) came from the Paris branch of M. Knoedler & Co. They were probably traced from plates in an 1876 edition of Letters and Notes, and several portraits, landscapes, or scenes of Indian activity often share the same page (fig. 158). John Cullum, another artist mentioned only in the entries, made watercolor copies of a number of Catlin paintings while they were on exhibit at Egyptian Hall. Unlike the Bonheur estate drawings, they could never be mistaken for Catlin's work.

Each entry begins with an edited version of Catlin's commentary regarding that particular individual or scene. This not only serves to identify the subject, but it enables the reader to sample the direction of the artist's interests, as discussed in the previous chapters, and to discover the often close relationship between his notes and his paintings. Additional information may be found by delving further into Letters and Notes and Catlin's other writings. Anthropologists in particular are urged to do so. Much that would have been valuable to them has been omitted in reducing the commentaries to a reasonable length.

The reader must also keep in mind that the Smithsonian painting is assumed to be the original and to closely match the corresponding plate in Letters and Notes. When this is not the case, reasons are given in the remarks section following the references. Related cartoons are designated as belonging to either the American Museum of Natural History (AMNH) in New York or the National Gallery of Art (NGA) in Washington. Most of those that Paul Mellon purchased from the former institution in 1965, he donated to the latter. The AMNH catalogue number is given for the few cartoons that remain in its collection, and NGA cartoons are identified by the accession number appearing in the gallery's 1970 publication American Paintings and Sculpture: An Illustrated Catalogue. Only important or unusual replicas of individual cartoons have been mentioned. Those that are not listed appear to be adequately represented by the examples noted in the American Museum of Natural History or the National Gallery.

At the suggestion of Smithsonian anthropologists, the English equivalent of Indian proper names is used in most portrait entries. The transliterated names Catlin favored in his 1848 catalogue have been included in the index, however, to guide the reader to the proper painting. Titles, of necessity, have been shortened and revised, but with every effort to strike a balance between John Ewers's precedent in "George Catlin, Painter of Indians and the West" and the text of the original entries.

Abbreviations of major and frequently cited references follow on page 140. Additional exhibition catalogues have been included only if they provide original material or place Catlin in a significant context of nineteenth-century American artists.

Notes

1 Gilcrease Institute, Tulsa.

2. Loyd Haberly, *Pursuit of the Horizon,* p. 84.

3. Ibid.; Mary Bartlett Cowdrey, *American Academy of Fine Arts and American Art-Union,* vol. 2, p. 61. An additional fourteen watercolors appear in the Cornelius Michaelson sale, Rains Galleries, New York, May 8, 1935.

4. Catlin to Sir Thomas Phillipps, Nov. 27, 1854, Gilcrease Institute, Tulsa.

5. Paul A. Rossi and David C. Hunt, *The Art of the Old West,* p. 320. The authors make the unfortunate mistake of calling these field sketches. One glance at Catlin's hasty notes and sketches from the Upper Missouri (see fig. 156; no. 388) or the Upper Mississippi (see fig. 157; no. 312) reveals the difference.

6. Albums presently belong to the following institutions: British Museum; Gilcrease Institute, Tulsa; Henry E. Huntington Library, San Marino, Calif.; Heye Foundation, New York; Montana Historical Society, Helena; New-York Historical Society; New York Public Library; New York State Library, Albany; Newberry Library, Chicago; Rutgers University Library, New Brunswick, N.J.; Stark Museum of Art, Orange, Texas; Beinecke Library, Yale University, New Haven, Conn.

7. Catlin to Lady Phillipps, Feb. 16, 1848, Gilcrease Institute, Tulsa. Several years ago tracing sheets were discovered between identical cartoon drawings at the Library of Congress.

8. The Berlin paintings are illustrated in Horst Hartmann, "George Catlin und Balduin Möllhausen." Only a fragmentary provenance can be established for the Royal Ontario Museum paintings. Belgium's Leopold I is supposed to have purchased the group from an exhibition held by Catlin in London in 1859. Later they passed to Richard Smithill, Rockbeare, Hants, England, and by 1907 they were with a New York dealer, H. Williams, 307 Fifth Avenue. Shortly after, they were acquired at auction by Sir Edmund

Osler of Toronto, who presented them to the Royal Ontario Museum in 1912.

9. A few National Gallery of Art (NGA) cartoons are signed and dated "1861," but most were apparently done later (see Marjorie Catlin Roehm, *The Letters of George Catlin and His Family,* p. 369). The paperboard on which the cartoons were originally painted measures ca. 18½ by 24½ inches. This was subsequently mounted on heavier paperboard, measuring ca. 21⅝ by 27⅞ inches.

10. Philadelphia Centennial catalogue, part 2, dept. 4, no. 1139.

11. Henry to Harrison, Feb. 22, 1873 (SI Archives, vol. 32:633). For the discussion that follows, see Harrison to Henry, Feb. 20, 1873 (SI Archives, vol. 133: 312); Theodore L. Harrison to Baird, Feb. 18, 1878 (SI Archives, vol. 170: 386).

12. The Catlin paintings at the Smithsonian were restored, and all but a few mounted on aluminum panels, about fifteen years ago, but the specialist will wish to know that frequent liberties were taken in covering previous damage. Recent examination has confirmed heavy overpainting and some compositional changes in the following (those most extensively overpainted are underlined): Nos. 11, 42, 84, 180, 181, 188, 199, 207, 211, 212, 213, 219, 220, 221, 222, 223, 224, 225, 226, 227, 228, 229, 230, 248, 258, 260, 265, 267, 268, 269, 275, 298, 299, 312, 335, 337, 351, 426, 427, 439, 440, 444, 452, 453, 457, 464, 465, 472, 476, 477, 479, 535, 536, 545, 558, 563, 567, 579, 580, 590, 594, 598, 599, 600. Heavy overpaint has been applied to the background only in the following: 8, 15, 17, 51, 55, 56, 60, 68, 71, 76, 80, 97, 103, 105, 151, 160, 161, 167, 175, 178, 179, 195, 198, 214, 215, 217, 242, 253, 259, 292, 293, 310, 330, 339, 345, 346, 389, 419, 429, 431, 432, 433, 434, 435, 437, 442, 443, 447, 448, 450, 451, 458, 467, 468, 475, 487, 495, 496, 501, 532, 554, 561, 581, 586, 595, 596.

13. The pages in the SI sketchbook are 5⅞ by 3¾ inches; in the NCFA sketchbook, 6¼ by 8 inches.

ABBREVIATIONS

1837 catalogue	*Catalogue of Catlin's Indian Gallery*, New York, 1837.
1840 catalogue	*A Descriptive Catalogue of Catlin's Indian Gallery*, Egyptian Hall, London, 1840.
Galerie Indienne	*Catalogue Raisonné de la Galerie Indienne de Mr. Catlin*, Paris, 1845.
1848 catalogue	*A Descriptive Catalogue of Catlin's Indian Collection*, No. 6, Waterloo Place, London, 1848.
1871 catalogue	*Catalogue Descriptive and Instructive of Catlin's Indian Cartoons*, New York, 1871.
Letters and Notes	Catlin, *Letters and Notes on the Manners, Customs, and Condition of the North American Indians*, 2 vols., London, 1841.
Travels in Europe	Catlin, *Catlin's Notes of Eight Years' Travels and Residence in Europe*, 2 vols., London, 1848.
America as Art	Joshua C. Taylor, with a contribution by John G. Cawelti, *America as Art*, Washington, D.C., 1976.
Catlin, Bodmer, Miller	Joslyn Art Museum, Omaha, *Catlin, Bodmer, Miller: Artist Explorers of the 1830s*, 1963.
Coe	Charles H. Coe, *Red Patriots: The Story of the Seminoles*, Cincinnati, 1898.
DeVoto	Bernard DeVoto, *Across the Wide Missouri*, Boston, 1947.
Donaldson	Thomas Donaldson, "The George Catlin Indian Gallery," *Annual Report of the Smithsonian Institution for 1885*, part 5, Washington, D.C., 1886.
Ewers (1953)	John C. Ewers, "Charles Bird King, Painter of Indian Visitors to the Nation's Capitol," *Annual Report of the Smithsonian Institution for 1953*, Washington, D.C., 1954, pp. 463-73.
Ewers (1956)	John C. Ewers, "George Catlin, Painter of Indians and the West," *Annual Report of the Smithsonian Institution for 1955*, Washington, D.C., 1956, pp. 483-528.
Ewers (1965)	John C. Ewers, *Artists of the Old West*, New York, 1965.
Ewers (1968)	John C. Ewers, *Indian Life on the Upper Missouri*, Norman Okla., 1968.
Fundaburk	Emma L. Fundaburk, *Southeastern Indians: Life Portraits*, Metuchen, N.J. (Scarecrow Reprint), 1969.
Gilcrease catalogue	"Gilcrease Institute Collection of Works by George Catlin," *Catlin's Indian Gallery*, Tulsa, 1973.
Haberly	Loyd Haberly, *Pursuit of the Horizon*, New York, 1948.
Halpin	Marjorie Halpin, *Catlin's Indian Gallery*, Smithsonian Institution, Washington, D.C., 1965.
Hartmann	Horst Hartmann, "George Catlin und Balduin Möllhausen," *Baessler-Archiv Beiträge zur Völkerkunde*, Neue Folge Beiheft 3, Berlin, 1963.
Haverstock	Mary Sayre Haverstock, *Indian Gallery: The Story of George Catlin*, New York, 1973.
Kennedy catalogue	Kennedy Galleries, New York, *George Catlin: Paintings from the Collection of the American Museum of Natural History*, 1956.
McCracken	Harold McCracken, *George Catlin and the Old Frontier*, New York, 1959.
McKenney and Hall	Thomas L. McKenney and James Hall, *The Indian Tribes of North America*, 3 vols., ed. Frederick W. Hodge, Edinburgh, 1933.
Matthews	Washington Matthews, "The Catlin Collection of Indian Paintings," *Report of the National Museum for 1890*, Washington, D.C., 1892.
Mississippi Panorama	City Art Museum of St. Louis, *Mississippi Panorama*, 1949.
NCFA-NPG Library	Library of the National Collection of Fine Arts and National Portrait Gallery, Washington, D.C.
Paris (1963)	Centre Culturel Américain, Paris, *Georges Catlin*, 1963.
Quimby	George I. Quimby, *Indians of the Western Frontier: Paintings of George Catlin*, Chicago Natural History Museum, 1954.
Roehm	Marjorie Catlin Roehm, *The Letters of George Catlin and His Family*, Berkeley, Calif., 1966.
Rossi and Hunt	Paul A. Rossi and David C. Hunt, *The Art of the Old West*, New York, 1973.
Spokane exhibition	International Exposition, Spokane, *Our Land, Our Sky, Our Water*, 1974.
Westward the Way	City Art Museum of St. Louis, *Westward the Way*, 1954.

The original Indian Gallery paintings —
except for those unlocated —are illustrated in this catalogue
or in the earlier chapters, as designated in each entry.
Known versions of unlocated paintings also
appear as catalogue illustrations, with the source
cited below each. "Version" refers to replicas
and adaptations by Catlin; "copy" to works by other artists.
Dimensions are in inches, followed by centimeters
in parentheses; height precedes width.
Unless otherwise indicated, all
works are oil on canvas.

Formerly University Museum, Philadelphia.

Daguerreotype of Keokuk, 1847, National Anthropological Archives, Smithsonian Institution.

flourished about for a considerable part of the day in front of me, until the picture was completed. The horse that he rode was the best animal on the frontier. . . . He made a great display on this day, and hundreds of the dragoons and officers were about him, and looking on during the operation. His horse was beautifully caparisoned, and his scalps were carried attached to the bridle-bits" (*Letters and Notes*, vol. 2, pp. 149-50, 210, 212, pls. 280, 290).

References: 1837 catalogue, nos. 19, 28; Donaldson, pp. 13-22, pls. 10, 12; Matthews, p. 605, pl. 145; H. Chadwick Hunter, "The American Indian in Painting," *Art and Archaeology* 8 (March-April 1919): 89, reprod. p. 82; Haberly, p. 102, pl. 13; J. F. McDermott, "Another Coriolanus: Portraits of Keokuk, Chief of the Sac and Fox," *Antiques* 54 (August 1948): 94, reprod. p. 99; Ewers (1956), pp. 489, 522; Kennedy catalogue, p. 12; (SI)* University Museum, Philadelphia, *The Noble Savage* (1958), no. 15; (SI) Robert C. Smith, "The Noble Savage in Painting and Prints," *Antiques* 74 (July 1958): 59; (SI) *Apollo* 68 (October 1958): 126; McCracken, pp. 19, 170, 179, 185, reprod. p. 20; Hartmann, p. 43; (SI) Catlin, Bodmer, Miller; (SI) Paris (1963), no. 1; Halpin, reprod. p. 4; Roehm, pp. 47, 65; Metropolitan Musem of Art, New York, *19th Century America: Paintings and Sculpture* (1970), no. 42, reprod.; Richard Dorment, "American Mythologies in Painting," *Arts Magazine* 46 (September 1971), reprod. p. 46; Emily Wasserman, "The Artist-Explorers," *Art in America* 60 (July 1972), reprod. p. 50; (SI) Hirschl & Adler Galleries, New York, *Faces and Places: Changing Images of 19th Century America* (1972), no. 11; Rossi and Hunt, pp. 61, 320; Gilcrease catalogue, p. 49; Haverstock, pp. 152-53; John Wilmerding, ed., *The Genius of American Painting* (New York, 1973), reprod. p. 126.

Versions:

Smithsonian Institution, 24 x 29

University Museum, Philadelphia (until 1971); Hirschl & Adler Galleries, New York (1972), 22⅛ x 26⅜, signed lower left: G. Catlin. 1836.

Gilcrease Institute, NAI sketchbook (4776.37 and .62), pen and ink

Copy:

M. Knoedler & Co., New York (until 1971), pencil and watercolor, signed lower right: Rosa B- [Bonheur]

Painted at the Sauk and Fox village in 1835, according to *Letters and Notes.* Donaldson gives the wrong date for Catlin's visit to the village, and Roehm is incorrect in assuming that the portrait was done at Jefferson Barracks (see no. 2). Keokuk was the most prominent chief on the frontier in the 1830s, an impressive, overbearing, portly man whom Catlin flattered in two of the most elaborately painted portraits of his western travels. A

1. Keokuk (The Watchful Fox), chief of the tribe
Sauk and Fox, 1835
29 x 24 (73.7 x 60.9)

"*Kee-o-kuk* . . . is the present chief of the tribe, a dignified and proud man, with a good share of talent, and vanity enough to force into action all the wit and judgment he possesses, in order to command the attention and respect of the world. At the close of the 'Black Hawk War,' in 1832 . . . *Kee-o-kuk* was acknowledged chief of the Sacs and Foxes by General Scott, who held a treaty with them at Rock Island. His appointment as chief was in consequence of the friendly position he had taken during the war, holding two-thirds of the warriors neutral, which was no doubt the cause of the sudden and successful termination of the war, and the means of saving much bloodshed. Black Hawk and his two sons [see nos. 2,3,4], as well as his principal advisers and warriors, were brought into Saint Louis in chains, and *Kee-o-kuk* appointed chief with the assent of the tribe. In his portrait I have represented him in the costume precisely in which he was dressed when he stood for it, with his shield on his arm and his staff (insignia of office) in his left hand. There is no Indian chief on the frontier better known at this time, or more highly appreciated for his eloquence, as a public speaker, than Kee-o-kuk, as he has repeatedly visited Washington and others of our Atlantic towns, and made his speeches before thousands, when he has been contending for his people's rights, in their stipulations with the United States Government, for the sale of their lands. . . .

"After I had painted the portrait of this . . . man at full length . . . he had the vanity to say to me, that he made a fine appearance on horseback, and that he wished me to paint him thus. So I prepared my canvass in the door of the hospital which I occupied, in the dragoon cantonment; and he

*Designates Smithsonian Institution version.

daguerreotype of Keokuk taken in 1847 (illustrated here) makes one wonder if he could have cut such a fine figure twelve years earlier, although Catlin has given some indication of incipient corpulence in both examples.

The standing portrait is based on a classical pose that the artist used frequently for important subjects (see nos. 128, 152), and Keokuk's proportions are as firm and well-articulated as any of Catlin's full-length figures. The profusion of costume accessories is the most striking aspect of the portrait, however. They have been reproduced with unusual clarity, probably in deference to Keokuk's wishes, and with a decorative skill that Catlin did not attempt in his earlier work. Yet their lavish appearance somewhat dilutes the image of strength and independence that was literally proclaimed in the Upper Missouri portraits (where Catlin did edit costume details, see no. 128). He was admittedly biased toward frontier chiefs, who had the trappings, if not the substance, of political authority, and one senses that in the eyes of the artist, Keokuk had been compromised by civilized indulgence—the pride and freedom of the Upper Missouri had been exchanged for an image more Roman than savage.

The facial features and the technique of the two Smithsonian portraits are so close that one tends to believe they were painted on the same occasion, as Catlin maintains. In the Smithsonian version (fig. 26), Keokuk sits heavily astride a horse descended from a baroque monument, and wears the same elaborate costume. Why the equestrian portrait is included only in the 1837 catalogue, and as plate 290 in *Letters and Notes,* remains a mystery.

The draftsmanship of the unfinished University Museum version (a similar equestrian, illustration 1b) is unusually tight and accomplished for 1836, and Keokuk's furrowed face is in marked contrast to his impassive expression in the original portrait. In spite of the signature, the version more likely comes from the late 1840s or early 1850s, when Catlin was busily engaged in copying other paintings from his original collection (see no. 504). Additional examples of his arbitrary dating methods are discussed in numbers 31 and 99.

Prominent chiefs on the frontier sat to numerous artists, and McDermott mentions portraits of Keokuk by James Otto Lewis, Peter Rindisbacher, Charles Bird King, John Mix Stanley, and Ferdinand Pettrich, and the daguerreotype of 1847. Donaldson says that Charles Deas also had a chance to observe the chief. The standing portrait of Keokuk is repeated in cartoon 15 (NGA 2054), with his wife and another Sauk chief. The cartoon is based on a watercolor (pl. 44) in the Gilcrease *Souvenir* album, and an oil-on-canvas version of the composition is in the Museum für Völkerkunde, Berlin. The equestrian portrait is repeated in cartoon 16 (NGA 2055).

2. Black Hawk, prominent Sauk chief
Sauk and Fox, 1832
29 x 24 (73.7 x 60.9)
[Figure 21]

Formerly University Museum, Philadelphia.

"The Black Hawk is the man to whom I have alluded, as the leader of the 'Black Hawk war,' who was defeated by General Atkinson, and held a prisoner of war, and sent through Washington and other Eastern cities, with a number of others, to be gazed at.

"This man, whose name has carried a sort of terror through the country where it has been sounded, has been distinguished as a speaker or counselor rather than as a warrior; and I believe it has been pretty generally admitted that 'Nahpope' [no. 8] and the 'Prophet' [no. 7] were, in fact, the instigators of the war, and either of them with much higher claims for the name of warrior than Black Hawk ever had.

"When I painted this chief, he was dressed in a plain suit of buckskin, with a string of wampum in his ears and on his neck, and held in his hand his medicine-bag, which was the skin of a black hawk, from which he had taken his name, and the tail of which made him a fan, which he was almost constantly using" (*Letters and Notes,* vol. 2, p. 211, pl. 283).

Catlin painted Black Hawk and his warriors when they were prisoners at Jefferson Barracks near St. Louis in October 1832 (see no. 1). They were described at the time in the following unidentified passage from Donaldson:

"We were immediately struck with admiration at the gigantic and symmetrical figures of most of these warriors, who seemed, as they reclined in native ease and gracefulness, with their half naked bodies exposed to view, rather like statues from some master hand than like beings of a race whom we had heard characterized as degenerate and debased. . . . They were clad in leggings and moccasins of buckskin, and wore blankets, which were thrown around them in the manner of the Roman toga, so as to leave their right arm bare. The youngest among them were painted on their necks with a bright vermilion color, and had their faces transversely streaked with alternate red and black stripes. From their bodies and from their faces and eyebrows they pluck out the hair with the most assiduous care. They also shave or pull it out from their heads, with the exception of a tuft of about three fingers width, extending from between the forehead and crown to the back of the head. This they sometimes plait into a queue on the crown, and cut the edges of it down to an inch in length, and plaster it with vermilion, which keeps it erect and gives it the appearance of a cock's comb" (Donaldson, p. 25).

References: 1837 catalogue, no. 18; Donaldson, pp. 22-29, pl. 13; Matthews, p. 605, pl. 146; H. Chadwick Hunter, "The American Indian in Painting," *Art and Archaeology* 8 (March-April

3

1919): 89, reprod. on cover; Haberly, pp. 78, 83-84; Quimby, pp. 8-9; *Westward the Way*, no. 52, reprod. p. 86; Ewers (1956), p. 522, pl. 3; McCracken, pp. 119, 123-25, reprod. p. 164; Roehm, pp. 64-65; Rossi and Hunt, pp. 59, 320; Gilcrease catalogue, p. 49.

Versions:
University Museum, Philadelphia (until 1971); Kennedy Galleries, New York, 28½ x 23¼

Field Museum of Natural History, ca. 28 x 23

Gilcrease Institute, watercolor, 6 x 5, signed lower left: Geo Catlin Pt

Gilcrease Institute, NAI sketchbook (4776.23), pen and ink

Copy:
Chemung County Historical Society, Elmira, New York, ca. 29 x 24

Catlin's visit to Jefferson Barracks must have taken place shortly after he returned from the Upper Missouri (see no. 69). With the experience of his most productive summer behind him, he turned to the Sauk prisoners, painting them with a sure economy that emphasizes the oval geometry of their features and their shaven skulls. In the portraits of Black Hawk and Sturgeon's Head (no. 18), perhaps the best of the group, an astonishing dimension is achieved with relatively simple brushwork, and the facial contours form an unusually bold and effective design.

The Smithsonian portrait, plate 283 in *Letters and Notes*, and the Gilcrease watercolor are almost identical in detail, although the latter may be the sketch that in an 1833 Philadelphia newspaper Audubon challenged as a bad likeness (see Haberly). A deerhair crest has been added to Black Hawk's roach and minor changes have been made in the arrangement of the beaded necklaces in the University Museum portrait (illustrated here), suggesting that it is a later version (see no. 504). The Field Museum portrait incorporates these same changes, but the roach and facial features have been overpainted with crude, flat strokes that obscure the original likeness (see no. 3).

Black Hawk also appears, full length, in cartoon 14 (NGA 2053) with his fellow prisoners at Jefferson Barracks, and in cartoon 232 (NGA 2272), exhorting Keokuk to join forces with him against the whites. Black Hawk toured the East after his imprisonment and was painted by John Wesley Jarvis (fig. 112), Robert Sully, and Charles Bird King (see McKenney and Hall, vol. 2, p. 95). Catlin's portrait compares favorably to all three likenesses.

3. Whirling Thunder, eldest son of Black Hawk
Sauk and Fox, 1832
29 x 24 (73.7 x 60.9)

"A very handsome young warrior, and one of the finest-looking Indians I ever saw. There is a strong party in the tribe that is anxious to put this young man up; and I think it more than likely that *Keokuk* as chief may fall ere long by his hand, or by some of the tribe who are anxious to reinstate the family of Black Hawk" (*Letters and Notes*, vol. 2, p. 211, pl. 284).

Whirling Thunder had distinguished himself in the Black Hawk War, but Catlin's prophecy did not come true (see no. 6).

References: 1837 catalogue, no. 23; Donaldson, pp. 29-30, pl. 13; Quimby, pp. 20-21; Ewers (1956), p. 522; McCracken, p. 125; *Catlin, Bodmer, Miller;* Paris (1963), no. 2.

Versions:
Field Museum of Natural History, ca. 28 x 23

Gilcrease Institute, NAI sketchbook (4776.23), pen and ink

Painted at Jefferson Barracks in October 1832 (see no. 2). The Smithsonian portrait and plate 284 in *Letters and Notes* are identical except for the deerhair crest worn by Whirling Thunder in the former. The crest does not appear in the Field Museum portrait, but that version differs from the others in that only a single metal loop is about Whirling Thunder's neck, and his features have not the definition or finish of the Smithsonian portrait. Except where noted, the remaining portraits in the O'Fallon collection at the Field Museum of Natural History follow this same pattern—they lack the detail and conviction of life portraits, and they are best accepted as versions painted by the artist a year or two after the originals (see no. 182). Catlin was a frequent guest at the St. Louis home of Major Benjamin O'Fallon, nephew of William Clark and principal of the American Fur Company, who commissioned a group of Indian paintings from the artist in the early 1830s. The O'Fallon collection was sold to Chicago's Field Museum in 1894.

Whirling Thunder appears again, full length, in cartoon 14 (NGA 2053), with other Sauk and Fox prisoners at Jefferson Barracks, and he was later painted with his father by Charles Bird King and John Wesley Jarvis.

4. Roaring Thunder, youngest son of Black Hawk
Sauk and Fox, 1832
29 x 24 (73.7 x 60.9)

References: 1837 catalogue, no. 24; *Letters and Notes,* vol. 2, p. 212; Donaldson, p. 30; Quimby, pp. 10-11; Ewers (1956), p. 522; McCracken, p. 125; Fine Arts Museum of New Mexico, Santa Fe, *The Artist in the American West 1800-1900* (1961), no. 7.

Version:
Field Museum of Natural History, ca. 28½ x 22½

Painted at Jefferson Barracks in October 1832 (see no. 2). The Field Museum portrait lacks the necklace strands, feathers pendant from each ear, and details on the breast ornament (see no. 3). Roaring Thunder also appears, full length, in cartoon 14 (NGA 2053).

5. Wife of Keokuk
Sauk and Fox, 1835
29 x 24 (73.7 x 60.9)

"Plate 281 is a portrait of the wife of *Kee-o-kuk,* and plate 282 of his favorite son [no. 6], whom he intends to be his successor. These portraits are both painted . . . in the costumes precisely in which they were dressed. This woman was the favorite one (I think) of seven whom he had living (*apparently* quite comfortably and peaceably) in his wigwam, where General Street and I visited him in his village on the Des Moines River. And, although she was the oldest of the 'lot,' she seemed to be the favorite one on this occasion—the only one that could be painted—on account, I believe, of her being the mother of his favorite son. Her dress, which was of civilized stuffs, was fashioned and ornamented by herself, and was truly a most splendid affair, the upper part of it being almost literally covered with silver brooches" (*Letters and Notes,* vol. 2, p. 210, pl. 281).

References: 1837 catalogue, no. 29; Donaldson, p. 30, pl. 14; Ewers (1956), p. 522; McCracken, p. 171, reprod. p. 161; *America as Art,* no. 170.

Version:
Gilcrease Institute, NAI sketchbook (4776.37), pen and ink

Painted at the Sauk and Fox village in 1835. Keokuk's wife also appears in cartoon 15 (NGA 2054), wearing a somewhat different costume (see nos. 1, 6). The cartoon figure is based on a watercolor (pl. 44) in the Gilcrease *Souvenir* album.

6. Deer's Hair, favorite son of Keokuk
Sauk and Fox, 1835
29 x 24 (73.7 x 60.9)

References: 1837 catalogue, no. 31; *Letters and Notes,* vol. 2, p. 210, pl. 282; Donaldson, pp. 30-31, pl. 15; Ewers (1956), p. 522.

Version:
Gilcrease Institute, NAI sketchbook (4776.37), pen and ink

Copy:
M. Knoedler & Co., New York (until 1971), pencil and watercolor, signed lower right:
Rosa B-[Bonheur]

Painted at the Sauk and Fox village in 1835. Deer's Hair succeeded his father as chief of the Sauk and Fox in 1848 (see nos. 1, 5). He also appears in cartoon 13 (NGA 2052).

7. White Cloud (called The Prophet), adviser to Black Hawk
Sauk and Fox, 1832
29 x 24 (73.7 x 60.9)

Donaldson quotes the following passage in his description of White Cloud: "The Prophet . . . is about 40 years old, and nearly 6 feet high, stout, and athletic. . . . He was by one side a Winnebago, and the other a Sac or Saukie. He has a large, broad face, short blunt nose, large full eyes, broad mouth, thick lips, with a full suit of hair. . . . He was clothed in very white dressed deer-skins, fringed at the seams with short cuttings of the same. . . . He carries with him a huge pipe, a yard in length, with the stem ornamented with the neck feathers of a duck, and beads and ribands of various colors. To its center is attached a fan of feathers. He wears his hair long all over his head" (Samuel G. Drake, *Book of the Indians of North America*, part 4 [Boston, 1832], p. 163).

The Prophet, along with Soup (no. 8), was apparently responsible for plotting the Black Hawk War.

References: 1837 catalogue, no. 20; *Letters and Notes*, vol. 2, p. 211, pl. 285; Donaldson, pp. 31-33, pl. 16; Haberly, reprod. opp. p. 97; Quimby, pp. 22-23; Ewers (1956), p. 522; McCracken, pp. 124-25, reprod. p. 164; Paris (1963), no. 3; *Catlin, Bodmer, Miller*; Los Angeles County Museum of Art, *The American West* (1972), no. 22, reprod. p. 55; Haverstock, reprod. p. 104.

Versions:
Field Museum of Natural History, ca. 28 x 23
Gilcrease Institute, NAI sketchbook (4776.23), pen and ink

Copy:
British Museum, London, by John Cullum, watercolor, 12⅛ x 9¾ (1842-1844)

Painted at Jefferson Barracks in October 1832 (see no. 2). The Smithsonian portrait and plate 285 in *Letters and Notes* are almost identical, but in the Field Museum version The Prophet wears no necklace and the arrangement of feathers on his pipe is somewhat different (see no. 3). He appears again, full length, in cartoons 14 and 232 (NGA 2053, 2272).

The broad, sensuous features of the sitter provide a telling parallel to Drake's description and to other Upper Missouri portraits done by Catlin that summer (see no. 182). The Prophet was painted a year later by Robert Sully.

8. Soup, adviser to Black Hawk
Sauk and Fox, 1832
29 x 24 (73.7 x 60.9)

Donaldson quotes the following passage in describing the portrait: "When Mr. Catlin, the artist, was about taking the portrait of . . . [Soup], he seized the ball and chain that were fastened to his leg, and, raising them on high, exclaimed, with a look of scorn, 'Make me so, and show me to the Great Father.' On Mr. Catlin's refusing to paint him as he wished, he kept varying his countenance with grimaces to prevent him from catching a likeness" (Samuel G. Drake, *Book of the Indians of North America*, part 4 [Boston, 1832], p. 163).

Soup was second in command to Black Hawk during the war and brother of The Prophet (no. 7), with whom he conspired to bring about the conflict.

References: 1837 catalogue, no. 26; *Letters and Notes*, vol. 2, p. 211; Donaldson, pp. 33-34; Quimby, pp. 24-25; Ewers (1956), p. 522; McCracken, pp. 124-25.

Version:
Field Museum of Natural History, ca. 28 x 23

Painted at Jefferson Barracks in October 1832 (see no. 2). The Smithsonian and Field Museum portraits are similar in detail, but the modeling of the facial structure is stronger in the former (see no. 3). Soup also appears, full length, in cartoon 14 (NGA 2053), as a prisoner at Jefferson Barracks.

9. The Whale, one of Keokuk's principal braves
Sauk and Fox, 1835
29 x 24 (73.7 x 60.9)

Catlin describes the subject as "holding a handsome war-club in his hand" (1848 catalogue, p. 9).

References: 1837 catalogue, no. 32; *Letters and Notes*, vol. 2, p. 211, pl. 287; Donaldson, p. 34; Ewers (1956), p. 522; McCracken, p. 170, reprod. p. 163; Paris (1963), no. 4.

Version:
Gilcrease Institute, NAI sketchbook (4776.37), pen and ink

Copy:
M. Knoedler & Co., New York (until 1971), pencil and watercolor, signed lower right:
Rosa B-[Bonheur]

Painted at the Sauk and Fox village in 1835. The Whale's display of costume accessories and weapons rivals that of Keokuk (see no. 1). The subject, holding the same war club, appears again in cartoon 13 (NGA 2052), with his wife (no. 10).

10. The Buck's Wife, wife of The Whale
Sauk and Fox, 1835
29 x 24 (73.7 x 60.9)

References: 1837 catalogue, no. 30; *Letters and Notes*, vol. 2, p. 211, pl. 288; Donaldson, p. 34; Ewers (1956), p. 522.

Version:
Gilcrease Institute, NAI sketchbook (4776.24), pen and ink

Copy:
M. Knoedler & Co., New York (until 1971), pencil and watercolor, signed lower right:
Rosa B-[Bonheur]

Painted at the Sauk and Fox village in 1835 (see no. 1). The Buck's Wife, wrapped in her Mackinaw blanket, also appears in cartoon 13 (NGA 2052), with her husband (no 9).

11. Little Stabbing Chief, a venerable Sauk chief
Sauk and Fox, 1835
29 x 24 (73.7 x 60.9)

Described by Catlin as "a very old man, holding his shield, staff and pipe in his hands; has long been the head civil chief of this tribe; but . . . has resigned his office to those younger and better qualified" *(Letters and Notes*, vol. 2, p. 211, pl. 289).

Little Stabbing Chief sided with Keokuk during the Black Hawk War.

References: 1837 catalogue, no. 22; Donaldson, pp. 34-36, pl. 17; Ewers (1956), p. 522; McCracken, pp. 170-71.

9

11

10

Copies:
M. Knoedler & Co., New York (until 1971), pencil and watercolor, signed lower right:
Rosa B-[Bonheur]
British Museum, London, by John Cullum, watercolor, 12½ x 9 (1842-1844)

Painted at the Sauk and Fox village in 1835 (see no. 1). Little Stabbing Chief appears in cartoon 15 (NGA 2054), which is based on a watercolor (pl. 44) in the Gilcrease *Souvenir* album. Some years earlier the subject had sat for Charles Bird King in Washington (see McKenney and Hall, vol. 1, pp. 195-96).

References: 1837 catalogue, no. 25; *Letters and Notes*, vol. 2, p. 212; Donaldson, p. 36; Quimby, pp. 16-17; Ewers (1956), p. 522.

Version:
Field Museum of Natural History, ca. 28 x 23

Painted at Jefferson Barracks in October 1832 (see no. 2). The Swimmer wears no necklaces or bracelet in the Field Museum portrait (see no. 3). He appears again, full length, in cartoon 14 (NGA 2053), with other prisoners from Jefferson Barracks, and by himself in cartoon 121 (unlocated), which may be an oil-on-canvas version of the original portrait.

14. Bear's Fat
Sauk and Fox, 1832
Unlocated

References: 1837 catalogue, no. 27; *Letters and Notes*, vol. 2, p. 212; Donaldson, p. 36.

Probably painted at Jefferson Barracks in October 1832, as Catlin includes the subject in a list of Black Hawk's warriors (see no. 2).

12. The Ioway, one of Black Hawk's principal warriors
Sauk and Fox, 1832
29 x 24 (73.7 x 60.9)

Catlin describes the subject as having "his body curiously ornamented with his 'war-paint'" (*Letters and Notes*, vol. 2, p. 212).

References: 1837 catalogue, no. 21; Donaldson, p. 36; Quimby, pp. 18-19; Ewers (1956), p. 522.

Version:
Field Museum of Natural History, ca. 28 x 23

Painted at Jefferson Barracks in October 1832 (see no. 2). The Ioway has no goatee in the Field Museum version; otherwise, the two portraits are almost identical (see no. 3).

15. Little Stabbing Chief the Younger, one of Black Hawk's braves
Sauk and Fox, 1832
29 x 24 (73.7 x 60.9)

References: 1837 catalogue, no. 33; *Letters and Notes*, vol. 2, p. 212; Donaldson, p. 36; Quimby, pp. 14-15; Ewers (1956), p. 522.

Versions:
Field Museum of Natural History, ca. 28 x 23
Gilcrease Institute, NAI sketchbook (4776.24), pen and ink

Painted at Jefferson Barracks in October 1832 (see no. 2). Catlin has added a necklace, arm band, and bracelet to the Field Museum version, but the facial features and forehead structure are more convincing in the Smithsonian portrait (see no. 3).

13. The Swimmer, one of Black Hawk's warriors
Sauk and Fox, 1832
29 x 24 (73.7 x 60.9)

Donaldson quotes the following description of the subject: "Fast-Swimming Fish is a short, thick-set, good-natured old brave, who bears his misfortunes with a philosophy worthy of the ancients" (Samuel G. Drake, *Book of the Indians of North America*, part 4 [Boston, 1832], p. 164).

16. Bear's Track
   Sauk and Fox, 1835
   29 x 24 (73.7 x 60.9)

References: 1837 catalogue, no. 34; *Letters and Notes,* vol. 2, p. 212; Donaldson, p. 36; Ewers (1956), p. 522; McCracken, p. 170, reprod. p. 172; Museum of Fine Arts, Houston, *Home on the Range* (1972), no. 28, reprod. p. 43.

Probably painted at the Sauk and Fox village in 1835. Catlin seems not to have made full-length portraits of any of the prisoners at Jefferson Barracks in 1832 (see no. 2), and Bear's Track's pose is similar to numbers 9 and 11.

17. The Fire, a Fox medicine man
   Sauk and Fox, 1835
   29 x 24 (73.7 x 60.9)

References: 1837 catalogue, no. 35; Donaldson, p. 36; Ewers (1956), p. 522.

Probably painted at the Sauk and Fox village in 1835 (see no. 16).

18. Sturgeon's Head, a Fox warrior
   Sauk and Fox, 1832
   29 x 24 (73.7 x 60.9)

"This man held a spear in his hand when he was being painted, with which he assured me he killed four white men during the war; though I have some doubts of the fact" (*Letters and Notes,* vol. 2, p. 211, pl. 286).
   Sturgeon's Head was one of Black Hawk's principal warriors.

References: 1837 catalogue, no. 36; Donaldson, p. 36, pl. 16; Quimby, pp. 12-13; Ewers (1956), p. 522; Haverstock, reprod. p. 114.

Versions:
Field Museum of Natural History, ca. 28 x 23
Gilcrease Institute, NAI sketchbook (4776.23), pen and ink

Painted at Jefferson Barracks in October 1832 (see no. 2). The carefully described ear pendants in the Smithsonian portrait, which match those in plate 286 of *Letters and Notes,* are repeated only in cursory form in the Chicago version (see no. 3). The original portrait is also distinguished by simplified oval contours, which Catlin has transformed into a striking classical bust.

16

18

17

19-21

19-21. Three Fox Indians
   Sauk and Fox, possibly 1837-1839
   29 x 24 (73.7 x 60.9)

References: Donaldson, p. 36; Ewers (1956), p. 522.

The painting is not listed in the 1837 catalogue, but does appear in the Egyptian Hall catalogue of January 1840, perhaps indicating that it was finished during the interval (see no. 147).

22

24

23

and Louise Barry convincingly challenge Haberly's research and Catlin's romantic recollections.

In the fall of 1832, Catlin did stay several weeks at Fort Leavenworth, where he encountered numerous members of the tribe and must have painted the following series of Kansa portraits. Each is modeled with broad firm strokes that give a vigorous dimension to the facial structure, yet the costume accessories are done with a technique turned surprisingly facile. The series appears to have much in common with Upper Missouri portraits painted earlier in the summer (see nos. 69, 149) and represents a marked achievement over Catlin's efforts in 1830 (see nos. 237-55).

The Wolf appears again, full length, in cartoon 1 (NGA 2269), with his wife and child, and three Kansa warriors.

23. Cannot Be Thrown Down, a warrior
Kansas, 1832
29 x 24 (73.7 x 60.9)

References: 1837 catalogue, no. 45; Donaldson, p. 39; Ewers (1956), p. 512; Time-Life Books, ed., *The Chroniclers* (New York, 1976), reprod. p. 104.

Probably painted at Fort Leavenworth in 1832 (see no. 22). This portrait closely resembles plate 135 in *Letters and Notes,* and the possibility remains that it should be catalogued as number 27, *Man of Good Sense,* rather than number 23.

24. No Fool, a great fop
Kansas, 1832
29 x 24 (73.7 x 60.9)

Catlin says that No Fool "used half the day in painting his face, preparing to sit for his picture" (*Letters and Notes,* vol. 2, p. 23, pl. 136).

References: 1837 catalogue, no. 46; Donaldson, p. 40, pl. 18; Haberly, p. 44; Ewers (1956), p. 512; McCracken, pp. 19, 34; *Catlin, Bodmer, Miller;* Paris (1963), no. 5; M. Knoedler & Co., New York, *The American Indian Observed* (1972), no. 28, reprod. p. 21.

Version:
Gilcrease Institute, NAI sketchbook (4776.10), pen and ink

Copy:
M. Knoedler & Co., New York (until 1971), pencil and watercolor, signed lower right:
Rosa B-[Bonheur]

Probably painted at Fort Leavenworth in 1832 (see no. 22). No Fool also appears, full length, in cartoon 1 (NGA 2269).

22. The Wolf, a chief
Kansas, 1832
29 x 24 (73.7 x 60.9)

"A chief of some distinction, with a bold and manly outline of head; exhibiting, like most of his tribe, an European outline of features, signally worth the notice of the inquiring world. The head of this chief was most curiously ornamented, and his neck bore a profusion of wampum strings" (*Letters and Notes,* vol. 2, p. 23, pl. 133).

References: 1837 catalogue, no. 44; Donaldson, p. 39, pl. 18; Haberly, pp. 43-44; Ewers (1956), pp. 485, 512; McCracken, pp. 19, 34; Roehm, pp. 55-57; Louise Barry, *The Beginning of the West* (Topeka, Kans., 1972), pp. 218-20.

Version:
Gilcrease Institute, NAI sketchbook (4776.10), pen and ink

Copy:
M. Knoedler & Co., New York (until 1971), pencil and watercolor, signed lower right:
Rosa B-[Bonheur]

Haberly, followed by Ewers and McCracken, states that Catlin visited the Kansa villages with General Clark in 1830, but Catlin recalls the visit taking place with Major John Dougherty in the spring of 1831 (Donaldson, p. 425). Unfortunately, there is no mention of a trip in either year in the Clark or Dougherty papers at the Kansas State Historical Society, and both Dale Morgan (see Roehm)

25. Little White Bear, a distinguished brave
Kansas, 1832
29 x 24 (73.7 x 60.9)

Catlin describes the subject's head as having a "bold and Roman outline" (*Letters and Notes*, vol. 2, p. 23, pl. 134).

References: 1837 catalogue, no. 47; Donaldson, p. 40, pl. 18; Ewers (1956), p. 512; McCracken, pp. 19, 29, 34; Halpin, reprod. p. 10; Gilcrease catalogue, p. 49.

Versions:
Gilcrease Institute, watercolor, 6 x 5, signed lower left: Geo. Catlin Pt.
and lower right (on mount): Geo. Catlin
Gilcrease Institute, NAI sketchbook (4776.10), pen and ink

Copy:
M. Knoedler & Co., New York (until 1971), pencil and watercolor, signed lower right: Rosa B-[Bonheur]

Probably painted at Fort Leavenworth in 1832 (see no. 22). The Smithsonian oil and the Gilcrease watercolor are identical in detail, but the face of the former is more forcefully modeled, indicating its status as the life portrait.

Little White Bear also appears, full length, in cartoon 1 (NGA 2269).

26. Bear-catcher, a celebrated warrior
Kansas 1832
29 x 24 (73.7 x 60.9)

References: 1837 catalogue, no. 48; Donaldson, p. 40; Ewers (1956), p. 512.

Probably painted at Fort Leavenworth in 1832 (see nos. 22, 28).

27. Man of Good Sense, a young warrior
Kansas, 1832
Unlocated

Catlin calls the subject "a handsome young warrior" whose headdress resembles a "Grecian helmet" (1848 catalogue, p. 10).

"The custom of shaving the head, and ornamenting it with the crest of deer's hair, belongs to this tribe; and also to the Osages, the Pawnees, the Sacs, and Foxes, and Ioways. . . . In Plate 135, is a fair exhibition of this very curious custom—the hair being cut as close to the head as possible, except a tuft the size of the palm of the hand, on the crown of the head, which is left of two inches in length: and in the centre of which is fastened a beautiful crest made of the hair of the deer's tail (dyed red) and horsehair, and oftentimes surmounted with the war-eagle's quill. In the centre

of the patch of hair, which I said was left of a couple of inches in length, is preserved a small lock, which is never cut, but cultivated to the greatest length possible, and uniformly kept in braid, and passed through a piece of curiously carved bone; which lies in the centre of the crest, and spreads it out to its uniform shape, which they study with great care to preserve. . . . This little braid is called in these tribes, the 'scalp-lock' and is scrupulously preserved in this way, and offered to their enemy if they can get it, as a trophy" (*Letters and Notes*, vol. 2, pp. 23-24, pl. 135).

References: 1837 catalogue, no. 49; Donaldson, p. 40, pl. 18; Ewers (1956), p. 512; McCracken, pp. 19, 34.

Version:
Gilcrease Institute, NAI sketchbook (4776.10), pen and ink

Copy:
M. Knoedler & Co., New York (until 1971), pencil and watercolor, signed lower right:
Rosa B-[Bonheur]

Probably painted at Fort Leavenworth in 1832 (see no. 22). The portrait now assigned to number 522 was originally catalogued as number 27. It did not, however, match Catlin's description or plate 135 in *Letters and Notes,* and the style of the portrait more nearly resembles the Iowa series painted in London. Plate 135 is illustrated in place of the original (see no. 23).

Man of Good Sense also appears, full length, in cartoon 1 (NGA 2269).

Harold McCracken, Cody, Wyoming, pencil, 4¾ x 3⅛

Gilcrease Institute, NAI sketchbook (4776.13), pen and ink

Painted at Fort Gibson in 1834. The Gilcrease watercolor is only three-quarter length and lacks the detail and firmness of the Smithsonian portrait. The McCracken drawing may be a study for plate 150 in *Letters and Notes.* Clermont also appears in cartoon 52 (NGA 2027), with his wife and child, and two Osage warriors.

Catlin demonstrates a sureness and control in the Osage portraits that was perhaps gained the previous year finishing the numerous paintings of the Upper Missouri series. The full-length subjects stand or move with an ease often lacking in his earlier, more rigidly posed figures, and despite some lapses, anatomical passages are done with an improved sense of proportion (see nos. 284, 288, 294).

30. Wáh-chee-te, wife of Clermont, and child
Osage, 1834
29 x 24 (73.7 x 60.9)

"She [Clermont's wife] was richly dressed in costly cloths of civilized manufacture, which is almost a solitary instance among the Osages, who so studiously reject every luxury and every custom of civilized people" (*Letters and Notes,* vol. 2, p. 41, pl. 151).

References: 1837 catalogue, no. 12; Donaldson, p. 42; Ewers (1956), p. 514; McCracken, pp. 129, 138, 139; Gilcrease catalogue, p. 49; *America as Art,* no. 168, reprod. p. 163.

Versions:
Gilcrease Institute, watercolor, 7 x 6, signed lower right (on mount): Geo. Catlin. 1836

Harold McCracken, Cody, Wyoming, pencil, 4¾ x 3⅛

Gilcrease Institute, NAI sketchbook (4776.13), pen and ink

Painted at Fort Gibson in 1834 (see no. 29). Donaldson's date must be based on Catlin's faulty itinerary (see nos. 31, 46). The Smithsonian and Gilcrease portraits are almost identical, and the subject appears again in cartoon 52 (NGA 2027).

28. Hón-je-a-pút-o, wife of Bear-catcher
Kansas, 1832
29 x 24 (73.7 x 60.9)

References: 1837 catalogue, no. 49½; Donaldson, p. 40; Ewers (1956), p. 512.

Probably painted at Fort Leavenworth in 1832 (see nos. 22 and 26).

29. Clermont, first chief of the tribe
Osage, 1834
29 x 24 (73.7 x 60.9)

"The head-chief of the Osages at this time, is a young man by the name of Clermont, the son of a very distinguished chief of that name, who recently died; leaving his son his successor, with the consent of the tribe. I painted the portrait of this chief at full length, in a beautiful dress, his leggings fringed with scalp-locks, and in his hand his favourite and valued war club" (*Letters and Notes,* vol. 2, p. 41, pl. 150).

References: 1837 catalogue, no. 6; Donaldson, p. 42, pl. 19; Ewers (1956), p. 514; McCracken, pp. 138, 139, reprod. p. 136; Halpin, reprod. p. 11; Gilcrease catalogue, p. 49.

Versions:
Gilcrease Institute, watercolor, 8½ x 7½, signed lower right: Geo Catlin/1836

Rains Galleries, New York, Cornelius Michaelson sale, May 8, 1935, no. 71, watercolor, 9 x 8½

31. Black Dog, second chief
Osage, 1834
29 x 24 (73.7 x 60.9)

"Amongst the chiefs of the Osages, and probably the next in authority and respect in the tribe, is . . . the black dog, whom I painted also at full length, and with his pipe in one hand, and his tomahawk in the other; his head shaved, and ornamented with a beautiful crest of deer's hair, and his body wrapped in a huge mackinaw blanket.

"This dignitary, who is blind in the left eye, is one of the most conspicuous characters in all this country, rendered so by his large size (standing in height and girth above all of his tribe), as well as by his extraordinary life. . . . His height, I think, is seven feet, and his limbs full and rather fat, making his bulk formidable, and weighing, perhaps, some 250 or 300 pounds" (*Letters and Notes*, vol. 2, p. 42, pl. 152).

John Mix Stanley, who painted Black Dog in 1843, recorded his height as six feet six inches.

References: 1837 catalogue, no. 1; Donaldson, pp. 42-43, 475, pl. 20; Haberly, p. 87; Mary C. Withington, *A Catalogue of Manuscripts in the Collection of Western Americana Founded by William Robertson Coe* (Yale University Library, New Haven, Conn., 1952), no. 67; Ewers (1956), p. 514; Hartmann, pp. 42-43; Los Angeles County Museum of Art, *The American West* (1972), no. 24, reprod. p. 89; Gilcrease catalogue, p. 49.

Versions:
Gilcrease Institute, watercolor, 11 x 8, signed lower right: Geo Catlin 1836

Rains Galleries, New York, Cornelius Michaelson sale, May 8, 1935, no. 71, watercolor, 9 x 8½

Gilcrease Institute, NAI sketchbook (4776.13), pen and ink

Copy:
M. Knoedler & Co., New York (until 1971), pencil and watercolor, signed lower right:
Rosa B-[Bonheur]

Landscape additions have been made to the Gilcrease watercolor, but Black Dog has no tomahawk. With few exceptions, the modeling of the Osage portraits at the Gilcrease lacks the strength and detail of the Smithsonian originals (see no. 29).

Painted from life in the presence of General Leavenworth at Fort Gibson in 1834, according to an original certificate in Smithsonian files. Donaldson's date of 1836 for this portrait must be based on Catlin's mistaken recollection of when the dragoon expedition took place (see 1871 catalogue, pp. 17, 90). Black Dog also appears in cartoon 51 (NGA 2026), which is based on a watercolor (pl. 36) in the Gilcrease *Souvenir* album (fig. 151). The best of several versions of this cartoon is in the Museum für Völkerkunde, Berlin.

32. Tál-lee, a warrior of distinction
Osage, 1834
29 x 24 (73.7 x 60.9)

"Amongst the many brave and distinguished warriors of the tribe, one of the most noted and respected is Tal-lee, painted at full length, with his lance in his hand—his shield on his arm, and his bow and quiver slung upon his back.

"In this portrait, there is a fair specimen of the Osage figure and dress, as well as of the facial outline, and shape and character of the head, and mode of dressing and ornamenting it with helmet crest, and the eagle's quill" (*Letters and Notes*, vol. 2, p. 42, pl. 153).

References: 1837 catalogue, no. 2; Donaldson, pp. 43-44; Ewers (1956), p. 514; McCracken, p. 138, reprod. p. 163; *Catlin, Bodmer, Miller;* Paris (1963), no. 6, pl. 1; M. Knoedler & Co., New York, *The American Indian Observed* (1972), no. 29, reprod. p. 22; Gilcrease catalogue, p. 49.

Version:
Gilcrease Institute, NAI sketchbook (4776.13), pen and ink

Copy:
M. Knoedler & Co., New York (until 1971), pencil and watercolor, signed lower right: Rosa B-[Bonheur]

Painted at Fort Gibson in 1834 (see nos. 29, 31). Tál-lee also appears as *An Osage Warrior* in plate 1 of *Catlin's North American Indian Portfolio,* first published in 1844, and in cartoon 51 (NGA 2026).

33. Wa-ho-béck-ee, a handsome brave
Osage, 1834
29 x 24 (73.7 x 60.9)
[Figure 110]

Catlin describes the subject as "a brave; said to be the handsomest man in the nation; with a profusion of wampum on his neck, and a fan in his hand made of the eagle's tail" (1848 catalogue, pp. 10-11).

References: 1839 catalogue, no. 11; *Letters and Notes,* vol. 2, p. 43; Donaldson, p. 43; Ewers (1956), p. 514; Gilcrease catalogue, p. 49.

Version:
Gilcrease Institute, watercolor, 6 x 6, signed lower right (on mount): Geo. Catlin

Painted at Fort Gibson in 1834 (see no. 29). The Gilcrease portrait is half-length, and the position of the subject's arms (his hands are not included) is even more awkward than in the Smithsonian original (see no. 31).

31

32

34-36

38-40

Versions:
Harold McCracken, Cody, Wyoming, pen and ink, 7¼ x 9⅞

Gilcrease Institute, NAI sketchbook (4776.14), pen and ink

Copy:
M. Knoedler & Co., New York (until 1971), pencil and watercolor, signed lower right:
Rosa B-[Bonheur]

Painted at Fort Gibson in 1834 (see nos. 29, 31). The McCracken drawing may be a study for plate 154-56 in *Letters and Notes.* The subjects appear again in cartoons 51 and 52 (NGA 2026, 2027).

37. Constant Walker
Osage, 1834
Unlocated

References: 1837 catalogue, no. 7; *Letters and Notes,* vol. 2, p. 43; Donaldson, p. 44.

Probably painted at Fort Gibson in 1834.

34-36. He Who Is Not Afraid, Big Crow, and Man of the Bed, three young warriors
Osage, 1834
29 x 24 (73.7 x 60.9)

"These portraits set forth fairly the modes of dress and ornaments of the young men of the tribe, from the tops of their heads to the soles of their feet. The only dress they wear in warm weather is the breech-cloth, leggings, and moccasins of dressed skins, and garters worn immediately below the knee, ornamented profusely with beads and wampum.

"These three distinguished and ambitious young men were of the best families in the Osage Nation; and, as they explained to me, having formed a peculiar attachment to each other—they desired me to paint them all on one canvas, in which wish I indulged them" (*Letters and Notes,* vol. 2, p. 43, pl. 154-56).

The three also served as guides on the dragoon expedition of 1834.

References: 1837 catalogue, nos. 3-5; Donaldson, pp. 43-44, pl. 21; Ewers (1956), p. 514; McCracken, p. 139; Gilcrease catalogue, p. 49.

38-40. He Who Takes Away, War, and Mink-chésk, three distinguished young men
Osage, 1834
29 x 24 (73.7 x 60.9)

References: 1837 catalogue, nos. 8-10; *Letters and Notes,* vol. 2, p. 43; Donaldson, p. 44; Ewers (1956), p. 514; Gilcrease catalogue, p. 49.

Painted at Fort Gibson in 1834 (see nos. 29, 31). The subjects of three watercolors in the Gilcrease Institute have been mistakenly identified as the three Indians in this portrait. The Gilcrease watercolors represent, instead, numbers 43, 44, and 45.

41. Mad Buffalo, murderer of two white men
Osage, 1834
29 x 24 (73.7 x 60.9)

Mad Buffalo "was tried and convicted for the murder of two white men during Adams's administration, and was afterwards pardoned, and still lives, though in disgrace in his tribe, as one whose life has been forfeited" (*Letters and Notes*, vol. 2, p. 43).

References: 1837 catalogue, no. 13; Donaldson, p. 44; Ewers (1956), p. 514; Gilcrease catalogue, p. 49.

Version:
Gilcrease Institute, watercolor, 11 x 8, signed lower right (on mount): Geo. Catlin

Painted at Fort Gibson in 1834 (see nos. 29, 31). Mad Buffalo has no bow and quiver in the Gilcrease watercolor (illustration 41a), but his features are carefully and decisively modeled. Both portraits may have been taken from life, although the studied strokes of the watercolor lack the spontaneous appeal of the Smithsonian oil.

42. Madman, a distinguished warrior
Osage, 1834
29 x 24 (73.7 x 60.9)

References: 1837 catalogue, no. 14; *Letters and Notes*, vol. 2, p. 43; Donaldson, p. 44; Ewers (1956), p. 514; Gilcrease catalogue, p. 49.

Version:
Gilcrease Institute, watercolor, 6 x 6, signed lower right (on mount): Geo Catlin

Painted at Fort Gibson in 1834 (see no. 29). The Gilcrease portrait is three-quarter length, and the facial features differ somewhat from those in the Smithsonian original (see no. 31).

43. White Hair, the Younger, a Band chief
Osage, 1834
29 x 24 (73.7 x 60.9)

"White Hair is another distinguished leader of the Osages. . . . I believe it has been generally agreed that his claims [to the title of Head Chief] are third in the tribe. . . . The portrait of this man, I regret to say, I did not get" (*Letters and Notes*, vol. 2, p. 42).

References: 1837 catalogue, no. 15; Donaldson, p. 44; Ewers (1956), p. 514; Gilcrease catalogue, p. 49.

Version:
Gilcrease Institute, watercolor, 9 x 4, signed lower right (on mount): Geo. Catlin

Probably painted at Fort Gibson in 1834 (see no.

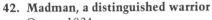
Gilcrease Institute, Tulsa.

29), although Catlin's remark may indicate a later date. The subject of the Gilcrease watercolor is incorrectly identified as Wa-másh-ee-sheek (He Who Takes Away, no. 38) in the Gilcrease catalogue. The Smithsonian painting and the watercolor closely resemble one another, but even the slight knowledge of anatomy demonstrated in the former has disappeared in the latter (see no. 31).

Painted at Fort Gibson in 1834 (see no. 29). The subject of the Gilcrease watercolor is incorrectly identified as Mink-chésk (no. 40) in the Gilcrease catalogue. The figures in the watercolor and the Smithsonian original are similar in detail, with anatomical problems that are a repeat of numbers 43 and 44.

46. Bow and Quiver, first chief of the tribe
Comanche, 1834
29 x 24 (73.7 x 60.9)

"A mild and pleasant looking gentleman, without anything striking or peculiar in his looks; dressed in a very humble manner, with very few ornaments upon him, and his hair carelessly falling about his face and over his shoulders. . . . The only ornaments to be seen about him were a couple of beautiful shells worn in his ears, and a boar's tusk attached to his neck, and worn on his breast" (*Letters and Notes*, vol. 2, pp. 66-67, pl. 168).

References: 1837 catalogue, no. 50; Donaldson, p. 47, pl. 22; Ewers (1956), p. 509; McCracken, p. 173; Gilcrease catalogue, p. 49.

Versions:
Gilcrease Institute, watercolor, 6¾ x 5⅝, signed lower right (on mount): Geo. Catlin 1834.

Gilcrease Institute, NAI sketchbook (4776.15), pen and ink

Painted at the Comanche village in 1834. The subject's right hand and forearm are included in the Gilcrease watercolor, but the handling of the facial features in the Smithsonian oil is more lively and vigorous, indicating its status as the life portrait (it also matches plate 168 in *Letters and Notes*). The Comanche series in the Gilcrease Institute is again based on the Smithsonian originals, and the dates Catlin used on this series (and on other Gilcrease watercolors) are no more reliable than those he arbitrarily assigned to the cartoon collection (see no. 31).

Bow and Quiver appears again in cartoon 43 (NGA 2006), with three Comanche warriors.

44. Handsome Bird
Osage, 1834
29 x 24 (73.7 x 60.9)

Catlin describes Handsome Bird as "a splendid-looking fellow, six feet eight inches high; with war club and quiver" (1848 catalogue, p. 11).

References: 1837 catalogue, no. 16; *Letters and Notes*, vol. 2, p. 43; Donaldson, p. 44; Haberly, p. 95; Ewers (1956), p. 514; Gilcrease catalogue, p. 49.

Version:
Gilcrease Institute, watercolor, 9 x 4, signed lower right (on mount): Geo. Catlin

Painted at Fort Gibson in 1834 (see no. 29). The subject of the Gilcrease watercolor is incorrectly identified as Wa-chésh-uk (War, no. 39) in the Gilcrease catalogue. The Smithsonian painting and the watercolor are alike in detail, but the figure is badly drawn in the latter (see no. 43).

45. Little Chief
Osage, 1834
29 x 24 (73.7 x 60.9)

References: 1837 catalogue, no. 17; *Letters and Notes*, vol. 2, p. 43; Donaldson, p. 44; Ewers (1956), p. 514; Gilcrease catalogue, p. 49.

Version:
Gilcrease Institute, watercolor, 9 x 4, signed lower right (on mount): Geo. Catlin

47. Mountain of Rocks, second chief of the tribe
Comanche, 1834
29 x 24 (73.7 x 60.9)

"This man received the United States Regiment of Dragoons with great kindness at his village, which was beautifully situated at the base . . . of the [Wichita Mountains]" (1848 catalogue, p. 11).

Catlin described Mountain of Rocks as "the largest and fattest Indian I ever saw. . . . A perfect personification of Jack Falstaff, in size and in figure, with an African face, and a beard on his chin of two or three inches in length. His name . . . he got from having conducted a large party of Camanchees through a secret and subterraneous passage, entirely through the mountain of granite rocks, which lies back of their village; thereby saving their lives" (*Letters and Notes,* vol. 2, p. 67, pl. 169).

References: 1837 catalogue, no. 51; Donaldson, p. 47, pl. 22; Ewers (1956), p. 509; McCracken, p. 152, reprod. p. 157; Gilcrease catalogue, p. 49.

Versions:
Gilcrease Institute, watercolor, 7½ x 6, signed lower right (on mount): Geo. Catlin

Gilcrease Institute, NAI sketchbook (4776.15), pen and ink

Painted at the Comanche village in 1834. Mountain of Rocks is seated with his hands visible in the Gilcrease watercolor, but the Smithsonian oil differs from plate 169 in *Letters and Notes* only in the addition of a feather headdress (see no. 46). Catlin matches the full, sensuous appeal of the sitter with brushwork as bold as any used in the dragoon expedition portraits.

The subject appears again, full length, in cartoon 42 (NGA 2005), with a Comanche warrior and a woman and child. The cartoon is based on a watercolor (pl. 40) in the Gilcrease *Souvenir* album.

48. He Who Carries a Wolf, a distinguished brave
   Comanche, 1834
   29 x 24 (73.7 x 60.9)

A man of some standing in the tribe who "piloted the dragoons to the Camanchee village, and received a handsome rifle from Colonel Dodge for so doing." He was named "from the circumstance of his carrying a *medicine-bag* made of the skin of a wolf; he holds a whip in his hand" (1848 catalogue, pp. 11-12).

References: 1837 catalogue, no. 52; *Letters and Notes,* vol. 2, p. 67, pl. 170; Donaldson, p. 47, pl. 22; Ewers (1956), p. 509; *Catlin, Bodmer, Miller;* Paris (1963), no. 7; Haverstock, reprod. p. 128; Gilcrease catalogue, p. 49.

47

48

Versions:
Gilcrease Institute, watercolor, 5½ x 4½, signed lower right (on mount): Geo. Catlin

Gilcrease Institute, NAI sketchbook (4776.15), pen and ink

Painted at the Comanche village in 1834. The Smithsonian portrait and plate 170 in *Letters and Notes* are almost identical (the shield is missing in the plate), but the Gilcrease watercolor is only bust length (see no. 46).

The subject appears again, full length, in cartoon 43 (NGA 2006).

49. Hair of the Bull's Neck, a chief
   Comanche, 1834
   29 x 24 (73.7 x 60.9)

References: 1837 catalogue, no. 53; *Letters and Notes,* vol. 2, p. 68; Donaldson, p. 47; Ewers (1956), p. 509; Gilcrease catalogue, p. 49.

Version:
Gilcrease Institute, watercolor, 6¼ x 5¼, signed lower right (on mount): Geo. Catlin

Painted at the Comanche village in 1834. The subject is half-length in the Gilcrease watercolor, he has no gun and shield, and his costume accessories differ noticeably from those in the Smithsonian portrait (see no. 46).

49

50

52

50. Wolf Tied with Hair, a chief
Comanche, 1834
29 x 24 (73.7 x 60.9)

Catlin describes the subject as holding a "pipe in his hand" (1848 catalogue, p. 12).

References: 1837 catalogue, no. 54; *Letters and Notes,* vol. 2, p. 67, pl. 171; Donaldson, p. 47, pl. 22; Ewers (1956), p. 509; Gilcrease catalogue, p. 49.

Versions:
Gilcrease Institute, watercolor, 6 x 5, signed lower right (on mount): Geo. Catlin

Gilcrease Institute, NAI sketchbook (4776.15), pen and ink

Painted at the Comanche village in 1834 (see no. 64). The Smithsonian portrait and plate 171 in *Letters and Notes* are identical, but the subject has no pipe in the Gilcrease watercolor, and he wears additional jewelry and a feather headdress (see no. 46).

Wolf Tied with Hair appears again in cartoon 43 (NGA 2006).

51. Little Spaniard, a warrior
Comanche, 1834
29 x 24 (73.7 x 60.9)
[Figure 86]

"A gallant little fellow . . . represented to us as one of the leading warriors of the tribe; and no doubt . . . one of the most extraordinary men at present living in these regions. He is half Spanish, and being a half-breed, for whom they generally have the most contemptuous feelings, he has been all his life thrown into the front of battle and danger; at which posts he has signalized himself, and commanded the highest admiration and respect of the tribe for his daring and adventurous career. This is the man of whom I have before spoken, who dashed out so boldly from the war-party, and came to us with the white flag raised on the point of his lance [see no. 488]. . . . I have here represented him as he stood for me, with his shield on his arm, with his quiver slung, and his lance of fourteen feet in length in his right hand. This extraordinary little man, whose figure was light, seemed to be all bone and muscle, and exhibited immense power, by the curve of the bones in his legs and his arms. We had many exhibitions of his extraordinary strength, as well as agility; and of his gentlemanly politeness and friendship we had as frequent evidences" (*Letters and Notes,* vol. 2, pp. 67-68, pl. 172).

References: 1837 catalogue, no. 55; Donaldson, pp. 47-48, pl. 23; Mary C. Withington, *A Catalogue of Manuscripts in the Collection of Western Americana Founded by William Robertson Coe* (Yale University Library, New Haven, Conn., 1952), no. 67; Ewers (1956), pp. 495, 509, pl.

5; McCracken, p. 148, reprod. p. 154; Halpin, reprod. p. 19; Haverstock, reprod. p. 29; Gilcrease catalogue, p. 49.

Versions:
Gilcrease Institute, watercolor, 10 x 8, signed lower right: Geo Catlin / 1836

Beinecke Library, Yale University, New Haven, Connecticut, oil on cardboard, 30 x 43½ cm, signed on back: Geo. Catlin p. 1848.

Gilcrease Institute, NAI sketchbook (4776.16), pen and ink

Copy:
M. Knoedler & Co., New York (until 1971), pencil and watercolor, signed lower right:
Rosa B-[Bonheur]

Painted at the Comanche village in 1834. Landscape details have been added to the Gilcrease watercolor; otherwise, it is identical to plate 172 of *Letters and Notes* and the Smithsonian portrait (see no. 46). The latter is one of Catlin's most skillfully articulated full-length figures, and the powerful curve of Little Spaniard's legs and torso does indeed suggest great physical energy.

The Yale painting is a weak version of the cartoon figure (see cartoon 42, NGA 2005), which in turn is based on a watercolor (pl. 40) in the Gilcrease *Souvenir* album.

52. The Beaver, a warrior
Comanche, 1834
29 x 24 (73.7 x 60.9)

Catlin describes The Beaver as "a warrior of terrible aspect, and also of considerable distinction" (*Letters and Notes,* vol. 2, p. 68).

References: 1837 catalogue, no. 56; Donaldson, p. 48; Ewers (1956), p. 509; McCracken, p. 147; Gilcrease catalogue, p. 49.

Version:
Gilcrease Institute, watercolor, 6½ x 5½

Painted at the Comanche village in 1834. The Beaver is shown bust length in the Gilcrease watercolor, and wears different jewelry and fewer feathers in his headdress (see no. 46). He appears again in cartoon 43 (NGA 2006), in a different pose and costume.

53-54. Two Comanche girls
    Comanche, 1834
    24 x 29 (60.9 x 73.7)

The scene consists of "the wigwam of the Chief, his dogs, and his five children" (1848 catalogue, p. 12).

References: 1837 catalogue, nos. 57, 58; *Letters and Notes,* vol. 2, p. 64, pl. 165; Donaldson, p. 48, pl. 24; Ewers (1956), p. 509; Roehm, p. 73; *America as Art,* no. 167, reprod. p. 162.

Version:
Gilcrease Institute, NAI sketchbook (4776.14), pen and ink

Copy:
M. Knoedler & Co., New York (until 1971), pencil and watercolor, signed lower right: Rosa B-[Bonheur]

Painted at the Comanche village in 1834. An almost identical scene is repeated in cartoon 44 (NGA 2007), which in turn is based on a watercolor (pl. 42) in the Gilcrease *Souvenir* album.

53-54

55

remains in the more fussy Gilcrease version. The latter is clearly taken from the original oil, however, as are the other Wichita portraits in the Gilcrease series (see no. 46).

The subject also appears, full length, in cartoon 45 (NGA 2014), with two Wichita women and a warrior.

55. Wee-tá-ra-shá-ro, head chief of the tribe
    Wichita, 1834
    29 x 24 (73.7 x 60.9)

"This man embraced Colonel Dodge and others of the dragoon officers in council, in his village, and otherwise treated them with great kindness, theirs being the first visit ever made to them by white people" (1848 catalogue, p. 12).

The subject was over ninety years old, according to Catlin.

References: 1837 catalogue, no. 37; *Letters and Notes,* vol. 2, p. 73, pl. 174; Donaldson, p. 50, pl. 25; Ewers (1956), p. 515; McCracken, p. 156, reprod. p. 159; Gilcrease catalogue, p. 50.

Versions:
Gilcrease Institute, watercolor, 6 x 5½, signed lower right (on mount): G. C. p.
Gilcrease Institute, NAI sketchbook (4776.18), pen and ink

Copy:
M. Knoedler & Co., New York (until 1971), pencil and watercolor, signed lower right: Rosa B-[Bonheur]

Painted at the Comanche village in 1834, according to *Letters and Notes.* Catlin's illness prevented him from accompanying the dragoons to the Wichita village (see no. 492).

The Smithsonian portrait and plate 174 in *Letters and Notes* are identical, but the subject has fewer necklaces and no fur robe in the Gilcrease watercolor. The Smithsonian portrait is a carefully brushed, moving study of the old chief's wrinkled features, and a suggestion of this image

56. Sky-se-ró-ka, second chief of the tribe
    Wichita, 1834
    29 x 24 (73.7 x 60.9)

Catlin describes the subject as "a fine-looking and remarkably shrewd and intelligent man" (1848) catalogue, p. 12).

References: 1837 catalogue, no. 40; *Letters and Notes,* vol. 2, p. 73, pl. 175; Donaldson, p. 50; Ewers (1956), p. 515; McCracken, p. 156, reprod. p. 159; Paris (1963), no. 8; Gilcrease catalogue, p. 50.

Versions:
Gilcrease Institute, watercolor, 7½ x 7, signed lower right: Geo. Catlin / 1836
Rains Galleries, New York, Cornelius Michaelson sale, May 8, 1935, no. 71, watercolor, 9 x 8½
Gilcrease Institute, NAI sketchbook (4776.18), pen and ink

Copy:
M. Knoedler & Co., New York (until 1971), pencil and watercolor, signed lower left: Rosa B[Bonheur]

Painted at the Comanche village in 1834. The sensitive modeling of Sky-se-ró-ka's features compares favorably to Catlin's best work on the dragoon expedition (see nos. 284, 288).

Landscape details have been added to the Gilcrease watercolor, and the subject is three-quarter length with a pipe in his left hand. The Smithsonian portrait and plate 175 in *Letters and Notes* are almost identical (see no. 55). Sky-se-ró-ka also appears, full length, in cartoon 45 (NGA 2014).

56

57

60

58

57. Kid-á-day, a distinguished brave
Wichita, 1834
29 x 24 (73.7 x 60.9)

References: 1837 catalogue, no. 41; Donaldson, p. 50; Ewers (1956), p. 515.

Painted at the Comanche village in 1834 (see no. 55).

58. Thighs, a Wichita woman

59. Wild Sage, a Wichita woman [Figure 91]
Wichita, 1834
29 x 24 each (73.7 x 60.9)

"Amongst the women of this tribe, there were many that were exceedingly pretty in feature and in form; and also in expression, though their skins are very dark. . . . [They] are always decently and comfortably clad, being covered generally with a gown or slip, that reaches from the chin quite down to the ankles, made of deer or elk skins. . . .

In plates 176 and 177, I have given the portraits of . . . [Thighs and Wild Sage], the two . . . women who had been held as prisoners by the Osages, and purchased by the Indian Commissioner, the Reverend Mr. Schemmerhom, and brought home to their own people" (*Letters and Notes*, vol. 2, pp. 73, 74, pls. 176, 177).

References: 1837 catalogue, nos. 38, 39; Donaldson, p. 51; (59) Haberly, reprod. opp. p. 112; Ewers (1956), p. 515; (59) Ewers (1965), reprod. p. 88.

Versions:
Gilcrease Institute, NAI sketchbook (4776.18), pen and ink

Copy:
M. Knoedler & Co., New York (until 1971), pencil and watercolor, signed lower left:
Rosa B-[Bonheur]

Probably painted at Fort Gibson in 1834 (see nos. 66-67). Thighs and Wild Sage also appear, full length, in cartoon 45 (NGA 2014) as the daughters of the chief (see no. 55). Presumably Catlin did not consult his earlier publications when he wrote the entry in the 1871 catalogue.

The sensual appeal of these two portraits suggests that the artist was not always an objective observer of Indian life.

60. Rotten Foot, a noted warrior
Wichita, 1834
29 x 24 (73.7 x 60.9)

References: 1837 catalogue, no. 42; Donaldson, p. 51; Ewers (1956), p. 515; Gilcrease catalogue, p. 50.

Versions:
Gilcrease Institute, watercolor, 8½ x 7½, signed lower right: Geo. Catlin 1836
Rains Galleries, New York, Cornelius Michaelson sale, May 8, 1935, no. 71, watercolor, 9 x 8½

Painted at the Comanche village in 1834. Landscape details have been added to the Gilcrease watercolor and the subject is wrapped in a different blanket (see nos. 46, 55).

61. Mad Elk, a great warrior
Wichita, 1834
Unlocated

References: 1837 catalogue, no. 43; Donaldson, p. 51.

Probably painted at the Comanche village in 1834 (see no. 55).

62. Téh-tóot-sah (better known as Tohausen, Little Bluff), first chief
Kiowa, 1834
29 x 24 (73.7 x 60.9)

"The head chief of the Kioways . . . we found to be a very gentlemanly and high minded man, who treated the dragoons and officers with great kindness while in his country. His long hair, which was put up in several large clubs, and ornamented with a great many silver broaches, extended quite down to his knees" (*Letters and Notes*, vol. 2, p. 74, pl. 178).

References: 1837 catalogue, no. 61; Donaldson, p. 51, pl. 25; Ewers (1956), p. 513; Gilcrease catalogue, p. 50.

Versions:
Gilcrease Institute, watercolor, 8 x 7, signed lower right: Geo. Catlin 1836

Gilcrease Institute, NAI sketchbook (4776.18), pen and ink

Copy:
(58) M. Knoedler & Co., New York (until 1971), pencil and watercolor, signed lower left: Rosa B-[Bonheur]

Painted at the Comanche village in 1834, according to *Letters and Notes* (see no. 64). Landscape details have been added to the Gilcrease watercolor, and the subject, wearing a feather headdress, is three-quarter length. The Smithsonian portrait is the more convincing likeness, however, as in the Wichita series (see no. 55).

Téh-tóot-sah appears again, full length, in cartoon 69 (NGA 2002), with a Kiowa warrior and two children.

63. Smoked Shield, a distinguished warrior
Kiowa, 1834
29 x 24 (73.7 x 60.9)

Catlin describes Smoked Shield as "another of the extraordinary men of this tribe, near seven feet in stature, and distinguished, not only as one of the greatest warriors, but the swiftest on foot, in the nation. This man, it is said, runs down a buffalo on foot, and slays it with his knife or his lance, as he runs by its side" (*Letters and Notes*, vol. 2, p. 75, pl. 182).

References: 1837 catalogue, no. 59; Donaldson, p. 51, pl. 26; Ewers (1956), p. 513.

Versions:
Rains Galleries, New York, Cornelius Michaelson sale, May 8, 1935, no. 71, watercolor, 9 x 8½

Gilcrease Institute, NAI sketchbook (4776.16), pen and ink

62

63

Copy:
M. Knoedler & Co., New York (until 1971), pencil and watercolor, signed lower right: Rosa B-[Bonheur]

Painted at the Comanche village in 1834 (see no. 55).

64. New Fire, a Band chief
Kiowa, 1834
29 x 24 (73.7 x 60.9)

Catlin calls New Fire "a very good man" and describes the ornaments hanging on his breast as a boar's tusk and a war whistle (*Letters and Notes*, vol. 2, p. 74, pl. 179).

References: 1837 catalogue, no. 60; Donaldson, p. 52; Ewers (1956), p. 513; Haverstock, p. 26; Gilcrease catalogue, p. 50.

Versions:
Gilcrease Institute, watercolor, 7½ x 7, signed lower right: Geo. Catlin

Rains Galleries, New York, Cornelius Michaelson sale, May 8, 1935, no. 71, watercolor, 9 x 8½

Gilcrease Institute, NAI sketchbook (4776.18), pen and ink

Copy:
M. Knoedler & Co., New York (until 1971), pencil and watercolor, signed lower right: Rosa B-[Bonheur]

Painted at the Comanche village in 1834 (see no. 55). The subject's broadly brushed features have much in common with number 62 and several Comanche portraits (see nos. 47, 50).

In the Gilcrease watercolor, New Fire is shown three-quarter length, seated in a landscape (see no. 62). He appears again, full length, in cartoon 69 (NGA 2002).

64

65

68

66-67

was taken the whole distance with us, on horseback, to the Pawnee village, and there delivered to her friends . . . the fine little boy was killed at the Fur Trader's house on the banks of the Verdigris, near Fort Gibson, the day after I painted his portrait, and only a few days before he was to have started with us on the march" (*Letters and Notes*, vol. 2, p. 73, pl. 181).

References: 1837 catalogue, nos. 62, 63; Donaldson, p. 52; Ewers, p. 513; McCracken, reprod. p. 141; Rossi and Hunt, pp. 262, 320; Haverstock, pp. 26, 120; Gilcrease catalogue, p. 50; *America as Art*, no. 163.

Versions:

(Thunderer) Gilcrease Institute, watercolor, 5½ x 5, signed lower right (on mount): G. C. pt.

(White Weasel) Gilcrease Institute, watercolor, 5¾ x 5, signed lower right (on mount): G. C. 1836.

Gilcrease Institute, NAI sketchbook (4776.18), pen and ink

Painted at Fort Gibson in 1834, according to *Letters and Notes*. To counter certain myths about Indian relationships, Catlin often wrote of or painted family situations in which members were bound by ties of affection no different from those experienced by their white counterparts.

The costumes and accessories in the Smithsonian portrait become greatly simplified in the Gilcrease watercolors (see no. 62). The two figures appear again in cartoon 69 (NGA 2002).

65. Stone Shell, a brave
Kiowa, 1834
29 x 24 (73.7 x 60.9)

Stone Shell "is another fair specimen of the warriors of this tribe," Catlin writes, "and . . . somewhat allied to the mysteries and arcana of the healing art, from the close company he keeps with my friend Dr. Findley, who is surgeon to the regiment, and by whom I have been employed to make a copy of my portrait of this distinguished personage" (*Letters and Notes*, vol. 2, p. 75, pl. 180).

References: 1837 catalogue, no. 64; Donaldson, p. 52; Ewers (1956), p. 513; Gilcrease catalogue, p. 50.

Versions:

Gilcrease Institute, watercolor, 6½ x 5, signed lower right (on mount): Geo. Catlin

Gilcrease Institute, NAI sketchbook (4776.18), pen and ink

Painted at the Comanche village in 1834 (see no. 55). Stone Shell lacks his knife in the Gilcrease watercolor, no skin lodges appear behind him, and his headdress and jewelry are greatly changed (see no. 62).

66-67. Thunderer, a boy, and White Weasel, a girl
Kiowa, 1834
29 x 24 (73.7 x 60.9)

Catlin describes the brother and sister as "two Kiowas who were purchased from the Osages, to be taken to their tribe by the dragoons. The girl

68. He Who Fights with a Feather, chief of the tribe
Waco, 1834
29 x 24 (73.7 x 60.9)

Described by Catlin as "a very polite and polished Indian, in his manners, and remarkable for his mode of *embracing* the officers and others in council" (*Letters and Notes*, vol. 2, p. 75, pl. 183).

References: 1837 catalogue, no. 65; Donaldson, p. 53; Haberly, p. 95; Ewers (1956), p. 515; Gilcrease catalogue, p. 50.

Versions:

Gilcrease Institute, watercolor, 5½ x 5, signed lower right (on mount): Geo Catlin

Gilcrease Institute, NAI sketchbook (4776.16), pen and ink

Copies:

M. Knoedler & Co., New York (until 1971), pencil and watercolor, signed lower left:
Rosa B-[Bonheur]

British Museum, London, by John Cullum, watercolor, 11⅞ x 10¼ (1842-1844)

Painted at the Comanche village in 1834, according to *Letters and Notes.* Costume and accessories differ somewhat between the Smithsonian and Gilcrease portraits. The latter is half-length and a pleasing, if less vigorous, edition of the former (see no. 55).

The subject appears again, full length, in cartoon 46 (NGA 2059), with his wife and child, and a Waco warrior.

69. One Horn, head chief of the Miniconjou tribe
Teton Dakota (Western Sioux), 1832
29 x 24 (73.7 x 60.9)
[Figure 81]

"Amongst . . . [the Sioux encamped at Fort Pierre] there were twenty or more of the different bands, each one with their chief at their head. . . . [One Horn was] a middle-aged man, of middling stature, with a noble countenance, and a figure almost equalling the Apollo, and I painted his portrait. . . . [He] has risen rapidly to the highest honours in the tribe, from his own extraordinary merits, even at so early an age. He told me he took the name of 'One Horn' (or shell) from a simple small shell that was hanging on his neck, which descended to him from his father, and which, he said, he valued more than anything he possessed; affording a striking instance of the living affection which these people often cherish for the dead. . . . His costume was a very handsome one, and will have a place in my Indian Gallery by the side of his picture. It is made of elk skins beautifully dressed, and fringed with a profusion of porcupine quills and scalp-locks; and his hair, which is very long and profuse, divided into two parts, and lifted up and crossed, over the top of his head, with a simple tie, giving it somewhat the appearance of a Turkish turban.

"This extraordinary man, before he was raised to the dignity of chief, was the renowned of his tribe for his athletic achievements. In the chase he was foremost; he could run down a buffalo, which he often had done, on his own legs, and drive his arrow to the heart. He was the fleetest in the tribe; and in the races he had run, he had always taken the prize.

"It was proverbial in his tribe, that Ha-won-je-tah's bow never was drawn in vain, and his wigwam was abundantly furnished with scalps that he had taken from his enemies' heads in battle" (*Letters and Notes,* vol. 1, pp. 211, 220, pl. 86; see no. 591).

References: 1837 catalogue, no. 66; Donaldson, p. 54, pl. 27; Museum of Modern Art, New York, *Romantic Painting in America* (1943), no. 44, reprod. p. 60; E. P. Richardson, *American Romantic*

Painting (New York, 1944), pl. 68; Quimby, pp. 30-31; Ewers (1956), p. 511; McCracken, pp. 48-49, reprod. p. 43; William Hayes Ackland Memorial Art Center, Chapel Hill, N.C., *Arts of the Young Republic* (1968), no. 87; Daniel M. Mendelowitz, *A History of American Art* (New York, 1970), p. 215; Haverstock, pp. 57-58; Seattle Art Museum, *Lewis and Clark's America* (1976), no. 34.

Versions:
Field Museum of Natural History, ca. 28 x 23
Gilcrease Institute, NAI sketchbook (4776.38), pen and ink

Among the first portraits painted by Catlin on his upriver voyage in 1832 were those of the Sioux encamped at Fort Pierre. This series and the others that followed on the Upper Missouri reveal an increasingly controlled brush and a bolder definition of contour than Catlin had attempted in 1830 (see nos. 22, 78). The solid and imposing appearance of One Horn became, in essence, the formula for the great portraits of that summer and fall (see nos. 99, 117, 149, 182).

The Smithsonian and Field Museum portraits are much alike and both match plate 86 in *Letters and Notes.* Catlin perhaps took more pains with the version of One Horn than any of the others he painted for O'Fallon. Even so, the fine fringe detail of the triangular neck piece is missing, and the subject's right ear is attached at an awkward angle. A more conclusive indication of the original, however, can be seen in the superior modeling about the cheek and eyes of One Horn in the Smithsonian portrait (see no. 3).

The chief also appears, seated, in cartoon 9 (NGA 1961), with his wife and child, another Sioux chief, and a counselor.

70. Big Eagle (or Black Dog), chief of the O-hah-kas-ka-toh-y-an-te Band
Eastern Dakota (Eastern Sioux), 1835
29 x 24 (73.7 x 60.9)

References: 1837 catalogue, no. 70; *Letters and Notes,* vol. 2, p. 134, pl. 234; Donaldson, p. 54; Ewers (1956), p. 510; McCracken, p. 166, reprod. p. 169; Paris (1963), no. 9.

Version:
Gilcrease Institute, NAI sketchbook (4776.20), pen and ink

Copies:
M. Knoedler & Co., New York (until 1971), pencil and watercolor, signed lower right:
Rosa B-[Bonheur]
British Museum, London, by John Cullum, watercolor, 11¾ x 10¼ (1842-1844)

70

Painted at Fort Snelling in 1835. Catlin's somewhat hasty and indifferent portraits of the Eastern Sioux seem to reflect his lack of interest in those tribes living on the fringe of civilization (see no. 69).

Big Eagle also appears, full length, in cartoon 6 (NGA 2301), with his wife and child, another Sioux chief, and a medicine man; and by himself in cartoon 117 (unlocated), which may be an oil-on-canvas version of the original portrait.

71

73

72

color; it was decorated with small tufts of owl's feathers and others of various hues. . . . A splendid necklace, formed of about sixty claws of the grizzly bear, imparted a manly character to his whole appearance. His leggins, jacket, and moccasins were in the real Dakota fashion, being made of white skins, profusely decorated with human hair! His moccasins were variegated with the plumage of several birds" (W.H. Keating, *Narrative of an Expedition to the Source of the St. Peter's River*, vol. 1 [Philadelphia, 1824], pp. 429-37).

References: 1837 catalogue, no. 86; *Letters and Notes*, vol. 1, p. 223, pl. 91; Ewers (1956), p. 512; Fogg Art Museum, Harvard University, Cambridge, Mass, *American Art at Harvard* (1972), no. 48; Gilcrease catalogue, p. 50; Parke-Bernet Galleries, New York, Redwood Library Collection (May 21, 1970), no. 8.

Version:
Peabody Museum, Harvard University, Cambridge, Massachusetts, oil on paper, 16½ x 11¾, signed on back: Geo. Catlin, p. 1868

Painted at Fort Pierre in 1832. Donaldson's date is incorrect (see nos. 69, 71). The Peabody version is a repetition of the figure of Wán-ee-ton from cartoon 8 (NGA 1960), in which the chief appears with his daughter and a Sioux warrior. The cartoon is based on a watercolor (pl. 14) in the Gilcrease *Souvenir* album.

King had painted a somewhat similar standing portrait of Wán-ee-ton in 1826 (see Parke-Bernet catalogue), and Catlin lists the subject among those paintings commissioned by Louis Philippe in 1845 (see no. 449).

71. Tobacco, an Oglala chief
Teton Dakota (Western Sioux), 1832
29 x 24 (73.7 x 60.9)

Described by Catlin as "a desperate warrior, and . . . one of the most respectable and famous chiefs of the tribe" (*Letters and Notes*, vol. 1, p. 222, pl. 92).

References: 1837 catalogue, no. 72; Donaldson, p. 54; Ewers (1956), pp. 486, 511; McCracken, p. 50, reprod. p. 43; Paris (1963), no. 10; Ewers, "The Opening of the West," *The Artist in America* (New York, 1967), reprod. p. 45.

Version:
Gilcrease Institute, NAI sketchbook (4776.38), pen and ink

Painted at Fort Pierre in 1832, according to *Letters and Notes* (see nos. 69, 78). Donaldson's date is incorrect. Tobacco appears again, seated, in cartoon 9 (NGA 1961).

73. Blue Medicine, a medicine man of the Ting-ta-to-ah Band
Eastern Dakota (Eastern Sioux), 1835
29 x 24 (73.7 x 60.9)

Described by Catlin as a noted doctor or medicine man, "with his *medicine* or mystery drum and rattle in his hands, his looking-glass on his breast, his rattle of antelope's hoofs, and drum of deer-skins" (1848 catalogue, p. 14).

References: 1837 catalogue, no. 67; *Letters and Notes*, vol. 2, p. 134, pl. 233; Donaldson, p. 55; Haberly, reprod. opp. p. 60; *Westward the Way*, no. 58, reprod. p. 92; Ewers (1956), p. 510; McCracken, pp. 57, 166, reprod. p. 169; Rena N. Coen, *Painting and Sculpture in Minnesota, 1820-1914* (Minneapolis, 1976), p. 8, reprod., p. 10.

Version:
Gilcrease Institute, NAI sketchbook (4776.20), pen and ink

72. Wán-ee-ton, chief of the tribe
Yanktonai Dakota, 1832
29 x 24 (73.7 x 60.9)

Donaldson (pp. 54-55) quotes the following passage in his description of Wán-ee-ton:
"He was dressed in the full habit of an Indian chief. We have never seen a more dignified person, or a more becoming dress. The most prominent part of his apparel was a splendid cloak or mantle of buffalo skin, dressed so as to be of a fine white

Copy:
M. Knoedler & Co., New York (until 1971), pencil and watercolor, signed lower right: Rosa B-[Bonheur]

Painted at Fort Snelling in 1835 (see no. 70). Blue Medicine appears again, full length, in cartoon 6 (NGA 2301).

74. He Who Stands on Both Sides, a distinguished ball player

75. Red Man, a distinguished ball player
Eastern Dakota (Eastern Sioux), 1835
29 x 24 each (73.7 x 60.9)

"The two most distinguished ballplayers in the Sioux tribe. . . . Both of these young men stood to me for their portraits, in the dresses precisely in which they are painted; with their ball-sticks in their hands, and in the attitudes of the play. We have had several very spirited plays here within the past few days; and each of these young men came from the ball-play ground to my painting-room, in the dress in which they had just struggled in the play" (*Letters and Notes*, vol. 2, p. 134, pls. 235, 236).
See numbers 299, 428, 429, and 430.

References: 1837 catalogue, nos. 68, 69; Donaldson, pp. 55-56; Ewers (1956), p. 510; McCracken, pp. 167, 181; Gilcrease catalogue, p. 50; *America as Art*, nos. 175, 176, reprod. p. 164.

Versions:
Gilcrease Institute, NAI sketchbook (4776.33), pen and ink

Copies:
M. Knoedler & Co., New York (until 1971), pencil and watercolor, signed lower right: Rosa B-[Bonheur]

Painted at Fort Snelling in 1835. The structure and movement of the two figures represent some improvement over the Osage series (see nos. 43-45).
Both subjects appear again in plate 21 of *Catlin's North American Indian Portfolio*, first published in 1844, and in cartoon 82 (NGA 2085). The cartoon is based on a watercolor (pl. 50) in the Gilcrease *Souvenir* album.

76. Shell Man, an Oglala brave
Teton Dakota (Western Sioux), 1832
29 x 24 (73.7 x 60.9)

References: 1837 catalogue, no. 71; *Letters and Notes*, vol. 1, p. 223; Donaldson, p. 56; Ewers (1956), p. 511.

Painted at Fort Pierre in 1832 (see nos. 69, 78).

74

76

75

77

77. Torn Belly, a distinguished brave
Yankton Dakota, 1832
29 x 24 (73.7 x 60.9)

References: 1837 catalogue, no. 72; *Letters and Notes*, vol. 1, p. 223; Donaldson, p. 56; Ewers (1956), p. 511.

Painted at Fort Pierre in 1832 (see nos. 69, 78), and a superior example of Catlin's ability to render accurately the intricacies of quill and bead decoration.

79

80

81

quite down to his feet, and surmounted on the top with a pair of horns denoting him . . . head leader or war-chief of his band.

"This man has been a constant and faithful friend of Mr. M'Kenzie and others of the Fur Traders. . . . So highly was the Black Rock esteemed . . . and his beautiful daughter admired and respected by the Traders, that Mr. M'Kenzie employed me to make him copies of their two portraits, which he has hung up in Mr. Laidlaw's trading-house, as valued ornaments and keepsakes" (*Letters and Notes*, vol. 1, pp. 222, 224, pl. 91).

References: 1837 catalogue, no. 76; Donaldson, p. 56, pl. 28; Quimby, pp. 34-35; Ewers (1956), p. 511; McCracken, p. 50, reprod. p. 41; Hartmann, pp. 32-34; Gilcrease catalogue, p. 50.

Versions:
Field Museum of Natural History, ca. 28 x 23

Gilcrease Institute, NAI sketchbook (4776.40), pen and ink

Copy:
M. Knoedler & Co., New York (until 1971), pencil and watercolor, signed lower right: Rosa B-[Bonheur]

Painted at Fort Pierre in 1832. Donaldson's date is incorrect (see nos. 69, 71). Black Rock's features are distinctly flat and expressionless in the Field Museum version, and his robe lacks certain minor details that appear in the Smithsonian portrait (see no. 3). Skin lodges are included in the background of both the Field Museum version and plate 91 in *Letters and Notes*.

Black Rock appears again in cartoon 5 (AMNH 85), with his wife and daughter, and by himself in cartoon 123 (unlocated), which may be the oil-on-canvas portrait originally commissioned by Louis Philippe (see no. 449). The former cartoon is based on a watercolor (pl. 12) in the Gilcrease *Souvenir* album, and an oil-on-canvas version of the composition is in the Museum für Völkerkunde, Berlin.

78. Corn, a Miniconjou (?) warrior
Teton Dakota (Western Sioux), 1832
29 x 24 (73.7 x 60.9)
[Figure 101]

References: 1837 catalogue, no. 74; *Letters and Notes*, vol. 1, p. 223; Donaldson, p. 56; Haberly, reprod. opp. p. 81; Ewers (1956), p. 511.

Painted at Fort Pierre in 1832 (see no. 69). Catlin modeled the faces of these Sioux subjects with a new awareness of planar structure.

79. No Heart, chief of the Wah-ne-watch-to-nee-nah Band
Teton Dakota (Western Sioux), 1832
29 x 24 (73.7 x 60.9)

References: 1837 catalogue, no. 75; *Letters and Notes*, vol. 1, p. 223; Donaldson, p. 56; Ewers (1956), p. 511.

Painted at Fort Pierre in 1832 (see no. 69).

80. Black Rock, a Two Kettle (?) chief
Teton Dakota (Western Sioux), 1832
29 x 24 (73.7 x 60.9)

Described by Catlin as "a tall and fine looking man, of six feet or more in stature; in a splendid dress, with his lance in his hand; with his pictured robe thrown gracefully over his shoulders, and his headdress made of war-eagles' quills and ermine skins, falling in a beautiful crest over his back,

81. Red Thing that Touches in Marching, daughter of Black Rock
Teton Dakota (Western Sioux), 1832
29 x 24 (73.7 x 60.9)

"She is an unmarried girl, and much esteemed by the whole tribe, for her modesty, as well as beauty. She was beautifully dressed in skins, ornamented profusely with brass buttons and beads. Her hair was plaited, her ears supported a great profusion of curious beads—and over her other dress she wore a handsomely garnished buffalo robe" (*Letters and Notes*, vol. 1, p. 224, pl. 94).

References: 1837 catalogue, no. 81; Donaldson, p. 56, pl. 27; Haberly, p. 95; Ewers (1956), p. 51¹ *Catlin, Bodmer, Miller.*

Painted at Fort Pierre in 1832 (see nos. 69, 80). The subject appears again, full length, in cartoon 5 (AMNH 85).

82. Stone with Horns, a chief
Yankton Dakota, 1832
29 x 24 (73.7 x 60.9)

The subject was reputed to be, according to Catlin, "the principal and most eloquent *orator* of the nation. The neck, and breast, and shoulders of this man, were curiously tattooed, by pricking in gunpowder and vermilion, which in this extraordinary instance, was put on in such elaborate profusion as to appear at a little distance like a beautifully embroidered dress. In his hand he held a handsome pipe, the stem of which was several feet long, and all the way wound with ornamented braids of the porcupine quills. Around his body was wrapped a valued robe, made of the skin of the grizzly bear, and on his neck several strings of *wampum*. . . . I was much amused with the excessive vanity and egotism of this notorious man, who, whilst sitting for his picture, took occasion to have the interpreter constantly explaining to me the wonderful effects which his oratory had at different times produced on the minds of the chiefs and people of his tribe" (*Letters and Notes,* vol. 1, pp. 222-23, pl. 93).

References: 1837 catalogue, no. 77; Donaldson, pp. 56-57; Ewers (1956), p. 511; McCracken, p. 137.

Version:
Gilcrease Institute, NAI sketchbook (4776.39), pen and ink

Copy:
British Museum, London, by John Cullum, watercolor, 12 x 10¼ (1842-1844)

Painted at Fort Pierre in 1832 (see nos. 69, 78). The subject also appears in cartoon 9 (NGA 1961).

83. Grizzly Bear that Runs without Regard, a Hunkpapa brave
Teton Dakota (Western Sioux), 1832
Unlocated

References: 1837 catalogue, no. 78; *Letters and Notes,* vol. 1, p. 223; Donaldson, p. 57; Haberly, p. 95.

Probably painted at Fort Pierre in 1832. There are eight unidentified portraits in the Quimby catalogue (pp. 38, 40, 64, 66, 68, 70, 74, 76), several of which (pp. 38, 40) closely resemble other Teton Dakota portraits in the Smithsonian collection. Since the remaining Catlin paintings in O'Fallon's collection were Upper Missouri subjects (see no. 3), the unidentified portraits could be later versions of originals missing from the Teton Dakota series in the Smithsonian (nos. 83, 87, 88, 91), or from other Upper Missouri tribes. No cartoons, copies, or plates from *Letters and Notes* are known that would otherwise establish the identity of these missing Smithsonian portraits.

84. Little Bear, a Hunkpapa brave
Teton Dakota (Western Sioux), 1832
29 x 24 (73.7 x 60.9)

References: 1837 catalogue, no. 79; *Letters and Notes,* vol. 1, p. 223; vol. 2, pp. 190-94, pl. 273; Donaldson, p. 57, pl. 29; Haberly, p. 53; Quimby, pp. 36-37; Ewers (1956), p. 511; McCracken, pp. 57-59, 61; Roehm, p. 60; Haverstock, pp. 59, 61.

Versions:
Field Museum of Natural History, ca. 28 x 23

Gilcrease Institute, NAI sketchbook (4776.25), pen and ink

Painted at Fort Pierre in 1832 (see nos. 69, 86). The Field Museum version, although identified on the stretcher as White Bear that Goes Out (no. 88), matches plate 273 in *Letters and Notes* and the Smithsonian portrait (see no. 3). Catlin confused his characters in several paintings (see nos. 182, 189).

85. The Dog, chief of the Bad Arrow Points Band
Teton Dakota (Western Sioux), 1832
29 x 24 (73.7 x 60.9)
[Figure 106]

References: 1837 catalogue, no. 84; *Letters and Notes,* vol. 1, p. 223; vol. 2, pp. 190-94, pl. 275; Donaldson, p. 57, pl. 29; Haberly, p. 53; Ewers (1956), p. 511; McCracken, pp. 57-59, 61; Roehm, p. 60; Haverstock, pp. 59, 61, 100.

Version:
Gilcrease Institute, NAI sketchbook (4776.25), pen and ink

Painted at Fort Pierre in 1832 (see nos. 69, 86). The Dog appears again, full length, in cartoon 7 (NGA 1959).

82

84

86. Steep Wind, a brave of the Bad Arrow Points Band
Teton Dakota (Western Sioux), 1832
29 x 24 (73.7 x 60.9)

"These three distinguished men [nos. 84, 85, 86] were all killed in a private quarrel (while I was in the country), occasioned by my painting only *one-half* of the face of the first (no. 84); ridicule followed, and resort to fire-arms, in which that side of the face which I had left out was blown off in a few moments after I had finished the portrait; and sudden and violent revenge for the offense soon laid the other two in the dust, and imminently endangered my own life" (1848 catalogue, p. 15).

See *Letters and Notes*, vol. 2, pages 190-94, for a full account of this episode.

References: 1837 catalogue, no. 82; *Letters and Notes*, vol. 1, p. 223; vol. 2, pl. 274; Donaldson, p. 57, pl. 29; Ewers (1956), p. 511; McCracken, pp. 59, 61, reprod. p. 55; Halpin, reprod. p. 7; Roehm, p. 60.

Version:
Gilcrease Institute, NAI sketchbook (4776.25), pen and ink

Painted at Fort Pierre in 1832 (see nos. 69, 78). Catlin's energetic brushwork was remarkably effective in recording the details of Indian costume. Steep Wind also appears, full length, in cartoon 7 (NGA 1959).

87. Elk's Head, chief of the Ee-ta-sip-show Band
Teton Dakota (Western Sioux), 1832
Unlocated

References: 1837 catalogue, no. 80; *Letters and Notes*, vol. 1, p. 223; Donaldson, p. 57.

Probably painted at Fort Pierre in 1832 (see no. 83).

88. White Bear that Goes Out, chief of the Blackfoot tribe
Teton Dakota (Western Sioux), 1832
Unlocated

References: 1837 catalogue, no. 85; *Letters and Notes*, vol. 1, p. 223; Donaldson, p. 57.

Probably painted at Fort Pierre in 1832 (see nos. 83, 84).

89. Sand Bar, wife of the trader François Chardon
Teton Dakota (Western Sioux), 1832
29 x 24 (73.7 x 60.9)

Catlin describes Sand Bar as "very richly dressed, the upper part of her garment being almost literally covered with brass buttons; and her hair, which was inimitably beautiful and soft, and glossy as silk, fell over her shoulders in great profusion, and in beautiful waves, produced by the condition in which it is generally kept in braids, giving to it, when combed out, a waving form, adding much to its native appearance, which is invariably straight and graceless.

"This woman is at present the wife of a white man by the name of Chardon, a Frenchman, who has been many years in the employment of the American Fur Company, in the character of a Trader and Interpreter" (*Letters and Notes*, vol. 1, p. 224, pl. 95).

References: 1837 catalogue, no. 83; Donaldson, p. 57; Quimby, pp. 32-33; Ewers (1956), p. 511.

Versions:
Field Museum of Natural History, ca. 28 x 23
Gilcrease Institute, NAI sketchbook (4776.39), pen and ink

Painted at Fort Pierre in 1832 (see no. 69). The Field Museum and Smithsonian portraits are almost identical, but the face in the latter has more solid and convincing proportions (see no. 3).

Sand Bar also appears, full length, in cartoon 9 (NGA 1961) as the wife of One Horn (no. 69). Catlin seems to have adjusted the identity of his cartoon figures at will (see nos. 58, 59).

90. The Leaf, a Band chief
Eastern Dakota (Eastern Sioux), 1835
Unlocated

Catlin describes the subject as "blind in one eye" (1848 catalogue, p. 15).

References: 1837 catalogue, no. 87; *Letters and Notes*, vol. 2, p. 132; Donaldson, p. 57.

Probably painted at Fort Snelling in 1835. An earlier portrait of The Leaf, after an original by James Otto Lewis, is illustrated in McKenney and Hall (vol. 1, pp. 112-13).

91. Horse Dung, a Band chief
Teton Dakota (Western Sioux), 1832
Unlocated

Described by Catlin as "a great conjuror and magician" (*Letters and Notes*, vol. 1, p. 223).

References: 1837 catalogue, no. 88; Donaldson, p. 58.

Probably painted at Fort Pierre in 1832, as Horse Dung is listed in *Letters and Notes* among other Teton Dakota notables (see no. 83). He appears in the 1837 catalogue as "Upper Mississippi," however, indicating that the location of the subject in entries 88 and 89 of the catalogue was mistakenly reversed (see no. 92).

92. Walking Buffalo, Red Wing's son
Eastern Dakota (Eastern Sioux), 1835
Unlocated

References: 1837 catalogue, no. 89; Donaldson, p. 58.

Catlin lists the painting as "Upper Missouri" in his 1837 catalogue, but Red Wing was an Eastern Dakota Band chief who resided on the Upper Mississippi (see cartoon 6 and *Letters and Notes,* vol. 2, p. 131). Presumably the painting was done at Fort Snelling in 1835, and Donaldson's date of 1832 is based on the error in the 1837 catalogue (see no. 91).

93. Iron, a brave of distinction
Eastern Dakota (Eastern Sioux), 1835
Unlocated

References: 1837 catalogue, no. 90; Donaldson, p. 58.

Probably painted at Fort Snelling in 1835, as the subject is listed in the 1837 and 1848 catalogues as "St. Peters" (see *Letters and Notes,* vol. 2, p. 131). Donaldson's date of 1832 would then be incorrect (see no. 94).

94. The Swift
Eastern Dakota (Eastern Sioux), 1835
Unlocated

Described by Catlin as "an ill-visaged and ill-natured fellow, though reputed a desperate warrior" (1848 catalogue, p. 15).

References: 1837 catalogue, no. 91; Donaldson, p. 58.

Probably painted at Fort Snelling in 1835, as the subject is listed in the 1837 catalogue as "St. Peters" (see *Letters and Notes,* vol. 2, p. 131). Donaldson's date of 1832 would then be incorrect (see no. 93).

95. The Smoke, chief of the tribe
Ponca, 1832
29 x 24 (73.7 x 60.9)

"The chief, who was wrapped in a buffalo robe, is a noble specimen of native dignity and philosophy. I conversed much with him; and from his dignified manners, as well as from the soundness of his reasoning, I became fully convinced that he deserved to be the sachem of a more numerous and prosperous tribe. He related to me with great coolness and frankness, the poverty and distress of his nation; and with the method of a philosopher, predicted the certain and rapid extinction of his tribe, which he had not the power to avert. . . . He sat upon the deck of the steamer, overlooking the little cluster of his wigwams mingled amongst the trees; and, like Caius Marius, weeping over the ruins of Carthage, shed tears as he was descanting on the povery of his ill-fated little community" (*Letters and Notes,* vol. 1, pp. 212-13, pl. 87).

References: 1837 catalogue, no. 92; Donaldson, pp. 63-64; Quimby, pp. 42-43; Ewers (1956), p. 515; McCracken, p. 44; Denver Art Museum, *The Western Frontier,* 1966.

Versions:
Field Museum of Natural History, ca. 28 x 23
Gilcrease Institute, NAI sketchbook (4776.35), pen and ink

Painted at the Ponca village in 1832, apparently on the upriver voyage (see no. 69). The landscape in the background differs between the Smithsonian and Field Museum portraits, and a skin lodge has been added to plate 87 in *Letters and Notes* (see no. 3).

The Smoke has similar, but more detailed, features in Bodmer's half-length portrait of 1833 (see Reuben Gold Thwaites, ed., *Early Western Travels 1748-1846,* pl. 40), and he appears again in cartoon 55 (NGA 2064), with his family (see no. 96).

96. Pure Fountain, wife of The Smoke
Ponca, 1832
29 x 24 (73.7 x 60.9)

Catlin describes Pure Fountain as "a young and very pretty woman . . . her neck and arms were curiously tattooed, which is a very frequent mode of ornamenting the body amongst this and some other tribes . . . done by pricking into the skin, gun-powder and vermilion" (*Letters and Notes,* vol. 1, p. 212, pl. 88).

References: 1837 catalogue, no. 94; Donaldson, p. 64; Haberly, p. 95; Quimby, pp. 44-45; Ewers (1956), p. 515.

Versions:
Field Museum of Natural History, ca. 28 x 23
Gilcrease Institute, NAI sketchbook (4776.7), pen and ink

Painted at the Ponca village in 1832 (see no. 95). The pose of Pure Fountain has been reversed in the Field Museum version and plate 88 in *Letters and Notes,* but the necklace arrangement and landscape details in the latter agree with the Smithsonian portrait (see no. 3). Quimby notes an ambiguous inscription on the back of the stretcher that suggests Catlin confused the subject with one of her daughters-in-law (no. 98).

Pure Fountain also appears in cartoon 54 (NGA 2063), with her son Great Chief (no. 97).

95

96

97

98

97. Great Chief, son of The Smoke
Ponca, 1832
29 x 24 (73.7 x 60.9)

Catlin describes Great Chief as "a youth of eighteen years . . . [who] distinguished himself in a singular manner the day before our steamer reached their village, by taking to him *four wives in one day!* This extraordinary and unprecedented freak of his, was just the thing to make him the greatest sort of *medicine* in the eyes of his people; and probably he may date much of his success and greatness through life, to this bold and original step, which suddenly raised him into notice and importance" (*Letters and Notes*, vol. 1, pp. 213-15, pl. 90).

References: 1837 catalogue, no. 93; Donaldson, p. 64; Ewers (1956), p. 515; Hartmann, p. 32; Gilcrease catalogue, p. 50.

Versions:
Peabody Museum, Harvard University, Cambridge, Massachusetts, oil on paper, 16½ x 11¾, signed on back: Geo. Catlin

Gilcrease Institute, NAI sketchbook (4776.39), pen and ink

Painted at the Ponca village in 1832 (see no. 95). the quiver has been omitted in plate 90 of *Letters and Notes.*

The Peabody version is a repetition of the figure of Great Chief from cartoon 54 (NGA 2063), in which he appears with his mother and a wife (see no. 96). The cartoon is based on a watercolor (pl. 8) in the Gilcrease *Souvenir* album, and an oil-on-canvas version of the composition is in the Museum für Völkerkunde, Berlin.

98. Bending Willow, wife of Great Chief
Ponca, 1832
29 x 24 (73.7 x 60.9)

"I visited the wigwam of [Great Chief, no. 97] . . . several times, and saw his four modest little wives seated around the fire, where all seemed to harmonize very well, . . . I selected [Bending Willow] . . . for her portrait, and painted it . . . in a very pretty dress of deer skins, and covered with a young buffalo's robe, which was handsomely ornamented, and worn with much grace and pleasing effect" (*Letters and Notes*, vol. 1, p. 214, pl. 89).

References: 1837 catalogue, no. 95; Donaldson, p. 65; Haberly, p. 95; Ewers (1956), p. 515; *America as Art*, no. 166.

Version:
Gilcrease Institute, NAI sketchbook (4776.39), pen and ink

Painted at the Ponca village in 1832 (see no. 95). Bending Willow appears again in cartoon 54 (NGA 2063), with her husband (no. 97).

99. Horse Chief, Grand Pawnee head chief
Pawnee, 1832
29 x 24 (73.7 x 60.9)
[Figure 20]

References: 1837 catalogue, no. 288; *Letters and Notes*, vol. 2, p. 27, pl. 138; Donaldson, pp. 68, 475, pl. 30; Haberly, p. 47, reprod. opp. p. 80; Ewers (1956), pp. 485-86, 515; McCracken, pp. 35, 129-30; Roehm, pp. 55-56; Halpin, reprod. p. 21; Corcoran Gallery of Art, Washington, D.C., *Wilderness* (1971), no. 49.

Version:
Gilcrease Institute, NAI sketchbook (4776.8), pen and ink

Copy:
M. Knoedler & Co., New York (until 1971), pencil and watercolor, signed lower right:
Rosa B-[Bonheur]

Haberly, followed by Ewers and McCracken, maintains that Catlin accompanied Major John Dougherty up the Missouri and Platte rivers in the spring of 1831 to visit the Pawnee, Omaha, Oto, and Missouri tribes, but Dale Morgan (see Roehm) thinks the paintings were done in 1832 at Fort Leavenworth (see no. 22). Donaldson's dates for the Pawnee series are based on Catlin's improbable recollections (see no. 31 and 1871 catalogue, p. 90).

The portrait of Horse Chief has a compelling dimension and presence, probably indicating that it came shortly after Catlin's painting experience on the Upper Missouri. Although the remaining portraits in the Pawnee series are less ambitious, they also appear to have more in common with Upper Missouri examples than with the portraits painted near Fort Leavenworth in 1830 (see nos. 237-55).

Horse Chief appears again, full length, in cartoon 22 (NGA 2017), with a Missouri chief.

100. Buffalo Bull, a Grand Pawnee warrior
Pawnee, 1832
29 x 24 (73.7 x 60.9)
[Figure 109]

Described by Catlin "as a warrior of great distinction," Buffalo Bull appears "with his *medicine* or *totem* (the head of a buffalo) painted on his breast and his face, with bow and arrow in his hands" (*Letters and Notes*, vol. 2, p. 27, pl. 140).

References: 1837 catalogue, no. 289; Donaldson, p. 68, pl. 31; Ewers (1956), p. 515; McCracken, pp. 35, 36, reprod. p. 38; Paris (1963), no. 11; Museum of Fine Arts, Houston, *Days on the Range* (1972), no. 29, reprod. p. 42; Haverstock, reprod. p. 99; *America as Art*, no. 162, reprod. p. 162.

Version:
Gilcrease Institute, NAI sketchbook (4776.12), pen and ink

Copy:
M. Knoedler & Co., New York (until 1971), pencil and watercolor, signed lower right:
Rosa B-[Bonheur]

Probably painted at Fort Leavenworth in 1832 (see no. 99). Several unfinished portraits in the Pawnee series show the rapid oil strokes that Catlin used to block in figure and costume at the initial sitting, and what color and detail remained to be filled in after he returned to St. Louis.
    Buffalo Bull appears again in cartoon 23 (NGA 2018), with his wife and children, and two Pawnee warriors.

101. Medicine Horse, a Grand Pawnee brave
Pawnee, 1832
29 x 24 (73.7 x 60.9)

References: 1837 catalogue, no. 290; *Letters and Notes*, vol. 2, p. 27; Donaldson, p. 68; Ewers (1956), p. 515.

Probably painted at Fort Leavenworth in 1832 (see nos. 99, 100).

102. Little Chief, a Tapage Pawnee warrior
Pawnee, 1832
29 x 24 (73.7 x 60.9)
[Figure 111]

References: 1837 catalogue, no. 291; *Letters and Notes*, vol. 2, p. 27; Donaldson, p. 68; Ewers (1956), p. 515.

Probably painted at Fort Leavenworth in 1832 (see no. 99). Even the blanket does not obscure Catlin's inability to render correctly the proportions of a seated figure. Little Chief also sat to Charles Bird King in Washington (see Ewers [1953], p. 471).

101

103

103. Bird that Goes to War, a Tapage Pawnee
Pawnee, 1832
29 x 24 (73.7 x 60.9)

References: 1837 catalogue, no. 292; *Letters and Notes*, vol. 2, p. 27; Donaldson, p. 68; Ewers (1956), p. 515; McCracken, p. 36.

Probably painted at Fort Leavenworth in 1832 (see nos. 99, 100). The subject is supposed to appear again in cartoon 23 (NGA 2018), but that figure more closely resembles Big Elk (no. 108). Catlin seems to have made numerous errors in identifying the cartoon figures (see nos. 104, 113).

104. Mole in the Forehead, chief of the Republican Pawnee
Pawnee, 1832
29 x 24 (73.7 x 60.9)

References: 1837 catalogue, no. 293; *Letters and Notes*, vol. 2, p. 27; Donaldson, p. 68; Ewers (1956), p. 515; McCracken, p. 36.

Probably painted at Fort Leavenworth in 1832 (see no. 99). The subject is supposed to appear again in cartoon 23 (NGA 2018), but that figure more closely resembles Big Elk (no. 114). See numbers 103 and 113.

104

105. Man Chief, a Republican Pawnee
Pawnee, 1832
29 x 24 (73.7 x 60.9)

References: 1837 catalogue, no. 294; *Letters and Notes,* vol. 2, p. 27; Donaldson, p. 68; Ewers (1956), p. 515.

Probably painted at Fort Leavenworth in 1832 (see nos. 99, 100).

106. War Chief, a Republican Pawnee
Pawnee, 1832
29 x 24 (73.7 x 60.9)

References: 1837 catalogue, no. 295; Donaldson, p. 68; Ewers (1956), p. 515.

Probably painted at Fort Leavenworth in 1832 (see no. 99). Catlin may have finished the robe and legs long after the original sketch of the head and shoulders, thus the dwarflike appearance of the subject (see no. 102).

107. The Cheyenne, a Republican Pawnee
Pawnee, 1832
29 x 24 (73.7 x 60.9)

Described by Catlin as "a fine-looking fellow, with a pipe in one hand and his whip in the other" (1848 catalogue, p. 17).

References: 1837 catalogue, no. 296; *Letters and Notes,* vol. 2, p. 27; Donaldson, p. 68; Ewers (1956), p. 515; *New York Times,* Aug. 20, 1967, p. D27; Montreal Museum of Fine Arts, *The Painter and the New World* (1967), no. 179, reprod. pl. 179; Gilcrease catalogue, p. 50.

Versions:
Gilcrease Institute, watercolor, 10 x 8¼, signed lower right: Geo. Catlin. 1836.
Rains Galleries, New York, Cornelius Michaelson sale, May 8, 1935, no. 71, watercolor, 9 x 8½

Probably painted at Fort Leavenworth in 1832 (see nos. 99, 100). The figure of The Cheyenne is much the same in both the Gilcrease and Smithsonian portraits, but a background landscape with skin lodges has been added to the former. The egg-shaped appearance of the subject's head in the watercolor reveals its status as a later version of the Smithsonian original (see nos. 46, 55, 62).

108. Big Elk, chief of the Skidi (Wolf) Pawnee
Pawnee, 1832
29 x 24 (73.7 x 60.9)

References: 1837 catalogue, no. 297; *Letters and Notes,* vol. 2, p. 27, pl. 141; Donaldson, p. 69; Ewers (1956), p. 515; *Catlin, Bodmer, Miller;* Gilcrease catalogue, p. 50.

Version:
Gilcrease Institute, NAI sketchbook (4776.12), pen and ink

Probably painted at Fort Leavenworth in 1832 (see no. 99). The feathers are missing from Big Elk's roach in plate 141 of *Letters and Notes,* and two lodges have been added to the landscape behind him. He later sat to Charles Bird King in Washington (see Ewers [1953], p. 471).

Big Elk supposedly appears again in cartoon 24 (NGA 2019), but the Smithsonian painting is so unlike the cartoon figure that the latter must be mislabeled (see nos. 109, 111, 113). A figure that does resemble the Smithsonian painting stands beside Buffalo Bull in cartoon 23, but he is incorrectly identified in the 1871 catalogue as Bird that Goes to War (no. 103).

Cartoon 24 is based on a watercolor (pl. 34) in the Gilcrease *Souvenir* album, which also appears to be mislabeled.

109. Big Chief, a Skidi (Wolf) Pawnee
Pawnee, 1832
Unlocated

References: 1837 catalogue, no. 298; *Letters and Notes,* vol. 2, p. 27; Donaldson, p. 69.

Probably painted at Fort Leavenworth in 1832 (see no. 99). Big Chief supposedly appears again in cartoon 24 (NGA 2019). As the identity of the other two figures in that cartoon is questionable, however, all three may have been mislabeled (see nos. 108, 111, 113).

110. Brave Chief, a Skidi (Wolf) Pawnee
Pawnee, 1832
29 x 24 (73.7 x 60.9)

Catlin describes Brave Chief as having "impressions of hands painted on his breast" (1848 catalogue, p. 17).

References: 1837 catalogue, no. 299; *Letters and Notes,* vol. 2, p. 27; Donaldson, p. 69; Ewers (1956), p. 515; Corcoran Gallery of Art, Washington, D.C., *Wilderness* (1971), no. 47.

Probably painted at Fort Leavenworth in 1832 (see no. 99).

108

110

111. Ill-natured Man, a Skidi (Wolf) Pawnee
Pawnee, 1832
29 x 24 (73.7 x 60.9)

References: 1837 catalogue, no. 248; *Letters and Notes,* vol. 2, p. 27; Donaldson, p. 69; Ewers (1956), p. 515.

Probably painted at Fort Leavenworth in 1832 (see no. 99). The subject supposedly appears again in cartoon 24 (NGA 2019), but the Smithsonian painting is so unlike the cartoon figure that the latter must be mislabeled (see nos. 108, 109, 113.).

112. Little Soldier, a brave
Omaha, 1832
Unlocated

References: 1837 catalogue, no. 248; *Letters and Notes,* vol. 2, p. 27; Donaldson, p. 72.

Version:
Rains Galleries, New York, Cornelius Michaelson sale, May 8, 1935, no. 71, watercolor, 9 x 8½

Probably painted at Fort Leavenworth in 1832 (see no. 99). The Omaha portraits generally follow the style of the Pawnee series.

Little Soldier supposedly appears in cartoon 20 (AMNH 165). As the identity of the other two figures in that cartoon is questionable, however, all three may have been mislabeled (see nos. 114, 116).

111

black, for war" (*Letters and Notes*, vol. 2, pp. 27-28, pl. 146).

References: 1837 catalogue, no. 250; Donaldson, pp. 72-73, pl. 32; Haberly, reprod. opp. p. 49; Ewers (1956), p. 514; McCracken, p. 35, reprod. p. 37; Paris (1963), no. 12; Matthew Baigell, *A History of American Painting* (New York, 1971), reprod. p. 127; Haverstock, reprod. p. 94.

Version:
Gilcrease Institute, NAI sketchbook (4776.12), pen and ink

Copy:
M. Knoedler & Co., New York (until 1971), pencil and watercolor, signed lower right:
Rosa B-[Bonheur]

Probably painted at Fort Leavenworth in 1832 (see nos. 112, 99). Plate 146 in *Letters and Notes* is a duplicate of the Smithsonian painting, but the figure of Big Elk in cartoon 20 (AMNH 165) is so unlike the latter that the cartoon must be mislabeled (see nos. 112, 116). The Smithsonian painting actually resembles a figure at the extreme right of cartoon 23, who is identified in the 1871 catalogue as Mole in the Forehead (no. 104).

Big Elk sat for Charles Bird King some years earlier in Washington (see McKenney and Hall, vol. 1, pp. 281-82).

113. Brave Chief, chief of the tribe
Omaha, 1832
29 x 24 (73.7 x 60.9)

References: 1837 catalogue, no. 249; *Letters and Notes*, vol. 2, p. 27, pl. 145; Donaldson, p. 72; Ewers (1956), p. 514; McCracken, p. 183; Gilcrease catalogue, p. 50.

Version:
Gilcrease Institute, NAI sketchbook (4776.12), pen and ink

Probably painted at Fort Leavenworth in 1832 (see nos. 112, 99). Brave Chief later sat to Charles Bird King in Washington (see Ewers [1953], p. 470).

The subject is supposed to appear again in cartoon 21 (NGA 2271), but the Smithsonian portrait actually matches the central figure in cartoon 24, who is identified in the 1871 catalogue as Ill-Natured Man (no. 111). Either Catlin selected the wrong figures in composing these two cartoons, or they have since become mislabeled (see nos. 108, 109, 111, 115). Cartoon 21 is based on a watercolor (pl. 16) in the Gilcrease *Souvenir* album, which apparently is also mislabeled.

115. There He Goes, a brave
Omaha, 1832
29 x 24 (73.7 x 60.9)

References: 1837 catalogue, no. 251; *Letters and Notes*, vol. 2, p. 28; Donaldson, p. 73; Ewers (1956), p. 514.

Probably painted at Fort Leavenworth in 1832 (see nos. 112, 99). The subject supposedly appears again in cartoon 21 (NGA 2271), but the Smithsonian painting is so unlike the cartoon figure that the latter must be mislabeled (see nos. 111, 113).

114. Big Elk, a famous warrior
Omaha, 1832
29 x 24 (73.7 x 60.9)

Big Elk sat for his portrait, according to Catlin, "with his tomahawk in his hand, and face painted

116. Double Walker, a brave
Omaha, 1832
29 x 24 (73.7 x 60.9)

References: 1837 catalogue, no. 252; *Letters and Notes,* vol. 2, p. 28; Donaldson, p. 73; Mary C. Withington, *A Catalogue of Manuscripts in the Collection of Western Americana Founded by William Robertson Coe* (Yale University Library, New Haven, Conn., 1952), no. 67; Ewers (1956), p. 514; *Catlin, Bodmer, Miller;* Gilcrease catalogue, p. 50.

Probably painted at Fort Leavenworth in 1832 (see nos. 112, 99). Double Walker is supposed to appear again in cartoon 20 (AMNH 165), but the Smithsonian painting is so unlike the cartoon figure that the latter must be mislabeled (see nos. 112, 114), as is the watercolor (pl. 18) in the Gilcrease *Souvenir* album, which is the original study for the cartoon.

The painting at Yale (see Withington), another version of the cartoon figure, is identified as Double Walker in an inscription on the back by the artist, but the costume is so different from the other Omaha portraits that one is reluctant to accept even such direct evidence. Catlin's mistakes in naming the characters of the cartoon collection are legion (see nos. 58, 59, 89, 113, 114).

117. The Surrounder, chief of the tribe
Oto, 1832
29 x 24 (73.7 x 60.9)
[Figure 82]

Described by Catlin as "quite an old man; his shirt made of the skin of a grizzly bear, with the claws on" (1848 catalogue, p. 17).

References: 1837 catalogue, no. 256; *Letters and Notes,* vol. 2, p. 27; Donaldson, p. 75; Ewers (1956), p. 514; Paris (1963), no. 13; Rossi and Hunt, pp. 59, 320; Gilcrease catalogue, p. 50.

Version:
Gilcrease Institute, watercolor, 5¾ x 5¼, signed lower left: Geo Catlin pt
and lower right (on mount): Geo. Catlin

Probably painted at Fort Leavenworth in 1832 (see nos. 99, 112). The Oto portraits generally follow the style of the Pawnee and Omaha series. Plate 33 in Donaldson is mistakenly identified as The Surrounder (see no. 120).

The Gilcrease and Smithsonian portraits are identical in detail, but the roughly brushed visage

of the latter is clearly the life study (see no. 107). The Surrounder ranks with Horse Chief (no. 99), whom he somewhat resembles, as one of Catlin's most powerfully modeled portraits, again indicating that the best date for the Oto series is probably 1832.

The Surrounder supposedly appears again in the center of cartoon 19 (NGA 2058), but the figure does not resemble the Smithsonian portrait (see nos. 116, 120). Charles Bird King's portrait of the subject is no longer extant (see Ewers [1953], p. 470).

118. No Heart, a distinguished brave
Oto, 1832
Unlocated

References: 1837 catalogue, no. 255; *Letters and Notes,* vol. 2, p. 27; Donaldson, pp. 75-76.

Probably painted at Fort Leavenworth in 1832 (see no. 117).

119. He Who Strikes Two at Once, a brave
Oto, 1832
29 x 24 (73.7 x 60.9)

Catlin describes this portrait as a "sketch quite unfinished; beautiful dress, trimmed with a profusion of scalp-locks and eagles' quills; pipe in his hand, and necklace of grisly bears' claws" (1848 catalogue, p. 17).

References: 1837 catalogue, no. 257; *Letters and Notes,* vol. 2, p. 27, pl. 143; Donaldson, p. 76; Ewers (1956), p. 514; McCracken, p. 35, reprod. p. 37.

Version:
Gilcrease Institute, NAI sketchbook (4776.12), pen and ink

Probably painted at Fort Leavenworth in 1832 (see nos. 117, 99). The degree of finish in this portrait perhaps represents what Catlin hoped to achieve in the single sitting he normally allowed his Indian subjects (see no. 100). Another portrait of He Who Strikes Two at Once is illustrated in McKenney and Hall (vol. 3, p. 16).

116

119

120

121

120. Loose Pipestem, a brave
Oto, 1832
29 x 24 (73.7 x 60.9)

Catlin describes the subject as "full length . . . in a tunic made of the entire skin of a grizzly bear, with a head-dress of war-eagle's quills" (*Letters and Notes*, vol. 2, p. 27, pl. 144).

References: 1837 catalogue, no. 258; Donaldson, p. 76, pl. 33; Ewers (1956), p. 514; Gilcrease catalogue, p. 50.

Version:
Gilcrease Institute, NAI sketchbook (4776.12), pen and ink.

Copy:
M. Knoedler & Co., New York (until 1971), pencil and watercolor, signed lower right:
Rosa B-[Bonheur]

Probably painted at Fort Leavenworth in 1832 (see nos. 117, 99). Plate 33 in Donaldson represents Loose Pipestem, and he appears again in cartoon 19 (NGA 2058), which is based on a watercolor (pl. 46) in the Gilcrease *Souvenir* album.

121. He Who Exchanges
Oto, 1832
29 x 24 (73.7 x 60.9)

The subject is described as having a "beautiful pipe in his hand" (1848 catalogue, p. 17).

References: 1837 catalogue, no. 259; *Letters and Notes*, vol. 2, p. 27; Donaldson, p. 76; Ewers (1956), p. 514; M. Knoedler & Co., New York, *The American Indian Observed* (1971), no. 27, reprod. p. 21.

Probably painted at Fort Leavenworth in 1832 (see nos. 117, 99). The subject later sat to Charles Bird King in Washington (see Ewers [1953], p. 471).

122. He Who Kills the Osages, chief of the tribe
Missouri, 1832
29 x 24 (73.7 x 60.9)
[Figure 83]

The subject is described as "an old man" with a "necklace of grisly bears' claws, and a handsome carved pipe in his hand" (1848 catalogue, p. 18).

References: 1837 catalogue, no. 260; *Letters and Notes*, vol. 2, p. 27, pl. 139; Donaldson, p. 76, pl. 34; Ewers (1956), p. 513; McCracken, reprod. p. 131.

Version:
Gilcrease Institute, NAI sketchbook (4776.8), pen and ink

Copies:
M. Knoedler & Co., New York (until 1971), pencil and watercolor, signed lower right:
Rosa B-[Bonheur]

British Museum, London, by John Cullum, watercolor, 13 x 10¼ (1842-1844)

Probably painted at Fort Leavenworth in 1832 (see nos. 99, 112, 117). The subject later sat to Charles Bird King in Washington (see Ewers [1953], p. 470), and he also appears, full length, in cartoon 22 (NGA 2017).

123. Bloody Hand, chief of the tribe
Arikara, 1832
29 x 24 (73.7 x 60.9)
[Figure 85]

Bloody Hand is described as having "his face painted with red vermilion, scalping-knife in his hand," and "wearing a beautiful dress" (1848 catalogue, p. 18).

References: 1837 catalogue, no. 180; *Letters and Notes*, vol. 1, p. 204, pl. 82; Donaldson, p. 78; Haberly, p. 95; Ewers (1956), p. 508; McCracken, pp. 111, 116; Haverstock, reprod. p. 91.

Version:
Gilcrease Institute, NAI sketchbook (4776.38), pen and ink

Copies:
M. Knoedler & Co., New York (until 1971), pencil and watercolor, signed lower right:
Rosa B-[Bonheur]

British Museum, London, by John Cullum, watercolor, 11⅞ x 10¼ (1842-1844)

Painted at the Arikara village in 1832. The broad modeling and strong features are typical of the Upper Missouri portraits. Bloody Hand also appears, full length, in cartoon 36 (NGA 2036), with his wife (no. 124).

124. The Twin, wife of Bloody Hand
Arikara, 1832
29 x 24 (73.7 x 60.9)

References: 1837 catalogue, no. 182; *Letters and Notes,* vol. 1, p. 204, pl. 81; Donaldson, p. 78; Ewers (1956), pp. 498, 508, pl. 11.

Version:
Gilcrease Institute, NAI sketchbook (4776.38), pen and ink

Copy:
M. Knoedler & Co., New York (until 1971), pencil and watercolor, signed lower right:
Rosa B-[Bonheur]

Painted at the Mandan village in 1832. Note the richly detailed treatment of the trade bead necklaces worn by The Twin. When time permitted and his interest was aroused, Catlin could vary his technique with considerable facility.

The Twin also appears, full length, in cartoon 36 (NGA 2036), with her husband (no. 123).

125. Sweet-scented Grass, twelve-year-old daughter of Bloody Hand
Arikara, 1832
29 x 24 (73.7 x 60.9)

This portrait, according to Catlin, gives "a very pretty specimen of the dress and fashion of the women in this tribe. The inner garment, which is like a slip or frock, is entire in one piece, and beautifully ornamented with embroidery and beads, with a row of elks' teeth passing across the breast, and a robe of the young buffalo's skin, tastefully and elaborately embroidered, gracefully thrown over her shoulders, and hanging down to the ground behind her" (*Letters and Notes,* vol. 1, p. 204, pl. 84).

References: 1837 catalogue, no. 183; Donaldson, p. 78; Ewers (1956), p. 508; McCracken, p. 116, reprod. p. 118; Paris (1963), no. 14; Gilcrease catalogue, p. 51; Time-Life Books, ed., *The Chroniclers* (New York, 1976), reprod. p. 104.

Versions:
Gilcrease Institute, 28 x 23
Gilcrease Institute, NAI sketchbook (4776.35), pen and ink

Painted at the Arikara village in 1832. The Smithsonian and Gilcrease portraits are identical, except for two earth lodges in the background of the former that are also included in plate 84 of *Letters and Notes.* The Gilcrease oils were done by Catlin

for Sir Thomas Phillips in the late 1840s and early 1850s, and they are clearly acknowledged as later versions of his original paintings. Sweet-scented Grass appears again in cartoon 37 (NGA 2048, see no. 126).

126. He Who Strikes, a distinguished brave
Arikara, 1832
Unlocated

References: 1837 catalogue, no. 181; *Letters and Notes,* vol. 1, pp. 203-4, pl. 83; Donaldson, p. 78; Gilcrease catalogue, p. 51.

Version:
Gilcrease Institute, NAI sketchbook (4776.35), pen and ink

Copy:
British Museum, London, by John Cullum, watercolor, 11⅞ x 10½ (1842-1844)

Painted at the Arikara village in 1832. Plate 83 of *Letters and Notes* is illustrated in place of the original.

The subject also appears in cartoon 37 (NGA 2048), with an Arikara warrior and a young girl. The cartoon is based on a watercolor (pl. 48) in the Gilcrease *Souvenir* album.

Plate 83, *Letters and Notes.*

127

127. Wolf Chief, head chief of the tribe
Mandan, 1832
29 x 24 (73.7 x 60.9)

"This man is head-chief of the nation, and famil-iarly known by the name of 'Chef de Loup,' as the French Traders call him; a haughty, austere, and overbearing man, respected and feared by his people rather than loved. The tenure by which this man holds his office, is that by which head-chiefs of most of the tribes claim, that of inheri-tance. . . . The dress of the chief was one of great extravagance, and some beauty; manufactured of skins, and a great number of quills of the raven, forming his stylish head-dress" (*Letters and Notes*, vol. 1, p. 92, pl. 49).

References: 1837 catalogue no. 105; Donaldson, pp. 80-81, pl. 35; Quimby, pp. 46-47; Ewers (1956), p. 513; McCracken, p. 93, reprod. p. 87; Paris (1963), no. 15; Nicholas B. Wainwright, "Joseph Harrison, Jr., a Forgotten Art Collector," *Antiques* 102 (October 1972), reprod. p. 664; Gilcrease catalogue, p. 50.

Versions:
Field Museum of Natural History, ca. 28 x 23
Gilcrease Institute, NAI sketchbook (4776.11), pen and ink

Painted at the Mandan village in 1832. The Smith-sonian portrait and plate 49 in *Letters and Notes* have in the background a Missouri River land-scape, but two Mandan earth lodges are behind Wolf Chief in the Field Museum version (see no. 3).

The subject appears again in cartoon 33 (NGA 2033), with his wife and child. The cartoon is based on a watercolor (pl. 4) in the Gilcrease *Souvenir* album.

128. Four Bears, second chief, in full dress
Mandan, 1832
29 x 24 (73.7 x 60.9)
[Figure 105]

"This extraordinary man, though second in office is undoubtedly the first and most popular man in the nation. Free, generous, elegant and gentle-manly in his deportment—handsome, brave and valiant; wearing a robe on his back, with the his-tory of his battles emblazoned on it; which would fill a book of themselves, if properly translated. This, readers, is the most extraordinary man, perhaps, who lives at this day, in the atmosphere of Nature's noblemen. . . .

"The dress of Mah-to-toh-pa . . . the greater part of which I have represented in his full-length portrait, and which I shall now describe, was pur-chased of him after I had painted his picture; and every article of it can be seen in my Indian Gallery by the side of the portrait, provided I succeed in getting them home to the civilized world without injury.

"Mah-to-toh-pa had agreed to stand before me for his portrait at an early hour of the next morn-ing, and on that day I sat with my palette of colours prepared, and waited till twelve o'clock, before he could leave his toilette with feelings of satisfac-tion as to the propriety of his looks and the ar-rangement of his equipments; and at that time it was announced, that 'Mah-to-toh-pa was coming in full dress!' I looked out of the door of the wig-wam, and saw him approaching with a firm and elastic step, accompanied by a great crowd of women and children, who were gazing on him with admiration, and escorting him to my room. No tragedian ever trod the stage, nor gladiator ever entered the Roman Forum, with more grace and manly dignity than did Mah-to-toh-pa enter the wigwam, where I was in readiness to receive him. He took his attitude before me, and with the st-ernness of a Brutus and the stillness of a statue, he stood until the darkness of night broke upon the solitary stillness. His dress, which was a very splendid one, was complete in all its parts, and consisted of a shirt or tunic, leggings, moccasins, head-dress, necklace, shield, bow and quiver, lance, tobacco-sack, and pipe; robe, belt, and knife; medicine-bag, tomahawk, and war-club, or *po-ko-mo-kon.*

"The shirt, of which I have spoken, was made of two skins of the mountain-sheep, beautifully dressed, and sewed together by seams which rest-ed upon the arms; one skin hanging in front, upon the breast, and the other falling down upon the back; the head being passed between them, and they falling over and resting on the shoulders. Across each shoulder, and somewhat in the form of an epaulette, was a beautiful band; and down each arm from the neck to the hand was a similar one, of two inches in width (and crossing the other at right angles on the shoulder) beautifully em-broidered with porcupine quills worked on the dress, and covering the seams. To the lower edge of these bands the whole way, at intervals of half an inch, were attached long locks of black hair, which he had taken with his own hand from the heads of his enemies whom he had slain in battle, and which he thus wore as a trophy, and also as an or-nament to his dress. The front and back of the shirt were curiously garnished in several parts with porcupine quills and paintings of the battles he had fought, and also with representations of the victims that had fallen by his hand. The bottom of the dress was bound or hemmed with ermine skins, and tassels of ermines' tails were suspended from the arms and the shoulders.

"The *Leggings*, which were made of deer skins, beautifully dressed, and fitting tight to the leg, extended from the feet to the hips, and were fastened to a belt which was passed around the waist. These, like the shirt, had a similar band, worked with porcupine quills of richest dyes, passing down the seam on the outer part of the leg, and fringed also the whole length of the leg, with the scalp-locks taken from his enemies' heads. . . .

"The *Head-dress*, which was superb and truly magnificent, consisted of a crest of war-eagles' quills, gracefully falling back from the forehead over the back part of the head, and extending quite down to his feet; set the whole way in a profusion of ermine, and surmounted on the top of the head, with the horns of the buffalo, shaved thin and highly polished. . . .

"Such was the dress of Mah-to-toh-pa when he entered my wigwam to stand for his picture; but such I have not entirely represented it in his portrait; having rejected such trappings and ornaments as interfered with the grace and simplicity of the figure. He was beautifully and extravagantly dressed; and in this he was not alone, for hundreds of others are equally elegant. In plumes, and arms, and ornaments, he is not singular; but in laurels and wreaths he stands unparalleled. His breast has been bared and scarred in defence of his country, and his brows crowned with honours that elevate him conspicuous above all of his nation. There is no man amongst the Mandans so generally loved, nor any one who wears a robe so justly famed and honourable as that of Mah-to-toh-pa" (*Letters and Notes*, vol. 1, pp. 92, 114-17, 145-54, pl. 64).

References: 1837 catalogue, no. 106; *Travels in Europe*, p. 316; Donaldson, p. 81, pl. 36; Matthews, pp. 602-4; Haberly, pp. 70-71; Oliver LaFarge, "George Catlin: Wild West Witness," *Art News* 52 (October 1953), reprod. p. 32; Ewers (1956), pp. 496-97, 513, pl. 8; McCracken, pp. 14, 93, 95-97, 109, 116; Hartmann, pp. 39-41; Ewers (1965), reprod. p. 69; Halpin, reprod. p. 15; Everson Museum of Art, Syracuse, N.Y., *American Painting from 1830* (1965), no. 43, reprod. p. 56; Ewers, "Fact and Fiction in the Documentary Art of the American West," *The Frontier Re-examined*, ed. J. F. McDermott (Urbana, Ill., 1967), pp. 91-92, fig. 13; Ewers (1968), pp. 103-5, 193, 196-7, pl. 17; M. Knoedler & Co., New York, *The American Indian Observed* (1971), no. 20; Haverstock, pp. 80-81, 83, 93, 158, 218; Rossi and Hunt, pp. 50, 320; Gilcrease catalogue, p. 51; National Portrait Gallery, Washington, D.C., *American Self-Portraits* (1974), no. 33; Peter Hassrick, *The Way West: Art of Frontier America* (New York, 1977), reprod. p. 36.

Versions:
Gilcrease Institute, watercolor, 10½ x 8½, signed lower right: Geo. Catlin/1836.
Rains Galleries, New York, Cornelius Michaelson sale, May 8, 1935, no. 71, watercolor, 9 x 8½
Gilcrease Institute, NAI sketchbook (4776.1 and 41), pen and ink

Copy:
M. Knoedler & Co., New York (until 1971), pencil and watercolor, signed lower right:
Rosa B-[Bonheur]

Painted at the Mandan village in 1832. Four Bears (Máh-to-tóh-pa) was the most publicized Indian of the Upper Missouri in the 1830s, and the subject among all of Catlin's portraits whom the artist most favored. The two communicated often and at length during Catlin's stay at Mandan village, and the full-length portrait of Four Bears is one of the finest, and certainly the most widely known, in the collection. Calm, dignified, splendidly costumed (and stripped of certain encumbering "ornaments and trappings"), the chief is presented by Catlin with all the pomp of an imperial portrait, and Ewers (1968) points out how that image of Four Bears became over the years a symbol of the North American Indian. Ewers (1956) also comments on the accuracy of the portrait by comparing the features to those of Four Bears' son, and the costume details to the original costume, which is in the Smithsonian anthropology collections. The deliberate brushwork and Karl Bodmer's well-known portraits of Four Bears (see Reuben Gold Thwaites, ed., *Early Western Travels 1748-1846*, pls. 46, 47) are a further guarantee that Catlin's likeness is generally correct.

The Gilcrease watercolor incorporates most of the detail of the original (see no. 107), and the half-length portrait of Four Bears in the Smithsonian (no. 131) is a less imposing, but more sympathetic and descriptive record of his features. Catlin also lists a painting of the subject among those commissioned by Louis Philippe (see *Travels in Europe*). Four Bears appears again, full length, in plate 28 of the *North American Indian Portfolio*, first published in 1844, and in several cartoons that Catlin reproduced with some frequency. The most popular are those in which the chief poses with his family (cartoon 30, NGA 2030), and before the astonished members of his tribe as the artist paints his portrait (cartoon 191, NGA 2142). A superior version of the former is in the Museum für Völkerkunde, Berlin, and the cartoon itself is based on a watercolor (pl. 2) in the Gilcrease *Souvenir* album. Another cartoon (133, NGA 2038), which was taken from plate 62 in *Letters and Notes*, shows Catlin feasting in Four Bears' lodge, and a fourth (cartoon 194, NGA 2044) illustrates the buffalo robe upon which the chief, who was also an artist, depicted his triumphs in battle.

129. Old Bear, a medicine man
Mandan, 1832
29 x 24 (73.7 x 60.9)
[Figure 99]

At twelve o'clock, "having used the whole of the fore-part of the day at his toilette," Old Bear arrived at Catlin's lodge "bedaubed and streaked with paints of various colours, with bear's grease and charcoal, with medicine-pipes in his hands and foxes tails attached to his heels . . . [and] with a train of his own profession, who seated themselves around him. . . . He took his position in the middle of the room, waving his eagle calumets in each hand, and singing his medicine-song . . . looking me full in the face until I completed his picture, which I painted at full length" *Letters and Notes*, vol. 1, pp. 92, 110-11, 155, 161, pl. 55).

References: 1837 catalogue, no. 107; Donaldson, pp. 81-82, pl. 37; Oliver LaFarge, "George Catlin: Wild West Witness," *Art News* 52 (October 1953), reprod. p. 31; Ewers (1956), p. 513; McCracken, pp. 94, 100, 102-4, reprod. p. 110; Perry T. Rathbone, "Rediscovery," *Art in America* 49 (1961), no. 1, reprod. p. 83; James T. Flexner, *That Wilder Image* (Boston, 1962), reprod. p. 85; Paris (1963), no. 16, pl. 4; Halpin, reprod. p. 14; *American Heritage* 18 (October 1967), reprod. p. 30; Haverstock, pp. 86-87; Museum of Fine Arts, Boston, *Frontier America: The Far West* (1976), no. 32, reprod. p. 50; National Museum of Man, Ottawa, *"Bo'jou, Neejee!": Profiles of Canadian Indian Art* (1976), reprod. p. 186.

Version:
Gilcrease Institute, NAI sketchbook (4776.11), pen and ink

Copies:
Robert L. Stolper, London, 15 x 13, false monogram lower left
M. Knoedler & Co., New York (until 1971), pencil and watercolor, signed lower right:
Rosa B-[Bonheur]

Painted at the Mandan village in 1832. Old Bear, flanked by two arcs of feathers, is one of Catlin's most successfully designed full-length figures.

The subject also appears in cartoon 184 (NGA 2043), practicing his medicine before a "crying and howling" crowd, and in plate 30 of the Gilcrease *Souvenir* album.

130

131

132

130. Rushes through the Middle, a brave
Mandan, 1832
29 x 24 (73.7 x 60.9)

References: 1837 catalogue, no. 108; *Letters and Notes*, vol. 1, p. 92, pl. 50; Donaldson, p. 82, pl. 38; Ewers (1956), p. 513.

Version:
Gilcrease Institute, NAI sketchbook (4776.5), pen and ink [fig. 148]

Copy:
M. Knoedler & Co., New York (until 1971), pencil and watercolor, signed lower right:
Rosa B-[Bonheur]

Painted at the Mandan village in 1832. The subject appears again, full length, in cartoon 31 (NGA 2031), in a different pose and costume (see no. 132).

131. Four Bears, second chief, in mourning
Mandan, 1832
29 x 24 (73.7 x 60.9)

Described by Catlin as Four Bears "in *undress,* being in mourning, with a few locks of hair cut off. His hair put up in plaits or slabs, with glue and red paint, a custom of the tribe.

"The scars on his breast, arms, and legs, show that he has several times in his life submitted to the propitiatory tortures represented in four paintings, nos. 504, 505, 506, 507" (1848 catalogue, p. 19).

References: 1837 catalogue, no. 109; Donaldson, p. 82; Ewers (1956), p. 513; Fine Arts Museum of New Mexico, Santa Fe, *The Artist in the American West, 1800-1900* (1961), no. 8, reprod.; Denver Art Museum, *The Western Frontier,* 1966; Haverstock, reprod. p. 30; Gilcrease catalogue, p. 51.

Version:
Gilcrease Institute, watercolor, 5¾ x 5¼, signed lower center: Geo. Catlin pt
and lower right (on mount): Geo. Catlin

Painted at the Mandan village in 1832. The Mandan portraits, like those of the Sioux, are brushed with strong, even strokes that form solid and distinctive facial characteristics (see no. 69).

The Smithsonian and Gilcrease portraits are identical, but the former is clearly the life study (see no. 107). Catlin also painted Four Bears full length (see no. 128).

132. Mouse-colored Feather, a noted brave
Mandan, 1832
29 x 24 (73.7 x 60.9)

The subject posed "with a beautiful pipe in his hand," and his hair was "quite yellow" (1848 catalogue, no. 19).

References: 1837 catalogue, no. 110; *Letters and Notes,* vol. 1, p. 92, pl. 51; Donaldson, p. 82, pl. 38; Ewers (1956), p. 513; McCracken, p. 93, reprod. p. 85; Paris (1963), no. 17; Ewers (1968), pp. 106-7, pl. 22.

Version:
Gilcrease Institute, NAI sketchbook (4776.5), pen and ink [fig. 148]

Copy:
M. Knoedler & Co., New York (until 1971), pencil and watercolor, signed lower right:
Rosa B-[Bonheur]

Painted at the Mandan village in 1832 (see no. 131). Ewers (1968) notes the similarity between Catlin's portrait of Mouse-colored Feather and the watercolor done by Karl Bodmer a year and a half later.

The subject also appears, full length, in cartoon 31 (NGA 2031), in a different pose and costume. The cartoon is based on a watercolor (pl. 6) in the Gilcrease *Souvenir* album.

133. Mink, a beautiful girl
Mandan, 1832
29 x 24 (73.7 x 60.9)

Catlin notes that Mink posed in a "Mountain-sheep skin dress, ornamented with porcupine quills, beads, and elk's teeth" (1848 catalogue, p. 19).

References: 1837 catalogue, no. 111; *Letters and Notes,* vol. 1, p. 92, pl. 53; Catlin, *Life Amongst the Indians* (London, 1861), pp. 140-41; Donaldson, p. 82, pl. 38; Ewers (1956), p. 513; McCracken, pp. 31, 116; *Catlin, Bodmer, Miller,* Paris (1963), no. 18; Gilcrease catalogue, p. 51; Time-Life Books, ed., *The Chroniclers* (New York, 1976), reprod. p. 105.

Version:
Gilcrease Institute, NAI sketchbook (4776.6), pen and ink

Copy:
M. Knoedler & Co., New York (until 1971), pencil and watercolor, signed lower right:
Rosa B-[Bonheur]

Painted at the Mandan village in 1832. The female portraits are much like those of the Sioux (see nos. 131, 81).

In *Life Amongst the Indians,* Catlin says he gave the original back to Mink as he was leaving the village. The subject also appears, full length, in cartoon 30 (NGA 2030) as "the favorite wife" of Four Bears (no. 128).

134. Mint, a pretty girl
Mandan, 1832
29 x 24 (73.7 x 60.9)
[Figure 62]

"A very pretty and modest girl, twelve years of age, with *grey hair! peculiar to the Mandans* . . . about one in twelve, of both sexes and of all ages, have . . . hair of a bright silvery grey, and exceedingly coarse and harsh" (1848 catalogue, p. 19).

References: 1837 catalogue, no. 112; *Letters and Notes,* vol. 1, pp. 92, 94, pl. 52; Donaldson, p. 82, pl. 38; Haberly, p. 70; Oliver LaFarge, "George Catlin: Wild West Witness," *Art News* 52 (October 1953), reprod. p. 32; Quimby, pp. 48-49; Ewers (1956), p. 513; McCracken, reprod. p. 85; Ewers (1965), reprod. p. 68; Rossi and Hunt, pp. 59, 320; Haverstock, reprod. p. 84; Gilcrease catalogue, p. 51.

Versions:
Field Museum of Natural History, ca. 28 x 23
Gilcrease Institute, watercolor, 5½ x 5, signed lower right (on mount): Geo. Catlin 1832

Gilcrease Institute, NAI sketchbook (4776.6), pen and ink

Copies:
M. Knoedler & Co., New York (until 1971), pencil and watercolor, signed lower right:
Rosa B-[Bonheur]
Chemung County Historical Society, Elmira, New York, ca. 29 x 24

Painted at the Mandan village in 1832. The Smithsonian and Gilcrease portraits are similar to plate 52 in *Letters and Notes,* but the Field Museum version shows Mint with dark hair and a slightly different variety of necklaces. The hair color in this last portrait does not agree with Catlin's description of Mint in the 1848 catalogue, and the date of the Gilcrease watercolor cannot be taken seriously (see nos. 3, 46, 107). Another portrait of Mandan children with gray hair is illustrated in Quimby (pp. 50-51), but the female figure does not resemble Mint.

Catlin's technique has a considerable range in the Smithsonian portrait, from the broad strokes of the flowing gray hair to the delicate touches of highlight on the costume accessories (see nos. 131, 133).

135. Long Fingernails, a brave
Mandan, 1832
Unlocated

References: 1837 catalogue, no. 113; Donaldson, p. 82.

Painted at the Mandan village in 1832. The subject also appears in cartoon 31 (NGA 2031). As the other two figures in the cartoon do not resemble the Smithsonian originals, however, there is no reason to suppose that this one would (see nos. 130, 132, 116). An unidentified portrait in the O'Fallon collection may be a later version of this subject (see no. 83).

136. One Who Rushes through the Middle
Mandan, 1832
Unlocated

References: 1837 catalogue, no. 114; Donaldson, p. 82.

Painted at the Mandan village in 1832. As Catlin makes a slight distinction between the Indian names of numbers 130 and 136, one must assume that they were two separate subjects. An unidentified portrait in the O'Fallon collection may be a later version of this subject (see no. 83).

133

Plate 54, *Letters and Notes.*

143

137-142. Deceiving Wolf and five other Mandan
Mandan, 1832
Unlocated

"The hair of the men is uniformly all laid over from the forehead backwards; carefully kept above and resting on the ear, and thence falling down over the back, in these flattened bunches, and painted red, extending oftentimes quite on to the calf of the leg. . . . In the portrait of [Deceiving Wolf] . . . where he is represented at full length, with several others of his family around him in a group, there will be seen a fair illustration of these and other customs of these people" (*Letters and Notes,* vol. 1, p. 95, pl. 54).

References: 1837 catalogue, nos. 116-21; Donaldson, p. 82, pl. 39; Gilcrease catalogue, p. 51.

Versions:
Gilcrease Institute, 11 x 14

Gilcrease Institute, NAI sketchbook (4776.4), pen and ink

Copy:
M. Knoedler & Co., New York (until 1971), pencil and watercolor, signed lower right:
Rosa B-[Bonheur]

Painted at the Mandan village in 1832. Plate 54 in *Letters and Notes* is illustrated in place of the original. The figures in the Gilcrease painting lack the detail of those in plate 54 and cartoon 32 (NGA 2032), in which the scene is repeated (see no. 125).

143. Wolf on the Hill, chief of the tribe
Cheyenne, 1832
29 x 24 (73.7 x 60.9)

"The chief . . . was clothed in a handsome dress of deer skins, very neatly garnished with broad bands of porcupine quill-work down the sleeves of his shirt and his leggings, and all the way fringed with scalp-locks. His hair was very profuse, and flowing over his shoulders; and in his hand he held a beautiful Sioux pipe, which had just been presented to him by Mr. M'Kenzie, the Trader. This was one of the finest looking and most dignified men that I have met in the Indian country; and from the account given of him by the Traders a man of honour and strictest integrity" (*Letters and Notes,* vol. 2, p. 2, pl. 115).

References: 1837 catalogue, no. 189; Donaldson, pp. 88-89, 475, pl. 40; Haberly, p. 95; Ewers (1956), p. 509; McCracken, p. 59; Haverstock, p. 100.

Version:
Gilcrease Institute, NAI sketchbook (4776.8), pen and ink

Copy:
British Museum, London, by John Cullum, watercolor, 12 x 10½ (1842-1844)

Painted at Fort Pierre in 1832, as Catlin clearly indicates in *Letters and Notes.* Donaldson's date is incorrect (see no. 69). The basic modeling for such boldly painted Upper Missouri portraits must have been completed in a remarkably short time (see nos. 78, 100).

Wolf on the Hill appears again, full length, in cartoon 48 (NGA 1994), with his wife (no. 144) and another Cheyenne.

144. She-Who Bathes Her Knees, wife of the chief
Cheyenne, 1832
29 x 24 (73.7 x 60.9)
[Figure 95]

"The woman was comely, and beautifully dressed; her dress of the mountain-sheep skins, tastefully ornamented with quills and beads, and her hair plaited in large braids, that hung down on her breast" (*Letters and Notes,* vol. 2, p. 2, pl. 116).

References: 1837 catalogue, no. 190; Donaldson, p. 89; Ewers (1956), p. 509; McCracken, p. 59, reprod. p. 55; Haverstock, p. 100.

Version:
Gilcrease Institute, NAI sketchbook (4776.8), pen and ink

Painted at Fort Pierre in 1832 (see no. 143). Judging from Catlin's itinerary that summer, the bead and jewelry detail were probably later additions.

The subject also appears, full length, in cartoon 48 (NGA 1994), with her husband.

145. Rabbit's Skin Leggings, a brave
[Figure 94]

146. No Horns on His Head, a brave
Nez Perce, 1832
29 x 24 each (73.7 x 60.9)

"These two men, when I painted them, were in beautiful Sioux dresses . . . [they] were part of a delegation that came across the Rocky Mountains to St. Louis, a few years since . . . I travelled two thousand miles, companion with these . . . young fellows, towards their own country, and became much pleased with their manners and dispositions" (*Letters and Notes,* vol. 2, pp. 108-9, pls. 207, 208).

References: 1837 catalogue, nos. 184, 185; Donaldson, pp. 94-95, pl. 41; Ewers (1956), p. 525; (145) *Catlin, Bodmer, Miller;* (145) Paris (1963), no. 19; (145) Gilcrease catalogue, p. 51.

Versions:
Gilcrease Institute, watercolor, 5½ x 5, signed lower right (on mount): Geo. Catlin
Gilcrease Institute, NAI sketchbook (4776.32), pen and ink

The two portraits were probably painted in St. Louis or aboard the steamboat *Yellowstone* in 1832. They appear to be closely related to the Sioux series (see no. 69).

The Gilcrease watercolor is mistakenly identified as No Horns on His Head (no. 146). Instead, it represents Rabbit's Skin Leggings (no. 145), and closely resembles plate 207 in *Letters and Notes* and the Smithsonian original (see nos. 62, 107). The subjects also appear, full length, in cartoon 92 (NGA 1992).

147. Woman and child, showing how the heads of children are flattened
Chinook, possibly 1837-1839
29 x 24 (73.7 x 60.9)

"Portrait of a Chinook woman, with her child in her arms, her own head flattened, and the infant undergoing the process . . . which is done by placing its back on a board . . . to which it is lashed with thongs, to a position from which it cannot escape, and the back of the head supported by a pillow, made of moss or rabbit skins, with an inclined piece . . . resting on the forehead of the child" (*Letters and Notes,* vol. 2, pp. 110-11, pl. 210).

References: Donaldson, pp. 99-100, pl. 42; Ewers (1956), p. 525; *Catlin, Bodmer, Miller.*

Version:
Gilcrease Institute, NAI sketchbook (4776.32), pen and ink

This painting is not listed in the 1837 catalogue, but does appear in the Egyptian Hall catalogue of

January 1840, perhaps indicating that it was executed in the interval (see no. 19-21). Donaldson gives no justification for his date of 1832, and Catlin did not visit the Northwest Coast until 1855.

The subject appears again in cartoon 90 (NGA 2108).

148. Hee-doh'ge-ats, a young man
Chinook, possibly 1837-1839
29 x 24 (73.7 x 60.9)

Described by Catlin as a "Chinook boy, of fifteen or eighteen years of age" whose head had never been flattened (*Letters and Notes,* vol. 2, p. 110, pl. 209).

References: Donaldson, p. 99; Ewers (1956), p. 525; Gilcrease catalogue, p. 51.

Version:
Gilcrease Institute, watercolor, 5½ x 5, signed lower left: Geo. Catlin pt.
and lower right (on mount): Geo. Catlin

See number 147 for explanation of the date. The feather headdress has been omitted and the subject is wrapped in a blanket in both the Gilcrease portrait and plate 209 of *Letters and Notes* (see no. 107). He wears a Plains Indian shirt in the Smithsonian original, which Catlin may have later recognized as an inconsistency.

The subject appears full length in cartoon 92 (NGA 1992), again wrapped in a blanket. His true identity is probably anyone's guess, although a Chinook boy of similar appearance is illustrated in McKenney and Hall (vol. 2, p. 276). This boy (or young man), whose name was Stumanu, toured Atlantic Coast cities in 1838 and 1839 to help raise funds for an Oregon mission.

149

Engraving of Buffalo Bull's Back Fat, after a watercolor by Karl Bodmer.

149. Buffalo Bull's Back Fat, head chief, Blood tribe
Blackfoot, 1832
29 x 24 (73.7 x 60.9)
[Figure 15]

"I have this day been painting a portrait of the head chief of the [Blood tribe] . . . he is a good-looking and dignified Indian, about fifty years of age, and superbly dressed; whilst sitting for his picture he has been surrounded by his own braves and warriors, and also gazed at by his enemies, the Crows and the Knisteneaux, Assinneboins and Ojibbeways; a number of distinguished personages of each of which tribes have laid all day around the sides of my room; reciting to each other the battles they have fought, and pointing to the scalp-locks, worn as proofs of their victories, and attached to the seams of their shirts and leggings. . . .

"The name of this dignitary of whom I have just spoken is Stu-mick-o-sucks (the buffalo's back fat), i.e., the 'hump' or 'fleece,' the most delicious part of the buffalo's flesh. . . . The dress . . . of the chief . . . consists of a shirt or tunic, made of two deerskins finely dressed, and so placed together with the necks of the skins downwards, and the skins of the hind legs stitched together, the seams running down on each arm, from the neck to the knuckles of the hand; this seam is covered with a band of two inches in width, of very beautiful embroidery of porcupine quills, and suspended from the under edge of this, from the shoulders to the hands, is a fringe of the locks of black hair, which he has taken from the heads of victims slain by his own hand in battle. . . . In his hand he holds a very beautiful pipe, the stem of which is four or five feet long, and two inches wide, curiously wound with braids of the porcupine quills of various colours; and the bowl of the pipe ingeniously carved by himself from a piece of red steatite of an interesting character, and which they all tell me is procured somewhere between this place and the Falls of St. Anthony, on the head waters of the Mississippi" (Letters and Notes, vol. 1, pp. 29-31, pl. 11).

References: 1837 catalogue, no. 132; Paris, Musée Royal, Salon de 1846, no. 315; Charles Baudelaire, Art in Paris 1845-1862, ed. and trans. Jonathan Mayne (London, 1965), pp. 70-71; Donaldson, pp. 101-2, pl. 43; Haberly, p. 59; Ewers, "An Anthropologist Looks at Early Pictures of North American Indians," New-York Historical Society Quarterly Bulletin 33 (October 1949), reprod. p. 232; Ewers (1956), pp. 504, 508, pl. 20; McCracken, pp. 67-68, reprod. p. 73; Robert Beetem, "George Catlin in France: His Relationship to Delacroix and Baudelaire," Art Quarterly 24 (Summer 1961): 140-41; Paris (1963), no. 20, pl. 3; Ewers (1965), reprod. p. 77; Halpin, reprod. on cover; Denys Sutton, "The Luminous Point,"

Apollo 85 (March 1967): 217; Montreal Museum of Fine Arts, The Painter and the New World (1967), no. 178; Paris, Petit Palais, Baudelaire (1969), no. 178, reprod.; Denys Sutton, "The Baudelaire Exhibition," Apollo 89 (March 1969): 180-81, reprod. p. 183; Haverstock, reprod. p. 68; Museum of Art, Pennsylvania State University, University Park, Portraits USA 1776-1976 (1976), p. 46, reprod. p. 47; Time-Life Books, ed., The Chroniclers (New York, 1976), reprod. p. 105.

Versions:
Pennypacker Auction Centre, Reading, Pennsylvania, April 8, 1968, no. 151, watercolor, 12 x 16, signed Geo Catlin
Gilcrease Institute, NAI sketchbook (4776.2), pen and ink

Copy:
M. Knoedler & Co., New York (until 1971), pencil and watercolor, signed lower right:
Rosa B-[Bonheur]

Painted at Fort Union in 1832. Catlin believed that in the Blackfoot and Crow tribes he had at last found the perfection of aboriginal life, and his month-long visit to the mouth of the Yellowstone was perhaps the most satisfying and productive time of his western travels. In full command of his craft, and inspired by the rich costumes and splendid physical appearance of his subjects, he painted some of his finest portraits, and one that may well rank as his masterpiece, Buffalo Bull's Back Fat. Broadly yet firmly modeled, with incisive detail and bold color, the portrait is as accomplished as any painted on the Missouri River voyage. But more compelling is Catlin's measure of the impassive, brooding stare of the chief, who seems perplexed and challenged, in spite of his imposing appearance, by the unfamiliar circumstances in which he finds himself.

Catlin must also have recognized the importance of the work, as it was one of two he entered in the Salon of 1846, perhaps after some additional finishing. Both paintings made a lasting impression on Baudelaire, who praised the noble and spirited character of the Indians, and the primitive strength of Catlin's reds and greens (see Beetem and no. 521). Ewers (1949) compares the portrait to Karl Bodmer's watercolor of the same subject (illustrated here), in which the features are recorded with extreme detail. Catlin's work seems accurate enough by comparison and conveys a far greater range of drama and insight.

Buffalo Bull's Back Fat becomes a full-length seated figure in plate 11 of Letters and Notes and cartoon 39 (NGA 1986). He is accompanied by his wife (no. 150) and a Blackfoot medicine man in the latter.

150. Crystal Stone, wife of the chief
Blackfoot, 1832
29 x 24 (73.7 x 60.9)

"I have also placed upon my canvass [Crystal Stone]; her countenance is rather pleasing, which is an uncommon thing amongst the Blackfeet— her dress is made of skins, and being the youngest of a bevy of six or eight, and the last one taken under his [the chief's] guardianship, was smiled upon with great satisfaction" (*Letters and Notes*, vol. 1, p. 30, pl. 13).

References: 1837 catalogue, no. 127; Donaldson, p. 102; Haberly, p. 59; Ewers (1956), p. 508; *Catlin, Bodmer, Miller,* reprod. p. 11.

Version:
Gilcrease Institute, NAI sketchbook (4776.3), pen and ink

Copy:
British Museum, London, by John Cullum, watercolor, 13 x 10¼ (1842-1844)

Painted at Fort Union in 1832. Crystal Stone also appears, full length, in cartoon 39 (NGA 1986), with her husband (no. 149).

151. Buffalo's Child, a warrior
Blackfoot, 1832
29 x 24 (73.7 x 60.9)

Described by Catlin as "a warrior, full-length, with *medicine-bag* of otter-skin" (1848 catalogue, p. 20).

References: 1837 catalogue, no. 122; *Letters and Notes,* vol. 1, pp. 30, 34, pl. 16; Donaldson, p. 103; Ewers (1956), p. 509; Gilcrease catalogue, p. 51.

Versions:
Gilcrease Institute, watercolor, 10 x 8, signed lower right: Geo Catlin/1836
Rains Galleries, New York, Cornelius Michaelson sale, May 8, 1935, no. 71, watercolor, 9 x 8½
Gilcrease Institute, NAI sketchbook (4776.4), pen and ink

Painted at Fort Union in 1832. Catlin mistakenly identifies plate 16 in *Letters and Notes* as Iron Horn (no. 153), but then describes the same figure as Buffalo's Child in the 1848 catalogue. The subject appears again as the central figure in cartoon 38 (NGA 1985), which is based on a watercolor (pl. 22) in the Gilcrease *Souvenir* album.
The Gilcrease watercolor listed above, which has always been labeled *Buffalo's Child,* is identical to plate 16 in *Letters and Notes* and the Smithsonian oil. A comparison of the facial expression in the Gilcrease and Smithsonian portraits reveals, as usual, that the latter is the life study (see nos. 62, 107). In his letters from Fort Union, Catlin often refers to the canvases upon which he painted his portraits.

150

151

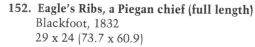

152. Eagle's Ribs, a Piegan chief (full length)
Blackfoot, 1832
29 x 24 (73.7 x 60.9)

"This man is one of the extraordinary men of the Blackfoot tribe; though not a chief, he stands here in the Fort, and deliberately boasts of eight scalps, which he says he has taken from the heads of trappers and traders with his own hand. His dress is really superb, almost literally covered with scalplocks, of savage and civil.
"I have painted him at full length, with a headdress made entirely of ermine skins and horns of the buffalo. This custom of wearing horns beautifully polished and surmounting the head-dress, is a very curious one, being worn only by the bravest of the brave; by the most extraordinary men in the nation. . . . When he stood for his picture, he also held a lance and two 'medicine-bags' in his hand" (*Letters and Notes,* vol. 1, pp. 30, 34, pl. 14).

References: 1837 catalogue, no. 131, p. 36; Donaldson, p. 103, pl. 44; Haberly, p. 59; Ewers (1956), p. 509; McCracken, pp. 66, 68, 70; Hartmann, p. 34; Ewers (1965), reprod. p. 78; Rossi and Hunt, pp. 69, 320; Gilcrease catalogue, p. 51.

Version:
Gilcrease Institute, NAI sketchbook (4776.3), pen and ink

Copy:
M. Knoedler & Co., New York (until 1971), pencil and water color, signed lower right:
Rosa B-[Bonheur]

Painted from life at Fort Union in 1832, according to a certificate signed by John Sanford, Indian

152

agent, that survives in Smithsonian files. The certificate also states that Catlin accurately reproduced the costume worn by the sitter.
Eagle's Ribs appears again in cartoon 40 (AMNH 120), with his wife and a Blackfoot warrior. The cartoon is based on a watercolor (pl. 20) in the Gilcrease *Souvenir* album, and an oil-on-canvas version of the composition is in the Museum für Völkerkunde, Berlin.

153

157

155

155. Woman Who Strikes Many
Blackfoot, 1832
29 x 24 (73.7 x 60.9)

Described by Catlin as a full-length portrait, with the subject "in a beautiful dress of the mountain-goats' skins, and her robe of the young buffalo's hide" (*Letters and Notes*, vol. 1, p. 34, pl. 17).

References: 1837 catalogue, no. 129; Donaldson, p. 103; Quimby, pp. 62-63; Ewers (1956), p. 509; *Catlin, Bodmer, Miller*; Gilcrease catalogue, p. 51.

Versions:
Field Museum of Natural History, 28 x 23

Gilcrease Institute, NAI sketchbook (4776.3), pen and ink

Painted at Fort Union in 1832. The markings on the subject's buffalo robe and the height of the skin lodge in the background vary slightly between the Field Museum and Smithsonian portraits (see·no. 3). The latter more closely matches plate 17 in *Letters and Notes*.

Woman Who Strikes Many appears again in cartoon 38 (NGA 1985, see no. 151).

156. The Hill
Blackfoot, 1832
Unlocated

References: 1837 catalogue, no. 130; Donaldson, p. 103.

Painted at Fort Union in 1832. One of several unidentified portraits in the O'Fallon collection may be a later version of this subject (see no. 83).

157. Bear's Child
Blackfoot, 1832
29 x 24 (73.7 x 60.9)

The subject holds a war club, according to Catlin (1848 catalogue, p. 21).

References: 1837 catalogue, no. 126; *Letters and Notes*, vol. 1, p. 30; Donaldson, p. 103; Haberly, p. 59; Ewers (1956), p. 509.

Painted at Fort Union in 1832.

153. Iron Horn, a warrior
Blackfoot, 1832
29 x 24 (73.7 x 60.9)

Catlin describes Iron Horn as a "warrior, in a splendid dress" (1848 catalogue, p. 20).

References: 1837 catalogue, no. 133; *Letters and Notes*, vol. 1, pp. 30, 34; Donaldson, p. 103; Haberly, p. 59; Ewers (1956), p. 509; McCracken, pp. 68, 155, reprod. p. 69; Gilcrease catalogue, p. 51.

Painted at Fort Union in 1832 (see no. 149). Certain Blackfoot portraits are closely related to the Sioux series (see no. 85). Catlin apparently confused the names of Iron Horn and Buffalo's Child (no. 151) when identifying plate 16 in *Letters and Notes*. Iron Horn also appears, full length, in cartoon 38 (NGA 1985), in a different pose and costume.

154. He Who Runs Down the Hill
Blackfoot, 1832
Unlocated

References: 1837 catalogue, no. 128; Donaldson, p. 103; McCracken, p. 70; Gilcrease catalogue, p. 51.

Painted at Fort Union in 1832. One of several unidentified portraits in the O'Fallon collection (see no. 83) may be a later version of this subject, who also appears, full length, in cartoon 40 (AMNH 120, see no. 152).

158. White Buffalo, an aged medicine man
   Blackfoot, 1832
   29 x 24 (73.7 x 60.9)

"I have also transferred to my canvass the 'looks and very resemblance' of an aged chief, who combines with his high office, the envied title of mystery or medicine-man, i.e. doctor—magician—prophet—soothsayer—jongleur—and high priest, all combined in one person, who necessarily is looked upon as 'Sir Oracle' of the nation. . . . on his left arm he presents his mystery-drum or tambour, in which are concealed the hidden and sacred mysteries of his healing art" (*Letters and Notes*, vol. 1, p. 34, pl. 15).

References: 1837 catalogue, no. 124; Donaldson, p. 103; Ewers (1956), p. 509; McCracken, p. 68, reprod. p. 17; Museum of Fine Arts, Boston, *Frontier America: The Far West* (1975), no. 35.

Version:
Gilcrease Institute, NAI sketchbook (4776.3), pen and ink

Copy:
M. Knoedler & Co., New York (until 1971), pencil and watercolor, signed lower right:
Rosa B-[Bonheur]

Painted at Fort Union in 1832 (see nos. 149, 161). White Buffalo also appears in cartoon 39 (NGA 1986).

159. Grandson of Buffalo Bull's Back Fat
   Blackfoot, 1832
   29 x 24 (73.7 x 60.9)
   [Figure 89]

"The grandson also of this sachem, a boy of six years of age, and too young as yet to have acquired a name, has stood forth like a tried warrior; and I have painted him at full length, with his bow and quiver slung, and his robe made of a raccoon skin. The history of this child is somewhat curious and interesting; his father is dead, and in case of the death of the chief . . . he becomes hereditary chief of the tribe. This boy has been twice stolen away by the Crows by ingenious stratagems, and twice re-captured by the Blackfeet, at considerable sacrifice of life, and at present he is lodged with Mr. M'Kenzie, for safe keeping and protection, until he shall arrive at the proper age to take the office to which he is to succeed" (*Letters and Notes*, vol. 1, p. 30, pl. 12).

References: 1837 catalogue, no. 125; Donaldson, p. 103; Ewers (1956), p. 509; McCracken, p. 68, reprod. p. 62; *Catlin, Bodmer, Miller*; Gilcrease catalogue, p. 51.

Versions:
Gilcrease Institute, 28 x 23
Gilcrease Institute, NAI sketchbook (4776.3), pen and ink

Painted at Fort Union in 1832. The true proportions of such a diminutive figure were still beyond Catlin's reach, but the appealing roundness of the little boy effectively conveys his age. The face and figure in the Gilcrease portrait are only a stylized approximation of the original (see no. 125).

160. Eagle's Ribs, a Piegan chief (half-length)
   Blackfoot, 1832
   29 x 24 (73.7 x 60.9)

References: 1837 catalogue, no. 123; Donaldson, pp. 103-4; Ewers (1956), p. 509; Paris (1963), no. 21.

Painted at Fort Union in 1832 (see nos. 149, 153). Eagle's Ribs is also the subject of a more elaborate full-length portrait by Catlin (see no. 152).

161

162

prod. p. 74; Emily Wasserman, "The Artist Explorers," *Art in America* 60 (July 1972), reprod. p. 48; Paris (1963), no. 22, pl. 5; Ewers (1965), p. 82; Haverstock, reprod. p. 60; Gilcrease catalogue, p. 51; National Museum of Man, Ottawa, *"Bo'jou, Neejee!": Profiles of Canadian Indian Art* (1976), reprod. p. 185.

Version:
Gilcrease Institute, NAI sketchbook (4776.4), pen and ink

Copy:
M. Knoedler & Co., New York (until 1971), pencil and watercolor, signed lower right:
Rosa B-[Bonheur]

Painted at Fort Union in 1832. The medicine man also appears in a watercolor (pl. 30, labeled *White Buffalo)* in the Gilcrease *Souvenir* album, and in cartoon 185 (AMNH 122), practicing his ritual before a crowd of Indians. The scene must have inspired a somewhat similar painting at Beaver House in London by the British artist C. P. Manley.

161. Medicine man, performing his mysteries over a dying man
Blackfoot, 1832
29 x 24 (73.7 x 60.9)

"[The medicine man] approached the ring [of spectators] with his body in a crouching position, with a slow and tilting step—his body and head were entirely covered with the skin of a yellow bear, the head of which (his own head being inside of it) served as a mask; the huge claws of which also, were dangling on his wrists and ancles; in one hand he shook a frightful rattle, and in the other brandished his medicine-spear or magic wand; to the rattling din and discord of all of which, he added the wild and startling jumps and yelps of the Indian, and horrid and appalling grunts, and snarls, and growls of the grizzly bear, in ejaculatory and guttural incantations to the Good and Bad Spirits, in behalf of his patient; who was rolling and groaning in the agonies of death, whilst he was dancing around him, jumping over him, and pawing him about, and rolling him in every direction" (*Letters and Notes*, vol. 1, pp. 39-41, pl. 19).

References: 1837 catalogue, nos. 134, 487; Donaldson, p. 104, pl. 45; Haberly, pp. 61-62; Ewers (1956), p. 509; McCracken, pp. 70-72, re-

162. Four Wolves, a chief in mourning
Crow, 1832
29 x 24 (73.7 x 60.9)

"A fine looking fellow, six feet in stature, and whose natural hair sweeps the grass as he walks; he is beautifully clad, and carries himself with the most graceful and manly mien—he is in mourning for a brother; and according to their custom, has cut off a number of locks of his long hair, which is as much as a man can well spare of so valued an ornament, which he has been for the greater part of his life cultivating" (*Letters and Notes*, vol. 1, p. 50, pl. 24).

References: 1837 catalogue, no. 96; Donaldson, p. 107; Ewers (1956), p. 510.

Version:
Gilcrease Institute, NAI sketchbook (4776.6), pen and ink

Painted at Fort Union in 1832 (see no. 149). The style of several Crow portraits is again similar to the Sioux series (see nos. 153, 85). Four Wolves also appears, full length, in cartoon 27 (NGA 1978).

163. He Who Ties His Hair Before

164. Two Crows, a Band chief
Crow, 1832
29 x 24 each (73.7 x 60.9)

"I have also secured portraits of [the two subjects] . . . fine and fair specimens of this tribe, in both of which are exhibited the extraordinary instances of the natural hair reaching to the ground, peculiarities belonging almost exclusively to this tribe. . . . The Crows are generally handsome, and comfortably clad; every man in the nation oils his hair with a profusion of bear's grease, and promotes its growth to the utmost of his ability. . . .

"In a former letter I gave some account of the head peculiar to this tribe, which may well be recorded as a national characteristic. . . . This striking peculiarity is quite conspicuous in the two portraits of which I have just spoken, exhibiting fairly, as they are both in profile, the *semi-lunar* outline of the face. . . . The greater part of the men are thus strongly marked with a bold and prominent anti-angular nose, with a clear and rounded arch, and a low and receding forehead" (*Letters and Notes*, vol. 1, p. 193, pls. 77, 78).

References: 1837 catalogue, nos. 97, 98; Donaldson, p. 107; (163) Quimby, pp. 72-73; Ewers (1956), p. 510; (164) McCracken, p. 75; (163) *Catlin, Bodmer, Miller;* (163) Paris (1963), no. 23; (163) Gilcrease catalogue, p. 52.

Versions:
(163) Field Museum of Natural History, 28 x 23
(163) Gilcrease Institute, watercolor, 10½ x 8½, signed lower right: Geo. Catlin 1836
(163) Rains Galleries, New York, Cornelius Michaelson sale, May 8, 1935, no. 71, 9 x 8½
Gilcrease Institute, NAI sketchbook (4776.11), pen and ink

Copy:
M. Knoedler & Co., New York (until 1971), pencil and watercolor, signed lower right:
Rosa B-[Bonheur]

Painted at the Hidatsa village in 1832. These two portraits, among the finest of the Upper Missouri series, represent the sum of Catlin's admiration for the tall and elegant Crow warriors (see no. 149).
In the Field Museum version, the robe of the subject (fig. 142; no. 163) lacks certain decorative details and his profile is a hasty caricature of the Smithsonian original (see no. 3). Otherwise, the two oils and the Gilcrease watercolor closely resemble one another and plate 77 in *Letters and Notes* (see no. 151). Cartoon 122 (unlocated) may be another oil-on-canvas version of number 163.
Catlin must have inadvertently reversed the plate numbers for the two subjects in his text. He describes Two Crows correctly in the 1848 catalogue as wearing a "head-dress made of the ea-

gle's skin entire" and holding "his lance and two *medicine*-bags."
Two Crows appears again in cartoon 27 (NGA 1978), with his wife and several Crow warriors. He Who Ties His Hair Before is shown in cartoon 25 (formerly AMNH), which is based on a watercolor (pl. 24) in the Gilcrease *Souvenir* album.

165. Hó-ra-tó-a, a brave
Crow, 1832
29 x 24 (73.7 x 60.9)

Described by Catlin as "a brave, wrapped in his robe, and his hair reaching to the ground; his spear in his hand, and bow and quiver slung" (1848 catalogue, p. 22).

References: 1837 catalogue, no. 99; Donaldson, p. 107; Ewers (1956), p. 510.

Painted at Fort Union in 1832. The subject also appears in cartoon 27 (NGA 1978), in a different costume.

166. Woman Who Lives in a Bear's Den
Crow, 1832
29 x 24 (73.7 x 60.9)

Catlin describes the subject as having her hair cut off in mourning (1848 catalogue, p. 22).

References: 1837 catalogue, no. 100; *Letters and Notes*, vol. 1, p. 50, pl. 25; Donaldson, p. 107; Ewers (1956), p. 510; McCracken, reprod. p. 79; *America as Art*, no. 158, reprod. p. 159.

Version:
Gilcrease Institute, NAI sketchbook (4776.6), pen and ink

Copy:
M. Knoedler & Co., New York (until 1971), pencil and watercolor, signed lower right:
Rosa B-[Bonheur]

Painted at Fort Union in 1832. The full, strong features and direct gaze indicate a surprising rapport between subject and artist. The woman appears again, full length, in cartoon 27 (NGA 1978), with a blanket wrapped around her.

166

167

168

as in the present instance" (*Letters and Notes,* vol. 1, p. 50, pl. 27).

References: 1837 catalogue, no. 102; Donaldson, p. 108; Ewers (1956), p. 510; Ewers (1965), reprod. p. 83.

Version:
Gilcrease Institute, NAI sketchbook (4776.34), pen and ink

Copy:
M. Knoedler & Co., New York (until 1971), pencil and watercolor, signed lower right:
Rosa B-[Bonheur]

Painted at Fort Union in 1832. Note how simply, but firmly, Catlin establishes the planes of Two Crow's unorthodox skull structure.

The subject also appears, full length, in cartoon 27 (NGA 1978).

169. Very Sweet Man
Crow, 1832
29 x 24 (73.7 x 60.9)

The subject wears over his temples a pair of hair bows, decorated with beads imported from Venice in the 1830s by white traders on the Upper Missouri (Ewers, 1968).

References: 1837 catalogue, no. 103; Donaldson, p. 108; Haberly, p. 95; Ewers (1956), p. 510; McCracken, reprod. p. 69; Ewers (1968), pp. 94-96.

Painted at Fort Union in 1832. Very Sweet Man is supposed to appear again in cartoon 25 (formerly AMNH), but the designated figure is unrelated to the Smithsonian portrait (see no. 163).

170. He Who Jumps over Everyone
Crow, 1832-1833
Unlocated

"I have said that no part of the human race could present a more picturesque and thrilling appearance on horseback than a party of Crows. . . . They may be justly said to be the most beautifully clad of all the Indians in these regions. . . .

"From amongst these showy fellows who have been entertaining us and pleasing themselves with their extraordinary feats of horsemanship, I have selected one of the most conspicuous, and transferred him and his horse, with arms and trappings, as faithfully as I could to the canvass. . . .

"I have painted him as he sat for me, balanced on his leaping wild horse with his shield and quiver slung on his back, and his long lance decorated with the eagle's quills, trailed in his right hand. His shirt and his leggings, and moccasins, were of the mountain-goat skins; beautifully dressed; and

167. Red Bear, a distinguished warrior
Crow, 1832
29 x 24 (73.7 x 60.9)

References: 1837 catalogue, no. 101; *Letters and Notes,* vol. 1, p. 50, pl. 26; Donaldson, p. 107; Ewers (1956), p. 510.

Copies:
M. Knoedler & Co., New York (until 1971), pencil and watercolor, signed lower right:
Rosa B-[Bonheur]

British Museum, London, by John Cullum, watercolor, 12¾ x 10¼ (1842)

Painted at Fort Union in 1832. Red Bear appears again, full length, in cartoon 27 (NGA 1978).

168. Two Crows, the younger
Crow, 1832
29 x 24 (73.7 x 60.9)

"I have also painted [Two Crows, the younger] . . . one of the most extraordinary men in the Crow nation; not only for his looks, from the form of his head, which seems to be distortion itself—and curtailed of all its fair proportions; but from his extraordinary sagacity as a counsellor and orator, even at an early stage of his life.

"There is something very uncommon in this outline, and sets forth the striking peculiarity of the Crow tribe, though rather in an exaggerated form. The semi-lunar outline of the Crow head, with an exceedingly low and retreating forehead, is certainly a very peculiar . . . characteristic . . . though not so strongly marked in most of the tribe their seams everywhere fringed with a profusion of scalp-locks taken from the heads of his enemies slain in battle. His long hair, which reached almost to the ground whilst he was standing on his feet, was now lifted in the air, and floating in black waves over the hips of his leaping charger. On his head, and over his shining black locks, he wore a magnificent crest or head-dress, made of the quills of the war-eagle and ermine skins; and on his horse's head also was another of equal beauty and precisely the same in pattern and material. Added to these ornaments there were yet many others which contributed to his picturesque appearance, and amongst them a beautiful netting of various colours, that completely covered and almost obscured the horse's head and neck, and extended over its back and its hips, terminating in a most extravagant and magnificent crupper, embossed and fringed with rows of beautiful shells and porcupine quills of various colours" (*Letters and Notes*, vol. 1, pp. 191-93, pl. 76).

References: 1837 catalogue, no. 104; Donaldson, p. 111; Haberly, p. 58; Kennedy catalogue, p. 8; McCracken, pp. 18, 77-78, 92; Hartmann, p. 35; Ewers (1965), p. 90; Ewers (1968), p. 196; Rossi and Hunt, pp. 60, 320; Gilcrease catalogue, p. 52.

Versions:
Museum für Völkerkunde, Berlin, 48 x 67 cm, signed lower right: Catlin./54
Collection of Mr. and Mrs. Paul Mellon, Upperville, Virginia, 1850s, 21⅜ x 26¾, signed lower right: G. Catlin
Gilcrease Institute, NAI sketchbook (4776.35 and .62), pen and ink

Copy:
M. Knoedler & Co., New York (until 1971), pencil and watercolor, signed lower right: Rosa B-[Bonheur]

Sketched at the Hidatsa village in 1832. The splendor of the equestrian performance Catlin describes must have inspired him to attempt his most elaborate portrait. The original was clearly a studio composition, painted with a print of Titian's *Charles V at Mühlberg* not far away. Ewers (1968) points out how Catlin's portrait and other ideal images of Plains culture came to represent the North American Indian (see no. 128).

The same horse and rider are repeated in cartoon 28, although with decorative accessories somewhat different from those in plate 76 of *Letters and Notes.* The Mellon version (fig. 98; formerly AMNH 179) was apparently exhibited with the cartoon collection. A similar watercolor, plate 28 in the Gilcrease *Souvenir* album, appears to be the source for both the Mellon and Berlin versions. The subject appears again, as a full-length standing figure, in cartoons 25 and 26 (formerly AMNH; NGA 1977), which are based on watercolors (pls. 24, 26) in the Gilcrease *Souvenir* album.

171. Black Moccasin, aged chief
Hidatsa, 1832
29 x 24 (73.7 x 60.9)
[Figure 88]

169

"The chief sachem of this tribe is a very ancient and patriarchal looking man . . . and counts, undoubtedly, more than an hundred *snows.* I have been for some days an inmate of his hospitable lodge, where he sits tottering with age, and silently reigns sole monarch of his little community around him, who are continually dropping in to cheer his sinking energies, and render him their homage. His voice and his sight are nearly gone; but the gestures of his hands are yet energetic and youthful, and freely speak the language of his kind heart.

"I have . . . painted his portrait as he was seated on the floor of his wigwam, smoking his pipe, whilst he was recounting over to me some of the extraordinary feats of his life, with a beautiful Crow robe wrapped around him, and his hair wound up in a conical form upon his head, and fastened with a small wooden pin, to keep it in its place.

"This man has many distinct recollections of Lewis and Clark, who were the first explorers of this country, and who crossed the Rocky Mountains thirty years ago" (*Letters and Notes*, vol. 1, pp. 186-87, pl. 72).

References: 1837 catalogue, no. 158; Donaldson, p. 115, pl. 46; Matthews, p. 604, pl. 142; Ewers (1956), pp. 494, 512, pl. 4; McCracken, pp. 112, 115; Ewers (1965), reprod. p. 70; Gilcrease catalogue, p. 52.

Versions:
Gilcrease Institute, 28 x 23
Gilcrease Institute, watercolor, 9 x 6½, signed lower right (on mount): Geo Catlin
Gilcrease Institute, NAI sketchbook (4776.35), pen and ink

Painted at the Hidatsa village in 1832. The sightless attention of Black Moccasin's ancient head, and the shriveled body that supports it, are portrayed by Catlin with a deep sympathy for the chief's age and position (see no. 55). Although the artist committed his usual anatomical indiscretions in the process, Matthews says that the portrait was easily recognized by Black Moccasin's descendants.

The Smithsonian and Gilcrease oils, and plate 72 in *Letters and Notes,* are almost identical; but the post on which the arms and ornaments hang has been left out of the Gilcrease watercolor, and the torso and blanket are badly drawn (see nos. 125, 151).

Black Moccasin also appears, for some unexplained reason, in number 503 *(Interior of a Mandan Lodge),* and in cartoon 34 (NGA 2034), surrounded by his family.

172

174

173

172. Red Thunder, son of Black Moccasin
Hidatsa, 1832
29 x 24 (73.7 x 60.9)

"The son of Black Moccasin . . . who is reputed one of the most desperate warriors of his tribe, I have also painted at full length, in his war-dress, with his bow in his hand, his quiver slung, and his shield upon his arm. In this plight, *sans* headdress, *sans* robe, and *sans* everything that might be an useless incumbrance—with the body chiefly naked, and profusely bedaubed with red and black paint, so as to form an almost perfect disguise, the Indian warriors invariably sally forth to war" (*Letters and Notes*, vol. 1, p. 187, pl. 73).

References: 1837 catalogue, no. 159; Donaldson, pp. 115-16; Ewers (1956), p. 512; McCracken, p. 65; *Catlin, Bodmer, Miller,* reprod. p. 11; Gilcrease catalogue, p. 52.

Versions:
Gilcrease Institute, watercolor, 7 x 5¼, signed lower right (on mount): Geo. Catlin

Gilcrease Institute, NAI sketchbook (4776.46), pen and ink

Copy:
M. Knoedler & Co., New York (until 1971), pencil and watercolor, signed lower right:
Rosa B-[Bonheur]

Painted at the Hidatsa village in 1832. The Gilcrease portrait is only three-quarter length, and Red Thunder's figure is weakly drawn (see no. 171). He appears again in cartoon 35 (NGA 2035), which is based on a watercolor (pl. 38) in the Gilcrease *Souvenir* album.

173. Two Crows, a chief
Hidatsa, 1832
29 x 24 (73.7 x 60.9)

The subject was dressed, according to Catlin, in "a handsome shirt, ornamented with ermine, and necklace of grisly bear's claws" (1848 catalogue, p. 22).

References: 1837 catalogue, no. 160; Donaldson, p. 116; Ewers (1956), p. 512.

Painted at the Hidatsa village in 1832. The portrait follows the style of the Sioux series (see no. 69). Karl Bodmer made two full-length watercolors of the subject a year and a half later (see Reuben Gold Thwaites, ed., *Early Western Travels 1748-1846,* pls. 50, 56). Catlin's portrait somewhat resembles the figure in plate 50.

174. Wife of Two Crows
Hidatsa, 1832
29 x 24 (73.7 x 60.9)

References: 1837 catalogue, no. 162½; Donaldson, p. 116; Ewers (1956), p. 512.

Painted at the Hidatsa village in 1832 (see no. 173).

175. Midday Sun, a pretty girl
Hidatsa, 1832
29 x 24 (73.7 x 60.9)

"Besides chiefs and warriors to be admired in this little tribe, there are many beautiful and voluptuous looking women, who are continually crowding in throngs, and gazing upon a stranger. . . .
"The one whom I have painted is a descendant from the old chief; and though not the most beautiful, is yet a fair sample of them, and dressed in a beautiful costume of the mountain-sheep skin, handsomely garnished with porcupine quills and beads. This girl was almost *compelled* to stand for her picture by her relatives who urged her on, whilst she modestly declined, offering as her excuse that 'she was not pretty enough, and that her picture would be laughed at.' This was either ignorance or excessive art on her part; for she was more than comely" (*Letters and Notes*, vol. 1, pp. 187-88, pl. 74).

References: 1837 catalogue, no. 162; Donaldson, p. 116; Ewers (1956), p. 512; Gilcrease catalogue, p. 52.

Versions:
Gilcrease Institute, watercolor, 9 x 7, signed lower right: Geo C[atlin 183]6
Rains Gallery, New York, Cornelius Michaelson sale, May 8, 1935, no. 71, watercolor, 9 x 8½
Gilcrease Institute, NAI sketchbook (4776.7), pen and ink

Copy:
M. Knoedler & Co., New York (until 1971), watercolor, signed lower right:
Rosa B-[Bonheur]

Painted at the Hidatsa village in 1832. Jewelry and costume details vary between the Gilcrease and Smithsonian portraits (see no. 151). The latter is identical to plate 74 in *Letters and Notes*, except for the earth lodges in the background, which are missing from the plate.

Midday Sun also appears in cartoon 35 (NGA 2035), which is based on a watercolor (pl. 38) in the Gilcrease *Souvenir* album.

176. He Who Has Eyes Behind Him (also known as Broken Arm), a foremost brave
Plains Cree, 1831
29 x 24 (73.7 x 60.9)

The subject wears over his temples a pair of "hair pipes," Bahamian conch shell ornaments distributed in the 1830s by white traders on the Upper Missouri (Ewers, 1968).

References: 1837 catalogue, no. 278; *Letters and Notes*, vol. 1, p. 57, pl. 30; Donaldson, p. 118; Ewers (1956), p. 510; Ewers (1965), reprod. p. 68; Ewers (1968), pp. 79-80, 88-90, pl. 10.

Version:
Gilcrease Institute, NAI sketchbook (4776.34), pen and ink

Painted in St. Louis in 1831 (Ewers, 1968). Donaldson's date is incorrect. Broken Arm accompanied The Light on his ill-fated journey to Washington (see nos. 179, 474).

The subject appears again, full length, in cartoon 76 (NGA 2082), with his wife and child.

177. Great Wonder, carrying her baby in her robe
Plains Cree, 1832
29 x 24 (73.7 x 60.9)

Described by Catlin as a "full length portrait of a young woman with a child on her back, showing fairly the fashion of cutting and ornamenting the

 175

 176

dresses of the females in this tribe" (*Letters and Notes*, vol. 1, pp. 57-58, pl. 33).

References: 1837 catalogue, no. 276; Donaldson, p. 118; Haberly, p. 95; Ewers (1956), p. 510; *Catlin, Bodmer, Miller.*

Version:
Gilcrease Institute, NAI sketchbook (4776.34), pen and ink

Copy:
British Museum, London, by John Cullum, watercolor, 12⅝ x 10¼ (1842-1844)

Painted at Fort Union in 1832. Catlin mistakenly labels a small boy in cartoon 76 as *Great Wonder, son of Broken Arm* (no. 176). The incorrect identification of cartoon figures has been frequently noted (see nos. 89, 116).

 177

garnished with quills of the porcupine, and fringed with locks of scalps, taken from his enemies' heads. Over these floated his long hair in plaits, that fell nearly to the ground" (*Letters and Notes,* vol. 1, pp. 55-57, pl. 28; vol. 2, p. 196).

See number 474 for additional biographical information.

References: 1837 catalogue, no. 187; Donaldson, pp. 118-19; Ewers (1956), pp. 498, 508, pl. 11; McCracken, pp. 42-43; Ewers (1968), pp. 78-79, pl. 9; Montreal Museum of Fine Arts, *The Painter and the New World* (1967), no. 178a, reprod.; Parke-Bernet Galleries, New York, Redwood Library Collection (May 21, 1970), no. 18.

Version:
Gilcrease Institute, NAI sketchbook (4776.34), pen and ink

Painted in St. Louis in the fall of 1831, when The Light was enroute to Washington. Donaldson's date is incorrect. Ewers (1956) comments on the accuracy with which Catlin reproduced the three-row quillwork design on the subject's sleeve. The rendering of detail does seem more certain in this portrait than in the 1830 series (nos. 237-55), and the firm modeling of the subject's head marks a progression toward the style of Upper Missouri portraits (see no. 69). The Light was painted by Charles Bird King in Washington (see Parke-Bernet catalogue), and he appears again, full length, in cartoon 75 (NGA 1990), with his wife and children.

178. Tow-ée-ka-wet, a Cree woman
Plains Cree, 1832
29 x 24 (73.7 x 60.9)

References: 1837 catalogue, no. 277; *Letters and Notes,* vol. 1, p. 57, pl. 31; Donaldson, p. 118; Ewers (1956), p. 510.

Version:
Gilcrease Institute, NAI sketchbook (4776.7), pen and ink

Painted at Fort Union in 1832. The subject's name has been changed in cartoon 76 (NGA 2082), where she appears as the wife of Broken Arm (no. 176).

179. Pigeon's Egg Head (The Light), a distinguished young warrior
Assiniboin, 1831
29 x 24 (73.7 x 60.9)

"*Wi-jun-jon* [The Light] . . . appeared as sullen as death in my painting-room—with eyes fixed like those of a statue, upon me, though his pride had plumed and tinted him in all the freshness and brilliancy of an Indian's toilet. In his nature's un-cowering pride he stood a perfect model; but superstition had hung a lingering curve upon his lip, and pride had stiffened it into contempt. . . .
"He was dressed in his native costume, which was classic and exceedingly beautiful; his leggings and shirt were of the mountain-goat skin, richly

180. Fire Bug that Creeps, wife of The Light
Assiniboin, 1832
29 x 24 (73.7 x 60.9)

"A fine looking squaw, in a handsome dress of the mountain-sheep skin, holding in her hand a stick curiously carved, with which every woman in this country is supplied; for the purpose of digging up the . . . prairie turnip" (*Letters and Notes,* vol. 1, p. 56, pl. 29).

References: 1837 catalogue, no. 186; Donaldson, p. 120; Ewers (1956), p. 508; McCracken, p. 63, reprod. p. 62; Paris (1963), no. 25.

Version:
Gilcrease Institute, NAI sketchbook (4776.7), pen and ink

Painted at Fort Union in 1832. The subject appears again, full length, in cartoon 75 (NGA 1990), with her husband (no. 179).

181. Assiniboin woman and child
Assiniboin, 1832
29 x 24 (73.7 x 60.9)

"The women of this tribe are often comely, and sometimes pretty; in plate 34, will be seen a fair illustration of the dresses of the women and children, which are usually made of the skins of the mountain-goat, and ornamented with porcupine's quills and rows of elk's teeth" (*Letters and Notes*, vol. 1, p. 57, pl. 34).

References: 1837 catalogue, no. 188; Donaldson, p. 120; Quimby, pp. 26-27; Ewers (1956), p. 508.

Versions:
Field Museum of Natural History, ca. 28 x 23
Gilcrease Institute, NAI sketchbook (4776.34), pen and ink

Painted at Fort Union in 1832. Although number 159 is a notable exception, Catlin's small children often look like shrunken adults. The Field Museum and Smithsonian portraits are alike, except for the seated child and skin lodges in the background of the latter (see no. 3). That same background is repeated in plate 34 of *Letters and Notes*.

182. The Six, chief of the Plains Ojibwa
Plains Ojibwa, 1832
29 x 24 (73.7 x 60.9)
[Figure 104]

"The chief of that part of the Ojibbeway tribe who inhabit these northern regions . . . is a man of huge size; with dignity of manner, and pride and vanity, just about in proportion to his bulk. He sat for his portrait in a most beautiful dress, fringed with scalp locks in profusion; which he had snatched, in his early life from his enemies' heads, and now wears as proud trophies and proofs of what his arm has accomplished in battles with his enemies. His shirt of buckskin is beautifully embroidered and painted in curious hieroglyphics, the history of his battles and charts of his life" (*Letters and Notes*, vol. 1, p. 58, pl. 35).

The Six wears a pair of "hair pipes" over his temples (see no. 176).

References: 1837 catalogue, no. 163; Donaldson, p. 122, pl. 47; Quimby, pp. 28-29; Ewers (1956), p. 514; *Catlin, Bodmer, Miller;* Paris (1963), no. 26; National Museum of Man, Ottawa, *"Bo'jou, Neejee!": Profiles of Canadian Indian Art* (1976), reprod. p. 189.

Versions:
Field Museum of Natural History, ca. 28 x 23
Gilcrease Institute, NAI sketchbook (4776.5), pen and ink (fig. 148)

Copy:
M. Knoedler & Co., New York (until 1971), pencil and watercolor, signed lower right:
Rosa B-[Bonheur]

Painted at Fort Union in 1832. The strongly modeled features of The Six remind one of the portraits of Horse Chief (no. 99) and The Surrounder (no. 117), other outstanding examples from the Upper Missouri series. The Six's expression in the Field Museum version is bland by comparison, although his costume seems to have been reproduced with comparable detail (see no. 3).

An inscription by the artist on the stretcher of the Field Museum version names the sitter as He Who Walks on the Sea (no. 190), but all of Catlin's publications confirm the present identification. The inscription does suggest, however, that Catlin was still delivering portraits to O'Fallon in 1835, the year in which he is supposed to have painted number 190.

The Six also appears, full length, in cartoon 12 (NGA 2051), with his wife and children.

183. Kay-a-gís-gis, a young woman
Plains Ojibwa, 1832
29 x 24 (73.7 x 60.9)
[Figure 93]

Described by Catlin as "a beautiful young woman pulling her hair out of braid" (1848 catalogue, p. 23).

References: 1837 catalogue, no. 175; Donaldson, p. 122; Ewers (1956), p. 514.

Painted at Fort Union in 1832, and one of Catlin's first attempts at facial expression in an Indian portrait. The smile, somewhat forced, but engagingly shy and self-conscious, is an indication of the artist's growing perception of individual qualities among subjects whose appearance had not been critically examined before.

184. Meeting Birds, a brave
Ojibwa, 1835-1836
29 x 24 (73.7 x 60.9)

Described by Catlin as "a brave, with his war-club in his hand" (1848 catalogue, p. 24).

References: 1837 catalogue, no. 164; Donaldson, p. 122; Ewers (1956), p. 520; M. Knoedler & Co., New York, *The American Indian Observed* (1971), no. 29, reprod. p. 22.

Painted at Fort Snelling in 1835, or near Sault Ste. Marie in 1836.

Copy:
M. Knoedler & Co., New York (until 1971), pencil and watercolor, signed lower right: Rosa B-[Bonheur]

Painted at Fort Snelling in 1835. Donaldson's date is again based on Catlin's faulty recollections (see no. 99). The subject also appears in cartoon 11 (NGA 2050), which is based on a watercolor (pl. 10) in the Gilcrease *Souvenir* album.

187. He Who Sits Everywhere, a brave
Ojibwa, 1835
29 x 24 (73.7 x 60.9)

"I have painted amongst the chippeways at this place, two distinguished young men [nos. 187, 189] . . . both . . . at full length, in full dress, and just as they were adorned and equipped, even to a quill and a trinket" (*Letters and Notes*, vol. 2, p. 139, pl. 242).

References: 1837 catalogue, no. 167; Donaldson, pp. 122-23; Ewers (1956), p. 520.

Version:
Gilcrease Institute, NAI sketchbook (4776.33), pen and ink

Copy:
M. Knoedler & Co., New York (until 1971), pencil and watercolor, signed lower right: Rosa B-[Bonheur]

Painted at Fort Snelling in 1835 (see no. 186). The subject supposedly appears again in cartoon 10 (NGA 2049), but he actually matches the central figure in cartoon 11, who is identified in the 1871 catalogue as The Ottaway (no. 188). Catlin frequently mislabeled the cartoon collection (see no. 116), and, in this instance, he also mislabeled plate 10 in the Gilcrease *Souvenir* album (see no. 186.)

188. The Ottaway, a warrior
Ojibwa, 1835
29 x 24 (73.7 x 60.9)

Described by Catlin as a "portrait of a warrior . . . with his pipe in his hand" (*Letters and Notes*, vol. 2, p. 139, pl. 244).

References: 1837 catalogue, no. 168; Donaldson, p. 123; Ewers (1956), p. 520.

Version:
Gilcrease Institute, NAI sketchbook (4776.20), pen and ink

185. He Who Tries the Ground with His Foot
Ojibwa, 1836
29 x 24 (73.7 x 60.9)

References: 1837 catalogue, no. 165; *Letters and Notes*, vol. 2, p. 162; Donaldson, p. 122; Ewers (1956), p. 520.

Painted near Sault Ste. Marie in 1836, and one of Catlin's more perfunctory portraits.

186. Jú-ah-kıs-gaw, woman with her child in a cradle
Ojibwa, 1835
29 x 24 (73.7 x 60.9)
[Figure 84]

Described by Catlin as "the portrait of a Chippeway woman . . . with her child in its crib or cradle . . . [the umbilicus] hanging before the child's face for its supernatural protector.
"The woman's dress was mostly made of civilized manufactures, but curiously decorated and ornamented according to Indian taste" (*Letters and Notes*, vol. 2, p. 139, pl. 245).

References: 1837 catalogue, no. 166; Donaldson, p. 122; Ewers (1956), p. 520; McCracken, reprod. p. 161; Haverstock, p. 136, reprod. p. 138; Gilcrease catalogue, p. 52; *America as Art*, no. 164, reprod. p. 163; National Museum of Man, Ottawa, *"Bo'jou, Neejee!": Profiles of Canadian Indian Art* (1976), reprod. p. 196.

Version:
Gilcrease Institute, NAI sketchbook (4776.32), pen and ink

Copy:
M. Knoedler & Co., New York (until 1971), pencil and watercolor, signed lower right:
Rosa B-[Bonheur]

Painted at Fort Snelling in 1835 (see no. 186). The Ottaway supposedly appears again in cartoon 11 (NGA 2050), but Catlin apparently mislabeled the figure (see no. 187).

189. He Who Travels Everywhere, a warrior
Ojibwa, 1835
29 x 24 (73.7 x 60.9)

See number 187. "The first of these two young men," Catlin continues, "is, no doubt, one of the most remarkable of his age to be found in the tribe. Whilst he was standing for his portrait, which was in one of the officer's quarters in the Fort, where there were some ten or fifteen of his enemies the Sioux, seated on the floor around the room; he told me to take particular pains in representing eight quills which were arranged in his head-dress, which he said stood for so many Sioux scalps that he had taken with his left hand, in which he was grasping his war-club, with which hand he told me he was in the habit of making all his blows" (*Letters and Notes*, vol. 2, p. 139, pl. 241).

References: 1837 catalogue, no. 169; Donaldson, p. 123; Ewers (1956), p. 514; Ewers, "The Opening of the West," *The Artist in America* (New York, 1967), p. 45; Denver Art Museum, *American Panorama* (1968), reprod. p. 19; Gilcrease catalogue, p. 52.

Version:
Gilcrease Institute, NAI sketchbook (4776.33), pen and ink

Copies:
M. Knoedler & Co., New York (until 1971), pencil and watercolor, signed lower right:
Rosa B-[Bonheur]
British Museum, London, by John Cullum, watercolor, 12¾ x 10¼ (1842-1844)

Catlin writes in *Letters and Notes* that the subject was painted at Fort Snelling in 1835, and the costume would seem to be that of an Eastern Ojibwa. In the Smithsonian files, however, is an original certificate for a life portrait of Ka-bés-hunk (He Who Travels Everywhere) painted at Fort Union in 1832 (see Ewers, 1967). The certificate is signed by Kenneth McKenzie, who was in charge of the fort during Catlin's visit. Perhaps the artist confused his characters again (see no. 187).
Cartoon 125 (unlocated) may be another version of the Smithsonian oil. The subject also appears in cartoon 11 (NGA 2050), which is based on a watercolor (pl. 10) in the Gilcrease *Souvenir* album.

190. He Who Walks on the Sea
Ojibwa, 1835-1836
Unlocated

References: 1837 catalogue, no. 170; Donaldson, p. 123.

Probably painted at Fort Snelling in 1835, or near Sault Ste. Marie in 1836.

191. Point that Remains Forever, an aged chief
Ojibwa, 1836
Unlocated

References: 1837 catalogue, no. 171; *Letters and Notes*, vol. 2, p. 162, pl. 269; Donaldson, p. 123; McCracken, p. 165; Gilcrease catalogue, p. 52.

Versions:
Gilcrease Institute, watercolor, 5½ x 5, signed lower right (on mount): G Catlin p
Gilcrease Institute, NAI sketchbook (4776.36), pen and ink

Painted from life in the presence of James L. Schoolcraft at Sault Ste. Marie in 1836, according to an original certificate in Smithsonian files. Plate 269 in *Letters and Notes* and the Gilcrease watercolor (illustrated here) are somewhat similar, although in the latter the subject is half length, and he wears a feather headdress and no necklaces (see no. 107).
The subject appears again in cartoon 10 (NGA 2049), with three Ojibwa warriors.

189

191

Gilcrease Institute, Tulsa.

192

194

192a.

Gilcrease Institute, Tulsa.

References: 1837 catalogue, no. 173; Donaldson, p. 123; Ewers (1956), p. 520; Gilcrease catalogue, p. 52.

Versions:
Gilcrease Institute, watercolor, 10 x 8

Gilcrease Institute, NAI sketchbook (4776.36), pen and ink

Copy:
M. Knoedler & Co., New York (until 1971), pencil and watercolor, signed lower right:
Rosa B-[Bonheur]

Painted from life in the presence of James L. Schoolcraft at Sault Ste. Marie in 1836, according to an original certificate in Smithsonian files. The Gilcrease and Smithsonian portraits are identical, except for bracelets and body paint designs, in which the latter matches plate 268 of *Letters and Notes* (see no. 151).

The Crow appears again in cartoon 10 (NGA 2049).

192. He Who Halloes
Ojibwa, 1836
29 x 24 (73.7 x 60.9)

The subject is described by Catlin as "civilized" (1848 catalogue, p. 24).

References: 1837 catalogue, no. 172; *Letters and Notes*, vol. 2, p. 162; Donaldson, p. 123, pl. 4; Ewers (1956), p. 520; Gilcrease catalogue, p. 52.

Version:
Gilcrease Institute, watercolor, 6 x 5, signed lower right (on mount): Geo. Catlin 1834

Painted from life in the presence of James L. Schoolcraft at Sault Ste. Marie in 1836, according to an original certificate in Smithsonian files (see Donaldson).

In the Gilcrease watercolor (illustration 192a), the subject is half-length, his shirt is plain, he wears no necklaces, and his features, though firmly modeled, differ somewhat from those in the Smithsonian portrait. The former may also be a life study, but the dates on the watercolors cannot be trusted (see no. 46).

193. The Crow, a dandy
Ojibwa, 1836
29 x 24 (73.7 x 60.9)
[Figure 107]

Described by Catlin as "a young man of distinction, in an extravagant and beautiful costume" (*Letters and Notes*, vol. 2, p. 162, pl. 268).

194. Male Caribou, a brave
Ojibwa, 1836
29 x 24 (73.7 x 60.9)

Described by Catlin as "a brave, with a war-club in his hand" (1848 catalogue, p. 24).

References: 1837 catalogue, no. 174; *Letters and Notes*, vol. 2, p. 162; Donaldson, p. 123; Ewers (1956), p. 520.

Painted from life in the presence of James L. Schoolcraft at Sault Ste. Marie in 1836, according to an original certificate in Smithsonian files. Male Caribou supposedly appears again in cartoon 10, but the designated figure bears no resemblance to the Smithsonian painting.

195. Wife of The Six
Plains Ojibwa, 1832
29 x 24 (73.7 x 60.9)
[Figure 90]

"Not the most agreeable" of The Six's several wives, according to Catlin (*Letters and Notes*, vol. 1, p. 58, pl. 36).

References: 1837 catalogue, no. 176; Donaldson, p. 123; Ewers (1956), p. 520.

Version:
Gilcrease Institute, NAI sketchbook (4776.5), pen and ink [fig. 148]

Copy:
M. Knoedler & Co., New York (until 1971), pencil and watercolor, signed lower right:
Rosa B-[Bonheur]

Painted at Fort Union in 1832. Donaldson must not have realized that the subject was the wife of a Plains Ojibwa. Catlin made few compromises in representing the blunt, heavy features and powerful contours of this woman's superbly aboriginal head. Such studies among the more civilized eastern tribes, whom he painted three or four years later, are rare (see nos. 184-94).

The subject appears again, full length, in cartoon 12 (NGA 2051), with her husband (no. 182).

196. Nót-to-way, a chief
Iroquois, 1835-1836
29 x 24 (73.7 x 60.9)

"Of this tribe I have painted but one. . . . This was an excellent man, and was handsomely dressed for his picture. . . . He seemed to be quite ignorant of the early history of his tribe, as well as of the position and condition of its few scattered remnants, who are yet in existence. . . . though he was an Iroquois, which he was proud to acknowledge to me . . . he wished it to be generally thought, that he was a Chippeway" (*Letters and Notes*, vol. 2, p. 107, pl. 206).

References: 1837 catalogue, no. 177; Donaldson, p. 125, pl. 48; Ewers (1956), p. 519; Gilcrease catalogue, p. 52.

Version:
Gilcrease Institute, NAI sketchbook (4776.30), pen and ink

Copy:
M. Knoedler & Co., New York (until 1971), pencil and watercolor, signed lower right:
Rosa B-[Bonheur]

Probably painted at Fort Snelling in 1835, or near Sault Ste. Marie in 1836, as Catlin seems to imply that the subject was living with the Ojibwa. Furthermore, the relaxed stance and costume of the figure are similar to several portraits in the Ojibwa series (see nos. 187, 189, 193), and the painting follows that series in numerical sequence in both the 1837 and 1848 catalogues. Donaldson's date of 1831 must again be based on Catlin's fictitious itinerary (see nos. 99, 31).

Nót-to-way also appears as *An Iroquois* in plate 1 of *Catlin's North American Indian Portfolio*, first published in 1844, and in cartoon 3 (NGA 2047), with his wife (no. 197) and an Iroquois warrior, although Catlin said he painted only one member of the tribe. The original version of the cartoon figure is in the Gilcrease *Souvenir* album (pl. 32).

197. Chée-ah-ká-tchée, wife of Nót-to-way
Iroquois, 1835-1836
29 x 24 (73.7 x 60.9)

References: 1837 catalogue, no. 178; Donaldson, pp. 125-26; Ewers (1956), p. 519; *Catlin, Bodmer, Miller; America as Art*, no. 171, reprod. p. 163.

See number 196 for explanation of the date. Catlin describes in detail similar cradles among the Eastern Sioux and Ojibwa (see no. 186). The subject supposedly appears again in cartoon 3 (NGA 2047), but the designated figure bears no resemblance to the Smithsonian painting.

198. Big Sail, a chief
Ottawa, probably 1836
29 x 24 (73.7 x 60.9)
[Figure 108]

Catlin describes Big Sail as "blind in one eye. The effects of whiskey and civilization are plainly discernible in this instance" (1848 catalogue, p. 24).

References: 1837 catalogue, no. 243; Donaldson, p. 126; Ewers (1956), pp. 485, 521; Haverstock, reprod. p. 43; *America as Art*, no. 160, reprod. p. 161.

Donaldson and Ewers maintain that the portrait was painted during a visit to Niagara Falls. The former thinks the visit occurred in 1831, and the latter, in the winter of 1829-30; but Catlin's circuit of 1831 was apparently limited to St. Louis, Philadelphia, Albany, and Great Bend, Pennsylvania, and during the winter of 1829-30 he stayed in Washington and Richmond. In the absence of other evidence, it seems safer to assume that the portrait was painted at Mackinac in 1836, where a remnant of the Ottawa tribe remained, interspersed among the Ojibwa. It is more likely, too, that such a perceptive and sympathetic response to Indian dissipation would have come at the end of Catlin's travels. In 1830 and 1831, his sustaining ambition was to paint those tribes untouched by the effects of civilization.

196

197

199-206

207

208

209

This hastily sketched group may have been one of Catlin's first attempts at Indian portraiture in the West. Later that summer he apparently worked in the neighborhood of Fort Leavenworth, with more encouraging results (see no. 237).

207. Man Who Puts All Out of Doors
Winnebago, 1835
29 x 24 (73.7 x 60.9)

Described by Catlin as "the largest man of the tribe, with rattle-snakes' skins on his arms, and his war-club in his hand" (*Letters and Notes,* vol. 2, p. 146, pl. 255).

References: 1837 catalogue, no. 206; Donaldson, p. 128; Ewers (1956), p. 523; *Catlin, Bodmer, Miller,* Paris (1963), no. 29.

Version:
Gilcrease Institute, NAI sketchbook (4776.26), pen and ink

Probably painted at Prairie du Chien in 1835, as the figure seems more closely related to the Eastern Sioux and Ojibwa series than to the previous portrait. The solid anatomy and stance of the subject, along with the more skillfully rendered costume details show Catlin making a marked improvement in the years that separate this painting from numbers 209 through 217 in the Winnebago series.

The subject also appears in cartoon 4 (AMNH 201).

208. The Wonder
Winnebago, 1835
29 x 24 (73.7 x 60.9)

References: 1837 catalogue, no. 216; Donaldson, *Notes,* vol. 2, p. 146; Donaldson, p. 128; Ewers (1956), p. 523.

Probably painted at Prairie du Chien in 1835, as the figure is more closely related to number 207 than to numbers 209 through 217.

199-206. Du-cór-re-a, chief of the tribe, and his family
Winnebago, probably 1830
24 x 29 (60.9 x 73.7)

References: 1837 catalogue, nos. 208-15; Donaldson, pp. 127-28; Ewers (1956), p. 523.

Probably painted at Prairie du Chien in 1830, as the size and style are noticeably different from the earlier Winnebago portraits (see no. 209). The chief died in 1834, so Catlin could not have seen him on one of his later visits to the Upper Mississippi.

209. Wood, former chief of the tribe
Winnebago, 1828
18½ x 14⅛ (47 x 35.7)

Described by Catlin as "the portrait of an old chief, who died a few years since; and who was for many years the head chief of the tribe. . . . This man has been much distinguished in his time, for his eloquence; and he desired me to paint him in the attitude of an orator, addressing his people" (*Letters and Notes,* vol. 2, p. 146, pl. 254).

References: 1837 catalogue, no. 216; Donaldson, pp. 128-29, pl. 49; Ewers (1956), p. 524; Roehm, p. 43.

Version:
Gilcrease Institute, NAI sketchbook (4776.26), pen and ink

Probably painted in Washington in the autumn of 1828, when a Winnebago delegation that included Wood visited several cities on the East Coast. According to Roehm, Catlin was in Washington at the time, having gone "south" (meaning Washington or Richmond) for his health in the winter of 1828-29. The portrait is unlike the style of number 199-206, and much less accomplished than the Fort Leavenworth series of 1830 (see nos. 237-55), or the Winnebago subjects Catlin painted at Prairie du Chien in 1835 (see no. 107). Besides, Wood died in 1833, a fact that must have escaped Donaldson when he assigned a date of 1835 to numbers 209 through 217, all of which have remarkably similar style characteristics.

These numbers in the Winnebago series are of uniformly smaller dimensions than the average Catlin portrait in the Smithsonian (see no. 218), and they are noticeably weak in technique and style. Each consists of a standing figure whose anatomy is ill-proportioned and partially obscured by a coarse blanket. Expressionless faces, built up with labored strokes, and costumes outlined in a harsh and perfunctory manner further contribute to their unsatisfactory appearance. The portraits are perhaps more reminiscent of Red Jacket (no. 263) than of future developments.

Charles Bird King painted a more detailed portrait of Wood in Washington (see McKenney and Hall, vol. 1, pp. 153-54), and the subject appears again in cartoon 4 (AMNH 201), with three Winnebago warriors.

210. Káw-kaw-ne-chóo-a, a brave
Winnebago, 1828
18⅜ x 14⅛ (46.7 x 35.7)

Described by Catlin, along with The Snake (no. 213), as full-length portraits and "fair specimens of the tribe, who are generally a rather short and thick-set, square shouldered set of men" (*Letters and Notes*, vol. 2, p. 146, pl. 256).

References: 1837 catalogue, no. 217; Donaldson, p. 129; Ewers (1956), p. 524.

Version:
Gilcrease Institute, NAI sketchbook (4776.26), pen and ink

Probably painted in Washington in the autumn of 1828 (see no. 209). Note the scale of the head and the absence of anatomy beneath the nondescript blanket.

At the extreme left of cartoon 4 (AMNH 201) is a figure who resembles the Smithsonian portrait, but he is incorrectly identified as Wood (no. 209) in the 1871 catalogue (see nos. 211, 215). Catlin often mislabeled the cartoon collection (see nos. 113-16).

210

211. He Who Comes on the Thunder
Winnebago, 1828
18½ x 14⅛ (47 x 35.7)
[Figure 80]

References: 1837 catalogue, no. 218; *Letters and Notes*, vol. 2, pp. 146-47; Donaldson, p. 129; Ewers (1956), p. 524.

Probably painted in Washington in the autumn of 1828 (see no. 209). The subject supposedly appears again in cartoon 4 (AMNH 201), but the Smithsonian portrait does not resemble either of the possible figures (see nos. 210, 213).

212. The Soldier
Winnebago, 1828
18½ x 14⅛ (47 x 35.7)

References: 1837 catalogue, no. 219; *Letters and Notes*, vol. 2, p. 147; Donaldson, p. 129; Ewers (1956), p. 524.

Probably painted in Washington in the autumn of 1828 (see no. 209).

213. The Snake
Winnebago, 1828
18½ x 14 (46.8 x 35.5)

See number 210 for Catlin's description.

References: 1837 catalogue, no. 220; *Letters and Notes*, vol. 2, p. 146, pl. 257; Donaldson, p. 129; Ewers (1956), p. 524.

212

213

Version:
Gilcrease Institute, NAI sketchbook (4776.26), pen and ink

Probably painted in Washington in the autumn of 1828 (see no. 209). James Otto Lewis made an earlier portrait of The Snake (see McKenney and Hall, vol. 2, p. 315), and at the extreme right of cartoon 4 (AMNH 201) is a figure who resembles the Smithsonian portrait, but he is incorrectly identified in the 1871 catalogue (see nos. 211, 215).

214

216

215

217

214. The Spaniard
Winnebago, 1828
18½ x 14⅛ (47 x 35.7)

References: 1837 catalogue, no. 221; *Letters and Notes,* vol. 2, p. 147; Donaldson, p. 130; Ewers (1956), p. 524.

Probably painted in Washington in the autumn of 1828 (see no. 209).

215. Little Elk
Winnebago, 1828
18½ x 14⅛ (47 x 35.7)

References: 1837 catalogue, no. 222; *Letters and Notes,* vol. 2, p. 147; Donaldson, p. 130; Ewers (1956), p. 524.

Probably painted in Washington in the autumn of 1828 (see no. 209). Note the broad and clumsy brushwork.

James Otto Lewis made an earlier portrait of Little Elk (see McKenney and Hall, vol. 2, p. 307), and the subject supposedly appears again in cartoon 4 (AMNH 201), but the Smithsonian portrait does not resemble either of the possible figures (see nos. 210, 213).

216. He Who Breaks the Bushes
Winnebago, 1828
18½ x 14⅛ (47 x 35.7)

References: 1837 catalogue, no. 223; *Letters and Notes,* vol. 2, p. 147; Donaldson, p. 130; Ewers (1956), p. 524.

Probably painted in Washington in the autumn of 1828 (see no. 209).

217. He Who Moistens the Wood
Winnebago, 1828
18½ x 14⅛ (47 x 35.7)

References: 1837 catalogue, no. 224; *Letters and Notes,* vol. 2, p. 147; Donaldson, p. 130; Ewers (1956), p. 524.

Probably painted in Washington in the autumn of 1828 (see no. 209).

218. Grizzly Bear, chief of the tribe
Menominee, 1831
21¼ x 16½ (53.8 x 40.9)
[Figure 11]

Described by Catlin as a dignified chief who "commanded great respect for his eloquence, and . . . deportment." Grizzly Bear was painted with "a handsome pipe in his hand, and wampum on his neck" (*Letters and Notes,* vol. 2, p. 147, pl. 258; 1848 catalogue, p. 25).

References: 1837 catalogue, no. 135; Donaldson, p. 132, pl. 50; Ewers (1956), p. 520; Roehm, pp. 50-51.

Version:
Gilcrease Institute, NAI sketchbook (4776.20), pen and ink

Probably painted in Washington in January 1831, when Grizzly Bear and thirteen members of his tribe visited the capital to negotiate the sale of a portion of their tribal lands. A treaty signed by the Menominee on February 8, 1831, includes the names of eleven of the twelve male subjects listed in the 1848 catalogue between numbers 218 and 231. Catlin's presence in Washington in January 1831 is certain (see Roehm), and the Menominee portraits are very different from the one Winnebago example (no. 199-206), apparently painted at Prairie du Chien in the summer of 1830 (see no. 222). They have more in common with the Fort Leavenworth series of the fall of that year (see nos. 237-55), and their small size connects them with other groups that must have been painted in Washington (see nos. 209-17, 264-69).

The portrait of Grizzly Bear is painted with a flourish and fullness of expression that distinguishes it among the Menominee group. Were it not for its size (the uniform dimensions of nos. 218-31), and the schematic modeling of eyes and lips, one would be tempted to assign it to one of Catlin's later visits to Prairie du Chien (see nos. 232-36). The succeeding portraits in this group, which Donaldson incorrectly dates 1835 or 1836, are modeled with heavier, less vigorous strokes, and costume details sometimes lack a sharp and careful definition. The unfortunate condition of several portraits further contributes to their uneven appearance.

Grizzly Bear appears again in cartoon 17 (NGA 2056), with his wife (no. 219) and son (no. 220).

219. Wounded Bear's Shoulder, wife of the chief
Menominee, 1831
21⅛ x 16½ (53.5 x 41.9)

References: 1837 catalogue, no. 142; *Letters and Notes,* vol. 2, p. 147, pl. 259; Donaldson, p. 132, pl. 50; Ewers (1956), p. 520.

Version:
Gilcrease Institute, NAI sketchbook (4776.21), pen and ink

Probably painted in Washington in January 1831. Although the technique seems more hesitant than in the previous portrait, Catlin gives every indication that the couple was painted at the same time (see no. 218).

The subject appears again, full length, in cartoon 17 (NGA 2056).

220. Great Cloud, son of Grizzly Bear
Menominee, 1831
21⅛ x 16⅝ (53.6 x 42)

Described by Catlin as "an ill-natured and insolent fellow who has since been killed for some of his murderous deeds" (*Letters and Notes,* vol. 2, p. 147, pl. 260).

References: 1837 catalogue, no. 143; Donaldson, p. 132; Ewers (1956), p. 520; Parke-Bernet Galleries, New York, Redwood Library Collection (May 21, 1970), no. 20.

Version:
Gilcrease Institute, NAI sketchbook (4776.21), pen and ink

Probably painted in Washington in January 1831 (see no. 218). Charles Bird King did a similar portrait several years later (see Parke-Bernet catalogue), and Great Cloud appears again, full length, in cartoon 17 (NGA 2056), with his parents.

219

220

221

223

222

224

221. Little Whale, a brave
Menominee, 1831
21⅛ x 16⅝ (53.6 x 42)

Described by Catlin as "a brave, with his *medicine-wand,* his looking-glass, and scissors" (1848 catalogue, p. 25).

References: 1837 catalogue, no. 136; *Letters and Notes,* vol. 2, p. 147; Donaldson, p. 132; Ewers (1956), p. 520.

Probably painted in Washington in January 1831 (see no. 218).

222. The South, a noted warrior
Menominee, 1831
21⅛ x 16⅝ (53.6 x 42)

References: 1837 catalogue, no. 137; *Letters and Notes,* vol. 2, p. 147; Donaldson, p. 132; Ewers (1956), p. 520.

According to an original certificate in Smithsonian files, The South (Sha-wá-no) was painted at Prairie du Chien. No date is given, but one would have to assume 1830, rather than 1835, on the basis of style. Equally strong evidence points to January 1831 in Washington as the time and place of the portrait (see no. 218). Changing the date of one example in this series would make it necessary to change the date of others, but more reliable evidence is needed before this can be done. At least one of Catlin's "original" certificates is incorrect (see no. 189), and he confused the identity of other sitters (see no. 239).

223. Másh-kee-wet, a great dandy
Menominee, 1831
21⅛ x 16⅝ (53.5 x 42)

References: 1837 catalogue, no. 138; *Letters and Notes,* vol. 2, p. 147; Donaldson, p. 132; Ewers (1956), p. 520.

Probably painted in Washington in January 1831 (see no. 218).

224. Pah-shee-náu-shaw, a warrior
Menominee, 1831
21⅛ x 16⅝ (53.6 x 42)

References: 1837 catalogue, no. 141; *Letters and Notes,* vol. 2, p. 147; Donaldson, p. 132; Ewers (1956), p. 520.

Probably painted in Washington in January 1831 (see no. 218).

225. Great Chief, a boy
Menominee, 1831
21⅛ x 16½ (53.6 x 41.9)

References: 1837 catalogue, no. 139; *Letters and Notes,* vol. 2, p. 147, pl. 261; Donaldson, p. 133; Ewers (1956), p. 520; McCracken, p. 174, reprod. p. 187; *America as Art,* no. 155, reprod. p. 156.

Version:
Gilcrease Institute, NAI sketchbook (4776.21), pen and ink

Probably painted in Washington in January 1831 (see no. 218), although McCracken says that Catlin encountered Great Chief on the trip to Pipestone Quarry in 1836. Numbers 232, 233, and 235-236 in the Menominee series may have been done at that time, but this portrait is clearly of a different style.

226. One Sitting in the Clouds, a boy
Menominee, 1831
21⅛ x 16⅝ (53.5 x 42)

References: 1837 catalogue, no. 140; *Letters and Notes,* vol. 2, p. 147; Donaldson, p. 133; Ewers (1956), p. 520; *America as Art,* no. 156, reprod. p. 157.

Probably painted in Washington in January 1831 (see no. 218).

227. Earth Standing, an old and valiant warrior
Menominee, 1831
21⅛ x 16½ (53.6 x 41.9)

References: 1837 catalogue, no. 144; *Letters and Notes,* vol. 2, p. 147; Donaldson, p. 133; Ewers (1956), p. 520.

Probably painted in Washington in January 1831 (see no. 218). The pigment surface was badly cracked and blistered before a recent restoration, and the effects are still noticeable.

228. Big Wave, an old and distinguished chief
Menominee, 1831
21⅛ x 16½ (53.7 x 41.8)

References: 1837 catalogue, no. 145; *Letters and Notes,* vol. 2, p. 147; Donaldson, p. 133; Ewers (1956), p. 520.

Probably painted in Washington in January 1831 (see no. 218). Past damage to the portrait is considerable (see no. 227).

225

227

226

228

232. The Owl, an aged chief
Menominee, 1836
29 x 24 (73.7 x 60.9)

Described by Catlin as "a very aged and emaciated chief, whom I painted at Green Bay, in Fort Howard. He had been a distinguished man, but now in his dotage, being more than 100 years old—and a great pet of the surgeon and officers of the post" (Letters and Notes, vol. 2, pp. 147, 160, pl. 262).

References: 1837 catalogue, no. 146; Donaldson, p. 133; Ewers (1956), p. 520; Gilcrease catalogue, p. 52; America as Art, no. 161; reprod. p. 162.

Versions:
Gilcrease Institute, watercolor, 8 x 7, signed lower right (on mount): Geo. Catlin 1837
Gilcrease Institute, NAI sketchbook (4776.36), pen and ink

Painted in 1836 when Catlin stopped at Green Bay on his way to the Pipestone Quarry (see Letters and Notes). Donaldson's date is incorrect. Like the Eastern Sioux and Ojibwa portraits of 1835-1836, numbers 232, 233, and 235-236 in the Menominee series have standard dimensions (see nos. 209, 218), and the subjects are shown in quiet, relaxed attitudes. The careful draftsmanship of this painting is less typical of the series than the hasty contours of the numbers that follow.

The Gilcrease and Smithsonian portraits are almost identical, but the face in the latter, as befits the original, is handled with greater conviction (see no. 151). The Owl also appears in cartoon 18 (NGA 2057), with two young men of the tribe.

229. Small Whoop, a distinguished warrior
Menominee, 1831
21⅛ x 16⅝ (53.7 x 42)

Described by Catlin as "a hard-visaged warrior, of most remarkable distinction" (1848 catalogue, p. 26).

References: 1837 catalogue, no. 148; Letters and Notes, vol. 2, p. 147; Donaldson, p. 133; Ewers (1956), p. 520.

Probably painted in Washington in January 1831 (see no. 218). Past damage to the portrait is considerable (see no. 227).

230. Ah-yaw-ne-tah-cár-ron, a warrior
Menominee, 1831
21⅛ x 16½ (53.7 x 41.9)

References: 1837 catalogue, no. 149; Donaldson, p. 133; Ewers (1956), p. 520.

Probably painted in Washington in January 1831 (see no. 218).

231. Female Bear
Menominee, 1831
Unlocated

Described by Catlin as the wife of number 230 (1848 catalogue, p. 26).

References: 1837 catalogue, no. 150; Letters and Notes, vol. 2, p. 147; Donaldson, p. 133.

Probably painted in Washington in January 1831, with her husband (see no. 218).

233. Wáh-chees, a brave
Menominee, 1835 or 1836
29 x 24 (73.7 x 60.9)

References: 1837 catalogue, no. 147; Donaldson, p. 133; Ewers (1956), p. 520; Gilcrease catalogue, p. 52.

Version:
Gilcrease Institute, watercolor, 7½ x 5½, signed lower right (on mount): Geo. Catlin

Probably painted at Prairie du Chien or Green Bay in 1835 or 1836 (see no. 232). The figure in the Gilcrease watercolor is three-quarter length and wears a feather headdress (see no. 151).

Wáh-chees supposedly appears again in cartoon 18 (NGA 2057), but the designated figure actually matches one of two young men in number 235-236.

234. He Who Sings the War Song
Menominee, 1835
Unlocated

References: 1837 catalogue, no. 151; *Letters and Notes,* vol. 2, p. 147; Donaldson, p. 133, pl. 4.

Painted from life at Prairie du Chien in 1835, according to an original certificate illustrated in Donaldson (see no. 232). The subject supposedly appears again in cartoon 18 (NGA 2057), but the designated figure actually matches one of two young men in number 235-236.

235-236. Two young men
Menominee, 1835 or 1836
29 x 24 (73.7 x 60.9)

Described by Catlin as "two Menominee youths at full length, in beautiful dresses . . . one with his war-club in his hand, and the other blowing on his 'courting flute' " (*Letters and Notes,* vol. 2, p. 147, pl. 263).

References: 1837 catalogue, no. 151½; Donaldson, p. 133; Ewers (1956), p. 520; *Catlin, Bodmer, Miller;* Paris (1963), no. 30.

Version:
Gilcrease Institute, NAI sketchbook (4776.36), pen and ink

Probably painted at Prairie du Chien or Green Bay in 1835 or 1836 (see no. 232). The two figures appear again in cartoon 18 (NGA 2057), although Catlin has mislabeled them (see nos. 233, 234, 210).

237. The Sauk, in the act of praying
Potawatomi, 1830
29 x 24 (73.7 x 60.9)

Catlin describes The Sauk as "in the act of praying; his prayer written in characters on a maple stick" (1848 catalogue, p. 26). See number 240.

References: 1837 catalogue, no. 195; *Letters and Notes,* vol. 2, p. 100, pl. 189; Donaldson, p. 134, pl. 50; Haberly, pp. 42, 43; Ewers (1956), pp. 485, 521; McCracken, p. 32; Gilcrease catalogue, p. 52; Roehm, p. 48.

Versions:
Gilcrease Institute, watercolor, 6 x 5½
Gilcrease Institute, NAI sketchbook (4776.27), pen and ink

Probably painted at Fort Leavenworth in 1830. No mention is made of Catlin visiting the Potawatomi in Illinois or Indiana. As the tribe was in the process of removing to lands near the fort, one would assume that numbers 237 through 239 were painted there, although neither Haberly nor

233

235-236

more recent scholars (Ewers, McCracken, and Roehm) offer evidence to support their claim that Catlin and General Clark traveled together through Kansas in 1830 (see no. 22). The artist was in the St. Louis area that summer and fall, however, and it is possible that he could have made the trip to Leavenworth without attracting local attention. Records of the Bureau of Indian Affairs show that at least two subjects (nos. 248, 279) Catlin painted among these Great Lakes tribes were already living west of the Mississippi in 1830.

The technique of the Potawatomi portraits is much superior to the Winnebago series (nos 209-17), but less assured than the vigorous Upper Missouri portraits of 1832. Thus, a date of 1830 seems reasonable for Catlin's visit to this tribe, and other Great Lakes tribes who were then settling near Fort Leavenworth. It must be acknowledged, however, that the artist made a well-documented stop at the fort on his voyage down the Missouri in 1832, and he later claimed that he visited the Kansa villages, beyond Leavenworth, in the spring of 1831, although his travel recollections are notoriously inaccurate (see nos. 31, 99). Catlin's rapid improvement over these years is manifest in annual styles that may be a more dependable guide to the dates and locations of his paintings than any previously proposed schedule of his travels.

The Sauk's right hand and his necklaces have been omitted from the Gilcrease portrait, but feathers and braids have been added to his hair. The Smithsonian original is identical to plate 189 in *Letters and Notes,* and is a more vital and convincing likeness than the Gilcrease watercolor (see no. 232). The Sauk also appears, full length, in cartoon 73 (NGA 2080).

237

name in cartoon 73 (NGA 2080) is not at all similar to the subject of the watercolor, however, making one question the identity of both (see no. 189).

240. Foremost Man, chief of the tribe
Kickapoo, 1830
29 x 24 (73.7 x 60.9)

"The present chief of this tribe . . . usually called the . . . *Prophet*, is a very shrewd and talented man. When he sat for his portrait, he took his attitude as seen in the picture, which was that of prayer. And I soon learned that he was a very devoted Christian. . . . It was told to me in the tribe by the Traders (though I am afraid to vouch for the whole truth of it), that while a Methodist preacher was soliciting him for permission to preach in his village, the Prophet refused him the privilege, but secretly took him aside and supported him until he learned from him his creed, and his system of teaching it to others; when he discharged him, and commenced preaching amongst his people himself; pretending to have had an interview with some . . . inspired personage; ingeniously resolving, that if there was any honour . . . or influence to be gained by the promulgation of it, he might as well have it as another person; and with this view he commenced preaching and instituted a prayer, which he ingeniously carved on a maplestick of an inch and a half in breadth, in characters somewhat resembling Chinese letters. These sticks, with the prayers on them, he has introduced into every family of the tribe, and into the hands of every individual; and as he has necessarily the manufacturing of them all, he sells them at his own price; and has thus added lucre to fame, and in two essential and effective ways, augmented his influence in his tribe" (*Letters and Notes*, vol. 2, pp. 98-99, pl. 185).

References: 1837 catalogue, no. 267; Donaldson, pp. 136-37, pl. 51; Ewers (1956), p. 519; Haverstock, p. 31; Gilcrease catalogue, p. 53.

Versions:
Gilcrease Institute, watercolor, 6½ x 5½, signed lower right (on mount): Geo. Catlin

Gilcrease Institute, NAI sketchbook (4776.19), pen and ink

Probably painted at Fort Leavenworth in 1830 (see no. 237). Catlin makes no mention of visiting the Kickapoo in Illinois.

Foremost Man must at first have been shown delivering a sermon, such as the one mentioned in *Letters and Notes*. The gesturing hands have been overpainted by the artist in the Smithsonian portrait, but they remain, ill-proportioned and awkwardly poised, in plate 185 of *Letters and Notes* and the Gilcrease watercolor. The Smithsonian portrait and plate 185 are otherwise identical, but the subject wears a feather headdress in the Gilcrease watercolor.

238. Bear Traveling at Night, a chief
Potawatomi, 1830
29 x 24 (73.7 x 60.9)

References: 1837 catalogue, no. 196; *Letters and Notes*, vol. 2, p. 100, pl. 190; Donaldson, p. 134, pl. 50; Ewers (1956), p. 520; Gilcrease catalogue, p. 52.

Versions:
Gilcrease Institute, watercolor, 6 x 4½

Gilcrease Institute, NAI sketchbook (4776.27), pen and ink

Probably painted at Fort Leavenworth in 1830 (see no. 237). Catlin still could not represent crossed arms in their proper position.

The subject is only bust length in the Gilcrease portrait, and the feathers project from his headdress at a different angle. Plate 190 in *Letters and Notes* is similar to the Smithsonian original. The subject appears again, full length, in cartoon 73 (NGA 2080).

239. Kée-se, a woman
Potawatomi, 1830
Unlocated

References: 1837 catalogue, no. 197; Donaldson, p. 134; Gilcrease catalogue, p. 52.

Version:
Gilcrease Institute, watercolor, 5½ x 5, signed lower right (on mount): G. C. 1834.

Probably painted at Fort Leavenworth in 1830 (see no. 237). The Gilcrease watercolor is illustrated in place of the original. The figure with the same

Foremost Man is incorrectly identified as Kee-mo-rá-nia (No English, no. 253) in the Gilcrease catalogue and Haverstock. He appears again, full length and with gesturing hands, in cartoon 72 (NGA 2079), accompanied by his wife (no. 244) and a Kickapoo disciple.

241. Cock Turkey, repeating his prayer
Kickapoo, 1830
29 x 24 (73.7 x 60.9)

Described by Catlin as "another Kickapoo of some distinction, and a disciple of the Prophet [no. 240]; in the attitude of prayer also, which he is reading off from characters cut upon a stick that he holds in his hands" (*Letters and Notes*, vol. 2, p. 98, pl. 186).

References: 1837 catalogue, no. 263; Donaldson, pp. 137-38, pl. 51; Ewers (1956), p. 519; *Catlin, Bodmer, Miller*; Corcoran Gallery of Art, Washington, D.C., *Wilderness* (1971), no. 41; Gilcrease catalogue, p. 53.

Versions:
Gilcrease Institute, watercolor, 7 x 5½, signed lower right (on mount): Geo. Catlin
Gilcrease Institute, NAI sketchbook (4776.19), pen and ink

Probably painted at Fort Leavenworth in 1830 (see no. 237). The portrait of Cock Turkey is either one of Catlin's best efforts at the fort that year, or it was mostly finished at a later date. The motif of the prayer stick, repeated in other Potawatomi and Kickapoo portraits, would probably indicate a date of 1830, but the hands are so skillfully articulated that one wonders why those of the Prophet (no. 240) came off so badly. The head is modeled with broad, flowing strokes that gracefully define the skull structure and facial features, a technique not often used by the artist before 1832, and the decorative tufts on the dress of the subject have been painted with astonishing speed and facility (see no. 245).
Cock Turkey's costume in the Gilcrease watercolor (fig. 144) lacks many of the details that enliven the Smithsonian portrait. He appears again, full length, in cartoon 72 (NGA 2079).

242. Elk's Horn, a subchief
Kickapoo, 1830
29 x 24 (73.7 x 60.9)

Described by Catlin as "a Sub-Chief, in the act of prayer" (1848 catalogue, p. 27). See number 240.

References: 1837 catalogue, no. 262; *Letters and Notes*, vol. 2, p. 99; Donaldson, p. 138; Ewers (1956), p. 519; Gilcrease catalogue, p. 53.

Version:
Gilcrease Institute, watercolor, 6 x 5½, signed lower right (on mount): Geo. Catlin./1834.

Probably painted at Fort Leavenworth in 1830 (see no. 237). The Gilcrease watercolor again lacks the costume details of the Smithsonian original, and the date on the watercolor is not reliable (see no. 46).

243. Big Bear
Kickapoo, 1830
29 x 24 (73.7 x 60.9)

Catlin describes the subject as having "wampum on his neck and [a] red flag in his hand, the symbol of war or 'blood'" (1848 catalogue, p. 27).

References: 1837 catalogue, no. 266; *Letters and Notes*, vol. 2, p. 99; Donaldson, p. 138; Ewers (1956), p. 519; Gilcrease catalogue, p. 53.

Version:
Gilcrease Institute, watercolor, 6 x 5½, signed lower right (on mount): Geo. Catlin/1835.

Probably painted at Fort Leavenworth in 1830 (see no. 237). The appearance of Big Bear's costume suggests that Catlin's broad brushwork was sometimes out of control in this period.
The figure in the Gilcrease watercolor is only bust length, and he wears a somewhat different costume and headdress (see no. 242).

244

246

245

References: 1837 catalogue, no. 265; Donaldson, p. 138; Ewers (1956), p. 519.

Probably painted at Fort Leavenworth in 1830 (see no. 237). Note the similar, but more skillfully executed tufts on the dress of Cock Turkey (no. 241).

246. Little Chief, a chief
Kaskaskia, 1830
29 x 24 (73.7 x 60.9)

Catlin describes the subject as "half-civilized, and, I should think, half-breed . . . This young man is chief of the tribe; and I was told by one of the Traders, that his mother and his son, were his only subjects" (*Letters and Notes,* vol. 2, p. 100, pl. 191).

References: 1837 catalogue, no. 272; Donaldson, p. 139, pl. 51; Haberly, reprod. opp. p. 48; Ewers (1956), p. 519; Gilcrease catalogue, p. 53.

Version:
Gilcrease Institute, watercolor, 5½ x 5, signed lower right (on mount): Geo. Catlin

Probably painted at Fort Leavenworth in 1830 (see no. 237). Donaldson suggests the right location but wrong date.

Catlin often used a more conventional pose in his portraits of civilized Indians. Little Chief is shown half-length in the Gilcrease watercolor, and he appears again, full length, in cartoon 50 (NGA 2061), with his mother (no. 247) and child.

244. A'h-tee-wát-o-mee, a woman
Kickapoo, 1830
29 x 24 (73.7 x 60.9)

Described by Catlin as a "woman, with wampum and silver brooches in profusion on her neck" (1848 catalogue, p. 27).

References: 1837 catalogue, no. 264; *Letters and Notes,* vol. 2, p. 99; Donaldson, p. 138; Ewers (1956), p. 519; Gilcrease catalogue, p. 53.

Version:
Gilcrease Institute, watercolor, 6 x 5, signed lower right (on mount): Geo. Catlin

Probably painted at Fort Leavenworth in 1830 (see no. 237). The subject holds a prayer stick, in place of her fan, in the Gilcrease watercolor. She is supposed to appear again in cartoon 72 (NGA 2079), but there is no apparent relation between the designated figure and the Smithsonian portrait. Catlin identifies her as the wife of the Prophet (no. 240) in the 1871 catalogue.

245. Shee-náh-wee
Kickapoo, 1830
29 x 24 (73.7 x 60.9)

The subject is described as a woman in *Letters and Notes* (vol. 2, p. 99), but no qualifying remarks follow the entry in the 1848 catalogue (p. 27).

247. Wah-pe-séh-see, mother of the chief
Kaskaskia, 1830
29 x 24 (73.7 x 60.9)

Described by Catlin as "a very aged woman" (*Letters and Notes*, vol. 2, p. 100, pl. 192).

References: 1837 catalogue, no. 273; Donaldson, p. 139, pl. 51; Ewers (1956), p. 519; Gilcrease catalogue, p. 53.

Versions:
Gilcrease Institute, watercolor, 6 x 5½, signed lower right (on mount): Geo. Catlin

Gilcrease Institute, NAI sketchbook (4776.27), pen and ink

Probably painted at Fort Leavenworth in 1830 (see no. 237). Only the necklace arrangement differs between the Gilcrease and Smithsonian portraits.

The subject appears again, full length, in cartoon 50 (NGA 2061), with her son (no. 246).

247

248

248. Stands by Himself, a distinguished brave
Wea, 1830
29 x 24 (73.7 x 60.9)

The subject is described by Catlin as having an "intelligent European head," and holding a hatchet in his hand (*Letters and Notes*, vol. 2, p. 99, pl. 187; 1848 catalogue, p. 27).

References: 1837 catalogue, no. 270; Donaldson, p. 140; Ewers (1956), p. 523; Gilcrease catalogue, p. 53.

Versions:
Gilcrease Institute, watercolor, 6 x 5, signed lower right (on mount): Geo. Catlin 1841

Gilcrease Institute, NAI sketchbook (4776.19), pen and ink

Probably painted at Fort Leavenworth in 1830 (see nos. 237, 279; records of the Bureau of Indian Affairs show that the subject was living west of the Mississippi by that year). Donaldson suggests the right location but wrong date. The broad sweeps of pigment are close to the technique Catlin used in the Potawatomi and Kickapoo portraits.

The subject is bust length in the Gilcrease watercolor, and his features have a somewhat different appearance than in the Smithsonian original, which matches plate 187 in *Letters and Notes*. He appears again, full length, in cartoon 66 (NGA 2075), with a Wea warrior and a woman.

249. The Swan, a warrior
Wea, 1830
29 x 24 (73.7 x 60.9)

Described by Catlin as a woman in the 1837 catalogue (no. 271), and as a "fine-looking fellow, with an European countenance" in the 1848 catalogue (p. 27). See number 245.

References: *Letters and Notes*, vol. 2, p. 99, pl. 188; Donaldson, p. 140, pl. 52; Ewers (1956), p. 523; Gilcrease catalogue, p. 53.

Versions:
Gilcrease Institute, watercolor, 6 x 5, signed lower right (on mount): Geo. Catlin

Gilcrease Institute, NAI sketchbook (4776.19), pen and ink

Probably painted at Fort Leavenworth in 1830 (see nos. 237, 248). The Swan is bust length in the Gilcrease watercolor, and without face paint. The Smithsonian portrait matches plate 188 in *Letters and Notes*.

The subject appears again, full length, in cartoon 66 (NGA 2075).

249

Gilcrease Institute, Tulsa.

Catlin further describes the subject as having a "remarkably fine head" (1848 catalogue, p. 27).

References: 1837 catalogue, no. 246; Donaldson, p. 140, pl. 52; Ewers (1956), p. 521; Gilcrease catalogue, p. 53.

Versions:
Gilcrease Institute, watercolor, 6 x 5½, signed lower right (on mount): Geo. Catlin/1835
Gilcrease Institute, NAI sketchbook (4776.28), pen and ink

Probably painted at Fort Leavenworth in 1830 (see no. 237). The broad sweeps of pigment are again close to the technique used by Catlin in the Potawatomi and Kickapoo portraits (see no. 248).

Although the subject is only half-length and costume details are somewhat different, the Gilcrease watercolor is a close interpretation of the Smithsonian original. The latter matches plate 193 in *Letters and Notes.* Man Who Tracks appears again, full length, in cartoon 58 (NGA 2067), with his wife and a Peoria "dandy."

250. The White
Wea, 1830
29 x 24 (73.7 x 60.9)

References: 1837 catalogue, no. 274; Donaldson, p. 140; Ewers (1956), p. 525; Gilcrease catalogue, p. 53.

Version:
Gilcrease Institute, watercolor, 6 x 5, signed lower right (on mount): Geo. Catlin

Probably painted at Fort Leavenworth in 1830 (see nos. 237, 248). The White is listed as Kaskaskia in the 1837 catalogue, and as an unidentified southeastern Indian in Ewers. The Smithsonian portrait closely resembles the Gilcrease watercolor, however, which is labeled *Wáh-pe-say, the White.*

251. Man Who Tracks, a chief
Peoria, 1830
29 x 24 (73.7 x 60.9)

"Of this tribe I painted the portraits of . . . [Man Who Tracks and No English, no. 253]. These are said to be the most influential men in the tribe, and both were very curiously and *well* dressed, in articles of civilized manufacture" (*Letters and Notes,* vol. 2, p. 101, pl. 193).

252. Wap-sha-ka-náh, a brave
Peoria, 1830
Unlocated

References: 1837 catalogue, no. 245; Donaldson, p. 140; Gilcrease catalogue, p. 53.

Version:
Gilcrease Institute, watercolor, 5½ x 5, signed lower right (on mount): Geo. Catlin

Probably painted at Fort Leavenworth in 1830 (see nos. 237, 251). The Gilcrease watercolor is illustrated in place of the original.

253. No English, a dandy
Peoria, 1830
29 x 24 (73.7 x 60.9)

See number 251. Catlin further describes No English as "a beau; his face curiously painted, and looking-glass in his hand" (1848 catalogue, p. 27).

References: 1837 catalogue, no. 244; *Letters and Notes,* vol. 2, p. 101, pl. 194; Donaldson, p. 140, pl. 52; Ewers (1956), p. 521; McCracken, reprod. p. 131; Haverstock, p. 31; Gilcrease catalogue, p. 53.

Versions:
Gilcrease Institute, watercolor, 7 x 5, signed lower right (on mount): Geo. Catlin

Gilcrease Institute, NAI sketchbook (4776.28), pen and ink

Probably painted at Fort Leavenworth in 1830 (see nos. 237, 251). The subject is incorrectly identified as Kee-án-ne-kuk (Foremost Man, no. 240) in the Gilcrease catalogue.

The Smithsonian and Gilcrease portraits are identical except for minor changes in the arrangement of the necklaces. The former matches plate 194 in *Letters and Notes.* No English appears again, full length, in cartoon 58 (NGA 2067).

254. Fix with the Foot, a brave
Piankashaw, 1830
29 x 24 (73.7 x 60.9)

References: 1837 catalogue, no. 199; *Letters and Notes,* vol. 2, p. 101, pl. 196; Donaldson, p. 141, pl. 53; Ewers (1956), p. 521; Gilcrease catalogue, p. 53.

Versions:
Gilcrease Institute, watercolor, 6 x 5, signed lower right (on mount): Geo. Catlin

Gilcrease Institute, NAI sketchbook (4776.28), pen and ink

Probably painted at Fort Leavenworth in 1830 (see nos. 237, 251). Catlin mislabeled plates 195 and 196 in *Letters and Notes* (see no. 255), and the subject is listed twice (once under the wrong tribe) in the Gilcrease catalogue.

Costumes differ between the Gilcrease and Smithsonian portraits, and the former is only bust length. The latter matches plate 196 in *Letters and Notes.* The subject appears again, full length, in cartoon 47 (NGA 2060).

253

254

255. Left Hand, a warrior
Piankashaw, 1830
29 x 24 (73.7 x 60.9)

Described by Catlin as "a fierce-looking and very distinguished warrior, with a stone-hatchet in his hand" (*Letters and Notes,* vol. 2, p. 101, pl. 195).

References: 1837 catalogue, no. 198; Donaldson, p. 141, pl. 53; Ewers (1956), p. 521; Gilcrease catalogue, p. 53.

Versions:
Gilcrease Institute, watercolor, 6 x 5, signed lower right (on mount): G. Catlin p.

Gilcrease Institute, NAI sketchbook (4776.28), pen and ink

Probably painted at Fort Leavenworth in 1830 (see nos. 237, 251). Catlin mislabeled plates 195 and 196 in *Letters and Notes* (see no. 254).

The subject is bust length in the Gilcrease watercolor, and his face is a simplified version of the Smithsonian portrait, which matches plate 195 in *Letters and Notes* (see no. 232). Left Hand appears again, full length, in cartoon 47 (NGA 2060), with his wife and a Piankashaw brave.

255

256

257

256. No Heart (called White Cloud), chief of the tribe
Iowa, 1832
29 x 24 (73.7 x 60.9)

No Heart (or White Cloud II) was the son of a distinguished chief of the same name, according to Catlin, but Frederick W. Hodge (McKenney and Hall, vol. 1, p. 294) thinks that No Heart may have been the brother of White Cloud I, and therefore uncle of White Cloud II, principal chief of the fourteen Iowa Indians who visited England and France in 1844 and 1845 (see no. 517). Hodge also speculates that No Heart and White Cloud II were brothers. Unfortunately, Charles Bird King's portraits of White Cloud I and No Heart (Notchimine) only add to the confusion, as neither appears to resemble this subject.

Catlin describes No Heart as "tastefully dressed with a buffalo robe wrapped around him, with a necklace of grizzly bear's claws on his neck; with shield, bow, and quiver on, and a profusion of wampum strings on his neck" (*Letters and Notes,* vol. 2, p. 22, pl. 129).

References: 1837 catalogue, no. 229; McKenney and Hall, vol. 1, pp. 294-95, 308-11; vol. 2, p. 114; Donaldson, p. 142, pl. 54; Haberly, p. 95; Ewers (1956), p. 512; McCracken, p. 32, reprod. p. 31; Rossi and Hunt, pp. 262, 320; Gilcrease catalogue, p. 33.

Versions:
Gilcrease Institute, watercolor, 9½ x 8, signed lower right: Geo. Catlin 1836
Rains Galleries, New York, Cornelius Michaelson sale, May 8, 1935, no. 71, watercolor, 9 x 8½
Gilcrease Institute, NAI sketchbook (4776.9), pen and ink

Probably painted at Fort Leavenworth in 1832. Catlin's portraits of the civilized tribes settled near Leavenworth (Delaware, Shawnee and nos. 237-55) were apparently painted before those of the more primitive tribes living some distance beyond the fort (Iowa, Kansas, Missouri, Omaha, Oto, and Pawnee). Although the Iowa portraits do not have the robust dimension of the Upper Missouri series, anatomy and costume details are more clearly articulated than in the loosely painted portraits of the civilized tribes. Under the circumstances, it seems best to assign the Iowa group to 1832, when Catlin encountered numerous members of the tribe encamped about Leavenworth (see nos. 22, 237).

The Gilcrease watercolor is an elaborately detailed version of the Smithsonian original (see no. 46). No Heart holds an arrow in his right hand in the watercolor and plate 129 of *Letters and Notes.* He appears again, full length, in cartoon 2 (NGA 2046), with his son and an Iowa brave.

257. Shooting Cedar, a brave
Iowa, 1832
29 x 24 (73.7 x 60.9)

"[Shooting Cedar and Busy Man (no. 260)] are also distinguished warriors of the tribe; tastefully dressed and equipped, the one with his war-club on his arm, the other with bow and arrows in his hand; both wore around their waists beautiful buffalo robes, and both had turbans made of vari-coloured cotton shawls, purchased of the Fur Traders. Around their necks were necklaces of the bears' claws, and a profusion of beads and wampum. Their ears were profusely strung with beads; and their naked shoulders curiously streaked and daubed with red paint" (*Letters and Notes,* vol. 2, p. 23, pl. 131).

References: 1837 catalogue, no. 225; Donaldson, p. 142, pl. 54; Ewers (1956), p. 512; Gilcrease catalogue, p. 53.

Versions:
Gilcrease Institute, watercolor, 7½ x 6, signed lower right (on mount): Geo. Catlin
Gilcrease Institute, NAI sketchbook (4776.9), pen and ink

Probably painted at Fort Leavenworth in 1832 (see no. 256). The Gilcrease and Smithsonian portraits are similar in appearance, but the former is a weak version of the latter (see no. 232). The subject is incorrectly identified as Wos-cóm-mun (Busy Man, no. 260) in the Gilcrease catalogue.

Shooting Cedar appears again, full length, in cartoon 2 (NGA 2046).

258. Walks in the Rain, a warrior
     Iowa, 1832
     29 x 24 (73.7 x 60.9)

Described by Catlin as a "warrior, with his pipe and tobacco-pouch in his hand" (1848 catalogue, p. 28). The subject may be the same as Walking Rain (no. 518).

References: 1837 catalogue, no. 226; Donaldson, p. 142; Ewers (1956), p. 512.

Version:
Glenbow-Alberta Institute, Calgary, pencil and watercolor, 8 x 6¼

Probably painted at Fort Leavenworth in 1832 (see no. 256). The Glenbow sketch closely resembles the Smithsonian portrait, but like the Gilcrease examples, it is most likely a later version. No preliminary drawings are known for any of the paintings in the 1848 catalogue.

259. Man of Sense, a brave
     Iowa, 1832
     29 x 24 (73.7 x 60.9)

"Man of Sense is another of this tribe, much distinguished for his bravery and early warlike achievements. His head was dressed with a broad silver band passing around it, and decked out with the crest of horsehair" (*Letters and Notes*, vol. 2, p. 22, pl. 130).

Catlin further describes the subject as having "a handsome pipe in his hand, and bears' claw necklace on his neck" (1848 catalogue, p. 28).

References: 1837 catalogue, no. 227; Donaldson, p. 142, pl. 54; Ewers (1956), p. 512; Haverstock, p. 31; Gilcrease catalogue, p. 53.

Versions:
Gilcrease Institute, watercolor, 9½ x 7½, signed lower right: Geo. Catlin 1836
Gilcrease Institute, NAI sketchbook (4776.9), pen and ink

Probably painted at Fort Leavenworth in 1832 (see no. 256). Donaldson incorrectly identifies the subject in plate 54 as Walks in the Rain (see nos. 258, 260).

The Gilcrease watercolor is a more finished version of the Smithsonian original, but its date is not to be trusted (see no. 46). Man of Sense appears again, full length, in cartoon 2 (NGA 2046).

260. Busy Man, a brave
     Iowa, 1832
     29 x 24 (73.7 x 60.9)

See number 257 for Catlin's description.

References: 1837 catalogue, no. 228; *Letters and Notes*, vol. 2, p. 23, pl. 132; Donaldson, p. 142, pl. 54; Ewers (1956), p. 512.

Version:
Gilcrease Institute, NAI sketchbook (4776.9), pen and ink

Probably painted at Fort Leavenworth in 1832 (see no. 256). Donaldson incorrectly identifies the subject in plate 54 as Man of Sense (no. 259).

261. This number does not appear in any catalogue of Catlin's collection published between 1840 and 1848.

262

263

Plate 205, *Letters and Notes.*

262. Mún-ne-o-ye, a woman
Iowa, 1832
29 x 24 (73.7 x 60.9)

References: Donaldson, p. 142; Ewers (1956), p. 512; Gilcrease catalogue, p. 53.

Version:
Gilcrease Institute, watercolor, 6 x 4½, signed lower right (on mount): Geo. Catlin

Probably painted at Fort Leavenworth in 1832 (see no. 256), although for some unexplained reason the subject is not included in the 1837 catalogue. This is the weakest portrait in the Iowa group, and the Gilcrease watercolor is only a fumbling equivalent of the original.

263. Red Jacket, a noted chief
Seneca, 1826-1828
Unlocated (described as "life size" in the 1848 catalogue)

"The Senecas . . . have . . . an aged and very distinguished chief, familiarly known throughout the United States, by the name of *Red Jacket.* I painted this portrait from the life, in the costume in which he is represented; and indulged him also, in the wish he expressed, 'that he might be seen standing on the Table Rock, at the Falls of Niagara; about which place he thought his spirit would linger after he was dead'. . . . he has been for many years the head chief of the scattered remnants of that once powerful compact, the Six Nations; a part of whom reside on their reservations in the vicinity of the Senecas, amounting perhaps in all, to about four thousand, and owning some two hundred thousand acres of fine lands. . . .

"Red Jacket has been reputed one of the greatest orators of his day; and, no doubt, more distinguished for his eloquence and his influence in council, than as a warrior, in which character I think history has not said much of him. This may be owing, in a great measure, to the fact that the wars of his nation were chiefly fought before his fighting days; and that the greater part of his life and his talents have been spent with his tribe, during its downfall; where, instead of the horrors of Indian wars, they have had a more fatal and destructive enemy to encounter, in the insidious encroachments of pale faces, which he has been for many years exerting his eloquence and all his talents to resist. Poor old chief—not all the eloquence of Cicero and Demosthenes would be able to avert the calamity, that awaits his declining nation—to resist the despoiling hand of mercenary white man, that opens and spreads liberally, but to entrap the unwary and ignorant within its withering grasp" (*Letters and Notes,* vol. 2, pp. 104-5, pl. 205).

References: American Academy of Fine Arts, New York, 1828, no. 68 *(Red Jacket, a sketch);* 1837 catalogue, no. 230; Donaldson, pp. 154-74, pl. 55; Matthews, pp. 604-5, pl. 143; Mary W. Kenway, "Portraits of Red Jacket," *Antiques* 54 (August 1948): 100-101, reprod. p. 101; Haberly, pp. 26-30, reprod. opp. p. 32; Ewers (1956), p. 485; McCracken, pp. 21, 25, 26; Halpin, p. 7; Ewers (1965), p. 72; Roehm, pp. XVI, 31, 45; Marie Hewett, "Pictorial Reporter: George Catlin in Western New York," *Niagara Frontier* 17 (Winter 1970): 101, 102; Haverstock, p. 41, reprod. p. 40; Gilcrease catalogue, p. 53.

Versions:
Gilcrease Institute, 28 x 22, signed lower right: Buffalo 1826/G Catlin

L. B. Goodrich, Oneonta, New York, 27 x 22

Gilcrease Institute, watercolor, 14 x 10

Gilcrease Institute, watercolor, 11 x 7, signed lower right: G. C. Buffalo 1827.

Rains Gallery, New York, Cornelius Michaelson sale, May 8, 1935, no. 71, watercolor, 9 x 8½

Gilcrease Institute, NAI sketchbook (4776.30), pen and ink

Catlin may have first attempted Indian portraiture in the context of a historical scene, as Haberly suggests, but all that remains is the 1826 oil sketch of Red Jacket at the Gilcrease Institute (fig. 4). Catlin had been in the vicinity of Buffalo the previous year preparing lithographs of the Erie Canal, and Hewett (whose dates for the artist's portraits are mostly incorrect) suggests that he met Red Jacket at the home of their mutual friend Gen. Peter B. Porter. Kenway states that Catlin was the first artist of note to persuade Red Jacket to pose for a portrait, but there is a drawing by Henry Inman of Red Jacket's head and shoulders at the Albany Institute dated 1823. Portraits by Charles Bird King, Robert Weir (fig. 60), and John Neagle followed shortly after Catlin's oil sketch.

Red Jacket was about seventy in 1826, confounded and disillusioned by the growing influence of white men's institutions among the Seneca, and in Catlin's words "as great a drunkard as some of our most distinguished law-givers and law-makers." The ravages of time and failure are visible in the Gilcrease sketch (fig. 4), yet Red Jacket also maintains a certain dignity, at least in the eyes of the artist. The technique, however, barely sustains the image. The features are without expression, drawn in a brusque and crude manner that reminds one of the only slightly improved Winnebago portraits of 1828 (see nos. 209-217). Judging from plate 205 of *Letters and Notes* (illustrated here), the full-length portrait was more carefully painted, with the Gilcrease watercolor of 1827 (if the date can be trusted) probably serving as a general model for the pose and costume. An awkward stance and stiff limbs are common to both figures, but Catlin somewhat modified the pose in the final portrait.

The Goodrich version appears to be a more finished edition of the Gilcrease oil sketch, and the unsigned Gilcrease watercolor shows the same portrait framed in a wide molding that is supported from behind by a collection of Indian armaments. Red Jacket appears again in cartoon 53 (NGA 2062), with two Seneca warriors and Niagara Falls in the background.

264. Deep Lake, an old chief
Seneca, 1831
21⅛ x 16½ (53.6 x 41.9)

References: 1837 catalogue, no. 233; Donaldson, p. 174; Ewers (1956), p. 523.

Probably painted in Washington in February 1831, when a delegation of Ohio Seneca that included numbers 266, 267, and 269 were there to negotiate a treaty for the sale of their lands south of Lake Erie. Catlin's presence in Washington in January 1831 has already been established (see no. 218), and the unusual size of the portraits matches those numbers in the Menominee series that were presumably painted in the capital. Moreover, the heavy, full strokes in the Seneca portraits are much like those used by the artist in recording the Menominee subjects (see nos. 218-31).

265. Round Island, a warrior
Seneca, 1831
21⅛ x 16½ (53.7 x 41.8)
[Figure 102]

Described by Catlin as "half-blood. A very handsome fellow" (1848 catalogue, p. 28).

References: 1837 catalogue, no. 231; Donaldson, p. 174; Ewers (1956), p. 523.

Probably painted in Washington in February 1831 (see no. 264).

266. Hard Hickory, an amiable man
Seneca, 1831
21⅛ x 16½ (53.6 x 41.9)

Described by Catlin as "a very ferocious-looking, but a mild and amiable man" (1848 catalogue, p. 28).

264

266

References: 1837 catalogue, no. 232; *Letters and Notes,* vol. 2, pp. 104-5, pl. 204; Donaldson, p. 174; Ewers (1956), p. 523.

Version:
Gilcrease Institute, NAI sketchbook (4776.30), pen and ink

Probably painted in Washington in February 1831 (see no. 264). Hard Hickory also appears, full length, in cartoon 53 (NGA 2062).

267

267. Good Hunter, a warrior
Seneca, 1831
21⅛ x 16½ (53.6 x 41.9)

References: 1837 catalogue, no. 234; *Letters and Notes,* vol. 2, pp. 104-5, pl. 203; Donaldson, p. 174; Ewers (1956), p. 523.

Version:
Gilcrease Institute, NAI sketchbook (4776.30), pen and ink

Copy:
British Museum, London, by John Cullum, watercolor, 12 x 10¼ (1842-1844)

Probably painted in Washington in February 1831 (see no. 264). Good Hunter also appears, full length, in cartoon 53 (NGA 2062).

References: 1837 catalogue, no. 237; Donaldson, p. 176; Haberly, p. 33, reprod.; Ewers (1956), p. 521; M. Knoedler & Co., New York, *The American Indian Observed* (1971), no. 23, reprod. p. 20; *America as Art*, no. 157, reprod. p. 158.

Version:
Gilcrease Institute, NAI sketchbook (4776.27), pen and ink

Probably painted in Washington in early 1831, as the size and style of the portrait so closely match the Seneca and Menominee series (see nos. 264, 218). Moreover, Bread's name appears on a treaty signed in Washington January 20, 1831, to determine the removal of certain New York tribes to land west of Green Bay, where Catlin locates the chief in the 1837 catalogue.

The artist apparently devoted some time to painting Bread, as the portrait is one of the most perceptive and carefully finished of the period. The subject also appears, full length, in cartoon 62 (NGA 2071), with his sister and a Tuscarora missionary.

271. Cú-sick, son of the chief
Tuscarora, probably 1837-1839
29 x 24 (73.7 x 60.9)
[Figure 97]

Described by Catlin as "a very talented man—has been educated for the pulpit in some one of our public institutions, and is now a Baptist preacher, and I am told a very eloquent speaker" *(Letters and Notes,* vol. 2, p. 104, pl. 202).

References: Donaldson, pp. 177-78; Ewers (1956), p. 523; Haverstock, reprod. p. 28.

The portrait is not included in the 1837 catalogue, but does appear in the Egyptian Hall catalogue of January 1840, indicating that it may have been painted in the interval. Judging from Cú-sick's dress and manner, Catlin did not necessarily encounter him on the Tuscarora reservation near Buffalo, as Donaldson and others have suggested. Cú-sick's features are modeled with a fine, light touch that one sees in Catlin's portraits of white men of the late 1830s.

The subject has no arm bands, necklaces, or sash in plate 202 of *Letters and Notes.* He appears again, full length, in cartoon 62 (NGA 2071).

268. String, a renowned warrior
Seneca, 1831
21¼ x 16½ (53.8 x 41.9)

References: 1837 catalogue, no. 235; Donaldson, p. 174; Ewers (1956), p. 523.

Probably painted in Washington in February 1831 (see no. 264).

269. Seneca Steele, a great libertine
Seneca, 1831
21⅞ x 16¾ (55.3 x 42.5)

Catlin describes the subject as having a hatchet in his hand (1848 catalogue, p. 29).

References: 1837 catalogue, no. 236; Donaldson, p. 174; Ewers (1956), p. 523.

Probably painted in Washington in February 1831 (see no. 264).

270. Bread, chief of the tribe
Oneida, 1831
21¼ x 16½ (53.9 x 42)

"He is a shrewd and talented man, well educated—speaking good English—is handsome, and a polite and gentlemanly man in his deportment" *(Letters and Notes,* vol. 2, p. 103, pl. 201). Catlin also describes Bread as "half-blood" (1848 catalogue, p. 29).

272. Both Sides of the River, chief of the tribe
Mohegan (Stockbridge), 1836.
29 x 24 (73.7 x 60.9)

"The chief of this tribe . . . which I have painted at full length, with a psalm-book in one hand, and a cane in the other, is a very shrewd and intelligent man, and a professed, and I think, sincere Christian" *(Letters and Notes,* vol. 2, p. 103, pl. 199).

References: Donaldson, p. 196; Ewers (1956), p. 520.

Version:
Gilcrease Institute, NAI sketchbook (4776.29), pen and ink

Probably painted at Green Bay in 1836, where the Stockbridge had settled after leaving New York in 1833. Catlin records the Wisconsin location for the tribe in *Letters and Notes,* and the two portraits are clearly later works, resembling the Eastern Sioux and Ojibwa series. The faces and costumes are painted with thin, deft strokes that were beyond Catlin's range in 1830, the date suggested by Donaldson and others for Catlin's visit to the tribe.

The portraits are not listed in the 1837 catalogue, perhaps because they were not sufficiently finished at the time. The subject appears again in cartoon 57 (NGA 2066), with another civilized Mohegan, and in cartoon 64 (NGA 2073), which is apparently mislabeled (see nos. 273, 288).

273. John W. Quinney (The Dish), a missionary preacher
Mohegan (Stockbridge), 1836
29 x 24 (73.7 x 60.9)
[Figure 87]

"John W. Quinney, in civilized dress, is a civilized Indian, well-educated—speaking good English—is a Baptist missionary preacher, and a very plausible and eloquent speaker" *(Letters and Notes,* vol. 2, p. 103, pl. 200).

References: Donaldson, p. 196; Ewers (1956), pp. 485, 520, pl. 2.

Probably painted at Green Bay in 1836 (see no. 272). Ewers says that Catlin saw Quinney at Niagara Falls in the winter of 1829-30, but no evidence is given to support the claim (see no. 198).

The rapidly brushed outlines of Quinney's frock coat suggest the beginnings of a well-articulated figure (see no. 100). The subject was also painted by Charles Bird King in Washington (see Ewers, 1953, p. 472), and he appears again in cartoons 57 (NGA 2066) and 64 (NGA 2073). The latter is apparently mislabeled (see no. 288).

272

274

274. Bód-a-sin, chief of the tribe
Delaware, 1830
29 x 24 (73.7 x 60.9)

References: 1837 catalogue, no. 285; Donaldson, p. 198; Ewers (1956), p. 519.

Probably painted at Fort Leavenworth in 1830 (see no. 237). The broad, open brushwork has much in common with the technique of the Potawatomi and Kickapoo portraits (nos. 237-45).

Bód-a-sin appears again in cartoon 63 (NGA 2072), with his wife and another Delaware chief.

275. The Answer, second chief
Delaware, 1830
29 x 24 (73.7 x 60.9)

See number 276. Catlin further describes the subject as having "his bow and arrows in his hand" *(Letters and Notes,* vol. 2, pp. 102-3, pl. 197).

References: 1837 catalogue, no. 286; Donaldson, p. 198, pl. 56; Ewers (1956), p. 519; Gilcrease catalogue, p. 54.

Versions:
Gilcrease Institute, watercolor, 6½ x 6, signed lower right (on mount): Geo. Catlin
Gilcrease Institute, NAI sketchbook (4776.29), pen and ink

Probably painted at Fort Leavenworth in 1830 (see no. 274). Note the similar garments of tufted material in numbers 241 and 245.

The Gilcrease portrait is half-length, and costume details are different in the Smithsonian original, which matches plate 197 of *Letters and Notes.*

275

276

277

278

277. Goes Up the River, an aged chief
Shawnee, 1830
29 x 24 (73.7 x 60.9)

"The present chief of the tribe . . . is a very aged, but extraordinary man, with a fine and intelligent head, and his ears slit and stretched down to his shoulders, a custom highly valued in this tribe; which is done by severing the rim of the ear with a knife, and stretching it down by wearing heavy weights attached to it at times, to elongate it as much as possible, making a large orifice, through which, on parades, &c. they often pass a bunch of arrows or quills, and wear them as ornaments" (*Letters and Notes*, vol. 2, pp. 116-17, pl. 211).

References: 1837 catalogue, no. 152; Donaldson, pp. 200-201, pl. 56; Ewers (1956), p. 522; Fundaburk, p. 123, pl. 201; McCracken, p. 33, reprod. p. 31; *America as Art*, no. 159, reprod. p. 160.

Probably painted at Fort Leavenworth in 1830 (see no. 237). The style of the Shawnee portraits again corresponds to the Potawatomi and Kickapoo series (see no. 274).

The subject also appears, full length, in cartoon 74 (NGA 2081), with his daughter (no. 278) and other members of the tribe.

278. Female Eagle, daughter of the chief
Shawnee, 1830
28⅜ x 23¼ (72 x 59)
National Gallery of Art, Washington, D.C.
Paul Mellon Collection

Described by Catlin as "an agreeable-looking girl, of fifteen years of age, and much thought of by the tribe" (*Letters and Notes*, vol. 2, p. 117, pl. 212).

References: 1837 catalogue, no. 154; Donaldson, p. 201; National Gallery of Art, Washington, D.C., *American Paintings and Sculpture* (1970), p. 33, no. 2306.

Version:
Gilcrease Institute, NAI sketchbook (4776.16), pen and ink

Probably painted at Fort Leavenworth in 1830 (see no. 277). The portrait was apparently withheld from Joseph Harrison and other creditors in 1852, and was eventually sold to the American Museum of Natural History by Catlin's heirs.

Female Eagle also appears, full length, in cartoon 74 (NGA 2081), with her father.

276. Non-on-dá-gon, a chief
Delaware, 1830
29 x 24 (73.7 x 60.9)

"Non-on-dá-gon, with a silver ring in his nose, is another of the chiefs of distinction, whose history I admired very much. . . . In both of these . . . [portraits (nos. 275, 276)] their dresses were principally of stuffs of civilized manufacture; and their heads were bound with vari-coloured handkerchiefs or shawls, which were tastefully put on like a Turkish turban" (*Letters and Notes*, vol. 2, pp. 102-3, pl. 198).

References: 1837 catalogue, no. 287; Donaldson, p. 198, pl. 56; Ewers (1956), p. 519; Gilcrease catalogue, p. 54.

Versions:
Gilcrease Institute, watercolor, 6 x 5, signed lower right (on mount): Geo. Catlin

Gilcrease Institute, NAI sketchbook (4776.29), pen and ink

Probably painted at Fort Leavenworth in 1830 (see no. 274). The subject is bust length in the Gilcrease watercolor and his earrings and headdress have been modified (see no. 232). He appears again, full length, in cartoon 63 (NGA 2072).

279

280

281

279. The Open Door, known as The Prophet, brother of Tecumseh
Shawnee, 1830
29 x 24 (73.7 x 60.9)

"The '*Shawnee Prophet*,' is perhaps one of the most remarkable men, who has flourished on these frontiers for some time past. This man is brother of the famous Tecumseh, and quite equal in his *medicines* or mysteries, to what his brother was in arms; he was blind in his left eye, and in his right hand he was holding his '*medicine fire*,' and his '*sacred string of beads*' in the other. With these mysteries he made his way through most of the North Western tribes, enlisting warriors wherever he went, to assist Tecumseh in effecting his great scheme, of forming a confederacy of all the Indians on the frontier, to drive back the whites and defend the Indians' rights; which he told them could never in any way be protected. . . . [he] had actually enlisted some eight or ten thousand, who were sworn to follow him home; and in a few days would have been on their way with him, had not a couple of his political enemies from his own tribe . . . defeated his plans, by pronouncing him an imposter. . . .

"This, no doubt, has been a very shrewd and influential man, but circumstances have destroyed him . . . and he now lives respected, but silent and melancholy in his tribe" (*Letters and Notes*, vol. 2, pp. 117-18, pl. 214).

References: 1837 catalogue, no. 153; Donaldson, pp. 201-2, pl. 56; Ewers (1956), pp. 496, 522, pl. 3; Fundaburk, p. 123, pl. 198; McCracken, p. 32, reprod. p. 33; Paris (1963), no. 31; Gilcrease catalogue, p. 54.

Versions:
Gilcrease Institute, watercolor, 7½ x 6½, signed lower right (on mount): Geo. Catlin

Gilcrease Institute, NAI sketchbook (4776.32), pen and ink

Probably painted at Fort Leavenworth in 1830 (see nos. 237, 277; records of the Bureau of Indian Affairs show that The Prophet was living west of the Mississippi by that year). Catlin was undoubtedly moved by The Prophet's desperate and tragic experience; the portrait is one of the artist's best efforts during his first years west of the Mississippi.

The subject is bust length in the Gilcrease watercolor (fig. 147), and he lacks many of the costume accessories that he wears in the Smithsonian original. The latter matches plate 214 in *Letters and Notes*. Charles Bird King also painted The Prophet (see McKenney and Hall, vol. 1, p. 98), and he appears again, full length, in cartoon 74 (NGA 2081).

280. Straight Man, semicivilized
Shawnee, 1830
29 x 24 (73.7 x 60.9)

Described by Catlin as both "semicivilized," and "a warrior" who had "distinguished himself by his exploits; and when he sat for his picture, had painted his face in a very curious manner with black and red paint" (1848 catalogue, p. 30; *Letters and Notes*, vol. 2, p. 117, pl. 213).

References: 1837 catalogue, no. 155; Donaldson, p. 202; Ewers (1956), p. 522; Fundaburk, p. 123, pl. 200.

Version:
Gilcrease Institute, NAI sketchbook (4776.27), pen and ink

Probably painted at Fort Leavenworth in 1830 (see no. 277), although the brushwork and the modeling of the hand seem rather advanced for that date. Straight Man also appears, full length, in cartoon 74 (NGA 2081).

281. Grass, Bush, and Blossom, semicivilized
Shawnee, 1830
29 x 24 (73.7 x 60.9)

The subject is described by Catlin as "half civil, and *more than half* drunk" (1848 catalogue, p. 30).

References: 1837 catalogue, no. 156; *Letters and Notes*, vol. 2, p. 118; Donaldson, pp. 202-3; Ewers (1956), p. 522; Fundaburk, p. 123, pl. 199.

Probably painted at Fort Leavenworth in 1830 (see no. 277).

283

Plate 215, *Letters and Notes.*

282. The Indescribable, a woman
Shawnee, 1830
Unlocated

References: 1837 catalogue, no. 157; Donaldson, p. 203.

Probably painted at Fort Leavenworth in 1830 (see no. 277).

283. John Ross, chief of the tribe
Cherokee, probably 1837-1838
Unlocated

"[Two-thirds of] the Cherokees . . . are yet living in Georgia, under the Government of their chief, John Ross . . . with this excellent man, who has been for many years devotedly opposed to the Treaty stipulations for moving from their country, I have been familiarly acquainted; and notwithstanding the bitter invective and animadversions that have been by his political enemies heaped upon him, I feel authorized, and bound, to testify to the unassuming and gentlemanly urbanity of his manners, as well as to the rigid temperance of his habits, and the purity of his language, in which I never knew him to transgress for a moment, in public or private interviews" (*Letters and Notes,* vol. 2, pp. 119, 120, pl. 215).

Reference: Donaldson, pp. 205-6, pl. 57.

The portrait is not listed in the 1837 catalogue, but does appear in the Egyptian Hall catalogue of January 1840, suggesting that it was painted in the interval. Ross lived in Georgia, according to Catlin, but the two were frequently in Washington, where the sitting probably took place. Plate 215 in *Letters and Notes* (illustrated here) shows Ross dressed and posed in the fashionable style of white subjects Catlin painted in the late 1830s (see no. 271). A portrait of Ross also appears in McKenney and Hall (vol. 3, p. 312).

284. Dutch, a war chief
Cherokee, 1834
28¼ x 23⅛ (71.7 x 58.7)
Collection of Mr. and Mrs. Paul Mellon, Upperville, Virginia
[Figure 96]

"This is one of the most extraordinary men that lives on the frontiers at the present day, both for his remarkable history, and for his fine and manly figure, and character of face. . . . I had him for a constant companion for several months, and opportunities in abundance, for studying his true

character, and of witnessing his wonderful exploits in the different varieties of the chase. The history of this man's life has been very curious and surprising. . . .

"Some twenty years or more since, becoming fatigued and incensed with civilized encroachments . . . on the borders of the Cherokee country in Georgia, where he then resided . . . he beat up for volunteers to emigrate to the West, where he had designed to go, and colonize in a wild country beyond the reach and contamination of civilized innovations; and succeeded in getting several hundred men, women, and children, whom he led over the banks of the Mississippi, and settled upon the head waters of White River, where they lived until the appearance of white faces, which began to peep through the forests at them, when they made another move of 600 miles to the banks of the Canadian, where they now reside; and where, by the system of desperate warfare, which he has carried on against the Osages and the Camanchees, he has successfully cleared away from a large tract of fine country, all the enemies that could contend for it" (*Letters and Notes,* vol. 2, pp. 121-22, pl. 218).

References: 1837 catalogue, no. 191; 1871 catalogue, no. 118; Donaldson, pp. 206-7, pl. 57; Gilcrease catalogue, p. 54.

Versions:
Gilcrease Institute, watercolor, 6 x 5, signed lower left: Geo. Catlin pt.
and lower right (on mount): Geo. Catlin
Gilcrease Institute, NAI sketchbook (4776.32), pen and ink

Copy:
British Museum, London, by John Cullum, watercolor, 12⅞ x 10¼ (1842-1844)

Painted at Fort Gibson in 1834. Donaldson's date for the Cherokee series is incorrect (see no. 31). Catlin had rarely before handled his brush with such boldness and fluency, even in the Upper Missouri series. The technique of this portrait marks a new level of accomplishment, and the characterization of the Cherokee chief is one of the most inspired of the dragoon expedition.

The portrait was apparently withheld from Joseph Harrison and other creditors in 1852, and was eventually sold to the American Museum of Natural History, as cartoon 118, by Catlin's heirs. The Gilcrease watercolor is a careful version of the Mellon original, and both match plate 218 in *Letters and Notes.* An earlier portrait of Dutch is illustrated in McKenney and Hall (vol. 1, pp. 341-42), and he appears again, full length, in cartoon 71 (NGA 2078), with another Cherokee chief.

285. Cól-lee, a Band chief
Cherokee, 1834
29 x 24 (73.7 x 60.9)

"An aged and dignified chief. . . . This man . . . as well as a very great proportion of the Cherokee population, has a mixture of red and white blood in his veins, of which, in this instance, the first seems decidedly to predominate" (*Letters and Notes*, vol. 2, p. 119, pl. 217).

References: 1837 catalogue, no. 192; Donaldson, p. 207, pl. 57; Ewers (1956), p. 518; Fundaburk, p. 122, pl. 194; McCracken, pp. 137-38, reprod. p. 135; Gilcrease catalogue, p. 54 (as *Ah-hoo-loo-tak-kee, the Drum Thrower*).

Version:
Gilcrease Institute, watercolor, 6 x 5, signed lower right (on mount): G C.

Painted at Fort Gibson in 1834. Catlin refers to the subject as Jol-lee in *Letters and Notes*.

The oil portrait has been modeled with a vivacity and assurance that almost equals number 284, but the Gilcrease watercolor, for once, also looks much like a life study (fig. 146). The subject is half-length in the latter, and a chair back is visible behind his right shoulder. The Smithsonian portrait more closely resembles plate 217 in *Letters and Notes*.

Cól-lee appears again, full length, in cartoon 71 (NGA 2078).

286. Black Coat, a chief
Cherokee, 1834
29 x 24 (73.7 x 60.9)

References: 1837 catalogue, no. 193; *Letters and Notes*, vol. 2, p. 119; Donaldson, p. 207; Ewers (1956), p. 518; Fundaburk, p. 122, pl. 195; *Catlin, Bodmer, Miller*; Gilcrease catalogue, p. 54.

Version:
Gilcrease Institute, watercolor, 6 x 5, signed lower right (on mount): Geo. Catlin pt.

Painted at Fort Gibson in 1834 (see no. 284). The Gilcrease watercolor (fig. 145) again appears to be a life study, although the subject lacks many of the costume details that he wears in the Smithsonian portrait (see no. 285).

285

286

287. Ah-hee-te-wáh-chee, a pretty woman
Cherokee, 1834
Unlocated

References: 1837 catalogue, no. 194; *Letters and Notes*, vol. 2, p. 119, pl. 216; Donaldson, p. 208.

Probably painted at Fort Gibson in 1834. Plate 216 of *Letters and Notes* is illustrated in place of the original. Donaldson incorrectly identifies one of the figures in plate 57 as this subject (see no. 289).

287

288

290

288. Great King (called Ben Perryman), a chief
Creek, 1834
29 x 24 (73.7 x 60.9)

Numbers 288 and 289, Catlin writes, are "portraits of two distinguished men, and I believe, both chiefs. . . . These two men are brothers, and are fair specimens of the tribe, who are mostly clad in calicoes, and other cloths of civilized manufacture; tasselled and fringed off by themselves in the most fantastic way, and sometimes with much true and picturesque taste" (*Letters and Notes,* vol. 2, p. 122, pl. 219).

References: 1837 catalogue, no. 200; Donaldson, p. 210, pl. 58; Ewers (1956), pp. 495, 519, pl. 5; Fundaburk, pp. 121-22, pl. 188; McCracken, p. 138, reprod. p. 135; Gilcrease catalogue, p. 54.

Versions:
Gilcrease Institute, watercolor, 6 x 5, signed lower right (on mount): Geo. Catlin
Gilcrease Institute, NAI sketchbook (4776.32), pen and ink

Painted at Fort Gibson in 1834. Catlin shows a suavity and control in the Creek series that almost equals the technical accomplishment of the Cherokee portraits (nos. 284-86). Ewers points out the range of Catlin's subjects on the dragoon expedition, from the civilized Ben Perryman to Little Spaniard (no. 51), a Comanche warrior.

The gun has been left out of the Gilcrease watercolor, and the subject's expression is a schematic version of the Smithsonian original (see no. 232). The latter matches plate 219 in *Letters and Notes.* Ben Perryman supposedly appears again in cartoon 64 (NGA 2073), but the figures bear no relation to the Smithsonian portrait (see nos. 272, 273). Instead the portrait matches a figure in a cartoon labeled A/225 that formerly belonged to the American Museum of Natural History. This cartoon does not seem to correspond to an entry in the 1871 catalogue.

289. Sam Perryman
Creek, 1834
29 x 24 (73.7 x 60.9)
[Figure 92]

See number 288. Catlin also describes the subject as "a jolly companionable man" (1848 catalogue, p. 31).

References: 1837 catalogue, no. 204; *Letters and Notes,* vol. 2, p. 122, pl. 220; Donaldson, p. 210, pl. 57; *Westward the Way,* no. 60, reprod. p. 94; Ewers (1956), p. 519; Fundaburk, p. 122, pl. 189; Gilcrease catalogue, p. 54.

Version:
Gilcrease Institute, watercolor, 6 x 5, signed lower right (on mount): Geo. Catlin

Painted at Fort Gibson in 1834 (see no. 288). Catlin records Sam Perryman's round and mellow features with an appealing insight.

Donaldson incorrectly labels the subject in plate 57 (see no. 287). The Gilcrease watercolor is a careful version of the Smithsonian original, and Perryman supposedly appears again in cartoon 64 (NGA 2073), but instead the Smithsonian portrait matches a figure in an unidentified cartoon (see no. 288).

290. Wat-ál-le-go, a brave
Creek, 1834
29 x 24 (73.7 x 60.9)

References: 1837 catalogue, no. 201; Donaldson, p. 210; Ewers (1956), p. 519; Fundaburk, p. 122, pl. 193; Gilcrease catalogue, p. 54.

Version:
Gilcrease Institute, watercolor, 6 x 5½, signed lower right (on mount): Geo. Catlin 1832

Painted at Fort Gibson in 1834 (see no. 288). The subject's hands do not appear in the Gilcrease watercolor, and his expression is rather different from the Smithsonian original. The dates on the watercolors are not dependable (see no. 46).

291. Hose-put-o-káw-gee, a brave
Creek, 1834
29 x 24 (73.7 x 60.9)

References: 1837 catalogue, no. 202; Donaldson, p. 210; Ewers (1956), p. 519; Fundaburk, p. 122, pl. 190; Gilcrease catalogue, p. 54.

Version:
Gilcrease Institute, watercolor, 6 x 5½

Painted at Fort Gibson in 1834 (see no. 288). The subject's hands are not included in the Gilcrease watercolor, and his costume is more elaborate in the Smithsonian original.

292. Tchow-ee-pút-o-kaw, a woman
Creek, 1834
29 x 24 (73.7 x 60.9)

References: 1837 catalogue, no. 203; Donaldson, p. 210; Ewers (1956), p. 519; Fundaburk, p. 122, pl. 192; Gilcrease catalogue, p. 54.

Version:
Gilcrease Institute, watercolor, 5 x 4½, signed lower right (on mount): Geo. Catlin

Painted at Fort Gibson in 1834 (see no. 288). The subject's facial features are refined and glamorous in the Gilcrease watercolor, but quite plain in the Smithsonian original (see no. 232). She is shown bust length in the former.

293. Tel-maz-há-za, a warrior of distinction
Creek, 1834
29 x 24 (73.7 x 60.9)

References: 1837 catalogue, no. 205; Donaldson, p. 210; Ewers (1956), p. 519; Fundaburk, p. 122, pl. 191; Gilcrease catalogue, p. 54.

Version:
Gilcrease Institute, watercolor, 7½ x 6½

Painted at Fort Gibson in 1834 (see no. 288). Catlin's portraits of exotic Creek Indians remind one of Delacroix's Algerians.

The Gilcrease watercolor is a close version of the Smithsonian original, although the subject in the former is only half-length.

294. He Who Puts Out and Kills, chief of the tribe
Choctaw, 1834
29 x 24 (73.7 x 60.9)

Described by Catlin as a "famous and excellent chief" (*Letters and Notes,* vol. 2, p. 123, pl. 221).

References: 1837 catalogue, no. 280; Donaldson, p. 212, pl. 58; Ewers (1956), p. 518; Fundaburk, p. 125, pl. 213; Gilcrease catalogue, p. 54.

Version:
Gilcrease Institute, watercolor, 6 x 5, signed lower right (on mount): Geo. Catlin

Painted at Fort Gibson in 1834, and similar in style to the Cherokee and Creek portraits (nos. 283-93). Catlin developed a fuller and more subtle range of expression in the Fort Gibson series (see no. 289). Donaldson's date for Catlin's visit to the fort is incorrect (see no. 31).

The subject has a strangely bloated face in the Gilcrease watercolor, and his arms are more awkwardly arranged than in the Smithsonian original. The fan and pipe are not included in the watercolor or plate 221 of *Letters and Notes.* The subject appears again, full length, in cartoon 65 (NGA 2074), with another Choctaw.

291

293

292

294

295

297

296

295. How Did He Kill?, a noted brave
Choctaw, 1834
29 x 24 (73.7 x 60.9)

References: 1837 catalogue, no. 279; Donaldson, p. 212; Ewers (1956), p. 518; Fundaburk, p. 124, pl. 212; Gilcrease catalogue, p. 54.

Version:
Gilcrease Institute, watercolor, 5½ x 4½

Painted at Fort Gibson in 1834 (see no. 294). The subject is called Wa-pa-heo in the Gilcrease catalogue. He is shown half-length in the watercolor, and his garment is less elaborate than in the Smithsonian original.

296. Snapping Turtle, a half-breed
Choctaw, 1834
29 x 24 (73.7 x 60.9)

Described by Catlin as " a distinguished and very gentlemanly man, who has been well-educated, and who gave me much curious and valuable information, of the history and traditions of his tribe" (*Letters and Notes,* vol. 2, p. 123, pl. 222).

References: 1837 catalogue, no. 281; Donaldson, p. 212, pl. 58; Ewers (1956), p. 518; Fundaburk, p. 125, pl. 215; *Catlin, Bodmer, Miller;* Gilcrease catalogue, p. 54; National Portrait Gallery, Washington, D.C., *Abroad in America* (1976), no. 92.

Versions:
Gilcrease Institute, watercolor, 6 x 6, signed lower right (on mount): G Catlin. p
Gilcrease Institute, NAI sketchbook (4776.32), pen and ink

Painted at Fort Gibson in 1834 (see no. 294). The facial features in the Gilcrease watercolor appear too stiff and finished beside the Smithsonian original (see no. 232). Both portraits match plate 222 of *Letters and Notes.*

Charles Dickens, who had probably seen Catlin's Indian Gallery in London, recalls meeting Snapping Turtle in this country in 1842 (see National Portrait Gallery catalogue). The Indian praised Catlin's work and remarked to Dickens that his own portrait was in the collection. Snapping Turtle also appears, full length, in cartoon 65 (NGA 2074).

297. A Choctaw woman
Choctaw, 1834
29 x 24 (73.7 x 60.9)

The subject is described by Catlin as having her hair in braids and a "remarkable expression" (1848 catalogue, p. 31).

References: 1837 catalogue, no. 282; Donaldson, p. 212; Ewers (1956), p. 518; Fundaburk, p. 125, pl. 214; Gilcrease catalogue, p. 54.

Version:
Gilcrease Institute, watercolor, 6 x 5, signed lower right (on mount): Geo. Catlin

Painted at Fort Gibson in 1834 (see no. 294). The Gilcrease portrait is a more finished and voluptuous edition of the Smithsonian original.

298. Drinks the Juice of the Stone
Choctaw, 1834
29 x 24 (73.7 x 60.9)

See number 299.

References: 1837 catalogue, no. 283; Donaldson, p. 212; Haberly, p. 95; Ewers (1956), p. 518; Fundaburk, p. 125, pl. 216; Haverstock, reprod. p. 116; Gilcrease catalogue, p. 54.

Version:
Gilcrease Institute, watercolor, 6 x 5½, signed lower right (on mount): Geo. Catlin

Painted at Fort Gibson in 1834 (see no. 294). Costume details vary between the Gilcrease watercolor and the Smithsonian original. The subject appears to be standing in the former, and seated in the latter.

299. Drinks the Juice of the Stone, in ball-player's dress
Choctaw, 1834
29 x 24 (73.7 x 60.9)
[Figure 100]

"The most distinguished ball-player of the Choctaw nation, represented in his ball-play dress, with his ball-sticks in his hands. In every ball-play of these people, it is a rule of the play, that no man shall wear mocassins on his feet, or any other dress than his breech-cloth around his waist, with a beautiful bead belt, and a 'tail,' made of white horsehair or quills, and a '*mane*' on the neck, of horsehair dyed of various colors" (*Letters and Notes*, vol. 2, pp. 124-25, pl. 223).
See numbers 428 and 429.

References: 1837 catalogue, no. 284; Donaldson, p. 212, pl. 59; *Westward the Way*, no. 59, reprod. p. 93; Ewers (1956), p. 518; Fundaburk, p. 125, pl. 217; McCracken, pp. 140, 181, reprod. p. 141; Gilcrease catalogue, p. 54.

Versions:
Gilcrease Institute, watercolor, 6½ x 5½, signed lower right (on mount): G C.
Gilcrease Institute, NAI sketchbook (4776.51), pen and ink

Copy:
M. Knoedler & Co., New York (until 1971), pencil and watercolor, signed lower right:
Rosa B-[Bonheur]

Painted at Fort Gibson in 1834 (see no. 294). Catlin produces an effective design from the profile of the ballplayer and his equipment (see no. 129).
The Gilcrease watercolor is a faithful edition of the Smithsonian original, and the subject appears again in cartoon 82 (NGA 2085), with two other ballplayers. The original version of this cartoon is in the Gilcrease *Souvenir* album (pl. 50), which in turn is based on plate 21 of *Catlin's North American Indian Portfolio,* first published in 1844.

300. Mick-e-no-páh, chief of the tribe
Seminole, 1838
29 x 24 (73.7 x 60.9)

"*Mick-e-no-pah* is the head chief of the tribe, and a very lusty and dignified man. He took great pleasure in being present every day in my room, whilst I was painting the others; but positively refused to be painted, until he found that a bottle of whiskey, and another of wine, which I kept on my mantlepiece . . . were only to deal out their occasional kindnesses to those who sat for their portraits; when he at length agreed to be painted, 'if I could make a fair likeness of his *legs,*' which he had very tastefully dressed in a handsome pair of red leggings, and upon which I at once began, (as he sat cross-legged), by painting *them* on the lower part of the canvass, leaving room for his body and head above" (*Letters and Notes,* vol. 2, p. 221, pl. 305).
Catlin also mentions that the subject "owned 100 negroes when the [Seminole] war broke out, and was raising large and valuable crops of corn and cotton" (1848 catalogue, p. 31).

References: 1837 catalogue (addendum), no. 302; Donaldson, pp. 215-16, pl. 60; Coe, pp. 25-26, 105-8, reprod. opp. p. 26; Ewers (1956), p. 523; Fundaburk, p. 124, pl. 203; *Catlin, Bodmer, Miller;* Paris (1963), no. 32; University of Florida Gallery, Gainesville, *Artists of the Florida Tropics* (1965), no. 21, reprod.; Haverstock, reprod. p. 32.

Version:
Gilcrease Institute, NAI sketchbook (4776.24), pen and ink

Painted at Fort Moultrie, Charleston, South Carolina, in January 1838 (see nos. 301, 308). Catlin might have done better with the subject's proportions had he not started with his legs, but the face and costume are painted with an accomplishment that supersedes even the Cherokee and Creek portraits (nos. 283-93). Textures are more clearly distinguished from one another, details are vivid and accurate, and costume folds at last reveal an articulate, solid dimension beneath. The hand clutching the blanket and the face are painted with a similar conviction. Catlin uses full, firm strokes to model the jowls that surround the small eyes and heavy features of Mick-e-no-páh, whose face reveals a sensuous blend of black and Indian characteristics. Charles Bird King also painted Mick-e-no-páh (see McKenney and Hall, vol. 2, p. 347), and he appears again in cartoon 68 (NGA 2077), with his wife and other members of the Seminole tribe.

298

300

301. Osceola, the Black Drink, a warrior of great distinction
Seminole, 1838
30⅞ x 25⅞ (78.4 x 65.6)
[Figure 103]

"Os-ce-o-la, commonly called Powell . . . is generally supposed to be a half-breed, the son [grandson] of a white man . . . and a Creek woman.

"I have painted him precisely in the costume, in which he stood for his picture, even to a string and a trinket. He wore three ostrich feathers in his head, and a turban made of a vari-coloured cotton shawl—and his dress was chiefly of calicos, with a handsome bead sash or belt around his waist, and his rifle in his hand.

"This young man is, no doubt, an extraordinary character, as he has been for some years reputed, and doubtless looked upon by the Seminoles as the master spirit and leader of the tribe, although he is not a chief. From his boyhood, he had led an energetic and desperate sort of life, which had secured for him a conspicuous position in society; and when the desperate circumstances of war were agitating his country, he at once took a conspicuous and decided part; and . . . acquired an influence and a name that soon sounded to the remotest parts of the United States, and amongst the Indian tribes, to the Rocky Mountains.

"This gallant fellow, who was, undoubtedly, *captured* a few months since, with several of his chiefs and warriors, was at first brought in to Fort Mellon in Florida, and afterwards sent to this place [Fort Moultrie] for safe-keeping, where he is grieving with a broken spirit, and ready to die, cursing white man, no doubt, to the end of his breath.

"In stature he is about at mediocrity, with an elastic and graceful movement; in his face he is good looking, with rather an effeminate smile; but of so peculiar a character, that the world may be ransacked over without finding another just like it. In his manners, and all his movements in company, he is polite and gentlemanly, though all his conversation is entirely in his own tongue; and his general appearance and actions, those of a full-blooded and wild Indian" (*Letters and Notes,* vol. 2, pp. 219-20).

References: 1837 catalogue (addendum), no. 301; Catlin to C. A. Harris, Jan. 31, 1838, National Archives, M 234, film 289; *New York Evening Star,* Feb. 1, 1838, p. 2; Donaldson, p. 216; Matthews, p. 605, pl. 144; Coe, pp. 26-29, 105-8, frontispiece; H. Chadwick Hunter, "The American Indian in Painting," *Art and Archaeology* 8 (March-April 1919):89, reprod. p. 83; Haberly, pp. 104-5; Joseph E. McCarthy, "Portraits of Osceola and the Artists Who Painted Them," *Jacksonville Historical Society Papers* 2 (1949): 23-44; John M. Goggin, "Osceola: Portraits, Features, and Dress," *Florida Historical Quarterly* 33 (January-April 1955): 168-70, 179, pl. 5; Ewers (1956), pp. 490, 505, 523, pl. 6; Fundaburk, pp. 123-24, pl. 202; McCracken, pp. 186, 187, reprod. p. 190; Halpin, reprod. p. 22; University of Florida Gallery, Gainesville, *Artists of the Florida Tropics* (1965), no. 27, reprod.; Roehm, pp. 125, 127; National Portrait Gallery, Washington, D.C., *This New Man* (1968), p. 101, reprod.; Haverstock, pp. 154-55, 158; Gilcrease catalogue, p. 54.

Copy:
Gilcrease Institute, 25 x 19

Painted at Fort Moultrie in January 1838. See number 308 for further discussion of the Osceola portraits.

Catlin believed that the tragic conclusion of the Seminole war, and the subsequent death of Osceola, were glaring examples of the government's misguided and inhuman Indian removal policy. The portraits of Osceola became one of the artist's major efforts to dramatize the effects of that policy, when one or both were exhibited at the Stuyvesant Institute February 6, 1838 (see *New York Evening Star*).

Osceola's fair skin and refined, almost delicate features came from his paternal grandfather, a Scotsman who had married a Creek woman. Catlin has noted and adjusted these characteristics in such a way as to cast the Seminole warrior as a model of studio perfection, even if the likeness is somewhat in contrast to a bust after a death mask of Osceola illustrated in Matthews. With flawless, even-textured strokes, Catlin builds the head to a full, sculptural dimension that resembles neoclassical portraits of a generation earlier. The artist occasionally reverts to the broader brushwork of the other Seminole portraits in Osceola's costume, but textures and details stand out with an elegance and precision rarely matched in the series.

Catlin says little about the abrupt change of style in the Osceola portrait. Clearly he wished to achieve a work of solid academic merit, in contrast to the rapidly brushed studies that he had done in the West. But he must have also wished to present Osceola as something more acceptable to the public than an Upper Missouri savage. Catlin's solution was to convert the Seminole into a character who might have stepped from the pages of a Chateaubriand novel— a true *Chactas,* the prince of an exotic Indian nation. By so doing he hoped to create an image that would evoke sympathy from the public and from those responsible for a national policy that would eventually destroy such a distinctive culture.

Goggin reviews McCarthy's findings and discusses the portraits of Osceola by Catlin, J. R. Vinton, R. J. Curtis, and others. Catlin's work is accepted as a reasonably accurate description of the subject and his costume. Catlin says in the letter to C. A. Harris, Commissioner of Indian Affairs, that he intends to make copies of the Seminole portraits for the "Indian Department," but none are known today. The Gilcrease painting is a roughly executed copy by an unknown artist after the Smithsonian original.

302. King Phillip, second chief
Seminole, 1838
29 x 24 (73.7 x 60.9)

Described by Catlin as "a very aged chief, who has been a man of great notoriety and distinction in his time" (*Letters and Notes,* vol. 2, p. 220, pl. 300).

References: 1837 catalogue (addendum), no. 304; Donaldson, p. 216, pl. 61; Coe, pp. 105-8, reprod. opp. p. 26; Ewers (1956), p. 523; Fundaburk, p. 124, pl. 209; University of Florida Gallery, Gainesville, *Artists of the Florida Tropics* (1965), no. 22, reprod.; Haverstock, reprod. p. 151.

Version:
Gilcrease Institute, NAI sketchbook (4776.22), pen and ink

Painted at Fort Moultrie in January 1838 (see nos. 300, 301, 308). King Phillip appears again, full length, in cartoon 67 (NGA 2076), with other Seminole prisoners.

303. The Cloud, a chief
Seminole, 1838
29 x 24 (73.7 x 60.9)

Described by Catlin as "a Chief who distinguished himself in the war" and as "a very good-natured, jolly man, growing fat in his imprisonment" (1848 catalogue, p. 32; *Letters and Notes,* vol. 2, p. 220, pl. 299).

References: 1837 catalogue (addendum), no. 305; Donaldson, p. 216; Coe, pp. 105-8, reprod. opp. p. 26; Ewers (1956), p. 523; Fundaburk, p. 124, pl. 205; University of Florida Gallery, Gainesville, *Artists of the Florida Tropics* (1965), no. 23, reprod.; Haverstock, reprod. p. 27.

Version:
Gilcrease Institute, NAI sketchbook (4776.22), pen and ink

Painted at Fort Moultrie in January 1838 (see nos. 300, 301, 308). The Cloud appears again, full length, in cartoon 67 (NGA 2076).

302

303

304. Co-ee-há-jo, a chief
Seminole, 1838
29 x 24 (73.7 x 60.9)

Described by Catlin as a "chief who has been a long time distinguished in the tribe, having signalized himself very much by his feats in the present war" (*Letters and Notes,* vol. 2, p. 220, pl. 301).

References: 1837 catalogue (addendum), no. 303; Donaldson, p. 216; Coe, pp. 105-8, reprod. opp. p. 26; Ewers (1956), p. 523; Fundaburk, p. 124, pl. 204; *Catlin, Bodmer, Miller;* University of Florida Gallery, Gainesville, *Artists of the Florida Tropics* (1965), no. 24, reprod.

Version:
Gilcrease Institute, NAI sketchbook (4776.22), pen and ink

Painted at Fort Moultrie in January 1838 (see nos. 300, 301, 308). The subject appears again, full length, in cartoon 67 (NGA 2076).

304

305

307

306

Plate 304, *Letters and Notes.*

305. The Licker, called "Creek Billy"
Seminole, 1838
29 x 24 (73.7 x 60.9)

Described by Catlin as "a half-breed warrior" and "a very handsome fellow" (1848 catalogue, p. 32; *Letters and Notes,* vol. 2, p. 221, pl. 302).

References: 1837 catalogue (addendum), no. 306; Donaldson, p. 216; Coe, pp. 105-8, reprod. opp. p. 26; Ewers (1956), p. 523; Fundaburk, p. 124, pl. 211; University of Florida Gallery, Gainesville, *Artists of the Florida Tropics* (1965), no. 25, reprod.; Haverstock, reprod. p. 33.

Version:
Gilcrease Institute, NAI sketchbook (4776.22), pen and ink

Painted at Fort Moultrie in January 1838 (see nos. 300, 301, 308). The Licker appears again, full length, in cartoon 67 (NGA 2076).

306. How-ee-dá-hee, a woman
Seminole, 1838
Unlocated

References: 1837 catalogue (addendum), no. 307; *Letters and Notes,* vol. 2, p. 221, pl. 304; Donaldson, p. 216; Coe, pp. 105-8, reprod. opp. p. 26.

Version:
Gilcrease Institute, NAI sketchbook (4776.25), pen and ink

Painted at Fort Moultrie in January 1838 (see nos. 300, 301, 308). This portrait is probably reproduced in plate 304 of *Letters and Notes* (illustrated here), although the subject is not fully identified in the text (see no. 307). She appears again, in the same pose and a similar costume, in cartoon 68 (NGA 2077), as the wife of Mick-e-no-páh (no. 300).

307. A Seminole woman
Seminole, 1838
29 x 24 (73.7 x 60.9)

References: 1837 catalogue (addendum), no. 308; Donaldson, p. 216; Coe, pp. 105-8, reprod. opp. p. 26; Ewers (1956), p. 523; Fundaburk, p. 124, pl. 208; University of Florida Gallery, Gainesville, *Artists of the Florida Tropics* (1965), no. 26, reprod.; Haverstock, reprod. p. 32; *America as Art,* no. 169.

Painted at Fort Moultrie in January 1838 (see nos. 300, 301, 308). Donaldson is apparently mistaken in identifying this portrait as plate 304 in *Letters and Notes* (see no. 306). Catlin was forever unable to compose a seated figure.

308. Osceola, the Black Drink (full length)
Seminole, 1838
28 x 23⅛ (71.1 x 58.7)
American Museum of Natural History,
New York
[Figure 28]

See number 301 for description of Osceola.

References: 1837 catalogue (addendum), no. 309;
Letters and Notes, vol. 2, pp. 219-20, pl. 298; *Great
Exhibition of the Works of Industry of All Na-
tions*, Official Descriptive and Illustrated
Catalogue, London (1851), vol. 2, p. 834;
Donaldson, pp. 217-19, pl. 63; Coe, pp. 105-8;
Holger Cahill and Alfred H. Barr, Jr., *Art in
America* (New York, 1934), p. 41; E. P. Rich-
ardson, *American Romantic Painting* (New
York, 1944), p. 28, pl. 69; Frank Weitenkampf,
"Early Pictures of North American Indians," *Bul-
letin of the New York Public Library* 53 (De-
cember 1949): 610; John M. Goggin, "Osceola:
Portraits, Features, and Dress," *Florida Historical
Quarterly* 33 (January-April 1955): 168-70, 190;
Kennedy catalogue, p. 13; Fundaburk, p. 128, pl.
286; McCracken, pp. 186, 187, 212; Gilcrease
catalogue, p. 54.

Versions:
Harold McCracken, Cody, Wyoming, pen and ink,
7¼ x 9⅞

Gilcrease Institute, NAI sketchbook (4776.24),
pen and ink

Copies:
John K. Foster Antiques, North Hollywood,
California, 29⅝ x 24⅜

Statuette of Osceola, by Napoleon Montanari (see
Crystal Palace catalogue).

Haberly and McCracken have Catlin rushing off to
South Carolina to expose the Army's treacherous
capture of Osceola, but a letter from the artist to C.
A. Harris, Commissioner of Indian Affairs,
suggests that there may have been a commission
involved (see no. 301 for further discussion of the
Osceola portraits). Catlin arrived at Fort Moultrie
in Charleston, on January 17, 1838, according to
Goggin, and wrote to Harris that he was back in
New York by January 30. He painted at least ten

Seminole and Yuchi Indians during his approximately ten days at the fort, including a carefully
finished bust-length portrait of Osceola (no. 301),
which probably served as the model, along with
sketches and notes, for the full-length portrait.
Goggin and Fundaburk maintain that the latter
was completed at Fort Moultrie, but Catlin probably painted it for the February 6 exhibition at the
Stuyvesant Institute. The two portraits are almost
identical from the waist up, although Osceola's
sash in the Smithsonian portrait is replaced by a
pouch and powder horn in the full-length version,
and the technique of the latter does not appear to
be as polished as number 301.

The full-length portrait became widely known
through a lithograph (ca. 26¼ x 19½, illustrated
here) published by Catlin in New York in 1838. (A
half-length mezzotint [ca. 8¾ x 7½], more closely
resembling number 301, was published the same
year by John Sartain; see McCracken, p. 212.) The
lithograph, a detailed replica of the original, was
copied in all different media by Catlin's contemporaries.

The original portrait was apparently withheld
from Joseph Harrison and other creditors in 1852,
and was eventually sold to the American
Museum of Natural History by Catlin's heirs. The
McCracken drawing may be a study for plate 298
of *Letters and Notes,* and the Foster Antiques
copy, to which a tropical landscape has been
added, is after the lithograph. Osceola also appears
in cartoon 68 (NGA 2077), with other members of
the Seminole tribe. The original version of the cartoon is in the Gilcrease *Souvenir* album (pl. 32).

309. Deer without a Heart, a chief
Yuchi, 1838
29 x 24 (73.7 x 60.9)

References: 1837 catalogue (addendum), no. 310;
Donaldson, p. 221; Ewers (1956), p. 524; Fundaburk, p. 123, pl. 196.

Painted at Fort Moultrie in January 1848 (see no.
308). The Yuchi portraits appear to have been
composed and executed with greater haste than
those in the Seminole series.

308

Lithograph of Osceola.

309

310

312

310. Chee-a-ex-e-co, daughter of Deer without a Heart
Yuchi, 1838
29 x 24 (73.7 x 60.9)

References: 1837 catalogue (addendum), no. 311; Donaldson, p. 221; Ewers (1956), p. 524; Fundaburk, p. 123, pl. 197; *Catlin, Bodmer, Miller.*

Painted at Fort Moultrie in January 1838 (see no. 309).

311. St. Louis from the river below
1832-1833
19⅜ x 26⅞ (49.2 x 68.1)
[Figure 10]

"St. Louis . . . is a flourishing town, of 15,000 inhabitants, and destined to be the great emporium of the West. . . . [It] is the great depôt of all the Fur Trading Companies to the Upper Missouri and Rocky Mountains, and their starting-place; and also for the Santa Fe, and other Trading Companies, who reach the Mexican borders overland, to trade for silver bullion, from the extensive mines of that rich country.

"I have also made it *my* starting-point, and place of deposit, to which I send from different quarters, my packages of paintings and Indian articles, minerals, fossils, &c., as I collect them in various regions, here to be stored till my return; and where on my *last return*, if I ever make it, I shall hustle them altogether, and remove them to the East" (*Letters and Notes*, vol. 2, pp. 29-30).

References: 1837 catalogue, no. 321; Donaldson, p. 231; Haberly, p. 48; *Mississippi Panorama*, no. 27, p. 37, reprod. p. 71; Ewers (1956), pp. 486, 524; McCracken, pp. 39-40, reprod. p. 40; Roehm, pp. 57-58; J. F. McDermott, ed., *Travelers on the Western Frontier* (Urbana, Ill., 1970), pp. 38, 59, reprod. p. 51; Corcoran Gallery of Art, Washington, D.C., *Wilderness* (1971), no. 44; Haverstock, pp. 49-51; Peter Hassrick, *The Way West: Art of Frontier America* (New York, 1977), reprod. p. 35.

Probably painted in St. Louis in 1832. It is one of the two earliest views of the city, according to *Mississippi Panorama*, and it ranks with the Niagara Falls series as Catlin's most detailed landscape.

A lithograph after the painting is inscribed: "St. Louis in 1832./From an original Painting by Geo. Catlin in possession of the Mercantile Library Association." The association was not founded until 1846, however, and there is no record that such a painting was ever in its collection. Apparently the lithograph was taken from the Smithsonian painting, although the steamboat in the foreground of the former is not the *Yellowstone,* but a similar side-wheeler called the *St. Louis.* Catlin gives dates of 1833 and 1836 for the painting in, respectively, the 1837 and 1848 catalogues. There is no apparent justification for either date.

In the summer of 1832, with Catlin aboard, the *Yellowstone* made its historic voyage up the Missouri to Fort Union, the American Fur Company's trading post at the mouth of the Yellowstone River. The next summer, after carrying Prince Maximilian and Karl Bodmer to the same destination, the steamboat was destroyed by fire (see McDermott for Bodmer's watercolor of the *Yellowstone*).

312. View on the Upper Mississippi, beautiful prairie bluffs
1835-1836
19⅝ x 27⅝ (49.8 x 70.1)

References: 1837 catalogue, no. 322; Donaldson, p. 232; Ewers (1956), p. 524.

Catlin probably sketched most of the Upper Mississippi River landscapes on his canoe trip from the Falls of St. Anthony to Dubuque in 1835. He mentions frequently in *Letters and Notes* (vol. 2, pp. 141, 142, 144, 152) that he used pencil and paper to record certain views, and a sketchbook now owned by the National Collection of Fine Arts must have been one that he was carrying at the time. Several consecutive pages of pencil drawings in the NCFA sketchbook are of towns, forts, and scenery observed along the river (fig. 157) that reappear, in somewhat modified form, in Upper Mississippi paintings (see nos. 326, 327, 330, 333).

On the evidence of these sketches, and the lack of convincing light or atmospheric effects in the paintings, one must conclude that the Upper Mississippi landscapes (unlike those painted on the Upper Missouri, see nos. 373, 390) are studio productions, perhaps completed the following winter. They share a certain blandness of color and outline, when compared to the former series, and Catlin has reduced many of the distinctive features of the Mississippi shoreline to a simplified and convenient repetition of forms.

There is no apparent basis for the dates assigned to this series of landscapes by Donaldson, and this painting is not illustrated in *Letters and Notes*.

313. Bad Axe, above Prairie du Chien
1835-1836
Unlocated

Described by Catlin as the "battle-ground where Black Hawk was defeated by General Atkinson, above Prairie du Chien. Indians making defense and swimming the river" (1848 catalogue, p. 33).

References: 1837 catalogue, no. 323; Donaldson, p. 233; Gilcrease catalogue, p. 55.

Version:
Gilcrease Institute, 11 x 14

Probably sketched in 1835 (see no. 312). The Gilcrease version is illustrated in place of the original (see no. 125).

314. Ojibwa gathering wild rice near the source of the St. Peter's River
1836-1837
Unlocated

"A party of Sioux, in bark canoes . . . gathering the wild rice, which grows in immense fields around the shores of the rivers and lakes of these northern regions, and used by the Indians as an useful article of food. The mode of gathering it is curious . . . one woman paddles the canoe whilst another, with a stick in each hand, bends the rice over the canoe with one, and strikes it with the other, which shells it into the canoe, which is constantly moving along until it is filled" (*Letters and Notes,* vol. 2, p. 208, pl. 278).

References: 1837 catalogue, no. 324; Donaldson, p. 234; Gilcrease catalogue, p. 55.

Versions:
Gilcrease Institute, 11 x 14

Gilcrease Institute, NAI sketchbook (4776.78), pen and ink

Sketched in 1836 on the return trip from Pipestone Quarry, according to *Letters and Notes.* The Gilcrease version is illustrated in place of the original, and the scene is repeated in cartoon 192 (NGA 2096).

315. View near Prairie la Crosse, beautiful prairie bluffs
1835-1836
Unlocated

The scene is described by Catlin as "above Prairie du Chien, Upper Mississippi" (1848 catalogue, p. 33).

References: 1837 catalogue, no. 325; Donaldson, p. 234.

Probably sketched in 1835 (see no. 312). The landscape may be similar to number 317.

316. Cap à l'Ail (Garlic Cape), a bold promontory on the Upper Mississippi
1835-1836
Unlocated

Catlin describes the location of Garlic Cape as "about twenty miles above Prairie du Chien" (*Letters and Notes,* vol. 2, p. 143, pl. 250).

References: 1837 catalogue, no. 326; Donaldson, p. 234; Los Angeles County Museum of Art, *The American West* (1972), p. 93; Gilcrease catalogue, p. 55.

Versions:
Gilcrease Institute, 11 x 14

Gilcrease Institute, NAI sketchbook (4776.76), pen and ink

Probably sketched in 1835 (see no. 312). The Gilcrease version is illustrated in place of the original, and the scene is repeated in cartoon 362 (unlocated).

Seth Eastman did several watercolors of the same bluffs about twelve years later (see *The American West*).

317. Picturesque bluffs above Prairie du Chien
1835-1836
19½ x 27⅝ (49.7 x 70)
[Figure 118]

References: 1837 catalogue, no. 327; *Letters and Notes,* vol. 2, p. 130, pl. 228; Donaldson, p. 234; Ewers (1956), p. 524.

Probably sketched in 1835 (see nos. 312, 322). Despite Donaldson's claim to the contrary, the landscape does appear in *Letters and Notes* (see no. 329).

Gilcrease Institute, Tulsa.

314

Gilcrease Institute, Tulsa.

316

Gilcrease Institute, Tulsa.

Cartoon 239, National Gallery of Art, Washington, D.C. Paul Mellon Collection.

Cartoon 241, Collection of Mr. and Mrs. Paul Mellon, Upperville, Virginia.

Cartoon 434, National Gallery of Art, Washington, D.C. Paul Mellon Collection.

318. "Pike's Tent," the highest bluff on the Mississippi
1835-1836
Unlocated

The bluff is described by Catlin as "running up in the form of a tent; from which circumstance, and that of having first been ascended by Lieutenant Pike, it has taken the name" (*Letters and Notes*, vol. 2, p. 143, pl. 249).

References: 1837 catalogue, no. 328; Donaldson, p. 234.

Probably sketched in 1835 (see no. 312). The scene is repeated in cartoon 239 (NGA 2153, illustrated here).

319. View of "Cornice Rocks," Upper Mississippi
1835-1836
Unlocated

Catlin describes the rocks as a fisherman's paradise, 750 miles above St. Louis, with "Pikes Tent" (no. 318) in the distance (*Letters and Notes*, vol. 2, pp. 143-44, pl. 251; 1848 catalogue, p. 34).

References: 1837 catalogue, no. 329; Donaldson, p. 234.

Version:
Gilcrease Institute, NAI sketchbook (4776.76), pen and ink

Probably sketched in 1835 (see no. 312). The scene is repeated in cartoon 241 (Collection of Mr. and Mrs. Paul Mellon, illustrated here).

320. Lover's Leap, on Lake Pepin, Upper Mississippi
1835-1836
Unlocated

"The *Lover's Leap* is a bold and projecting rock, of six or seven hundred feet elevation on the East side of the Lake, from the summit of which, it is said, a beautiful Indian girl, the daughter of a chief, threw herself off in presence of her tribe, some fifty years ago, and dashed herself to pieces, to avoid being married to a man whom her father had decided to be her husband" (*Letters and Notes*, vol. 2, p. 143, pl. 248).

References: 1837 catalogue, no. 330; Donaldson, pp. 234-35; J. F. McDermott, *Seth Eastman*, pl. 95.

Version:
Gilcrease Institute, NAI sketchbook (4776.76), pen and ink

Probably sketched in 1835 (see no. 312). The scene is repeated in cartoon 363 (unlocated) and in car-

toon 434 (NGA 2286, illustrated here), an oil-on-canvas version from the LaSalle series.

Seth Eastman's watercolor of *Wenona's Leap*, painted about twelve years later (see McDermott), shows clearly that the bluff is a more complex structure than Catlin chose to record.

321. Falls of St. Anthony, 900 miles above St. Louis
1835-1836
Unlocated

"The Fall of St. Anthony . . . is the natural curiosity of this country . . . and, although a picturesque and spirited scene, is but a pigmy in size to Niagara, and other cataracts in our country—the actual perpendicular fall being but eighteen feet, though of half a mile or so in extent, which is the width of the river; with brisk and leaping rapids above and below, giving life and spirit to the scene" (*Letters and Notes*, vol. 2, p. 131, pl. 230).

References: 1837 catalogue, no. 331; Donaldson, p. 235; Matthews, p. 600, pl. 135; J. F. McDermott, *Seth Eastman*, pl. 86.

Versions:
Hanzel Galleries, Chicago (1976), oil on paperboard, 16 x 22, signed lower left: G. Catlin 1871.

Gilcrease Institute, NAI sketchbook (4776.75), pen and ink

Probably sketched in 1835 during Catlin's visit to Fort Snelling (see no. 312). The scene is repeated in cartoon 240 (Collection of Mr. and Mrs. Paul Mellon, fig. 25) and in cartoon 435 (NGA 2287) with Father Hennepin's party in the foreground. An Indian and his wife, carrying freshly caught fish, cross the center foreground of the Hanzel Galleries version.

Seth Eastman's view of the falls some twelve years later is remarkably close to Catlin's landscape (see McDermott). Matthews compares the solitude of the falls in 1835 to the industrial environment of Minneapolis that surrounded them by the late nineteenth century.

322. Madame Ferrebault's Prairie, above Prairie du Chien
1835-1836
19½ x 27½ (49.6 x 69.9)

References: 1837 catalogue, no. 332; Donaldson, p. 235; *Mississippi Panorama*, no. 28, reprod. p. 72; Ewers (1956), p. 524; McCracken, reprod. p. 166; Halpin, reprod. p. 2; Montreal Museum of Fine Arts, *The Painter and the New World* (1967), no. 230, reprod.

Probably sketched in 1835 (see no. 312). The reflections in the still surface of the Upper Mississippi are similar to those in number 317.

323. Little Falls, near the Falls of St. Anthony
1835-1836
Unlocated

References: 1837 catalogue, no. 333; Donaldson, p. 235; *Westward the Way*, p. 47; Haverstock, reprod. p. 73; Gilcrease catalogue, p. 55.

Version:
Gilcrease Institute, 11 x 14

Probably sketched in 1835 (see no. 312), and undoubtedly the same falls as Seth Eastman's *Laughing Waters* (see *Westward the Way*). The Gilcrease version is illustrated in place of the original.

324. La montagne que trempe l'eau, above Prairie du Chien
1835-1836
Unlocated

"This mountain, or rather pyramid, is an anomaly in this country, rising as it does, about seven hundred feet from the water, and washed at its base, all around, by the river; which divides and runs on each side of it. It is composed chiefly of rock, and all of its strata correspond exactly with those of the projecting promontories on either side of the river" (*Letters and Notes*, vol. 2, p. 209).

References: 1837 catalogue, no. 334; Donaldson, p. 235; J. F. McDermott, *Seth Eastman*, pl. 58.

Probably sketched in 1835 (see no. 312), and later repeated in cartoon 364 (unlocated). Seth Eastman recorded the same scene several years later (see McDermott).

325. Cassville, below Prairie du Chien
1835-1836
Unlocated

Described by Catlin as "a small village just commenced, in 1835" (1848 catalogue, p. 34).

References: 1837 catalogue, no. 335; Donaldson, p. 235; Los Angeles County Museum of Art, *The American West* (1972), p. 94; Gilcrease catalogue, p. 55.

Version:
Gilcrease Institute, 11 x 14

Probably sketched in 1835 (see no. 312). The Gilcrease version is illustrated in place of the original. Seth Eastman painted a distant view of Cassville some twelve years later (see *The American West*).

326. Dubuque, a town in the lead mining country
1835-1836
Unlocated

"It is a small town of 200 houses, built entirely within the last two years, on one of the most delightful sights on the river, and in the heart of the richest and most productive parts of the mining region; having this advantage over most other mining countries, that immediately over . . . the lead mines; the land on the surface produces the finest corn, and all other vegetables that may be put into it" (*Letters and Notes*, vol. 2, p. 149).

References: 1837 catalogue, no. 336; Donaldson, pp. 235-36.

Probably sketched in 1835 (see number 312). On a page labeled "Dubuque" in the NCFA sketchbook is a faint drawing of several houses on an irregular shoreline.

327. Galena, a small town on the Upper Mississippi
1835-1836
Unlocated

References: 1837 catalogue, no. 337; *Letters and Notes*, vol. 2, p. 148; Donaldson, p. 236.

Probably sketched in 1835 (see no. 312). On a page labeled "Galena" in the NCFA sketchbook is a drawing of a small town at the bend of a river, surrounded by rolling hills (illustrated here).

Gilcrease Institute, Tulsa.

Gilcrease Institute, Tulsa.

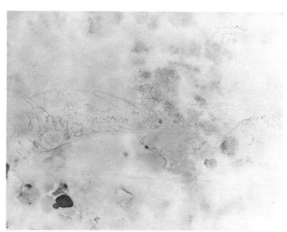
Galena, NCFA sketchbook.

328. Rock Island, United States garrison
1835-1836
19⅝ x 27⅝ (49.7 x 70.2)

References: 1837 catalogue, no. 338; *Letters and Notes,* vol. 2, p. 148; Donaldson, p. 236; Ewers (1956), p. 524; J. F. McDermott, *Seth Eastman,* pl. 60.

Probably sketched in 1835 (see no. 312). The scene is repeated in cartoon 365 (unlocated).

In the NFCA sketchbook is a drawing that appears to be the opposite side of Fort Armstrong. The fort was abandoned in 1836, but was still standing in 1848, according to the date on a drawing by Seth Eastman (see McDermott).

329. Beautiful prairie bluffs, Upper Mississippi
1835-1836
19½ x 27½ (49.6 x 69.9)

References: 1837 catalogue, no. 339; Donaldson, p. 236; Ewers (1956), p. 524; Gilcrease catalogue, p. 55.

Version:
Gilcrease Institute, 11 x 14

Probably sketched in 1835 (see no. 312). Donaldson mistakenly identifies the landscape as plate 228 in *Letters and Notes* (see no. 317).

The right sides of the Gilcrease and Smithsonian landscapes are reasonably similar, but a steep hillside has been added at the left edge of the former. Catlin painted the small Gilcrease oils between 1851 and 1853 (see no. 125).

330. Dubuque's Grave, Upper Mississippi
1835-1836
19⅝ x 27⅝ (49.7 x 70)

"*Dubuque's Grave* is a place of great notoriety on this river, in consequence of its having been the residence and mining place of the first lead mining pioneer of these regions, by the name of Dubuque, who held his title under a grant from the Mexican Government (I think), and settled by the side of this huge bluff, on the pinnacle of which he erected the tomb to receive his own body, and placed over it a cross with his own inscription on it. . . .

"At the foot of this bluff, there is now an extensive smelting furnace, where vast quantities of lead are melted from the ores which are dug out of the hills in all directions about it" (*Letters and Notes,* vol. 2, p. 130, pl. 229).

References: 1837 catalogue, no. 340; Donaldson, pp. 236-38; Matthews, p. 600, pl. 134; Ewers (1956), p. 524.

Version:
Gilcrease Institute, NAI sketchbook (4776.75), pen and ink

Probably sketched in 1835 (see number 312). The scene is repeated in cartoon 366 (unlocated).

On a page labeled "Dubuque's Bluff" in the NCFA sketchbook is a drawing of rock formations that might be a detail of those below the grave site. Matthews says that the sepulcher had disappeared by 1857.

331. River bluffs, magnificent view, Upper Mississippi
1835-1836
Unlocated

References: 1837 catalogue, no. 341; Donaldson, p. 238.

Probably sketched in 1835 (see no. 312).

332. Fort Snelling, United States garrison at the mouth of the St. Peter's River
1835-1836
Unlocated

"On the point of land between the Mississippi and the St. Peters rivers, the United States' Government has erected a strong Fort, which has taken the name of Fort Snelling, from the name of a distinguished and most excellent officer of that name, who superintended the building of it. The site of this Fort is one of the most judicious that could have been selected in the country, both for health and defense; and being on an elevation of 100 feet or more above the water, has an exceedingly bold and picturesque effect" (*Letters and Notes,* vol. 2, p. 131, pl. 231).

References: 1837 catalogue, no. 342; Donaldson, pp. 238-39; McCracken, pp. 160, 162, 165-66; J. F. McDermott, *Seth Eastman,* pl. 22; Roehm, pp. 81-82; Haverstock, pp. 135-36; Gilcrease catalogue, p. 55.

Versions:
Gilcrease Institute, 11 x 14
Gilcrease Institute, NAI sketchbook (4776.75), pen and ink

Probably sketched in 1835 during Catlin's visit to Fort Snelling (see no. 312). The Gilcrease oil is illustrated in figure 24, and the scene is repeated in cartoon 367 (unlocated).

Seth Eastman painted a similar view of the fort three years later (see McDermott).

333. Prairie du Chien, United States garrison
1835-1836
19½ x 27⅝ (49.5 x 70)
[Figure 117]

"Prairie du Chien has been one of the earliest and principal trading posts of the Fur Company, and they now have a large establishment at that place; but doing far less business than formerly, owing to the great mortality of the Indians in its vicinity, and the destruction of the game, which has almost entirely disappeared in these regions. The prairie is a beautiful elevation above the river, of several miles in length, and a mile or so in width, with a most picturesque range of grassy bluffs encompassing it in the rear. The Government has erected there a substantial Fort, in which are generally stationed three or four companies of men, for the purpose . . . of keeping the peace amongst the hostile tribes, and also of protecting the frontier inhabitants from the attacks of the excited savages" (*Letters and Notes*, vol. 2, pp. 144-45, pl. 253).

References: 1837 catalogue, no. 343; Donaldson, p. 239; Ewers (1956), p. 524; J. F. McDermott, *Seth Eastman*, pl. 11; Los Angeles County Museum of Art, *The American West* (1972), no. 21, reprod. p. 87; Gilcrease catalogue, p. 55.

Versions:
Gilcrease Institute, 11 x 14

Gilcrease Institute, NAI sketchbook (4776.77), pen and ink

Probably sketched in 1835 during Catlin's visit to Prairie du Chien (see no. 312). The river channels are less clearly marked in the Gilcrease version (see no. 329), and the scene is repeated in cartoon 368 (unlocated).

In the NCFA sketchbook is a drawing of several military barracks on a level terrace above a river. The scene is somewhat similar to Seth Eastman's view of Fort Crawford in 1829 (see McDermott).

334. Ojibwa village and dog feast at the Falls of St. Anthony
1835-1836
Unlocated

"The encampment of the Chippeways, to which I have been a daily visitor, was built in the manner seen in plate 238; their wigwams made of birch bark, covering the framework, which was of slight poles stuck in the ground, and bent over at the top, so as to give a rooflike shape to the lodge, best calculated to ward off rain and winds" (*Letters and Notes*, vol. 2, p. 137, pl. 238).

References: 1837 catalogue, no. 344; Donaldson, pp. 239-40; Rena N. Coen, *Painting and Sculpture in Minnesota, 1820-1914* (Minneapolis, 1976), p. 8.

Version:
Gilcrease Institute, NAI sketchbook (4776.56), pen and ink

Probably sketched during Catlin's visit to Fort Snelling in 1835 (see no. 312). The scene is repeated in cartoon 127 (AMNH 240, illustrated here), to which Coen mistakenly assigns the date of the original.

335. Sioux village, Lake Calhoun, near Fort Snelling
1835-1836
19½ x 27½ (49.6 x 69.9)

References: 1837 catalogue, no. 345; Donaldson, p. 240; Ewers (1956), p. 510.

Probably sketched during Catlin's visit to Fort Snelling in 1835 (see no. 312). Cartoon 387 (Collection of Mr. and Mrs. Paul Mellon) is a related view.

336. Coteau des Prairies, headwaters of the St. Peter's River
1836-1837
Unlocated

The scene is described by Catlin as "My companion, Indian guide, and myself encamping at sunset, cooking by our fire, made of buffalo-dung" (1848 catalogue, p. 35).

The Coteau des Prairies is the dividing ridge between the Minnesota (St. Peter's) and Missouri rivers. It is "several hundred miles in length," the artist observes, "and varying from fifty to a hundred in width . . . perhaps the noblest mound of its kind in the world. It gradually and gracefully rises on each side, by swell after swell, without tree, bush or rock (save what are to be seen in the vicinity of Pipestone Quarry), and everywhere covered with green grass, affording the traveller, from its highest elevations, the most unbounded and sublime views of—nothing at all—save the blue and boundless ocean of prairies that lie beneath and all around him" (*Letters and Notes*, vol. 2, pp. 204-5).

References: 1837 catalogue, no. 346; Donaldson, p. 240.

Sketched in 1836 on Catlin's journey to the Pipestone Quarry (see no. 337). Cartoon 304 (unlocated) may be a related view.

334

Cartoon 127, American Museum of Natural History, New York.

335

338

Cartoon 200, Collection of Mr. and Mrs. Paul Mellon, Upperville, Virginia.

337. Pipestone Quarry, on the Coteau des Prairies
1836-1837
19½ x 27¼ (49.5 x 69.2)
[Figure 27]

"For many miles we had the Coteau in view in the distance before us [see no. 336], which looked like a blue cloud settling down in the horizon. . . .

"On the very top of this mound or ridge, we found the far-famed quarry or fountain of the Red Pipe, which is truly an anomaly in nature. The principal and most striking feature of this place, is a perpendicular wall of close-grained, compact quartz, of twenty-five and thirty feet in elevation, running nearly North and South with its face to the West, exhibiting a front of nearly two miles in length, when it disappears at both ends by running under the prairie. . . . The depression of the brow of the ridge at this place has been caused by the wash of a little stream, produced by several springs on the top, a little back from the Wall; which has gradually carried away the super-incumbent earth, and having bared the wall for the distance of two miles, is now left to glide for some distance over a perfectly level surface of quartz rock; and then to leap from the top of the wall into a deep basin below, and from thence seek its course to the Missouri, forming the extreme source of a noted and powerful tributary, called the 'Big Sioux.'

"This beautiful wall is horizontal, and stratified in several distinct layers of light grey, and rose or flesh-coloured quartz; and for most of the way, both on the front of the wall, and for acres of its horizontal surface, highly polished or glazed, as if by ignition.

"At the base of this wall there is a level prairie, of half a mile in width, running parallel to it; in any and all parts of which, the Indians procure the red stone for their pipes, by digging through the soil and several slaty layers of the red stone, to the depth of four or five feet. From the very numerous marks of ancient and modern diggings or excavations, it would appear that this place has been for many centuries resorted to for the red stone; and from the great number of graves and remains of ancient fortifications in its vicinity, it would seem, as well as from their actual traditions, that the Indian tribes have long held this place in high superstitious estimation; and also that it has been the resort of different tribes, who have made their regular pilgrimages here to renew their pipes. . . .

"At the base of the wall, and within a few rods of it, and on the very ground where the Indians dig for the red stone, rests a group of five stupendous boulders of gneiss, leaning against each other; the smallest of which is twelve or fifteen feet, and the largest twenty-five feet in diameter, altogether weighing, unquestionably, several hundred tons. . . .

"That these five immense blocks, of precisely the same character, and differing materially from all other specimens of boulders which I have seen in the great vallies of the Mississippi and Missouri, should have been hurled some hundreds of miles from their native bed, and lodged in so singular a group on this elevated ridge, is truly a matter of surprise for the scientific world, as well as for the poor Indian, whose superstitious veneration of them is such, that not a spear of grass is broken or bent by his feet, within three or four rods of them, where he stops, and in humble supplication, by throwing plugs of tobacco to them, solicits permission to dig and carry away the red stone for his pipes." (*Letters and Notes,* vol. 2, pp. 201-6, pl. 270).

References: 1837 catalogue, no. 347; Donaldson, pp. 240-53, pl. 64; Haberly, pp. 98-99; Ewers (1956), pp. 489, 501, 510, pl. 19; McCracken, pp. 174-78, reprod. p. 177; Roehm, pp. 92, 100-101; Corcoran Gallery of Art, Washington, D.C., *Wilderness* (1971), no. 51; Haverstock, pp. 141-47; Gilcrease catalogue, p. 56; Rena N. Coen, *Painting and Sculpture in Minnesota, 1820-1914* (Minneapolis, 1976), p. 8, pl. 3.

Versions:
Gilcrease Institute, 19 x 26, signed lower right: G. Catlin. 1848

Gilcrease Institute, NAI sketchbook (4776.77), pen and ink

Sketched in 1836, when Catlin made his well-documented journey to the Pipestone Quarry in southwestern Minnesota. He was not the first white man to visit the sacred quarry, but he was the first to record its appearance. This is one of his most detailed landscapes, and an interesting parallel to the descriptive passages in *Letters and Notes* that reveal his intense geological interest in the area. Ewers notes that Catlin has exaggerated the height of the ledge and moved the boulders far to the left of their actual location to include them in the picture. The artist occasionally used such devices to increase the dramatic or narrative effect of his landscapes.

The Indians wear leggings and are smaller in scale in the Gilcrease version of 1848.

338. Sault Ste. Marie, Indians catching whitefish
1836-1837
Unlocated

"The *white fish* . . . is caught in immense quantities by the scoop-nets of the Indians and Frenchman, amongst the foaming and dashing of the rapids, where it gains strength and flavour not to be found in the same fish in any other place. This unequalled fishery has long been one of vast importance to the immense number of Indians, who have always assembled about it; but of late, has been found by *money-making men* . . . who have dipped *their* nets til the poor Indian is styled an intruder" (*Letters and Notes,* vol. 2, pp. 161-62, pl. 266).

References: 1837 catalogue, no. 348; Donaldson, pp. 253-54; Porter Butts, *Art in Wisconsin* (Madison, 1936), p. 41; Gilcrease catalogue, p. 55.

Versions:
Gilcrease Institute, 11 x 14
Gilcrease Institute, NAI sketchbook (4776.77), pen and ink

Copy:
Schweitzer Gallery, New York, 50¾ x 67

Sketched in 1836 during Catlin's only visit to Sault Ste. Marie (see *Letters and Notes*, vol. 2, p. 160). The Gilcrease painting is a roughly executed version of plate 266 in *Letters and Notes*. The scene is repeated in cartoon 200 (Collection of Mr. and Mrs. Paul Mellon, see illustration), and in cartoon 233 (unlocated).

The Schweitzer copy is a large flat landscape in which neither the figures nor the foliage has the animated detail of Catlin's touch.

339. Sault Ste. Marie, showing the United States garrison in the distance
1836-1837
19⅝ x 27⅝ (49.7 x 70)

Described by Catlin as "a view of the *Sault de St. Marys*, taken from the Canada shore, near the missionary-house, which is seen in the foreground of the picture, and in the distance, the United States Garrison, and the Rapids; and beyond them the Capes at the outlet of Lake Superior" (*Letters and Notes*, vol. 2, p. 161, pl. 265).

References: 1837 catalogue, no. 349; Donaldson, p. 254; Ewers (1956), p. 524.

Sketched in 1836 (see no. 338). A nineteenth-century print after the painting was published in the *Sault Star*, January 27, 1967.

340. View on the St. Peter's River, twenty miles above Fort Snelling
1836-1837
Unlocated

References: 1837 catalogue, no. 350; *Letters and Notes*, vol. 2, p. 208; Donaldson, p. 254; National Gallery of Art, Washington, D.C., *American Paintings and Sculpture* (1970), p. 32, no. 2148.

Version:
National Gallery of Art, Washington, D.C., 14¾ x 22⅛ (sight)

Cartoon 242, National Gallery of Art, Washington, D.C. Paul Mellon Collection.

Probably sketched in 1836 on the journey to Pipestone Quarry (see no. 337). The landscape may be the same as plate 279 in *Letters and Notes*, which Catlin describes as "one of the many lovely prairie scenes we passed on the banks of the St. Peters river, near the Traverse de Sioux."

Number 242 in the 1871 catalogue (NGA 2148, see illustration) is an oil-on-canvas version of the scene.

341. View on the St. Peter's River, Sioux Indians pursuing a stag in their canoes
1836-1837
19½ x 27⅝ (49.5 x 70.1)

References: 1837 catalogue, no. 351; Donaldson, p. 254; Ewers (1956), p. 511; Henri Dorra, *The American Muse* (New York, 1961), reprod. p. 60; Paris (1963), no. 34; Halpin, reprod. p. 9; Montreal Museum of Fine Arts, *The Painter and the New World* (1967), no. 229, reprod.; Rena N. Coen, *Painting and Sculpture in Minnesota, 1820-1914* (Minneapolis, 1976), p. 8, pl. 2.

Sketched in 1836 on Catlin's journey to Pipestone Quarry (see no. 337). The painting is closely related to several Mississippi River landscapes of the previous year (see nos. 317, 322), and to number 347.

Gilcrease Institute, Tulsa.

Gilcrease Institute, Tulsa.

342. Salt meadows on the Upper Missouri, and great herds of buffalo
1832-1833
Unlocated

"Not many miles back of this range of hills . . . we came suddenly upon a great depression of the prairie, which extended for several miles, and as we stood upon its green banks, which were gracefully sloping down, we could overlook some hundreds of acres of the prairie which were covered with an incrustation of salt, that appeared the same as if the ground was everywhere covered with snow. . . . Through each of these meadows there is a meandering small stream which arises from salt springs, throwing out in the spring of the year great quantities of water, which flood over these meadows to the depth of three or four feet; and during the heat of summer, being exposed to the rays of the sun, entirely evaporates, leaving the incrustation of *muriate* on the surface, to the depth of one or two inches. . . . on approaching the banks of this place we stood amazed at the almost incredible numbers of [buffalo] . . . which were in sight on the opposite banks, at the distance of a mile or two from us, where they were lying in countless numbers, on the level prairie above, and stretching down by hundreds, to lick at the salt, forming in distance, large masses of black, most pleasingly to contrast with the snow white, and the vivid green" (*Letters and Notes*, vol. 1, pp. 219-20).

References: 1837 catalogue, no. 352; Donaldson, pp. 254-55; Gilcrease catalogue, p. 55.

Version:
Gilcrease Institute, 11 x 14

Probably sketched in 1832 near the mouth of the Teton River. The Gilcrease version is illustrated in place of the original.

343. Wichita village in Oklahoma, at the base of the Wichita Mountains
1834-1835
Unlocated

"We found here a very numerous village, containing some five or six hundred wigwams, all made of long prairie grass, thatched over poles which are fastened in the ground and bent in at the top; giving to them, in distance, the appearance of straw beehives, as in plate 173, which is an accurate view of it, shewing the Red River in front, and the '*mountains of rocks*' behind it" (*Letters and Notes*, vol. 2, p. 70, pl. 173).
    Catlin was referring to the North Fork of the Red River in the above passage. The original title for this painting, *Pawnee Village in Texas, at the base of a spur of the Rocky Mountains*, has been amended to correspond to present-day geographical designations (see no. 345).

References: 1837 catalogue, no. 353; Donaldson, pp. 255-57; Pauline A. Pinckney, *Painting in Texas* (Austin, 1967), pp. 35-36, note 23; Rossi and Hunt, pp. 54, 320; Gilcrease catalogue, p. 55.

Versions:
Gilcrease Institute, 11 x 14
Gilcrease Institute, NAI sketchbook (4776.61), pen and ink

Painted in Catlin's studio from a sketch made by Joe Chadwick at the Wichita village in 1834 (see *Letters and Notes*). The Gilcrease version, which matches plate 173 in *Letters and Notes*, is illustrated in place of the original. The scene is repeated in cartoon 140 (unlocated).

344. View on the Canadian River, in Oklahoma
1834-1835
Unlocated

References: 1837 catalogue, no. 354; Donaldson, p. 257.

Sketched in 1834 on the dragoon expedition.

345. View of the junction of the Red River and the False Washita, in Texas
1834-1835
19⅝ x 27⅝ (49.7 x 70)

"We are, at this place, on the banks of the Red River, having Texas under our eye on the opposite bank. Our encampment is on the point of land between the Red and False Washita rivers, at their junction; and the country about us is a panorama . . . of prairie and timber, alternating in the most delightful shapes and proportions that the eye of a connoisseur could desire. The verdure is everywhere of the deepest green" (*Letters and Notes*, vol. 2, p. 45).
    Presumably, this was the closest Catlin came on the dragoon expedition to the present boundaries of Texas (see no. 343).

References: 1837 catalogue, no. 354½; Donaldson, p. 257; Ewers (1956), p. 518.

Sketched in 1834 on the dragoon expedition. Although Catlin took his "canvass and painting apparatus" on the expedition (see *Letters and Notes*, vol. 2, p. 49), he seems to have reserved them for portraits rather than landscapes. The bland contours of this scene hardly indicate that it was painted on location (see no. 312).

346. Comanche village, women dressing robes and drying meat
1834-1835
20 x 27¼ (50.9 x 69.3)

"The village of the Camanchees . . . is composed of six or eight hundred skin-covered lodges, made of poles and buffalo skins, in the manner precisely as those of the Sioux and other Missouri tribes. . . . This village with its thousands of wild inmates, with horses and dogs, and wild sports and domestic occupations, presents a most curious scene; and the manners and looks of the people, a rich subject for the brush and the pen.

"In the view I have made of it, but a small portion of the village is shewn; which is as well as to shew the whole of it, inasmuch as the wigwams, as well as the customs, are the same in every part of it. In the foreground is seen the wigwam of the chief; and in various parts, crotches and poles, on which the women are drying meat, and *'graining'* buffalo robes" (*Letters and Notes*, vol. 2, p. 64, pl. 164).

The Comanche village visited by Catlin on the dragoon expedition was not in Texas, as he maintains in the original title of this painting, but in southwestern Oklahoma, at the foot of the Wichita Mountains (see nos. 343, 345).

References: 1837 catalogue, no. 355; Donaldson, p. 257, pl. 65; Ewers (1956), p. 509; McCracken, p. 152, reprod. p. 153; Ewers, "The Opening of the West," *The Artist in America* (New York, 1967), reprod. p. 58; M. Knoedler & Co., New York, *The American Indian Observed* (1971), no. 25, reprod. p. 20; Rossi and Hunt, pp. 54, 320.

Version:
Gilcrease Institute, NAI sketchbook (4776.61), pen and ink

Copy:
M. Knoedler & Co., New York (until 1971), pencil and watercolor, signed lower right:
Rosa B-[Bonheur]

Sketched at the Comanche village in 1834 (see no. 345). The women dressing robes and the drying racks are based on drawings in the SI sketchbook (see no. 377). Catlin's quick observation and his haste to recapture a scene led him to paint figures that often have only a planar dimension, composed of several flat strokes of alternating value.

The scene is repeated in cartoon 137 (AMNH 143), and cartoon 373 (unlocated) must be a similar subject.

347. View on the Wisconsin River, Winnebago shooting ducks
1836-1837
19½ x 27⅝ (49.6 x 70)

"The Ouisconsin, which the French most appropriately denominate 'La belle riviere,' may certainly vie with any other on the Continent . . . for its beautifully skirted banks and prairie bluffs. It may justly be said to be equal to the Mississippi about the Prairie du Chien in point of sweetness and beauty, but not on quite so grand a scale" (*Letters and Notes*, vol. 2, p. 163).

References: 1837 catalogue, no. 356; Donaldson, p. 257; Ewers (1956), pp. 489, 524.

Sketched in 1836 on Catlin's journey to the Pipestone Quarry (see no. 341).

348. Lac du Cygne (Swan Lake), near the Coteau des Prairies
1836-1837
19½ x 27⅝ (49.5 x 70)

"After having glutted our curiosity at the fountain of the Red Pipe, our horses brought us to the base of the Coteau, and then over the extended plain that lies between that and the Traverse de Sioux, on the St. Peters. . . .

"In this distance we passed some of the loveliest prairie country in the world, and I made a number of sketches—*'Laque du Cygne,* Swan Lake,' was a peculiar and lovely scene, extending for many miles, and filled with innumerable small islands covered with a profusion of rich forest trees" (*Letters and Notes*, vol. 2, p. 207, pl. 276).

References: 1837 catalogue, no. 357; Donaldson, p. 257; Ewers (1956), p. 524.

Sketched in 1836 on the return trip from Pipestone Quarry. The scene is repeated in cartoon 369 (unlocated).

346

347

348

349

350

351

349. Beautiful savannah in the pine woods of Florida
1834-1835
19½ x 27⅝ (49.6 x 70.1)

"Florida is, in a great degree, a dark and sterile wilderness, yet with spots of beauty and of loveliness, with charms that cannot be forgotten. Her swamps and everglades, the dens of alligators, and lurking places of the desperate savage, gloom the thoughts of the wary traveller, whose mind is cheered and lit to admiration, when in the solitary pine woods, where he hears nought but the echoing notes of the *sand-hill cranes,* or the howling wolf, he suddenly breaks out into the open savannahs, teeming with their myriads of wild flowers, and palmettos" (*Letters and Notes,* vol. 2, p. 33, pl. 147).

References: 1837 catalogue, no. 358; Donaldson, pp. 257-58; Ewers (1956), p. 524; Fundaburk, p. 124, pl. 206; University of Florida Gallery, Gainesville, *Artists of the Florida Tropics* (1965), no. 20, reprod.; Roehm, p. 76; Corcoran Gallery of Art, Washington, D.C., *Wilderness* (1971), no. 50; Gilcrease catalogue, p. 55.

Version:
Gilcrease Institute, 11 x 14

Painted in the winter of 1834-35 during Catlin's visit to Florida (see no. 354). The time sequence in *Letters and Notes* is misleading, but correspondence in Roehm confirms the artist's presence in Pensacola in January 1835. Catlin's description of the Florida wilderness is a heavy mixture of English landscape theory and Gothic novels.

Foreground plants differ somewhat between the Gilcrease landscape and the Smithsonian original. The latter matches plate 147 in *Letters and Notes,* and the scene is repeated in cartoon 370 (unlocated).

350. View on Lake St. Croix, Upper Mississippi
1835-1836
19½ x 26¾ (49.5 x 68)

References: 1837 catalogue, no. 359; Donaldson, p. 259; Art Institute of Chicago, *The Hudson River School and the Early American Landscape Tradition* (1945), no. 25; Ewers (1956), p. 524.

Probably sketched in 1835 (see no. 312). This appears to be one of the more topographically accurate landscapes of the Upper Mississippi series. The scene is repeated in cartoon 371 (unlocated).

351. View on the Canadian River, dragoons crossing
1834-1835
19½ x 27½ (49.5 x 69.9)

References: 1837 catalogue, no. 360; Donaldson, p. 259; Ewers (1956), p. 518.

Sketched in 1834 on the dragoon expedition (see no. 345).

352. Ta-wa-que-nah, or the Rocky Mountain, near the Comanche village
1834-1835
19⅝ x 27⅝ (49.7 x 70)
[Figure 120]

"Our Camanchee guides . . . pointed to their village at several miles distance, in the midst of one of the most enchanting valleys that human eyes ever looked upon . . . with a magnificent range of mountains rising in distance beyond . . . composed entirely of a reddish granite of gneiss" (*Letters and Notes,* vol. 2, p. 60).
   The Comanche village was not in Texas, as Catlin maintains in the original title of this painting (see no. 346).

References: 1837 catalogue, no. 361; Donaldson, p. 259; Ewers (1956), p. 518.

Sketched in 1834 at the Comanche village, or perhaps partially painted on location, an uncommon practice for Catlin on the dragoon expedition (see no. 345). It is the most topographically accurate landscape of the Southern Great Plains series, and a composition that is reminiscent of early Hudson River school paintings.
   The subject is repeated in cartoon 372 (unlocated).

353. Comanche warriors, with white flag, receiving the dragoons
1834-1835
24⅛ x 29⅛ (61.1 x 73.9)
[Figure 23]

"In the midst of this lovely valley [see no. 352], we could just discern amongst the scattering shrubbery that lined the banks of the watercourses, the tops of the Camanchee wigwams, and the smoke curling above them. The valley, for a mile distant about the village, seemed speckled with horses and mules that were grazing in it. The chiefs of the war-party requested the regiment to halt, until they could ride in, and inform their people who were coming. We then dismounted for an hour or so; when we could see them busily running and catching their horses; and at length, several hundreds of their braves and warriors came out at full speed to welcome us, and forming in a line in front of us, as we were again mounted, presented a formidable and pleasing appearance. As they wheeled their horses, they very rapidly formed in a line, and 'dressed' like well-disciplined cavalry. The regiment was drawn up in three columns, with a line formed in front, by Colonel Dodge and his staff, in which rank my friend Chadwick and I were also paraded; when we had a fine view of the whole manoeuvre, which was picturesque and thrilling in the extreme" (*Letters and Notes*, vol. 2, p. 61, pl. 163).

See number 488.

References: 1837 catalogue, no. 363; Donaldson, pp. 259-60; Ewers (1956), p. 509; McCracken, pp. 150-51; Haverstock, reprod. pp. 124-25.

Sketched in 1834 at the Comanche village. Note the dashes of pigment used to indicate the formations of dragoons and Comanche (see no. 346).

Catlin probably reserved his few healthy hours at the village for portraits. Landscapes of such detail must have been painted after his return to St. Louis and the East (see no. 345).

354. White sand bluffs, on Santa Rosa Island, near Pensacola
1834-1835
19⅝ x 27½ (49.6 x 69.9)

"This sketch was made on *Santa Rosa Island*, within a few miles of Pensacola. . . . The hills of sand are as *purely white as snow*, and fifty or sixty feet in height, and supporting on their tops, and in their sides, clusters of magnolia bushes—of myrtle—of palmetto and heather, all of which are evergreens, forming the most vivid contrast with the snow-white sand in which they are growing. On the beach a family of Seminole Indians are encamped, catching and drying red fish, their chief article of food" (*Letters and Notes*, vol. 2, p. 33, pl. 148).

References: 1837 catalogue, no. 363½; Donaldson, pp. 260-61; Ewers (1956), p. 523; Fundaburk, p. 124, pl. 207; University of Florida Gallery, Gainesville, *Artists of the Florida Tropics* (1965), no. 19, reprod.

Version:
Gilcrease Institute, NAI sketchbook (4776.59), pen and ink

Copy:
M. Knoedler & Co., New York (until 1971), pencil and watercolor, signed lower right:
Rosa B-[Bonheur]

Painted in the winter of 1834-35 during Catlin's visit to Florida (see no. 349).

355. View of the "Stone Man Medicine," Coteau des Prairies
1836-1837
Unlocated

Described by Catlin as "a human figure, of some rods in length, made on the top of a high bluff by laying flat stones on the grass. A great *mystery* or *medicine* place of the Sioux" (1848 catalogue, p. 36).

References: 1837 catalogue, no. 364; Donaldson, p. 261; Gilcrease catalogue, p. 55.

Version:
Gilcrease Institute, 11 x 14

Sketched in 1836 on Catlin's journey to the Pipestone Quarry (see nos. 336, 337). The Gilcrease version is illustrated in place of the original.

356. Fort Winnebago, on the Fox River, a United States outpost
1836-1837
Unlocated

References: 1837 catalogue, no. 365; *Letters and Notes*, vol. 2, p. 163; Donaldson, p. 261; Ewers (1956), p. 489.

Sketched in 1836 on Catlin's journey to the Pipestone Quarry (see no. 357).

357. Fort Howard, Green Bay, a United States outpost
1836-1837
Unlocated

References: 1837 catalogue, no. 366; *Letters and Notes*, vol. 2, pp. 160, 162; Donaldson, p. 261; Ewers (1956), p. 489.

Sketched in 1836 on Catlin's journey to the Pipestone Quarry. Since this was Catlin's only visit to Green Bay (and presumably to Fort Winnebago, no. 356), Donaldson's date is incorrect.

354

355

Gilcrease Institute, Tulsa.

Plate 264, *Letters and Notes.*

358. Fort Gibson, Arkansas, a United States outpost 700 miles west of the Mississippi River
1834
Unlocated

"Fort Gibson is the extreme south-western outpost on the United States frontier; beautifully situated on the banks of the river, in the midst of an extensive and lovely prairie" (*Letters and Notes,* vol. 2, p. 36).

References: 1837 catalogue, no. 367; Donaldson, p. 261; Ewers (1956), p. 488; McCracken, pp. 137-38; Roehm, pp. 71, 72.

Painted in 1834. Catlin spent about two months (early April through mid-June) at the fort before the dragoon expedition began.

359. The "Short Tower," Wisconsin
1836-1837
Unlocated

References: 1837 catalogue, no. 368; Donaldson, p. 261.

Probably sketched in 1836 on Catlin's journey to the Pipestone Quarry (see no. 357). The painting is entitled "Shot Tower" in the 1837 catalogue.

360. Passing the "Grand Chute" with bark canoe, Fox River
1836
Unlocated

"The many amusing little incidents which enlivened our transit up the sinuous windings of the Fox river, amid its rapids, its banks of loveliest prairies and 'oak openings,' and its boundless shores of wild rice . . . have been registered, perhaps for a future occasion" (*Letters and Notes,* vol. 2, p. 163).

References: 1837 catalogue, no. 369; Donaldson, p. 262.

Sketched in 1836 on Catlin's trip to the Pipestone Quarry (see no. 357).

361. View of Mackinaw, Lake Michigan, a United States outpost
1836-1837
Unlocated

References: 1837 catalogue, no. 370; *Letters and Notes,* vol. 2, p. 161, pl. 264; Donaldson, p. 262.

Sketched in 1836 on Catlin's journey to the Pipestone Quarry. This was his only visit to the Straits (see no. 357). Plate 264 in *Letters and Notes* is illustrated in place of the original.

362. View in the "Cross Timbers," Texas
1832 or 1834-1835
11¼ x 14⅜ (28.5 x 36.5)

References: 1837 catalogue, no. 371; Donaldson, p. 262; *Letters and Notes,* vol. 2, pp. 49, 79; Ewers (1956), p. 518.

Presumably sketched in 1834 on the dragoon expedition, although Catlin never crossed into Texas during the expedition and the timber for which the region is named has mysteriously disappeared from slopes bordering the Red River, or whatever river appears in the painting. The conformation of the bald hills resembles Catlin's earlier views of the Upper Missouri (nos. 364-403), and the painting is of the same small size as the other landscapes in that series. Perhaps the painting has been incorrectly catalogued, and should appear as number 393 *(Prairie bluffs, 1100 miles above St. Louis),* which is missing from the Smithsonian collection.

363. View on the Missouri, alluvial banks falling in, 600 miles above St. Louis
1832
11¼ x 14⅜ (28.5 x 36.4)

"For the distance of 1000 miles above St. Louis, the shores of this river . . . are filled with snags and rafts, formed of trees of the largest size, which have been undermined by the falling banks and cast into the stream; their roots becoming fastened in the bottom of the river, with their tops floating on the surface of the water, and pointing down the stream, forming the most frightful and discouraging prospect for the adventurous voyageur" (*Letters and Notes,* vol. 1, pp. 17-18, pl. 4).

References: 1837 catalogue, no. 372; Donaldson, p. 262; Matthews, p. 599; Ewers (1956), p. 517; Paris (1963), no. 35; Gilcrease catalogue, p. 55.

Versions:
Gilcrease Institute, 11 x 14

Gilcrease Institute, NAI sketchbook (4776.71), pen and ink

Painted in 1832 on the Missouri River voyage. Donaldson incorrectly states that the scene is not illustrated in *Letters and Notes,* and Matthews says that Catlin has accurately represented the river in flood stage.

The Gilcrease version closely resembles the Smithsonian original, and the scene is repeated in cartoon 243 (NGA 2154). Cartoon 311 (NGA 2167) is a related view of the lower Mississippi.

364. Blackbird's Grave on the Missouri River, 1100 miles above St. Louis
1832
Unlocated

"We landed our canoe, and spent a day in the vicinity of the '*Black Bird's Grave.*' This is a celebrated point on the Missouri, and a sort of telegraphic place, which all the travellers in these realms, both white and red, are in the habit of visiting: the one to pay respect to the bones of one of their distinguished leaders; and the others, to indulge their eyes on the lovely landscape that spreads out to an almost illimitable extent in every direction about it. This elevated bluff, which may be distinguished for several leagues in distance, has received the name of the 'Black Bird's Grave,' from the fact, that a famous chief of the O-ma-haws, by the name of the Black Bird, was buried on its top, at his own peculiar request; over whose grave a cedar post was erected by his tribe some thirty years ago, which is still standing" (*Letters and Notes,* vol. 2, pp. 5-6, pl. 117).

References: 1837 catalogue, no. 373; Donaldson, pp. 262-65, pl. 66; Matthews, p. 600, pl. 134; Gilcrease catalogue, p. 55.

Versions:
Gilcrease Institute, 11 x 14

Gilcrease Institute, NAI sketchbook (4776.66), pen and ink

Painted in 1832 on Catlin's Missouri River voyage (see nos. 365, 369, 373). The Gilcrease version, which matches plate 117 in *Letters and Notes,* is illustrated in place of the original. The scene is repeated in cartoon 374 (unlocated), and Karl Bodmer sketched a view of the grave a year later (see Reuben Gold Thwaites, ed., *Early Western Travels 1748-1846,* pl. 12).

365. Blackbird's Grave, a back view, prairies enameled with flowers
1832
11¼ x 14⅜ (28.5 x 36.6)

See number 364 for Catlin's description.

References: 1837 catalogue, no. 374; *Letters and Notes,* vol. 2, pp. 5-6; Donaldson, p. 265; Ewers (1956), p. 514.

Painted in 1832 on Catlin's Missouri River voyage.

366. "Brick Kilns," clay bluffs 1900 miles above St. Louis
1832
11¼ x 14⅜ (28.3 x 36.3)
[Figure 114]

"To this group of clay bluffs, which line the river for many miles in distance, the voyageurs have very appropriately given the name of 'the Brickilns'; owing to their red appearance, which may be discovered in a clear day at the distance of many leagues.

"By the action of water, or other power, the country seems to have been graded away; leaving occasionally a solitary mound or bluff, rising in a conical form to the height of two or three hundred feet, generally pointed or rounded at the top, and in some places grouped together in great numbers . . . the sides of these conical bluffs (which are composed of strata of different coloured clays), are continually washing down by the effect of the rains and melting of the frost; and the superincumbent masses of pumice and basalt are crumbling off, and falling down to their bases; and from thence, in vast quantities, by the force of the gorges of water which are often cutting their channels between them—carried into the river, which is close by. . . .

"The upper part of this layer of pumice is of a brilliant red; and when the sun is shining upon it, is as bright and vivid as vermilion. It is porous and open, and its specific gravity but trifling. These curious bluffs must be seen as they are in nature; or else in a painting, where their colours are faithfully given, or they lose their picturesque beauty, which consists in the variety of their vivid tints. The strata of clay are alternating from red to yellow—white—brown and dark blue; and so curiously arranged, as to form the most pleasing and singular effects" (*Letters and Notes,* vol. 1, pp. 69-70, pl. 37).

References: 1837 catalogue, no. 375; Donaldson, p. 266; Matthews, p. 599, pl. 132; Art Institute of Chicago, *The Hudson River School and the Early American Landscape Tradition* (1945), no. 24; Ewers (1956), p. 517; Gilcrease catalogue, p. 55.

Versions:
Gilcrease Institute, 11 x 14

Gilcrease Institute, NAI sketchbook (4776.73), pen and ink

Painted in 1832 on the Missouri River voyage. Catlin's method of recording landscapes on the Upper Missouri remains a puzzle. He mentions a sketchbook in *Letters and Notes,* and there is an outline of this scene with brief notes in the SI sketchbook, but it was made on the upriver voyage with a reminder to examine the formation on his return. Other passages make it clear that certain paintings were at least begun in the field or on the deck of the steamboat (see nos. 373, 386, 390). The small can-

Gilcrease Institute, Tulsa.

vases were easy to mount, colors were kept to a minimum, and the artist was a fast worker. Furthermore, the variety of topographical formations and the pattern of colors in this landscape would be difficult to reproduce even from a carefully annotated drawing.

Matthews observes that Catlin had an intuitive understanding of the geology of the area (see no. 337). The Gilcrease version includes more foliage on the domes, but is otherwise identical to the Smithsonian original, which matches plate 37 in *Letters and Notes.* The scene is repeated in cartoon 248 (unlocated).

367. Foot war party on the march, Upper Missouri
1832
11¼ x 14⅜ (28.5 x 36.5)

References: 1837 catalogue, no. 376; Donaldson, p. 266; Kennedy catalogue, p. 10; Ewers (1956), p. 517; Vernon Young, "George Catlin's Indian Gallery: The Wilderness in a Locket," *Arts* 31 (December 1956): 21; Haverstock, p. 72; Gilcrease catalogue, p. 55.

Version:
Gilcrease Institute, 11 x 14

Painted in 1832 on Catlin's Missouri River voyage. The Gilcrease version has a slightly different topographical arrangement, and the scene is repeated in cartoon 324 (NGA 2170), where the curving line of warriors is reversed.

368. Prairie bluffs at sunrise, near the mouth of the Yellowstone River
1832
11¼ x 14½ (28.5 x 36.6)

References: 1837 catalogue, no. 377; Donaldson, p. 266; Ewers (1956), p. 517; Paris (1963), no. 36.

Painted in 1832 on Catlin's Missouri River voyage.

369. Mouth of the Platte River, 900 miles above St. Louis
1832
11¼ x 14½ (28.5 x 36.6)

"The mouth of the Platte is a beautiful scene, and no doubt will be the site of a large and flourishing town, soon after the Indian titles shall have been extinguished to the lands in these regions. . . . The Platte is a long and powerful stream, pouring in from the Rocky Mountains" (*Letters and Notes,* vol. 2, p. 12, pl. 124).

Catlin's prediction almost came true. Omaha is located just north of the junction of the two rivers.

References: 1837 catalogue, no. 378; Donaldson, p. 266; Ewers (1956), p. 517; J. F. McDermott, ed.,

Travelers on the Western Frontier (Urbana, Ill., 1970), reprod. p. 54; Gilcrease catalogue, p. 55; Spokane exhibition, no. 35.

Versions:
Gilcrease Institute, 11 x 14
Gilcrease Institute, NAI sketchbook (4776.68), pen and ink
Copy:
M. Knoedler & Co., New York (until 1971), pencil and watercolor, Rosa Bonheur estate

Painted in 1832 on the Missouri River voyage. The topographical formula of Catlin's river panoramas suggests that he brushed the broad outlines directly on these small canvases (see no. 366). This procedure is corroborated by Catlin's own statements in *Letters and Notes* (see nos. 373, 390).

Topographical details in the Gilcrease landscape are less clearly defined than in the Smithsonian original, which matches plate 124 in *Letters and Notes.* The scene is repeated in cartoon 375 (unlocated).

370. Magnificent clay bluffs, 1800 miles above St. Louis
1832
11¼ x 14½ (28.4 x 36.7)

"The sketch of the bluffs denominated 'the Grand Dome,' of which I spoke but a few moments since, is a faithful delineation of the lines and character of that wonderful scene; and the reader has here a just and striking illustration of the ruin-like appearances, as I have formerly described, that are so often met with on the banks of this mighty river.

"This is, perhaps, one of the most grand and beautiful scenes of the kind to be met with in this country, owing to the perfect appearance of its several huge domes, turrets, and towers, which were everywhere as precise and as perfect in their forms as they are represented in the illustration. These stupendous works are produced by the continual washing down of the sides of these clay-formed hills; and although, in many instances, their sides, by exposure, have become so hardened, that their change is very slow" (*Letters and Notes,* vol. 1, pp. 76, 78, pl. 41).

Catlin describes the black line just above the river as "a streak of coal" (1848 catalogue, p. 37).

References: 1837 catalogue, no. 379; Donaldson, p. 266; *Mississippi Panorama,* no. 29; Ewers (1956), p. 517; Paris (1963), no. 37; Rossi and Hunt, pp. 76, 320; Spokane exhibition, no. 40.

Version:
Gilcrease Institute, NAI sketchbook (4776.70), pen and ink

Painted in 1832 on Catlin's Missouri River voyage (see nos. 366, 378). The scene is repeated in cartoon 244 (NGA 2149).

371. Cabane's trading house, 930 miles above St. Louis
1832
11¼ x 14⅜ (28.5 x 36.5)

References: 1837 catalogue, no. 380; Donaldson, p. 266; Ewers (1956), p. 517.

Painted in 1832 on Catlin's Missouri River voyage.

372. View in the Grand Detour, 1900 miles above St. Louis
1832
11¼ x 14⅜ (28.4 x 36.5)
[Figure 65]

Described by Catlin as "magnificent clay bluffs, with red pumice-stone resting on their tops, and a party of Indians approaching buffalo" (1848 catalogue, p. 37).

References: 1837 catalogue, no. 381; Donaldson, p. 266; Ewers (1956), p. 517.

Painted in 1832 on Catlin's Missouri River voyage (see nos. 366, 390).

373. Beautiful grassy bluffs, 110 miles above St. Louis
1832
11¼ x 14⅜ (28.4 x 36.6)

"We landed our canoe at the base of a beautiful series of grass-covered bluffs, which, like thousands and thousands of others on the banks of this river, are designated by no name, that I know of; and I therefore introduce them as fair specimens of the *grassy bluffs* of the Missouri. . . . As soon as we were ashore, I scrambled to their summits, and beheld, even to a line, what the reader has before him in plates 119 and 120. I took my easel, and canvass and brushes, to the top of the bluff, and painted the two views from the same spot; the one looking up, and the other down the river. The reader, by imagining these hills to be five or six hundred feet high, and every foot of them, as far as they can be discovered in distance, covered with a vivid green turf, whilst the sun is gilding one side, and throwing a cool shadow on the other, will be enabled to form something like an adequate idea of the shores of the Missouri. From this enchanting spot there was nothing to arrest the eye from ranging over its waters for the distance of twenty or thirty miles, where it quietly glides between its barriers, formed of thousands of green and gracefully sloping hills, with its rich and alluvial meadows, and woodlands—and its hundred islands, covered with stately cottonwood" (*Letters and Notes*, vol. 2, p. 8, pl. 120).

371

373

References: 1837 catalogue, no. 382; Donaldson, p. 266; Ewers (1956), p. 517.

Version:
Gilcrease Institute, NAI sketchbook (4776.67), pen and ink

Copy:
M. Knoedler & Co., New York (until 1971), pencil and watercolor, Rosa Bonheur estate

Painted in 1832 on Catlin's Missouri River voyage. In the 1837 catalogue, the scene is located 1,100 miles above St. Louis; and number 399 in the 1848 catalogue, supposedly painted from the same spot, is placed 1,320 miles above St. Louis.

Catlin tells us in the above passage that he painted some Upper Missouri landscapes from direct observation, carefully noting colors and shadows, and transcribing topography "even to a line." The vivid greens, which have been criticized as primitive technique, were probably a legitimate attempt to capture the rich color of prairie grass.

374. Prairie meadows burning
1832
11 x 14⅛ (27.8 x 35.7)

"There is yet another character of burning prairies [see no. 375] . . . the war, or hell of fires! where the grass is seven or eight feet high . . . and the flames are driven forward by the hurricanes, which often sweep over the vast prairies of this denuded country. There are many of these meadows on the Missouri, and the Platte, and the Arkansas, of many miles in breadth, which are perfectly level, with a waving grass, so high, that we are obliged to stand erect in our stirrups, in order to look over its waving tops, as we are riding through it. The fire in these, before such a wind, travels at an immense and frightful rate, and often destroys, on their fleetest horses, parties of Indians, who are so unlucky as to be overtaken by it" (*Letters and Notes*, vol. 2, pp. 17, 20-21, pl. 128).

References: 1837 catalogue, no. 383; Donaldson, pp. 266-69; Art Institute of Chicago, *The Hudson River School and the Early American Landscape Tradition* (1945), no. 25, reprod. p. 73; *Mississippi Panorama*, no. 39; *Westward the Way*, no. 4, reprod. p. 35; Ewers (1956), p. 517; Vernon Young, "George Catlin's Indian Gallery: The Wilderness in a Locket," *Arts* 31 (December 1956), reprod. p. 22; William Rockhill Nelson Gallery of Art, Kansas City, *The Last Frontier* (1957), no. 16; Henri Dorra, *The American Muse* (New York, 1961), reprod. p. 61; James T. Callow, *Kindred Spirits* (Chapel Hill, N.C., 1967), p. 156; Corcoran Gallery of Art, Washington, D.C., *Wilderness* (1971), no. 43; Haverstock, pp. 108-9; Gilcrease catalogue, p. 55; Spokane exhibition, no. 41; Fine Arts Museum of San Francisco, *American Art from the Collection of Mr. and Mrs. John D. Rockefeller 3rd* (1976), no. 25.

Versions:
Gilcrease Institute, 11 x 14

Gilcrease Institute, NAI sketchbook (4776.79), pen and ink

Private collection, New York, oil on paperboard, 18 x 24¼, signed lower left: G. Catlin. 1871.

Copy:
M. Knoedler & Co., New York (until 1971), pencil and watercolor, Rosa Bonheur estate

Painted in 1832 on Catlin's Missouri River voyage. Donaldson's date is incorrect. Callow includes the subject in a "terror and desolation" category of the sublime, where man is pursued by nature.

The smoke clouds and the formation of the riders in the Gilcrease version differ somewhat from the Smithsonian original. The scene is repeated in cartoon 317 (Collection of Mr. and Mrs. Paul Mellon), where the riders flee directly across the meadows, parallel to the picture plane, and this cartoon is the model for the 1871 painting. Cartoon 399 (unlocated) must be a similar subject.

375. Prairie bluffs burning
1832
11¼ x 14½ (28.6 x 36.7)

"The prairies burning form some of the most beautiful scenes that are to be witnessed in this country, and also some of the most sublime. Every acre of these vast prairies (being covered for hundreds and hundreds of miles, with a crop of grass, which dies and dries in the fall) burns over during the fall or early in the spring, leaving the ground of a black and doleful colour. . . .

"Over the elevated lands and prairie bluffs, where the grass is thin and short, the fire slowly creeps with a feeble flame, which one can easily step over; where the wild animals often rest in their lairs until the flames almost burn their noses, when they will reluctantly rise, and leap over it, and trot off amongst the cinders, where the fire has past and left the ground as black as jet" (*Letters and Notes*, vol. 2, pp. 16-17, pl. 127).

References: 1837 catalogue, no. 384; Donaldson, pp. 266-69; *Mississippi Panorama*, no. 30, reprod. p. 73; Ewers (1956), p. 517; McCracken, reprod. p. 145; Perry T. Rathbone, "Rediscovery," *Art in America* 49 (no. 1, 1961), reprod. p. 83; Paris (1963), no. 38; Allan Gussow, *A Sense of Place* (New York, 1971), reprod. p. 70; Whitney Museum of American Art, New York, *The American Frontier: Images and Myths* (1973), no. 13, reprod. p. 19; Gilcrease catalogue, p. 55.

Versions:
Gilcrease Institute, 11 x 14

Gilcrease Institute, NAI sketchbook (4776.79), pen and ink

Painted in 1832 on Catlin's Missouri River voyage. Scale and distance relationships have been changed in the Gilcrease version. The Smithsonian original matches plate 127 in *Letters and Notes*.

The scene is repeated in cartoon 316 (unlocated), and cartoon 251 (NGA 2152) is a related subject.

376. Floyd's Grave, where Lewis and Clark buried Sergeant Floyd in 1804
1832
11⅛ x 14⅜ (28.5 x 36.6)
[Figure 67]

" 'Floyd's Grave' is a name given to one of the most lovely and imposing mounds or bluffs on the Missouri River, about twelve hundred miles above St. Louis, from the melancholy fate of Serjeant Floyd, who was of Lewis and Clark's expedition, in 1806; who died on the way, and whose body was taken to this beautiful hill, and buried in its top, where now stands a cedar post, bearing the initials of his name.

"I landed my canoe in front of this grass-covered mound, and . . . several times ascended it and sat upon his grave, overgrown with grass and the most delicate wild flowers, where I . . . contemplated the solitude and stillness of this tenanted mound; and beheld from its top, the windings infinite of the Missouri, and its thousand hills and domes of green, vanishing into blue in distance, when nought but the soft-breathing winds were heard, to break the stillness and quietude of the scene. Where not the chirping of bird or sound of cricket, nor soaring eagle's scream, were interposed 'tween God and man; nor aught to check man's whole surrender of his soul to his creator" (*Letters and Notes*, vol. 2, pp. 4-5, pl. 118).

References: 1837 catalogue, no. 385; Donaldson, pp. 270-71; Matthews, p. 600, pl. 133; Ewers (1956), pp. 495, 517; Haverstock, pp. 101-2.

Version:
Gilcrease Institute, NAI sketchbook (4776.66), pen and ink

Painted in 1832 on the Missouri River voyage. The above passage reveals Catlin in one of his most transcendental moods.

Matthews says that Sioux City, Iowa, now covers the bluff on which the grave was located. The scene is repeated in cartoon 376 (unlocated).

377. Sioux encamped on the Upper Missouri, dressing buffalo meat and robes
1832
11¼ x 14½ (28.6 x 36.6)

"The Blackfeet and the Crows, like the Sioux and Assinneboins, have nearly the same mode of constructing their wigwam or lodge. . . . These lodges, or tents, are taken down in a few minutes by the squaws, when they wish to change their location, and easily transported to any part of the country where they wish to encamp; and they generally move some six or eight times in the course of the summer; following the immense herds of buffaloes, as they range over these vast plains, from east to west, and north to south. The objects for which they do this are two-fold,—to procure and dress their skins, which are brought in, in the fall and winter, and sold to the Fur Company, for white man's luxury; and also for the purpose of killing and drying buffalo meat, which they bring in from their hunts, packed on their horses' backs, in great quantities; making pemican, and preserving the marrow-fat for their winter quarters" (*Letters and Notes*, vol. 1, p. 43, pl. 22).

References: 1837 catalogue, no. 386; Donaldson, p. 271; Ewers (1956), p. 511; McCracken, p. 77; Gilcrease catalogue, p. 55; Spokane exhibition, no. 45.

Version:
Gilcrease Institute, 11 x 14

Copy:
M. Knoedler & Co., New York (until 1971), pencil and watercolor, signed lower right:
Rosa B-[Bonheur]

Painted in 1832 on Catlin's Missouri River voyage. Donaldson incorrectly states that the scene is not illustrated in *Letters and Notes*, and the women dressing robes and the drying racks are based on drawings in the SI sketchbook (see no. 346). Despite their improbable structure, the small figures in these landscapes go about their tasks with an animated conviction.

The Gilcrease version is almost identical to the Smithsonian original, and the scene is repeated in cartoon 128 (NGA 1962). Cartoons 301 (NGA 1970) and 414 (AMNH 107) are related views.

378. The Tower, 1100 miles above St. Louis
1832
11¼ x 14⅜ (28.5 x 36.6)

Described by Catlin as "a high and remarkable clay bluff, rising to the height of some hundreds of feet from the water, and having in distance, the castellated appearance of a fortification" (*Letters and Notes*, vol. 2, p. 9).

References: 1837 catalogue, no. 387; Donaldson, p. 271; Ewers (1956), p. 517.

Painted in 1832 on the Missouri River voyage (see no. 366). A brief drawing of the same view is in the SI sketchbook. Every bluff on the Upper Missouri reminded Catlin, a true student of the picturesque, of a castle, turret, or tower.

The scene is repeated in cartoon 377 (unlocated).

379. Distant view of the Mandan village
1832
11¼ x 14½ (28.5 x 36.7)

"This tribe is at present located on the west bank of the Missouri, about 1800 miles above St. Louis, and 200 below the Mouth of Yellow Stone river. . . . The site of the lower (or principal) town . . . is one of the most beautiful and pleasing that can be seen in the world, and even more beautiful than imagination could ever create. In the very midst of an extensive valley (embraced within a thousand graceful swells and parapets or mounds of interminable green, changing to blue, as they vanish in distance) . . . on an extensive plain . . . without tree or bush . . . are to be seen rising from the ground, and towards the heavens, domes—(not 'of gold,' but) of dirt—and the thousand spears (not 'spires') and scalp-poles, &c. &c., of the semi-subterraneous village of the hospitable and gentlemanly Mandans" (*Letters and Notes*, vol. 1, pp. 80-81, pl. 45).

Fort Clark, the American Fur Company outpost, is at the left of the village.

References: 1837 catalogue, no. 388; Donaldson, pp. 271-73, pl. 67; *Mississippi Panorama*, no. 31, reprod. p. 74; Ewers (1956), p. 513; Ewers (1965), p. 115.

Painted in 1832 on Catlin's Missouri River voyage (see nos. 366, 373). The landscape details are remarkably close to Karl Bodmer's watercolor of the Mandan village in the winter of 1833-34 (see Ewers, 1965).

Cartoon 130 (NGA 2037) is a later edition of the Smithsonian painting, and cartoon 131 (Collection of Mr. and Mrs. Paul Mellon) is a related view.

380. Picturesque clay bluff, 1700 miles above St. Louis
1832
11¼ x 14½ (28.5 x 36.6)
[Figure 66]

"At the base of one of these [bluffs] . . . we with difficulty landed our canoe, and I ascended to its top, with some hours' labour; having to cut a foot-hold in the clay with my hatchet for each step, a great part of the way up its sides. So curious was this solitary bluff, standing alone as it did, to the height of 250 feet, with its sides washed down into hundreds of variegated forms—with large blocks of indurated clay, remaining upon pedestals and columns as it were, and with such a variety of tints; that I looked upon it as a beautiful picture, and devoted an hour or two with my brush, in transferring it to my canvass" (*Letters and Notes*, vol. 1, p. 78, pl. 43).

References: 1837 catalogue, no. 389; Donaldson, p. 271; Matthews, p. 599, pl. 132; Ewers (1956), p. 517; Corcoran Gallery of Art, Washington, D.C., *Wilderness* (1971), no. 42; Gilcrease catalogue, p. 55; Spokane exhibition, no. 39; Seattle Art Museum, *Lewis and Clark's America* (1976), no. 37, reprod. p. 33.

Versions:
Gilcrease Institute, 11 x 14

Gilcrease Institute, NAI sketchbook (4776.74), pen and ink

Painted in 1832 on the Missouri River voyage. Catlin claims again that he recorded the river topography directly on canvas (see no. 366).

The Gilcrease painting is a mannered version of the Smithsonian original, and the scene is repeated in cartoon 378 (unlocated).

381. Belle Vue, Indian agency of Major Dougherty, 870 miles above St. Louis
1832
11¼ x 14⅜ (28.5 x 36.6)

"*Belle Vue* is a lovely scene on the West bank of the river, about nine miles above the mouth of the Platte, and is the agency of Major Dougherty, one of the oldest and most effective agents on our frontiers. This spot is, as I said, lovely in itself; but doubly so to the eye of the weatherbeaten *voyageur* from the sources of the Missouri, who steers his canoe in, to the shore, as I did. . . . It was a pleasure to see again, in this great wilderness, a civilized habitation; and still more pleasant to find it surrounded with corn-fields, and potatoes, with numerous fruit-trees bending under the weight of their fruit" (*Letters and Notes*, vol. 2, p. 11, pl. 122).

References: 1837 catalogue, no. 390; Donaldson, p. 273, pl. 67; Ewers (1956), p. 517; Haverstock, pp. 102-3.

Copy:
M. Knoedler & Co., New York (until 1971), pencil, Rosa Bonheur estate

Painted in 1832 on Catlin's Missouri River voyage. Karl Bodmer did a closer view of Dougherty's agency the next summer (see Reuben Gold Thwaites, ed., *Early Western Travels 1748-1846*, pl. 31).

382. Beautiful clay bluffs, 1900 miles above St. Louis
1832
11¼ x 14½ (28.5 x 36.6)

References: 1837 catalogue, no. 391; Donaldson, p. 273; Ewers (1956), p. 517; Spokane exhibition, no. 44.

Painted in 1832 on Catlin's Missouri River voyage (see no. 370).

383. Hidatsa village, earth-covered lodges on the Knife River, 1810 miles above St. Louis
1832
11¼ x 14½ (28.5 x 36.6)

"The principal village of the Minatarees [Hidatsa] which is built upon the bank of the Knife river, contains forty or fifty earth-covered wigwams, from forty to fifty feet in diameter, and being elevated, overlooks the other two, which are on lower ground and almost lost amidst their numerous corn fields and other profuse vegetation which cover the earth with their luxuriant growth.

"The scenery along the banks of this little river, from village to village, is quite peculiar and curious; rendered extremely so by the continual wild and garrulous groups of men, women, and children, who are wending their way along its winding shores, or dashing and plunging through its blue waves, enjoying the luxury of swimming, of which both sexes seem to be passionately fond. Others are paddling about in their tub-like canoes, made of the skins of buffaloes" (*Letters and Notes*, vol. 1, p. 186, pl. 70).

References: 1837 catalogue, no. 392; Donaldson, pp. 273-74; *Mississippi Panorama*, no. 32, reprod. p. 75; Ewers (1956), p. 512; McCracken, p. 111, reprod. p. 113; Henri Dorra, "Parallel Trends in Literature and Art," *Art in America* 47 (Summer 1959), reprod. p. 30; Paris (1963), no. 39; Rossi and Hunt, pp. 76, 320; Gilcrease catalogue, p. 55.

Versions:
Gilcrease Institute, 11 x 14

Gilcrease Institute, NAI sketchbook (4776.57), pen and ink

Painted in 1832 on Catlin's Missouri River voyage (see no. 366). The Gilcrease version and the Smithsonian original both match plate 70 in *Letters and Notes*. The scene is repeated in cartoon 136 (Collection of Mr. and Mrs. Paul Mellon).

384. Fort Pierre, mouth of the Teton River, 1200 miles above St. Louis
1832
11¼ x 14½ (28.6 x 36.7)
[Figure 13]

"This Fort is undoubtedly one of the most important and productive of the American Fur Company's posts, being in the centre of the great Sioux country, drawing from all quarters an immense and almost incredible number of buffalo robes, which are carried to the New York and other Eastern markets, and sold at a great profit. This post is thirteen hundred miles above St. Louis, on the west bank of the Missouri, on a beautiful plain near the mouth of the Teton river which empties into the Missouri from the West, and the Fort has received the name of Fort Pierre, in compliment to Monsr. Pierre Chouteau, who is one of the partners in the Fur Company, residing in St. Louis. . . .

"The country about this Fort is almost entirely prairie, producing along the banks of the river and streams only, slight skirtings of timber. No site could have been selected more pleasing or more advantageous than this; the Fort is in the centre of one of the Missouri's most beautiful plains, and hemmed in by a series of gracefully undulating, grass-covered hills, on all sides; rising like a series of terraces, to the summit level of the prairies, some three or four hundred feet in elevation, which then stretches off in an apparently boundless ocean of gracefully swelling waves and fields of green. On my way up the river I made a painting of this lovely spot, taken from the summit of the bluffs, a mile or two distant, shewing an encampment of Sioux, of six hundred tents or skin lodges, around the Fort, where they had concentrated to make their spring trade; exchanging their furs and peltries for articles and luxuries of civilized manufactures" (*Letters and Notes*, vol. 1, p. 209, pl. 85).

Catlin occasionally contradicts himself in giving the distance above St. Louis of various points on the Upper Missouri (see no. 373).

References: 1837 catalogue, no. 393; Donaldson, p. 274; Ewers (1956), p. 517; McCracken, p. 47, reprod. p. 48; Paris (1963), no. 40; Roehm, pp. 58-60; J. F. McDermott, ed., *Travelers on the Western Frontier* (Urbana, Ill., 1970), reprod. p. 55; South Dakota Memorial Art Center, Brookings, *The Art of South Dakota* (1975), no. 25, reprod.

Catlin again implies that he was painting directly from nature on the Missouri River voyage of 1832 (see no. 373). Karl Bodmer's view of Fort Pierre the next summer is remarkably similar to Catlin's (see Reuben Gold Thwaites, ed., *Early Western Travels 1748-1846*, pl. 43). The scene is repeated in cartoon 201 (NGA 2097).

385. Nishnabottana Bluffs, 1070 miles above St. Louis
1832
11¼ x 14⅜ (28.5 x 36.6)

References: 1837 catalogue, no. 394; Donaldson, p. 274; *Mississippi Panorama*, no. 42; Ewers (1956), p. 517; Corcoran Gallery of Art, Washington, D.C., *Wilderness* (1971), no. 48.

Painted in 1832 on Catlin's Missouri River voyage (see no. 402). The scene is repeated in cartoon 306 (unlocated).

386. Arikara village of earth-covered lodges, 1600 miles above St. Louis
1832
11¼ x 14⅜ (28.5 x 36.5)

"Plate 80 gives a view of the Ricaree village, which is beautifully situated on the west bank of the river, 200 miles below the Mandans; and built very much in the same manner; being constituted of 150 earth-covered lodges, which are in part surrounded by an imperfect and open barrier of pickets set firmly in the ground, and ten or twelve feet in height.

"This village is built upon an open prairie, and the gracefully undulating hills that rise in the distance behind it are everywhere covered with a verdant green turf, without a tree or a bush anywhere to be seen. This view was taken from the deck of the steamer when I was on my way up the river" (*Letters and Notes*, vol. 1, p. 204, pl. 80).

References: 1837 catalogue, no. 395; Donaldson, p. 274; *Westward the Way*, no. 53, reprod. p. 87; Ewers (1956), pp. 494-95, 499, 508, pl. 12; McCracken, pp. 116-17; Ewers (1968), pl. 5.

Version:
Gilcrease Institute, NAI sketchbook (4776.57), pen and ink

Painted in 1832 on Catlin's Missouri River voyage. Ewers notes that the earth lodges are probably too regular in size and shape. A brief drawing of the lodges, apparently unrelated to the painting, appears in the SI sketchbook (see no. 366).

The scene is repeated in cartoon 135 (unlocated).

385

386

387. South side of Buffalo Island, showing buffalo berries in the foreground
1832
11¼ x 14½ (28.5 x 36.7)

References: 1837 catalogue, no. 396; Donaldson, p. 274; Ewers (1956), p. 517; Gilcrease catalogue, p. 55.

Version:
Gilcrease Institute, 11 x 14

Painted in 1832 on Catlin's Missouri River voyage. The Gilcrease version has flowers in the right foreground, and three white men (instead of the four Indians in the Smithsonian original) are debarking from the canoe. In the Gilcrease records, that version is called *Cedar Island*, but a drawing of the same title in the SI sketchbook does not resemble either painting. Cartoon 312 (NGA 2168) is a view over the prairie from the island bluffs.

388. Fort Union, mouth of the Yellowstone River, 2000 miles above St. Louis
1832
11¼ x 14⅜ (28.5 x 36.6)

"The American Fur Company have erected here, for their protection against the savages, a very substantial Fort, 300 feet square, with bastions armed with ordnance; and our approach to it under the continued roar of cannon for half an hour, and the shrill yells of the half-affrighted savages who lined the shores, presented a scene of the most thrilling and picturesque appearance. . . .

"The Fort . . . was built by Mr. McKenzie, who now occupies it. It is the largest and best-built establishment of the kind on the river, being the great or principal head-quarters and depôt of the Fur Company's business in this region. A vast stock of goods is kept on hand at this place; and at certain times of the year the numerous out-posts concentrate here with the returns of their season's trade, and refit out with a fresh supply of goods to trade with the Indians.

"The site for the Fort is well selected, being a beautiful prairie on the bank near the junction of the Missouri with the Yellow Stone rivers; and its inmates and its stores well protected from Indian assaults" (*Letters and Notes*, vol. 1, pp. 14, 21, pl. 3).

References: 1837 catalogue, no. 397; Donaldson, pp. 274-76, pl. 5; Haberly, p. 56; *Mississippi Panorama*, no. 41; Ewers (1956), pp. 501, 517, pl. 19; McCracken, pp. 65-66, reprod. p. 67; Ewers (1965), p. 100; Roehm, pp. 60-61; Haverstock, pp. 62-63; Spokane exhibition, no. 46; Peter Hassrick, *The Way West: Art of Frontier America* (New York, 1977), reprod. p. 34.

Version:
Gilcrease Institute, NAI sketchbook (4776.71), pen and ink

Painted in 1832 at the upriver terminus of Catlin's voyage on the *Yellowstone* (see no. 311). Roehm says the steamboat arrived at Fort Union June 5; other authorities give the date as June 16, on the basis of the Catlin letter cited in McCracken, and Catlin writes in the SI sketchbook that he reached the mouth of the Yellowstone June 25.

Audubon challenged the accuracy of this painting, stating that his colleague Sprague had "walked to the hills about two miles off, but could not see any portion of the Yellowstone River, which Mr. Catlin has given in his view, as if he had been in a balloon some thousands of feet over the earth" (see Ewers, 1956). Audubon was apparently unaware that Karl Bodmer's view of Fort Union, taken the next summer from approximately the same location, also shows the river (see Ewers, 1965).

Another view of the fort, from the riverbank, appears in the SI sketchbook (see fig. 156; Donaldson, pl. 5). Cartoon 206 (NGA 2144) is a later edition of the Smithsonian painting.

389. Iron Bluff, 1200 miles above St. Louis
1832
11¼ x 14½ (28.5 x 36.6)

Described by Catlin as "a beautiful subject for a landscape" (1848 catalogue, p. 38).

References: 1837 catalogue, no. 398; Donaldson, p. 276; Ewers (1956), p. 517; Spokane exhibition, no. 36.

Painted in 1832 on Catlin's Missouri River voyage (see no. 373). The scene is repeated in cartoon 379 (unlocated).

390. Big Bend on the Upper Missouri, 1900 miles above St. Louis
1832
11⅛ x 14⅜ (28.3 x 36.4)
[Figure 16]

"Saturday, fifth day of our voyage from the mouth of Yellow Stone. . . . Landed our canoe in the Grand Détour (or Big Bend) as it is called, at the base of a stately clay mound, and ascended, all hands, to the summit level, to take a glance at the picturesque and magnificent works of Nature that were about us. Spent the remainder of the day in painting a view of this grand scene; for which purpose Ba'tiste and Bogard carried my easel and canvass to the top of a huge mound, where they left me at my work. . . .

"Scarcely anything in nature can be found, I am sure, more exceedingly picturesque than the view from this place; exhibiting the wonderful manner in which the gorges of the river have cut out its deep channel through these walls of clay on either side, of two or three hundred feet in elevation; and the imposing features of the high table-lands in distance, standing as a perpetual anomaly in the country, and producing the indisputable, though astounding evidence of the fact, that there has been at some ancient period, a *super* surface to this country, corresponding with the elevation of these tabular hills, whose surface, for half a mile or more, on their tops, is perfectly level" (*Letters and Notes*, vol. 1, pp. 74-75, pl. 39).

References: 1837 catalogue, no. 399; Donaldson, p. 276; Haberly, ff. p. 128; *Mississippi Panorama*, no. 33, reprod. p. 76; Corcoran Gallery of Art, Washington, D.C., *American Processional* (1950), p. 119; Ewers (1956), p. 517; Kennedy catalogue, p. 11; National Collection of Fine Arts, Washington, D.C., *American Landscape: a Changing Frontier* (1966), pl. 13; Henry Gallery, University of Washington, Seattle, *The View and the Vision* (1968), no. 5, p. 18, reprod. p. 15; Rossi and Hunt, pp. 74, 320; Gilcrease catalogue, p. 55; Museum of Fine Arts, Boston, *Frontier America: The Far West* (1975), no. 30, reprod. p. 48.

Versions:

Gilcrease Institute, 11 x 14

Gilcrease Institute, NAI sketchbook (4776.70), pen and ink

Painted in 1832 on the downriver voyage. This is the most imposing landscape of the Upper Missouri series, and probably one of the most topographically accurate, as Catlin was attempting a treatise on erosion as well as a picturesque view. Much of it was painted from direct observation, one learns from the above passage. Consequently, the light has a fine clear quality rarely observed in Catlin's landscapes, and the transitions of color and shadow are more consistent than usual. The lone Indian symbolizes the untouched wilderness that spreads before him.

The Gilcrease version has less geological detail than the Smithsonian original, which matches plate 39 in *Letters and Notes*. The scene is repeated in cartoon 247 (Collection of Mr. and Mrs. Paul Mellon), with the addition of the steamboat *Yellowstone* puffing past the bluffs.

391. View in the Big Bend of the Upper Missouri

1832

11¼ x 14½ (28.5 x 36.6)

Described by Catlin as "magnificent clay bluffs, with high table-land in the distance" (1848 catalogue, p. 38).

References: 1837 catalogue, no. 400; Donaldson, p. 276; Ewers (1956), p. 517; Paris (1963), no. 41, pl. 6; Alfred Frankenstein, "American Art and American Moods," *Art in America* 54 (March 1966), reprod. p. 80; Spokane exhibition, no. 43.

Painted in 1832 on Catlin's Missouri River voyage (see nos. 366, 390). Frankenstein discusses the landscape as a manifestation of R. W. B. Lewis's Adamic dream.

392. Back view of Mandan village, showing the cemetery

1832

11⅛ x 14⅜ (28.5 x 36.6)

"These people never bury the dead, but place the bodies on slight scaffolds just above the reach of human hands, and out of the way of wolves and dogs; and they are there left to moulder and decay. This cemetery, or place of deposit for the dead, is just back of the village, on a level prairie; and with all its appearances, history, forms, ceremonies, &c. is one of the strangest and most interesting objects to be described in the vicinity of this peculiar race. . . .

"When the scaffolds on which the bodies rest, decay and fall to the ground, the nearest relations having buried the rest of the bones, take the skulls, which are perfectly bleached and purified, and place them in circles of an hundred or more on the prairie—placed at equal distances apart (some eight or nine inches from each other), with the faces all looking to the centre; where they are religiously protected and preserved in their precise positions from year to year. . . .

"There are several of these 'Golgothas' or circles of twenty or thirty feet in diameter, and in the centre of each ring or circle is a little mound of three feet high, on which uniformly rest two buffalo skulls (a male and female); and in the centre of the little mound is erected a "medicine pole," about twenty feet high, supporting many curious articles of mystery and superstition, which they suppose have the power of guarding and protecting this sacred arrangement" (*Letters and Notes,* vol. 1, pp. 89-90, pl. 48).

References: 1837 catalogue, no. 401; Donaldson, pp. 276-77, pls. 7, 68; Museum of Modern Art, New York, *Romantic Painting in America* (1943), no. 45; Ewers (1956), p. 513; McCracken, reprod. p. 99; Gilcrease catalogue, p. 55; Museum of Fine Arts, Boston, *Frontier America: The Far West* (1975), no. 31, reprod. p. 49.

391

392

Versions:

Gilcrease Institute, 11 x 14

Gilcrease Institute, NAI sketchbook (4776.52), pen and ink

Sketched and perhaps painted at the Mandan village in 1832 (see no. 379). A drawing of several scaffolds and a circle of skulls appears in the SI sketchbook (see Donaldson, pl. 7). Catlin's description of the cemetery represents a curious blend of anthropological and romantic interests.

Details of the Gilcrease version and the Smithsonian original differ slightly from plate 48 in *Letters and Notes.* The scene is repeated in cartoon 134 (unlocated), and Karl Bodmer sketched a similar circle of skulls during his visit to the village in the winter of 1833-34 (see Reuben Gold Thwaites, ed., *Early Western Travels 1748-1846,* pl. 14).

Plate 6, *Letters and Notes.*

393. Prairie bluffs, 1100 miles above St. Louis
1832
Unlocated

"Amongst these groups [of bluffs] may be seen tens and hundreds of thousands of different forms and figures, of the sublime and the picturesque; in many places for miles together, as the boat glides along, there is one continued appearance, before and behind us, of some ancient and boundless city in ruins—ramparts, terraces, domes, towers, citadels and castles may be seen,—cupolas, and magnificent porticoes, and here and there a solitary column and crumbling pedestal, and even spires of clay which stand alone—and glistening in distance, as the sun's rays are refracted back by the thousand crystals of gypsum which are imbedded in the clay of which they are formed" (*Letters and Notes*, vol. 1, p. 19, pl. 6).

References: 1837 catalogue, no. 402; Donaldson, p. 278.

Version:
Gilcrease Institute, NAI sketchbook (4776.72), pen and ink

This is the only unidentified landscape missing from the Upper Missouri series (nos. 364-403). Because plate 6 in *Letters and Notes* (see illustration) does not correspond to any other painting in the series, it might represent number 393, although the title seems vague for such a distinctive view. The landscape presently catalogued as no. 362 is another candidate for this entry.

Catlin again acknowledges his debt to English landscape theory in the above passage (see no. 378).

394. The Three Domes, clay bluffs 15 miles above the Mandan village
1832
11¼ x 14½ (28.6 x 36.7)

References: 1837 catalogue, no. 403; *Letters and Notes,* vol. 1, p. 78, pl. 44; Donaldson, p. 278; Ewers (1956), p. 517; Corcoran Gallery of Art,

Washington, D.C., *Wilderness* (1971), no. 45; Gilcrease catalogue, p. 55; Seattle Art Museum, *Lewis and Clark's America* (1976), no. 35, reprod. p. 32.

Versions:
Gilcrease Institute, 11 x 14
Gilcrease Institute, NAI sketchbook (4776.74), pen and ink

Painted in 1832 on Catlin's Missouri River voyage (see no. 366). A herd of buffalo charge across the foreground of the Gilcrease version. The scene is repeated in cartoon 380 (unlocated).

395. Square Hills, 1200 miles above St. Louis
1832
11¼ x 14½ (28.5 x 36.6)

"An hundred miles above . . . [Belle Vue, no. 381], I passed a curious feature, called the 'Square Hills'. . . . On ascending them I found them to be two or three hundred feet high, and rising on their sides at an angle of 45 degrees; and on their tops, in some places, for half a mile in length, perfectly level, with a green turf, and corresponding exactly with the tabular hills spoken of above the Mandans [see no. 390]" (*Letters and Notes,* vol. 2, pp. 11-12, pl. 123).

Catlin again contradicts himself in giving the distance above St. Louis (see nos. 381, 384).

References: 1837 catalogue, no. 404; Donaldson, p. 278; Ewers (1956), p. 517; Gilcrease catalogue, p. 55; Spokane exhibition, no. 37.

Versions:
Gilcrease Institute, 11 x 14
Gilcrease Institute, NAI sketchbook (4776.68), pen and ink

Copy:
M. Knoedler & Co., New York (until 1971), pencil and watercolor, Rosa Bonheur estate

Painted in 1832 on the Missouri River voyage (see no. 390). The Gilcrease version has a canoe in the foreground and the arrangement of hills differs slightly from the Smithsonian original, which matches plate 123 in *Letters and Notes.*

The scene is repeated in cartoon 381 (unlocated).

396. River bluffs, with white wolves in the foreground, Upper Missouri
1832
11¼ x 14½ (28.5 x 36.6)

References: 1837 catalogue, no. 405; Donaldson, p. 278; *Mississippi Panorama,* no. 34, reprod. p. 77; Ewers (1956), p. 518; Spokane exhibition, no. 42.

Painted in 1832 on Catlin's Missouri River voyage.

397. Beautiful prairie bluffs above the Poncas, 1050 miles above St. Louis
1832
11¼ x 14½ (28.5 x 36.6)

"The summit level of the great prairies stretching off to the west and the east from the river, to an almost boundless extent, is from two to three hundred feet above the level of the river; which has formed a bed or valley for its course, varying in width from two to twenty miles. This channel or valley has been evidently produced by the force of the current, which has gradually excavated, in its floods and gorges, this immense space, and sent its debris into the ocean. By the continual overflowing of the river, its deposits have been lodged and left with a horizontal surface, spreading the deepest and richest alluvion over the surface of its meadows on either side; through which the river winds its serpentine course, alternately running from one bluff to the other, which present themselves to its shores in all the most picturesque and beautiful shapes and colours imaginable—some with their green sides gracefully slope down in the most lovely groups to the water's edge" (*Letters and Notes,* vol. 1, p. 19, pl. 5).

References: 1837 catalogue, no. 406; Donaldson, p. 278; Matthews, p. 600; Haberly, reprod. opp. p. 96; Ewers (1956), p. 518; *Mississippi Panorama,* no. 35, reprod. p. 78; Gilcrease catalogue, p. 55.

Versions:
Gilcrease Institute, 11 x 14

Gilcrease Institute, NAI sketchbook (4776.72), pen and ink

Painted in 1832 on the Missouri River voyage (see nos. 369, 390). Catlin's geological interests often determined his selection of subject matter. Matthews says the conformation of the hills is characteristic of that stretch of the river.

The Gilcrease version lacks the number and variety of hills in the Smithsonian original. The latter matches plate 5 in *Letters and Notes.* The scene is repeated in cartoon 246 (NGA 2151).

398. View from Floyd's Grave, 1300 miles above St. Louis
1832
11¼ x 14½ (28.5 x 36.6)

See number 376 for Catlin's description.

References: 1837 catalogue, no. 407; *Letters and Notes,* vol. 2, pp. 4-5; Donaldson, p. 278; Ewers (1956), p. 518; Corcoran Gallery of Art, Washington, D.C., *Wilderness* (1971), no. 46; Spokane exhibition, no. 38; Seattle Art Museum, *Lewis and Clark's America* (1976), no. 36, reprod. p. 36.

Painted in 1832 on Catlin's Missouri River voyage (see nos. 369, 373).

399. River bluffs, 1320 miles above St. Louis
1832
11¼ x 14½ (28.5 x 36.6)
[Figure 113]

See number 373 for Catlin's description.

References: 1837 catalogue, no. 408; *Letters and Notes,* vol. 2, p. 8, pl. 119; Donaldson, p. 278; Ewers (1956), p. 518; Paris (1963), no. 42.

Version:
Gilcrease Institute, NAI sketchbook (4776.67), pen and ink

Copy:
M. Knoedler & Co., New York (until 1971), pencil, Rosa Bonheur estate

Painted in 1832 on Catlin's Missouri River voyage (see nos. 369, 373).

400. Buffalo herds crossing the Upper Missouri
1832
11¼ x 14½ (28.5 x 36.6)

"Near the mouth of White River, we met the most immense herd crossing the Missouri River—and from an imprudence got our boat into imminent danger amongst them, from which we were highly delighted to make our escape. It was in the midst of the 'running season,' and we had heard the 'roaring' (as it is called) of the herd, when we were several miles from them. When we came in sight, we were actually terrified at the immense numbers that were streaming down the green hills on one side of the river, and galloping up and over the bluffs on the other. The river was filled, and in parts blackened, with their heads and horns, as they were swimming about . . . furiously hooking and climbing on to each other. I rose in my canoe, and by my gestures and hallooing, kept them from coming in contact with us, until we were out of their reach" (*Letters and Notes,* vol. 2, p. 13, pl. 126).

References: 1837 catalogue, no. 409; Donaldson, pp. 278-79, pl. 68; *Mississippi Panorama,* no. 36; Ewers (1956), p. 518; McCracken, p. 119, reprod. p. 120; Paris (1963), no. 43; Gilcrease catalogue, p. 55; Amon Carter Museum of Western Art, Fort Worth, *The Bison in Art* (1977), reprod. p. 101.

Versions:
Gilcrease Institute, 11 x 14

Gilcrease Institute, NAI sketchbook (4776.69), pen and ink

Copy:
M. Knoedler & Co., New York (until 1971), pencil, Rosa Bonheur estate

Painted in 1832 on Catlin's Missouri River voyage. The Smithsonian landscape matches plate 126 in *Letters and Notes,* but the terrain has been simplified in the Gilcrease version.

397

398

400

401. Clay bluffs, twenty miles above the Mandan
1832
11¼ x 14½ (28.6 x 36.7)

References: 1837 catalogue, no. 410; Donaldson, p. 279; Ewers (1956), p. 518.

Painted in 1832 on Catlin's Missouri River voyage.

402. Nishnabottana Bluffs, Upper Missouri
1832
11¼ x 14⅜ (28.6 x 36.6)

References: 1837 catalogue, no. 412; Donaldson, p. 279; Ewers (1956), p. 518.

Painted in 1832 on the Missouri River voyage (see no. 385). The rich carpet of prairie grass on the river bluffs was endlessly attractive to Catlin, but not altogether successful as the subject of a landscape.

Cartoon 289 (NGA 2161) is a related view.

403. Indians encamping at sunset, Upper Missouri
1832
11¼ x 14⅜ (28.5 x 36.5)

References: 1837 catalogue, no. 413; Donaldson, p. 279; Ewers (1956), p. 518; Paris (1963), no. 44; Gilcrease catalogue, p. 55.

Version:
Gilcrease Institute, 11 x 14

Painted in 1832 on Catlin's Missouri River voyage. The Gilcrease version has a simplified terrain, fewer shadows, and more figures than the Smithsonian original.

404. Buffalo bull, grazing on the prairie
1832-1833
24 x 29 (60.9 x 73.7)
[Figure 64]

"The American bison, or . . . buffalo, is the largest of the ruminating animals that is now living in America; and seems to have been spread over the plains of this vast country, by the Great Spirit, for the use and subsistence of the red men, who live almost exclusively on their flesh, and clothe themselves with their skins. . . .

"The buffalo bull often grows to the enormous weight of 2000 pounds, and shakes a long and shaggy black mane, that falls in great profusion and *confusion* over his head and shoulders; and oftentimes falling down quite to the ground. The horns are short, but very large, and have but one turn, *i.e.* they are a simple arch, without the least approach to a spiral form, like those of the common ox, or of the goat species. . . .

"One of the most remarkable characteristics of the buffalo, is the peculiar formation and expression of the eye, the ball of which is very large and white, and the iris jet black. The lids of the eye seem always to be strained quite open, and the ball rolling forward and down; so that a considerable part of the iris is hidden behind the lower lid, while the pure white of the eyeball glares out over it in an arch, in the shape of a moon at the end of its first quarter" (*Letters and Notes,* vol. 1, pp. 24, 247-48, pl. 7).

References: 1837 catalogue, no. 414; Donaldson, p. 283; Quimby, pp. 56-57; Ewers (1956), p. 516; McCracken, p. 122; Gilcrease catalogue, p. 56; Amon Carter Museum of Western Art, Fort Worth, *The Bison in Art* (1977), frontispiece.

Versions:
Field Museum of Natural History, ca. 21 x 28

Gilcrease Institute, 20 x 25, signed lower right: Catlin./54.

H. Williams, New York, 1907, no. 14, 19 x 27 (exhibited in London, 1859)

Copy:
M. Knoedler & Co., New York (until 1971), pencil, signed lower right: Rosa B-[Bonheur]

Sketched on the Upper Missouri in 1832. Catlin writes of filling a notebook with drawings of a wounded buffalo in various positions (see no. 406). The paintings were probably composed the following winter and spring. In spite of Catlin's limited experience, the proportions of the buffalo are reasonably accurate.

The Gilcrease version includes a cow, in profile, behind the bull. The eyes of the buffalo in the Smithsonian original are just as Catlin describes them in the above passage, but in the Field Museum version they have less detail (see no. 3). Both paintings match plate 7 in *Letters and Notes.* The buffalo bull appears again as plate 2 of *Catlin's North American Indian Portfolio,* first published in 1844, and as plate 54 of the Gilcrease *Souvenir* album.

405. Buffalo cow, grazing on the prairie
1832-1833
24 x 29 (60.9 x 73.7)

"The cow is less in stature [than the bull], and less ferocious . . . and always distinguishable by the peculiar shape of the horns, which are much smaller and more crooked, turning their points more in towards the centre of the forehead" (*Letters and Notes*, vol. 1, pp. 24, 248, pl. 8). See number 404.

References: 1837 catalogue, no. 415; Donaldson, p. 283; Quimby, pp. 58-59; Ewers (1956), p. 516; Paris (1963), no. 45.

Version:
Field Museum of Natural History, ca. 21 x 28

Copy:
M. Knoedler & Co., New York (until 1971), pencil, signed lower right: Rosa B-[Bonheur]

Sketched on the Upper Missouri in 1832 (see no. 404). The Field Museum version closely resembles the Smithsonian original (see no. 3).

406. Wounded buffalo, strewing his blood over the prairies
1832-1833
24 x 29 (60.9 x 73.7)
[Figure 123]

"I found that my shot had entered him a little too far forward, breaking one of his shoulders, and lodging in his breast, and from his very great weight it was impossible for him to make much advance upon me. As I rode up within a few paces of him, he would bristle up with fury enough in his *looks* alone, almost to annihilate me; and making one lunge at me, would fall upon his neck and nose, so that I found the sagacity of my horse alone enough to keep me out of reach of danger: and I drew from my pocket my sketch-book, laid my gun across my lap, and commenced taking his likeness. He stood stiffened up, and swelling with awful vengeance, which was sublime for a picture, but which he could not vent upon me. I rode around him and sketched him in numerous attitudes, sometimes he would lie down, and I would then sketch him; then throw my cap at him, and rousing him on his legs, rally a new expression, and sketch him again. . . .

"No man on earth can imagine what is the look and expression of such a subject before him as this was. I defy the world to produce another animal than can look so frightful as a huge buffalo bull, when wounded as he was, turned around for battle,

and swelling with rage;—his eyes bloodshot, and his long shaggy mane hanging to the ground,—his mouth open, and his horrid rage hissing in streams of smoke and blood from his mouth and through his nostrils, as he is bending forward to spring upon his assailant" (*Letters and Notes*, vol. 1, pp. 26-27, pl. 10).

References: 1837 catalogue, no. 416; Ewers (1956), p. 516.

Copy:
M. Knoedler & Co., New York (until 1971), pencil and watercolor, signed lower right:
Rosa B-[Bonheur]

Sketched in 1832 on the Upper Missouri. The above passage is one of Catlin's most detailed accounts of his field technique (see nos. 404, 407).

The subject is repeated in plate 16 of Catlin's *North American Indian Portfolio*, first published in 1844, and in cartoon 292 (NGA 2163). The buffalo faces the opposite direction in both compositions, and in the former he stands in a winter landscape.

407. Dying buffalo, shot with an arrow
1832-1833
24 x 29 (60.9 x 73.7)

The animal is described by Catlin as "sinking down on his haunches" (1848 catalogue, p. 39). See number 406.

References: 1837 catalogue, no. 417; *Letters and Notes*, vol. 1, pp. 26-27; Donaldson, pp. 285-86; Quimby, pp. 60-61; Ewers (1956), p. 516.

Version:
Field Museum of Natural History, ca. 21 x 28

The sketches of buffalo made by Catlin on the Upper Missouri in 1832 (see nos. 404, 406) were developed into his most effective animal paintings. Like an untutored Barye, he moved from direct observation to dramatic compositions in which the appearance and movement of the animals conveyed a full range of primitive emotion.

The Field Museum version is in poor condition and the mouth of the buffalo is distorted; otherwise, it closely matches the Smithsonian original (see no. 3). The subject is repeated in cartoon 293 (NGA 2164), where the buffalo faces the opposite direction. Cartoon 291 (NGA 2162) is a related scene, and the same bull expires in a snowdrift, with a trail of hunters and buffalo behind, in plate 17 of *Catlin's North American Indian Portfolio*, first published in 1844, and plate 78 of the Gilcrease *Souvenir* album. Paintings by the artist of this last subject (at the Joslyn Art Museum [illustration 407a], the Royal Ontario Museum, and cartoon 263 at the National Gallery) would seem to fit the description of number 423 in the 1848 catalogue, but so does another Smithsonian example.

Buffalo Hunt, 19 x 26½, Joslyn Art Museum, Omaha.

408

408a.

Gilcrease Institute, Tulsa.

408. Buffalo chase, a single death
1832-1833
24 x 29 (60.9 x 73.7)

"In the chase of the buffalo, or other animal, the Indian generally 'strips' himself and his horse, by throwing off his shield and quiver, and every part of his dress, which might be an encumbrance to him in running; grasping his bow in his left hand, with five or six arrows drawn from his quiver, and ready for instant use. . . .

"These horses are so trained, that the Indian has little use for the rein, which hangs on the neck, whilst the horse approaches the animal on the right side, giving his rider the chance to throw his arrow to the left; which he does at the instant when the horse is passing—bringing him opposite to the heart, which receives the deadly weapon 'to the feather'. . . .

"In plate 107, I have fairly represented the mode of *approaching*, at the instant the arrow is to be thrown; and the striking disparity between the size of a huge bull of 2000 pounds weight, and the Indian horse, which, it will be borne in mind, is but a pony" (*Letters and Notes*, vol. 1, pp. 251-52, pl. 107).

References: 1837 catalogue, no. 418; Donaldson, pp. 286-87; Ewers (1956), p. 16; J. F. McDermott, *Seth Eastman*, pl. 109; Gilcrease catalogue, p. 56.

Versions:
Gilcrease Institute, 25 x 31, signed lower right: Catlin 1847

Royal Ontario Museum, 18¾ x 26⅛

H. Williams, New York, 1907, no. 4, 19 x 27 (exhibited in London, 1859)

Copies:
M. Knoedler & Co., New York (until 1971), pencil and watercolor, signed lower right:
Rosa B-[Bonheur]

John Howell, San Francisco, oil on wood, 4 x 6

Sketched on the Upper Missouri in 1832 (see nos. 404, 406). The horse and rider, and the landscape are more detailed in the Gilcrease and Ontario versions (see nos. 411, 413). The technique and size of the former (illustration 408a) is reminiscent of the Louis Philippe series, although the subject is not included in the *Travels in Europe* list (see no. 449). The latter painting may be the same as the H. Williams version. The Smithsonian original appears to be unfinished, and has two additional buffalo in the background. The Howell copy is by an amateur who has reversed the composition.

The subject is repeated in plate 5 of *Catlin's North American Indian Portfolio*, first published in 1844; in plate 60 of the Gilcrease *Souvenir* album; and in cartoon 144 (NGA 2133).

Peter Rindisbacher painted a similar buffalo hunting scene in St. Louis in about 1833 (see Parke-Bernet, New York, April 19, 1972, no. 85a), and Eastman reversed the composition for a *Buffalo Chase* he did some years later (see McDermott).

409. Buffalo chase, a surround by the Hidatsa
1832-1833
24 x 29 (60.9 x 73.7)

"We soon descried at a distance, a fine herd of buffaloes grazing, when a halt and a council were ordered and the mode of attack was agreed upon. I had armed myself with my pencil and my sketchbook only, and consequently took my position generally in the rear, where I could see and appreciate every manoeuvre.

"The plan of attack, which in this country is familiarly called a '*surround*,' was explicitly agreed upon, and the hunters who were all mounted on their 'buffalo horses' and armed with bows and arrows or long lances, divided into two columns, taking opposite directions, and drew themselves gradually around the herd at a mile or more distance from them; thus forming a circle of horsemen at equal distances apart, who gradually closed in upon them with a moderate pace, at a signal given. The unsuspecting herd at length 'got the wind' of the approaching enemy and fled in a mass in the greatest confusion. . . . I had rode up in the rear and occupied an elevated position at a few rods distance, from which I could . . . survey from my horse's back, the nature and the progress of the grand mêleé . . . a cloud of dust was soon raised, which in parts obscured the throng where the hunters were galloping their horses around and driving the whizzing arrows or their long lances to the hearts of these noble animals; which in many instances, becoming infuriated with deadly wounds in their sides, erected their shaggy manes over their blood-shot eyes and furiously plunged forwards at the sides of their assailants' horses, sometimes goring them to death at a lunge, and putting their dismounted riders to flight for their lives; sometimes their dense crowd was opened, and the blinded horsemen, too intent on their prey amidst the cloud of dust, were hemmed and wedged in amidst the crowding beasts, over whose backs they were obliged to leap for security, leaving their horses to the fate that might await them" (*Letters and Notes*, vol. 1, pp. 199-200, pl. 79).

References: 1837 catalogue, no. 419; Donaldson, pp. 287-89, pl. 69; Matthews, p. 601; Quimby, pp. 54-55; Ewers (1956), p. 516; Fine Arts Museum of New Mexico, Santa Fe, *The Artist in the American West 1800-1900* (1961), no. 10; Haverstock, reprod. pp. 64-65; Museum of Fine Arts, Boston, *Frontier America: The Far West* (1975), no. 33; *Antiques* 107 (February 1975), reprod. p. 282.

Versions:
Field Museum of Natural History, ca. 21 x 28

Gilcrease Institute, NAI sketchbook (4776.55), pen and ink

Copy:
M. Knoedler & Co., New York (until 1971), pencil and watercolor, Rosa Bonheur estate

Sketched on the Upper Missouri in 1832 (see no. 404). Noting how carefully the small figures were painted, Matthews observes that Catlin was better than a camera. Quimby says the subject is mentioned in an 1837 letter from Catlin to O'Fallon.

The Field Museum version has less detail than the Smithsonian original (see no. 3), but both compositions match plate 79 in *Letters and Notes*. The scene is repeated in plate 9 of *Catlin's North American Indian Portfolio*, first published in 1844, and in cartoon 382 (unlocated).

410. Buffalo chase with bows and lances
1832-1833
24 x 29 (60.9 x 73.7)

"In plate 108, I have represented a party of Indians in chase of a herd, some of whom are pursuing with lance and others with bows and arrows. The group in the foreground shews the attitude at the instant after the arrow has been thrown and driven to the heart; the Indian at full speed, and the *laso* dragging behind his horse's heels. . . . In running the buffaloes, or in time of war, the *laso* drags on the ground at the horse's feet, and sometimes several rods behind, so that if a man is dismounted, which is often the case, by the tripping or stumbling of the horse, he has the power of grasping to the laso, and by stubbornly holding on to it, of stopping and securing his horse" (*Letters and Notes*, vol. 1, p. 253, pl. 108).

References: 1837 catalogue, no. 420; Donaldson, p. 289; Ewers (1956), p. 516; Halpin, reprod. p. 8.

Version:
Gilcrease Institute, NAI sketchbook (4776.55), pen and ink

Copy:
M. Knoedler & Co., New York (until 1971), pencil and watercolor, signed lower right:
Rosa B-[Bonheur]

Sketched on the Upper Missouri in 1832 (see no. 404). Donaldson incorrectly states that the subject is not illustrated in *Letters and Notes*.

411. Buffalo chase over prairie bluffs
1832-1833
24 x 29 (60.9 x 73.7)
[Figure 127]

References: 1837 catalogue, no. 421; Donaldson, p. 290; *Antiques* 54 (August 1948): 97; *Westward the Way*, no. 54, reprod. p. 88; Ewers (1956), p.

516; Vernon Young, "George Catlin's Indian Gallery: The Wilderness in a Locket," *Arts* 31 (December 1956), reprod. p. 23; McCracken, reprod. p. 46; Newark Museum, *Classical America* (1963), no. 231; Ewers (1965), reprod. p. 80; Oliver Jensen, ed., *Great Stories of American Businessmen* (New York, 1972), pp. 88-93; Rena M. Coen, "The Last of the Buffalo," *American Art Journal* 5 (November 1973): 88, reprod. p. 87; Gilcrease catalogue, p. 56; Rena M. Coen, *Painting and Sculpture in Minnesota, 1820-1914* (Minneapolis, 1976), pp. 6, 8.

Versions:
Royal Ontario Museum, 18½ x 26, signed lower right: Catlin
American Museum of Natural History, New York, 18 x 25¼, signed lower right: Geo. Catlin/55
H. Williams, New York, 1907, no. 24, 19 x 27 (exhibited in London, 1859)

Sketched on the Upper Missouri in 1832 (see no. 404). The title has been changed to avoid confusion with number 410. Catlin's horses and buffalo have only one running position in the original paintings of this series, but in later versions he represented swiftly moving animals with greater variety and accuracy (see no. 413). Coen (1976) describes the apparent contradiction between Catlin's energetic hunting scenes and his concern over the inevitable destruction of the buffalo, but misdates the Museum of Natural History painting.

The scene is repeated in plate 6 of *Catlin's North American Indian Portfolio* (fig. 128), first published in 1844; in plate 62 of the Gilcrease *Souvenir* album; and in cartoon 145 (AMNH 90). Catlin used a similar composition, based on a painting in the Knoedler collection, for the buffalo hunt in the *Colt Firearm Series* of about 1860 (see *Antiques* and *Great Stories of American Businessmen*).

The Ontario version (fig. 129, which probably came from H. Williams) more closely resembles the cartoon than the Smithsonian original, in which the animals are rather badly proportioned. Several of the Royal Ontario Museum paintings are dated in the mid-1850s, and the others are so similar in style that they must have been done at the same time. Catlin had sharpened his technique on the South American cartoons, which he had begun a year or two earlier. A few of the same subjects (and his improved draftsmanship) reappear in the Ontario series.

409

410

412

413

414

412. Buffalo chase, bull protecting a cow and calf

1832-1833

24 x 29 (60.9 x 73.7)

"During the season of the year whilst the calves are young, the male seems to stroll about by the side of the dam, as if for the purpose of protecting the young, at which time it is exceedingly hazardous to attack them, as they are sure to turn upon their pursuers, who have often to fly to each others assistance" (*Letters and Notes,* vol. 1, p. 255, pl. 112).

References: 1837 catalogue, no. 422; Donaldson, pp. 290-91; John I. H. Baur, "After Catlin," *Brooklyn Museum Bulletin* 5 (no. 1, 1948): 17-20; Ewers (1956), p. 516; Ewers, "Not Quite Redmen: The Plains Indian Illustrations of Felix O. C. Darley," *American Art Journal* 3 (Fall 1972): 92-93; Whitney Museum of American Art, *The American Frontier: Images and Myths* (1973), no. 12, reprod. p. 20; Paul C. Mills, "The Buffalo Hunter," *Archivero* I (Santa Barbara Museum of Art, 1973): 138-45.

Copy:
M. Knoedler & Co., New York (until 1971), pencil and watercolor, signed lower right:
Rosa B-[Bonheur]

Sketched on the Upper Missouri in 1832 (see no. 404). Baur and Ewers note that Darley based one of his compositions (fig. 141) on this painting, and Mills carries on the investigation by showing Catlin's work in a progression of nineteenth-century American buffalo hunting scenes. The subject is repeated in cartoon 153 (NGA 2137).

413. Buffalo chase, bulls making battle with men and horses

1832-1833

24 x 29 (60.9 x 73.7)

"The buffalo is a very timid animal, and shuns the vicinity of man with keenest sagacity; yet, when overtaken, and harassed or wounded, turns upon its assailants with the utmost fury, who have only to seek safety in flight. In their desperate resistance the finest horses are often destroyed; but the Indian, with his superior sagacity and dexterity, generally finds some effective mode of escape" (*Letters and Notes,* vol. 1, pp. 254-55, pl. 111).

References: 1837 catalogue, no. 423; Donaldson, p. 291, pl. 70; Ewers (1956), p. 516; McCracken, reprod. p. 146; *The Old Print Shop Portfolio* 30 (April 1971): 189; M. Knoedler & Co., New York, *The American Indian Observed* (1971), no. 24, reprod. p. 20; Gilcrease catalogue, p. 56.

Versions:
Gilcrease Institute, 25 x 32

National Cowboy Hall of Fame, Oklahoma City, 25¾ x 32

Copies:
Sotheby & Co., London, December 6, 1967, no. 58, 49.5 x 59.5 cm, inscribed lower left: C Catlin/1881

M. Knoedler & Co., New York (until 1971), pencil and watercolor, signed lower right:
Rosa B-[Bonheur]

Sketched on the Upper Missouri in 1832 (see no. 404). The animals in the Gilcrease and Oklahoma City paintings are more detailed and convincing than those in the Smithsonian original. In later versions of his buffalo hunting scenes, Catlin seems to have been guided by the superior draftsmanship of the lithographer of his *North American Indian Portfolio,* first published in 1844 (see figs. 127-29).

The scene is repeated in plate 7 of the *Portfolio,* which was also issued as a Currier & Ives lithograph (11½ x 17½, see *Old Print Shop Portfolio*); in plate 64 of the Gilcrease *Souvenir* album; and in an unnumbered cartoon belonging to Mr. and Mrs. Paul Mellon. Cartoon 146 (NGA 2134) is a related subject.

414. Buffalo hunt under the wolf-skin mask

1832-1833

24 x 29 (60.9 x 73.7)

"The poor buffaloes have their enemy *man,* besetting and beseiging them at all times of the year, and in all the modes that man in his superior wisdom has been able to devise for their destruction. They struggle in vain to evade his deadly shafts, when he dashes amongst them over the plains on his wild horse—they plunge into the snow-drifts where they yield themselves an easy prey to their destroyers, and they also stand unwittingly and behold him, unsuspected under the skin of a white wolf, insinuating himself and his fatal weapons into close company, when they are peaceably grazing on the level prairies, and shot down before they are aware of their danger" (*Letters and Notes,* vol. 1, p. 254, pl. 110).

References: 1837 catalogue, no. 424; Donaldson, p. 291; Museum of Modern Art, New York, *Romantic Painting in America* (1943), no. 46; Ewers (1956), p. 516; Paris (1963), no. 46, pl. 7; Rossi and Hunt, pp. 52, 320; Gilcrease catalogue, p. 56.

Copy:
M. Knoedler & Co., New York (until 1971), pencil and watercolor, Rosa Bonheur estate

Sketched on the Upper Missouri in 1832 (see no. 404). The painting is closely related to number 590, and the subject is repeated in plate 13 of *Catlin's North American Indian Portfolio,* first published in 1844, and in plate 68 of the Gilcrease *Souvenir* album.

415. Buffalo chase, mouth of the Yellowstone
1832-1833
24 x 29 (60.9 x 73.7)

Catlin describes the scene as "animals dying on the ground passed over; and my man Batiste swamped in crossing a creek" (1848 catalogue, p. 39).

References: 1837 catalogue, no. 425; Donaldson, p. 291; *Mississippi Panorama,* no. 37, reprod. p. 80; Ewers (1956), p. 516; McCracken, reprod. p. 64; Gilcrease catalogue, p. 56; Peter Hassrick, *The Way West: Art of Frontier America* (New York, 1977), reprod. p. 38.

Version:
Gilcrease Institute, 11 x 14

Sketched on the Upper Missouri in 1832 (see no. 404). Catlin must have put together a variety of buffalo and landscape studies to compose such a painting. The Gilcrease version is a hasty edition of the Smithsonian original.

416. Buffalo chase in winter, Indians on snowshoes
1832-1833
24 x 29 (60.9 x 73.7)

See number 417 for Catlin's description.

References: 1837 catalogue, no. 426; Donaldson, p. 291; Ewers (1956), pp. 500, 516; McCracken, reprod. p. 133; Fine Arts Museum of New Mexico, Santa Fe, *The Artist in the American West 1800-1900* (1961), no. 9, reprod.; Paris (1963), no. 47; Indiana University Art Gallery, Bloomington, *The American Scene 1920-1900* (1970), no. 61, reprod.; Seattle Art Museum, *Lewis and Clark's America* (1976), no. 33, reprod. p. 39.

Painted in Catlin's studio during the winter of 1832-33. Ewers points out that the Indians are wading through the snow in summer war dress because Catlin had never seen a winter buffalo hunt on the Great Plains. Nevertheless, the landscape is a delightful conceit, with soft colors and deep, flowing space dissolving into fanciful sweeps of pigment.

417. Buffalo chase in snowdrifts, Indians pursuing on snowshoes
1832-1833
24 x 29 (60.9 x 73.7)
[Figure 131]

"In the dead of the winters, which are very long and severely cold in this country, where horses cannot be brought into the chase with any avail, the Indian runs upon the surface of the snow by the aid of his snow shoes, which buoy him up, while the great weight of the buffaloes, sinks them down to the middle of their sides, and completely stopping their progress, ensures them certain and easy victims to the bow or lance of their pursuers. . . . This is the season in which the greatest number of these animals are destroyed for their robes—they are most easily killed at this time, and their hair or fur being longer and more abundant, gives greater value to the robe" (*Letters and Notes,* vol. 1, p. 253, pl. 109).

References: 1837 catalogue, no. 427; Donaldson, pp. 291-92; Matthews, pp. 601-2, pl. 139; Haberly, reprod. opp. p. 161; Kennedy catalogue, p. 11; Ewers (1956), pp. 500, 516; Vernon Young, "The Legend and the Loss: Paintings of the Old West," *Arts* 30 (September, 1956), reprod. p. 47; Perry T. Rathbone, "Rediscovery," *Art in America* 49 (no. 1, 1961), reprod. p. 83; J. F. McDermott, *Seth Eastman,* pl. 89; Rossi and Hunt, pp. 176, 320; Gilcrease catalogue, p. 56.

Versions:
Gilcrease Institute, 25 x 32
Royal Ontario Museum, 19¼ x 26¾
H. Williams, New York, 1907, no. 25, 19 x 27 (exhibited in London, 1859)

Copies:
Gilcrease Institute, 15 x 17
M. Knoedler & Co., New York (until 1971), pencil and watercolor, Rosa Bonheur estate

Painted in Catlin's studio during the winter of 1832-33 (see no. 416). The Smithsonian and Gilcrease paintings have similar compositions, and the latter may be the "Buffalo-hunt on snowshoes" that appears on the *Travels in Europe* list (see no. 449). The Ontario version (which probably once belonged to H. Williams) and cartoon 147 (NGA 2087) more closely follow the arrangement of buffalo in plate 15 of *Catlin's North American Indian Portfolio,* first published in 1844 (see nos. 411, 413). Plate 76 in the Gilcrease *Souvenir* album, and the Gilcrease copy, which is not by Catlin, are also based on the *Portfolio* lithograph.

Catlin may have been inspired by Peter Rindisbacher's scenes of Indians hunting buffalo on snowshoes, and Seth Eastman painted a similar subject several years later (see McDermott).

415

416

418

419

420

Gilcrease Institute, Tulsa.

418. Grizzly bears attacking Indians on horseback
1832-1833
24 x 29 (60.9 x 73.7)

References: 1837 catalogue, p. 428; Donaldson, p. 292; Ewers (1956), p. 516; McCracken, p. 15; *Catlin, Bodmer, Miller;* Paris (1963), no. 48; Denver Art Museum, *The Western Frontier,* 1966; Haverstock, pp. 160-61; Gilcrease catalogue, p. 56.

Versions:
Royal Ontario Museum, 18⅝ x 26¼

Christie, Manson & Woods, London, 1960, no. 128, 35½ x 51

H. Williams, New York, 1907, no. 26, 19 x 27 (exhibited in London, 1859)

Painted in the artist's studio during the winter of 1832-33. Catlin encountered several grizzly bears on the Upper Missouri, but for obvious reasons he never attempted a sketch. The arrangement of the figures along two intersecting diagonals is a more formal composition than usual.

The Ontario version, which probably once belonged to H. Williams, has an additional horse and rider behind the two bears (see no. 411). The scene is repeated in plate 19 of *Catlin's North American Indian Portfolio,* first published in 1844; in plate 84 of the Gilcrease *Souvenir* album; and in cartoon 155 (NGA 2139). The authenticity of the Christie version cannot be confirmed at this time.

419. Antelope shooting, decoyed up
1832-1833
19⅝ x 27⅝ (49.7 x 70.2)

"This little animal seems to be endowed, like many other gentle and sweet-breathing creatures, with an undue share of curiosity, which often leads them to destruction; and the hunter who wishes to entrap them, saves himself the trouble of travelling after them. When he has been discovered, he has only to elevate above the tops of the grass his red or yellow handkerchief on the end of his gun-rod, which he sticks in the ground, and to which they are sure to advance, though with great coyness and caution; whilst he lies close, at a little distance, with his rifle in hand; when it is quite an easy matter to make sure of two or three at a shot, which he gets in range of his eye, to be pierced with one bullet" (*Letters and Notes,* vol. 1, p. 76, pl. 40).

References: 1837 catalogue, no. 429; Donaldson, p. 292; Ewers (1956), p. 516; National Gallery of Art, Washington, D.C., *American Paintings and Sculpture* (1970), p. 24, no. 1993; Gilcrease catalogue, p. 57; Anschutz Collection, Denver, *American Masters in the West* (1974), p. 9.

Versions:
Royal Ontario Museum, 18½ x 26

National Gallery of Art, Washington, D.C., 17½ x 23½ (sight)

H. Williams, New York, 1907, no. 27, 19 x 27 (exhibited in London, 1859)

Copies:
Anschutz Collection, Denver, by James Walker, 20 x 35

Earle B. DeLaittre, Minneapolis, by James Walker, oil on paperboard, 10½ x 17 (sight)

John Howell, San Francisco, oil on wood, 4 x 6

Sketched in 1832 on Catlin's Missouri River voyage. The details of the Ontario version and number 264 in the 1871 catalogue (NGA 1993) are much alike, but differ somewhat from the Smithsonian original, which matches plate 40 in *Letters and Notes* (see nos. 411, 413). The scene is repeated in plate 20 of *Catlin's North American Indian Portfolio,* first published in 1844, and in plate 86 of the Gilcrease *Souvenir* album.

The Royal Ontario Museum version probably once belonged to H. Williams, and the James Walker copies are acknowledged as such in the Anschutz catalogue.

420. Sioux taking muskrats near the St. Peter's River
1836-1837
Unlocated

"Plate 277 exhibits the Indian mode of taking muskrats, which dwell in immense numbers in these northern prairies, and build their burrows in shoal water, of the stalks of the wild rice. They are built up something of the size and form of haycocks, having a dry chamber in the top, where the animal sleeps above water, passing in and out through a hole beneath the water's surface. The skins of these animals are sought by the Traders, for their fur, and they constitute the staple of all these regions, being caught in immense numbers by the Indians, and vended to the Fur Traders. The mode of taking them is seen in the drawing; the women, children and dogs attend to the little encampments, while the men wade to their houses or burrows, and one strikes on the backs of them, as the other takes the inhabitants in a rapid manner with a spear, while they are escaping from them" (*Letters and Notes,* vol. 2, p. 207, pl. 277).

References: 1837 catalogue, no. 430; Donaldson, p. 292; Gilcrease catalogue, p. 56.

Versions:
Gilcrease Institute, 11 x 14

Gilcrease Institute, NAI sketchbook (4776.78), pen and ink

Sketched in 1836 on Catlin's return from the Pipestone Quarry (see no. 337). The Gilcrease version, which matches plate 277 in *Letters and Notes,* is illustrated in place of the original.

421. Batiste and I running buffalo, mouth of the Yellowstone
1832-1833
24 x 29 (60.9 x 73.7)

"Amidst the trampling throng, Mons. Chardon had wounded a stately bull, and at this moment was passing him again with his piece levelled for another shot; they were both at full speed and I also, within the reach of the muzzle of my gun, when the bull instantly turned and receiving the horse upon his horns, and the ground received poor Chardon, who made a frog's leap of some twenty feet or more over the bull's back, and almost under my horse's heels" (*Letters and Notes*, vol. 1, p. 26, pl. 9).

References: 1837 catalogue, no. 431; Donaldson, p. 292; Matthews, p. 601, pl. 136; Ewers (1956), p. 516.

Copy:
M. Knoedler & Co., New York (until 1971), pencil, signed lower right: Rosa B-[Bonheur]

Sketched in 1832 on Catlin's Missouri river voyage (see no. 404). Donaldson incorrectly lists this painting as number 405a.

422. "My turn now," Batiste and I, and a buffalo bull, Upper Missouri
1837-1839
Unlocated

Reference: Donaldson, p. 292.

The subject is not included in the 1837 catalogue, but does appear in the Egyptian Hall catalogue of January 1840, indicating that it may have been painted in the interval (see nos. 423, 472). Plate 12 in the *North American Indian Portfolio*, showing Catlin's friend Charles Murray being chased by a wounded buffalo bull, may be a variation on this subject (see no. 421). In a later painting, *Chasing Back*, based on the lithograph, Catlin places an Indian instead of Murray on the horse fleeing before the wounded buffalo (see illustration and Gilcrease catalogue, p. 56).

423. Dying buffalo bull in a snowdrift
1837-1839
20⅛ x 27⅜ (50.9 x 69.4)
[Figure 126]

References: Donaldson, p. 292; Ewers (1956), p. 516; Paris (1963), no. 49.

The scene is not included in the 1837 catalogue, but does appear in the Egyptian Hall catalogue of January 1840, indicating that it was painted in the interval. The title of this entry would seem more appropriate for another winter buffalo hunt (see no. 407), but there is no alternate title for this painting in the 1848 catalogue, and it apparently came to the Smithsonian in frame 423.

424. Buffalo bulls fighting in running season, Upper Missouri
1837-1839
24 x 29 (60.9 x 73.7)
[Figure 124]

"The '*running season*,' which is in August and September, is the time when they [the buffalo] congregate into such masses in some places, as literally to blacken the prairies for miles together. It is no uncommon thing at this season, at these gatherings, to see several thousands in a mass, eddying and wheeling about under a cloud of dust, which is raised by the bulls as they are pawing in the dirt, or engaged in desperate combats, as they constantly are, plunging and butting at each other in the most furious manner. In these scenes, the males are continually following the females, and the whole mass are in constant motion; and all bellowing (or 'roaring') in deep and hollow sounds; which, mingled altogether, appear, at the distance of a mile or two, like the sound of distant thunder" (*Letters and Notes*, vol. 1, p. 249, pl. 105).
　See numbers 548, 606, and 607.

References: Donaldson, pp. 292-93; Ewers (1956), p. 516.

Copy:
M. Knoedler & Co., New York (until 1971), pencil and watercolor, signed lower right:
Rosa B-[Bonheur]

The scene is not included in the 1837 catalogue, but does appear in the Egyptian Hall catalogue of January 1840, indicating that it was painted in the interval (see no. 423). Numbers 424 and 425 are similar in style, and both are based on buffalo sketches made by Catlin on the Upper Missouri in 1832 (see no. 406).
　The scene is repeated in cartoon 154 (NGA 2138).

421

422

Buffalo Chasing Back, 25 x 32, Gilcrease Institute, Tulsa.

425. Buffalo bulls in a wallow
1837-1839
24 x 29 (60.9 x 73.7)

"In the heat of summer, these huge animals, which no doubt, suffer very much with the great profusion of their long and shaggy hair or fur, often graze on the low grounds in the prairies, where there is a little stagnant water lying amongst the grass, and the ground underneath being saturated with it, is soft, into which the enormous bull, lowered down upon one knee, will plunge his horns, and at last his head, driving up the earth, and soon making an excavation in the ground, into which the water filters from amongst the grass, forming for him in a few moments, a cool and comfortable bath, into which he plunges like a hog in his mire.

"In this *delectable* laver, he throws himself flat upon his side, and forcing himself violently around, with his horns and his huge hump on his shoulders presented to the sides, he ploughs up the ground by his rotary motion, sinking himself deeper and deeper in the ground, continually enlarging his pool, in which he at length becomes nearly immersed; and the water and mud about him mixed into a complete mortar, which changes his colour, and drips in streams from every part of him as he rises up upon his feet, a hideous monster of mud and ugliness, too frightful and too eccentric to be described" (*Letters and Notes*, vol. 1, pp. 249-50, pl. 106).

References: Donaldson, pp. 293-94; Ewers (1956), p. 516; *Catlin, Bodmer, Miller.*

Copy:
M. Knoedler & Co., New York (until 1971), pencil and watercolor, signed lower right:
Rosa B-[Bonheur]

See number 424. The scene is repeated in cartoon 152 (NGA 2136).

426. Grouse shooting on the Missouri prairies
1837-1839
19⅝ x 27⅝ (49.7 x 70)

References: Donaldson, p. 294; Ewers (1956), p. 517.

Not included in the 1837 catalogue (see no. 424). The painting must have been a last-minute attempt by Catlin to add variety to the Upper Missouri hunting scenes.

427. Ball-play Dance, Choctaw
1834-1835
19⅝ x 27⅝ (49.7 x 70)

"The ground having been all prepared and preliminaries of the game all settled, and the bettings all made, and the goods all 'staked,' night came on . . . a procession of lighted flambeaux was seen coming from each encampment, to the ground where the players assembled around their respective byes; and at the beat of the drums and chaunts of the women, each party of players commenced the 'ball-play dance.' Each party danced for a quarter of an hour around their respective byes, in their ball-play dress; rattling their ball-sticks together in the most violent manner, and all singing as loud as they could raise their voices; whilst the women of each party, who had their goods at stake, formed into two rows on the line between the two parties of players, and danced also, in an uniform step, and all their voices joined in chaunts to the Great Spirit; in which they were soliciting his favour in deciding the game to their advantage; and also encouraging the players to exert every power they possessed, in the struggle that was to ensue. In the mean time, four old *medicine-men*, who were to have the starting of the ball, and who were to be judges of the play, were seated at the point where the ball was to be started; and busily smoking to the Great Spirit for their success in judging rightly, and impartially, between the parties in so important an affair" (*Letters and Notes*, vol. 2, p. 125, pl. 224).

References: 1837 catalogue, no. 432; Donaldson, p. 300, pl. 71; Ewers (1956), p. 518; Fundaburk, p. 126, reprod. pl. 222.

Version:
Gilcrease Institute, NAI sketchbook (4776.51), pen and ink

Copy:
Schweitzer Gallery, New York, 50¾ x 66

Sketched near Fort Gibson in 1834. Catlin produced a lively rhythm in the ball-play scenes by repeating the pose of figures engaged in a similar action.

The subject is repeated in plate 22 of *Catlin's North American Indian Portfolio*, first published in 1844, and in cartoon 175 (NGA 2095). The Schweitzer copy lacks Catlin's animated touch (see no. 338).

428. Ball-play of the Choctaw—ball up
1834-1835
19½ x 27½ (49.6 x 70)
[Figure 22]

See number 427. "In the morning," Catlin continues, "the game commenced, by the judges throwing up the ball at the firing of a gun; when an instant struggle ensued between the players, who were some six or seven hundred in numbers, and were mutually endeavouring to catch the ball in their sticks, and throw it home and between their respective stakes; which, whenever successfully done, counts one for game. In this game every player was dressed alike, that is, *divested* of all dress, except the girdle and the tail, which I have before described; and in these desperate struggles for the ball, when it is *up* (where hundreds are running together and leaping, actually over each other's heads, and darting between their adversaries' legs, tripping and throwing, and foiling each other in every possible manner, and every voice raised to the highest key, in shrill yelps and barks)! there are rapid successions of feats, and of incidents, that astonish and amuse far beyond the conception of any one who has not had the singular good luck to witness them. In these struggles, every mode is used that can be devised, to oppose the progress of the foremost, who is likely to get the ball; and these obstructions often meet desperate individual resistance, which terminates in a violent scuffle" (*Letters and Notes,* vol. 2, pp. 125-26, pl. 225).

References: 1837 catalogue, no. 433; *Travels in Europe,* vol. 2, p. 316; Donaldson, p. 300, pl. 72; Matthews, p. 601, pl. 137; Ewers (1956), p. 518; McCracken, p. 142, reprod. p. 143; Fundaburk, pp. 125-26, pl. 219; Halpin, reprod. p. 12; *America as Art,* nos. 172, 173, reprod. p. 165.

Versions:
Smithsonian Institution, 25¾ x 32

Musée de la Coopération Franco-Américaine de Blérancourt, Compiègne, 65 x 80 cm

Gilcrease Institution, NAI sketchbook (4776.60), pen and ink

Sketched near Fort Gibson in 1834. Catlin's figures all run in the same position (see no. 427). A line of skin lodges has been added, across the far side of the playing field, to the Smithsonian (see illustration) and Blérancourt versions, and in the latter, at lower left, Catlin sits on horseback beside a gentleman in a tall hat who may represent Louis Philippe. The subject appears on the *Travels in Europe* list, and the Blérancourt version, presumably, was destined for the King's collection (see no. 449).

The Smithsonian original matches plate 225 in *Letters and Notes,* and the scene is repeated in plate 23 of *Catlin's North American Indian Portfolio,* first published in 1844, and in cartoon 176 (AMNH 251).

429. Ball-play of the Choctaw—ball down
1834-1835
19⅝ x 27⅝ (49.7 x 70.1)

"There are times, when the ball gets to the ground, and such a confused mass rushing together around it, and knocking their sticks together, without the possibility of any one getting or seeing it, for the dust that they raise, that the spectator loses his strength, and everything else but his senses; when the condensed mass of ball-sticks, and shins, and bloody noses, is carried around the different parts of the ground, for a quarter of an hour at a time, without any one of the mass being able to see the ball; and which they are often thus scuffling for, several minutes after it has been thrown off, and played over another part of the ground" (*Letters and Notes,* vol. 2, p. 126, pl. 226).

References: 1837 catalogue, no. 434; Donaldson, pp. 301-3, pl. 73; Ewers (1956), p. 518; McCracken, p. 142; Fundaburk, p. 126, pl. 221.

Version:
Gilcrease Institute, NAI sketchbook (4776.60), pen and ink

Sketched near Fort Gibson in 1834 (see nos. 427, 428).

430. Ball-play of the women, Prairie du Chien
Eastern Dakota (Eastern Sioux)
1835-1836
19½ x 27⅝ (49.7 x 70)

"In the ball-play of the women, they have two balls attached to the ends of a string, about a foot and half long; and each woman has a short stick in each hand, on which she catches the string with the two balls, and throws them, endeavouring to force them over the goal of her own party. The men are more than half drunk, when they feel liberal enough to indulge the women in such an amusement; and take infinite pleasure in rolling about on the ground and laughing to excess, whilst the women are tumbling about in all attitudes, and scuffling for the ball" (*Letters and Notes,* vol. 2, p. 146, pl. 252).

References: 1837 catalogue, no. 435; Donaldson, pp. 303-4; Oliver LaFarge, "George Catlin: Wild West Witness," *Art News* 52 (October 1953), reprod. p. 30; Ewers (1956), p. 511; J. F. McDermott, *Seth Eastman,* pl. 46; Paris (1963), no. 55; *America as Art,* no. 174, reprod. p. 165.

Version:
Gilcrease Institute, NAI sketchbook (4776.50), pen and ink

Sketched at Prairie du Chien in 1835 (see nos. 427, 428). The subject is repeated in cartoon 177 (NGA 1965).

Seth Eastman recorded a similar scene while stationed at Fort Snelling (see McDermott).

428

429

430

431. Tchung-kee, a Mandan game played with a ring and pole
1832-1833
19½ x 27⅝ (49.7 x 70)

"The game of Tchung-kee [is] a beautiful athletic exercise, which they seem to be almost unceasingly practicing whilst the weather is fair, and they have nothing else of moment to demand their attention. This game is decidedly their favourite amusement, and is played near to the village on a pavement of clay, which has been used for that purpose until it has become as smooth and hard as a floor. . . . The play commences with two (one from each party), who start off upon a trot, abreast of each other, and one of them rolls in advance of them, on the pavement, a little ring of two or three inches in diameter, cut out of a stone; and each one follows it up with his 'tchung-kee' (a stick of six feet in length, with little bits of leather projecting from its sides of an inch or more in length), which he throws before him as he runs, sliding it along upon the ground after the ring, endeavouring to place it in such a position when it stops, that the ring may fall upon it, and receive one of the little projections of leather through it" (*Letters and Notes*, vol. 1, p. 132, pl. 59).

References: 1837 catalogue, no. 436; Donaldson, p. 304, pl. 74; Matthews, p. 601, pl. 136; Ewers (1956), p. 513.

Sketched at the Mandan village in 1832. Catlin often set the principal figures in motion with a few hasty strokes, and then left the remainder of the painting almost unfinished. Matthews says that many Indians he has known have been favorably impressed by Catlin's representation of the game.
The scene is repeated in cartoon 173 (AMNH 189).

432. Horseracing on a course behind the Mandan village
1832-1833
19⅝ x 27⅝ (49.7 x 70)

"*Horse-racing* here, as in all more enlightened communities, is one of the most exciting amusements, and one of the most extravagent modes of gambling.
"I have been this day a spectator . . . on a course which they have, just back of their village; and although I never had the least taste for this cruel amusement in my own country, yet, I must say, I have been not a little amused and pleased with the thrilling effect which these exciting scenes have produced amongst so wild and picturesque a group.
"I have made a sketch of the ground and the group, as near as I could; shewing the manner of 'starting' and 'coming out,' which vary a little from the customs of the *knowing* world; but in other respects, I believe a horse-race is the same all the world over" (*Letters and Notes*, vol. 1, p. 143, pl. 61).

References: 1837 catalogue, no. 437; Donaldson, pp. 304-5, pl. 75; Ewers (1956), p. 513; McCracken, p. 96.

Version:
Gilcrease Institute, NAI sketchbook (4776.49), pen and ink

Copy:
M. Knoedler & Co., New York (until 1971), pencil and watercolor, signed lower right:
Rosa B-[Bonheur]

Sketched at the Mandan village in 1832 (see no. 431). The scene is repeated in cartoon 179 (NGA 2141).

433. Footrace behind the Mandan village
1832-1833
19⅝ x 27⅝ (49.7 x 70)

References: 1837 catalogue, no. 438; Donaldson, p. 305; Ewers (1956), p. 513.

Sketched at the Mandan village in 1832 (see no. 431). The scene is repeated in cartoon 334 (unlocated).

434. Canoe race near Sault Ste. Marie
Ojibwa
1836-1837
19½ x 27⅝ (49.7 x 70)

"In plate 267 is seen one of their favourite amusements at this place, which I was lucky enough to witness a few miles below the Sault, when high bettings had been made, and a great concourse of Indians had assembled to witness an *Indian regatta* or *canoe race*, which went off with great excitement, firing of guns, yelping, &c. The Indians in this vicinity are all Chippeways, and their canoes all made of birch bark, and chiefly of one model; they are exceedingly light, as I have before described, and propelled with wonderful velocity" (*Letters and Notes*, vol. 2, p. 162, pl. 267).

References: 1837 catalogue, no. 439; Donaldson, p. 305; Porter Butts, *Art in Wisconsin* (Madison, 1936), p. 41; Ewers (1956), p. 521.

Version:
Gilcrease Institute, NAI sketchbook (4776.58), pen and ink

Sketched on Catlin's journey to the Pipestone Quarry in 1836 (see no. 338). The scene is repeated in cartoon 335 (unlocated).

435. Archery of the Mandan
1835-1837
19½ x 27½ (49.6 x 70)
[Figure 134]

"I have seen a fair exhibition of their archery this day, in a favourite amusement which they call the *'game of the arrow,'* where the young men who are the most distinguished in this exercise, assemble on the prairie at a little distance from the village, and having paid, each one, his 'entrance-fee,'such as a shield, a robe, a pipe, or other article, step forward in turn, shooting their arrows into the air, endeavouring to see who can get the greatest number flying in the air at one time, thrown from the same bow" (*Letters and Notes,* vol. 1, pp. 141-42, pl. 60).

References: 1837 catalogue, no. 440; Donaldson, pp. 305-6, pl. 76; Ewers (1956), p. 513; McCracken, pp. 96, 98; Paris (1963), no. 56.

Version:
Gilcrease Institute, NAI sketchbook (4776.48), pen and ink

Copy:
M. Knoedler & Co., New York (until 1971), pencil and watercolor, signed lower right:
Rosa B-[Bonheur]

Probably sketched in 1832 at the Mandan village, but the style of the painting is closer to the dance scenes (see no. 437). Catlin has turned the game into a major anatomy demonstration. The frieze of contestants, all looking like young Apollos, is the most carefully arranged and balanced group to be found in any of the artist's paintings.

The scene is repeated in plate 24 of *Catlin's North American Indian Portfolio,* first published in 1844, and in cartoon 174 (NGA 2041), with a less formal arrangement of figures.

436. Dance of the chiefs, mouth of the Teton River
Teton Dakota (Western Sioux), 1832-1833
24 x 29 (60.9 x 73.7)

"The dancing is generally done by the young men, and considered undignified for the chiefs or doctors to join in. Yet so great was my *medicine,* that chiefs and medicine-men turned out and agreed to compliment me with a dance. I looked on with great satisfaction; having been assured by the Interpreters and Traders, that this was the highest honour they had ever known them to pay to any stranger amongst them.

"This dance, which I have called 'the dance of the chiefs,' for want of a more significant title, was given by fifteen or twenty chiefs and doctors; many of whom were very old and venerable men. All of them came out in their head-dresses of war-eagle quills, with a spear or staff in the left hand, and a rattle in the right. It was given in the midst of the Sioux village, in front of the head chief's lodge, and beside the medicine-man who beat on the drum, and sang for the dance, there were four young women standing in a row, and chanting a sort of chorus for the dancers; forming one of the very few instances that I ever have met, where the women are allowed to take any part in the dancing, or other game or amusement, with the men" (*Letters and Notes,* vol. 1, p. 237, pl. 100).

References: 1837 catalogue, no. 441; Donaldson, pp. 306-7; Ewers (1956), p. 511; McCracken, pp. 50-51; *Catlin, Bodmer, Miller;* Paris (1963), no. 57.

Version:
Gilcrease Institute, NAI sketchbook (4776.64), pen and ink

Sketched near Fort Pierre in 1832, or perhaps painted there, in great haste. The scene is repeated in cartoon 164 (unlocated, see no. 443).

437. Dog Dance at Fort Snelling
Eastern Dakota (Eastern Sioux), 1835-1837
19⅝ x 27⅝ (49.7 x 70)

"Considerable preparation was made for the occasion, and the Indians informed me, that if they could get a couple of dogs that were of no use about the garrison, they would give us their favourite, the *'dog dance.'* The two dogs were soon produced by the officers, and in presence of the whole assemblage of spectators, they butchered them and placed their two hearts and livers entire and uncooked, on a couple of crotches about as high as a man's face. These were then cut into strips, about an inch in width, and left hanging in this condition, with the blood and smoke upon them. A spirited dance then ensued; and , in a confused manner, every one sung forth his own deeds of bravery in ejaculatory gutturals, which were almost deafening; and they danced up, two at a time to the stakes, and after spitting several times upon the liver and hearts, catched a piece in their mouths, bit it off and swallowed it. This was all done without losing the step (which was in time to their music), or interrupting the times of their voices" (*Letters and Notes,* vol. 2, pp. 136-37, pl. 237).

References: 1837 catalogue, no. 442; Donaldson, pp. 307-8; Ewers (1956), p. 511; J. F. McDermott, *Seth Eastman,* pl. 78; Rossi and Hunt, pp. 57, 320.

Version:
Gilcrease Institute, NAI sketchbook (4776.65), pen and ink

Sketched at Fort Snelling in 1835. Most figures in Catlin's dance groups assume a similar half-crouching position that is repeated, at various angles and with different gestures, as the dancers move around a loosely defined circle. The individual figures often have a fixed or static appear-

436

437

ance, but the repetition of similar poses does generate a lively rhythm in the groups that becomes a substitute for motion. A corresponding effect may be observed in Catlin's hunting and sporting scenes.

Individual figures and ritual details are described in the dance scenes with a thinly painted, linear clarity unusual for the artist at this period. The technique is much the same throughout the series, indicating a date of execution after 1835, when Catlin saw the dances at Fort Snelling and the Sauk and Fox village (see no. 455). The cartoons that he began painting in the 1850s are of a somewhat similar style.

The Dog Dance is repeated in cartoon 170 (NGA 1964). Seth Eastman sketched the same dance while stationed at Fort Snelling several years later (see McDermott).

438

438a.

Smithsonian Institution.

439

438. Scalp Dance, mouth of the Teton River

Teton Dakota (Western Sioux), 1835-1837
20⅛ x 27⅜ (50.9 x 69.4)

"The *Scalp-dance* is given as a celebration of a victory; and amongst this tribe, as I learned whilst residing with them, danced in the night, by the light of their torches, and just before retiring to bed. When a war party returns from a war excursion, bringing home with them the scalps of their enemies, they generally 'dance them' for fifteen nights in succession, vaunting forth the most extravagant boasts of their wonderful prowess in war, whilst they brandish their war weapons in their hands. A number of young women are selected to aid (though they do not actually join in the dance), by stepping into the centre of the ring, and holding up the scalps that have been recently taken, whilst the warriors dance (or rather *jump*), around in a circle, brandishing their weapons, and barking and yelping in the most frightful manner, all jumping on both feet at a time, with a simultaneous stamp, and blow, and thrust of their weapons; with which it would seem as if they were actually cutting and carving each other to pieces. During these frantic leaps, and yelps, and thrusts, every man distorts his face to the utmost of his muscles, darting about his glaring eye-balls and snapping his teeth, as if he were in the heat (and actually breathing through his inflated nostrils the very hissing death) of battle! No description that can be written, could ever convey more than a feeble outline of the frightful effects of these scenes enacted in the dead and darkness of night, under the glaring light of their blazing flambeaux" (*Letters and Notes*, vol. 1, pp. 245-6, pl. 104).

References: 1837 catalogue, no. 443; Donaldson, pp. 308-9, pl. 77; McCracken, *Portrait of the Old West* (New York, 1952), p. 58; *Westward the Way*, no. 56, reprod. p. 90; Ewers (1956), p. 511; McCracken, pp. 52, 54; Ewers (1965), p. 74; Halpin, reprod. p. 8; Rossi and Hunt, pp. 76, 320; *America as Art*, no. 181.

Versions:
Smithsonian Institution, 26⅜ x 32¾

Gilcrease Institute, NAI sketchbook (4776.65), pen and ink

Copy:
Schweitzer Gallery, New York, 48 x 66½

Sketched near Fort Pierre in 1832 (see no. 437). The Smithsonian version (illustration 438a), which in size and finish closely resembles the paintings commissioned by Louis Philippe (see no. 449), appears to be the night scene described by Catlin in the above passage. A moon and torches illuminate the circle of dancers, who are surrounded by other members of the tribe. Skin lodges and trees loom in the background. The dramatic setting was meant to appeal to European audiences, who may have found the Smithsonian original, with its absence of stage props, a bit too anthropological. The latter matches plate 104 in *Letters and Notes*.

The scene is repeated in plate 27 of *Catlin's North American Indian Portfolio* (fig. 35), first published in 1844, and in cartoon 166 (NGA 1963). The Schweitzer painting is a copy of the lithograph.

439. Begging Dance, Sauk and Fox

1835-1837
19⅝ x 27⅝ (49.7 x 70)

"The *Begging Dance* is a frequent amusement, and one that has been practiced with some considerable success at this time, whilst there have been so many distinguished and liberal visitors here. It is got up by a number of desperate and long-winded fellows, who will dance and yell their visitors into liberality; or, if necessary, laugh them into it, by their strange antics, singing a song of importunity, and extending their hands for presents, which they allege are to gladden the hearts of the poor, and ensure a blessing to the giver" (*Letters and Notes*, vol. 2, p. 214, pl. 293).

References: 1837 catalogue, no. 444; Donaldson, p. 309, pl. 78; Ewers (1956), p. 522; Rossi and Hunt, pp. 57, 320.

Version:
Gilcrease Institute, NAI sketchbook (4776.65), pen and ink

Sketched at the Sauk and Fox village in 1835 (see no. 437). The scene is repeated in cartoon 156 (NGA 2088).

440. Buffalo Dance, Mandan
1835-1837
20⅛ x 27⅜ (50.9 x 69.4)
[Figure 132]

The [buffalo] mask is put over the head, and generally has a strip of the skin hanging to it, of the whole length of the animal, with the tail attached to it, which, passing down over the back of the dancer, is dragging on the ground. When one becomes fatigued of the exercise, he signifies it by bending quite forward, and sinking his body towards the ground; when another draws a bow upon him and hits him with a blunt arrow, and he falls like a buffalo—is seized by the bye-standers, who drag him out of the ring by the heels, brandishing their knives about him; and having gone through the motions of skinning and cutting him up, they let him off, and his place is at once supplied by another, who dances into the ring with his mask on; and by this taking of places, the scene is easily kept up night and day, until the desired effect has been produced, that of 'making buffalo come' " (*Letters and Notes*, vol. 1, p. 128, pl. 56).

References: 1837 catalogue, no. 445; Donaldson, pp. 309-12, pl. 79; Ewers (1956), p. 513; McCracken, pp. 97, 103; Wendell D. Garrett, *The Arts in America: The Nineteenth Century* (New York, 1969), reprod. p. 185; Gilcrease catalogue, p. 57; *America as Art*, no. 177, reprod. p. 167.

Version:
Gilcrease Institute, NAI sketchbook (4776.64), pen and ink

Sketched in 1832 at the Mandan village (see no. 437). The scene is repeated in plate 8 of *Catlin's North American Indian Portfolio,* first published in 1844; in plate 70 of the Gilcrease *Souvenir* album; and in cartoon 171 (NGA 2040).
Karl Bodmer saw the same dance during his visit to the village in 1833-34 (see Reuben Gold Thwaites, ed., *Early Western Travels 1748-1846,* pl. 51).

441. Ball-play Dance, Choctaw
1834-1835
Unlocated

References: 1837 catalogue, no. 446; Donaldson, p. 312.

Probably sketched near Fort Gibson in 1834 (see no. 427).

442. Dance to the berdash
Sauk and Fox, 1835-1837
19⅝ x 27⅝ (49.6 x 70)

"*Dance to the Berdashe* is a very funny and amusing scene, which happens once a year or oftener, as they choose, when a feast is given to the 'Berdashe,' as he is called in French . . . who is a man dressed in woman's clothes, as he is known to be all his life, and for extraordinary privileges which he is known to possess, he is driven to the most servile and degrading duties, which he is not allowed to escape; and he being the only one of the tribe submitting to this disgraceful degradation, is looked upon as *medicine* and sacred, and a feast is given to him annually" (*Letters and Notes,* vol. 2, pp. 214-15, pl. 296).

References: 1837 catalogue, no. 447; Donaldson, p. 313, pl. 80; Ewers (1956), p. 522.

Sketched at the Sauk and Fox village in 1835 (see no. 437). The scene is repeated in cartoon 162 (NGA 2091).

443. Beggar's Dance, mouth of the Teton River
Teton Dakota (Western Sioux), 1835-1837
19½ x 27⅝ (49.5 x 70)

"This spirited dance was given, not by a set of *beggars* . . . but by the first and most independent young men in the tribe, beautifully dressed, (*i.e.,* not dressed at all, except with their breech clouts or *kelts,* made of eagles' and ravens' quills) with their lances, and pipes, and rattles in their hands, and a medicine-man beating the drum, and joining in the song at the highest key of his voice. In this dance every one sings as loud as he can halloo; uniting his voice with the others, in an appeal to the Great Spirit, to open the hearts of the bystanders to give to the poor, and not to themselves; assuring them that the Great Spirit will be kind to those who are kind to the helpless and poor" (*Letters and Notes,* vol. 1, p. 245, pl. 103).

References: 1837 catalogue, no. 448; Donaldson, p. 313; Ewers (1956), p. 511; McCracken, p. 51, reprod. p. 45; National Gallery of Art, Washington, D.C., *American Paintings and Sculpture* (1970), p. 31, no. 1975; Rossi and Hunt, pp. 76, 320.

Version:
Gilcrease Institute, NAI sketchbook (4776.65), pen and ink

Sketched near Fort Pierre in 1832 (see no. 437). The scene is repeated in a cartoon (NGA 1975) incorrectly labeled *Chief's Dance—Sioux* in the National Gallery catalogue (see no. 436). Presumably, NGA 1975 is cartoon 157 in the 1871 catalogue.

442

443

444. Dance to the medicine bag of the brave
Sauk and Fox, 1835-1837
19⅝ x 27⅝ (49.7 x 70.1)

"This is a custom well worth recording, for the beautiful moral which is contained in it. In this plate is represented a party of Sac warriors who have returned victorious from battle, with scalps they have taken from their enemies, but having lost one of their party, they appear and dance in front of his wigwam, fifteen days in succession, about an hour on each day, when the widow hangs his *medicine-bag* on a green bush which she erects before her door, under which she sits and cries, whilst the warriors dance and brandish the scalps they have taken, and at the same time recount the deeds of bravery of their deceased comrade in arms, whilst they are throwing presents to the widow to heal her grief and afford her the means of a living" (*Letters and Notes,* vol. 2, p. 215, pl. 297).

References: 1837 catalogue, no. 449; Donaldson, pp. 313-14; Ewers (1956), p. 522; *America as Art,* no. 178, reprod. p. 167.

Version:
Gilcrease Institute, NAI sketchbook (4776.64), pen and ink

Sketched at the Sauk and Fox village in 1835 (see no. 437). The scene is repeated in cartoon 160 (AMNH 244).

445. Brave's Dance at Fort Snelling
Eastern Dakota (Eastern Sioux), 1835-1837
19⅝ x 27⅝ (49.7 x 70)

"[The Brave's Dance] is peculiarly beautiful, and exciting to the feelings in the highest degree.

"At intervals they stop, and one of them steps into the ring, and vociferates as loud as possible, with the most significant gesticulations, the feats of bravery which he has performed during his life—he boasts of the scalps he has taken—of the enemies he has vanquished, and at the same time carries his body through all the motions and gestures, which have been used during these scenes when they were transacted. At the end of his boasting, all assent to the truth of his story, and give in their approbation by the guttural 'waugh!' and the dance again commences. At the next interval, another makes his boasts, and another, and another, and so on" (*Letters and Notes,* vol. 2, pp. 135-36).

References: 1837 catalogue, no. 450; Donaldson, p. 314; Ewers (1956), p. 511.

Sketched at Fort Snelling in 1835 (see nos. 437, 452). The scene is repeated as a War Dance in plate 29 of *Catlin's North American Indian Portfolio,* first published in 1844.

446. Green Corn Dance, Hidatsa
1835-1837
19⅝ x 27⅝ (49.7 x 70)

"On the day appointed by the doctors, the villagers are all assembled, and in the midst of the group a kettle is hung over a fire and filled with the green corn, which is well boiled, to be given to the Great Spirit, as a sacrifice necessary to be made before any one can indulge the cravings of his appetite. Whilst this first kettleful is boiling, four medicine-men, with a stalk of the corn in one hand and a rattle . . . in the other, with their bodies painted with white clay, dance around the kettle, chanting a song of thanksgiving to the Great Spirit to whom the offering is to be made. At the same time a number of warriors are dancing around in a more extended circle, with stalks of the corn in their hands, and joining also in the song of thanksgiving, whilst the villagers are all assembled and looking on. During this scene there is an arrangement of wooden bowls laid upon the ground, in which the feast is to be dealt out, each one having in it a spoon made of the buffalo or mountain-sheep's horn.

"In this wise the dance continues until the doctors decide that the corn is sufficiently boiled; it then stops for a few moments, and again assumes a different form and a different song, whilst the doctors are placing the ears on a little scaffold of sticks, which they erect immediately over the fire where it is entirely consumed, as they join again in the dance around it" (*Letters and Notes,* vol. 1, p. 189, pl. 75).

References: 1837 catalogue, no. 451; Donaldson, pp. 314-16, pl. 6; Ewers (1956), p. 512; McCracken, pp. 114, 117; Rossi and Hunt, pp. 76, 320; *America as Art,* no. 179.

Version:
Gilcrease Institute, NAI sketchbook (4776.65), pen and ink

A faint drawing of the dance, made during Catlin's visit to the Hidatsa village in 1832, appears in the SI sketchbook (see Donaldson, pl. 6, and no. 437). The scene is repeated in cartoon 168 (NGA 2039).

447. Bear Dance, preparing for a bear hunt
Teton Dakota (Western Sioux), 1835-1837
19½ x 27⅝ (49.7 x 70)

"The Sioux, like all the others of these western tribes, are fond of bear's meat, and must have good stores of the 'bear's-grease' laid in, to oil their long and glossy locks, as well as the surface of their bodies. And they all like the fine pleasure of a bear hunt, and also a participation in the bear dance, which is given several days in succession, previous to their starting out, and in which they all join in a song to the *Bear Spirit;* which they think holds somewhere an invisible existence, and must be consulted and conciliated before they can enter upon their excursion with any prospect of success. For this grotesque and amusing scene, one of the chief medicine-men, placed over his body the entire skin of a bear, with a war-eagle's quill on his head, taking the lead in the dance, and looking through the skin which formed a masque that hung over his face. Many others in the dance wore masques on their faces, made of the skin from the bear's head; and all, with the motions of their hands, closely imitated the movements of that animal; some representing its motion in running, and others the peculiar attitude and hanging of the paws, when it is sitting upon its hind feet, and looking out for the approach of an enemy" (*Letters and Notes,* vol. 1, p. 245, pl. 102).

References: 1837 catalogue, no. 452; Donaldson, p. 316; Ewers (1956), p. 511; McCracken, p. 51, reprod. p. 49; Paris (1963), no. 58; Ewers, "The Opening of the West," *The Artist in America* (New York, 1967), reprod. p. 45; Rossi and Hunt, pp. 60, 320; Gilcrease catalogue, p. 57; Museum of Fine Arts, Boston, *Frontier America: The Far West* (1975), no. 34.

Versions:
Gilcrease Institute, 25 x 32, signed on tipi, left center: G. Catlin 1847

Gilcrease Institute, NAI sketchbook (4776.64), pen and ink

Sketched near Fort Pierre in 1832 (see no. 437). In the Gilcrease version, the dance takes place in a Sioux village, with members of the tribe looking on and skin lodges in the background. Although the subject does not appear on the *Travels in Europe* list, this version closely resembles other paintings commissioned by Louis Philippe (see no. 449). The Smithsonian original matches plate 102 in *Letters and Notes.*

The scene is repeated in plate 18 of *Catlin's North American Indian Portfolio,* first published in 1844; in plate 82 of the Gilcrease *Souvenir* album; and in cartoon 165 (NGA 2092).

448. Discovery Dance, Sauk and Fox
1835-1837
19½ x 27½ (49.5 x 69.9)

"The *Discovery Dance* has been given here, amongst various others, and pleased the bystanders very much; it was exceedingly droll and picturesque, and acted out with a great deal of pantomimic effect—without music, or any other noise than the patting of their feet, which all came simultaneously on the ground, in perfect time, whilst they were dancing forward two or four at a time, in a skulking posture, overlooking the country, and professing to announce the approach of animals or enemies which they have discovered, by giving the signals back to the leader of the dance" (*Letters and Notes,* vol. 2, p. 214, pl. 295).

References: 1837 catalogue, no. 453; Donaldson, p. 316, pl. 81; Ewers (1956), p. 522; *America as Art,* no. 180.

Version:
Gilcrease Institute, NAI sketchbook (4776.64), pen and ink

Sketched at the Sauk and Fox village in 1835 (see no. 437). The scene is repeated in cartoon 167 (NGA 2093).

Plate 18, *North American Indian Portfolio.*

Gilcrease Institute, Tulsa.

Cartoon 165, National Gallery of Art, Washington, D.C. Paul Mellon Collection.

449

450

449. Eagle Dance, Choctaw
1835-1837
19⅝ x 27⅝ (49.6 x 70)

"The *Eagle Dance*, a very pretty scene . . . [was] got up by their young men, in honour of that bird, for which they seem to have a religious regard. This picturesque dance was given by twelve or sixteen men, whose bodies were chiefly naked and painted white, with white clay, and each one holding in his hand the tail of the eagle, while his head was also decorated with an eagle's quill. Spears were stuck in the ground, around which the dance was performed by four men at a time, who had simultaneously, at the beat of the drum, jumped up from the ground where they had all sat in rows of four, one row immediately behind the other, and ready to take the place of the first four when they left the ground fatigued. . . .

"In this dance, the steps or rather jumps, were different from anything I had ever witnessed before, as the dancers were squat down, with their bodies almost to the ground, in a severe and most difficult posture, as will have been seen in the drawing" (*Letters and Notes*, vol. 2, pp. 126-27, pl. 227).

References: 1837 catalogue, no. 454; *Travels in Europe*, vol. 2, pp. 17, 316; Donaldson, pp. 316-17, pl. 82; Ewers (1956), p. 518; Fundaburk, p. 125, pl. 218.

Version:
Gilcrease Institute, NAI sketchbook (4776.63), pen and ink

Sketched near Fort Gibson in 1834 (see no. 437). The scene is repeated in cartoon 161 (NGA 2090).

In the Smithsonian Catlin collection (fig. 135; no. 386,440, 26⅛ x 32⅝ in.) is a Sauk and Fox or Iowa dance scene in which each Indian holds an eagle feather and wears another in his headdress. Their bodies are not painted white, however, nor is the position and arrangement of the dancers at all similar to number 449.

The subject was probably taken from the Eagle Dance performed by the Iowa troupe in London in 1844, and Catlin then filled in an appropriate background (see *Travels in Europe* and no. 517). Presumably the painting was destined for Louis Philippe, as an Eagle Dance appears on the list of fifteen paintings that the king commissioned from Catlin in 1845. Although the size of these is given as 30 by 36 inches, the frames may have been included in the dimensions. Even the present size is noticeably larger than the average dance or hunting scene in the 1848 catalogue, and the elaborate detail of the painting, which is much like the execution of the LaSalle series, would indicate that Catlin made a considerable effort to please the king. Except for a version of number 428, no Catlin paintings remain in the French national collections. This may mean that the group of fifteen were retrieved by the artist, along with the LaSalle series, after Louis was deposed in February 1848.

450. Slave Dance, Sauk and Fox
1835-1837
19⅝ x 27⅝ (49.7 x 70)

"The *slave-dance* is a picturesque scene, and the custom in which it is founded a very curious one. This tribe has a society which they call the '*slaves*,' composed of a number of the young men of the best families in the tribe, who volunteer to be slaves for the term of two years, and subject to perform any menial service that the chief may order, no matter how humiliating or how degrading it may be; by which, after serving their two years, they are exempt for the rest of their lives, on war-parties or other excursions, or wherever they may be—from all labour or degrading occupations, such as cooking, making fires, &c. &c.

"These young men elect one from their numbers to be their master, and all agree to obey his command whatever it may be, and which is given to him by one of the chiefs of the tribe. On a certain day or season of the year, they have to themselves a great feast, and preparatory to it the above-mentioned dance" (*Letters and Notes*, vol. 2, p. 213, pl. 291).

References: 1837 catalogue, no. 455; Donaldson, p. 317, pl. 83; Ewers (1956), p. 522.

Version:
Gilcrease Institute, NAI sketchbook (4776.64), pen and ink

Sketched at the Sauk and Fox village in 1835 (see no. 437). The scene is repeated in cartoon 158 (NGA 2089).

451. Snowshoe Dance, at the first snowfall
Ojibwa, 1835-1837
19½ x 26⅞ (49.5 x 68.2)
[Figure 133]

"The *snow-shoe dance* . . . is exceedingly picturesque, being danced with the snow shoes under the feet, at the falling of the first snow in the beginning of winter, when they sing a song of thanksgiving to the Great Spirit for sending them a return of snow, when they can run on their snow shoes in their valued hunts, and easily take the game for their food" (*Letters and Notes,* vol. 2, p. 139, pl. 243).

References: 1837 catalogue, no. 456; Donaldson, p. 317; *Westward the Way,* no. 57, reprod. p. 91; Ewers (1956), p. 521; McCracken, p. 165, reprod. p. 167; Rossi and Hunt, pp. 57, 320; Gilcrease catalogue, p. 57.

Version:
Gilcrease Institute, NAI sketchbook (4776.65), pen and ink

Copy:
M. Knoedler & Co., New York (until 1971), pencil, Rosa Bonheur estate

Details were probably sketched at Fort Snelling in 1835, but Catlin never saw the dance performed in winter (see nos. 437, 416). The scene is repeated in plate 14 of *Catlin's North American Indian Portfolio,* first published in 1844; in plate 74 of the Gilcrease *Souvenir* album; and in cartoon 169 (NGA 2094).

452. Brave's Dance, Ojibwa
1835-1837
19⅝ x 27⅝ (49.7 x 70)

See number 445. Catlin does not distinguish between the Sioux and Ojibwa Brave's Dance.

References: 1837 catalogue, no. 457; Donaldson, p. 317; Ewers (1956), p. 521.

Sketched at Fort Snelling in 1835 (see no. 437).

453. Pipe Dance, Assiniboin
1835-1837
19⅝ x 27⅝ (49.7 x 70)

"One of these scenes . . . appeared to me to be peculiar to this tribe, and exceedingly picturesque in its effect. . . . On a half-trodden pavement in front of their village . . . the young men, who were to compose the dance, had gathered themselves around a small fire, and each one seated on a buffalo-robe spread upon the ground. In the centre

and by the fire, was seated a dignitary, who seemed to be a chief . . . with a long pipe in his hand, which he lighted at the fire and smoked incessantly, grunting forth at the same time, in half-strangled gutturals, a sort of song. . . . While this was going on, another grim-visaged fellow in another part of the group, commenced beating on a drum or tambourine, accompanied by his voice; when one of the young men seated, sprang instantly on his feet, and commenced singing in time with the taps of the drum, and leaping about on one foot and the other in the most violent manner imaginable. In this way he went several times around the circle, bowing and brandishing his fists in the faces of each one who was seated, until at length he grasped one of them by the hands, and jerked him forcibly up upon his feet; who joined in the dance for a moment, leaving the one who had pulled him up, to continue his steps and his song in the centre of the ring; whilst he danced around in a similar manner, jerking up another . . . and so on . . . until all were upon their feet" (*Letters and Notes,* vol. 1, p. 55, pl. 32).

References: 1837 catalogue, no. 458; Donaldson, pp. 317-18; Ewers (1956), p. 508; McCracken, p. 180.

Version:
Gilcrease Institute, NAI sketchbook (4776.63), pen and ink

Copy:
M. Knoedler & Co., New York (until 1971), pencil and watercolor, signed lower right:
Rosa B-[Bonheur]

Sketched at Fort Union in 1832 (see no. 437). The scene is repeated in cartoon 159 (NGA 2140).

454. Straw Dance, Sioux
Unlocated

Catlin describes the scene as "Children made to dance with burning straws tied to their bodies, to make them tough and brave" (1848 catalogue, p. 42).

References: 1837 catalogue, no. 459; Donaldson, p. 318.

Probably sketched near Fort Pierre in 1832 (see no. 437). Cartoon 336 (unlocated) in the 1871 catalogue is labeled *Straw Dance-Mandans.*

452

453

455

457

457a.

Smithsonian Institution.

455. Sham fight, Mandan boys
1832-1833
19⅝ x 27⅝ (49.7 x 70)

"The *sham-fight* . . . of the Mandan boys . . . is a part of their regular exercise, and constitutes a material branch of their education. During the pleasant mornings of the summer, the little boys between the age of seven and fifteen are called out, to the number of several hundred, and being divided into two companies, each of which is headed by some experienced warrior . . . they are led out into the prairie at sunrise, where this curious discipline is regularly taught them. Their bodies are naked, and each one has a little bow in his left hand and a number of arrows made of large spears of grass, which are harmless in their effects . . . on the tops of their heads are slightly attached small tufts of grass, which answer as scalps, and in this plight, they follow the dictates of their experienced leaders . . . through the judicious evolutions of Indian warfare" (*Letters and Notes*, vol. 1, p. 131, pl. 57).

References: 1837 catalogue, no. 460; Donaldson, pp. 318-19, pl. 84; Ewers (1956), p. 513.

Sketched at the Mandan village in 1832. The scale relationships in the painting are impossible, and the anatomy of the mock warriors has been represented with great haste and little accuracy. The painting offers further proof that the dance scenes were executed after 1835 (see no. 437).

The scene is repeated in cartoon 337 (unlocated).

456. Sham Scalp Dance, Mandan boys
Unlocated

"After this exciting exhibition is ended [the sham fight, see no. 455], they all return to their village, where the chiefs and braves pay profound attention to their vaunting, and applaud them for their artifice and valour.

"Those who have taken scalps then step forward, brandishing them and making their boast as they enter into the *scalp-dance* (in which they are also instructed by their leaders or teachers), jumping and yelling—brandishing their scalps, and reciting their *sanguinary deeds*, to the great astonishment of their tender aged sweethearts, who are gazing with wonder upon them" (*Letters and Notes*, vol. 1, p. 132).

References: 1837 catalogue, no. 461; Donaldson, p. 319.

Sketched at the Mandan village in 1832.

457. War Dance, Sioux
Teton Dakota (Western Sioux), 1837-1839
19⅜ x 26⅝ (49 x 67.5)

"Each warrior, in turn, jumps through the fire, and then advances shouting and boasting, and taking his oath, as he 'strikes the *reddened post*' " (1848 catalogue, p. 42).

References: Donaldson, p. 319; Ewers (1956), p. 511.

Version:
Smithsonian Institution, 26⅛ x 32½

Probably sketched near Fort Pierre in 1832. The subject is not included in the 1837 catalogue, but does appear in the Egyptian Hall catalogue of January 1840, indicating that it was painted in the interval (see no. 422). Catlin transformed the Smithsonian original, an abrupt and hasty oil sketch, into an elaborately finished night scene. This final version (illustration 457a) has much in common with the paintings intended for Louis Philippe, but does not appear on the *Travels in Europe* list (see no. 449).

Although the title is similar, plate 29 in *Catlin's North American Indian Portfolio* represents another dancing group (see no. 445).

458. Foot war party in council, Mandan
1835-1837
19⅝ x 27⅝ (49.7 x 70.1)

"This party was made up of the most distinguished and desperate young men of the tribe, who had sallied out against the Riccarees, and taken the most solemn oath amongst themselves never to return without achieving a victory. They had wandered long and faithfully about the country, following the trails of their enemy; when they were attacked by a numerous party, and lost several of their men and all their horses. . . .

"In this plight, it seems, I had dropped my little canoe alongside of them, while descending from the Mouth of Yellow Stone to this place, not many weeks since; where they had bivouacked or halted, to smoke and consult on the best and safest mode of procedure. . . . Seated on their buffalo robes, which were spread upon the grass, with their respective weapons laying about them, and lighting their pipes at a little fire which was kindled in the centre—the chief or leader of the party, with his arms stacked behind him, and his long head-dress of war-eagles' quills and ermine falling down over his back, whilst he sat in a contemplative and almost desponding mood, was surely one of the most striking and beautiful illustrations of a natural hero that I ever looked upon" (*Letters and Notes*, vol. 1, pp. 143-44, pl. 63).

References: 1837 catalogue, no. 462; Donaldson, pp. 319-20; Ewers (1956), p. 513.

Version:
Gilcrease Institute, NAI sketchbook (4776.48), pen and ink

Probably sketched in 1832 on the Missouri River voyage, but the calculated arrangement of the figures (the chief clearly has a classical ancestor) and the linear style are more like the dance groups (see nos. 437, 435).
The scene is repeated in cartoon 182 (NGA 2042).

459. Comanche war party, chief discovering the enemy and urging his men at sunrise
1834-1835
19½ x 27½ (49.5 x 69.8)

References: 1837 catalogue, no. 463; Donaldson, p. 320; Ewers (1956), p. 509.

Probably painted in Catlin's studio during the winter following the dragoon expedition (see no. 345).

460. Self-torture in a Sioux religious ceremony
Teton Dakota (Western Sioux), 1835-1837
19⅝ x 27¼ (49.7 x 69.2)

"I was called upon by one of the clerks [at Fort Pierre] . . . to ride up a mile or so, near the banks of the Teton River . . . to see a man (as they said) *'looking at the sun!'* We found him naked, except his breech-cloth, with splints or skewers run through the flesh on both breasts, leaning back and hanging with the weight of his body to the top of a pole which was fastened in the ground, and to the upper end of which he was fastened by a cord which was tied to the splints. In this position he was leaning back, with nearly the whole weight of his body hanging to the pole, the top of which was bent forward, allowing his body to sink about half-way to the ground. . . . In this condition, with the blood trickling down over his body, which was covered with white and yellow clay, and amidst a great crowd who were looking on, sympathizing with and encouraging him, he was . . . to stand and look at the sun, from its rising in the morning 'till its setting at night; at which time, if his heart and his strength have not failed him, he is 'cut down,' receives the liberal donation of presents . . . and also the name and the style of a doctor, or *medicine-man*, which lasts him, and ensures him respect, through life" (*Letters and Notes*, vol. 1, p. 232, pl. 97).

References: 1837 catalogue, no. 464; Donaldson, pp. 320-21; Ewers (1956), p. 511; McCracken, pp. 53, 54.

A rough drawing of the scene, presumably made near Fort Pierre in 1832, appears in the SI sketchbook, but the technique of the painting is similar to that of the dance groups (see no. 437). Note the linear design of the seated Indians at lower left.
The scene is repeated in cartoon 187 (AMNH 305).

458

459

460

Gilcrease Institute, Tulsa.

Gilcrease Institute, Tulsa.

461. Dragoons on the march, with buffalo breaking through their ranks
1834-1835
Unlocated

"In one of those spirited scenes when the regiment were on the march, and the Indians with their bows and arrows were closely plying a band of these affrighted animals, they made a bolt through the line of the dragoons, and a complete breach, through which the whole herd passed, upsetting horses and riders in the most amusing manner, and receiving such shots as came from those guns and pistols that were *aimed,* and not fired off into the empty air" (*Letters and Notes,* vol. 2, p. 57, pl. 158).

References: 1837 catalogue, no. 465; Donaldson, p. 321; Rossi and Hunt, pp. 215, 320; Gilcrease catalogue, p. 57.

Versions:
Gilcrease Institute, 11 x 14

Gilcrease Institute, NAI sketchbook (4776.60), pen and ink

Sketched on the dragoon expedition in 1834. The Gilcrease version, which matches plate 158 in *Letters and Notes,* is illustrated in place of the original.

The scene is repeated in cartoon 338 (unlocated).

462. Prairie dog village
1832-1833
Unlocated

"The size of these curious little animals is not far from that of a very large rat, and they are not unlike in their appearance. As I have said, their burrows, are uniformly built in a lonely desert; and away, both from the proximity of timber and water. Each individual, or each family, dig their hole in the prairie to the depth of eight or ten feet, throwing up the dirt from each excavation, in a little pile, in the form of a cone, which forms the only elevation for them to ascend; where they sit, to bark and chatter when an enemy is approaching their village. These villages are sometimes of several miles in extent; containing (I would almost say) myriads of their excavations and little dirt hillocks, and to the ears of their visitors, the din of their barkings is too confused and too peculiar to be described" (*Letters and Notes,* vol. 1, pp. 76-78, pl. 42).

References: 1837 catalogue, no. 466; Donaldson, pp. 321-22; Gilcrease catalogue, p. 57.

Versions:
Gilcrease Institute, 11 x 14

Gilcrease Institute, NAI sketchbook (4776.78), pen and ink

Sketched near the mouth of the Yellowstone River in 1832. The Gilcrease version, which matches plate 42 in *Letters and Notes,* is illustrated in place of the original.

The scene is repeated in cartoon 202 (NGA 2143).

463. "Smoking horses," a curious custom of the Sauk and Fox
1835-1836
19⅝ x 27⅝ (49.7 x 70)

"When General Street and I arrived at Kee-o-kuk's village, we were just in time to see this amusing scene, on the prairie a little back of his village. The Foxes, who were making up a war-party to go against the Sioux, and had not suitable horses enough by twenty, had sent word to the Sacs, the day before (according to an ancient custom), that they were coming on that day, at a certain hour, to 'smoke' that number of horses, and they must not fail to have them ready. On that day, and at the hour, the twenty young men who were beggars for horses, were on the spot, and seated themselves on the ground in a circle, where they went to smoking. The villagers flocked around them in a dense crowd, and soon after appeared on the prairie, at half a mile distance, an equal number of young men of the Sac tribe, who had agreed, each to give a horse, and who were then galloping them about at full speed; and, gradually, as they went around in a circuit, coming in nearer to the centre, until they were at last close around the ring of young fellows seated on the ground. Whilst dashing about thus, each one, with a heavy whip in his hand, as he came within reach of the group on the ground, selected the one to whom he decided to present his horse, and as he passed him, gave him the most tremendous cut with his lash, over his naked shoulders; and as he darted around again he plied the whip as before and again and again, with a violent 'crack!' until the blood could be seen trickling down over his naked shoulders, upon which he instantly dismounted, and placed the bridle and whip in his hands . . . [the beggar] could afford to take the stripes and the scars as the price of the horse, and the giver could afford to make the present for the satisfaction of putting his mark upon the other, and of boasting of his liberality" (*Letters and Notes,* vol. 2, pp. 213-14, pl. 292).

References: 1837 catalogue, no. 467; Donaldson, pp. 322-23, pl. 85; Ewers (1956), p. 522.

Version:
Gilcrease Institute, NAI sketchbook (4776.49), pen and ink

Copy:
M. Knoedler & Co., New York (until 1971), pencil
and watercolor, signed lower right:
Rosa B-[Bonheur]

Sketched at the Sauk and Fox village in 1835. The
scene is repeated in cartoon 205 (Collection of Mr.
and Mrs. Paul Mellon).

464. Mandan attacking a party of Arikara
1832-1833
19⅝ x 27⅝ (49.7 x 70)

Catlin describes the location of the attack as "a
ravine, near the Mandan village" (1837 catalogue,
p. 43).

References: 1837 catalogue, no. 468; Donaldson,
p. 323; Ewers (1956), p. 513; Denver Art Museum,
The Western Frontier, 1966.

Catlin may have observed an Indian skirmish during his visit to the Mandan village in 1832, but the
painting is most likely a studio fabrication. The
scene is repeated in cartoon 339 (unlocated).

465. Ojibwa portaging around the Falls of St. Anthony
1835-1836
19½ x 27½ (49.7 x 70)

"The Chippeways . . . were swiftly propelled by
paddles to the Fall of St. Anthony, where we had
repaired to witness their mode of passing the
cataract, by '*making* (as it is called) *the portage,*'
which we found to be a very curious scene; and
was done by running all their canoes into an eddy
below the Fall, and as near as they could get by
paddling; when all were landed, and every thing
taken out of the canoes, and with them carried by
the women, around the Fall, and half a mile or so
above, where the canoes were put into the water
again; and goods and chattels being loaded in, and
all hands seated, the paddles were again put to
work, and the light and bounding crafts upon their
voyage" (*Letters and Notes,* vol. 2, p. 138, pl. 239).

References: 1837 catalogue, no. 469; Donaldson,
p. 323; Ewers (1956), p. 521; Paris (1963), no. 59.

Version:
Gilcrease Institute, NAI sketchbook (4776.56),
pen and ink

Sketched at the Falls of St. Anthony in 1835. The
scene is repeated in cartoon 340 (unlocated).

466. Comanche moving camp, dog fight enroute
1834-1835
19⅝ x 27⅝ (49.8 x 70)

"In speaking just above, of the mode of moving
their wigwams, and changing their encampments,
I should have . . . given to the reader, a sketch of
one of these extraordinary scenes, which I have
had the good luck to witness; where several
thousands were on the march, and furnishing one
of those laughable scenes which daily happen,
where so many dogs, and so many squaws, are
traveling in such a confused mass; with so many
conflicting interests, and so many local and individual rights to be pertinaciously claimed and
protected. Each horse drags his load, and each dog,
i.e. each dog that *will* do it (and there are many
that will *not*), also dragging his wallet on a couple
of poles; and each squaw with her load, and all together (notwithstanding their burthens) cherish-
ing their pugnacious feelings, which often bring
them into general conflict, commencing usually
amongst the dogs, and sure to result in fisticuffs of
the women; whilst the men, riding leisurely on
the right or the left, take infinite pleasure in overlooking these desperate conflicts, at which they
are sure to have a laugh, and in which, as sure
never to lend a hand" (*Letters and Notes,* vol. 2, pp.
64-65, pl. 166).
See number 482.

References: 1837 catalogue, no. 470; Donaldson,
pp. 323-24; Ewers (1956), p. 509.

Version:
Gilcrease Institute, NAI sketchbook (4776.51),
pen and ink

Copy:
M. Knoedler & Co., New York (until 1971), pencil
and watercolor, signed lower right:
Rosa B-[Bonheur]

Sketched at the Comanche village in 1834. The
scene is repeated in cartoon 194 (NGA 2011).

464

465

466

467

468

469

Plate 184, *Letters and Notes.*

467. White wolves attacking a buffalo bull
1832-1833
19⅝ x 27⅝ (49.7 x 70)

"Whilst the herd is together, the wolves never attack them, as they instantly gather for combined resistance, which they effectually make. But when the herds are travelling, it often happens that an aged or wounded one, lingers at a distance behind, and when fairly out of sight of the herd, is set upon by these voracious hunters, which often gather to the number of fifty or more, and are sure at last to torture him to death, and use him up at a meal. The buffalo, however, is a huge and furious animal, and when his retreat is cut off, makes desperate and deadly resistance, contending to the last moment for the right of life—and oftentimes deals death by wholesale, to his canine assailants, which he is tossing into the air or stamping to death under his feet" (*Letters and Notes,* vol. 1, p. 257, pl. 113).

References: 1837 catalogue, no. 471; Donaldson, p. 324; Ewers (1956), p. 517; Ewers (1965), p. 62; Denver Art Museum, *The Western Frontier,* 1966.

Copy:
M. Knoedler & Co., New York (until 1971), pencil and watercolor, signed lower right:
Rosa B-[Bonheur]

Sketched on the Upper Missouri in 1832 (see nos. 404, 407, 468). Catlin's ensuing reverie in *Letters and Notes* (pp. 258-64) would suggest that the subject of numbers 467 and 468 represented more to him than a simple contest of nature. The inevitable death of the bull symbolized the coming destruction of the buffalo herds and the primitive life of the Plains Indians. "Many are the rudenesses and wilds in Nature's works, which are destined to fall before the . . . desolating hands of cultivating man," he reflected, and then launched into the earliest known argument for a national park to preserve the Indians and buffalo in their natural habitat.

The scene may be repeated in cartoon 325 (unlocated).

468. Wounded buffalo bull surrounded by white wolves
1832–1833
19⅝ x 27⅝ (49.7 x 70)

See number 467. "We discovered at a distance," Catlin continues, "a huge bull, encircled with a gang of white wolves; we rode up as near as we could without driving them away, and being within pistol shot, we had a remarkable good view, where I sat for a few moments and made a sketch in my note-book; after which, we rode up and gave the signal for them to disperse, which they instantly did, withdrawing themselves to the distance of fifty or sixty rods, when we found, to our great surprise, that the animal had made desperate resistance, until his eyes were entirely eaten out of his head—the grizzle of his nose was mostly gone—his tongue was half eaten off, and the skin and flesh of his legs torn almost literally into strings. In this tattered and torn condition, the poor old veteran stood bracing up in the midst of his devourers, who had ceased hostilities for a few minutes, to enjoy a sort of parley, recovering strength and preparing to resume the attack in a few moments again. In this group, some were reclining, to gain breath, whilst others were sneaking about and licking their chops in anxiety for a renewal of the attack; and others, less lucky, had been crushed to death by the feet or the horns of the bull" (*Letters and Notes,* vol. 1, p. 258, pl. 114).

References: 1837 catalogue, no. 472; Donaldson, pp. 324-25; Ewers, p. 517.

Copy:
M. Knoedler & Co., New York (until 1971), pencil and watercolor, signed lower right:
Rosa B-[Bonheur]

Sketched on the Upper Missouri in 1832 (see nos. 404, 407, 467). The scene is repeated in plate 10 of *Catlin's North American Indian Portfolio,* first published in 1844; in plate 72 of the Gilcrease *Souvenir* album; and probably in cartoon 341 (unlocated).

469. Catlin and his horse Charley, encamped on the prairie at sunrise
1837-1839
Unlocated

Catlin describes the scene as typical of his journey from Fort Gibson to the Missouri River, at the conclusion of the dragoon expedition in 1834.

"My horse Charley was picketed near me at the end of his laso, which gave him room for his grazing; and thus we snored and nodded away the nights, and never were denied the doleful serenades of the gangs of sneaking wolves that were nightly perambulating our little encampment, and stationed at a safe distance from us at sun-rise in the morning—gazing at us, and impatient to pick up the crumbs and bones that were left, when we moved away from our feeble fire that had faintly flickered through the night" (*Letters and Notes,* vol. 2, p. 89, pl. 184).

References: Donaldson, pp. 325-27; B. F. Stevens & Brown, London, to the Secretary of the Smithsonian Institution, Feb. 23, 1907; Haverstock, pp. 130-31.

The scene is not included in the 1837 catalogue, but does appear in the Egyptian Hall catalogue of January 1840, indicating that it was painted in the interval (see no. 422). Plate 184 of *Letters and Notes* is illustrated in place of the original, which was offered for sale in the above letter by the Misses Shippard, descendants of the artist's family (see no. 478).

The scene is repeated in cartoon 282 (unlocated).

470. Sioux worshipping at the red boulders
Eastern Dakota (Eastern Sioux), 1837-1839
19⅝ x 27⅝ (49.7 x 70)

"A large boulder and two small ones, bearing some resemblance to a buffalo cow and two calves, painted red by the Indians, and regarded by them with superstitious reverence, near the 'Coteau des Prairies' "(1848 catalogue, p. 43).

References: Donaldson, p. 327; Ewers (1956), p. 511.

Probably sketched on Catlin's journey to the Pipestone Quarry in 1836, but the painting is not included in the 1837 catalogue (see nos. 469, 336). The scene is repeated in cartoon 342 (unlocated).

471. Comanche warrior lancing an Osage, at full speed
1837-1839
19⅝ x 27⅝ (49.7 x 70)

References: Donaldson, p. 327; Ewers (1956), p. 509.

The subject is not included in the 1837 catalogue, but does appear in the Egyptian Hall catalogue of January 1840, indicating that it was painted in the interval (see no. 422). The frantic appearance of the riders is greatly enhanced by the lively brushwork.

The scene is repeated in cartoon 303 (NGA 2029), where the horses gallop in the opposite direction.

472. Comanche giving arrows to the Medicine Rock
1837-1839
19⅝ x 27⅝ (49.7 x 70)

"A curious superstition of the Camanchees: going to war, they have no faith in their success, unless they pass a celebrated painted rock, where they appease the spirit of war (who resides there), by riding by it at full gallop, and sacrificing their best arrow by throwing it against the side of the ledge" (1848 catalogue, pp. 43-44).

References: Donaldson, pp. 327-28; Ewers (1956), p. 509.

The painting is not included in the 1837 catalogue, and the brushwork is the same as in number 471, indicating a similar date of execution. Catlin used a wide range of techniques in the late 1830s, depending on the subject and the time he wished to devote to an individual painting.

The scene is repeated in cartoon 343 (unlocated).

473. Batiste, Bogard, and I, approaching buffalo on the Missouri
1837-1839
19⅝ x 27⅝ (49.7 x 70)

"We met immense numbers of buffaloes in the early part of our voyage and used to land our canoe almost every hour in the day; and oftentimes all together approach the unsuspecting herds, through some deep and hidden ravine within a few rods of them, and at the word, 'pull trigger,' each of us bring down our victim" (*Letters and Notes,* vol. 2, p. 13, pl. 125).

References: Donaldson, p. 328; Ewers (1956), p. 516; McCracken, p. 126.

Versions:
Joslyn Art Museum, Omaha, 19 x 26½, signed lower right: Catlin 1854
H. Williams, New York, 1907, no. 5, 19 x 27 (exhibited in London, 1859)
Gilcrease Institute, NAI sketchbook (4776.69), pen and ink

Copy:
M. Knoedler & Co., New York (until 1971), pencil and watercolor, Rosa Bonheur estate

Sketched on the Upper Missouri in 1832, but the painting is not included in the 1837 catalogue. The style is similar to numbers 424 and 425.

The Joslyn version, which may have once belonged to H. Williams, has trees and two reclining buffalo on the right edge of the composition. The Smithsonian original matches plate 125 in *Letters and Notes.* The scene is repeated in plate 11 of *Catlin's North American Indian Portfolio,* first published in 1844; in plate 66 of the Gilcrease *Souvenir* album; and in cartoon 150 (NGA 2155).

470

471

472

473

475

476

474. Pigeon's Egg Head (The Light) going to and returning from Washington
1837-1839
29 x 24 (73.6 x 60.9)
[Figure 12]

"On his way home from St. Louis to this place, a distance of 2000 miles, I travelled with this gentleman, on the steamer Yellow-Stone; and saw him step ashore (on a beautiful prairie, where several thousands of his people were encamped), with a complete suit *en militaire*, a colonel's uniform of blue, presented to him by the President of the United States, with a beaver hat and feather, with epaulettes of gold—with sash and belt, and broad sword; with high-heeled boots—with a keg of whiskey under his arm, and a blue umbrella in his hand" (*Letters and Notes,* vol. 1, p. 56; vol. 2, pl. 271-72).

Catlin first painted The Light in St. Louis, when the latter was en route to Washington in the fall of 1831, as an official guest of the Secretary of War (see no. 179). The two met again next spring on the upriver voyage of the *Yellowstone,* and Catlin watched The Light debark from the steamboat at Fort Union, where he was scarcely recognized by the members of his own tribe. Astonishment and disbelief gradually turned into fear and hostility as The Light recounted his travel experiences, and in time he was killed by a young Indian who could not comprehend what was probably an accurate description of a building in Washington (see Ewers, 1968).

As far as Catlin was concerned, the episode illustrated the tragic gulf between Indian culture and white civilization, and he traced the steps of The Light's downfall through many pages of *Letters and Notes* (vol. 1, pp. 55-57; vol. 2, pp. 194-200).

References: Donaldson, pp. 328-32, pl. 86; Ewers (1956), p. 508; Kennedy catalogue, p. 19; McCracken, pp. 39, 61, 63, reprod. p. 56; Paris (1963), no. 24; Ewers (1965), reprod. p. 73; Ewers (1968), pp. 81-88, pl. 11; Rossi and Hunt, pp. 61, 320; Haverstock, p. 53, reprod. p. 52; Gilcrease catalogue, p. 52; *America as Art,* reprod. p. 168; Jean Lipman and Helen M. Franc, *Bright Stars: American Painting and Sculpture Since 1776* (New York, 1976), p. 44, reprod.

Version:
Gilcrease Institute, NAI sketchbook (4776.21), pen and ink

The subject is not included in the 1837 catalogue, but does appear in the Egyptian Hall catalogue of January 1840, indicating that it was painted in the interval (see no. 472). Catlin has finished both figures with unusual care, and The Light in uniform, whose swagger and vanity are an amusing change from a long line of stoic chiefs, is one of the artist's most successful characters.

The subject is repeated in plate 25 of *Catlin's North American Indian Portfolio,* first published in 1844; in plate 52 of the Gilcrease *Souvenir* album; and in cartoon 83 (NGA 1991).

475. Butte de Mort, Sioux burial ground, Upper Missouri
Teton Dakota (Western Sioux), 1837-1839
20⅛ x 27⅜ (50.9 x 69.4)

"Regarded by the Indians with great dread and superstition. There are several thousand buffalo and human skulls, perfectly bleached and curiously arranged about it" (1848 catalogue, p. 44).

References: Donaldson, p. 332; Ewers (1956), p. 511; McCracken, reprod. p. 145; Perry T. Rathbone, "Rediscovery," *Art in America* 49 (no. 1, 1961), reprod. p. 83; Paris (1963), no. 61.

Probably sketched in 1832, but the painting does not appear in the 1837 catalogue. The style is similar to numbers 471 and 472.

The scene is repeated in cartoon 344 (unlocated).

476. Rainmaking among the Mandan
1837-1839
19½ x 27 (49.5 x 68.6)

"Medicine-men performing their mysteries inside of the lodge, and young men volunteer to stand upon the lodge from sunrise until dawn, in turn, commanding it to rain.

"Each one has to hazard the disgrace which attaches (when he descends at sundown) to a fruitless attempt; and he who succeeds acquires a lasting reputation as a *Mystery* or *Medicine man*" (1848 catalogue, p. 44).

Catlin describes the ritual at great length in *Letters and Notes* (vol. 1, pp. 134-40, pl. 58).

References: Donaldson, pp. 332-36, pl. 87; Ewers (1956), p. 513.

Version:
Gilcrease Institute, NAI sketchbook (4776.53), pen and ink

A rough drawing of the scene, presumably made at the Mandan village in 1832, appears in the SI sketchbook, but the painting is not listed in the 1837 catalogue (see nos. 471, 472).

The scene is repeated in cartoon 186 (Collection of Mr. and Mrs. Paul Mellon) with additional figures and earth lodges.

477

477. Smoking the shield
Probably Teton Dakota (Western Sioux),
1837-1839
18¾ x 26¼ (47.5 x 66.6)

"The Sioux *shield* [is] made of the skin of the buffalo's neck, hardened with the glue extracted from the hoofs and joints of the same animal. . . . This skin is at first, twice as large as the size of the required shield; but having got his particular and best friends (who are invited on the occasion) into a ring, to dance and sing around it, and solicit the Great Spirit to instil into it the power to protect him harmless against his enemies . . . [the young man] spreads over it the glue, which is rubbed and dried in, as the skin is heated; and a second busily drives other and other pegs, inside of those in the gound, as they are gradually giving way and being pulled up by the contraction of the skin. By this curious process, which is most dexterously done, the skin is kept tight whilst it contracts to one-half of its size, taking up the glue and increasing in thickness until it is rendered as thick and hard as required" (*Letters and Notes*, vol. 1, p. 241).

References: Donaldson, pp. 336–37; Ewers (1956), p. 511; McCracken, pp. 51, 54.

The painting appears to be unfinished, and is not listed in the 1837 catalogue (see fig. 155 for an indication of previous damage, and nos. 471, 472). The scene is repeated in cartoon 188 (AMNH 145) with additional dancers and skin lodges.

478. Sioux approaching "The Thunder's Nest,"
Coteau des Prairies
Eastern Dakota (Eastern Sioux), 1837-1839
Unlocated

Near the Pipestone Quarry, in small bushes on a high mound, is the legendary "Thunder's nest" of the Sioux, Catlin relates, where "a very small bird sits upon her eggs during fair weather, and the skies are rent with bolts of thunder at the approach of a storm, which is occasioned by the hatching of her brood!" (*Letters and Notes*, vol. 2, p. 164). See number 336.

References: Donaldson, p. 337; B. F. Stevens & Brown, London, to the Secretary of the Smithsonian Institution, Feb. 23, 1907; McCracken, pp. 175-76.

The painting is not listed in the 1837 catalogue, but does appear in the Egyptian Hall catalogue of January 1840, indicating that it was executed in the interval. In the above letter, the "original painting" is offered for sale by the Misses Shippard, descendants of the artist's family (see no. 469).

479. Sauk and Fox sailing in canoes
1837-1839
19½ x 27½ (49.6 x 70.1)

"I was often amused at their freaks in their canoes, whilst travelling; and I was induced to make a sketch of one which I frequently witnessed, that of sailing with the aid of their blankets, which the men carry; and when the wind is fair, stand in the bow of the canoe and hold by two corners, with the other two under the foot or tied to the leg; while the women sit in the other end of the canoe, and steer it with their paddles" (*Letters and Notes*, vol. 2, p. 214, pl. 294).

References: Donaldson, p. 337, pl. 88; Ewers (1956), p. 522.

Version:
Gilcrease Institute, NAI sketchbook (4776.58), pen and ink

Sketched in 1835 near the Sauk and Fox village, but the painting is not included in the 1837 catalogue (see nos. 471, 472). The abbreviated technique is similar to number 477.
The scene is repeated in cartoon 199 (Collection of Mr. and Mrs. Paul Mellon).

480. Grand tournament of the Comanche
1837-1839
Unlocated

Described by Catlin as a "Sham Fight in a large encampment, on the borders of Texas" (1848 catalogue, p. 44).

References: Donaldson, p. 337; Gilcrease catalogue, p. 57.

Versions:
Royal Ontario Museum, 18⅞ x 26¼, signed lower right: Catlin.
Gilcrease Institute, 11 x 14
H. Williams, New York, 1907, no. 1, 19 x 27 (exhibited in London, 1859)

Sketched at the Comanche village in 1834, but the painting is not listed in the 1837 catalogue (see no. 471). With the exception of a few galloping riders, the Gilcrease and Ontario versions are almost the same. The latter, which probably once belonged to H. Williams, is illustrated in place of the original.
The scene is repeated in cartoon 138 (NGA 2008).

479

480

Royal Ontario Museum, Toronto.

481

482

485

481. Bogard, Batiste, and I, traveling through a Missouri bottom
1837-1839
19⅝ x 27⅝ (49.7 x 70)

See number 374.

References: Donaldson, p. 337; Ewers (1956), p. 518.

Probably sketched on the Upper Missouri in 1832, but the painting is not included in the 1837 catalogue (see nos. 471, 472, 486). The scene is repeated in cartoon 346 (unlocated).

482. Band of Sioux moving camp
Teton Dakota (Western Sioux), 1837-1839
19½ x 27½ (49.4 x 69.8)

"For this strange cavalcade, preparation is made in the following manner: the poles of a lodge are divided into two bunches, and the little ends of each bunch fastened upon the shoulder or withers of a horse, leaving the butt ends to drag behind on the ground on either side. Just behind the horse, a brace or pole is tied across, which keeps the poles in their respective places; and then upon that and the poles behind the horse, is placed the lodge or tent, which is rolled up, and also numerous other articles of household and domestic furniture, and on the top of all, two, three, and even (sometimes) four women and children! Each one of these horses has a conductress, who sometimes walks before and leads it, with a tremendous pack upon her own back; and at others she sits astride of its back, with a child, perhaps, at her breast, and another astride of the horse's back behind her, clinging to her waist with one arm, while it affectionately embraces a sneaking dog-pup in the other.

"In this way five or six hundred wigwams, with all their furniture, may be seen drawn out for miles, creeping over the grass-covered plains of this country; and three times that number of men, on good horses, strolling along in front or on the flank . . . and every cur . . . who is large enough, and not too cunning to be enslaved, is encumbered with a car or sled . . . on which he patiently drags his load (*Letters and Notes,* vol. 1, pp. 44-45, pl. 21).

See number 466.

References: Donaldson, p. 337; Ewers (1956), p. 511; McCracken, pp. 78-79, reprod. p. 78; Ewers (1965), p. 75; Halpin, reprod. p. 6.

Version:
Gilcrease Institute, NAI sketchbook (4776.50), pen and ink

Copy:
M. Knoedler & Co., New York (until 1971), pencil and watercolor, signed lower right:
Rosa B-[Bonheur]

Drawings of a horse and dog dragging poles supporting baggage are in the SI sketchbook (1832), but the painting is not included in the 1837 catalogue (see nos. 471, 472). The cursory technique is similar to other examples from the late 1830s (see nos. 477, 479, 485).

Cartoon 193 (AMNH 97) is a later edition of this scene, and cartoon 307 (NGA 1971) is a related view.

483. Bogard, Batiste, and I, descending the Missouri River
1837-1839
Unlocated

Reference: Donaldson, p. 337.

Probably sketched in 1832, but the painting is not included in the 1837 catalogue (see nos. 471, 472, 484).

484. Bogard, Batiste, and I, eating breakfast on a pile of driftwood, Upper Missouri
1837-1839
Unlocated

Reference: Donaldson, p. 337.

Probably sketched in 1832, but the painting is not included in the 1837 catalogue (see nos. 471, 472). The scene is repeated in cartoon 348 (unlocated), which is described in the 1871 catalogue (p. 58) as Catlin and his two companions "descending the Missouri river in a canoe, and breakfasting on a pile of drift wood" (see no. 483).

485. Medicine buffalo of the Sioux
Teton Dakota (Western Sioux), 1837-1839
19⅝ x 27⅝ (49.7 x 70)

Described by Catlin as "the figure of a buffalo cut out of the turf on the prairie, and visited by the Indians going on a buffalo-hunt" (1848 catalogue, p. 45).

References: Donaldson, p. 337; Ewers (1956), p. 511; Amon Carter Museum of Western Art, Fort Worth, *The Bison in Art* (1977), reprod. p. 97.

Probably sketched on the Upper Missouri in 1832, but the painting is not included in the 1837 catalogue (see nos. 471, 472).

486. Bogard, Batiste, and I, chasing buffalo in high grass on a Missouri bottom
1837-1839
19⅝ x 27⅝ (49.7 x 70)

References: Donaldson, p. 337; Ewers (1956), p. 516; Paris (1963), no. 62.

Probably sketched on the Upper Missouri in 1832, but the painting is not included in the 1837 catalogue (see nos. 471, 472). The subject and style are similar to number 481.

487. Comanche feats of horsemanship
1834-1835
24 x 29 (60.9 x 73.7)

"Amongst their feats of riding, there is one that has astonished me more than anything of the kind I have ever seen, or expect to see, in my life:—a stratagem of war, learned and practiced by every young man in the tribe; by which he is able to drop his body upon the side of his horse at the instant he is passing, effectually screened from his enemies' weapons as he lays in a horizontal position behind the body of his horse, with his heel hanging over the horses' back; by which he has the power of throwing himself up again, and changing to the other side of the horse if necessary. In this wonderful condition, he will hang whilst his horse is at fullest speed, carrying with him his bow and his shield, and also his long lance of fourteen feet in length, all or either of which he will wield upon his enemy as he passes; rising and throwing his arrows over the horse's back, or with equal ease and equal success under the horse's neck" (*Letters and Notes*, vol. 2, pp. 65-66, pl. 167).

References: 1837 catalogue, no. 474; Donaldson, pp. 338-39, pl. 89; Ewers (1956), p. 509; McCracken, pp. 149-50, reprod. p. 151; Ewers (1965), reprod. p. 94; Halpin, reprod. p. 20; Rossi and Hunt, pp. 54, 320.

Version:
Gilcrease Institute, NAI sketchbook (4776.61), pen and ink

Copy:
M. Knoedler & Co., New York (until 1971), pencil and watercolor, signed lower right:
Rosa B-[Bonheur]

Sketched on the dragoon expedition in 1834. Catlin never completely mastered the anatomy or movement of the horse, although his shortcomings were less noticeable when the animals were further removed from the foreground of the composition (see no. 411).

The scene is repeated in cartoon 196 (NGA 2009).

488. Comanche meeting the dragoons
1834-1835
24 x 29 (60.9 x 73.7)

"Col. Dodge ordered the command to halt, while he rode forward with a few of his staff, and an ensign carrying a white flag. I joined this advance, and the Indians stood their ground until we had come within half a mile of them, and could distinctly observe all their numbers and movements. We then came to a halt, and the white flag was sent a little in advance, and waved as a signal for them to approach; at which one of their party galloped out in advance of the war-party, on a milk white horse, carrying a piece of white buffalo skin on the point of his long lance in reply to our flag.

"This moment was the commencement of one of the most thrilling and beautiful scenes I ever witnessed. All eyes, both from his own party and ours, were fixed upon the manoeuvres of this gallant little fellow, and he well knew it.

"The distance between the two parties was perhaps half a mile, and that a beautiful and gently sloping prairie; over which he was for the space of a quarter of an hour, reining and spurring his maddened horse, and gradually approaching us by tacking to the right and the left, like a vessel beating against the wind. He at length came prancing and leaping along till he met the flag of the regiment, when he leaned his spear for a moment against it, looking the bearer full in the face, when he wheeled his horse, and dashed up to Col. Dodge with his extended hand, which was instantly grasped and shaken. We all had him by the hand in a moment, and the rest of the party seeing him received in this friendly manner, instead of being sacrificed, as they undoubtedly expected, started under 'full whip' in a direct line toward us" (*Letters and Notes*, vol. 2, pp. 55-56, pl. 157).

See numbers 51 and 353.

References: 1837 catalogue, no. 475; Donaldson, pp. 339-40; Ewers (1956), p. 509; McCracken, pp. 147-48, reprod. p. 181; *Catlin, Bodmer, Miller*; Ewers (1965), reprod. p. 93; Halpin, reprod. p. 18.

Version:
Gilcrease Institute, NAI sketchbook (4776.59), pen and ink

Copy:
M. Knoedler & Co., New York (until 1971), pencil and watercolor, signed lower right:
Rosa B-[Bonheur]

Sketched on the dragoon expedition in 1834 (see no. 487). Catlin often communicated the visual impact of such events more effectively in his written descriptions than in his paintings.

The scene is repeated in cartoon 190 (unlocated).

486

487

488

490

Cartoon 234, National Gallery of Art, Washington, D.C. Paul Mellon Collection.

491

492

493

489. An Assiniboin wedding, young man making presents to the father of the girl
1832-1837
Unlocated

References: 1837 catalogue, no. 476; Donaldson, p. 340.

Probably sketched on the Upper Missouri in 1832. The scene is repeated in cartoon 347 (unlocated).

490. A Crow at his toilet, oiling his long hair with bear's grease
1832-1837
Unlocated

References: 1837 catalogue, no. 477; Donaldson, p. 340.

Probably sketched on the Upper Missouri in 1832. The scene is repeated in cartoon 234 (NGA 1980), which is illustrated in place of the original.

491. Crow lodge of twenty-five buffalo skins
1832-1833
24 x 29 (60.9 x 73.7)

"The Crows, of all the tribes in this region . . . make the most beautiful lodge . . . they oftentimes dress the skins of which they are composed almost as white as linen, and beautifully garnish them with porcupine quills, and paint and ornament them in such a variety of ways, as renders them exceedingly picturesque and agreeable to the eye. I have procured a very beautiful one of this description, highly-ornamented, and fringed with scalp-locks, and sufficiently large for forty men to dine under. The poles which support it are about thirty in number, of pine, and all cut in the Rocky Mountains, having been some hundred years, perhaps, in use. This tent, when erected, is about twenty-five feet high, and has a very pleasing effect" (*Letters and Notes,* vol. 1, pp. 43-44, pl. 20).

References: 1837 catalogue, no. 478; Donaldson, p. 340, pl. 90; Ewers (1956), p. 510; McCracken, p. 78, reprod. p. 76; Halpin, reprod. p. 5; Rossi and Hunt, pp. 63, 320; Gilcrease catalogue, p. 57.

Versions:
Gilcrease Institute, 11 x 14
Gilcrease Institute, NAI sketchbook (4776.54), pen and ink

Copy:
M. Knoedler & Co., New York (until 1971), pencil and watercolor, signed lower right:
Rosa B-[Bonheur]

Sketched, or perhaps painted, at Fort Union in 1832. No figures appear in the Gilcrease version, and the designs on the lodge are different. The Smithsonian original matches plate 20 in *Letters and Notes,* and the scene is repeated in cartoon 349 (unlocated).

492. Wichita lodge, thatched with prairie grass
1834-1835
24 x 29 (60.9 x 73.7)

See number 343.

References: 1837 catalogue, no. 479; Donaldson, p. 340; Ewers (1956), p. 515; Gilcrease catalogue, p. 57.

Version:
Gilcrease Institute, 11 x 14

Painted in Catlin's studio from a sketch made by Joe Chadwick (see no. 343). The figures are arranged differently in the Gilcrease version.
The scene is repeated in cartoon 350 (unlocated).

493. Comanche lodge of buffalo skins
1834-1835
24 x 29 (60.9 x 73.7)

See number 346.

References: 1837 catalogue, no. 480; Donaldson, p. 340; Ewers (1956), p. 509.

Sketched at the Comanche village in 1834.

494. Sioux Dog Feast
Teton Dakota (Western Sioux), 1832-1837
24 x 29 (60.9 x 73.7)
[Figure 14]

"Some few days after the steamer had arrived, it was announced that a grand feast was to be given to the *great white chiefs*, who were visitors amongst them; and preparations were made accordingly for it. The two chiefs . . . brought their . . . tents together, forming the two into a semi-circle, enclosing a space sufficiently large to accommodate 150 men; and sat down with that number of the principal chiefs and warriors of the Sioux nation; with Mr. Chouteau, Major Sanford, the Indian agent, Mr. M'Kenzie, and myself, whom they had invited in due time, and placed on elevated seats in the centre of the crescent; while the rest of the company all sat upon the ground, and mostly cross-legged, preparatory to the feast being dealt out.

"In the centre of the semi-circle was erected a flag-staff, on which was waving a white flag, and to which also was tied the calumet, both expressive of their friendly feelings towards us. Near the foot of the flag-staff were placed in a row on the ground, six or eight kettles, with iron covers on them, shutting them tight, in which were prepared the viands for our *voluptuous* feast. Near the kettles, and on the ground also, bottomside upwards, were a number of wooden bowls, in which the meat was to be served out. And in front, two or three men, who were there placed as waiters, to light the pipes for smoking, and also to deal out the food" (*Letters and Notes*, vol. 1, pp. 228-31, pl. 96).

Catlin continues with a lengthy account of the ritual—speeches, presents and feasting—and concludes that it is a "religious ceremony, wherein the poor Indian sees fit to sacrifice his faithful companion to bear testimony to the sacredness of his vows of friendship."

References: 1837 catalogue, no. 481; Donaldson, pp. 341-43; Ewers (1956), p. 511; *Catlin, Bodmer, Miller*; Paris (1963), no. 63; Nicholas B. Wainwright, "Joseph Harrison, Jr., a Forgotten Art Collector," *Antiques* 102 (October 1972), reprod. p. 664.

Version:
Gilcrease Institute, NAI sketchbook (4776.46), pen and ink

Probably sketched at Fort Pierre in 1832, but the clarity of space and figure relationships, and the flexible brushwork, indicate a later date for the painting. Catlin notes in the SI sketchbook that the feast took place May 7.
The subject is repeated in cartoon 189 (NGA 1966).

495. Sioux Indian council, chiefs in profound deliberation
Teton Dakota (Western Sioux), 1832-1837
19½ x 27½ (49.4 x 70)

References: 1837 catalogue, no. 482; Donaldson, p. 343; Ewers (1956), p. 511; *America as Art*, no. 184, reprod. p. 166.

Catlin may have observed a similar scene on the Upper Missouri in 1832, but the painting is most likely a studio fabrication. The same softly brushed foliage appears in the landscapes dated between 1835 and 1837.

496. Comanche war party, mounted on wild horses
1834-1837
19⅝ x 27⅝ (49.7 x 70)

References: 1837 catalogue, no. 483; Donaldson, p. 343; Ewers (1956), p. 510; Paris (1963), no. 64.

Probably painted in Catlin's studio between 1835 and 1837. The sketchy figures are unlike other examples from the dragoon expedition, and the foliage is similar to number 495.
The scene is repeated in cartoon 286 (NGA 2012), with the riders in a somewhat different formation.

497. Sioux scalping an enemy
Teton Dakota (Western Sioux), 1832-1837
Unlocated

Described by Catlin as "showing the mode of taking the scalp" (1848 catalogue, p. 45).

References: 1837 catalogue, no. 485; *Letters and Notes*, vol. 1, p. 240, pl. 101; Donaldson, p. 344; McCracken, p. 108; Gilcrease catalogue, p. 57.

Versions:
Gilcrease Institute, 11 x 14
Gilcrease Institute, NAI sketchbook (4776.81), pen and ink

Copy:
British Museum, London, by John Cullum, watercolor, 20½ x 25½ (1842-1844)

Painted in Catlin's studio, perhaps at the same time as number 498. The scalping scene from the bottom of plate 101 in *Letters and Notes* (see illustration) is repeated in the Cullum copy, thus indicating the appearance of the original. In the Gilcrease version, the scalper plants his foot upon the chest of the prostrate victim, while riders circle in the background.
Cartoon 351 (unlocated) is probably a later edition of the original scene.

Plate 101, *Letters and Notes*.

498

499

500

Gilcrease Institute, Tulsa.

Copy:
M. Knoedler & Co., New York (until 1971), pencil and watercolor, signed lower right:
Rosa B-[Bonheur]

Sketched on the dragoon expedition in 1834, but probably painted in Catlin's studio between 1835 and 1837. Bold contours over a thinly brushed background, and the repetitive positioning of the horses reminds one of the style of the dance groups (see nos. 437, 500, 501).

The scene is repeated in plate 3 of *Catlin's North American Indian Portfolio,* first published in 1844; in plate 56 of the Gilcrease *Souvenir* album; and in cartoon 142 (Collection of Mr. and Mrs. Paul Mellon).

498. Mandan scalping an enemy
1835-1837
19⅝ x 27⅝ (49.6 x 70)

Described by Catlin as the "Conqueror conquered. From a story of the Mandans—took place in front of the Mandan village" (1848 catalogue, p. 45).

References: 1837 catalogue, no. 486; Donaldson, p. 344; Ewers (1956), p. 513.

Painted in Catlin's studio between 1835 and 1857. The style of the figures is similar to those in the dance groups (see no. 437).

499. Wild horses at play
1834-1837
19½ x 27⅝ (49.7 x 70)

"There is no other animal on the prairies so wild and so sagacious as the horse. . . . I made many attempts to approach them by stealth, when they were grazing and playing their gambols, without ever having been more than once able to succeed. In this instance, I left my horse, and with my friend Chadwick, skulked through a ravine for a couple of miles; until we were at length brought within gun-shot of a fine herd of them, when I used my pencil for some time, while we were under cover of a little hedge of bushes which effectually screened us from their view. In this herd we saw all the colours, nearly, that can be seen in a kennel of English hounds. Some were milk white, some jet black—others were sorrel, and bay, and cream colour—many were of an iron grey; and others were pied, containing a variety of colours on the same animal. Their manes were very profuse, and hanging in the wildest confusion over their necks and faces—and their long tails swept the ground" (*Letters and Notes,* vol. 2, p. 57, pl. 160).

References: 1837 catalogue, no. 488; Donaldson, p. 344; Ewers (1956), p. 517; Paris (1963), no. 50; *America as Art,* no. 185, reprod. p. 166.

500. Lassoing a wild horse
Comanche, 1834-1837
Unlocated

"The usual mode of taking the wild horses, is, by throwing the *laso,* whilst pursuing them at full speed, and dropping a noose over their necks, by which their speed is soon checked, and they are 'choked down.' The laso is a thong of rawhide, some ten or fifteen yards in length, twisted or braided, with a noose fixed at the end of it; which, when the coil of the laso is thrown out, drops with great certainty over the neck of the animal, which is soon conquered" (*Letters and Notes,* vol. 2, p. 58, pl. 161).

References: 1837 catalogue, no. 489; Donaldson, p. 344; McCracken, pp. 148-49; Gilcrease catalogue, p. 56.

Versions:
Gilcrease Institute, 11 x 14
H. Williams, New York, 1907, no. 20, 19 x 27 (exhibited in London, 1859)
Gilcrease Institute, NAI sketchbook (4776.59), pen and ink

Copy:
M. Knoedler & Co., New York (until 1971), pencil and watercolor, signed lower right:
Rosa B-[Bonheur]

Sketched on the dragoon expedition in 1834 (see no. 499). The Gilcrease version, which matches plate 161 in *Letters and Notes,* is illustrated in place of the original.

501. Breaking down the wild horse
Comanche, 1834-1837
19⅝ x 27⅝ (49.7 x 70)

See number 500. When the lasso falls over the neck of a wild horse, Catlin continues, the Indian "instantly dismounts, leaving his own horse, and runs as fast as he can, letting the laso pass out gradually and carefully through his hands, until the horse falls for want of breath, and lies helpless on the ground; at which time the Indian advances slowly towards the horse's head, keeping his laso tight upon its neck, until he fastens a pair of hobbles on the animal's two forefeet, and also loosens the laso (giving the horse chance to breathe), and gives it a noose around the under jaw, by which he gets great power over the affrighted animal, which is rearing and plunging when it gets breath; and by which, as he advances, hand over hand, towards the horse's nose, he is able to hold it down and prevent it from throwing itself over on its back, at the hazard of its limbs. By this means he gradually advances, until he is able to place his hand on the animal's nose, and over its eyes; and at length to breathe in its nostrils, when it soon becomes docile and conquered; so that he has little else to do than to remove the hobbles from its feet, and lead or ride it into camp" (*Letters and Notes,* vol. 2, p. 58, pl. 162).

References: 1837 catalogue, no. 490; Donaldson, p. 344; Ewers (1956), p. 510; McCracken, p. 149; Paris (1963), no. 65; Rossi and Hunt, pp. 62-63, 320; Gilcrease catalogue, p. 57.

Versions:
University Museum, Philadelphia (until 1971); Graham Gallery, New York (1973), 25¾ x 32
Royal Ontario Museum, 18¾ x 26¼, signed lower right: Catlin.
Gilcrease Institute, 12 x 16
H. Williams, New York, 1907, no. 16, 19 x 27 (exhibited in London, 1859)
Gilcrease Institute, NAI sketchbook (4776.59), pen and ink

Copy:
M. Knoedler & Co., New York (until 1971), pencil and watercolor, signed lower right:
Rosa B-[Bonheur]

Sketched on the dragoon expedition in 1834, but the original was probably painted in Catlin's studio between 1835 and 1837 (see no. 499). The mountain range in the background of the University Museum version (illustration 501a) is one of Catlin's finest landscape passages, and the size and finish of the painting are much like those intended for Louis Philippe (see nos. 449, 504). The other two versions and the cartoon also have mountains in the background, and more horses and riders chasing across the prairie than in the Smithsonian original. The latter is the least detailed of all, but matches plate 162 in *Letters and Notes.* The Ontario version probably once belonged to H. Williams (see nos. 411, 413).

The scene is repeated in plate 4 of *Catlin's North American Indian Portfolio,* first published in 1844; in plate 58 of the Gilcrease *Souvenir* album; and in cartoon 143 (NGA 2024).

502. Bird's-eye view of the Mandan village, 1800 miles above St. Louis
1837-1839
24⅛ x 29 (61.2 x 73.6)
[Figure 17]

"I have this morning, perched myself upon the top of one of the earth-covered lodges . . . and having the whole village beneath and about me, with its sachems—its warriors—its dogs—and its horses in motion—its medicines (or mysteries) and scalp-poles waving over my head—its piquets—its green fields and prairies, and river in full view, with the din and bustle of the thrilling panorama that is about me. I shall be able, I hope, to give some sketches more to the life than I could have done from any effort of recollection. . . .

"The groups of lodges around me present a very curious and pleasing appearance, resembling in shape (more nearly than anything else I can compare them to) so many potash-kettles inverted. On the tops of these are to be seen groups standing and reclining, whose wild and picturesque appearance it would be difficult to describe. Stern warriors, like statues, standing in dignified groups, wrapped in their painted robes, with their heads decked and plumed with quills of the war-eagle. . . . In another direction, the wooing lover. . . . On other lodges, and beyond these, groups are engaged in games of the 'moccasin,' or the 'platter.' Some are to be seen manufacturing robes and dresses, and others, fatigued with amusements or occupations, have stretched their limbs to enjoy the luxury of sleep, whilst basking in the sun."

Catlin continues the description of the village over several pages of *Letters and Notes* (vol. 1, pp. 87–89, pl. 47), noting, in addition, the drumlike shrine in the center of the open area, the medicine lodge, the paraphernalia and trophies of Indian life, and the scaffolds of the Mandan cemetery in the distance.

References: Donaldson, pp. 349-50, pls. 7, 91; Ewers (1956), pp. 499, 513, pl. 12; McCracken, pp. 85-86, reprod. p. 82; Halpin, reprod., p. 17; Ewers (1965), reprod. pp. 84-85; Daniel M. Mendelowitz, *A History of American Art* (New York, 1970), reprod. p. 215; J. F. McDermott, ed., *Travelers on the Western Frontier* (Urbana, Ill., 1970), reprod. p. 56; Haverstock, reprod. pp. 78-79.

Version:
Gilcrease Institute, NAI sketchbook (4776.54), pen and ink

501

501a.

Formerly University Museum, Philadelphia.

Copy:
M. Knoedler & Co., New York (until 1971), pencil, Rosa Bonheur estate

The subject is not included in the 1837 catalogue, but does appear in the Egyptian Hall catalogue of January 1840, indicating that it was painted in the interval (see no. 472). Audubon thought Catlin had represented the earth lodges as too regular in size and shape (see Ewers, 1956); otherwise, the scene appears to be a unique and vivid account of Mandan village life. The painting is unusually detailed for the late 1830s, and apparently unrelated to a brief drawing of Mandan lodges in the SI sketchbook (see Donaldson, pl. 7). The scene is repeated in cartoon 129 (unlocated).

503

503. Interior of a Mandan lodge
1832-1833
23¼ x 28 (59 x 71.1)
Mrs. J. Roy Osborne, Augusta, Georgia;
Kennedy Galleries, New York, 1975

"Their lodges are closely grouped together . . . and appear from without, to be built entirely of dirt; but one is surprised when he enters them, to see the neatness, comfort, and spacious dimensions of these earth-covered dwellings. They all have a circular form, and are from forty to sixty feet in diameter. Their foundations are prepared by digging some two feet in the ground, and forming the floor of earth, by levelling the requisite size for the lodge. . . . The superstructure is then produced, by arranging, inside of this circular excavation, firmly fixed in the ground and resting against the bank, a barrier or wall of timbers, some eight or nine inches in diameter, of equal height (about six feet) placed on end, and resting against each other, supported by a formidable embankment of earth raised against them outside; then, resting upon the tops of these timbers or piles, are others of equal size and equal in numbers, of twenty or twenty-five feet in length, resting firmly against each other, and sending their upper or smaller ends towards the centre and top of the lodge; rising at an angle of forty-five degrees to the apex or sky-light, which is about three or four feet in diameter, answering as a chimney and sky-light at the same time. . . .

"In the centre, and immediately under the sky-light is the fire-place—a hole of four or five feet in diameter, of a circular form, sunk a foot or more below the surface, and curbed around with stone. Over the fire-place, and suspended from the apex of diverging props or poles, is generally seen the pot or kettle, filled with buffalo meat; and around it are the family, reclining in all the most picturesque attitudes and groups, resting on their buffalo-robes and beautiful mats of rushes. . . . They all sleep on bedsteads similar in form to ours, but generally not quite so high; made of round poles rudely lashed together with thongs" (*Letters and Notes*, vol. 1, pp. 80-83, pl. 46).

See number 502. The ceiling timbers were covered with an impervious clay.

References: 1837 catalogue, no. 473; Quimby, pp. 52-53; McCracken, pp. 84-85, 86; *Kennedy Quarterly* 14 (June 1975): 123-24, reprod. p. 99.

Versions:
Field Museum of Natural History, ca. 23 x 28
Gilcrease Institute, NAI sketchbook (4776.47), pen and ink

Copy:
M. Knoedler & Co., New York (until 1971), pencil and watercolor, Rosa Bonheur estate

Sketched at the Mandan village in 1832. Mrs. Osborne's painting, which may have come from Eng-

land, would seem to be the original. The style is similar to numbers 504 and 506, and the details match plate 46 in *Letters and Notes*. For some unknown reason, Catlin has placed the aged Hidatsa chief, Black Moccasin, on the left side of the fire smoking his long pipe (see no. 171).

The Field Museum version (fig. 143) lacks the consistent detail and finish of the original (see no 3). The doorway opening off the right side of the lodge in the former is not included in cartoon 132 (AMNH 183), a later edition of the scene. The lodge interior is repeated, with some modifications, in numbers 504 and 506, and in cartoon 133 (NGA 2038). Karl Bodmer painted a similar scene at the Mandan village (see Reuben Gold Thwaites, ed., *Early Western Travels 1748-1846*, pl. 52).

504. Interior view of the medicine lodge, Mandan O-kee-pa ceremony
1832
23 x 27¾ (58.4 x 70.5)
University Museum, Philadelphia (until 1971); Anschutz Collection

" 'Now we have it!' (exclaimed my host . . .) the grand ceremony has commenced. . . . I seized my sketch-book, and all hands of us were in an instant in front of the medicine-lodge, ready to see and hear all that was to take place. . . . There were on this occasion about fifty young men who entered the lists, and as they went into the sacred lodge, each one's body was chiefly naked, and covered with clay of different colours; some were red, others were yellow, and some were covered with white clay, giving them the appearance of white men. Each one of them carried in his right hand his *medicine-bag*—on his left arm, his shield of the bull's hide—in his left hand, his bow and arrows, with his quiver slung on his back.

"When all had entered the lodge, they placed themselves in reclining postures around its sides, and each one had suspended over his head his respective weapons and *medicine*, presenting altogether, one of the most wild and picturesque scenes imaginable . . . the medicine or mystery-man . . . was left sole conductor and keeper; and according to those injunctions, it was his duty to lie by a small fire in the centre of the lodge, with his medicine-pipe in his hand, crying to the Great Spirit incessantly, watching the young men, and preventing entirely their escape from the lodge, and all communication whatever with people outside, for the space of four days and nights, during which time they were not allowed to *eat*, to *drink*, or to *sleep*, preparatory to the excruciating self-tortures which they were to endure on the fourth day.

"I mentioned that I had made four paintings of these strange scenes, and the first one exhibits the interior of the medicine-lodge at this moment; with the young men all reclining around its sides, and the conductor or mystery-man lying by the fire, crying to the Great Spirit. It was just at this juncture that I was ushered into this sacred temple of their worship, with my companions, which was undoubtedly, the first time that their devotions had ever been trespassed upon by the presence of pale faces . . . we returned every morning at sunrise, and remained until sun-down for four days, the whole time which these strange scenes occupied.

"In addition to the preparations and arrangements of the interior of this sanctuary, as above described, there was a curious, though a very strict arrangement of buffalo and human skulls placed on the floor of the lodge, and between them (which were divided into two parcels), and in front of the reclining group of young candidates, was a small and very delicate scaffold. . . .

"Immediately under the little frame or scaffold . . . on the floor of the lodge was placed a knife, and by the side of it a bundle of splints or skewers, which were kept in readiness for the infliction of the cruelties directly to be explained. There were seen also, in this stage of the affair, a number of cords of rawhide hanging down from the top of the lodge, and passing through its roof, with which the young men were to be suspended by the splints passed through their flesh, and drawn up by men placed on the top of the lodge for the purpose" (*Letters and Notes*, vol. 1, pp. 158-64, pl. 66).

Catlin was not the first white man to witness this major religious ceremony of the Mandan, but he was the first to make a pictorial record of the strange and primitive scenes that comprised the annual event. Fortunately, it began about a week after his arrival at the Mandan village, and through his own "medicine" power as a portrait painter, he gained admission to the sacred lodge. The O-kee-pa ceremony was both a gruesome test of manhood and a fertility rite that was almost unknown to the public before Catlin's letter of August 5 to the *New-York Commercial Advertiser* and the subsequent long chapter in *Letters and Notes*, published some nine years later. His voluminous notes on the Mandan and these four scenes from the O-kee-pa ceremony have proven to be his most valuable ethnological contribution, although during his lifetime several prominent scholars challenged their accuracy (see Ewers [1967], who discusses the history of the ceremony and all aspects of the controversy). This led to the publication in 1867 of an illustrated book (*O-Kee-Pa, a Religious Ceremony and Other Customs of the Mandans*), in which Catlin described the self-torture and dance scenes in even greater detail, and included an appendix with testimonials from others who had witnessed the event. Unhappily, however, the book was not widely distributed, and Catlin became convinced that the doubt cast upon his scholarship finally prevented the sale of his collection to the government.

References: 1837 catalogue, no. 491; Donaldson, pp. 350-58, pl. 92; Matthews, pp. 605-6, pl. 147; Haberly, pp. 72-76; Ewers (1956), pp. 499, 513; McCracken, pp. 101-2; Paris (1963), no. 67, pl. 8; Roehm, pp. 64, 123, 344-45; Catlin, *O-Kee-Pa, a Religious Ceremony and Other Customs of the Mandans*, London, 1867 (reprinted with an introduction by Ewers, Yale University Press, New Haven, Conn., 1967); *American Heritage* (October 1967): 31-37, 69-75; Haverstock, reprod. pp. 88-89; Anschutz Collection, *American Masters in the West* (1976), reprod. p. 6.

Versions:
Smithsonian Institution, 24 x 29
Gilcrease Institute, NAI sketchbook (4776.53), pen and ink

Copy:
M. Knoedler & Co., New York (until 1971), pencil and watercolor, signed lower right:
Rosa B-[Bonheur]

Two sets of paintings of the ceremony are presently known, one of which was executed at the Mandan village in 1832, according to Catlin's account in *Letters and Notes* (vol 1, p. 155):

"I took my sketch-book with me, and have made many and faithful drawings of what we saw, and full notes of everything as translated to me by the interpreter; and since the close of that horrid and frightful scene, which was a week ago or more, I have been closely ensconced in an earth-covered wigwam, with a fine sky-light over my head, with my palette and brushes, endeavouring faithfully to put the whole of what we saw upon canvass, which my companions all agree to be critically correct, and of the fidelity of which they have attached their certificates to the backs of the paintings. I have made four paintings of these strange scenes, containing several hundred figures, representing the transactions of each day; and if I live to get them home, they will be found to be exceedingly curious and interesting."

Catlin did get these four paintings home (if we can trust the above passage) and then to London, where they were claimed by Joseph Harrison, along with the rest of the original collection, in 1852. After Harrison's death, however, the four paintings and several other Catlin duplicates (see nos. 1, 2, 501, 562) were separated from the Smithsonian gift, and sold to John Wanamaker in Philadelphia, who eventually gave them to the University Museum, where they remained until 1971. This set appears to have been painted under the conditions Catlin describes in *Letters and Notes*. The figures in the dance scenes (nos. 505, 507) are either unfinished or roughly sketched, and those in the medicine lodge (nos. 504, 506) are only slightly more composed. The same abrupt and incomplete treatment has been given the architectural details in the four scenes. Nevertheless, as

504

504a.

the first set of paintings taken from the sketchbooks, they are a more authentic representation of the ceremony than the O-kee-pa series belonging to the Smithsonian. Number 506 is missing from this latter series, but the others are carefully finished and dramatically staged versions which Catlin probably painted in the late 1830s.

None of the group is of great interest esthetically, and the medicine lodge scene perhaps least of all. The simple arrangement of figures in the original has become an unbroken semicircle of contrived poses in the Smithsonian version (illustration 504a). The two front posts supporting the ceiling timbers have disappeared, and the rear posts have been conveniently tucked behind the figures, who bask in a ghoulish light cast from the opening above.

The Smithsonian version is repeated in plate 66 of *Letters and Notes*. Cartoon 417 (NGA 2045) is a mixture of both paintings, and the basis for plate 3 in the original edition of *O-Kee-Pa*.

505

505. Bull Dance, Mandan O-kee-pa ceremony
1832
23¼ x 28 (59 x 71.1)
University Museum, Philadelphia (until 1971); Anschutz Collection

See number 504. "During the three first days of this solemn conclave," Catlin continues, "there were many very curious forms and amusements enacted in the open area in the middle of the village, and in front of the medicine-lodge, by other members of the community, one of which formed a material part or link of these strange ceremonials. This very curious and exceedingly grotesque part of their performance, which they denominated . . . the bull-dance, of which I have before spoken, as one of the avowed objects for which they held this annual féte; and to the strictest observance of which they attribute the coming of buffaloes to supply them with food during the season—is repeated four times during the first day, eight times on the second day, twelve times on the third day, and sixteen times on the fourth day; and always around the curb, or 'big canoe' [the drum-like shrine in the center of the open area].

"This subject I have selected for my second picture, and the principal actors in it were eight men, with the entire skins of buffaloes thrown over their backs, with the horns and hoofs and tails remaining on; their bodies in a horizontal position, enabling them to imitate the actions of the buffalo, whilst they were looking out of its eyes as through a mask.

"The bodies of these men were chiefly naked and all painted in the most extraordinary manner, with the nicest adherence to exact similarity; their limbs, bodies and faces, being in every part covered, either with black, red, or white paint. Each one of these strange characters had also a lock of buffalo's hair tied around his ankles—in his right hand a rattle, and a slender white rod or staff, six feet long, in the other; and carried on his back, a bunch of green willow boughs about the usual size of a bundle of straw. These eight men, being divided into four pairs, took their positions on the four different sides of the curb or big canoe, representing thereby the four cardinal points; and between each group of them, with the back turned to the big canoe, was another figure, engaged in the same dance, keeping step with them, with a similar staff or wand in one hand and a rattle in the other, and (being four in number) answering again to the four cardinal points. The bodies of these four young men were chiefly naked, with no other dress upon them than a beautiful kelt (or quartz-

quaw), around the waist, made of eagles quills and ermine, and very splendid headdresses made of the same materials. Two of these figures were painted entirely black with pounded charcoal and grease, whom they called the 'firmament or night,' and the numerous white spots which were dotted all over their bodies, they called 'stars.' The other two were painted from head to foot as red as vermilion could make them; these they said represented the day, and the white streaks which were painted up and down over their bodies, were 'ghosts which the morning rays were chasing away' " (*Letters and Notes*, vol. 1, pp. 164-66, pl. 67).

References: 1837 catalogue, no. 492; Donaldson, pp. 358-62, pl. 93; Matthews, pp. 606-7, pl. 148; Haberly, pp. 72-76; Ewers (1956), p. 499, 513; McCracken, pp. 101, 103-4, 128, reprod. p. 127; James T. Flexner, *That Wilder Image* (Boston, 1962), reprod. p. 89; Paris (1963), no. 68, pl. 9; Catlin, *O-Kee-Pa* (see no. 504); *American Heritage* 18 (October 1967), reprod. p. 33; Anschutz Collection, *American Masters in the West* (1974), pp. 7-8, reprod. p. 17; (1976), p. 6, reprod. p. 7; *America as Art*, no. 182; Seattle Art Museum, *Lewis and Clark's America* (1976), no. 42.

Versions:
Smithsonian Institution, 24 x 29
Gilcrease Institute, NAI sketchbook (4776.52), pen and ink

Painted at the Mandan village in 1832 (see no. 504). There are additional dancers, spectators, and lodges in the Smithsonian version (fig. 63), and Catlin has described costumes, ritual accessories, and gestures with a clarity noticeably lacking in the original. The later version must have been painted as a text illustration for *Letters and Notes*, where it appears as plate 67.

The Smithsonian version, minus the foreground spectators, is repeated as cartoon 418 (AMNH 196), and the cartoon, in turn, became the source for plate 4 in *O-Kee-Pa*.

506. The Cutting Scene, Mandan O-kee-pa ceremony
1832
23⅝ x 27⅞ (60 x 70.8)
University Museum, Philadelphia (until 1971); Harmsen Collection, Denver
[Figure 19]

See number 504 for a description of the previous phase of the ceremony.

"Around the sides of the lodge are seen, still reclining . . . a part of the group, whilst others of them have passed the ordeal of self-tortures, and have been removed out of the lodge; and others still are seen in the very act of submitting to them, which were inflicted in the following manner:— After having removed the . . . little scaffold . . . and having removed also the buffalo and human skulls from the floor, and attached them to the posts of the lodge; and two men having taken their positions near the middle of the lodge, for the purpose of inflicting the tortures—the one with the scalping-knife, and the other with the bunch of splints (which I have before mentioned) in his hand; one at a time of the young fellows, already emaciated with fasting, and thirsting, and waking, for nearly four days and nights, advanced from the side of the lodge, and placed himself on his hands and feet, or otherwise, as best suited for the performance of the operation, where he submitted to the cruelties in the following manner:—An inch or more of the flesh on each shoulder, or each breast was taken up between the thumb and finger by the man who held the knife in his right hand; and the knife, which had been ground sharp on both edges, and then hacked and notched with the blade of another, to make it produce as much pain as possible, was forced through the flesh below the fingers, and being withdrawn, was followed with a splint or skewer, from the other, who held a bunch of such in his left hand, and was ready to force them through the wound. There were then two cords lowered down from the top of the lodge (by men who were placed on the lodge outside, for the purpose), which were fastened to these splints or skewers, and they instantly began to haul him up; he was thus raised until his body was suspended from the ground where he rested, until the knife and a splint were passed through the flesh or integuments in a similar manner on each arm below the shoulder . . . below the elbow . . . on the thighs . . . and below the knees. . . .

"In some instances they remained in a reclining position on the ground until this painful operation was finished, which was performed, in all instances, exactly on the same parts of the body and limbs; and which, in its progress, occupied some five or six minutes.

"Each one was then instantly raised with the cords, until the weight of his body was suspended by them, and then, while the blood was streaming down their limbs, the bystanders hung upon the splints each man's appropriate shield, bow and quiver, &c.; and in many instances; the skull of a buffalo with the horns on it, was attached to each lower arm and each lower leg, for the purpose, probably, of preventing by their great weight, the struggling, which might otherwise have taken place to their disadvantage whilst they were hung up.

"When these things were all adjusted, each one was raised higher by the cords, until these weights all swung clear from the ground, leaving his feet, in most cases, some six or eight feet above the ground. In this plight they at once became appalling and frightful to look at—the flesh, to support the weight of their bodies, with the additional weights which were attached to them, was raised six or eight inches by the skewers; and their heads sunk forward on the breasts, or thrown backwards, in a much more frightful condition, according to the way in which they were hung up" (*Letters and Notes,* vol. 1, pp. 169-73, pl. 68).

While the candidates remained in this hanging position, they were turned about until pain and exhaustion caused them to lose consciousness, after which the torture ceased and they were lowered to the ground. When they regained their senses, they crawled to a corner of the lodge, where the little finger of their left hand was abruptly chopped off as a sacrifice to the Great Spirit, and then they were led outside to participate in The Last Race (see no. 507).

References: 1837 catalogue, no. 493; Donaldson, pp. 362-65, pl. 94; Matthews, pp. 607-8, pl. 149; Haberly, pp. 72-76; Ewers (1956), p. 499, pl. 16; Vernon Young, "George Catlin's Indian Gallery: The Wilderness in a Locket," *Arts* 31 (December 1956), p. 20; University Museum, Philadelphia, *The Noble Savage* (1958), no. 12; McCracken, pp. 105-9, 128; Ewers (1965), reprod. pp. 86-87; Catlin, *O-Kee-Pa* (see no. 504); *American Heritage* 18 (October 1967), reprod. pp. 37-38; Emily Wasserman, "The Artist-Explorers," *Art in America* 60 (July 1972): 52; Arvada Center, Arvada, Colo., *Harmsen's Western Americana Art Collection* (1976), no. 35, reprod.

Painted at the Mandan village in 1832 (see no. 504). Plate 68 in *Letters and Notes* is not based upon the University Museum original, but on a more detailed version that closely followed Catlin's written account of the scene (see no. 505), and would have matched the other paintings in the Smithsonian O-kee-pa series. Unlike the original, the numerous figures in plate 68 are engaged in clearly defined actions that the architectural arrangement does not obscure.

The missing version is repeated in cartoon 419 (AMNH 197), and the cartoon is the source for plate 10 in *O-Kee-Pa.*

507

507a.

Smithsonian Institution.

507. The Last Race, Mandan O-kee-pa ceremony

1832

23⅜ x 28⅛ (58.8 x 71.3)

University Museum, Philadelphia (until 1971); Anschutz Collection

"The signal for the commencement of this part of the cruelties was given by the old master of ceremonies, who again ran out as in the buffalo-dance, and leaning against the big canoe, with his *medicine-pipe* in his hand, began to cry. This was done several times in the afternoon, as often as there were six or eight who had passed the ordeal just described within the lodge [see no. 506], who were then taken out in the open area, in the presence of the whole village, with the buffalo skulls and other weights attached to their flesh, and dragging on the ground! There were then in readiness, and prepared for the purpose, about twenty young men, selected of equal height and equal age; with their bodies chiefly naked, with beautiful (and similar) head-dresses of war eagles' quills, on their heads, and a wreath made of willow boughs held in the hands between them, connecting them in a chain or circle in which they ran around the *big canoe*, with all possible speed, raising their voices in screams and yelps to the highest pitch that was possible, and keeping the curb or big canoe in the centre, as their nucleus.

"Then were led forward the young men who were further to suffer, and being placed at equal distances apart, and outside of the ring just described, each one was taken in charge of two athletic young men, fresh and strong, who stepped up to him, one on each side, and by wrapping a broad leather strap around his wrists, without tying it, grasped it firm underneath the hand, and stood prepared for what they call the last race. . . .

"In this condition they stand, pale and ghastly, from abstinence and loss of blood, until all are prepared, and the word is given, when all start and run around, outside of the other ring; and each poor fellow, with his weights dragging on the ground, and his furious conductors by his side, who hurry him forward by the wrists, struggles in the desperate emulation to run longer without 'dying' (as they call it) than his comrades, who are fainting around him and sinking down, like himself, where their bodies are dragged with all possible speed, and often with their faces in the dirt. In the commencement of this dance or race they all start at a moderate pace, and their speed being gradually increased, the pain becomes so excruciating that their languid and exhausted frames give out, and they are dragged by their wrists until they are disengaged from the weights that were attached to their flesh, and this must be done by such violent force as to tear the flesh out with the splint, which (as they say) can never be pulled out endwise, without greatly offending the Great Spirit and defeating the object for which they have thus far suffered. . . . when they were freed from the last of the buffalo skulls and other weights, (which was often done by some of the bystanders throwing the weight of their bodies on to them as they were dragging on the ground) they were in every instance dropped by the persons who dragged them, and their bodies were left, appearing like nothing but a mangled and a loathsome corpse" (*Letters and Notes*, vol. 1, pp. 173-75, pl. 69).

Some minutes later, the battered candidates would arise from the dust and stagger to their respective lodges, where their family and friends were prepared to receive them.

References: 1837 catalogue, no. 494; Donaldson, pp. 366-68, pl. 95; Matthews, p. 609, pl. 150; Haberly, pp. 72-76; Ewers (1956), pp. 499, 513; McCracken, pp. 107-8; *Catlin, Bodmer, Miller;* University Museum, Philadelphia, *The Noble Savage* (1958), no. 9; Paris (1963), no. 69; Catlin, *O-Kee-Pa* (see no. 504); *American Heritage* 18 (October 1967): 74-75; Los Angeles County Museum of Art, *The American West* (1972), no. 23, reprod. p. 88; National Archives, Washington, D.C., *Indians and the American West* (1974), no. 32; reprod.; Seattle Art Museum, *Lewis and Clark's America* (1976), no. 38, reprod. p. 25.

Version:
Smithsonian Institution, 24 x 29

Copy:
Schweitzer Gallery, New York, 48 x 69

Painted at the Mandan village in 1832 (see no. 504). The Smithsonian version (illustration 507a) is again a close visual account of the passage in *Letters and Notes,* and a more detailed and finished painting than the original (see nos. 505, 506). The crude little figures in the latter, however, are less contrived and more expressive of the primitive drama of the scene. The Schweitzer copy lacks Catlin's animated touch (see no. 338).

The Smithsonian version matches plate 69 in *Letters and Notes,* and is repeated in cartoon 420 (collection of Mr. and Mrs. Paul Mellon), although the latter is lacking foreground spectators. The cartoon, in turn, is the basis for plate 12 in *O-Kee-Pa.*

508. Boy Chief
Ojibwa, 1843
28 x 23 (71.1 x 58.4)
National Gallery of Art, Washington, D.C.
Paul Mellon Collection

Described by Catlin as "an excellent old man, of seventy-five years, with an intelligent and benignant countenance, and . . . somewhat distinguished as a warrior in his younger days (*Travels in Europe*, vol. 1, pp. 108-10, 196, pl. 4)

The nine Ojibwa were brought to England by Arthur Rankin, a Canadian promoter, in the spring of 1843. When Catlin met the group in Manchester several days after their arrival, he quickly perceived the advantage of using real Indians, instead of a hired London troupe, in the *Tableaux Vivants* that had become the chief attraction of the Indian Gallery. Accompanied by the Ojibwa, he hurried back to London, planning a promotional appearance before Queen Victoria at Windsor Castle and a return engagement for the Indian Gallery at Egyptian Hall. For several months the Ojibwa performances did succeed in reviving interest in Catlin's collection, but eventually he and Rankin were accused by the British press of exploiting the group. Before the end of the year, Rankin had made other arrangements for the Indians, and Catlin apparently did not see them again.

References: Carolyn T. Foreman, *Indians Abroad*, pp. 166-73; Haberly, pp. 135-44; McCracken, pp. 192-93, 195; Roehm, pp. 261-62, 299; National Gallery of Art, Washington, D.C., *American Paintings and Sculpture* (1970), p. 29, no. 2307; Haverstock, pp. 173, 175-78; Gilcrease catalogue, p. 57; Rossi and Hunt, pp. 64, 320.

Painted in London in 1843. Catlin's European portraits generally lack the broad and spirited quality of his American work. They are carefully brushed and composed studio images in which extravagant costume details occasionally compete with an effective presentation of the individual.

This portrait was apparently withheld from Joseph Harrison and other creditors in 1852, and was eventually sold to the American Museum of Natural History by Catlin's heirs. The subject does not appear to be an "old man, of seventy-five years," but his face and costume closely resemble a figure of the same identity in Catlin's watercolor of the nine Ojibwa at the Gilcrease Institute (fig. 34), which was probably the source for plate 31 in the *North American Indian Portfolio* (1844). Cartoon 59 (NGA 2068) is a similar group portrait of the nine Indians, and plate 4 in *Travels in Europe* (1848) is a reduced and simplified version of the watercolor or *Portfolio* plate.

509. Driving Cloud, a war chief
Ojibwa, 1843
Unlocated

Described by Catlin as "a remarkably fine man of thirty-five years of age, and . . . distinguished . . . as a warrior in several battles in the war of 1812" (*Travels in Europe*, vol. 1, pp. 108-10, pl.4). Catlin is wrong either about Driving Cloud's age or the war in which he fought.

Painted in London in 1843 (see no. 508 for additional references and discussion). Driving Cloud appears again in the Gilcrease watercolor and cartoon 59 (NGA 2068).

510. Flying Gull, a medicine man
Ojibwa, 1843
Unlocated

Described by Catlin as "a sort of doctor or necromancer to the party, and a young fellow of much drollery and wit" (*Travels in Europe*, vol. 1, pp. 108-10, pl. 4).

Painted in London in 1843 (see no. 508 for additional references and discussion). Flying Gull appears again in the Gilcrease watercolor and cartoon 59 (NGA 2068).

511. Tobacco
Ojibwa, 1843
Unlocated

Described by Catlin as a "fine young man" (*Travels in Europe*, vol. 1, pp. 108-10, pl. 4).

Painted in London in 1843 (see no. 508 for additional references and discussion). Tobacco appears again in the Gilcrease watercolor and cartoon 59 (NGA 2068).

512. Moonlight Night
Ojibwa, 1843
Unlocated

Described by Catlin as a "fine young man" (*Travels in Europe*, vol. 1, pp. 108-10, pl. 4).

Painted in London in 1843 (see no. 508 for additional references and discussion). Moonlight Night appears again in the Gilcrease watercolor and cartoon 59 (NGA 2068).

508

517

513. Strong Wind
Ojibwa, 1843
Unlocated

Described by Catlin as "a half-caste, a young man of fine personal appearance and address" (*Travels in Europe*, vol. 1, pp. 108-10, pl. 4).

Reference: Ewers (1956), p. 520.

Painted in London in 1843, but the portrait previously catalogued as number 513 by the Smithsonian does not resemble the figure of the same identity in the Gilcrease watercolor or cartoon 59 (see no. 508). It has been reassigned to number 520 or 523.

514. Wos-see-ab-e-neuh-qua, a woman
Ojibwa, 1843
Unlocated

Reference: Travels in Europe, vol. 1, pp. 108-10, pl. 4.

Painted in London in 1843 (see no. 508 for additional references and discussion). The subject appears again in the Gilcrease watercolor and cartoon 59 (NGA 2068).

515. Nib-nab-ee-qua, a young girl
Ojibwa, 1843
Unlocated

Reference: Travels in Europe, vol. 1, pp. 108-10, pl. 4.

Painted in London in 1843 (see no. 508 for additional references and discussion). The subject appears again in the Gilcrease watercolor and cartoon 59 (NGA 2068).

516. Ne-bet-neuh-quat, a woman
Ojibwa, 1843
Unlocated

Reference: Travels in Europe, vol. 1, pp. 108-10, pl.4.

Painted in London in 1843 (see no. 508 for additional references and discussion). The subject appears again in the Gilcrease watercolor and cartoon 59 (NGA 2068).

517. White Cloud, chief of the tribe
Iowa, 1844
27¾ x 22¾ (70.5 x 57.8)
National Gallery of Art, Washington, D.C.
Paul Mellon Collection

"This young man, only 32 years of age, has, by several humane and noble acts since he inherited the office, proved himself well worthy of it, and has thereby gained the love of all his tribe, and also the admiration of the President of the United States, who has granted him the unusual permission to make the journey to Europe, and to select such a party as he chose to bring with him; and he, having chosen them according to merit, as warriors, has brought the aristocracy of the tribe.

"The stature of this man is about five feet ten inches, and he may generally be recognized . . . by his beautiful head-dress of war—eagles' quills—necklace of grizzly bears' claws, and the skin of a white wolf hanging down over his back. His features are roman, with a benignant expression, but rather embarrassed, from a defect in one of his eyes" (Catlin, *Fourteen Ioway Indians*, London, 1844, pp. 5-6).

Catlin claims in *Travels in Europe* that his earlier portrait of White Cloud was hanging in Egyptian Hall when the Iowa delegation arrived in London (see below), but Frederick W. Hodge (McKenney and Hall) thinks this earlier portrait is of No Heart (no. 256), and the present subject is his nephew or brother, White Cloud II. Charles Bird King's portrait of White Cloud II (Young Mahaskah) appears to be a younger version of this subject.

Shepherded by G. H. C. Melody, a sympathetic American, the fourteen Iowa began their European travels in London in the summer of 1844, and soon after they replaced the Ojibwa (see no. 508) as the performing troupe in Catlin's Indian Gallery (fig. 36). During their stay in the city, they were escorted to the usual attractions, had breakfast with Disraeli, danced in Vauxhall Gardens, and continued their performances at Egyptian Hall until late fall, when Catlin and Melody took them on a tour of the provinces, Edinburgh, and Dublin. Having exhausted British interest in his collection, Catlin moved on to Paris with the Iowa in April 1845, and engaged the Salle Valentino for several months. The French gave him a warm reception, and Louis Philippe, who had been in exile in America from 1797 to 1799, invited the troupe to perform at the Tuileries before the royal family. By midsummer, however, the death of Little Wolf's wife (see nos. 521, 527) had considerably lessened the Indians' curiosity about Europe, and they departed for home.

References: McKenney and Hall, vol. 1, pp. 294-95, 308-11; vol. 3, p. 114; Catlin, *Fourteen Ioway Indians,* London, 1844; *Travels in Europe,* vol. 2, pp. 2-3, 5, 13-14, 317, pl. 9; 1871 catalogue, no. 120; Carolyn T. Foreman, *Indians Abroad,* pp. 185-93; Haberly, pp. 145-67; Kennedy catalogue, reprod. p. 4; McCracken, pp. 193-95, reprod. p. 182; James T. Flexner, *That Wilder Image* (Boston 1962) p. 97; *Metropolitan Museum of Art Bulletin,* April 1965, reprod. p. 290; Roehm, pp. 299-300, 305-6; Jules D. Prown, *American Painting* (Geneva, 1969), p. 106, reprod. p. 108; National Gallery of Art, Washington, D.C., *American Paintings and Sculpture* (1970), p. 27, no. 2305, reprod. p. 25; Los Angeles County Museum of Art, *The American West* (1972), no. 19, reprod. p. 86; Haverstock, pp. 178-81.

Catlin would have had more time to paint the Iowa delegation in London than in any subsequent stop on their travels. Furthermore, numbers 522 and 530 were dead before the delegation reached Paris.

The technique of this portrait is much the same as number 508, but the costume accessories worn by the Iowa are less distracting. Numbers 517 through 530 are a somber, brooding lot, who rarely confront the spectator with the aggressive confidence of the Indians Catlin painted on native grounds. In place of that confidence, however, the Iowa portraits reflect a deeper recognition of the sitters as individuals, perplexed and dismayed, perhaps, by the experience of European travel.

The portrait was apparently withheld from Joseph Harrison and other creditors in 1852, and was eventually sold as cartoon 120 to the American Museum of Natural History by Catlin's heirs. The artist also lists a painting of the subject among those commissioned by Louis Philippe in 1845 (see no. 449 and *Travels in Europe*), and White Cloud appears again in cartoon 60 (NGA 2069), with his wife (no. 525) and other members of the Iowa delegation.

518. Walking Rain, war chief
Iowa, 1844
29 x 24 (73.7 x 60.9)

Catlin describes Walking Rain as "54 years of age, and nearly six feet and a half in height," and claims that his earlier portrait of the war chief (no. 258) was then hanging in Egyptian Hall (*Travels in Europe,* vol. 2, pp. 2-3, 14, pl. 9.

Reference: Ewers (1956), p. 512.

Probably painted in London in 1844 (see no. 517 for additional references and discussion). Walking Rain's appearance in this second portrait only distantly corresponds to the first, but he clearly resembles the Iowa chief Neomanni in Charles Bird King's 1837 portrait (see McKenney and Hall, vol. 2, p. 153). The technique of numbers 518 and 519 shows less studio restraint than the other exam-

ples in the Iowa series.
Walking Rain appears again in cartoon 60 (NGA 2069).

519. Blistered Feet, a medicine man
Iowa, 1844
28 x 22⅞ (71.1 x 58.1)
National Gallery of Art, Washington, D.C.
Paul Mellon Collection

Described by Catlin as "near 60 years of age." A portrait medallion of George III hangs from the subject's neck (Catlin, *Fourteen Ioway Indians,* London, 1844, p. 6).

References: *Travels in Europe,* vol. 2, p. 14, pl. 9; 1871 catalogue, no. 119; Kennedy catalogue, reprod. p. 4; McCracken, reprod. p. 182; *Metropolitan Museum of Art Bulletin,* April 1965, reprod. p. 291; National Gallery of Art, Washington, D.C., *American Paintings and Sculpture,* 1970, p. 27, no. 2304, reprod. p. 23; William Campbell, "The American Heritage at the National Gallery of Art," *Connoisseur* 178 (December 1971), reprod. p. 272; Los Angeles County Museum of Art, *The American West* (1972), no. 20, reprod. p. 86; *Apollo* 96 (August 1972), reprod. p. 153.

Probably painted in London in 1844 (see nos. 517 and 518 for additional references and discussion). The portrait was apparently withheld from Joseph Harrison and other creditors in 1852, and was eventually sold as cartoon 119 to the American Museum of Natural History by Catlin's heirs. Blistered Feet appears again in cartoon 60 (NGA 2069), with the other members of the Iowa party.

520. Fast Dancer, a warrior
Iowa, 1844
29 x 24 (73.7 x 60.9)

References: *Travels in Europe,* vol. 2, pp. 2-3, 13, pl. 9; Ewers, p. 520.

This portrait was previously catalogued as number 513, but the headdress and style more closely resemble the portraits of the Iowa delegation, which were probably painted in London in 1844 (see no. 517 for additional references and discussion). The subject might also be Foremost Man (no. 523).

Catlin claims that he painted an earlier portrait of Fast Dancer at the Iowa village (see *Travels in Europe*), but none is listed in the 1837 or 1848 catalogues. The subject appears again in cartoon 60 (NGA 2069).

522

524

521. Little Wolf, a famous warrior
Iowa, 1844
29 x 24 (73.7 x 60.9)
[Figure 40]

The wife and child of Little Wolf (nos. 527, 530) both died while abroad.

References: Travels in Europe, vol. 2, pp. 13, 15-16, 317, pl. 9; Paris, Musée Royal, Salon de 1846, no. 314; Charles Baudelaire, *Art in Paris 1845-1862*, ed. and trans. Jonathan Mayne (London, 1965), pp. 70-71; Ewers (1956), p. 512; Robert N. Beetem, "George Catlin in France: His Relationship to Baudelaire and Delacroix," *Art Quarterly* 24 (Summer 1961): 140-41; Paris (1963), no. 33, pl. 2; Denys Sutton, "The Luminous Point," *Apollo* 85 (March 1967): 217; University of Maryland Art Gallery, College Park, *Hommage à Baudelaire* (1968), p. 38, reprod. p. 39; Paris, Petit Palais, *Baudelaire* (1969), no. 177; Haverstock, reprod. p. 174.

Probably painted in London in 1844, but further retouching may have taken place in Paris (see no. 517 for additional references and discussion). The portrait is one of two Catlin entered in the Salon of 1846 (see no. 149), and it is surely the masterpiece of his European career. The balanced strength of the modeling and brushwork, which surpasses that of any of his American achievements, must represent an effort by the artist to conform, if only temporarily, to the academic standards of the Salon jury. Even the jewelry is more sharply finished than usual, and more skillfully designed as a setting for the imposing head of Little Wolf. The remote and thoughtful presence of the Indian might also reflect the civilized restrictions of London and Paris, rather than the primitive world of the Upper Missouri.

Catlin lists another portrait of Little Wolf among those commissioned by Louis Philippe in 1845 (see no. 449 and *Travels in Europe*), and the subject appears again in cartoon 60 (NGA 2069).

522. One Who Gives No Attention
Iowa, 1844
29 x 24 (73.7 x 60.9)

Described by Catlin as "the finest looking man of the party," having "elegant" limbs and a "Herculean" frame. The subject was also called "Roman Nose," and he died in Liverpool before the Iowa delegation departed for Paris (*Travels in Europe*, vol. 2, pp. 15-16, 21-22, 200-201, pl. 9).

Reference: Ewers (1956), p. 520.

Probably painted in London in 1844 (see no. 517 for additional references and discussion). The portrait was previously catalogued as number 27, but the headdress is identical to those worn by the Iowa delegation, and the name Roman Nose seems particularly appropriate for the sitter. The style is similar to numbers 517 through 519.

The subject appears again in cartoon 60 (NGA 2069).

523. Foremost Man
Iowa, 1844
Unlocated

Probably painted in London in 1844 (see no. 517 for references and discussion). The subject appears again in plate 9 of *Travels in Europe*, and in cartoon 60 (NGA 2069). The portrait presently catalogued as number 520 may be either Fast Dancer or Foremost Man.

524. Commanding General, a boy
Iowa, 1844
28 x 23 (71.1 x 58.4)
Historical Society of Pennsylvania

References: Travels in Europe, vol. 2, pp. 13, 317, pl. 9; William Sawitsky, *Catalogue of the Paintings and Miniatures in the Historical Society of Pennsylvania* (Philadelphia, 1942), p. 74.

Probably painted in London in 1844 (see no. 517 for additional references and discussion). Catlin lists another portrait of Commanding General among those commissioned by Louis Philippe in 1845 (see no. 449 and *Travels in Europe*), and the subject appears again in cartoon 60 (NGA 2069).

525. Strutting Pigeon, wife of White Cloud
Iowa, 1844
29 x 24 (73.7 x 60.9)

References: Travels in Europe, vol. 2, no. 13, pl. 9; Ewers (1956), p. 512; *America as Art*, no. 165, reprod. p. 163.

Probably painted in London in 1844 (see no. 517 for additional references and discussion). The subject appears again in cartoon 60 (NGA 2069).

526. Pigeon on the Wing
Iowa, 1844
29 x 24 (73.7 x 60.9)

References: Travels in Europe, vol. 2, p. 13, pl. 9;
Ewers (1956), p. 512.

Probably painted in London in 1844 (see no. 517 for
additional references and discussion). The subject
appears again in cartoon 60 (NGA 2069).

**527. Female Bear that Walks on the Back of
Another**
Iowa, 1844
Unlocated

Female Bear was the wife of Little Wolf (no. 521)
and mother of Corsair (no. 530). Her death in Paris
in June 1845 evoked great sympathy among prominent French artists and writers, as she had requested a Christian burial. Designs were begun for
a tomb, with Chopin and George Sand offering
suggestions to the sculptor Preault, but the project
was never carried out.

Probably painted in London in 1844 (see no. 517
for references and discussion). Female Bear appears again in plate 9 of *Travels in Europe*, and in
cartoon 60 (NGA 2069).

528. Female War Eagle
Iowa, 1844
29 x 24 (73.7 x 60.9)

References: Travels in Europe, vol. 2, p. 13, pl. 9;
Ewers (1956), p. 512; M. Knoedler & Co., New
York, *The American Indian Observed* (1971), no.
26, reprod. p. 21.

Probably painted in London in 1844 (see no. 517 for
additional references and discussion). The subject
appears again in cartoon 60 (NGA 2069).

529. Wisdom, a girl
Iowa, 1844
Unlocated

Probably painted in London in 1844 (see no. 517 for
references and discussion). The subject appears
again in plate 9 of *Travels in Europe*, and in cartoon 60 (NGA 2069).

530. Corsair, a papoose
Iowa, 1844
Unlocated

Corsair, who died in Scotland, was the son of Little
Wolf (no. 521) and Female Bear (no. 527). His
portrait was probably painted in London in 1844
(see no. 517 for references and discussion). The
papoose appears again in plate 9 of *Travels in
Europe*, and in cartoon 60 (NGA 2069).

525

528

526

531

Smithsonian Institution.

531. Great Hero, a chief
Ojibwa, 1845
Unlocated

Described by Catlin as a "half-caste," forty-one
years old, and "a remarkably fine man . . . in his
personal appearance" (*Travels in Europe*, vol. 2., p.
279, pl. 18). An unidentified and unfinished
portrait in the Smithsonian collection (see illustration; MNH 386,321; 29 x 24) may be either
Great Hero or Strong Rock (no. 533). The subject, a

middle-aged Indian, wears a heavy fur cap, two
large medals around his neck, and a robe or trade
blanket across his shoulders. He holds a decorated
pipe in his left hand.

Painted in Paris in 1845 (see no. 532 for additional references and discussion). Catlin lists
another portrait of Great Hero among those commissioned by Louis Philippe in 1845 (see no. 449
and *Travels in Europe*, vol. 2., p. 317), and the subject appears again in cartoon 61 (NGA 2070).

the Iowa group (see no. 517), and Catlin has not always probed the bland features of the subjects for an individual interpretation.

The Gilcrease version is taken from a slightly different angle than the Smithsonian portrait, costume details vary between the two, and the former is more carefully painted. If both portraits are life studies, the Gilcrease version must have been painted some years before the other examples that Catlin supplied to Sir Thomas Phillips (see no. 125). Catlin lists another portrait of Hail Storm among those commissioned by Louis Philippe in 1845 (see no. 449 and *Travels in Europe*).

The subject is incorrectly listed under the Osage tribe in the Gilcrease catalogue. He appears again in cartoon 61 (NGA 2070), with the entire Ojibwa delegation.

533. Strong Rock
Ojibwa, 1845
Unlocated

Painted in Paris in 1845 (see nos. 531, 532 for references and discussion). Strong Rock appears again in plate 18 of *Travels in Europe*, and in cartoon 61 (NGA 2070).

534. King of the Loons
Ojibwa, 1845
Unlocated

Painted in Paris in 1845 (see no. 532 for references and discussion). The subject appears again in plate 18 of *Travels in Europe*, and in cartoon 61 (NGA 2070).

535. Tempest Bird
Ojibwa, 1845
29 x 24 (73.7 x 60.9)

References: Travels in Europe, vol. 2, p. 279, pl. 18; Ewers (1956), p. 520.

Painted in Paris in 1845 (see no. 532 for additional references and discussion). Tempest Bird appears again in cartoon 61 (NGA 2070).

536. Bird of Thunder
Ojibwa, 1845
29 x 24 (73.7 x 60.9)

References: Travels in Europe, vol. 2, pp. 279, 317, pl. 18; Ewers (1956), p. 520.

Painted in Paris in 1845 (see no. 532 for additional references and discussion). Catlin lists another portrait of Bird of Thunder among those commissioned by Louis Philippe in 1845 (see no. 449 and *Travels in Europe*), and the subject appears again in cartoon 61 (NGA 2070).

532. Hail Storm, war chief
Ojibwa, 1845
29 x 24 (73.7 x 60.9)

Described by Catlin in *Travels in Europe* as "a fine and intelligent Indian," thirty-one years old.

The eleven Canadian Ojibwa (subsequently increased to twelve by the birth of a papoose) arrived in Paris in the late summer of 1845, having heard of the Iowa's successful engagement (see no. 517), and they soon replaced the latter on the stage of the Salle Valentino. In early October, the Ojibwa entertained Louis Philippe and the royal family at Saint-Cloud with ball games and dances, and the king reciprocated by asking Catlin to display the Indian Gallery in the Salle de Séance at the Louvre (fig. 42). After moving the collection to the palace, Catlin took the Ojibwa to Belgium for a series of appearances, but several contracted smallpox in Brussels, and the remainder of the tour was canceled. Catlin parted from the group in Antwerp in January 1846.

References: Travels in Europe, vol. 2, pp. 278-80, 299, 317, pl. 18; Carolyn T. Foreman, *Indians Abroad*, pp. 193-95; Haberly, pp. 168-70; Ewers (1956), p. 520; McCracken, pp. 196, 198; Roehm, p. 306; Gilcrease catalogue, p. 49; San Jose Museum of Art, *Americans Abroad: Painters of the Victorian Era*, 1975.

Version:
Gilcrease Institute, 11 x 14

Painted in Paris in 1845 (see no. 508). This series of Ojibwa portraits seems to have been executed with haste and some indifference. They have neither the finish nor the vigorous appearance of

537. Elk
Ojibwa, 1845
Unlocated

Painted in Paris in 1845 (see no. 532 for references and discussion). The subject appears again in plate 18 of *Travels in Europe*, and in cartoon 61 (NGA 2070).

538. Pelican, a boy
Ojibwa, 1845
29 x 24 (73.7 x 60.9)

References: Travels in Europe, vol. 2, p. 279, pl. 18; Ewers (1956), p. 520.

Painted in Paris in 1845 (see no. 532 for additional references and discussion). Pelican appears again in cartoon 61 (NGA 2070).

539. Furious Storm, four years old
Ojibwa, 1845
Unlocated

Painted in Paris in 1845 (see no. 532 for references and discussion). The subject appears again in plate 18 of *Travels in Europe*, and in cartoon 61 (NGA 2070).

540. Brave Warrior, three years old
Ojibwa, 1845
Unlocated

Painted in Paris in 1845 (see no. 532 for references and discussion). Brave Warrior appears again in plate 18 of *Travels in Europe*, and in cartoon 61 (NGA 2070).

541. Woman of the Upper World
Ojibwa, 1845
Unlocated

Painted in Paris in 1845 (see no. 532 for references and discussion). The subject appears again in plate 18 of *Travels in Europe*, and in cartoon 61 (NGA 2070).

542. Papoose, born in Paris
Ojibwa, 1845
Unlocated

Painted in Paris in 1845 (see no. 532 for references and discussion). The papoose appears again in plate 18 of *Travels in Europe*, and in cartoon 61 (NGA 2070).

543. Death of the white buffalo
1846-1848
Unlocated

Described by Catlin as "a feat of the Mandan chiefs" (1848 catalogue, p. 50).

The artist must have sensed a European preference for "Wild West" scenes over studies of Indian life as he turned out numbers 543 through 607, the final series in the 1848 catalogue and perhaps his last attempt to arouse interest in the Indian Gallery. The paintings had not been included in the *Galerie Indienne* catalogue of 1845, and presumably were not begun until early 1846, when Catlin returned from his Belgian tour (see no. 531). For the next two years he divided his time between these hunting and adventure scenes, and two series of paintings commissioned by Louis Philippe.

In February 1848, shortly after he completed these commissions, angry mobs took over the streets of Paris, and Catlin fled to London with his family and his collection. Some months later, at Number 6, Waterloo Place, where the Indian Gallery was again on display, he published the final catalogue of his original collection.

References: Roehm, pp. 311-13; Rossi and Hunt, pp. 187, 320; Gilcrease catalogue, p. 56.

Version:
Gilcrease Institute, 11 x 14

The Gilcrease version is illustrated in place of the original, and the scene is repeated in cartoon 352 (unlocated).

544. Sioux war council
Yanktonai Dakota, 1846-1848
Unlocated

"The Chief Waneton speaking, and asking of the head Chief a war-party to go against the Sacs and Foxes" (1848 catalogue, p. 50).

References: Travels in Europe, vol. 2, p. 316; *Kennedy Quarterly* 9 (June 1969): 21, reprod. p. 20; Gilcrease catalogue, p. 57; *Connoisseur* 192 (July 1976): 206.

Versions:
Gilcrease Institute, 25 x 32
Dietrich Foundation, Philadelphia, 21½ x 32

Painted in Paris 1846-1848 (see no. 543). Both versions are larger and more detailed than Catlin's European originals of this period, and both are similar in appearance. The Gilcrease painting, probably another of the group commissioned by Louis Philippe (see no. 449 and *Travels in Europe*), is illustrated in place of the original.

The subject is repeated in cartoon 353 (unlocated).

538

543

Gilcrease Institute, Tulsa.

544

Gilcrease Institute, Tulsa.

545

547

Royal Ontario Museum, Toronto.

545 Battle between Sioux and Sauk and Fox
Eastern Dakota, 1846-1848
26¼ x 32½ (66.7 x 82.6)

"The Sioux chief killed and scalped on his horse's back. An historical fact" (1848 catalogue, p. 50).

References: Donaldson, p. 385; Ewers (1956), p. 511.

Painted in Paris 1846-1848 (see no. 543). The style is similar to the series commissioned by Louis Philippe, but the subject does not appear on the *Travels in Europe* list (see no. 544).

A simplified version of the scene is repeated as cartoon 273 (NGA 2157).

546. Death of One Horn, head chief of the Miniconjou tribe
Teton Dakota (Western Sioux), 1846-1848
Unlocated

"Having been the accidental cause of the death of his only son . . . [One Horn] threw himself in the way of a buffalo bull" (1848 catalogue, p. 50; *Letters and Notes*, vol. 1, pp. 221-22). See numbers 69 and 591.

Painted in Paris 1846-1848 (see no. 543). Cartoon 354 (unlocated) is a similar or related scene.

547. The Long Speech
Iowa, 1846-1848
Unlocated

"It is an invariable rule amongst Indians, that while one speaks in council no one can rise. . . . Blistered Feet (no. 519), a great *medicine-man*, made his favourite boast, that when he once rose in an Ioway council of war it happened unfortunately for the council that 'he began to speak just as it began to snow' " (1848 catalogue, p. 50).

Versions:
Royal Ontario Museum, 18½ x 26
H. Williams, New York, 1907, no. 10, 19 x 27 (exhibited in London, 1859)

Painted in Paris 1846-1848 (see no. 543). The Ontario version, which probably once belonged to H. Williams, is illustrated in place of the original. The scene is repeated in cartoon 197 (Collection of Mr. and Mrs. Paul Mellon).

548. Battle of the buffalo bulls
1846-1848
Unlocated

Painted in Paris 1846-1848 (see nos. 543, 424, 606).

549. Buffalo crossing a ravine in a snowdrift
1846-1848
Unlocated

Painted in Paris 1846-1848 (see nos. 543, 556).

550. Buffalo crossing the Missouri on ice
1846-1848
Unlocated

Painted in Paris 1846-1848 (see nos. 543, 561). The scene is probably repeated in cartoon 259 (unlocated).

551. Grizzly bears attacking a buffalo bull
1846-1848
Unlocated

Painted in Paris 1846-1848 (see no. 543). Cartoons 355 (unlocated) and 388 (NGA 2176) may be related scenes.

552. Indians spearing salmon at night by torchlight
1846-1848
Unlocated

Painted in Paris 1846-1848 (see nos. 543, 575). Cartoons 235 (NGA 2099), 267 (unlocated), or 272 (unlocated) may be similar or related scenes.

553. Deer hunting by moonlight
1846-1848
Unlocated

Reference: Kennedy Quarterly 16 (June 1978), reprod. p. 95.

Versions:
Kennedy Galleries, New York, 18¾ x 26½
H. Williams, New York, 1907, no. 7, 19 x 27 (exhibited in London, 1859)

Painted in Paris 1846-1848 (see nos. 543, 544). The Kennedy version, which probably once belonged to H. Williams, is illustrated in place of the original.

554. Deer hunting by torchlight in bark canoes
1846-1848
19½ x 27⅝ (49.5 x 70)

References: Antiques 37 (January 1940): 35; Ewers (1956), p. 524; Paris (1963), no. 51; Gilcrease catalogue, p. 56.

Versions:
Royal Ontario Museum, 18½ x 26
Gilcrease Institute, 11 x 14
M. Knoedler & Co., New York, 1965 (property of Mrs. E. S. Cushman), 19 x 26¾
H. Williams, New York, 1907, no. 21, 19 x 27 (exhibited in London, 1859)

Painted in Paris 1846-1848. The first of Catlin's night scenes were done at this time, no doubt as a further attempt to interest European audiences (see no. 543).

The torch is mounted on a stationary pole in the Ontario, Gilcrease, and Knoedler versions, but background details vary widely among the three. The Ontario version probably once belonged to H. Williams, and the Knoedler version, in which Catlin and two white men replace the Indians, may be the source for a similar lithograph in the *Colt Firearm Series* of about 1860 (see no. 411 and *Antiques*).

Cartoons 268 and 269 (both unlocated) must be similar or related views.

555. War party attacked in their camp at night
1846-1848
Unlocated

Painted in Paris 1846-1848 (see no. 543).

556. Batiste, Bogard, and I, taking a shot at buffalo crossing a ravine, Upper Missouri
1846-1848
Unlocated

References: Art Digest 15 (June 1941): 10; Gilcrease catalogue, p. 56.

Versions:
Gilcrease Institute, 11 x 14
M. Knoedler & Co., New York, 19 x 26¾, signed lower left: Catlin.

Painted in Paris 1844-1846 (see no. 543). The Gilcrease and Knoedler versions, which closely resemble each other, may combine the settings of numbers 549 and 556. Hunters are not mentioned in the title of the former painting, nor snowdrifts in the title of the latter. Cartoon 260 (unlocated) has almost the same title as number 556.

The Knoedler version, which is illustrated in place of the original, is probably the source of a similar lithograph in the *Colt Firearm Series* of about 1860 (see no. 554).

557. Catlin shooting parakeets in Texas, among its gorgeous wildflowers
1846-1848
Unlocated

Reference: Gilcrease catalogue, p. 56.

Version:
Gilcrease Institute, 11 x 14

Painted in Paris 1846-1848 (see no. 543). Catlin did not travel in Texas until some years later (see nos. 345, 346). The Gilcrease version, which is illustrated here, is probably close to the appearance of the original.

Cartoons 256 and 356 (both unlocated) may be similar or related scenes.

553

Kennedy Galleries, New York.

554

556

M. Knoedler & Co., New York.

557

Gilcrease Institute, Tulsa.

558

559

Museum für Völkerkunde, Berlin.

561

Gilcrease Institute, Tulsa.

562

558. Assiniboin Indians pursuing buffalo on snowshoes
1846-1848
19⅝ x 27⅝ (49.6 x 70)

Reference: Ewers (1956), p. 508.

Painted in Paris 1846-1848 (see no. 416). Catlin must have produced over 100 pictures between 1846 and early 1848. Those intended for Louis Philippe were finished with great care (see no. 449), but others are little more than hasty sketches he painted to round out his collection for European audiences (see no. 543). Even at high speed, however, Catlin had a surprisingly delicate and sure touch, giving to his figures the animated presence of actors on a miniature stage. The setting is not the Great Plains or the Upper Missouri, but a land of fantastic foliage and bright pastel tones shaped by the artist's beguiling and fanciful memory.

559. Ojibwa village of skin lodges
1846-1848
Unlocated

The village, according to Catlin, was on the "St. Peter's [River] near the Traverse de Sioux" (1848 catalogue, p. 50*).

References: Hartmann, p. 38; Gilcrease catalogue, p. 56.

Versions:
Gilcrease Institute, 11 x 14
Museum für Völkerkunde, Berlin, 48.5 x 67.5 cm, signed lower right: Catlin./54

Painted in Paris 1846-1848 (see no. 543). The Gilcrease and Berlin versions are generally alike. The latter is illustrated in place of the original.

The scene is apparently repeated in cartoon 126 (unlocated), although Catlin describes a Plains Ojibwa village in the 1871 catalogue.

560. Band of elk crossing the Missouri, and the author and his two men in a bark canoe
1846-1848
Unlocated

Painted in Paris 1846-1848 (see no. 543). Cartoons 296 and 357 (both unlocated) may be similar or related views.

561. A herd of numerous buffalo crossing the Missouri on the ice
1846-1848
Unlocated

References: McCracken, p. 132; Gilcrease catalogue, p. 56.

Versions:
Gilcrease Institute, 19 x 26, signed lower right: Catlin/54.
Gilcrease Institute, 11 x 14
H. Williams, New York, 1907, no. 11, 19 x 27 (exhibited in London, 1859)

Painted in Paris 1846-1848 (see no. 543). The two Gilcrease versions, which are similar in appearance, have been listed under this entry, instead of number 550, because the title seems to describe more accurately the "numerous" buffalo that appear in each. The larger version, which probably once belonged to H. Williams, is illustrated in place of the original.

The scene may be repeated in cartoon 358 (unlocated).

562. Batiste is run over, and loses his bouillon, in the Nishnabottana meadows
1846-1848
19⅛ x 26¾ (48.5 x 67.9)
University Museum, Philadelphia (until 1971); Anschutz Collection

References: Apollo 97 (January 1973), reprod. p. 41; Anschutz Collection, *American Masters in the West* (1974), reprod. p. 7; Duncan Pollock, "The Philip Anschutz Collection of Western Painting," *American Art Review* 2 (September 1975), reprod. p. 105.

Painted in Paris 1846-1848 (see nos. 543, 504). The technique is raw and hasty, but similar to other originals in this last series (see no. 558).

The scene is repeated in cartoon 401 (Collection of Mr. and Mrs. Paul Mellon), and number 584 is a similar subject.

563. Weapons and physiognomy of the grizzly bear
1846-1848
26⅝ x 32⅝ (67.5 x 82.8)

Catlin describes the subject as "the exact size of life" (1848 catalogue, p. 50*).

References: Donaldson, p. 385; Ewers (1956), p. 516.

Version:
Smithsonian Institution, 19½ x 27⅝

Painted in Paris 1846-1848 (see no. 543). The awesome size and power of the American grizzly was a source of great fascination to European audiences (see no. 603). The Smithsonian version (illustration 563a) is a carefully finished close-up of the snout, teeth, and claws of the bear.

564. Comanche Indians chasing buffalo with lances and bows
1846-1848
19⅝ x 27⅝ (49.7 x 70)

Reference: Ewers (1956), p. 510.

Painted in Paris 1846-1848 (see nos. 543, 558). Number 571 and cartoon 291 (unlocated) may be similar subjects.

565. Sioux Indians on snowshoes lancing buffalo
Teton Dakota (Western Sioux), 1846-1848
20⅛ x 27⅜ (51 x 69.4)

References: Pennsylvania State University, University Park, *Pennsylvania Painters* (1955), no. 18, reprod.; Ewers (1956), p. 511; Whitney Museum of American Art, New York, *The American Frontier: Images and Myths* (1973), no. 14, reprod. p. 20.

Painted in Paris 1846-1848 (see nos. 543, 558). The scene may be repeated in cartoon 263 (unlocated).

566. Elk crossing the Upper Brazos, Texas
1846-1848
Unlocated

Reference: Gilcrease catalogue, p. 55.
Versions:
Royal Ontario Museum, 19 x 26½
Gilcrease Institute, 11 x 14
H. Williams, New York, 1907, no. 17, 19 x 27 (exhibited in London, 1859)

Painted in Paris 1846-1848 (see nos. 543, 557). The Gilcrease version is illustrated in place of the original. The Ontario version, in which elk wade across the river and the right bank is an open meadow, probably once belonged to H. Williams.
The scene is repeated in cartoon 359 (unlocated).

563

563a.

Smithsonian Institution.

564

565

566

Gilcrease Institute, Tulsa.

567

567. An Osage Indian lancing a buffalo
1846-1848
19½ x 27⅝ (49.7 x 70)

Reference: Ewers (1956), p. 514.

Painted in Paris 1846-1848 (see nos. 543, 558). The scene is repeated in cartoon 266 (NGA 1968), with fewer buffalo in the background.

Gilcrease Institute, Tulsa.

Royal Ontario Museum, Toronto.

568. Grizzly bear attacking a buffalo bull in a snowdrift
1846-1848
Unlocated

Reference: Gilcrease catalogue, p. 55.

Versions:
Joslyn Art Museum, Omaha, 19 x 26½, signed lower right: Catlin.
Gilcrease Institute, 11 x 14
H. Williams, New York, 1907, no. 19, 19 x 27 (exhibited in London, 1859)

Painted in Paris 1846-1848 (see no. 543). The Gilcrease and Joslyn versions are almost identical. The former is illustrated in place of the original, and the latter probably once belonged to H. Williams.

The scene is repeated in plate 80 of the Gilcrease *Souvenir* album, and in cartoon 270 (unlocated).

569. Caddo Indians chasing buffalo, Texas
1846-1848
Unlocated

Painted in Paris 1846-1848 (see nos. 543, 557, 589).

570. Party of Indians lunching, alarmed by a prairie fire
1846-1848
Unlocated

Versions:
Royal Ontario Museum, 18¾ x 26⅛, signed lower right: Catlin./54
H. Williams, New York, 1907, no. 8, 19 x 27 (exhibited in London, 1859)

Painted in Paris 1846-1848 (see no. 543). The Ontario version, which probably once belonged to H. Williams, is illustrated in place of the original. The scene is repeated in cartoon 198 (unlocated).

571. Comanche chasing buffalo
1846-1848
Unlocated

Painted in Paris 1846-1848 (see no. 543).

572. Ojibwa hunting deer by torchlight, Lake St. Croix
1846-1848
Unlocated

Painted in Paris 1846-1848 (see nos. 543, 554, 577). The scene may be repeated in cartoon 268 (unlocated).

573. Oneida spearing trout by torchlight, Seneca Lake
1846-1848
Unlocated

Painted in Paris 1846-1848 (see nos. 543, 552, 575). Cartoons 235 (NGA 2099) and 272 (unlocated) may be similar or related views.

574. Deer alarmed, a moonlight scene
1846-1848
Unlocated

Painted in Paris 1846-1848 (see no. 543).

575. Ojibwa spearing salmon by torchlight
1846-1848
19½ x 27½ (49.6 x 69.9)

References: Donaldson, p. 385; Porter Butts, *Art in Wisconsin* (Madison, 1936), p. 41; Ewers (1956), p. 521; J. Russell Harper, *Paul Kane's Frontier* (Austin, 1971), p. 179.

Painted in Paris 1846-1848 (see nos. 543, 554). This particular scene came to the Smithsonian in frame 575; otherwise, it might as well have been catalogued under number 552 or 576. Cartoon 267 (unlocated) may be a similar or related view.

The same subject was sketched by Paul Kane in 1845 on the Fox River. Harper also notes that salmon were unknown at this time in the Great Lakes above Niagara Falls.

576. Ojibwa spearing a salmon by torchlight
1846-1848
Unlocated

Reference: Gilcrease catalogue, p. 56.

Versions:
Joslyn Art Museum, Omaha, 19 x 26½
Gilcrease Institute, 11 x 14
H. Williams, New York, 1907, no. 23, 19 x 27 (exhibited in London, 1859)

Painted in Paris 1846-1848 (see no. 543). The Joslyn and Gilcrease versions have been listed under number 576, as they seem to represent the successful conclusion of the spearing operation begun in number 575. The versions are reasonably similar in appearance, although there is no moon in the latter. The Joslyn painting, which probably once belonged to H. Williams, is illustrated in place of the original.
   Cartoon 267 (unlocated) may be a similar or related view.

577. Deer hunting by torchlight
1846-1848
Unlocated

Painted in Paris 1846-1848 (see nos. 543, 554, 572). Cartoon 268 (unlocated) may be a similar or related view.

578. Deer hunting with a torch carried on the head
1846-1848
Unlocated

Painted in Paris 1846-1848 (see no. 543). An unidentified cartoon (formerly AMNH), which may be after the original, is illustrated here.

579. Catlin and party stalking buffalo, Upper Missouri
1846-1848
19⅝ x 27⅝ (49.7 x 70)

References: Donaldson, p. 385; Ewers (1956), p. 516.

Painted in Paris 1846-1848 (see nos. 543, 558).

576

Joslyn Art Museum, Omaha.

578

Formerly American Museum of Natural History, New York.

580. Elk and buffalo grazing among prairie flowers, Texas
1846-1848
19½ x 27⅝ (49.7 x 70)

References: Donaldson, p. 385; Ewers (1956), pp. 500, 516; *America as Art*, no. 183.

Painted in Paris 1846-1848 (see nos. 543, 558). Catlin never went south of Oklahoma in 1834 (see nos. 345, 346), and Ewers thinks that the animals are an unlikely combination for the Texas prairie.

581. Elk and buffalo making acquaintance, Texas
1846-1848
19⅝ x 27⅝ (49.7 x 70)
[Figure 130]

References: Donaldson, p. 385; Haberly, reprod. opp. p. 13; Ewers (1956), pp. 500, 516; Perry T. Rathbone, "Rediscovery," *Art in America* 49 (no. 1, 1961), reprod. p. 83; Paris (1963), no. 52; Pauline A. Pinckney, *Painting in Texas* (Austin, 1967), reprod. p. 38.

Painted in Paris 1846-1848 (see nos. 543, 558, 580). The scene is repeated in cartoon 361 (unlocated).

579

580

582

Royal Ontario Museum, Toronto.

584

Joslyn Art Museum, Omaha.

585

586

589

582. Cree Indians pursuing moose on snowshoes
1846-1848
Unlocated

References: Hartmann, p. 41; Gilcrease catalogue, p. 56.

Versions:
Royal Ontario Museum, 18½ x 26
Museum für Völkerkunde, Berlin, 48.5 x 67.5 cm, signed lower center: Catlin
Gilcrease Institute, 11 x 14
H. Williams, New York, 1907, no. 6, 19 x 27 (exhibited in London, 1859)

Painted in Paris 1846-1848 (see no. 543). The Ontario and Berlin versions are almost identical, but two Indians pursue two moose in a different landscape in the Gilcrease version. The Ontario painting, which probably once belonged to H. Williams, is illustrated in place of the original.

The scene is repeated in plate 98 of the Gilcrease *Souvenir* album, and in cartoon 253 (unlocated).

583. A Cheyenne tournament or sham fight
1846-1848
Unlocated

Painted in Paris 1846-1848 (see no. 543).

584. Batiste, Bogard, and I, run over in a Missouri meadow
1846-1848
Unlocated

References: McCracken, p. 123; Gilcrease catalogue, p. 56.

Versions:
Joslyn Art Museum, Omaha, 18¾ x 26½, signed lower right: Catlin. 1855
Gilcrease Institute, 11 x 14
H. Williams, New York, 1907, no. 9, 19 x 27 (exhibited in London, 1859)

Painted in Paris 1846-1848 (see no. 543). The Joslyn and Gilcrease versions are reasonably alike. The former, which probably once belonged to H. Williams, is illustrated in place of the original.

The scene is probably repeated in cartoon 151 (unlocated), and number 562 is a similar subject.

585. Catlin and his men in their canoe, urgently solicited to come ashore, Upper Missouri
1846-1848
19¼ x 26¾ (48.9 x 67.7)

References: Donaldson, p. 385; Ewers (1956), p. 516; Paris (1963), no. 53; Haverstock, reprod. pp. 168-69.

Painted in Paris 1846-1848 (see no. 543). Catlin often turned from description to entertainment in this final series, hoping to find a formula that would again arouse interest in the Indian Gallery.

The scene is repeated in cartoon 328 (unlocated).

586. Mounted war party scouring a thicket
Comanche, 1846-1848
20⅛ x 27¼ (50.9 x 69.2)

References: Donaldson, p. 385; Ewers (1956), p. 510.

Painted in Paris 1846-1848 (see nos. 543, 558). Cartoon 274 (NGA 2010) is a similar subject.

587. An "American Gentleman's" seat, near the Cross Timbers, Texas
1846-1848
Unlocated

Painted in Paris 1846-1848 (see nos. 543, 589).

588. A Delaware war party lunching, Texas
1846-1848
Unlocated

Painted in Paris 1846-1848 (see nos. 543, 557).

589. Caddo Indians chasing buffalo, Cross Timbers, Texas
1846-1848
19½ x 27⅝ (49.7 x 70)

References: Donaldson, p. 385; Ewers (1956), p. 509.

Painted in Paris 1846-1848 (see nos. 543, 558). The Cross Timbers area extends into southern Oklahoma, where Catlin saw many such chases (see nos. 557, 569).

Cartoon 360 (unlocated) is a similar or related view.

590. Catlin and his Indian guide approaching buffalo under white wolf skins
1846-1848
20 x 27⅛ (50.9 x 69.2)
[Figure 125]

See number 414 for Catlin's description.

References: Letters and Notes, vol. 1, p. 254; Donaldson, p. 385; E. P. Richardson, *American Romantic Painting* (New York, 1944), p. 28; *Westward the Way*, no. 55, reprod. p. 89; Ewers (1956), p. 516; William Rockhill Nelson Gallery of Art, Kansas City, *The Last Frontier* (1957), no. 13; McCracken, p. 72; Hartmann, p. 36; Haverstock, pp. 70-71.

Versions:
Royal Ontario Museum, 16 x 27, signed lower right: G. Catlin. 1857
Museum für Völkerkunde, Berlin, 48 x 67 cm, signed lower right: Catlin/54
Royal Ontario Museum, 18½ x 26, signed lower right: G. Catlin. 1857
H. Williams, New York, 1907, nos. 2, 3, 19 x 27 each (exhibited in London, 1859)

Painted in Paris 1846-1848 (see nos. 543, 558). The first Ontario and the Berlin versions are similar in detail and more carefully finished than the Smithsonian original. The scene is repeated in cartoon 148 (unlocated), and the subject is closely related to number 414.

In the second Ontario version (both probably once belonged to H. Williams), Catlin and his Indian guide have thrown off their wolf skins and begun shooting into the herd, the former with a Colt rifle and the latter with arrows. This may be another of the paintings Catlin prepared for the *Colt Firearm Series* of about 1860 (see nos. 554, 556). The scene is repeated in cartoon 149 (NGA 2135).

591. Death of One Horn on the Little Missouri
Teton Dakota (Western Sioux), 1846-1848
Unlocated

See number 546 for Catlin's description.

Reference: Letters and Notes, vol. 2, pp. 221-22.

Painted in Paris 1846-1848 (see no. 543). Cartoon 354 (unlocated) is a similar or related scene.

592. Sioux Indians at their breakfast, alarmed at the shadow of a war party
1846-1848
Unlocated

Reference: Gilcrease catalogue, p. 57.

Versions:
Royal Ontario Museum, 18½ x 26
Gilcrease Institute, 11 x 14
H. Williams, New York, 1907, no. 13, 19 x 27 (exhibited in London, 1859)

Painted in Paris 1846-1848 (see no. 543). The Ontario and Gilcrease versions are reasonably similar, but the latter has less detail. The former probably once belonged to H. Williams, and the latter is illustrated in place of the original.

The scene may be repeated as cartoon 295 (unlocated).

593. Caddo Indians gathering wild grapes, Texas
1846-1848
Unlocated

Reference: Gilcrease catalogue, p. 55.

Version:
Gilcrease Institute, 11 x 14

Painted in Paris 1846-1848 (see nos. 543, 557). The Gilcrease version is illustrated in place of the original, and cartoons 318 and 319 (NGA 2169, 2004) are related subjects.

594. Catlin and party stalking buffalo in Texas
1846-1848
20 x 27⅜ (50.8 x 69.4)

References: Donaldson, p. 385; Ewers (1956), p. 516.

Painted in Paris 1846-1848 (see nos. 543, 557, 558).

595. Indian family alarmed at the approach of a prairie fire
1846-1848
20 x 27⅜ (50.8 x 69.4)

References: Donaldson, p. 385; Ewers (1956), p. 518.

Painted in Paris 1846-1848 (see nos. 543, 558). Cartoon 399 (unlocated) may be a similar or related subject.

592

593
Gilcrease Institute, Tulsa.

594

595

Gilcrease Institute, Tulsa.

596. Comanche war party on the march, fully equipped
1846-1848
20 x 27⅜ (50.8 x 69.4)

References: Ewers (1956), p. 510; Pauline A. Pinckney, *Painting in Texas* (Austin, 1967), reprod. p. 37.

Painted in Paris 1846-1848 (see no. 543). In spite of Catlin's haste, the technique and palette are astonishingly delicate (see no. 558).

The scene is repeated in cartoon 300 (Collection of Mr. and Mrs. Paul Mellon), with the line of warriors moving in the opposite direction.

597. Indian encampment, Comanche (or Kiowa) dressing skins, Red River
1846-1848
19½ x 27⅝ (49.7 x 70)

References: Donaldson, p. 385; Ewers (1956), p. 510.

Painted in Paris 1846-1848 (see nos. 543, 558). Catlin was probably referring to the North Fork of the Red River in the title (see no. 343). Cartoons 139 (NGA 1996) and 414 (AMNH 107) are related views.

598. Elk grazing on an autumn prairie
1846-1848
20⅛ x 27⅜ (51 x 69.4)

References: Donaldson, p. 385; Ewers (1956), p. 517.

Painted in Paris 1846-1848 (see nos. 543, 558).

599. Stalking buffalo, Arkansas
1846-1848
20 x 27¼ (50.8 x 69.2)

Reference: Ewers (1956), p. 516.

Painted in Paris 1846-1848 (see nos. 543, 558).

600. Comanche Indians chasing buffalo
1846-1848
20 x 27¼ (50.8 x 69.2)

References: Donaldson, p. 385; Ewers (1956), p. 510.

Painted in Paris 1846-1848 (see nos. 543, 558).

601. Portraits of two grizzly bears, from life
1846-1848
Unlocated

Painted in Paris 1846-1848 (see no. 543). The grizzly bear series was probably based on the five studies of bears' heads on an unnumbered canvas (illustrated here; MNH 386, 502; 20 x 27⅜) in the Smithsonian Catlin collection. The most likely models for these studies were the two bears Catlin brought with him to England in the fall of 1839 (see *Travels in Europe,* vol. 1, pp. 1-11).

602. Two grizzly bears, life size
1846-1848
Unlocated

Painted in Paris 1846-1848 (see nos. 543, 601).

603. Portraits of two grizzly bears, life size
1846-1848
Unlocated

Painted in Paris 1846-1848 (see nos. 543, 601).

603*. Portraits of a grizzly bear and mouse, life size
1846-1848
26½ x 32½ (67.5 x 82.5)
[Figure 47]

References: Donaldson, p. 385; Ewers (1956), p. 516.

Painted in Paris 1846-1848 (see nos. 543, 601). Catlin designed the portrait for European audiences to dramatize the relative size of the grizzly bear (see no. 563).

604. A famous hunter lancing the grizzly bear
1846-1848
Unlocated

Painted in Paris 1846-1848 (see no. 543).

605. A famous hunter encamped at night in the snowdrifts of winter
1846-1848
Unlocated

Painted in Paris 1846-1848 (see no. 543).

606. Buffalo bulls fighting, Upper Missouri
1846-1848
Unlocated

Painted in Paris 1846-1848 (see nos. 543, 424, 548, 607).

607. Battle between buffalo bulls, a draw
1846-1848
Unlocated

Painted in Paris 1846-1848 (see nos. 543, 606).

600

601

Smithsonian Institution.

Bibliography

PUBLICATIONS BY CATLIN

(See Harold McCracken, *George Catlin and the Old Frontier*, pp. 212-14, for a complete checklist of publications by Catlin. Additional references appear in the catalogue entries.)

Catalogue of Catlin's Indian Gallery. New York (Piercy & Read), 1837.

A Descriptive Catalogue of Catlin's Indian Gallery. Egyptian Hall, London (C. and J. Adlard), 1840.

Letters and Notes on the Manners, Customs, and Condition of the North American Indians. 2 vols. London, 1841. Reprinted by Dover Publications, New York, 1973.

Unparalleled Exhibition. Fourteen Ioway Indians . . . just arrived from the Upper Missouri. London (W. S. Johnson), 1844.

Catlin's North American Indian Portfolio. London (Day & Hague), 1844.

Catalogue Raisonné de la Galerie Indienne de Mr. Catlin. Paris (Imprimerie de Wittersheim), 1845.

Catlin's Notes of Eight Years' Travels and Residence in Europe, with His North American Indian Collection. 2 vols. London, 1848.

A Descriptive Catalogue of Catlin's Indian Collection. No. 6, Waterloo Place, London, 1848.

Life Amongst the Indians. New York, 1857 (London, 1861).

The Breath of Life, or Mal-respiration. New York, 1861.

O-Kee-Pa: A Religious Ceremony. London, 1867. Reprinted (with an introduction by John C. Ewers) by Yale University Press, New Haven, Conn., 1967.

Last Rambles Amongst the Indians of the Rocky Mountains and the Andes. New York, 1867.

The Lifted and Subsided Rocks of America. London, 1870.

Catalogue Descriptive and Instructive of Catlin's Indian Cartoons . . . and 27 Canvas Paintings of LaSalle's Discoveries. New York (Baker & Godwin), 1871.

BOOKS

Adkins, N. F. *Fitz-Greene Halleck.* New Haven, Conn., 1930.

Babbitt, Irving. *Rousseau and Romanticism.* New York (Meridian Books), 1955.

Barnum, P. T. *Struggles and Triumphs; or, Forty Years' Recollections.* Buffalo, 1873.

Baudelaire, Charles. *The Mirror of Art.* New York (Doubleday Anchor Books), 1955.

Berkhofer, Robert F., Jr. *The White Man's Indian: Images of the American Indian from Columbus to the Present.* New York, 1978.

Bissell, Benjamin. *The American Indian in English Literature of the Eighteenth Century.* New York (Archon Books), 1968.

Block, E. Maurice. *George Caleb Bingham.* 2 vols. Berkeley, Calif., 1967.

Bourbourg, Brasseur de. *Quatre Lettres sur le Mexique.* Paris (Auguste Durand et Pedone, Éditeurs), 1868.

Brooks, Van Wyck. *The World of Washington Irving.* New York, 1944.

Chateaubriand, François-René Vicomte de. *Recollections of Italy, England and America.* Philadelphia, 1816.

——— *Atala & René.* New York (New American Library), 1961.

Coe, Charles H. *Red Patriots: The Story of the Seminoles.* Cincinnati, 1898.

Colden, Cadwallader D. *Memoir Prepared at the Request of a Committee of the Common Council of the City of New York.* New York, 1825.

Cooper, James Fenimore. *Notions of the Americans.* 2 vols. New York (Frederick Ungar), 1963.

———. *The Prairie.* New York (Rinehart Editions), 1950.

———. *The Leatherstocking Saga.* Edited by Allan Nevins. New York (Modern Library), 1966.

Coues, Elliott. *History of the Expedition Under the Command of Lewis and Clark.* 4 vols. New York, 1893.

Cowdrey, Mary Bartlett. *American Academy of Fine Arts and American Art-Union.* 2 vols. New York, 1953.

Daniels, George H. *American Science in the Age of Jackson.* New York, 1968.

Darley, F. O. C. *Scenes in Indian Life.* Philadelphia, 1843.

Davis, Frank. *Victorian Patrons of the Arts.* London, 1963.

DeVoto, Bernard. *Across the Wide Missouri.* Boston, 1947.

Dondere, Dorothy A. *The Prairie and the Making of Middle America: Four Centuries of Description.* Cedar Rapids, Iowa, 1926.

Dunlap, William. *History of the Rise and Progress of the Arts of Design in the United States.* Vol. 3. New York (Benjamin Bloom), 1965.

Ewers, John C. *Artists of the Old West.* New York, 1965.

———. "Fact and Fiction in the Documentary Art of the American West." In *The Frontier Re-examined,* edited by J. F. McDermott. Urbana, Ill., 1965.

———. *Indian Life on the Upper Missouri.* Norman, Okla., 1968.

———. "The Opening of the West." In *The Artist in America,* compiled by the editors of Art in America. New York, 1967.

———. "William Clark's Indian Museum." In *A Cabinet of Curiosities: Five Episodes in the Evolution of American Museums,* edited by Walter Muir Whitehill. Charlottesville, Va., 1967.

Fairchild, Hoxie N. *The Noble Savage.* New York, 1961.

Flexner, James T. *That Wilder Image.* Boston, 1962.

Flint, Timothy. *Recollections of the Past Ten Years . . . in the Valley of the Mississippi.* New York (Da Capo Press), 1968.

Foreman, Carolyn T. *Indians Abroad 1493-1938.* Norman, Okla., 1943.

Foreman, Grant. *The Last Trek of the Indians.* Chicago, 1946.

French, H. W. *Art and Artists in Connecticut.* New York, 1879.

Fundaburk, Emma L. *Southeastern Indians: Life Portraits.* Metuchen, N.J. (Scarecrow Reprint), 1969.

Gauss, Christian, ed. *Selections from the Works of Jean-Jacques Rousseau.* Princeton, N.J., 1914.

Godman, John D. *Addresses Delivered on Various Public Occasions.* Philadelphia, 1829.

———. *American Natural History.* 2 vols. Philadelphia, 1860.

Goetzmann, William H. *Exploration and Empire.* New York, 1966.

Greeley, Horace. *An Overland Journey, from New York to San Francisco in the Summer of 1859.* New York, 1860.

Haberly, Loyd. *Pursuit of the Horizon.* New York, 1948.

Halleck, Fitz-Greene. *The Poetical Works of Fitz-Greene Halleck.* New York (Greenwood Press), 1969.

Harper, J. Russell. *Paul Kane's Frontier.* Austin, Texas, 1971.

Harris, Neil. *Humbug; the Art of P. T. Barnum.* Boston, 1973.

Hassrick, Peter. *The Way West: Art of Frontier America.* New York, 1977.

Haverstock, Mary Sayre. *Indian Gallery: The Story of George Catlin.* New York, 1973.

Heckewelder, John. *History, Manners, and Customs of the Indian Nations Who Once Inhabited Pennsylvania and the Neighbouring States.* Philadelphia (Historical Society of Pennsylvania), 1876.

Honour, Hugh. *The New Golden Land.* New York, 1976.

Huth, Hans. *Nature and the American.* Berkeley, Calif., 1957.

Irving, Washington. *The Sketchbook.* New York (New American Library), 1961.

———. *A Tour of the Prairies.* New York (Putnam), 1895.

James, Edwin. *Account of an Expedition from Pittsburgh to the Rocky Mountains.* 2 vols. Ann Arbor, Mich. (University Microfilms), 1966.

Jameson, Anna B. *Winter Studies and Summer Rambles in Canada.* Toronto (Thomas Nelson and Sons), 1943.

Jones, Howard Mumford. *The Frontier in American Fiction.* Jerusalem, 1956.

———. *Ideas in America.* Cambridge, Mass., 1944.

Kappler, Charles J. *Indian Affairs, Laws and Treaties.* Vol. 2. Washington, D.C., 1904.

Keiser, Albert. *The Indian in American Literature.* New York, 1933.

King, Clarence. *Mountaineering in the Sierra Nevada.* New York (W. W. Norton), 1935.

Kinietz, W. Vernon. *John Mix Stanley.* Ann Arbor, Mich., 1942.

Lewis, R. W. B. *The American Adam.* Chicago, 1955.

Marx, Leo. *The Machine in the Garden.* New York, 1964.

May, Henry F. *The Enlightenment in America.* New York, 1976.

McCracken, Harold. *George Catlin and the Old Frontier.* New York, 1959.

McDermott, John Francis, ed. *Audubon in the West.* Norman, Okla., 1965.

McDermott, John Francis. *Seth Eastman: Pictorial Historian of the Indian.* Norman, Okla., 1961.

McDermott, John Francis, ed. *Travelers on the Western Frontier.* Urbana, Ill., 1970.

———. *The Western Journals of Washington Irving.* Norman, Okla., 1944.

McKenney, Thomas L., and Hall, James. *The Indian Tribes of North America.* 3 vols. Edited by Frederick W. Hodge. Edinburgh, 1933.

Miller, Perry. *Nature's Nation.* Cambridge, Mass., 1967.

Munby, A. L. *Phillipps Studies.* Vol. 4. Cambridge, England, 1956.

Murray, Charles Augustus. *Travels in North America during the Years 1834, 1835, & 1836.* 2 vols. London, 1839.

Nash, Roderick. *Wilderness and the American Mind.* New Haven, Conn., 1967.

Nevins, Allan, ed. *The Diary of Philip Hone 1828-1851.* New York, 1927.

New York State Historical Association. *James Fenimore Cooper: a Reappraisal.* Cooperstown, N.Y., 1954.

Nuttall, Thomas. *A Journal of Travels into the Arkansa Territory.* Ann Arbor, Mich. (University Microfilms), 1966.

Pearce, Roy Harvey. *The Savages of America.* Baltimore, 1953.

Peattie, Donald C., ed. *Audubon's America.* Boston, 1940.

Peterson, Merrill D., ed. *The Portable Thomas Jefferson.* New York (New American Library), 1961.

Pinckney, Pauline A. *Painting in Texas.* Austin, Texas, 1967.

Poesch, Jessie. *Titian Ramsay Peale 1799-1885.* Philadelphia, 1961.

Reingold, Nathan, ed. *Science in Nineteenth-century America.* New York, 1964.

Richardson, Edgar P. *American Romantic Painting.* New York, 1944.

Roehm, Marjorie Catlin. *The Letters of George Catlin and His Family.* Berkeley, Calif., 1966.

Ross, Marvin C., ed. *George Catlin: Episodes from Life Among the Indians and Last Rambles.* Norman, Okla., 1959.

———. *The West of Alfred Jacob Miller.* Norman, Okla., 1968.

Rossi, Paul A., and Hunt, David C. *The Art of the Old West.* New York, 1973.

Rutledge, Anna Wells, ed. *The Pennsylvania Academy of the Fine Arts: Cumulative Record of Exhibition Catalogues 1807-1870.* Philadelphia, 1955.

Schoolcraft, Henry R. *Algic Researches.* 2 vols. New York, 1839.

———. *Historical and Statistical Information Respecting the History, Condition and Prospects of the Indian Tribes of the United States.* 6 vols. Philadelphia, 1851-1857.

Sellers, Charles Coleman. *Charles Willson Peale.* New York, 1969.

Shepard, Paul. *Man in the Landscape.* New York, 1967.

Smallwood, William M. *Natural History and the American Mind.* New York, 1941.

Smith, Henry Nash. *American Emotional and Imaginative Attitudes toward the Great Plains and the Rocky Mountains 1803-1850.* Unpublished Ph.D. dissertation. Harvard University, 1940.

———. *Virgin Land.* Cambridge, Mass., 1970.

Taft, Robert. *Artists and Illustrators of the Old West 1850-1900.* New York, 1953.

Taylor, Joshua C., with a contribution by John G. Cawelti. *America as Art.* Washington, D.C., 1976.

Thomas, Davis, and Ronnefeldt, Karin, eds. *People of the First Man . . . Account of Prince Maximilian's Expedition up the Missouri River, 1833-34.* New York, 1976.

Thwaites, Reuben Gold, ed. *Early Western Travels 1748-1846.* Vol. 25 (Maximilian's Travels in the Interior of North America, 1832-1834). Cleveland, 1906.

Tuckerman, Henry T. *Book of the Artists.* New York (James F. Carr), 1966.

Viola, Herman J. *The Indian Legacy of Charles Bird King.* Washington, D.C., 1976.

Whitney, Lois. *Primitivism and the Idea of Progress in English Popular Literature of the Eighteenth Century.* Baltimore, 1934.

REPORTS, PERIODICALS, AND NEWSPAPERS

American Turf Register and Sporting Magazine 7 (August 1836): 554-55.

Beetem, Robert N. "George Catlin in France: His Relationship to Delacroix and Baudelaire." *Art Quarterly* 24 (Summer 1961): 129-44.

Cabinet of Natural History and American Rural Sports 2 (1832): 184-86.

Daily National Intelligencer, Washington, D.C., April 16 and May 18, 1838.

Donaldson, Thomas. "The George Catlin Indian Gallery." *Annual Report of the Smithsonian Institution for 1885,* part 5. Washington, D.C., 1886.

Ewers, John C. "Charles Bird King, Painter of Indian Visitors to the Nation's Capitol." *Annual Report of the Smithsonian Institution for 1953,* pp. 463-73. Washington, D.C., 1954.

———. "George Catlin, Painter of Indians and the West." *Annual Report of the Smithsonian Institution for 1955,* pp. 483-528. Washington, D.C., 1956.

Hartmann, Horst. "George Catlin und Balduin Möllhausen." *Baessler-Archiv Beiträge zur Völkerkunde,* pp. 11-58. Neue Folge Beiheft 3. Berlin, 1963.

Hewett, Marie. "Pictorial Reporter: George Catlin in Western New York." *Niagara Frontier* 17 (Winter 1970): 100-103.

"Historic Philadelphia, from the Founding until the Early Nineteenth Century." *Transactions of the American Philosophical Society*, vol. 43. Philadelphia, 1953.

"Indian Loving Catlin and His Buffalo Powder Horn." *Proceedings and Collections of the Wyoming Historical and Geological Society*, vol. 21. Wilkes-Barre, Pa., 1930.

LaFarge, Oliver. "George Catlin: Wild West Witness." *Art News* 52 (October 1953): 30-32.

Matthews, Washington. "The Catlin Collection of Indian Paintings." *Report of the National Museum for 1890*, pp. 593-610. Washington, D.C., 1892.

McDermott, John Francis. "Samuel Seymour: Pioneer Artist of the Plains and the Rockies." *Annual Report of the Smithsonian Institution for 1950*, pp. 497-509. Washington, D.C., 1951.

Mills, Paul C. *"The Buffalo Hunter* and Other Related Versions of the Subject in Nineteenth-century American Art and Literature." *Archivero* I, pp. 131-72. Santa Barbara Museum of Art, Calif., 1973.

Morse, Jedidiah. *Report to the Secretary of War.* New Haven, Conn., 1822.

New Orleans Courier, April 2, 1835, p. 3.

New York Commercial Advertiser. Photostat copies of letters by George Catlin describing the "Manners, Customs, and Condition of the North American Indians," July 24, 1832-Sept. 30, 1837. National Collection of Fine Arts/National Portrait Gallery Library, Washington D.C.

New York Evening Post, Oct. 23-Nov. 2, 1871.

New York Evening Star, Feb. 1, 1838, p. 2.

New York Times, Oct. 22-31, 1871.

North American Miscellany and Dollar Magazine 4 (July 1852): 271.

Rathbone, Perry T. "Rediscovery." *Art in America* 49 (no. 1, 1961): 82-83.

Russell, Jason A. "Cooper: Interpreter of the Real and Historical Indian." *Journal of American History* 22 (no. 1, 1928): 41-71.

Sellin, David. "Denis A. Volozan, Philadelphia Neoclassicist." *Winterthur Portfolio* 4 (1968): 119-28.

Senate Miscellaneous Documents, vol. 511, no. 152, July 1848.

Todd, Ruthven. "The Imaginary Indian in Europe." *Art in America* 60 (July-August 1972): 40-47.

Truettner, William H. "George Catlin, Frank Wilkin, and the Prince of Econchatti." *Apollo* 105 (February 1977): 124-26.

United States Democratic Review 11 (July 1842): 44-52.

Wainwright, Nicholas B. "Joseph Harrison, Jr., a Forgotten Art Collector." *Antiques* 102 (October 1972): 660-68.

Wasserman, Emily. "The Artist-Explorers." *Art in America* 60 (July-August 1972): 48-57.

Weitenkampf, Frank. "Early Pictures of North American Indians." *Bulletin of the New York Public Library* 53 (December 1949): 591-614.

Western Monthly Magazine 2 (November 1833): 535-38.

Wissler, Clark. "The American Indian and the American Philosophical Society." *Proceedings of the American Philosophical Society* 86 (September 1942): 189-204.

Young, Vernon. "The Wilderness in a Locket." *Arts* 31 (December 1956): 20-24.

CATALOGUES

Art Institute of Chicago. *The Hudson River School and the Early American Landscape Tradition*, 1945.

Butts, Porter. *Art in Wisconsin.* Madison Art Association, 1936.

Centre Culturel Américain, Paris. *Georges Catlin*, 1963.

City Art Museum of St. Louis. *Charles Wimar 1828-1862*, 1946.

———. *Mississippi Panorama*, 1949.

———. *Westward the Way*, 1954.

Fisher, Samuel H. *Litchfield Law School 1774-1833; Biographical Catalogue of Students.* New Haven, Conn., 1946.

"Gilcrease Institute Collection of Works by George Catlin." *Catlin's Indian Gallery.* Tulsa, 1973.

Halpin, Marjorie. *Catlin's Indian Gallery.* Smithsonian Institution, Washington, D.C., 1965.

Henry Gallery, University of Washington, Seattle. *The View and the Vision: Landscape Painting in Nineteenth-century America*, 1968.

Heritage Book Shop, Lake Zurich, Ill. Catalogue No. 2 (1970-1976?).

Honour, Hugh. *The European Vision of America.* Cleveland Museum of Art, 1975.

Indiana University Art Museum, Bloomington. *The American Scene 1820-1900*, 1970.

International Exposition, Spokane. *Our Land, Our Sky, Our Water*, 1974.

Joslyn Art Museum, Omaha. *Catlin, Bodmer, Miller: Artist Explorers of the 1830s*, 1963.

Kennedy Galleries, New York. *George Catlin: Paintings from the Collection of the American Museum of Natural History*, 1956.

Los Angeles County Museum of Art. *The American West*, 1972.

Memorial Art Gallery, Rochester, N.Y. *Thomas Cole*, 1969.

Montclair Art Museum, Montclair, N.J. *A. B. Durand, 1796-1886*, 1971.

Museum of Fine Arts, Boston. *Frontier America: The Far West*, 1975.

Museum of Modern Art, New York. *Romantic Painting in America*, 1943.

National Collection of Fine Arts, Washington, D.C. *National Parks and the American Landscape*, 1972.

National Gallery of Art, Washington, D.C. *American Paintings and Sculpture: An Illustrated Catalogue*, 1970.

Pennsylvania Academy of the Fine Arts, Philadelphia. *Catalogue of the Joseph and Sarah Harrison Collection*, 1974.

Philadelphia Centennial Catalogue, 1876, part 2, dept. 4, no. 1139.

Philadelphia Museum of Art. *Philadelphia: Three Centuries of American Art*, 1976.

Quimby, George I. *Indians of the Western Frontier: Paintings of George Catlin.* Chicago Natural History Museum, 1954.

University of Maryland Art Gallery, College Park. *Hommage à Baudelaire*, 1968.

University of Michigan Museum of Art, Ann Arbor, Mich. *John Mix Stanley: A Traveller in the West*, 1970.

University Museum, Philadelphia. *The Noble Savage: The American Indian in Art*, 1958.

Whitney Museum of American Art, New York. *The American Frontier: Images and Myths*, 1973.

ARCHIVAL SOURCES

Buffalo, N.Y. Buffalo and Erie County Historical Society. General Peter B. Porter Papers.

New York. Manuscript Division, New York Public Library. Catlin Correspondence.

St. Louis. Missouri Historical Society. Catlin Papers.

Tulsa. Thomas Gilcrease Institute of American History and Art. Phillipps Papers.

Washington, D. C. Library of the National Collection of Fine Arts and the National Portrait Gallery, Smithsonian Institution. Catlin Papers.

Washington, D. C. National Archives. Records of the Bureau of Indian Affairs (compiled by Edward E. Hill), 2 vols.

Washington, D. C. National Archives. Record Group 92. Quartermaster's Consolidated Correspondence File.

Washington, D. C. Smithsonian Institution Archives. Joseph Henry Papers.

Title Index

Catalogue numbers are in brackets.

General Index

Catalogue numbers are in brackets.